# Pokémon

## Ω RUBY · α SAPPHIRE
OMEGA · ALPHA

■ STORY : Hidenori Kusaka
■ ART : Satoshi Yamamoto

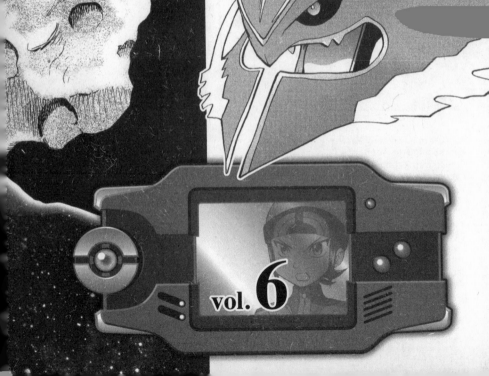

vol. 6

## Our Story Th

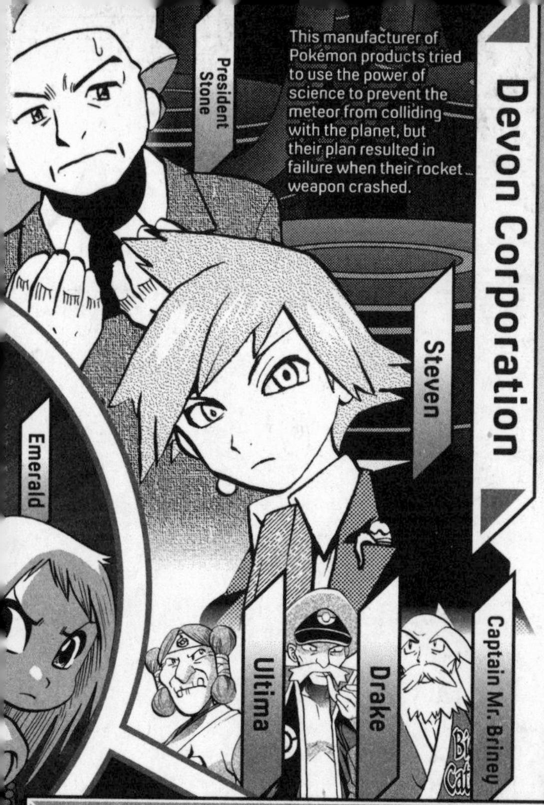
President Stone
This manufacturer of Pokémon products tried to use the power of science to prevent the meteor from colliding with the planet, but their plan resulted in failure when their rocket weapon crashed.
Devon Corporation
Steven
Emerald
Captain Mr. Briney
Drake
Ultima

A story about young people entrusted with Pokédexes by the world's leading Pokémon researchers. Together with their Pokémon, they travel, do battle and grow!

In order to power a rocket to prevent a huge approaching meteor from striking the planet, Steven Stone, president of the Devon Corporation, summons the three Pokédex holders of Hoenn to help him convert the life force of many Pokémon into Infinity Energy.

The rocket launch ends in failure due to sabotage by Zinnia, the Lorekeeper of the Draconid People. The Draconid have long predicted the arrival of the meteor and claim they know how to prevent it from striking the planet. During the battle with Zinnia, Sapphire mysteriously goes missing.

Ruby and Emerald are hit by the shockwave when Legendary Pokémon Groudon and Kyogre suddenly appear. Our heroes regain consciousness at Meteor Falls, where the Elder of the Draconid People provides them with clues to saving the world. Armed with new information, Ruby and his father head for Johto in search of Legendary Pokémon Rayquaza. Will they find Rayquaza and help it master its move, Dragon Ascent? They're about to run out of time...!

# CONTENTS

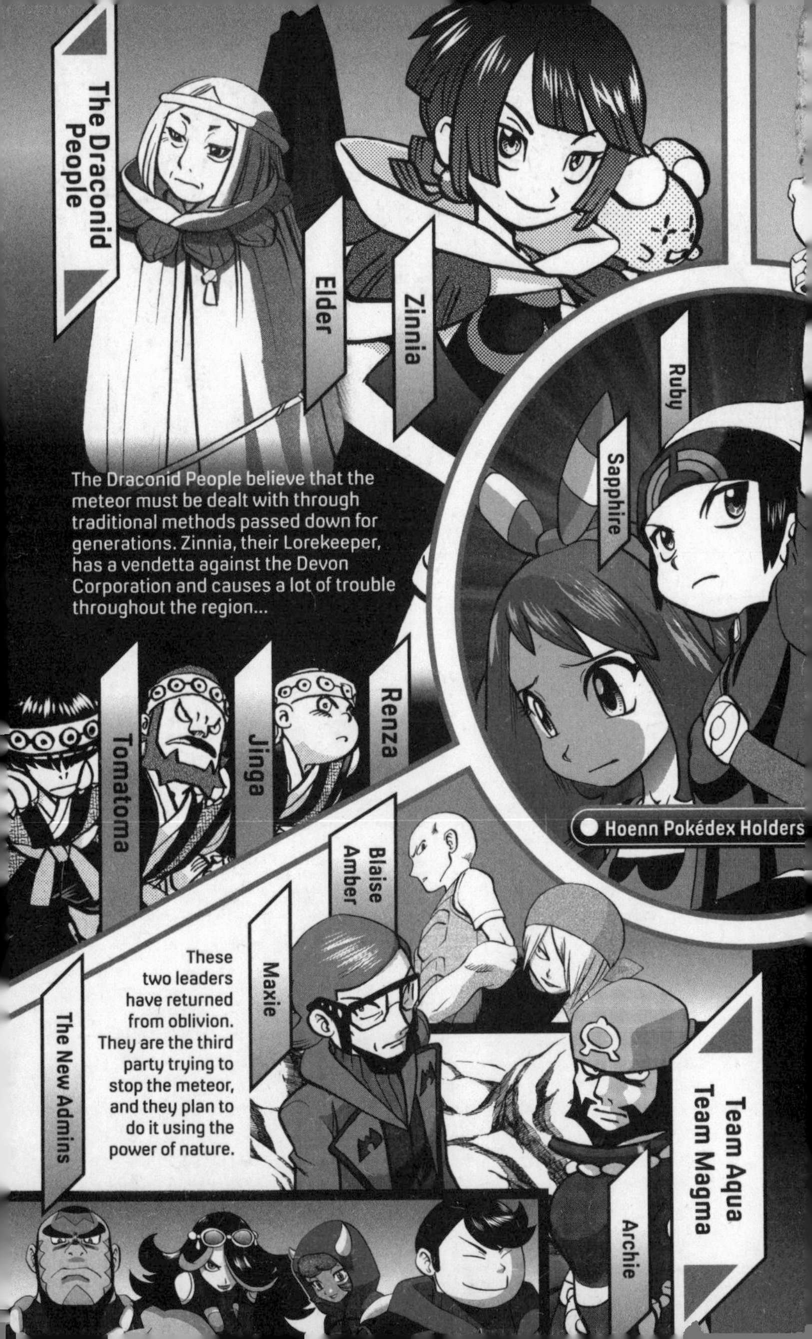
Ruby
Sapphire
Hoenn Pokédex Holders
Zinnia
Elder
The Draconid People
The Draconid People believe that the meteor must be dealt with through traditional methods passed down for generations. Zinnia, their Lorekeeper, has a vendetta against the Devon Corporation and causes a lot of trouble throughout the region...
Renza
Jinga
Tomatoma
Team Aqua
Team Magma
Archie
Blaise
Amber
Maxie
These two leaders have returned from oblivion. They are the third party trying to stop the meteor, and they plan to do it using the power of nature.
The New Admins

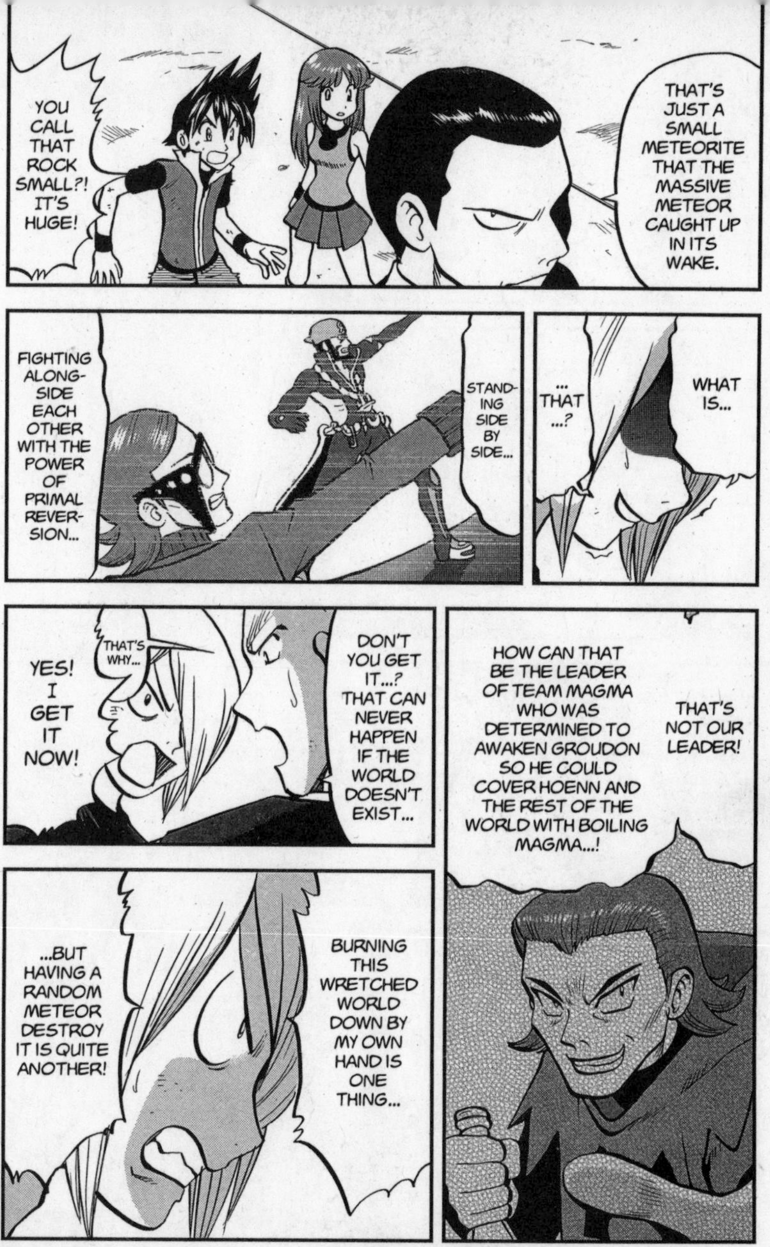
THAT'S JUST A SMALL METEORITE THAT THE MASSIVE METEOR CAUGHT UP IN ITS WAKE.
YOU CALL THAT ROCK SMALL?! IT'S HUGE!
WHAT IS...
...THAT ...?
STANDING SIDE BY SIDE...
FIGHTING ALONGSIDE EACH OTHER WITH THE POWER OF PRIMAL REVERSION...
THAT'S NOT OUR LEADER!
HOW CAN THAT BE THE LEADER OF TEAM MAGMA WHO WAS DETERMINED TO AWAKEN GROUDON SO HE COULD COVER HOENN AND THE REST OF THE WORLD WITH BOILING MAGMA...!
DON'T YOU GET IT...? THAT CAN NEVER HAPPEN IF THE WORLD DOESN'T EXIST...
THAT'S WHY...
YES! I GET IT NOW!
BURNING THIS WRETCHED WORLD DOWN BY MY OWN HAND IS ONE THING...
...BUT HAVING A RANDOM METEOR DESTROY IT IS QUITE ANOTHER!

# Omega Alpha Adventure 18

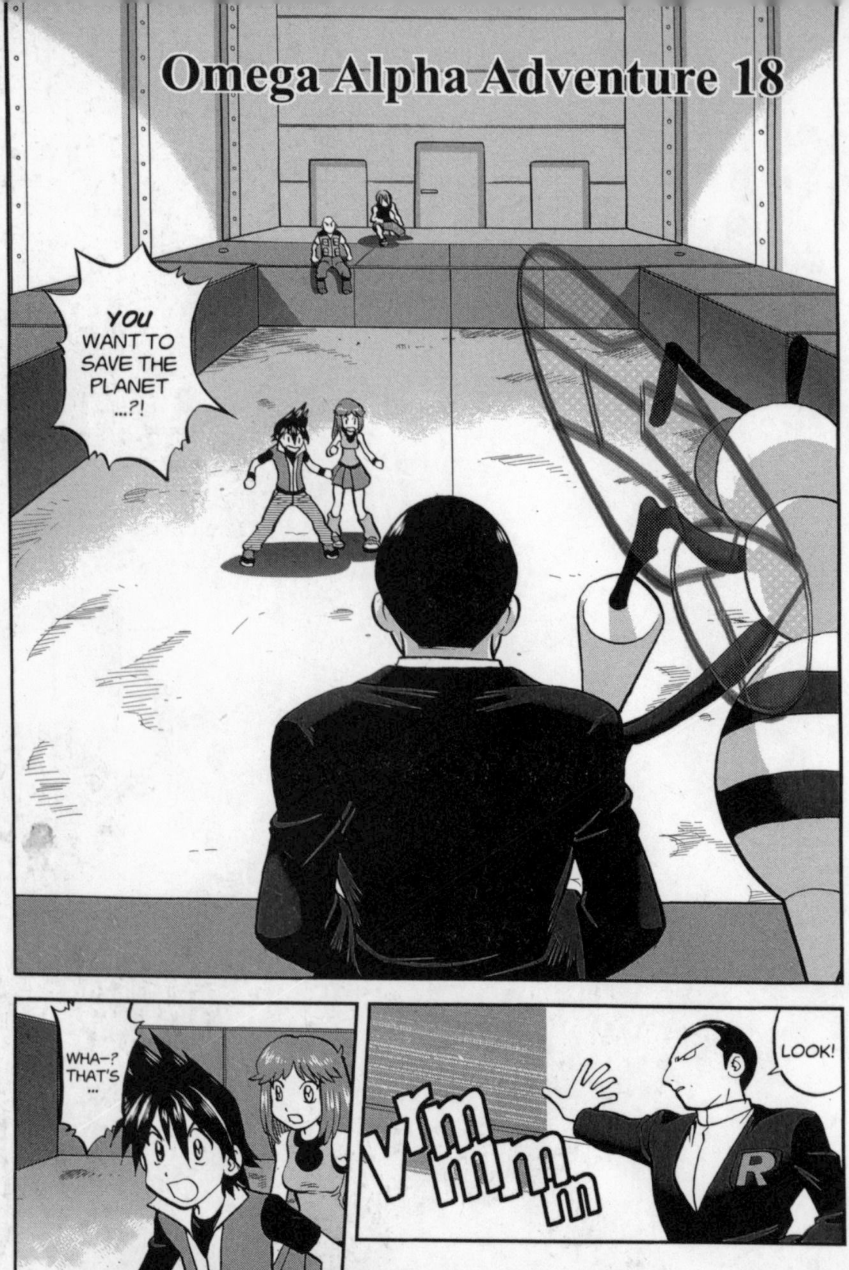
YOU WANT TO SAVE THE PLANET ...?!
LOOK!
vrmmmm
WHA-? THAT'S ...

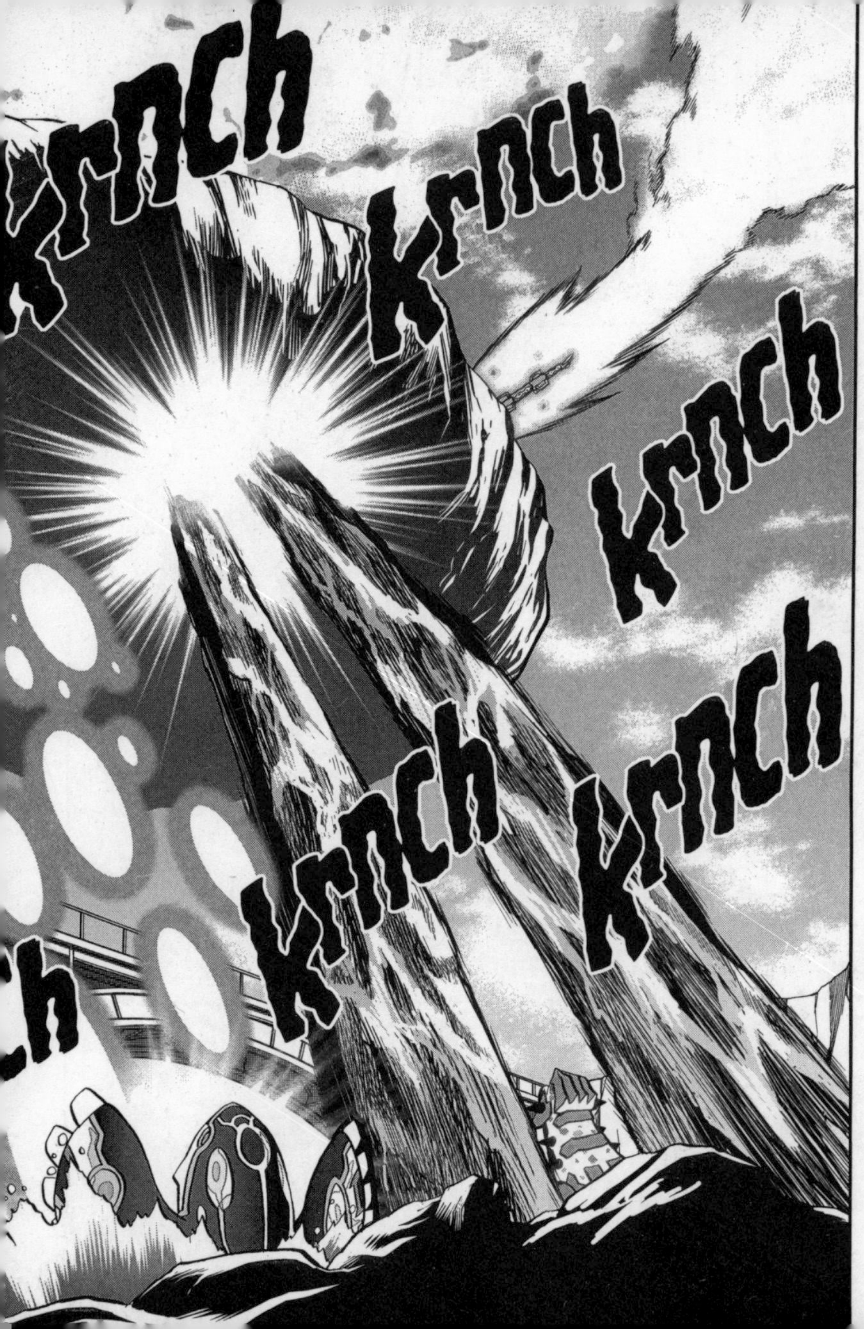

krnch
krnch
krnch
krnch
krnch
krnch

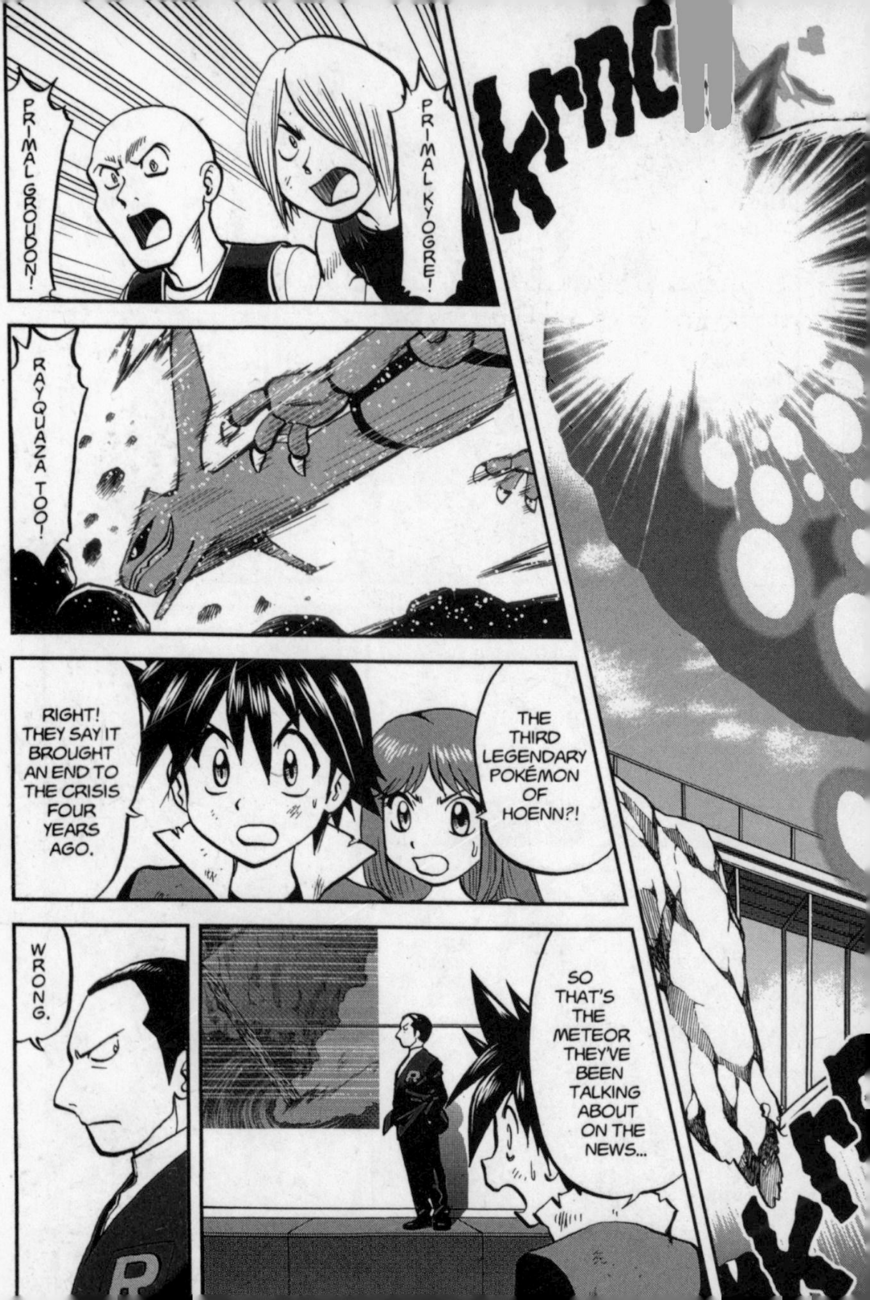
krnch
PRIMAL KYOGRE!
PRIMAL GROUDON!
RAYQUAZA TOO!
THE THIRD LEGENDARY POKÉMON OF HOENN?!
RIGHT! THEY SAY IT BROUGHT AN END TO THE CRISIS FOUR YEARS AGO.
SO THAT'S THE METEOR THEY'VE BEEN TALKING ABOUT ON THE NEWS...
WRONG.

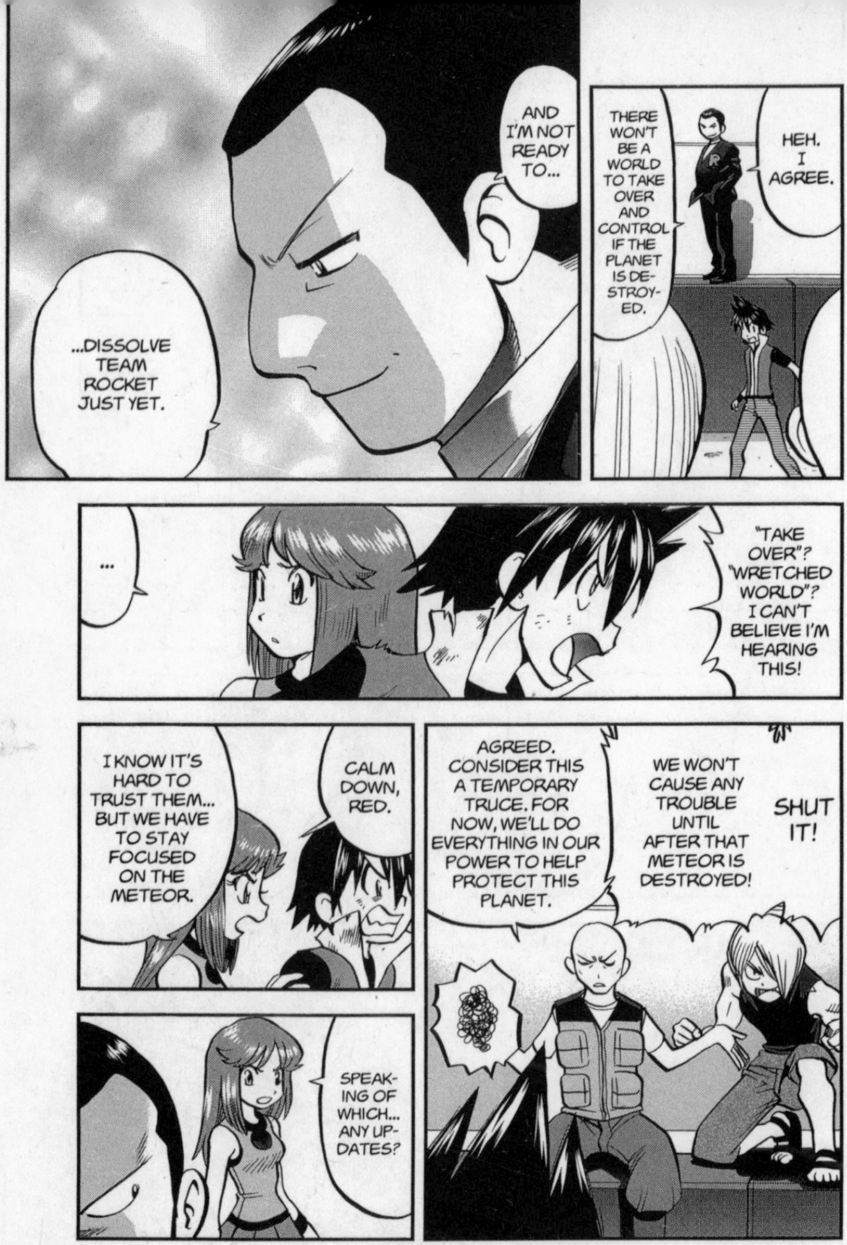
HEH. I AGREE.
THERE WON'T BE A WORLD TO TAKE OVER AND CONTROL IF THE PLANET IS DE-STROY-ED.
AND I'M NOT READY TO...
...DISSOLVE TEAM ROCKET JUST YET.
"TAKE OVER"? "WRETCHED WORLD"? I CAN'T BELIEVE I'M HEARING THIS!
...
SHUT IT!
WE WON'T CAUSE ANY TROUBLE UNTIL AFTER THAT METEOR IS DESTROYED!
AGREED. CONSIDER THIS A TEMPORARY TRUCE. FOR NOW, WE'LL DO EVERYTHING IN OUR POWER TO HELP PROTECT THIS PLANET.
CALM DOWN, RED.
I KNOW IT'S HARD TO TRUST THEM... BUT WE HAVE TO STAY FOCUSED ON THE METEOR.
SPEAK-ING OF WHICH... ANY UP-DATES?

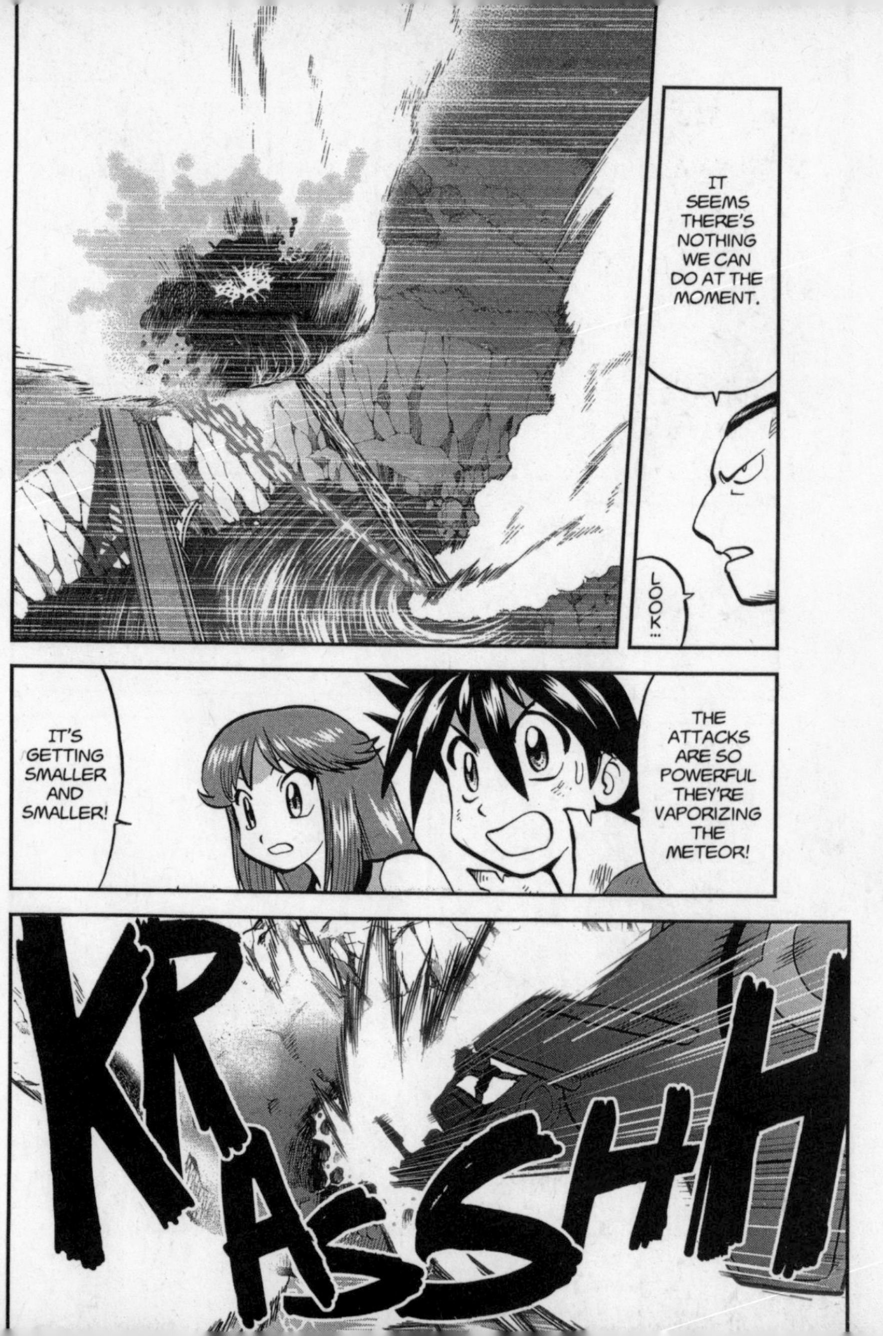
LOOK...
IT SEEMS THERE'S NOTHING WE CAN DO AT THE MOMENT.
THE ATTACKS ARE SO POWERFUL THEY'RE VAPORIZING THE METEOR!
IT'S GETTING SMALLER AND SMALLER!
KRASHH

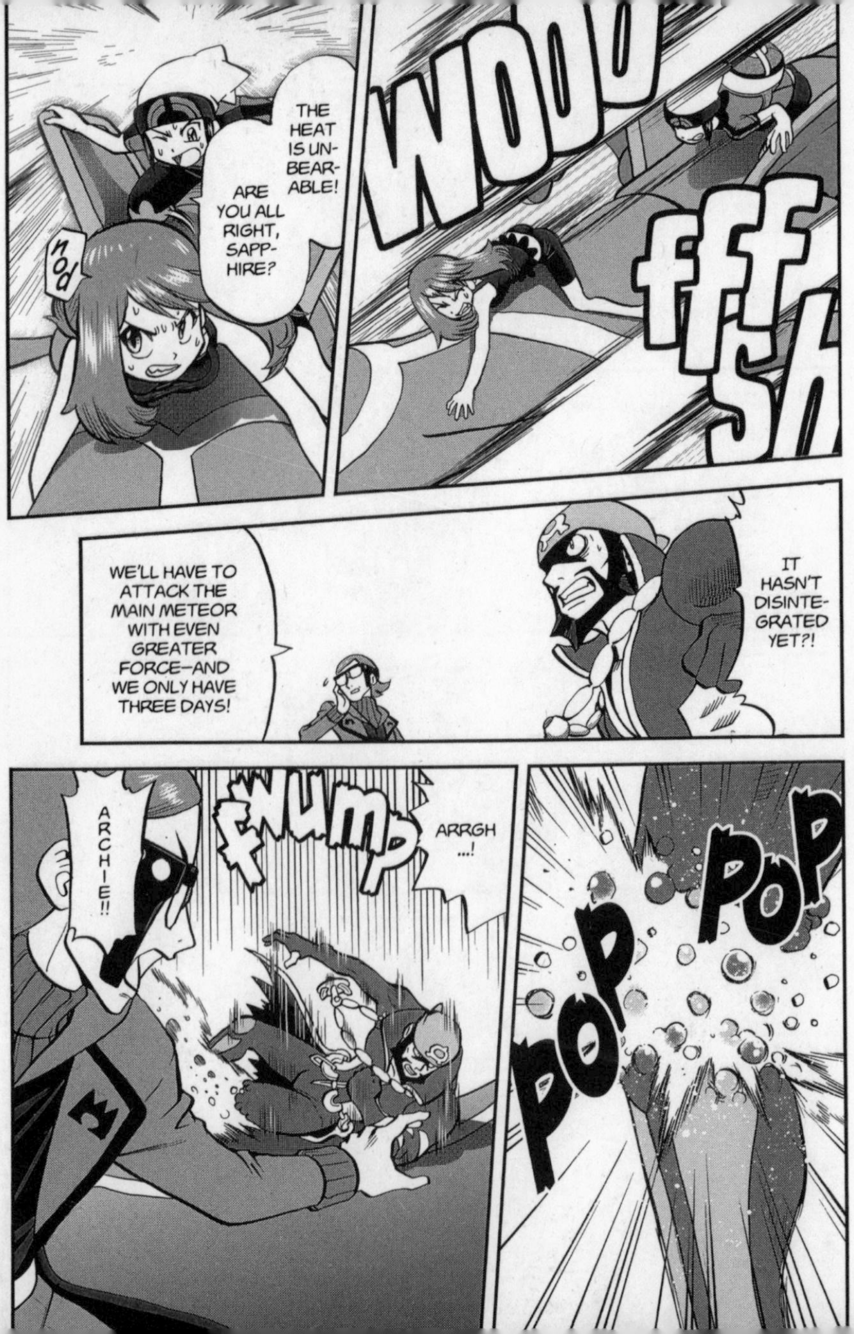
WOOO
fff
Sh
THE HEAT IS UN-BEARABLE!
nod
ARE YOU ALL RIGHT, SAPP-HIRE?
IT HASN'T DISINTE-GRATED YET?!
WE'LL HAVE TO ATTACK THE MAIN METEOR WITH EVEN GREATER FORCE—AND WE ONLY HAVE THREE DAYS!
POP
POP
POP
ARRGH ...!
THUMP
ARCHIE!!

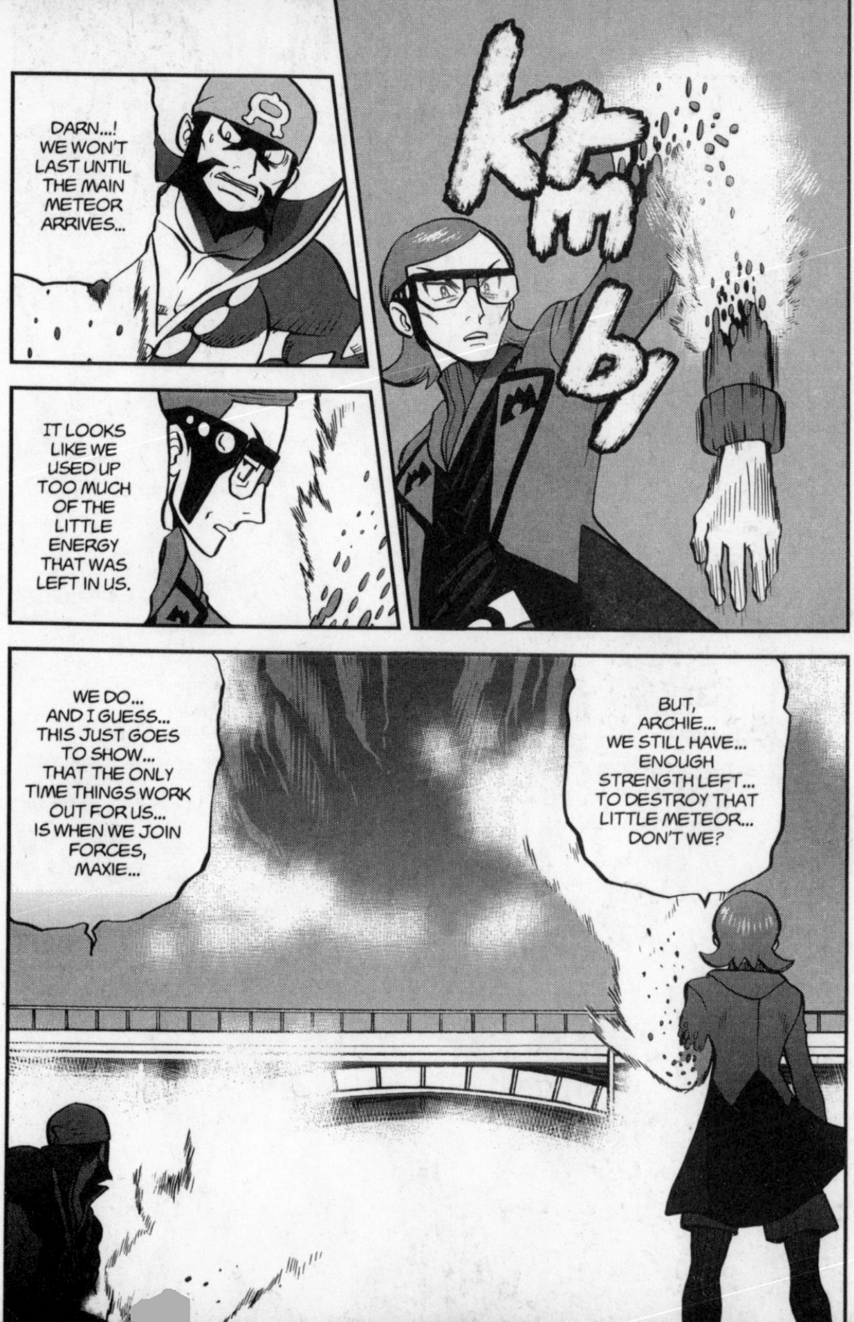
DARN...! WE WON'T LAST UNTIL THE MAIN METEOR ARRIVES...
IT LOOKS LIKE WE USED UP TOO MUCH OF THE LITTLE ENERGY THAT WAS LEFT IN US.
BUT, ARCHIE... WE STILL HAVE... ENOUGH STRENGTH LEFT... TO DESTROY THAT LITTLE METEOR... DON'T WE?
WE DO... AND I GUESS... THIS JUST GOES TO SHOW... THAT THE ONLY TIME THINGS WORK OUT FOR US... IS WHEN WE JOIN FORCES, MAXIE...

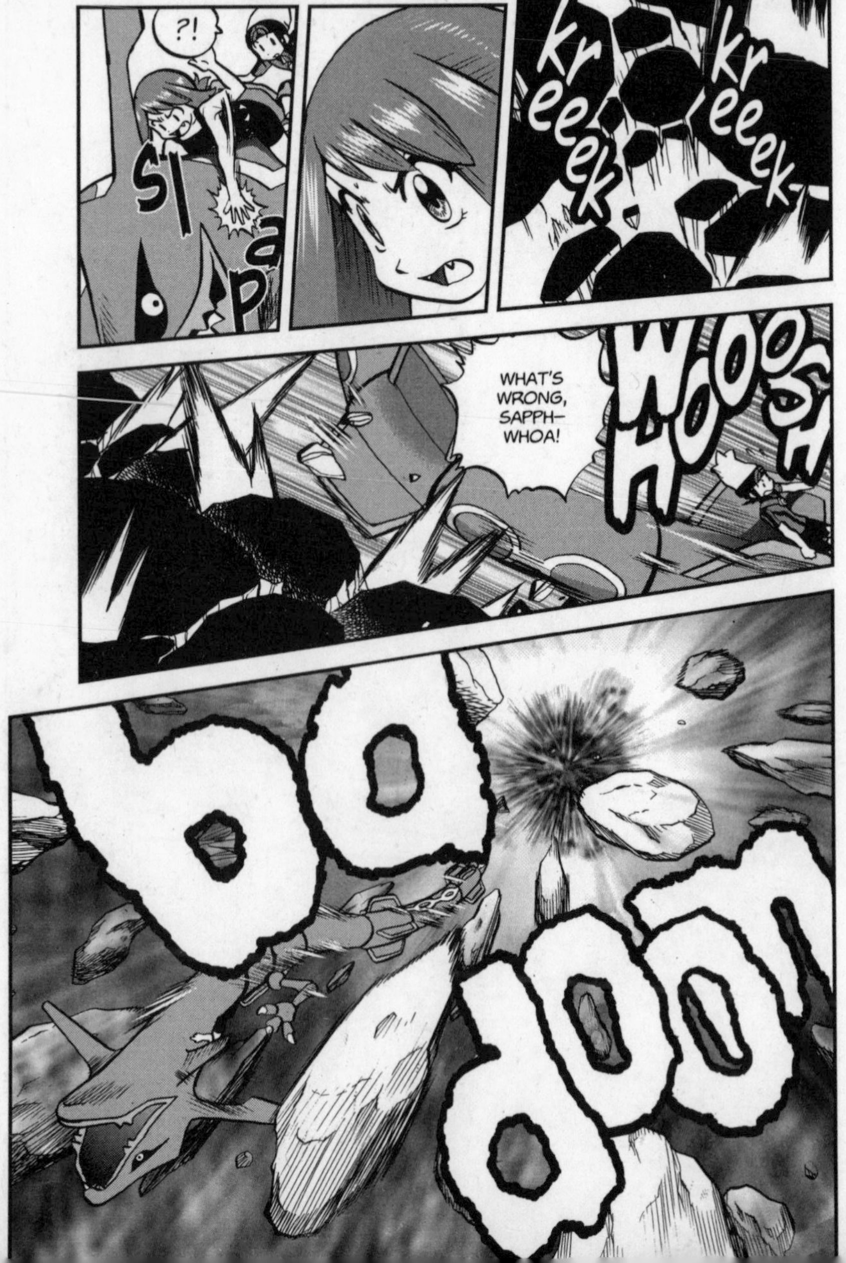
kreeeek-kreeeek
?!
slap
WHOOOSH
WHAT'S WRONG, SAPPH— WHOA!
bo
doom!

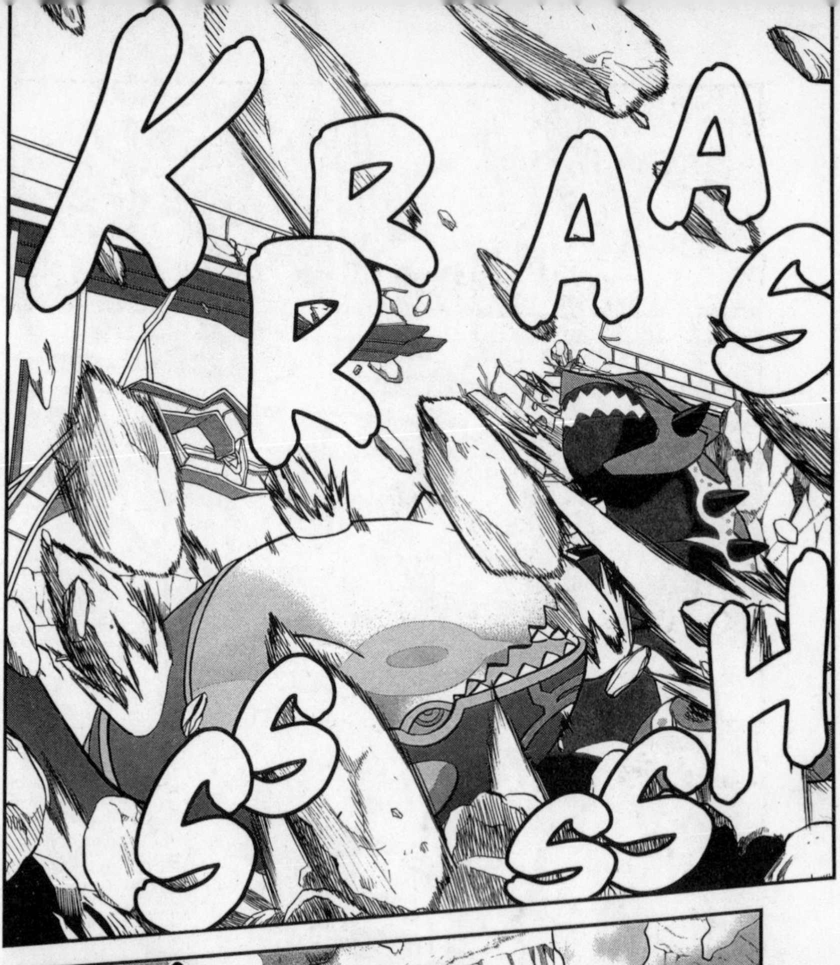
KRRAASSSSSH
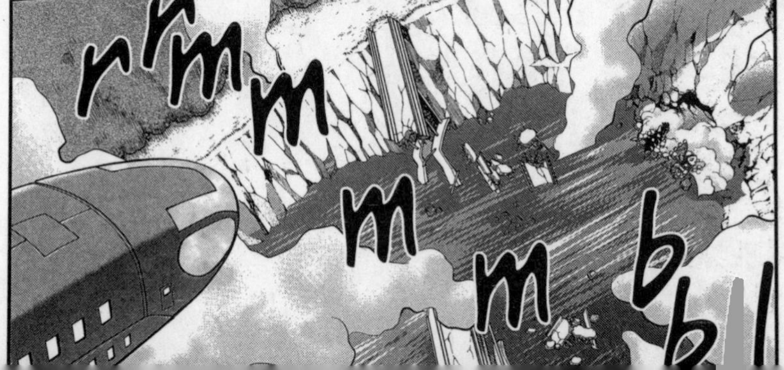
rrmmmmmbbl

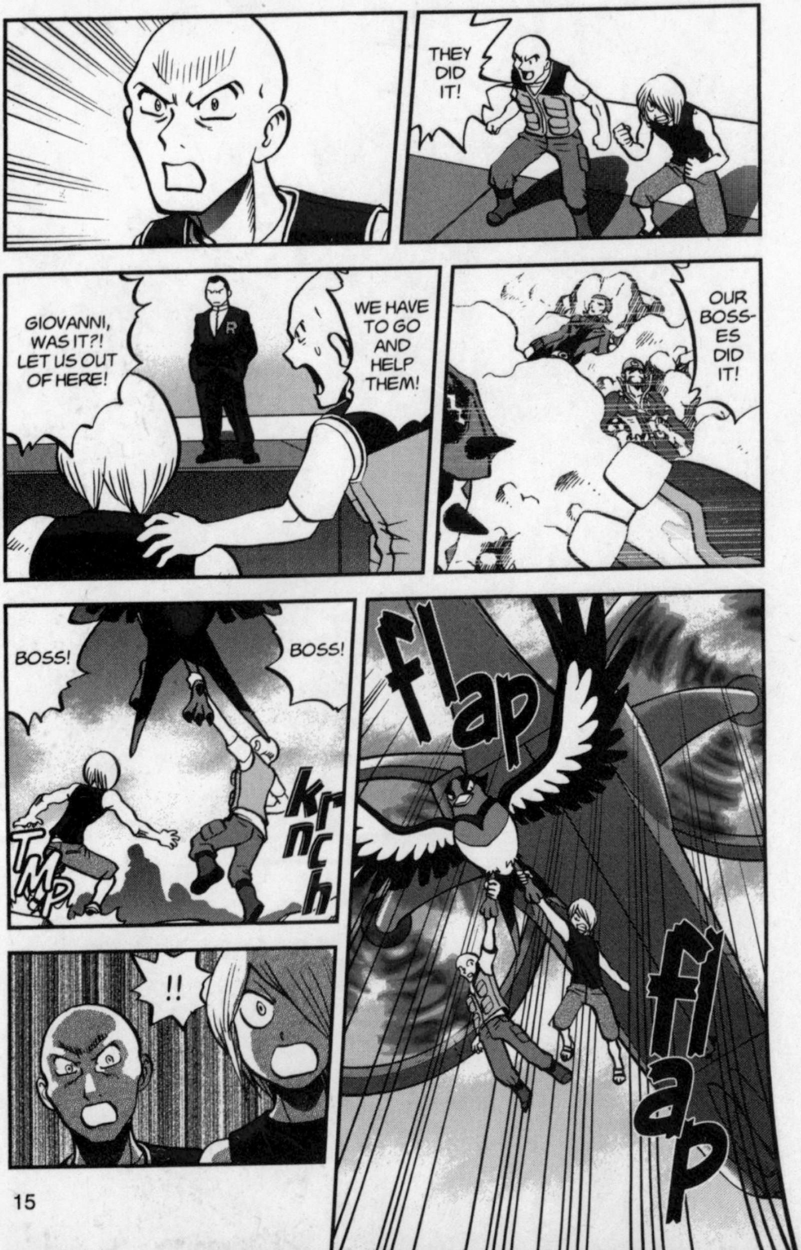
THEY DID IT!
OUR BOSS-ES DID IT!
WE HAVE TO GO AND HELP THEM!
GIOVANNI, WAS IT?! LET US OUT OF HERE!
flap
flap
BOSS!
BOSS!
krnch
TMP
!!

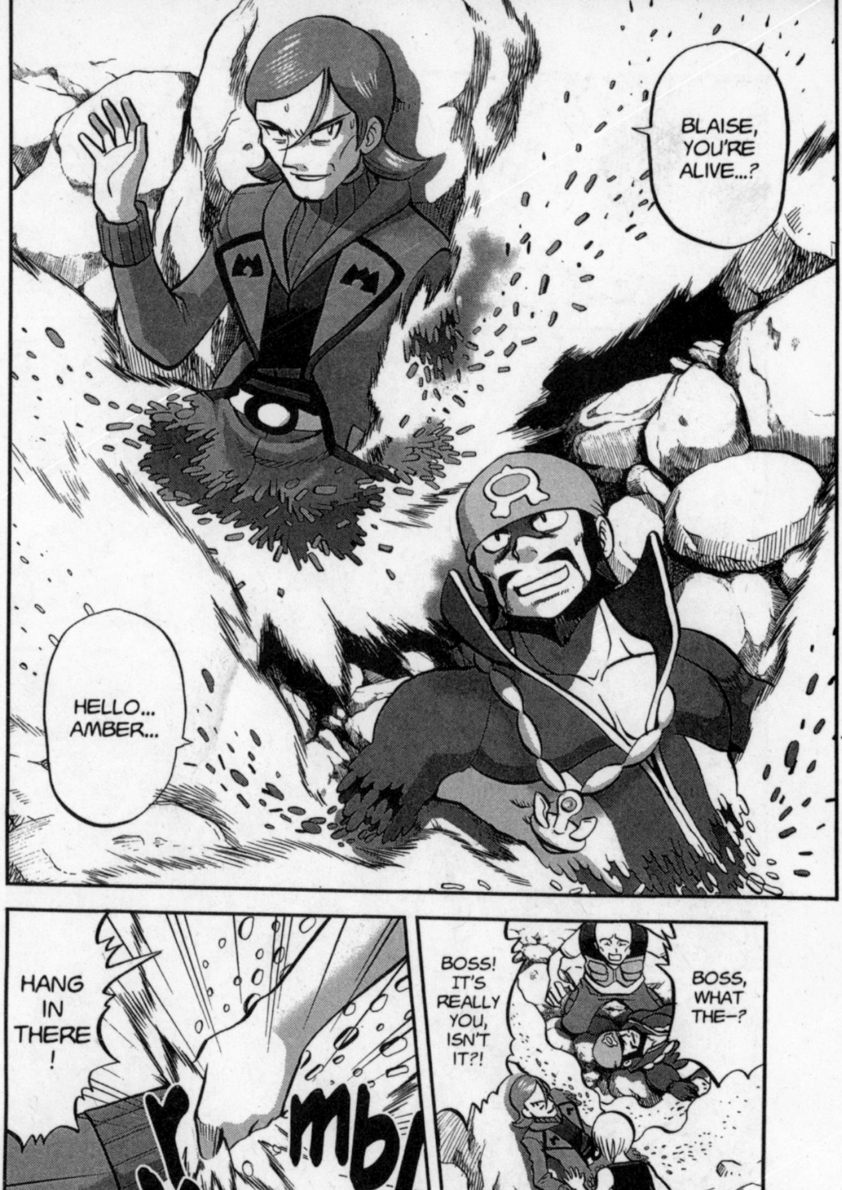
BLAISE, YOU'RE ALIVE...?
HELLO... AMBER...
BOSS, WHAT THE–?
BOSS! IT'S REALLY YOU, ISN'T IT?!
HANG IN THERE!
Krmbl

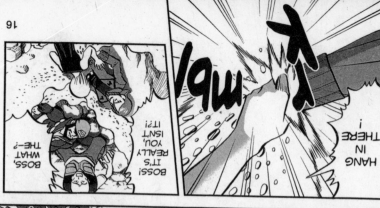

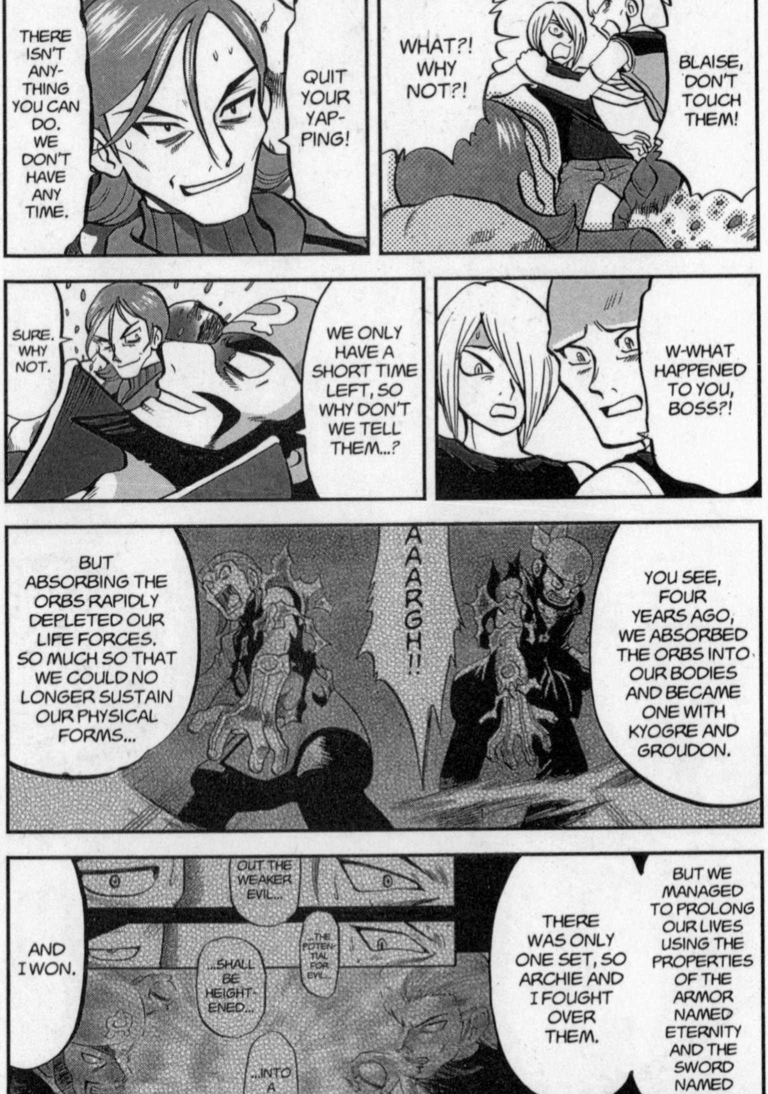
BLAISE, DON'T TOUCH THEM!
WHAT?! WHY NOT?!
QUIT YOUR YAP-PING!
THERE ISN'T ANY-THING YOU CAN DO. WE DON'T HAVE ANY TIME.
W-WHAT HAPPENED TO YOU, BOSS?!
WE ONLY HAVE A SHORT TIME LEFT, SO WHY DON'T WE TELL THEM...?
SURE. WHY NOT.
YOU SEE, FOUR YEARS AGO, WE ABSORBED THE ORBS INTO OUR BODIES AND BECAME ONE WITH KYOGRE AND GROUDON.
AAAARGH!!
BUT ABSORBING THE ORBS RAPIDLY DEPLETED OUR LIFE FORCES. SO MUCH SO THAT WE COULD NO LONGER SUSTAIN OUR PHYSICAL FORMS...
BUT WE MANAGED TO PROLONG OUR LIVES USING THE PROPERTIES OF THE ARMOR NAMED ETERNITY AND THE SWORD NAMED INSTANT.
THERE WAS ONLY ONE SET, SO ARCHIE AND I FOUGHT OVER THEM.
OUT THE WEAKER EVIL...
...THE POTEN-TIAL FOR EVIL...
...SHALL BE HEIGHT-ENED...
...INTO A PURER STATE.
AND I WON.

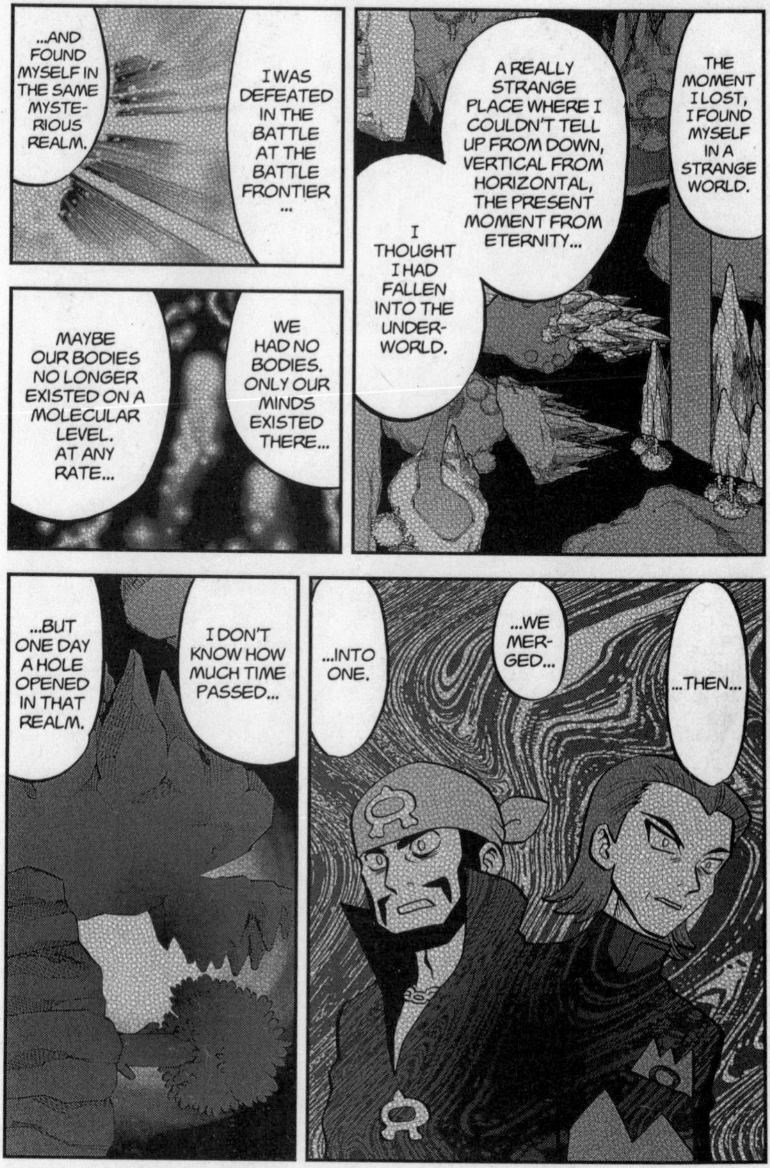
THE MOMENT I LOST, I FOUND MYSELF IN A STRANGE WORLD.
A REALLY STRANGE PLACE WHERE I COULDN'T TELL UP FROM DOWN, VERTICAL FROM HORIZONTAL, THE PRESENT MOMENT FROM ETERNITY...
I THOUGHT I HAD FALLEN INTO THE UNDER-WORLD.
I WAS DEFEATED IN THE BATTLE AT THE BATTLE FRONTIER...
...AND FOUND MYSELF IN THE SAME MYSTE-RIOUS REALM.
WE HAD NO BODIES. ONLY OUR MINDS EXISTED THERE...
MAYBE OUR BODIES NO LONGER EXISTED ON A MOLECULAR LEVEL. AT ANY RATE...
...THEN...
...WE MER-GED...
...INTO ONE.
I DON'T KNOW HOW MUCH TIME PASSED...
...BUT ONE DAY A HOLE OPENED IN THAT REALM.

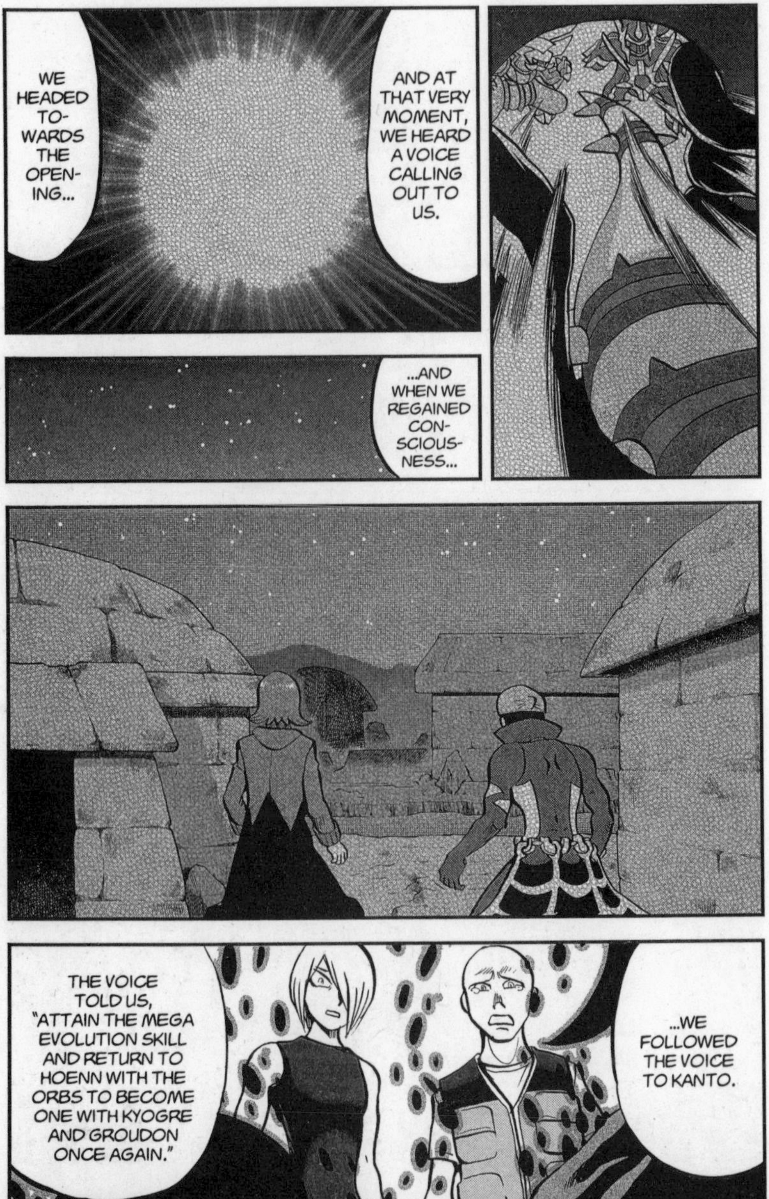
WE HEADED TO-WARDS THE OPEN-ING...
AND AT THAT VERY MOMENT, WE HEARD A VOICE CALLING OUT TO US.
...AND WHEN WE REGAINED CON-SCIOUS-NESS...
...WE FOLLOWED THE VOICE TO KANTO.
THE VOICE TOLD US, "ATTAIN THE MEGA EVOLUTION SKILL AND RETURN TO HOENN WITH THE ORBS TO BECOME ONE WITH KYOGRE AND GROUDON ONCE AGAIN."

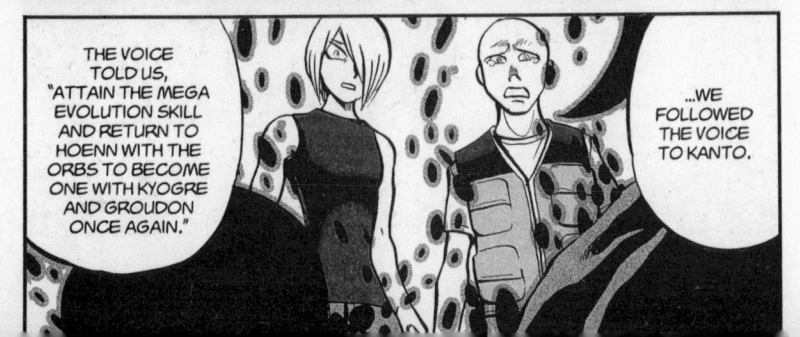

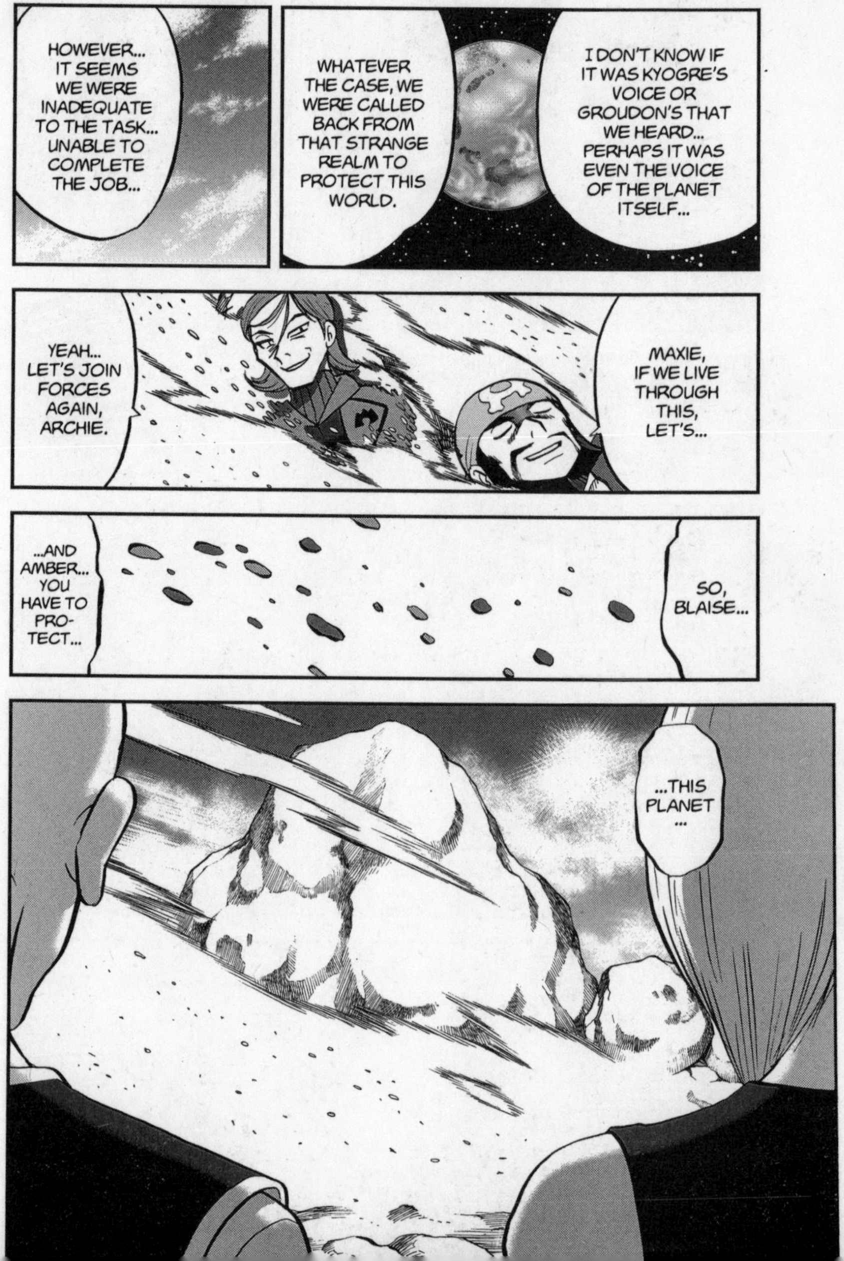
I DON'T KNOW IF IT WAS KYOGRE'S VOICE OR GROUDON'S THAT WE HEARD... PERHAPS IT WAS EVEN THE VOICE OF THE PLANET ITSELF...
WHATEVER THE CASE, WE WERE CALLED BACK FROM THAT STRANGE REALM TO PROTECT THIS WORLD.
HOWEVER... IT SEEMS WE WERE INADEQUATE TO THE TASK... UNABLE TO COMPLETE THE JOB...
MAXIE, IF WE LIVE THROUGH THIS, LET'S...
YEAH... LET'S JOIN FORCES AGAIN, ARCHIE.
SO, BLAISE...
...AND AMBER... YOU HAVE TO PRO-TECT...
...THIS PLANET ...

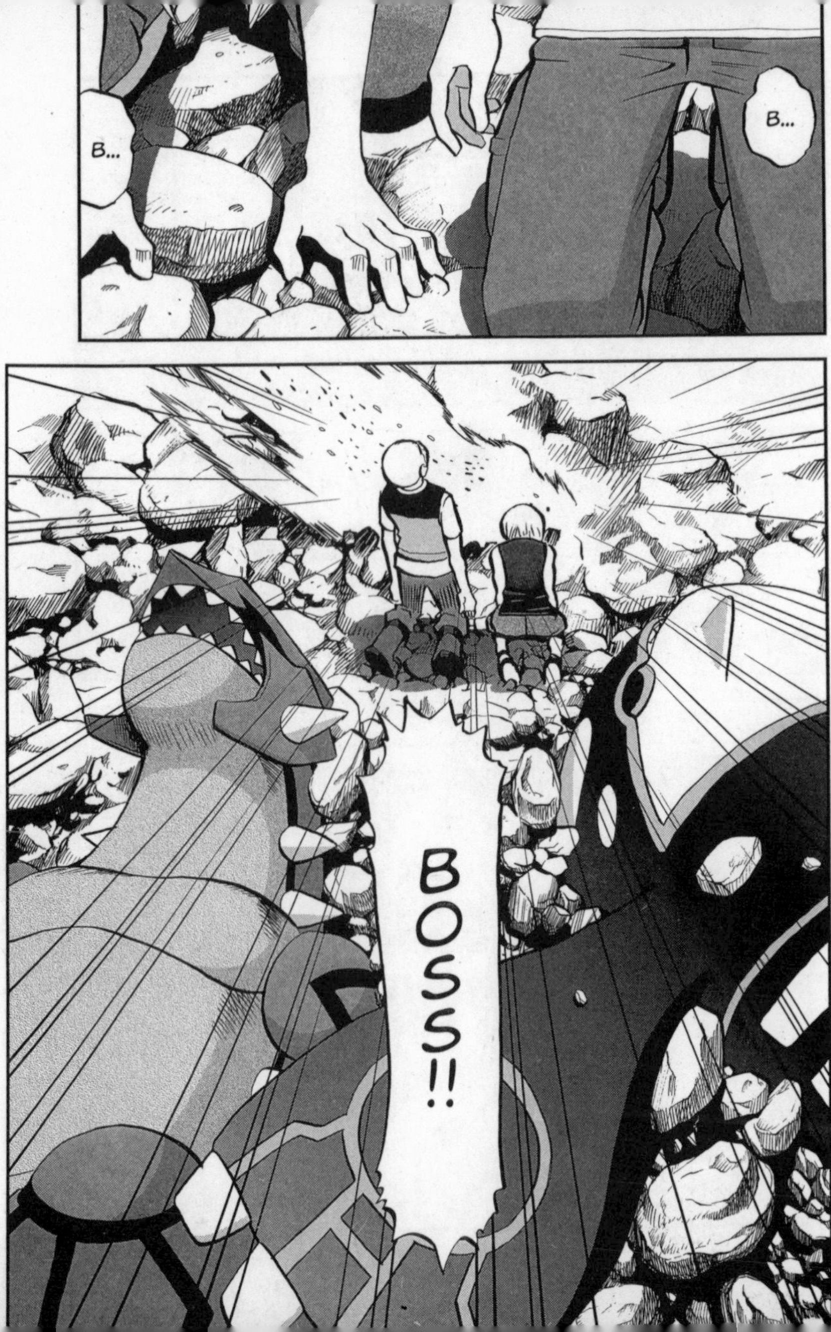
B...
B...
BOSS!!

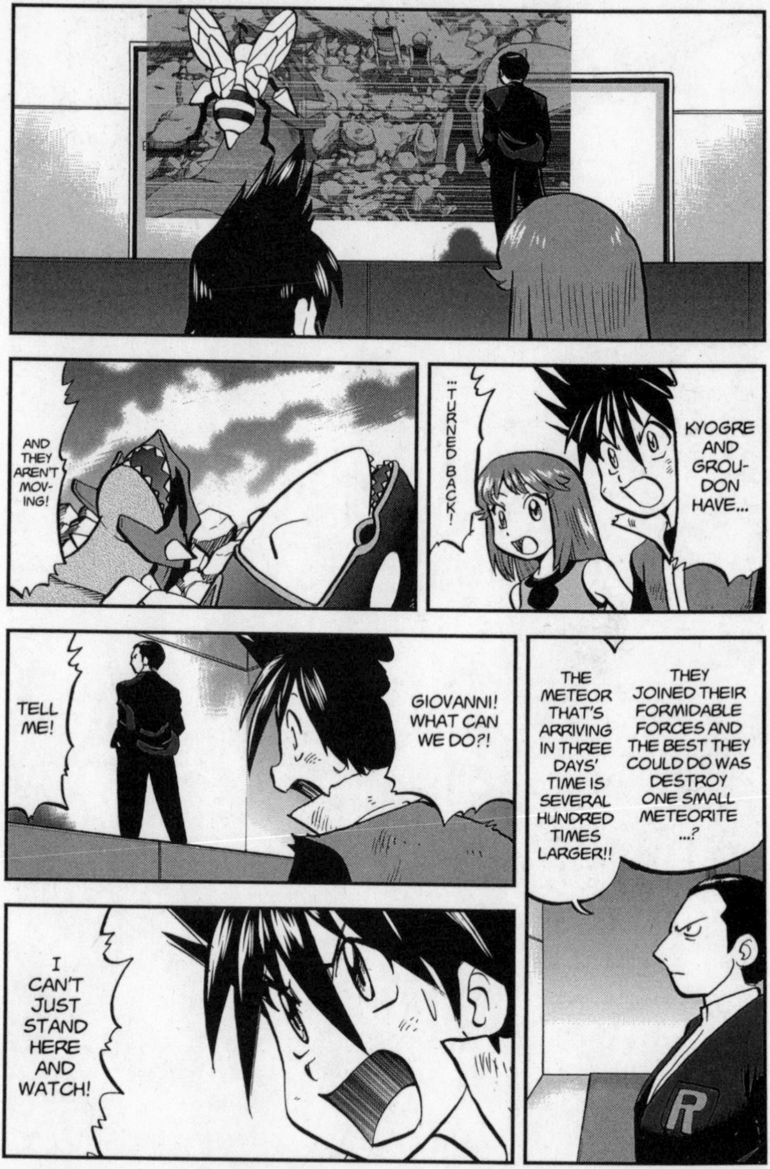
KYOGRE AND GROU-DON HAVE...
...TURNED BACK!
AND THEY AREN'T MOV-ING!
THEY JOINED THEIR FORMIDABLE FORCES AND THE BEST THEY COULD DO WAS DESTROY ONE SMALL METEORITE ...?
THE METEOR THAT'S ARRIVING IN THREE DAYS' TIME IS SEVERAL HUNDRED TIMES LARGER!!
GIOVANNI! WHAT CAN WE DO?!
TELL ME!
I CAN'T JUST STAND HERE AND WATCH!

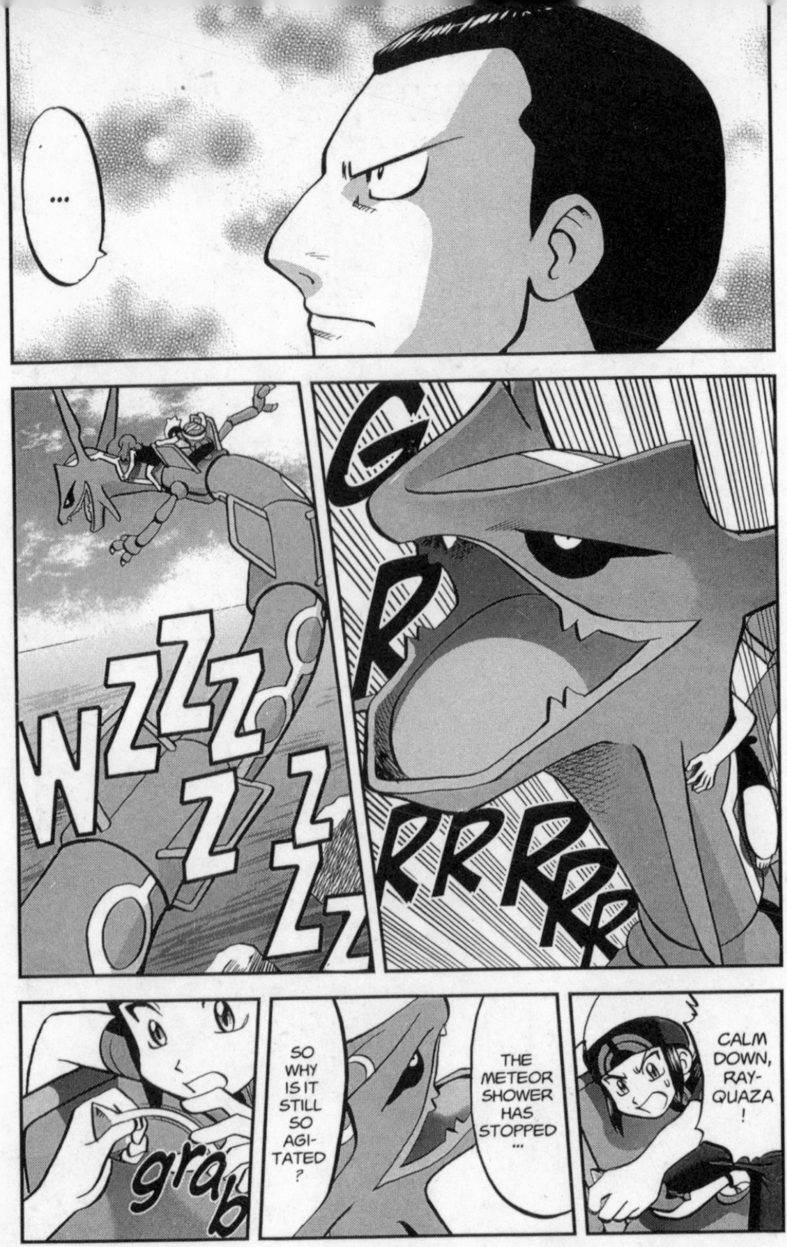
...
GRRRRRRR
WZZZZZZZZ
CALM DOWN, RAY-QUAZA!
THE METEOR SHOWER HAS STOPPED...
SO WHY IS IT STILL SO AGI-TATED?
grab

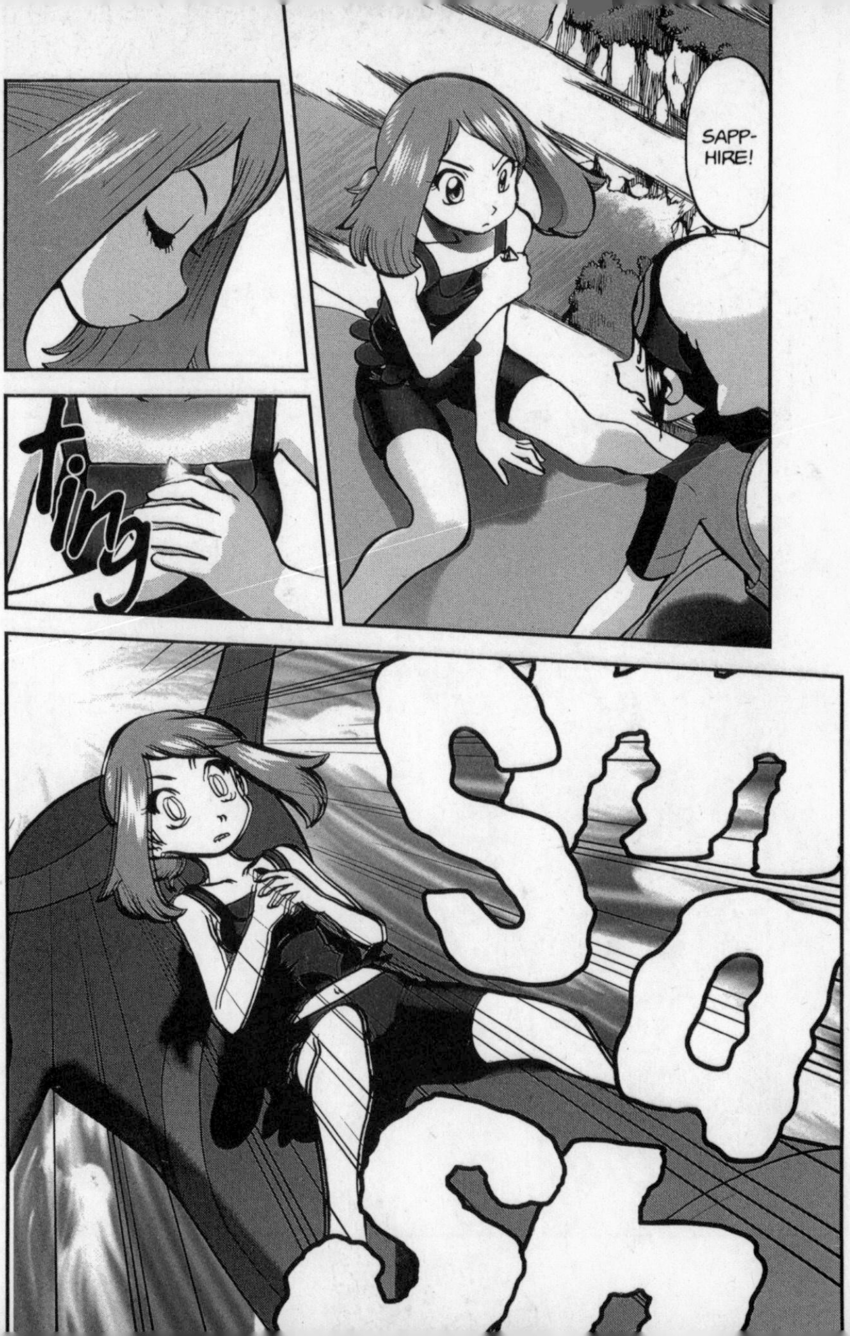
SAPP-
HIRE!
ting

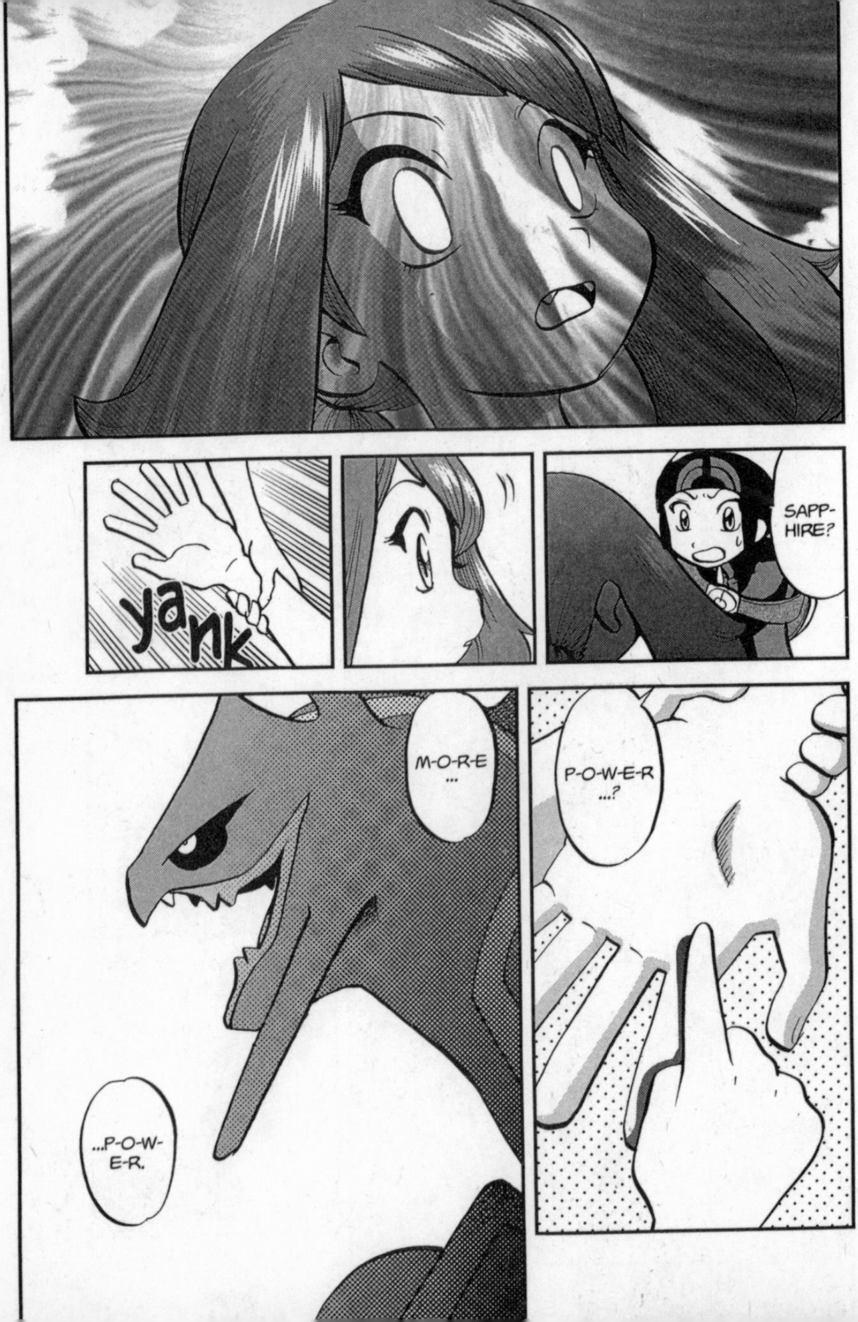
SAPP-
HIRE?
yank
P-O-W-E-R
...?
M-O-R-E
...
...P-O-W-
E-R.

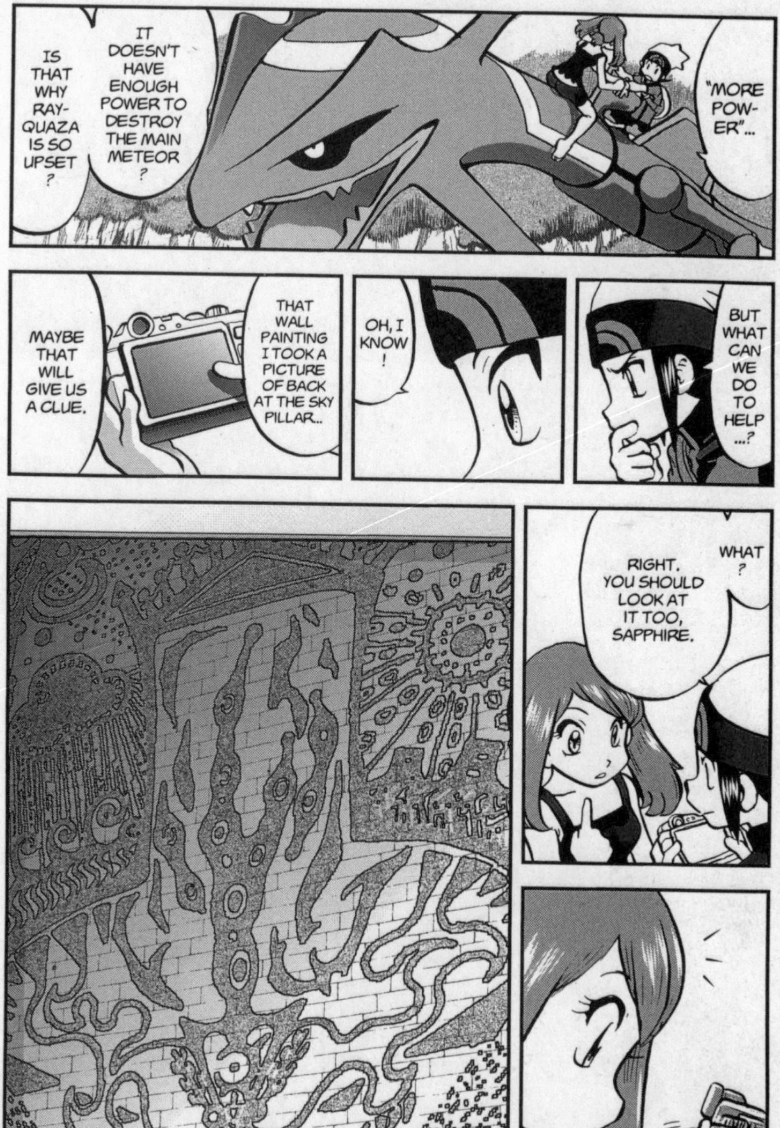
"MORE POW-ER"...
IT DOESN'T HAVE ENOUGH POWER TO DESTROY THE MAIN METEOR?
IS THAT WHY RAY-QUAZA IS SO UPSET?
BUT WHAT CAN WE DO TO HELP...?
OH, I KNOW!
THAT WALL PAINTING I TOOK A PICTURE OF BACK AT THE SKY PILLAR..
MAYBE THAT WILL GIVE US A CLUE.
WHAT?
RIGHT. YOU SHOULD LOOK AT IT TOO, SAPPHIRE.

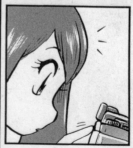

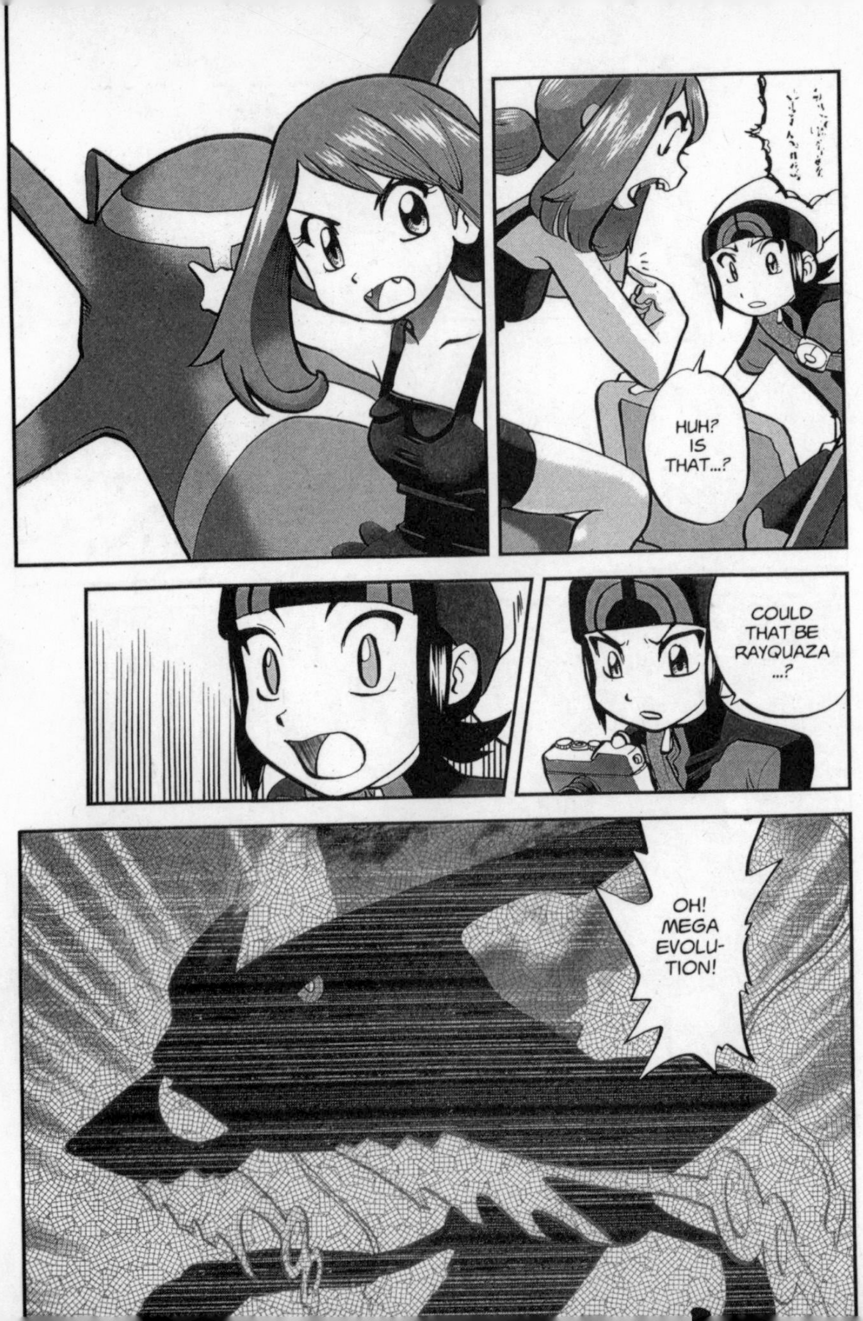
HUH? IS THAT...?
COULD THAT BE RAYQUAZA ...?
OH! MEGA EVOLU- TION!

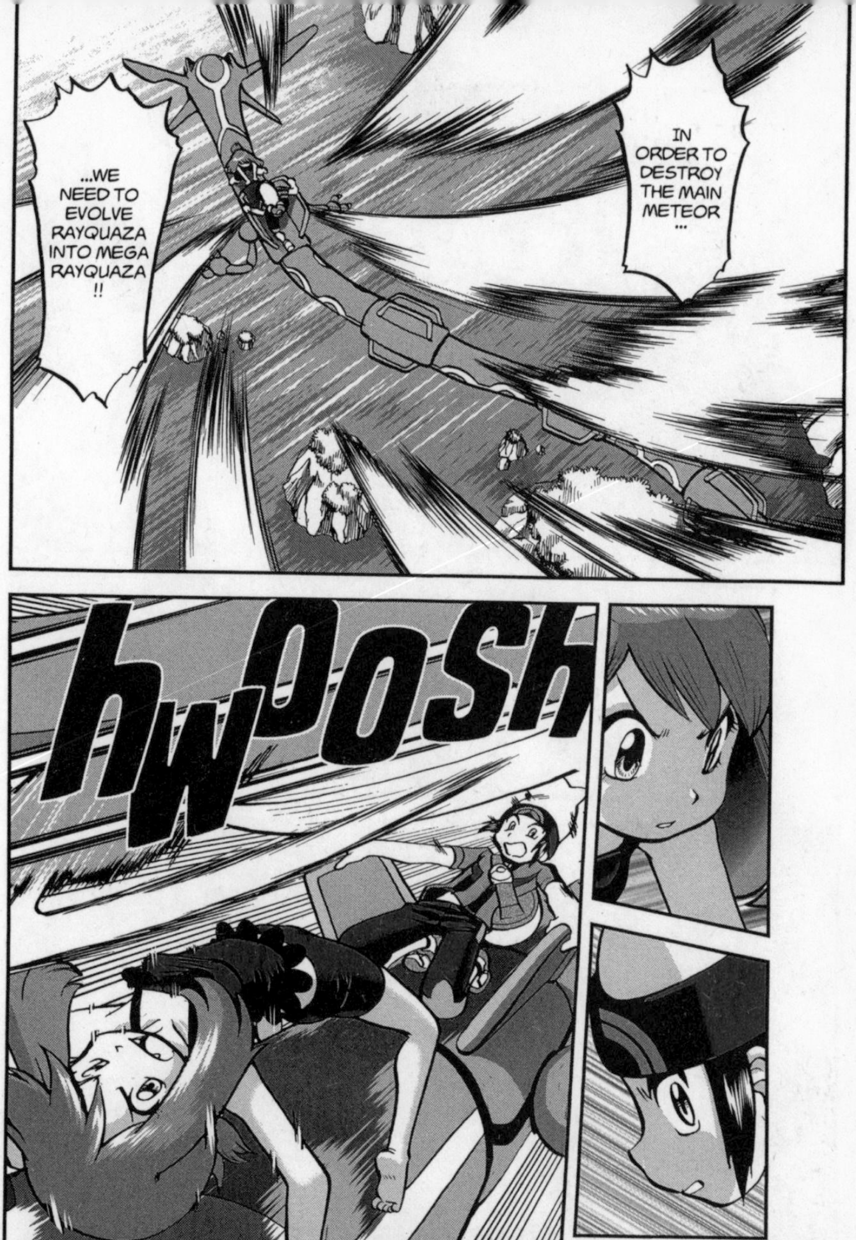
IN ORDER TO DESTROY THE MAIN METEOR ...
...WE NEED TO EVOLVE RAYQUAZA INTO MEGA RAYQUAZA !!
hwoosh

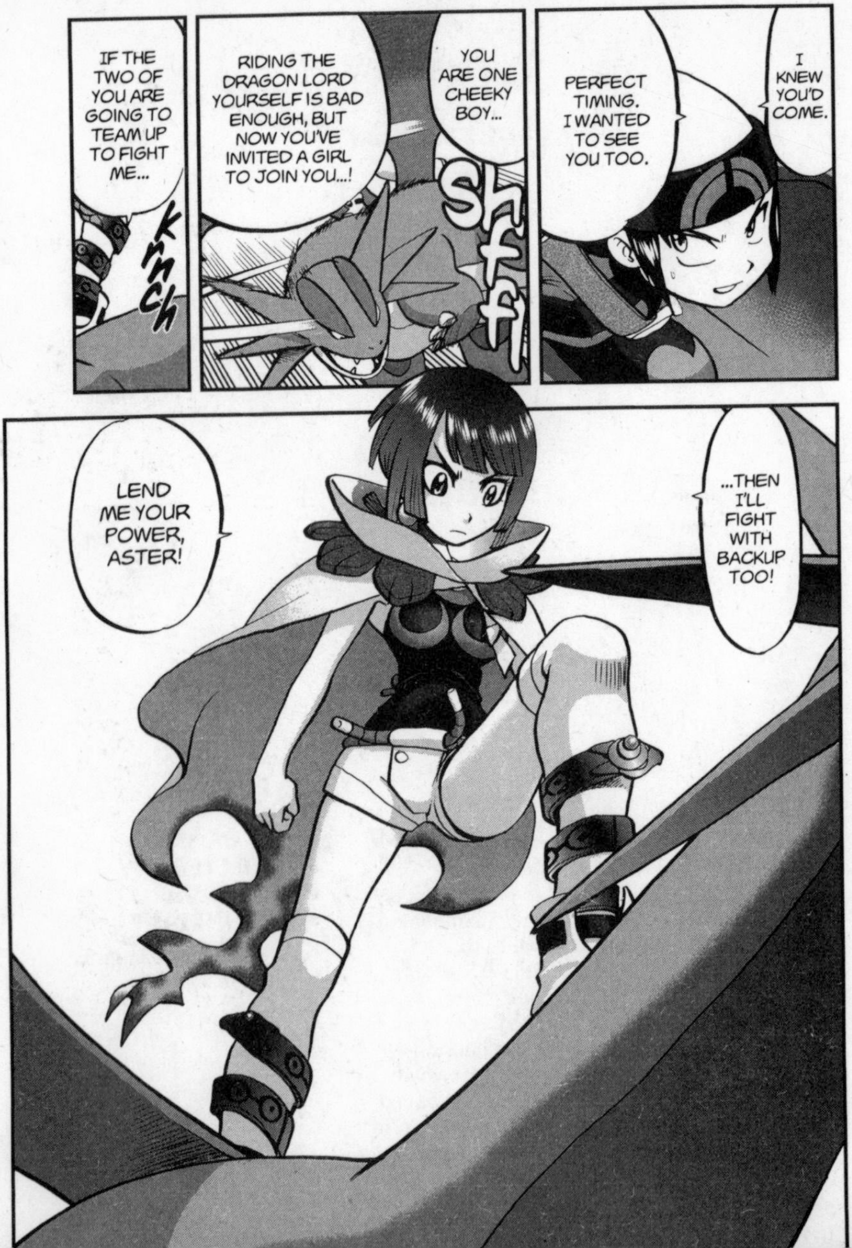
I KNEW YOU'D COME.
PERFECT TIMING. I WANTED TO SEE YOU TOO.
YOU ARE ONE CHEEKY BOY...
RIDING THE DRAGON LORD YOURSELF IS BAD ENOUGH, BUT NOW YOU'VE INVITED A GIRL TO JOIN YOU...!
Shff
IF THE TWO OF YOU ARE GOING TO TEAM UP TO FIGHT ME...
Krnch
...THEN I'LL FIGHT WITH BACKUP TOO!
LEND ME YOUR POWER, ASTER!

## THE DISTORTION WORLD

An alternate realm in which the common laws of this world have no meaning. There is a theory that it was named the Distortion World because it distorts reality and the five senses. It is a world that cannot be comprehended through logic. It is sometimes called "the Other Side of This World" or "the Antimatter World."

## A SUIT OF ARMOR NAMED ETERNITY AND A SWORD NAMED INSTANT

Archie and Maxie fought over these objects.

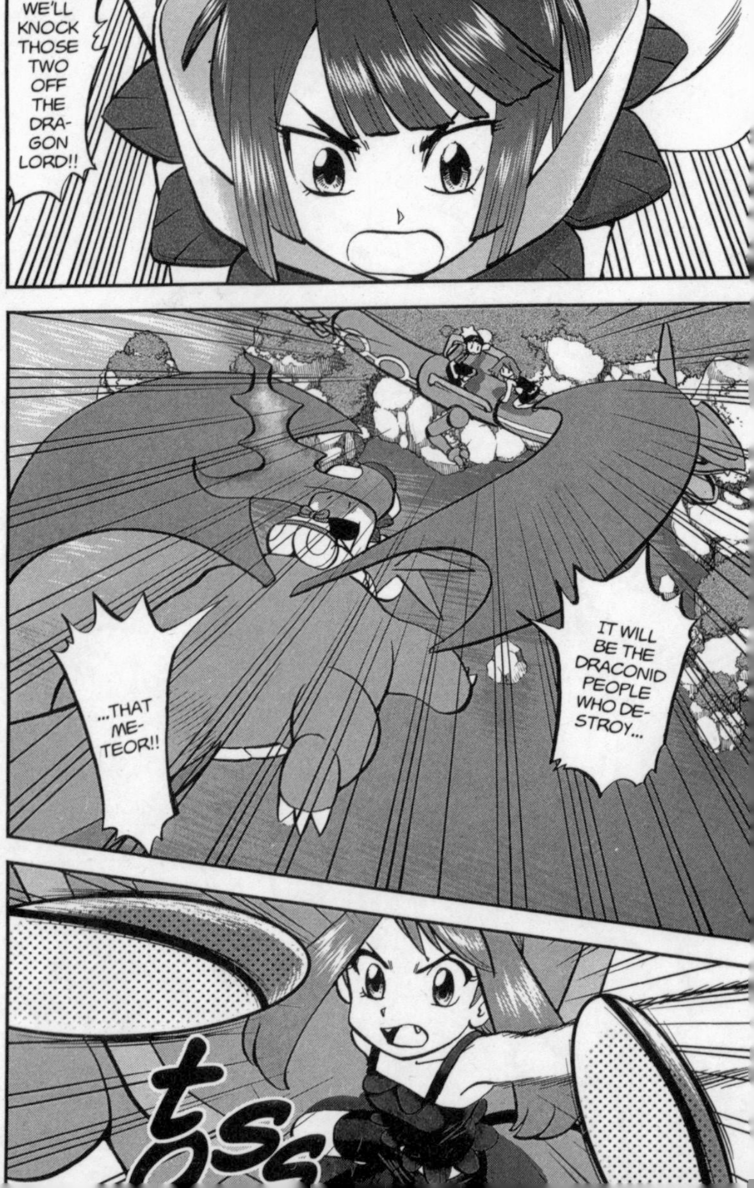
WE'LL KNOCK THOSE TWO OFF THE DRA-GON LORD!!
IT WILL BE THE DRACONID PEOPLE WHO DE-STROY...
...THAT ME-TEOR!!

# Omega Alpha Adventure 19

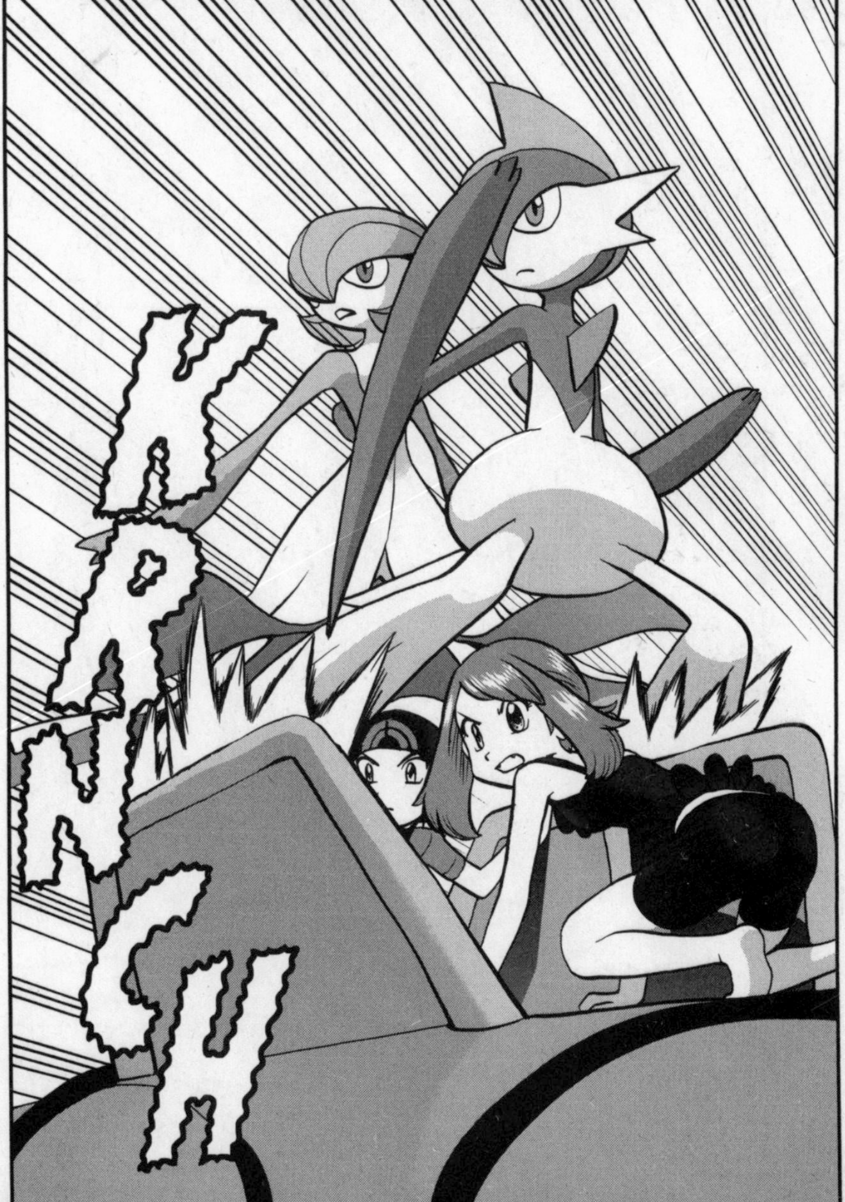

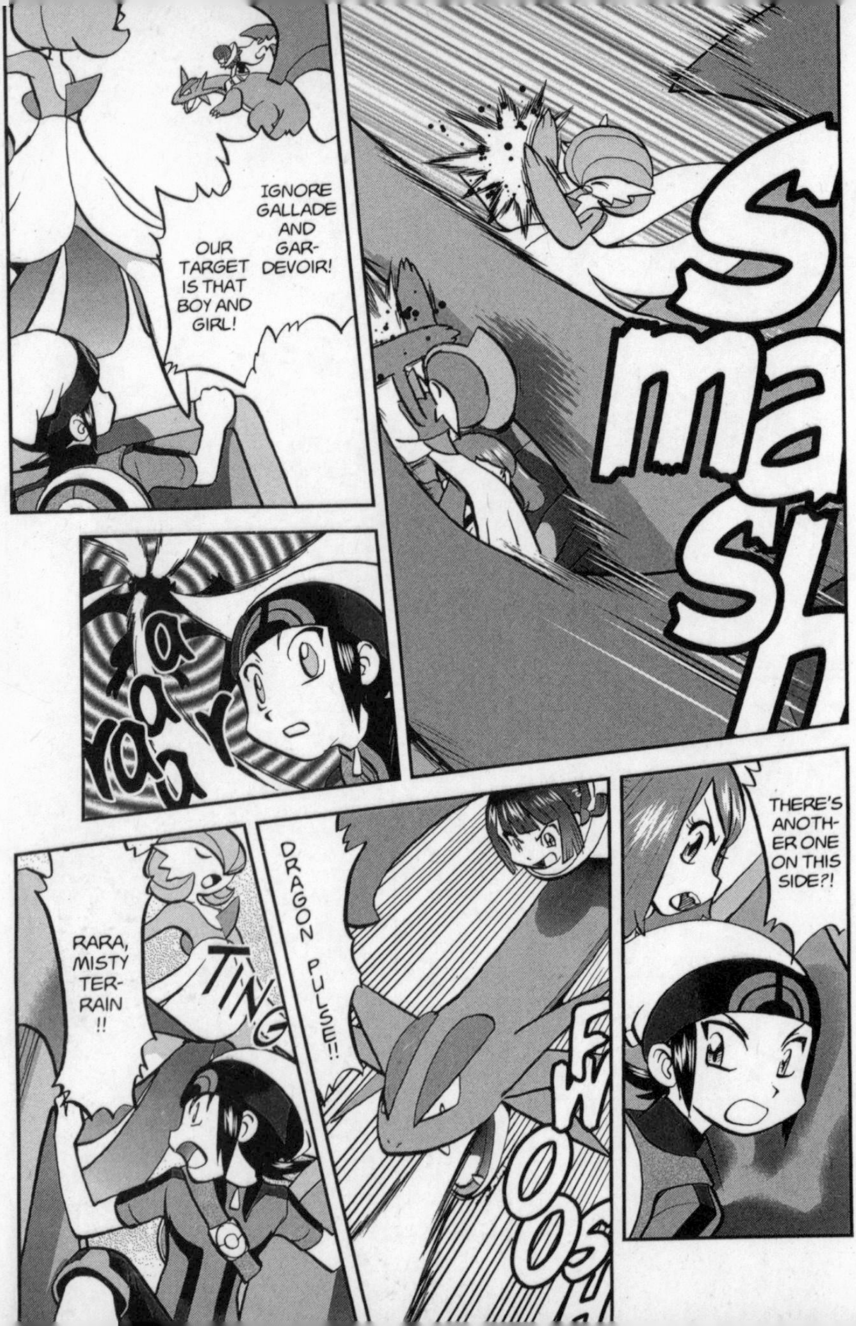
IGNORE GALLADE AND GAR-DEVOIR!
OUR TARGET IS THAT BOY AND GIRL!
THERE'S ANOTH-ER ONE ON THIS SIDE?!
DRAGON PULSE!!
RARA, MISTY TER-RAIN!!
TING

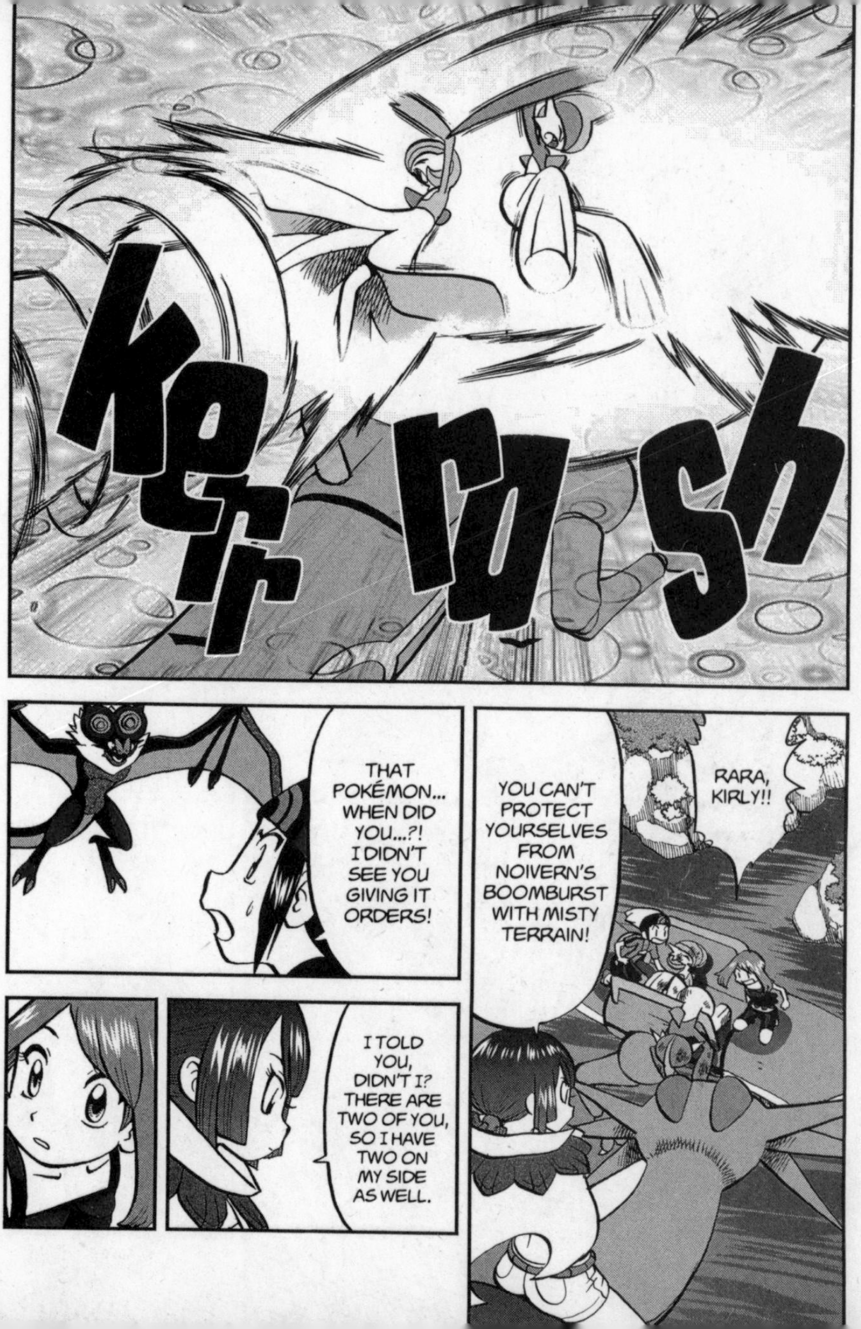
kerrrash
RARA, KIRLY!!
YOU CAN'T PROTECT YOURSELVES FROM NOIVERN'S BOOMBURST WITH MISTY TERRAIN!
THAT POKÉMON... WHEN DID YOU...?! I DIDN'T SEE YOU GIVING IT ORDERS!
I TOLD YOU, DIDN'T I? THERE ARE TWO OF YOU, SO I HAVE TWO ON MY SIDE AS WELL.

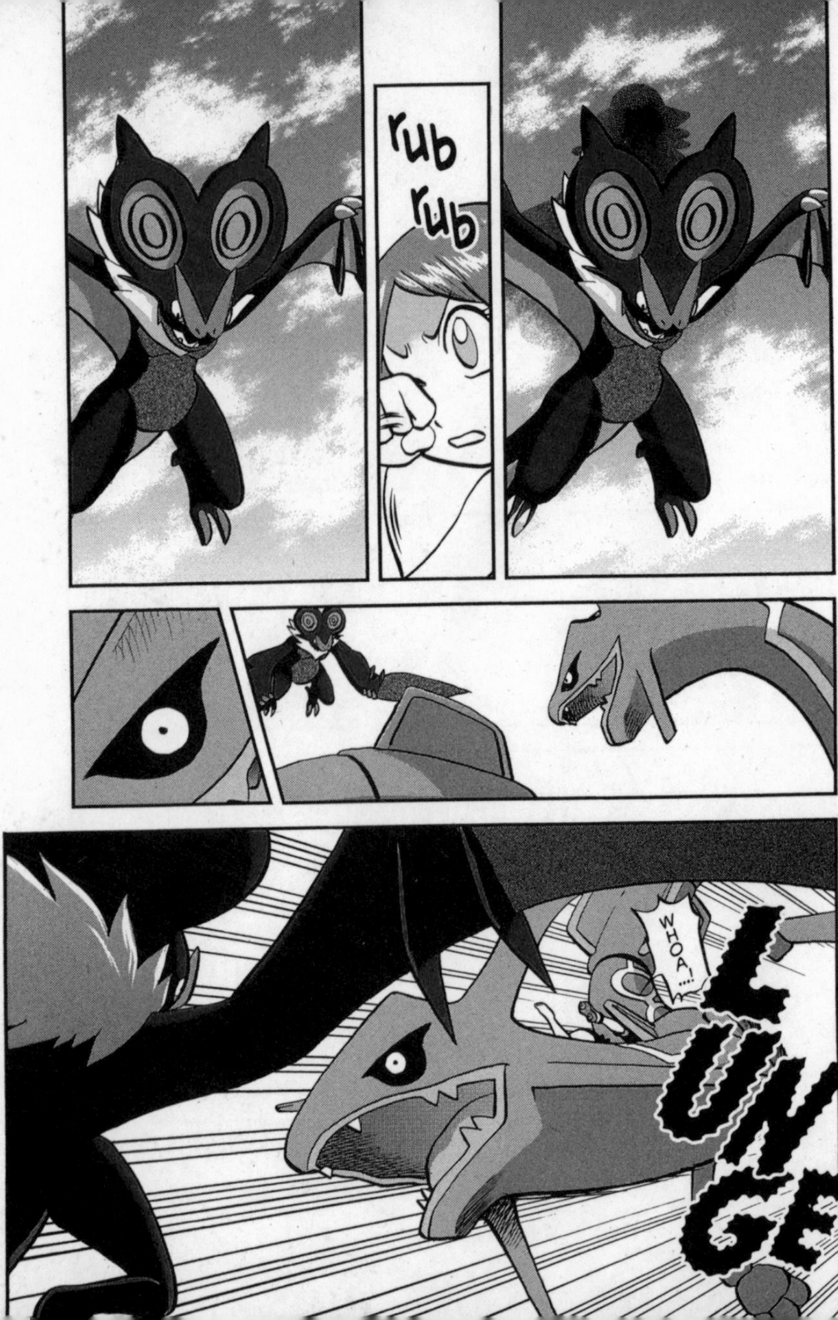
rub
rub
WHOA...!
LUNGE

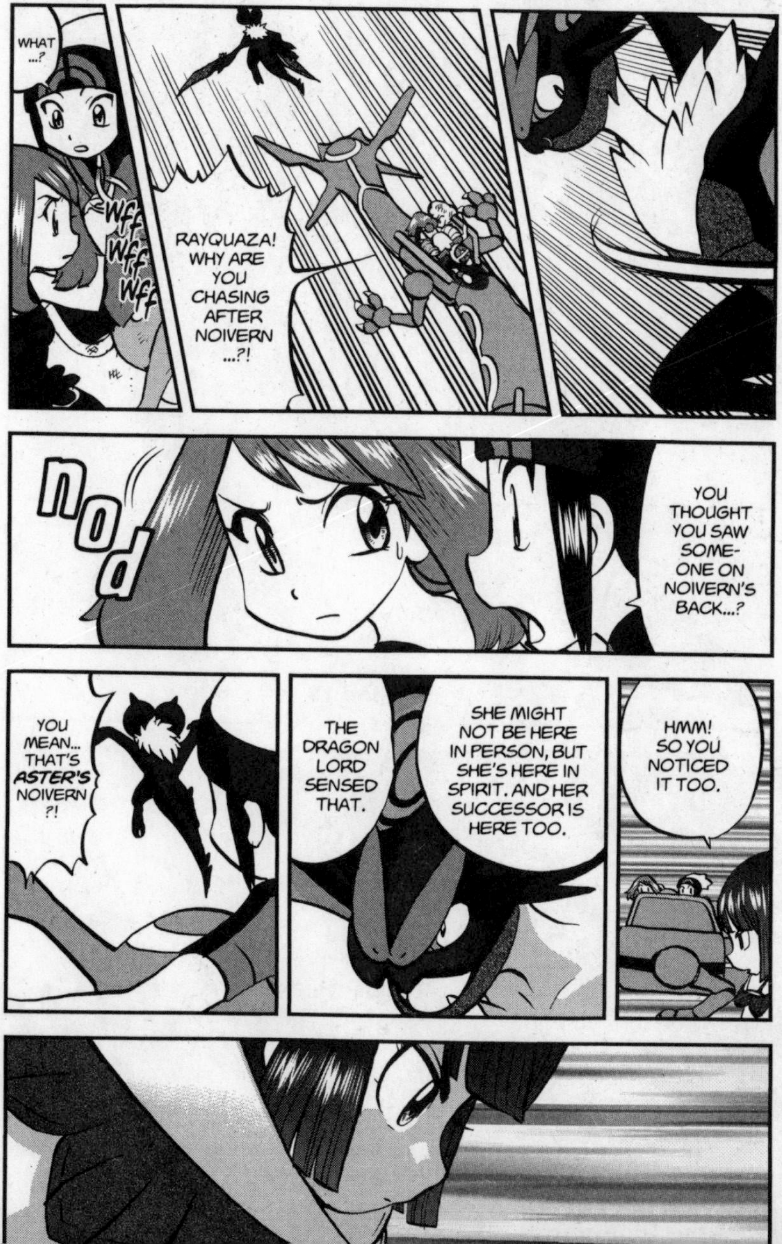
RAYQUAZA! WHY ARE YOU CHASING AFTER NOIVERN ...?!
WHAT ...?
Wff Wff Wff
YOU THOUGHT YOU SAW SOME-ONE ON NOIVERN'S BACK...?
nod
HMM! SO YOU NOTICED IT TOO.
SHE MIGHT NOT BE HERE IN PERSON, BUT SHE'S HERE IN SPIRIT. AND HER SUCCESSOR IS HERE TOO.
THE DRAGON LORD SENSED THAT.
YOU MEAN... THAT'S ASTER'S NOIVERN ?!

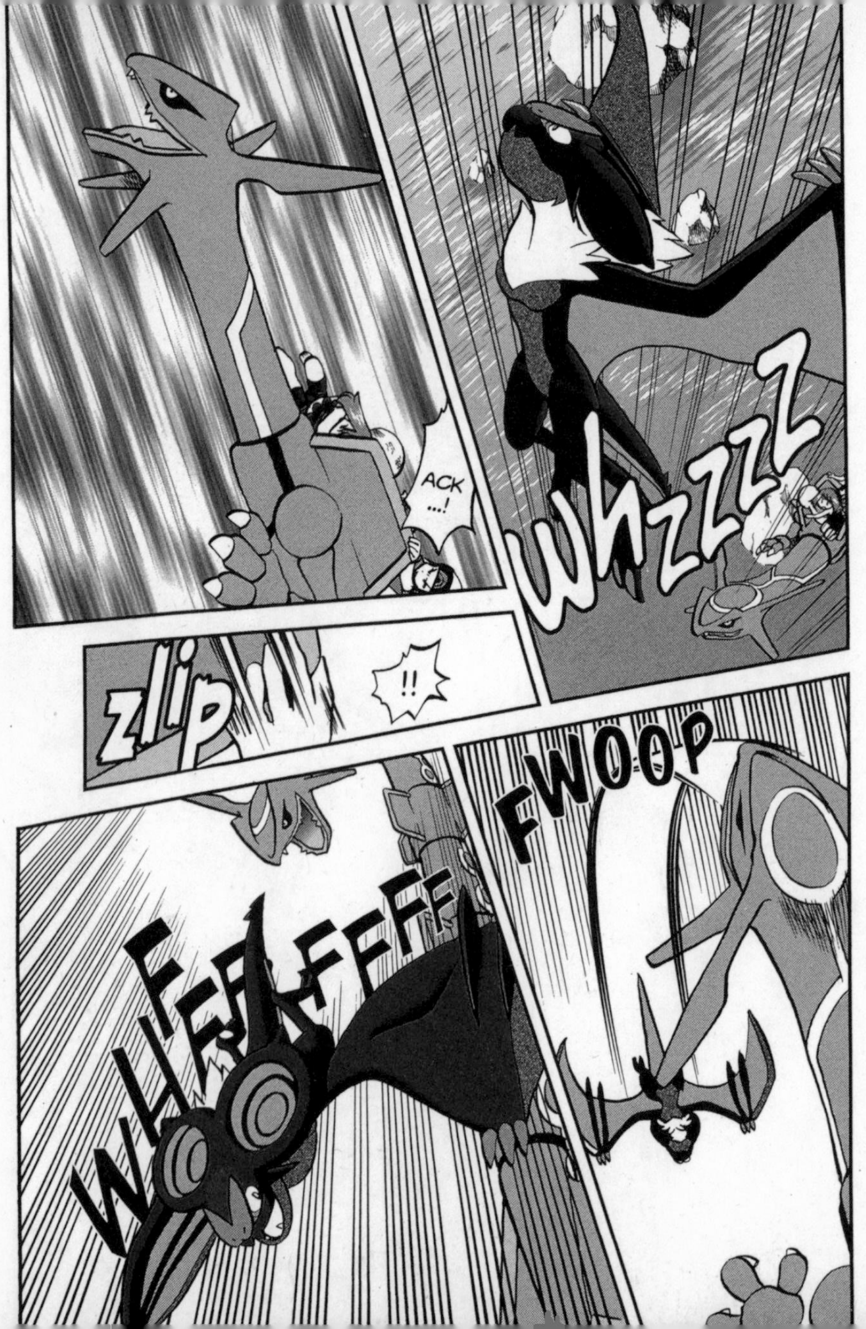
whzzzzz
ACK ...!
zlip
!!
FWOOP
WHRRFFFFF

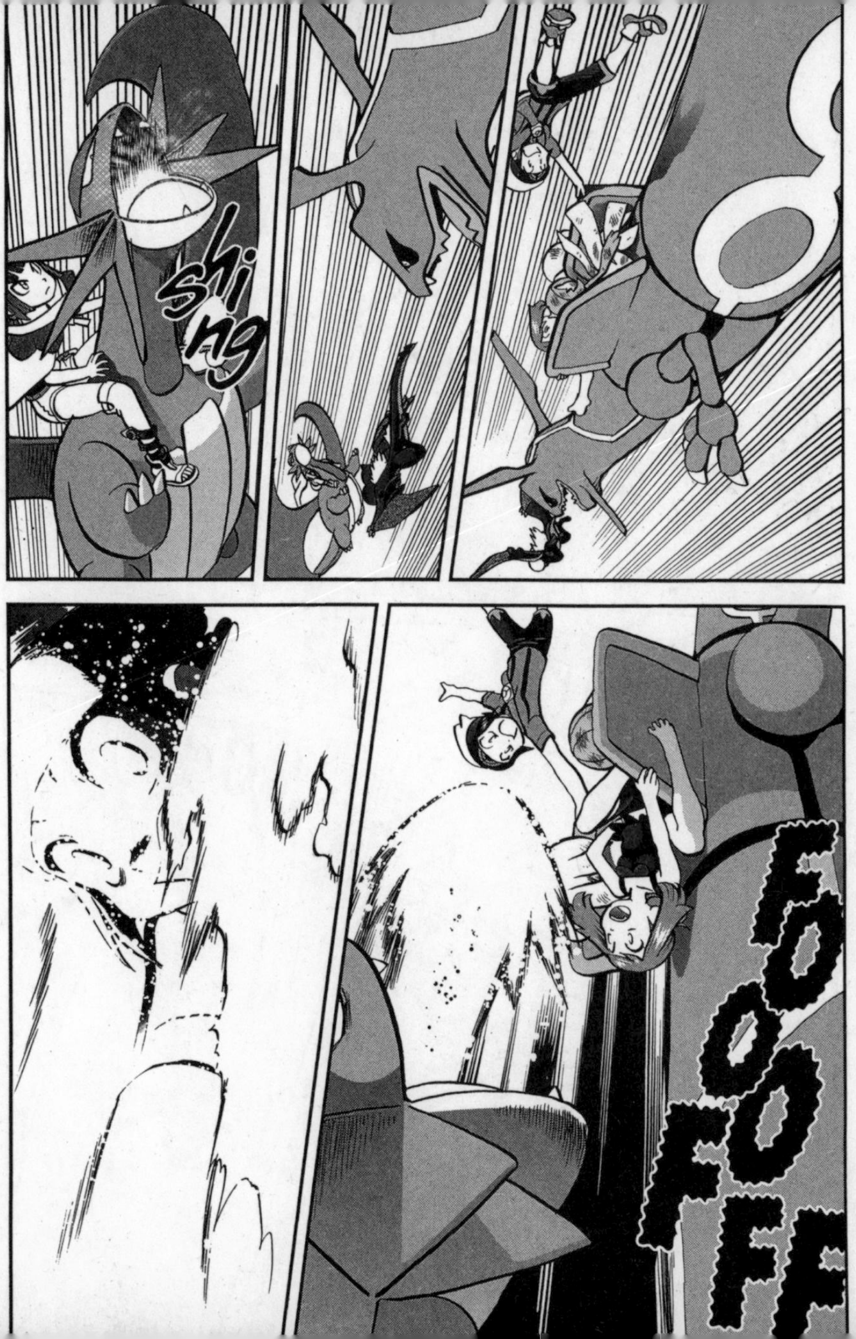
shing
FOOOFFF

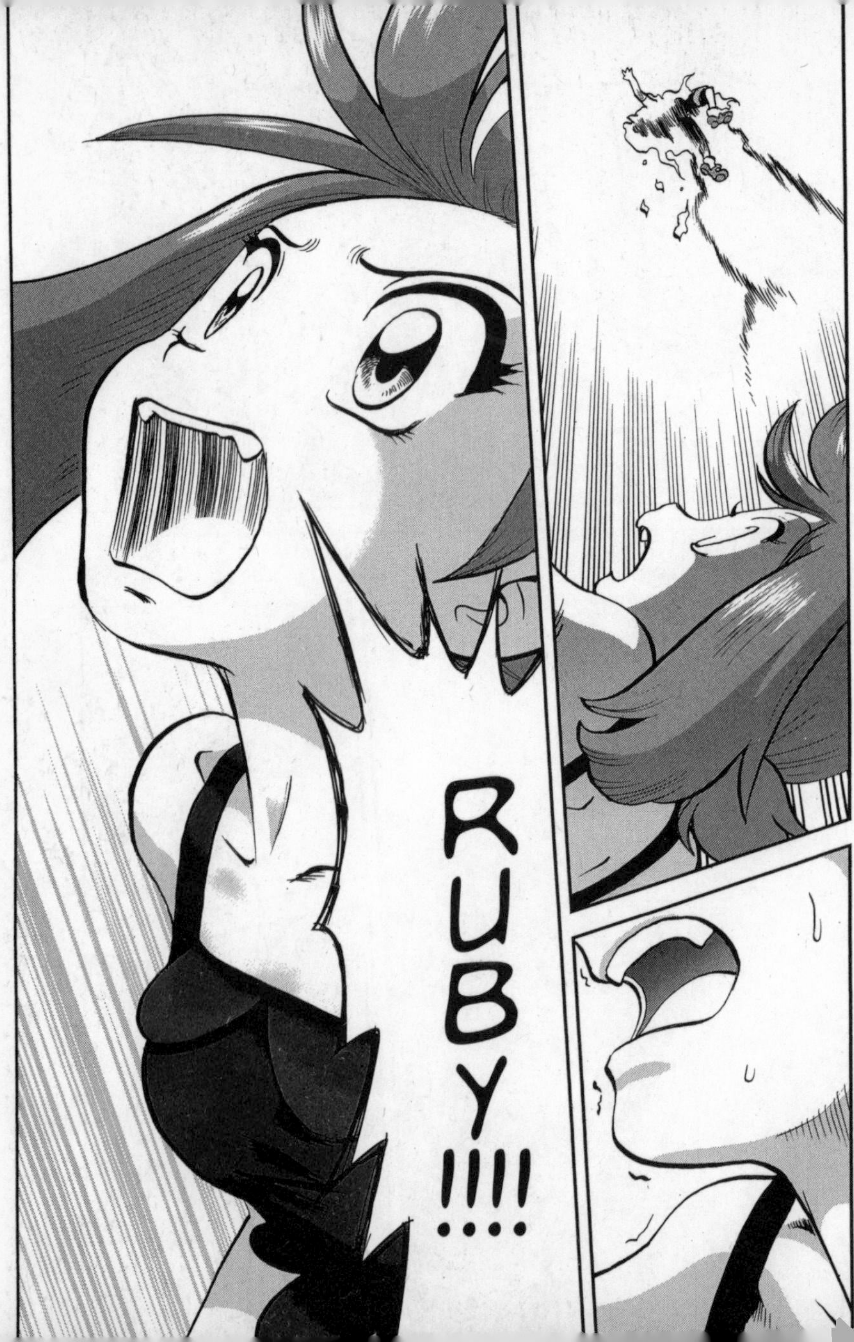
RUBY!!!!...

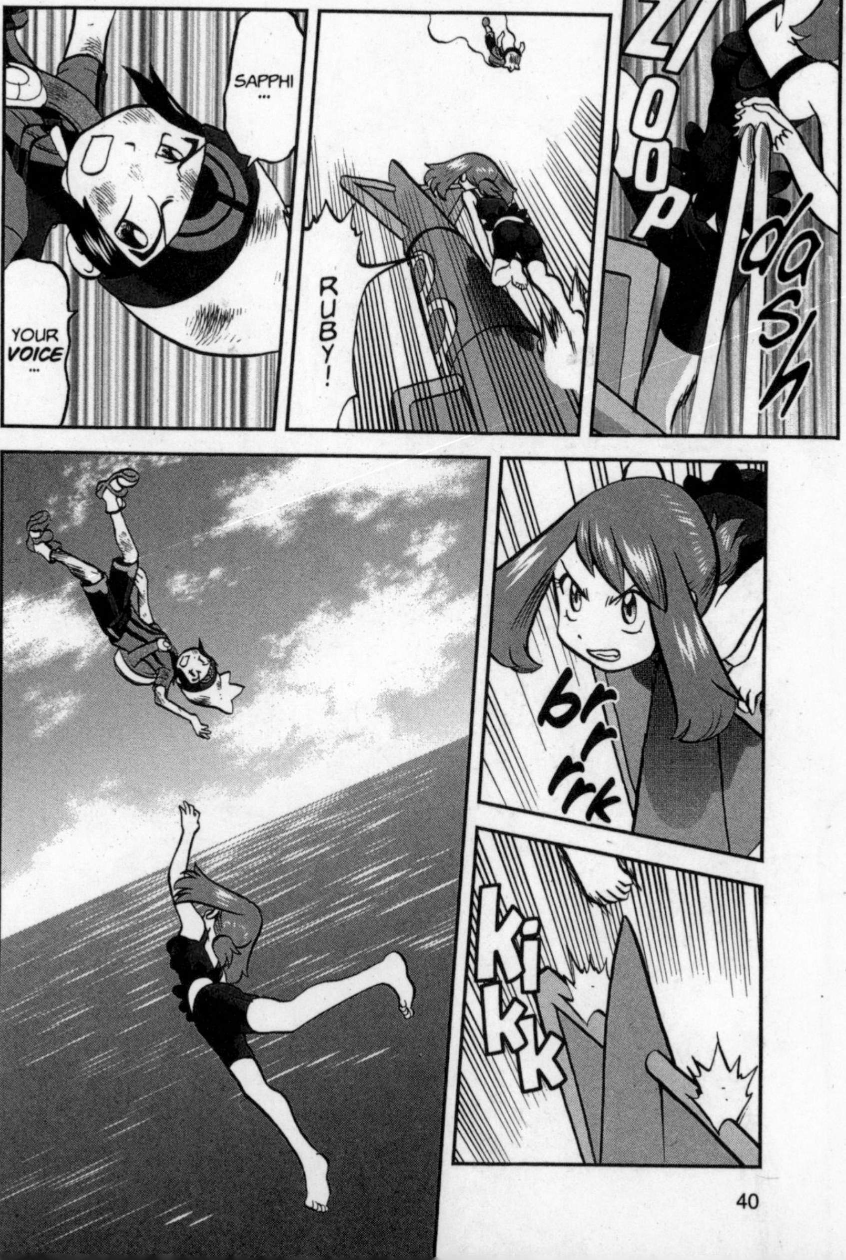
ZIOOP
dash
RUBY!
SAPPHI...
YOUR VOICE...
brrrrk
Kikkk

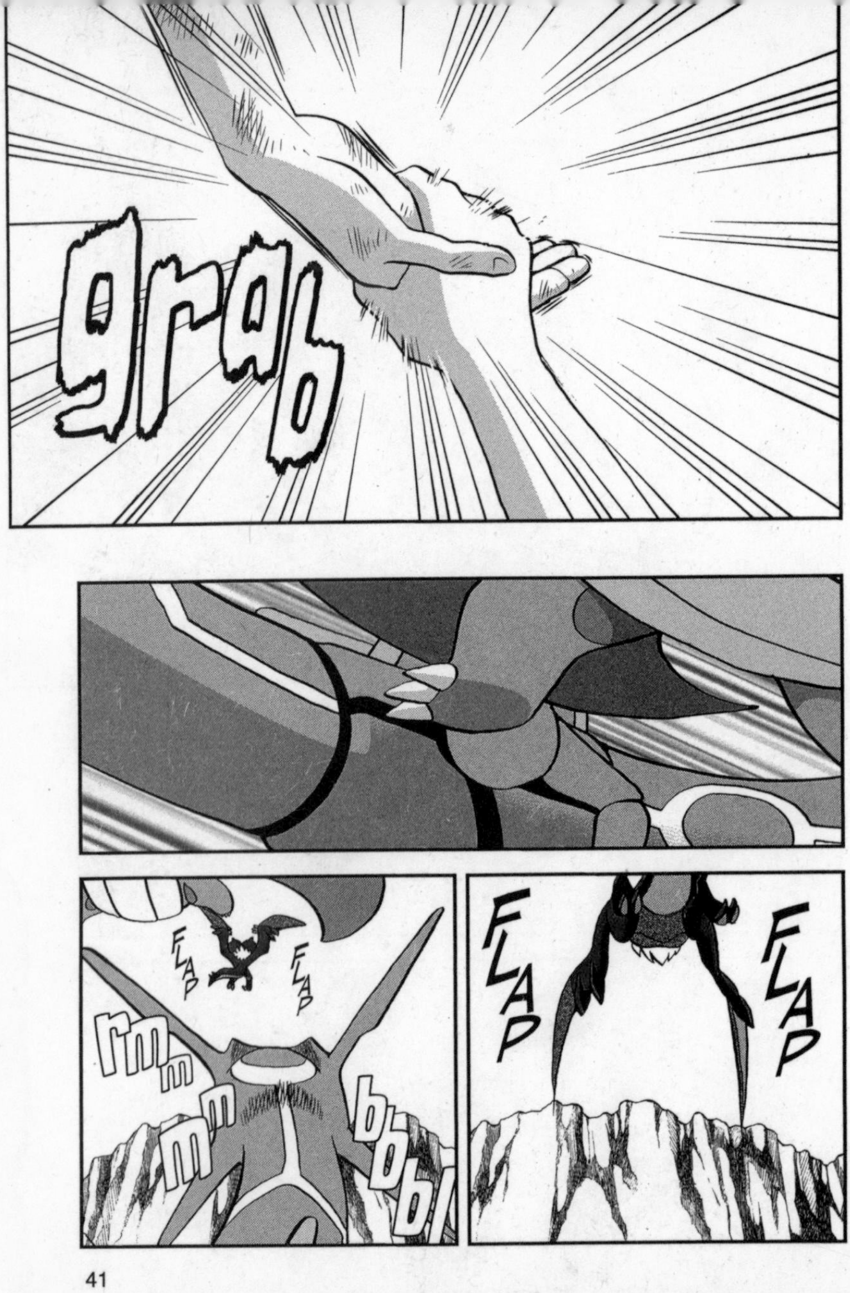
grab
FLAP
FLAP
FLAP
FLAP
rmmmm
bbbl

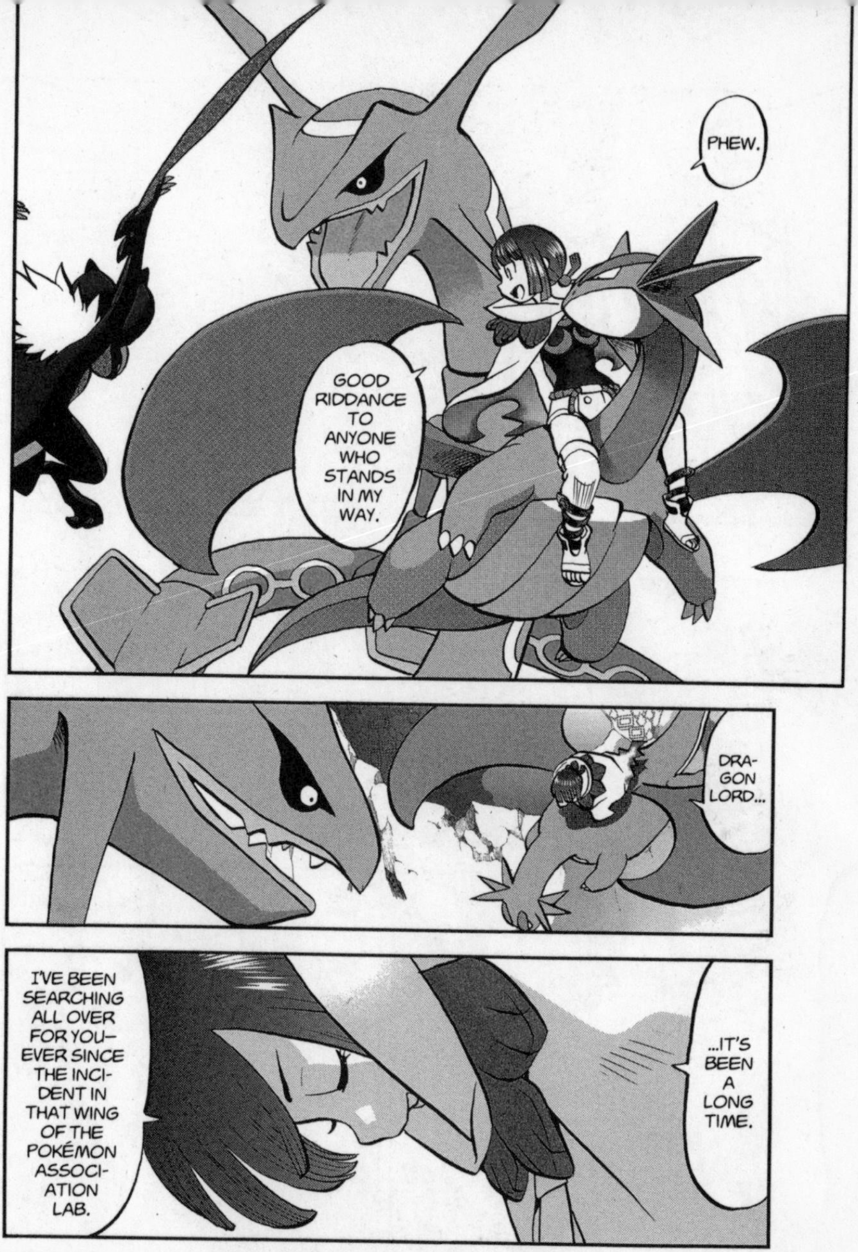
PHEW.
GOOD RIDDANCE TO ANYONE WHO STANDS IN MY WAY.
DRA-GON LORD...
...IT'S BEEN A LONG TIME.
I'VE BEEN SEARCHING ALL OVER FOR YOU—EVER SINCE THE INCI-DENT IN THAT WING OF THE POKÉMON ASSOCI-ATION LAB.

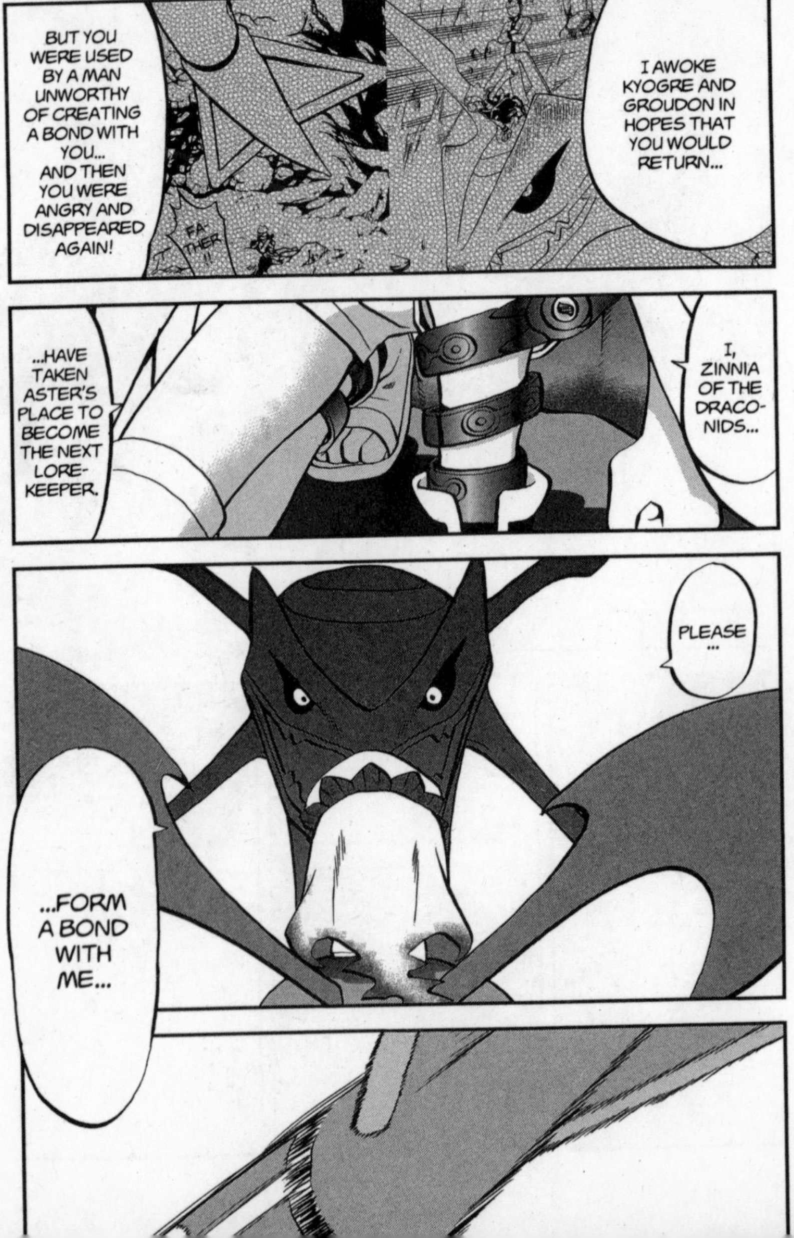
I AWOKE KYOGRE AND GROUDON IN HOPES THAT YOU WOULD RETURN...
BUT YOU WERE USED BY A MAN UNWORTHY OF CREATING A BOND WITH YOU... AND THEN YOU WERE ANGRY AND DISAPPEARED AGAIN!
FA-THER!!
I, ZINNIA OF THE DRACO-NIDS...
...HAVE TAKEN ASTER'S PLACE TO BECOME THE NEXT LORE-KEEPER.
PLEASE...
...FORM A BOND WITH ME...

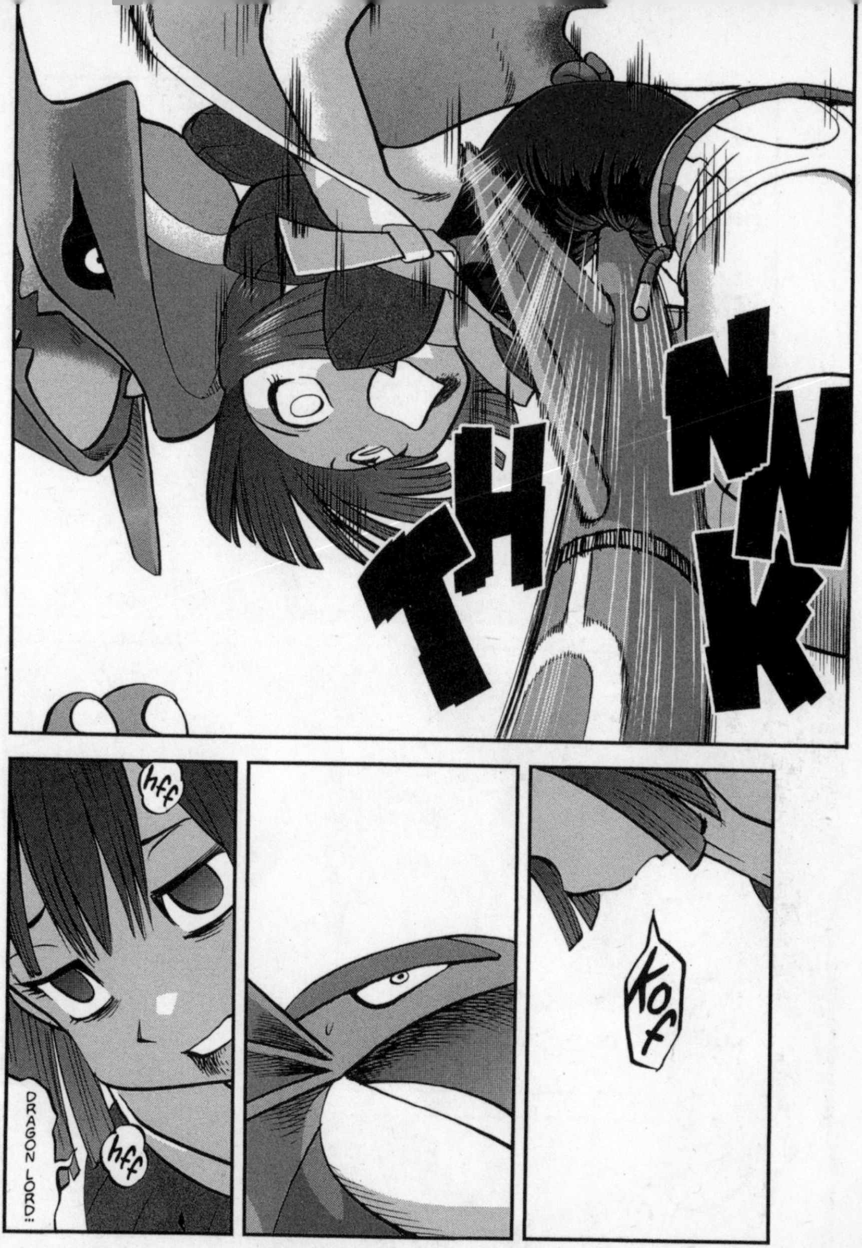
THNNK
kof
hff
hff
DRAGON LORD...!

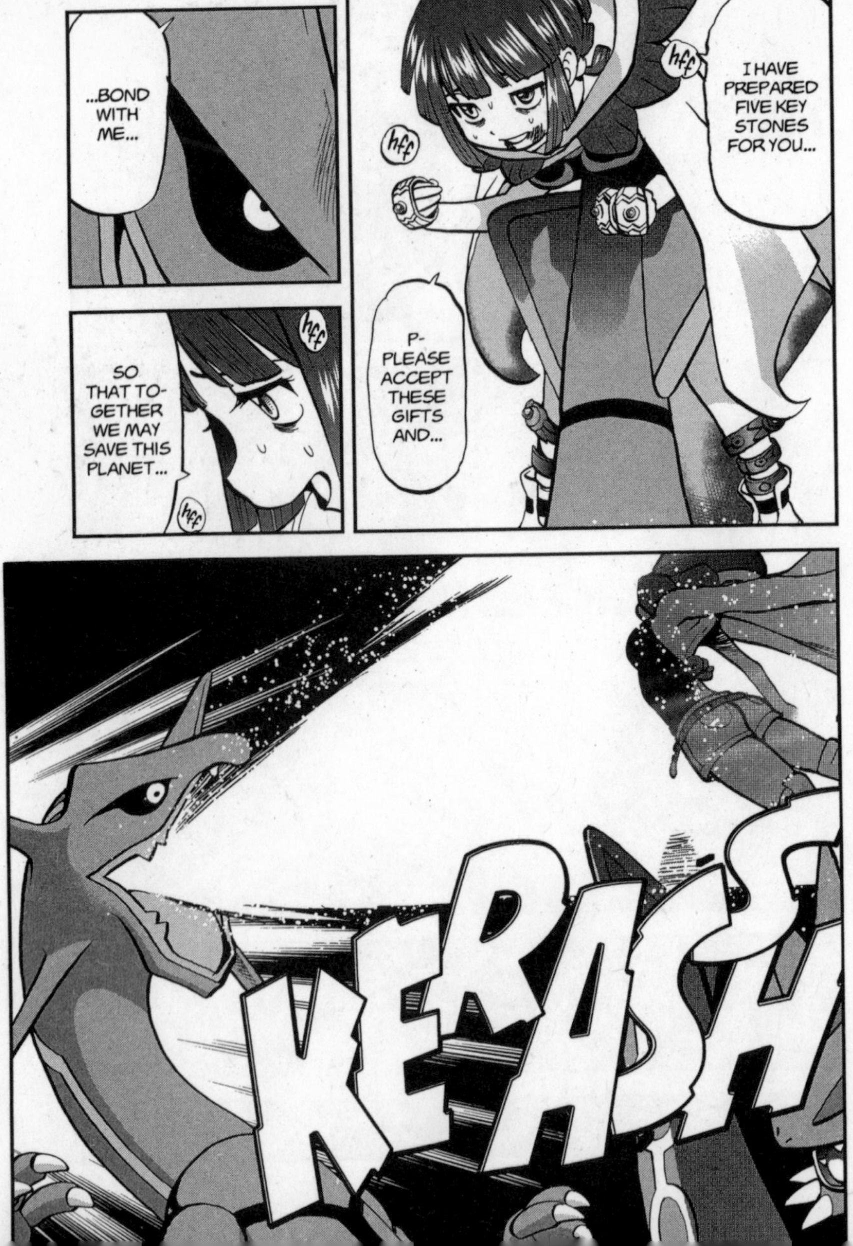
hff
I HAVE PREPARED FIVE KEY STONES FOR YOU...
hff
P-PLEASE ACCEPT THESE GIFTS AND...
...BOND WITH ME...
hff
SO THAT TO-GETHER WE MAY SAVE THIS PLANET...
hff
KERASH

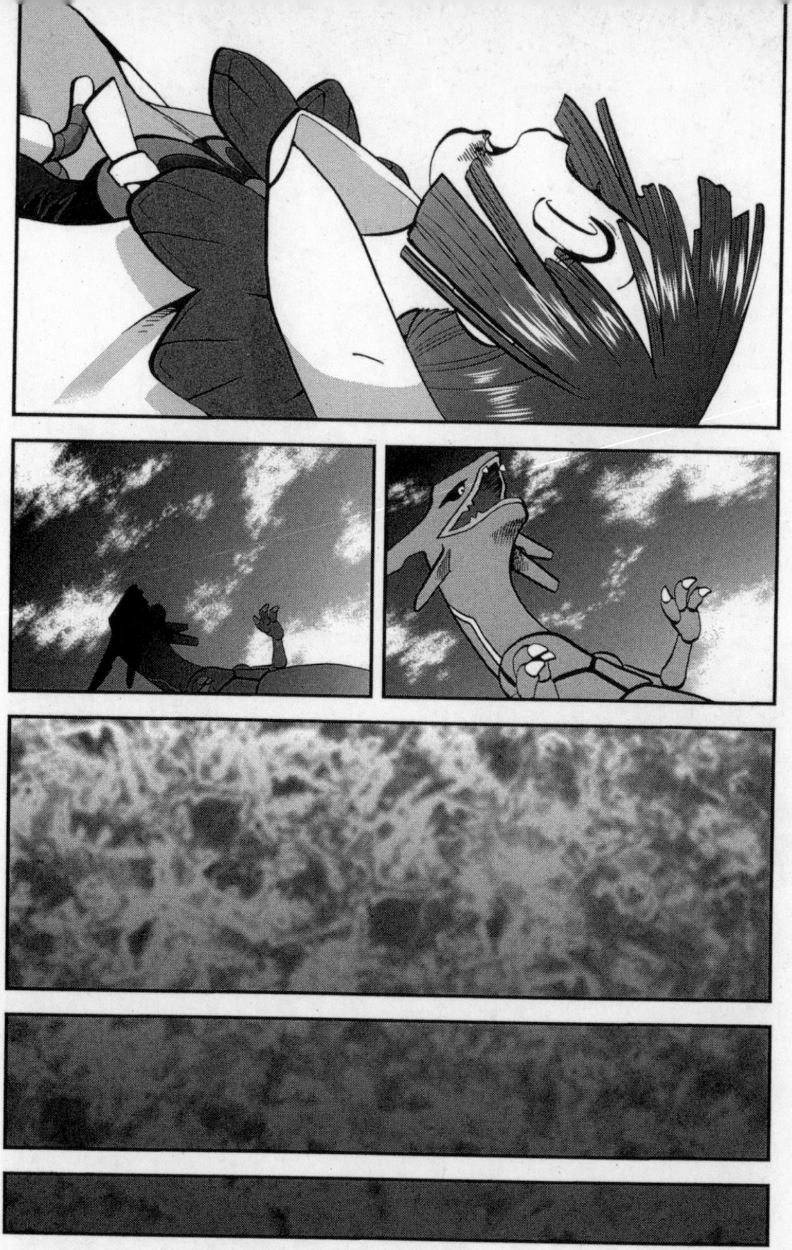

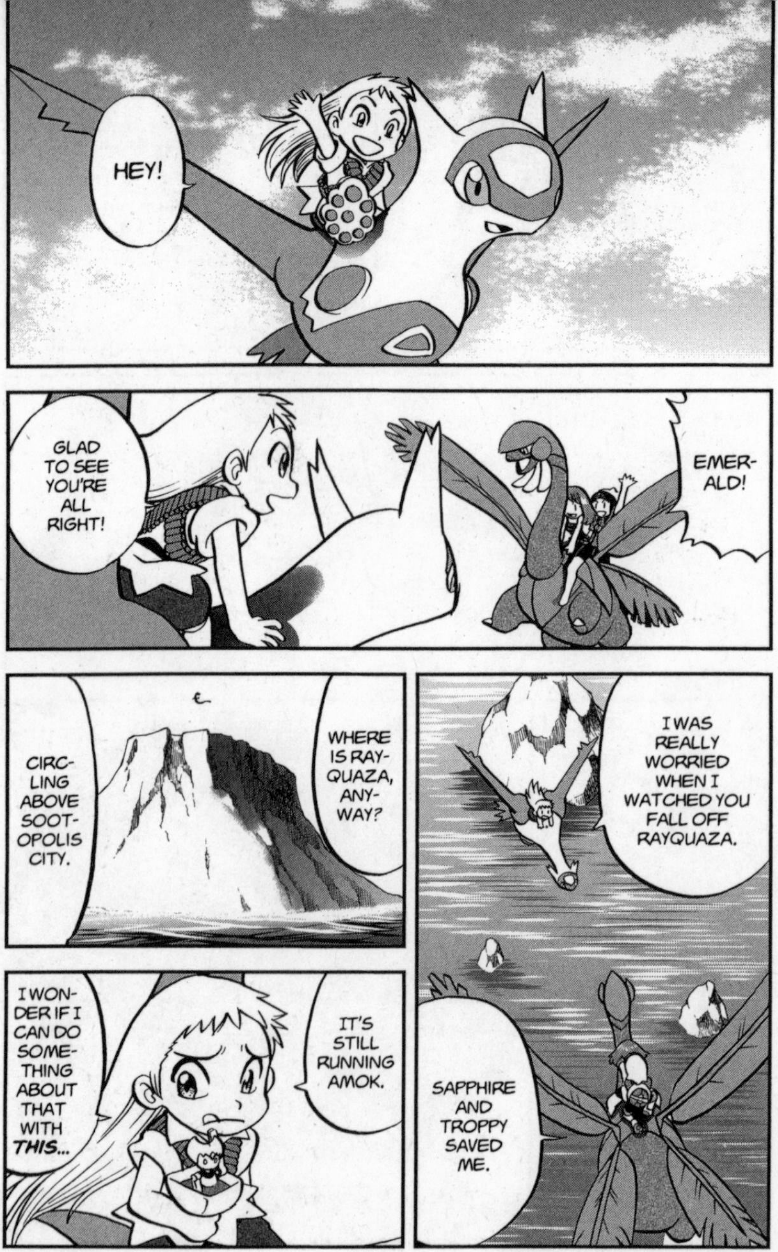
HEY!
EMERALD!
GLAD TO SEE YOU'RE ALL RIGHT!
I WAS REALLY WORRIED WHEN I WATCHED YOU FALL OFF RAYQUAZA.
SAPPHIRE AND TROPPY SAVED ME.
WHERE IS RAYQUAZA, ANYWAY?
CIRCLING ABOVE SOOTOPOLIS CITY.
IT'S STILL RUNNING AMOK.
I WONDER IF I CAN DO SOMETHING ABOUT THAT WITH ***THIS***...

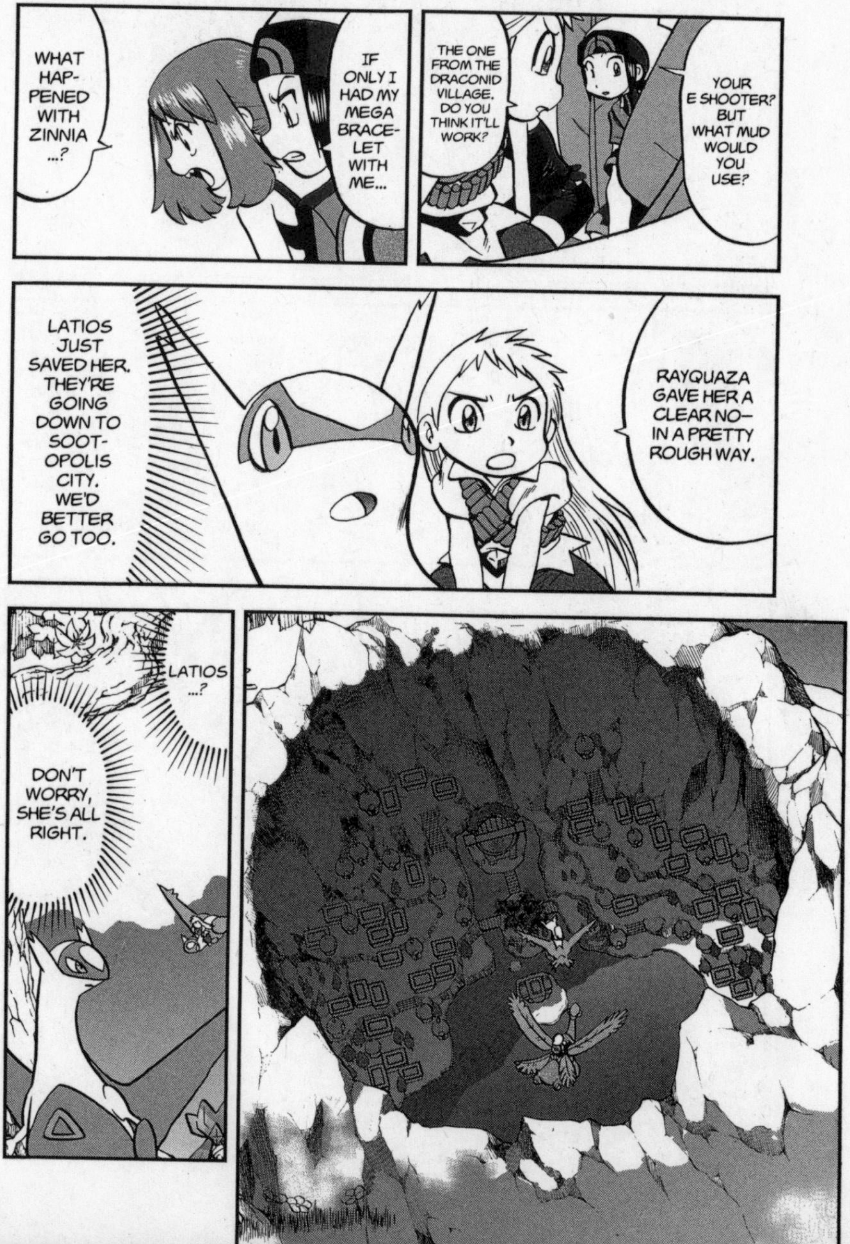
YOUR E SHOOTER? BUT WHAT MUD WOULD YOU USE?
THE ONE FROM THE DRACONID VILLAGE. DO YOU THINK IT'LL WORK?
IF ONLY I HAD MY MEGA BRACE-LET WITH ME...
WHAT HAP-PENED WITH ZINNIA ...?
RAYQUAZA GAVE HER A CLEAR NO— IN A PRETTY ROUGH WAY.
LATIOS JUST SAVED HER. THEY'RE GOING DOWN TO SOOT-OPOLIS CITY. WE'D BETTER GO TOO.
LATIOS ...?
DON'T WORRY, SHE'S ALL RIGHT.

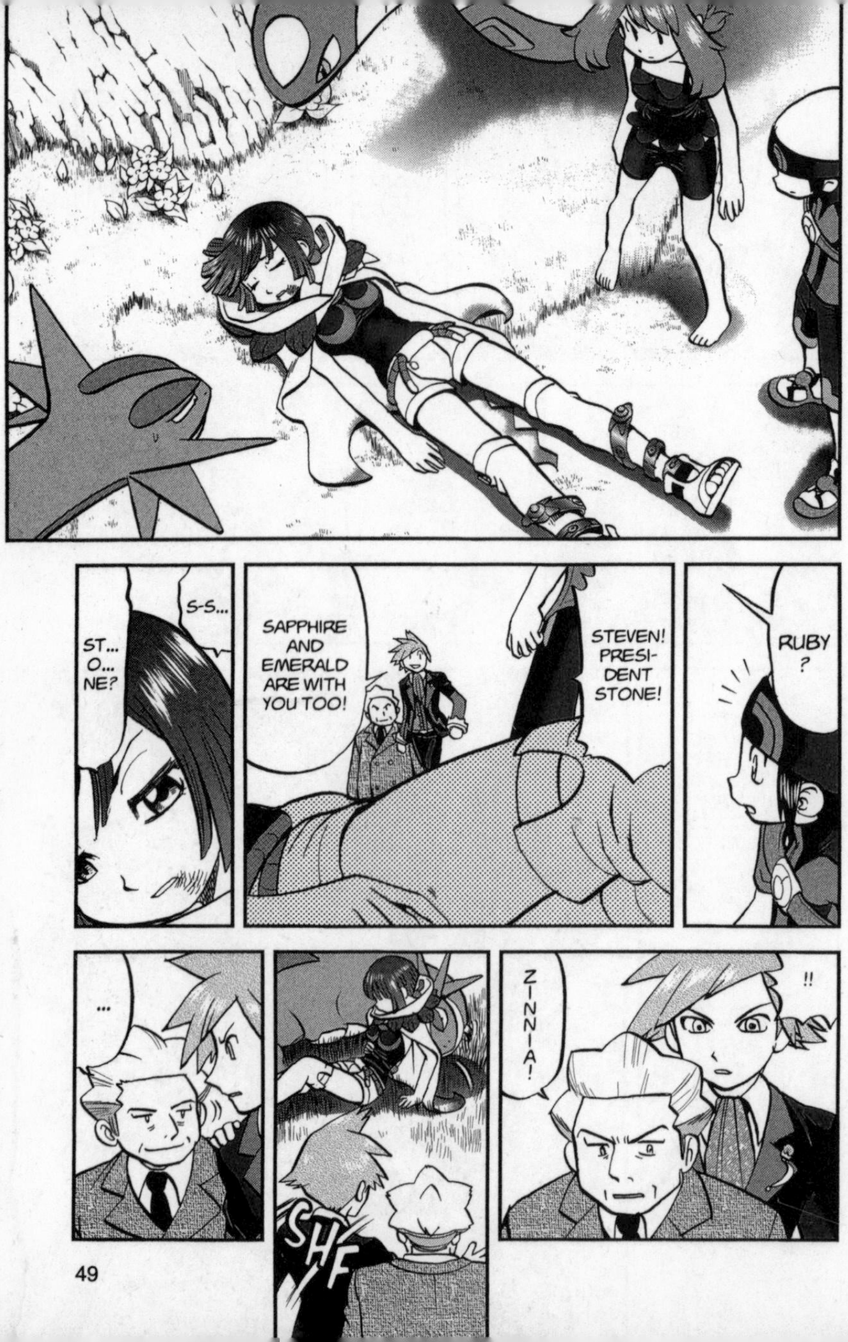
RUBY?
STEVEN! PRESI-DENT STONE!
SAPPHIRE AND EMERALD ARE WITH YOU TOO!
S-S...
ST... O... NE?
!!
ZINNIA!
SHF
...

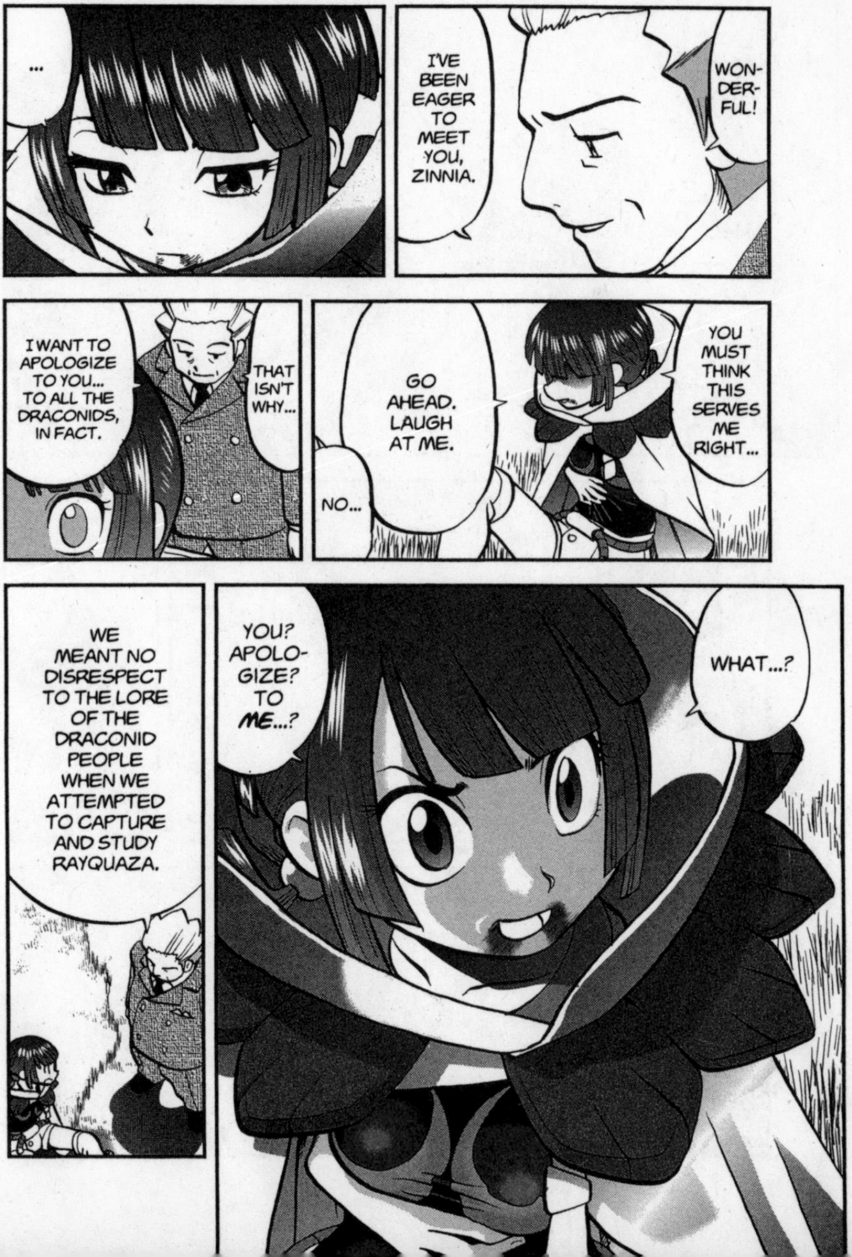
WON-DER-FUL!
I'VE BEEN EAGER TO MEET YOU, ZINNIA.
...
YOU MUST THINK THIS SERVES ME RIGHT...
GO AHEAD. LAUGH AT ME.
NO...
THAT ISN'T WHY...
I WANT TO APOLOGIZE TO YOU... TO ALL THE DRACONIDS, IN FACT.
WHAT...?
YOU? APOLOGIZE? TO ME...?
WE MEANT NO DISRESPECT TO THE LORE OF THE DRACONID PEOPLE WHEN WE ATTEMPTED TO CAPTURE AND STUDY RAYQUAZA.

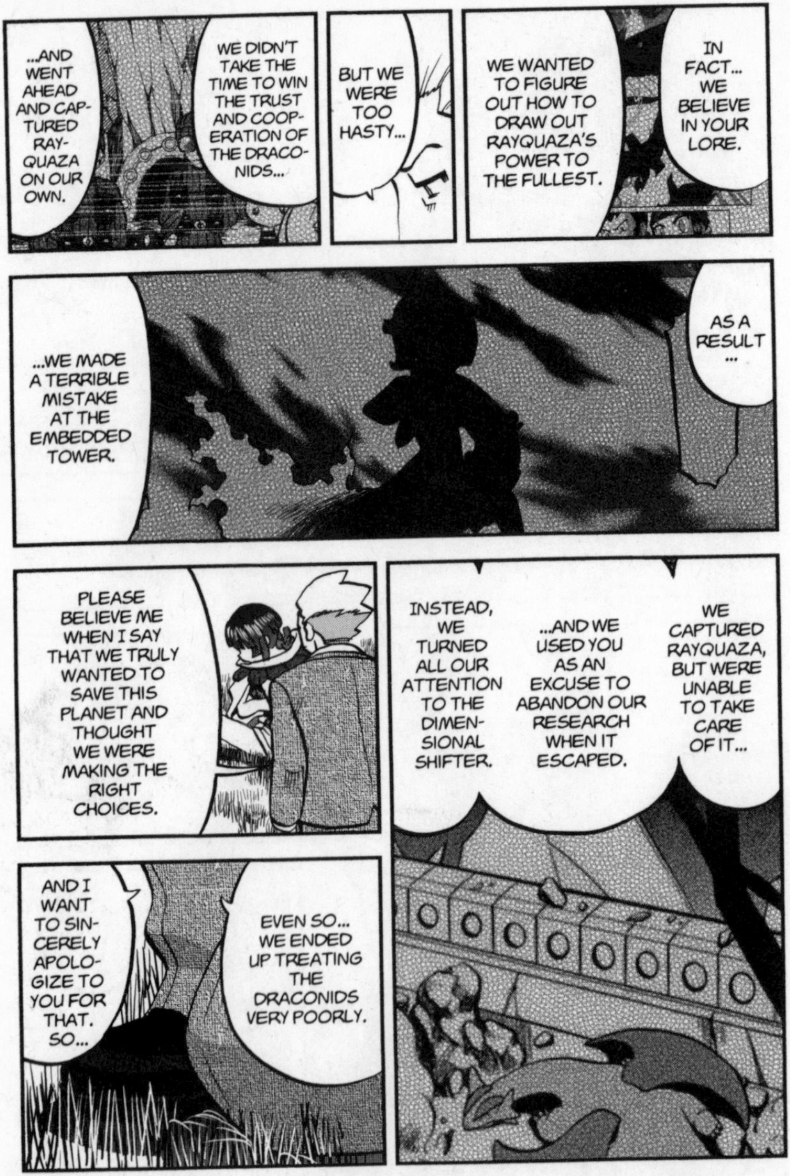
IN FACT... WE BELIEVE IN YOUR LORE.
WE WANTED TO FIGURE OUT HOW TO DRAW OUT RAYQUAZA'S POWER TO THE FULLEST.
BUT WE WERE TOO HASTY...
WE DIDN'T TAKE THE TIME TO WIN THE TRUST AND COOPERATION OF THE DRACONIDS...
...AND WENT AHEAD AND CAPTURED RAYQUAZA ON OUR OWN.
AS A RESULT...
...WE MADE A TERRIBLE MISTAKE AT THE EMBEDDED TOWER.
WE CAPTURED RAYQUAZA, BUT WERE UNABLE TO TAKE CARE OF IT...
...AND WE USED YOU AS AN EXCUSE TO ABANDON OUR RESEARCH WHEN IT ESCAPED.
INSTEAD, WE TURNED ALL OUR ATTENTION TO THE DIMENSIONAL SHIFTER.
PLEASE BELIEVE ME WHEN I SAY THAT WE TRULY WANTED TO SAVE THIS PLANET AND THOUGHT WE WERE MAKING THE RIGHT CHOICES.
EVEN SO... WE ENDED UP TREATING THE DRACONIDS VERY POORLY.
AND I WANT TO SINCERELY APOLOGIZE TO YOU FOR THAT. SO...

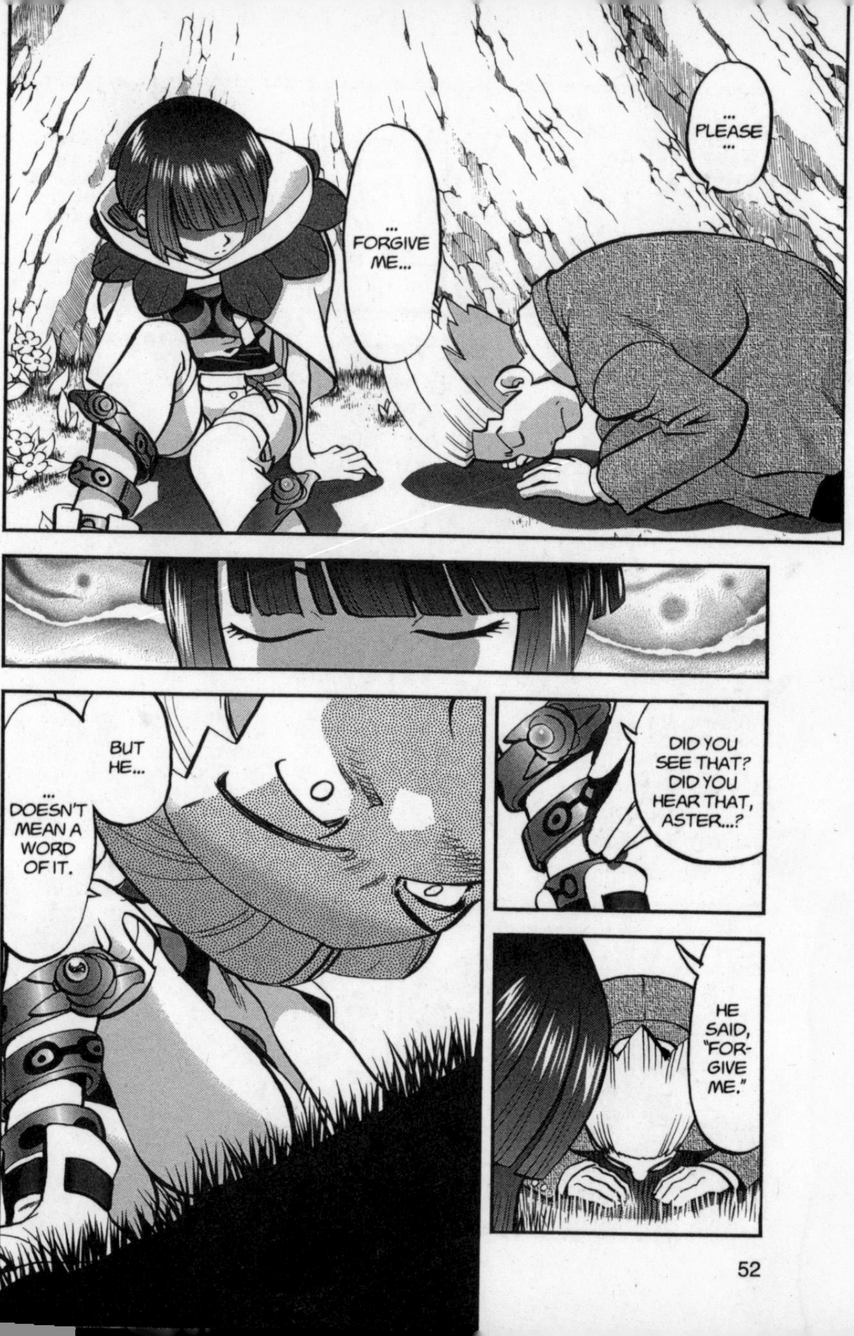
...PLEASE...
...FORGIVE ME...
DID YOU SEE THAT? DID YOU HEAR THAT, ASTER...?
HE SAID, "FOR-GIVE ME."
BUT HE...
...DOESN'T MEAN A WORD OF IT.

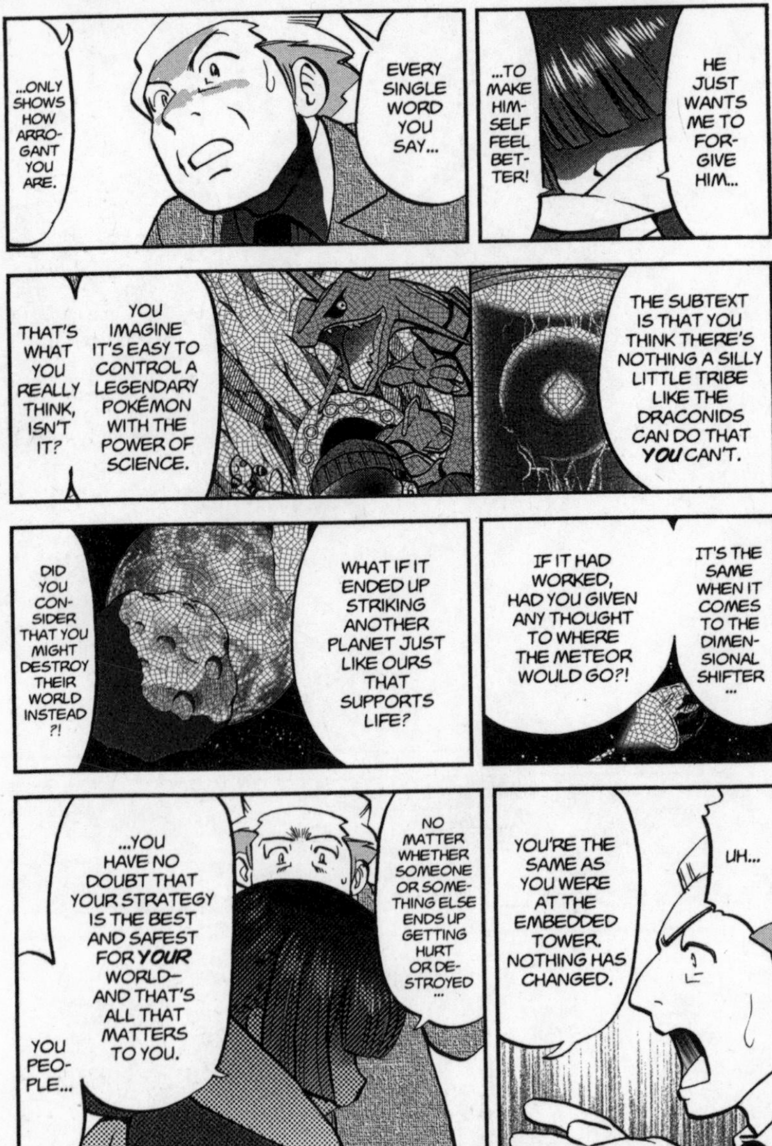
HE JUST WANTS ME TO FORGIVE HIM...
...TO MAKE HIMSELF FEEL BETTER!
EVERY SINGLE WORD YOU SAY...
...ONLY SHOWS HOW ARROGANT YOU ARE.
THE SUBTEXT IS THAT YOU THINK THERE'S NOTHING A SILLY LITTLE TRIBE LIKE THE DRACONIDS CAN DO THAT **YOU** CAN'T.
YOU IMAGINE IT'S EASY TO CONTROL A LEGENDARY POKÉMON WITH THE POWER OF SCIENCE.
THAT'S WHAT YOU REALLY THINK, ISN'T IT?
IT'S THE SAME WHEN IT COMES TO THE DIMENSIONAL SHIFTER...
IF IT HAD WORKED, HAD YOU GIVEN ANY THOUGHT TO WHERE THE METEOR WOULD GO?!
WHAT IF IT ENDED UP STRIKING ANOTHER PLANET JUST LIKE OURS THAT SUPPORTS LIFE?
DID YOU CONSIDER THAT YOU MIGHT DESTROY THEIR WORLD INSTEAD?!
UH...
YOU'RE THE SAME AS YOU WERE AT THE EMBEDDED TOWER. NOTHING HAS CHANGED.
NO MATTER WHETHER SOMEONE OR SOMETHING ELSE ENDS UP GETTING HURT OR DESTROYED...
...YOU HAVE NO DOUBT THAT YOUR STRATEGY IS THE BEST AND SAFEST FOR **YOUR** WORLD—AND THAT'S ALL THAT MATTERS TO YOU.
YOU PEOPLE...

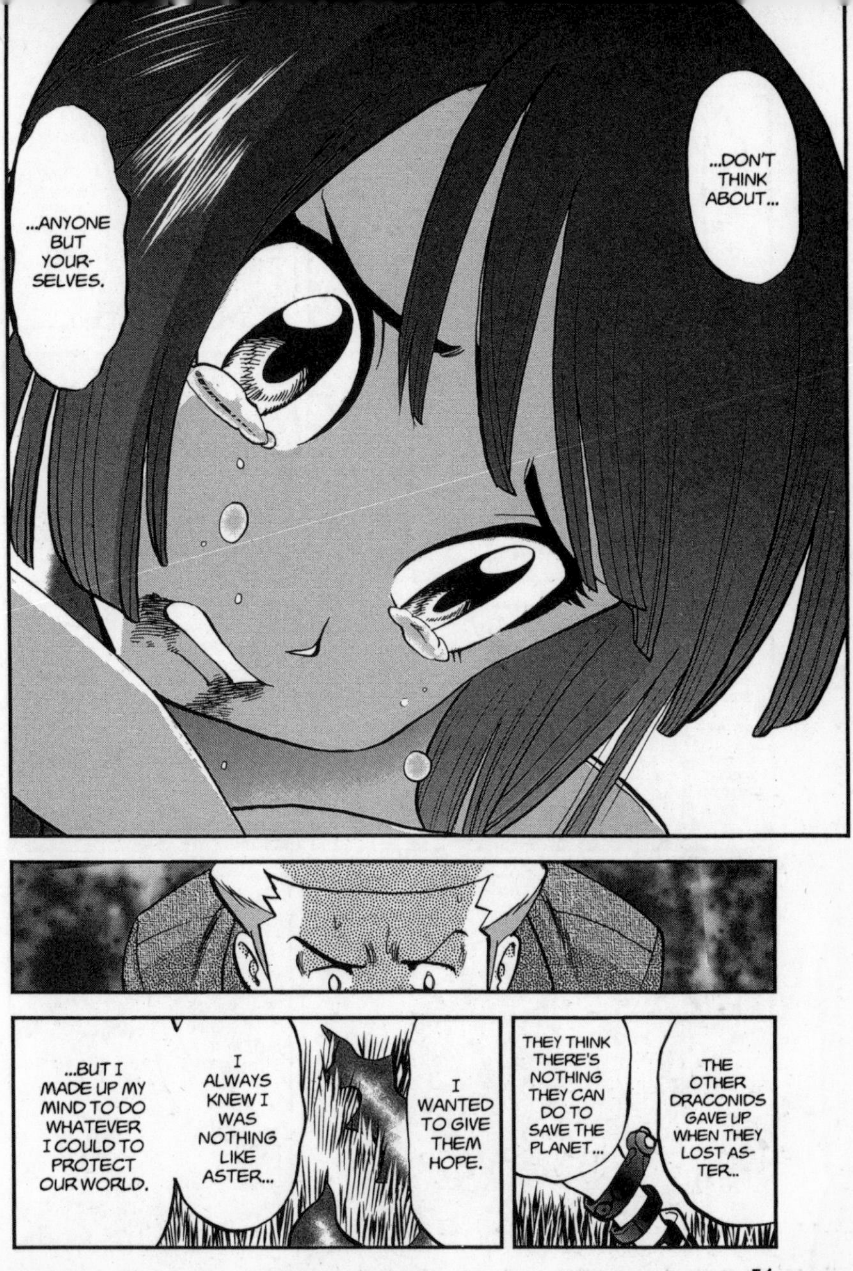
...DON'T THINK ABOUT...
...ANYONE BUT YOUR-SELVES.
THE OTHER DRACONIDS GAVE UP WHEN THEY LOST ASTER..
THEY THINK THERE'S NOTHING THEY CAN DO TO SAVE THE PLANET...
I WANTED TO GIVE THEM HOPE.
I ALWAYS KNEW I WAS NOTHING LIKE ASTER...
...BUT I MADE UP MY MIND TO DO WHATEVER I COULD TO PROTECT OUR WORLD.

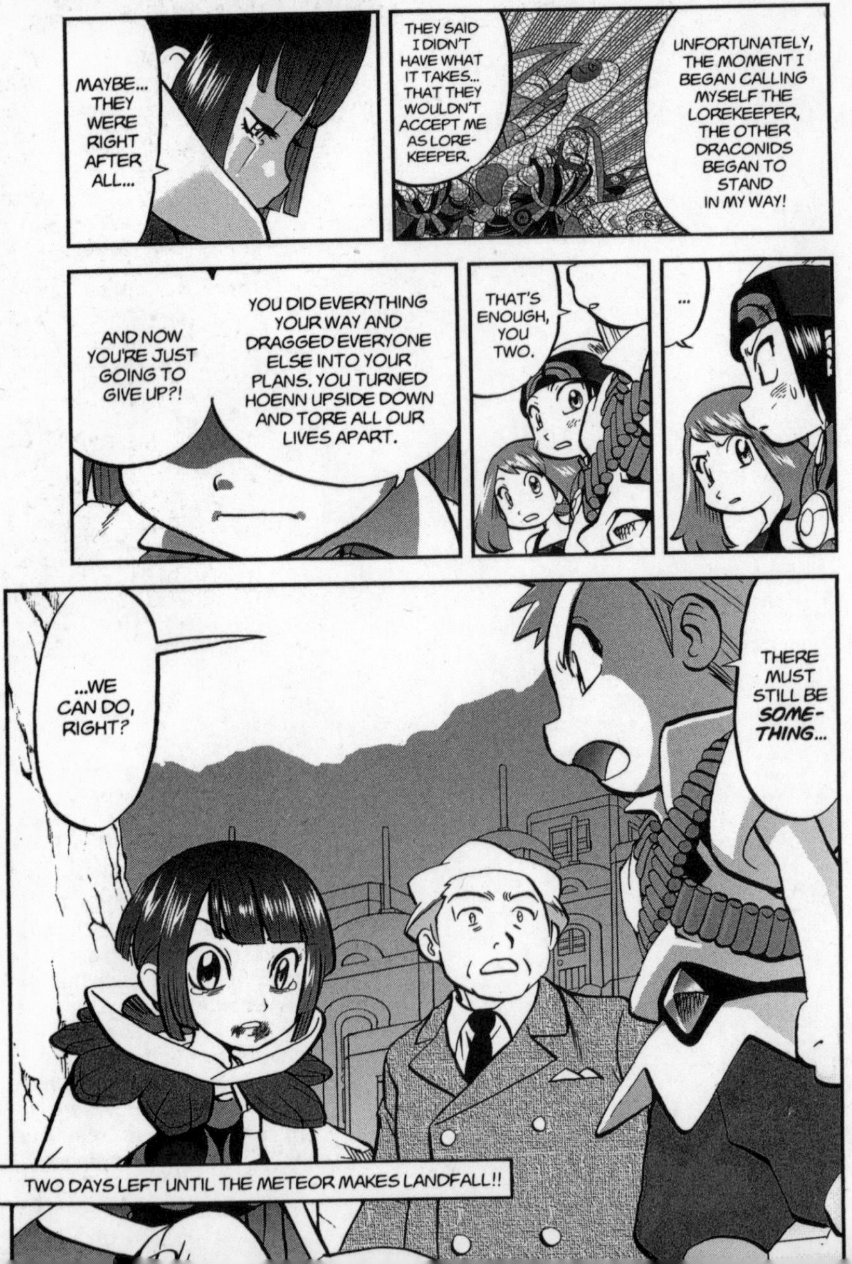
UNFORTUNATELY, THE MOMENT I BEGAN CALLING MYSELF THE LOREKEEPER, THE OTHER DRACONIDS BEGAN TO STAND IN MY WAY!
THEY SAID I DIDN'T HAVE WHAT IT TAKES... THAT THEY WOULDN'T ACCEPT ME AS LORE-KEEPER.
MAYBE... THEY WERE RIGHT AFTER ALL...
...
THAT'S ENOUGH, YOU TWO.
YOU DID EVERYTHING YOUR WAY AND DRAGGED EVERYONE ELSE INTO YOUR PLANS. YOU TURNED HOENN UPSIDE DOWN AND TORE ALL OUR LIVES APART.
AND NOW YOU'RE JUST GOING TO GIVE UP?!
THERE MUST STILL BE ***SOME-THING***...
...WE CAN DO, RIGHT?
TWO DAYS LEFT UNTIL THE METEOR MAKES LANDFALL!!

## THE EMBEDDED TOWER

A tower that soars into the sky along Route 47 in Johto. The tower is covered by rocks and the passages stretch out to the underground. It is said that the tower continues down into the sea. Some researchers believe that the tower connects the land, sea and sky. Although the tower is in Johto, there is a theory that it was created by the people of ancient Hoenn.

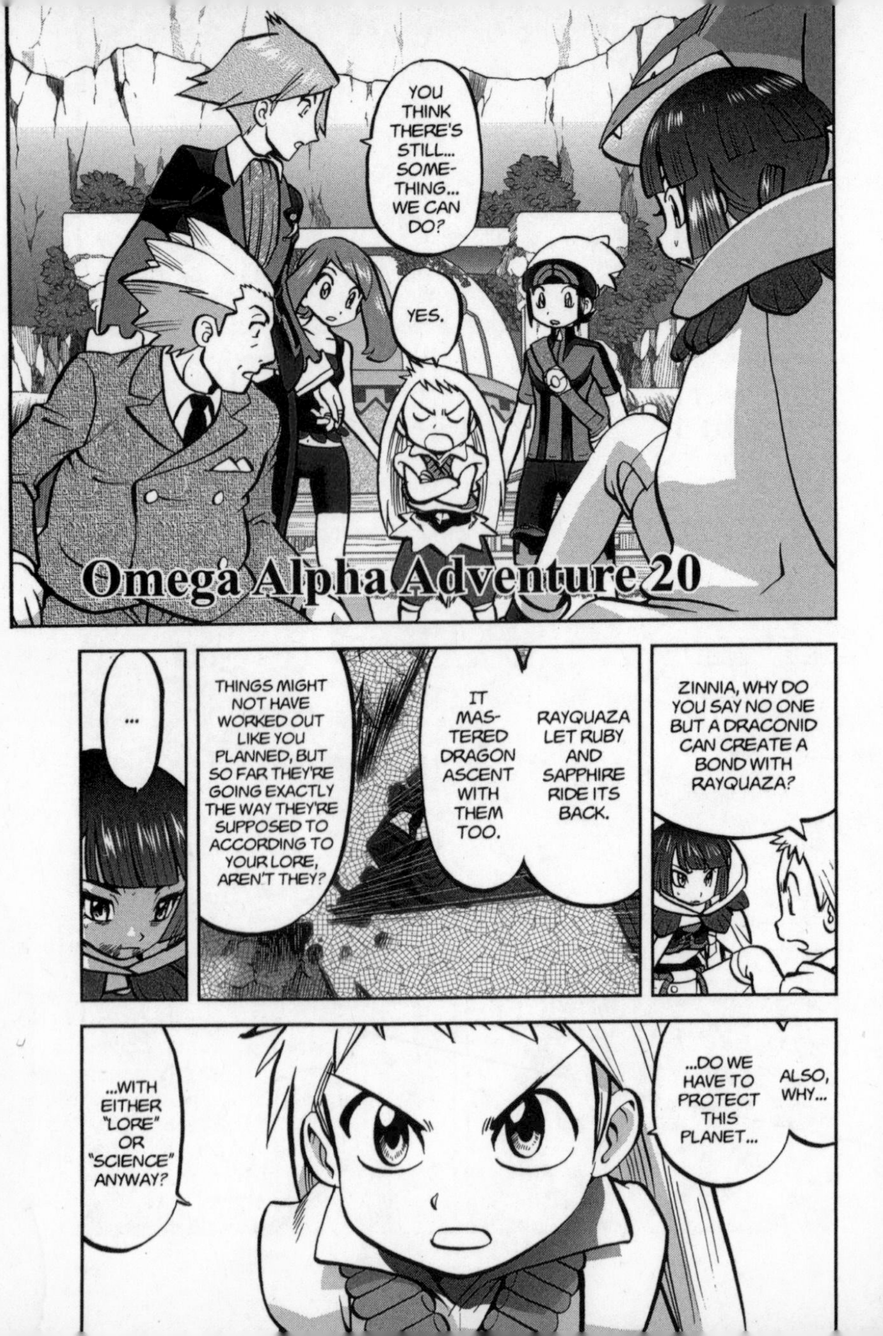
YOU THINK THERE'S STILL... SOME-THING... WE CAN DO?
YES.
Omega Alpha Adventure 20
ZINNIA, WHY DO YOU SAY NO ONE BUT A DRACONID CAN CREATE A BOND WITH RAYQUAZA?
RAYQUAZA LET RUBY AND SAPPHIRE RIDE ITS BACK.
IT MAS-TERED DRAGON ASCENT WITH THEM TOO.
THINGS MIGHT NOT HAVE WORKED OUT LIKE YOU PLANNED, BUT SO FAR THEY'RE GOING EXACTLY THE WAY THEY'RE SUPPOSED TO ACCORDING TO YOUR LORE, AREN'T THEY?
...
ALSO, WHY...
...DO WE HAVE TO PROTECT THIS PLANET...
...WITH EITHER "LORE" OR "SCIENCE" ANYWAY?

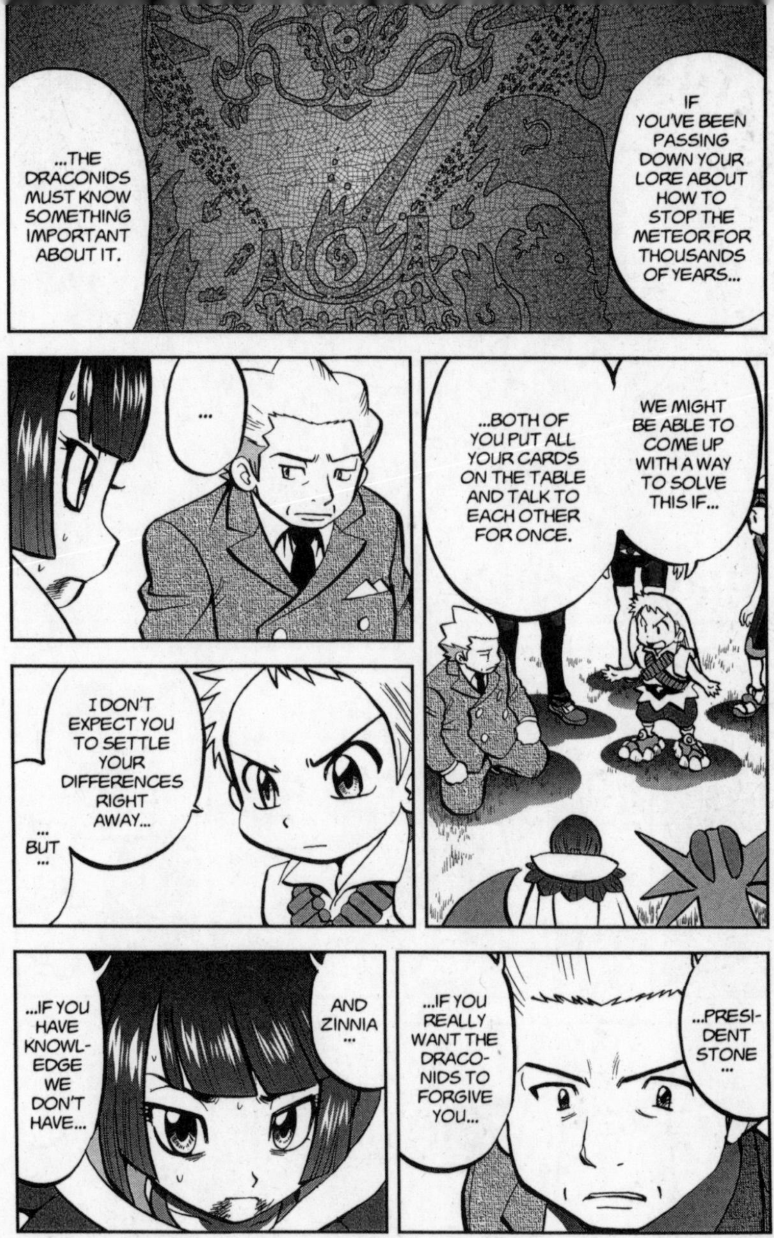
IF YOU'VE BEEN PASSING DOWN YOUR LORE ABOUT HOW TO STOP THE METEOR FOR THOUSANDS OF YEARS...
...THE DRACONIDS MUST KNOW SOMETHING IMPORTANT ABOUT IT.
WE MIGHT BE ABLE TO COME UP WITH A WAY TO SOLVE THIS IF...
...BOTH OF YOU PUT ALL YOUR CARDS ON THE TABLE AND TALK TO EACH OTHER FOR ONCE.
...
I DON'T EXPECT YOU TO SETTLE YOUR DIFFERENCES RIGHT AWAY...
...BUT...
...PRESI-DENT STONE...
...IF YOU REALLY WANT THE DRACO-NIDS TO FORGIVE YOU...
AND ZINNIA...
...IF YOU HAVE KNOWL-EDGE WE DON'T HAVE...

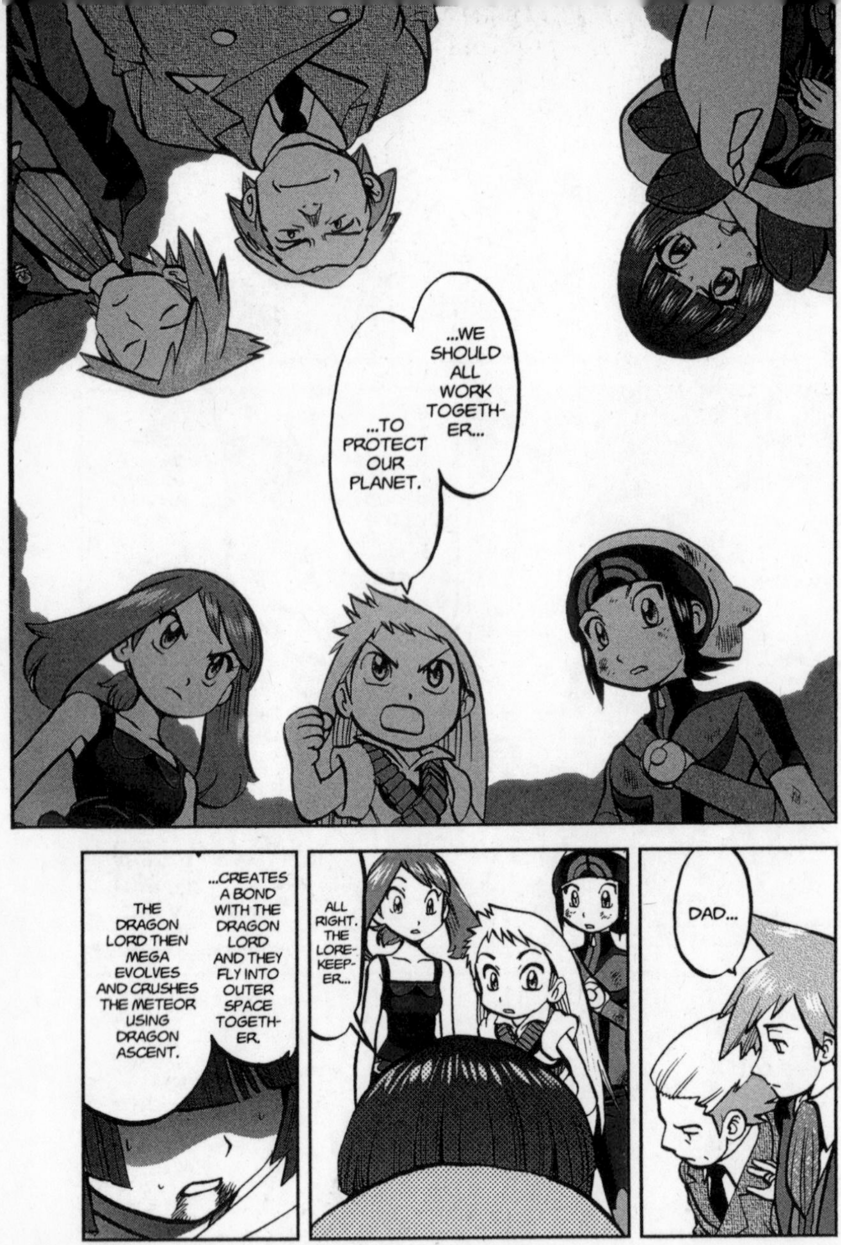
...WE SHOULD ALL WORK TOGETH-ER...
...TO PROTECT OUR PLANET.
DAD...
ALL RIGHT. THE LORE-KEEP-ER...
...CREATES A BOND WITH THE DRAGON LORD AND THEY FLY INTO OUTER SPACE TOGETH-ER.
THE DRAGON LORD THEN MEGA EVOLVES AND CRUSHES THE METEOR USING DRAGON ASCENT.

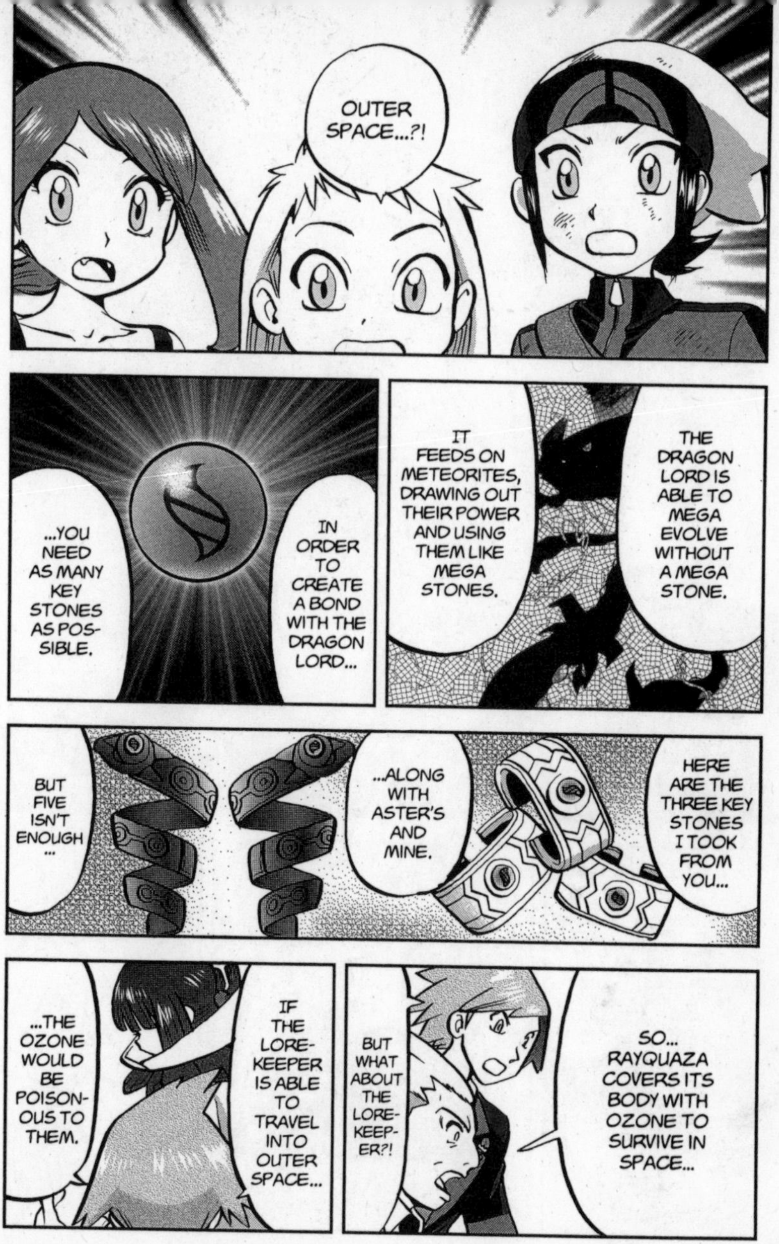
OUTER SPACE...?!
THE DRAGON LORD IS ABLE TO MEGA EVOLVE WITHOUT A MEGA STONE.
IT FEEDS ON METEORITES, DRAWING OUT THEIR POWER AND USING THEM LIKE MEGA STONES.
IN ORDER TO CREATE A BOND WITH THE DRAGON LORD...
...YOU NEED AS MANY KEY STONES AS POSSIBLE.
HERE ARE THE THREE KEY STONES I TOOK FROM YOU...
...ALONG WITH ASTER'S AND MINE.
BUT FIVE ISN'T ENOUGH...
SO... RAYQUAZA COVERS ITS BODY WITH OZONE TO SURVIVE IN SPACE...
BUT WHAT ABOUT THE LOREKEEPER?!
IF THE LOREKEEPER IS ABLE TO TRAVEL INTO OUTER SPACE...
...THE OZONE WOULD BE POISONOUS TO THEM.

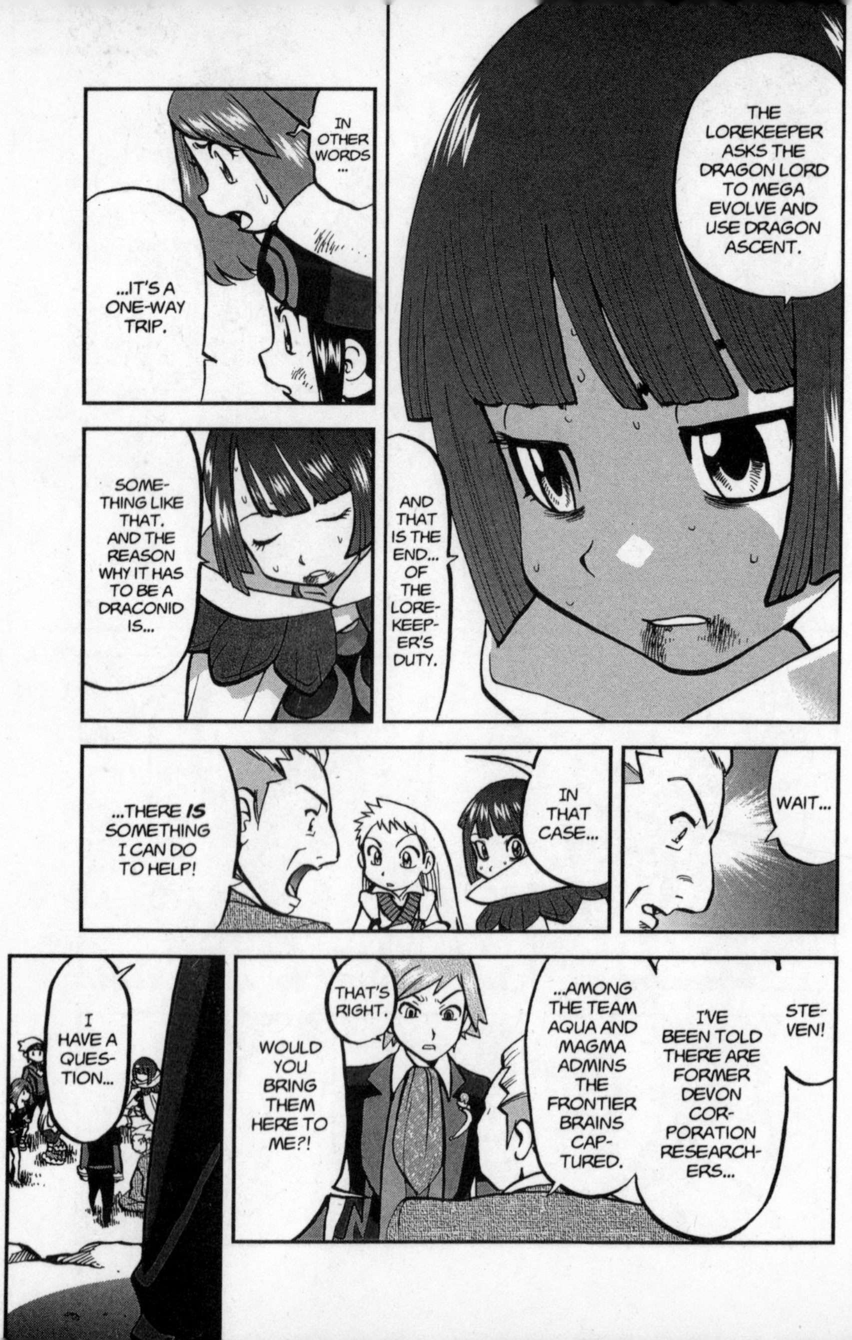
THE LOREKEEPER ASKS THE DRAGON LORD TO MEGA EVOLVE AND USE DRAGON ASCENT.
AND THAT IS THE END... OF THE LOREKEEPER'S DUTY.
IN OTHER WORDS...
...IT'S A ONE-WAY TRIP.
SOMETHING LIKE THAT. AND THE REASON WHY IT HAS TO BE A DRACONID IS...
WAIT...
IN THAT CASE...
...THERE *IS* SOMETHING I CAN DO TO HELP!
STEVEN!
I'VE BEEN TOLD THERE ARE FORMER DEVON CORPORATION RESEARCHERS...
...AMONG THE TEAM AQUA AND MAGMA ADMINS THE FRONTIER BRAINS CAPTURED.
THAT'S RIGHT.
WOULD YOU BRING THEM HERE TO ME?!
I HAVE A QUESTION...

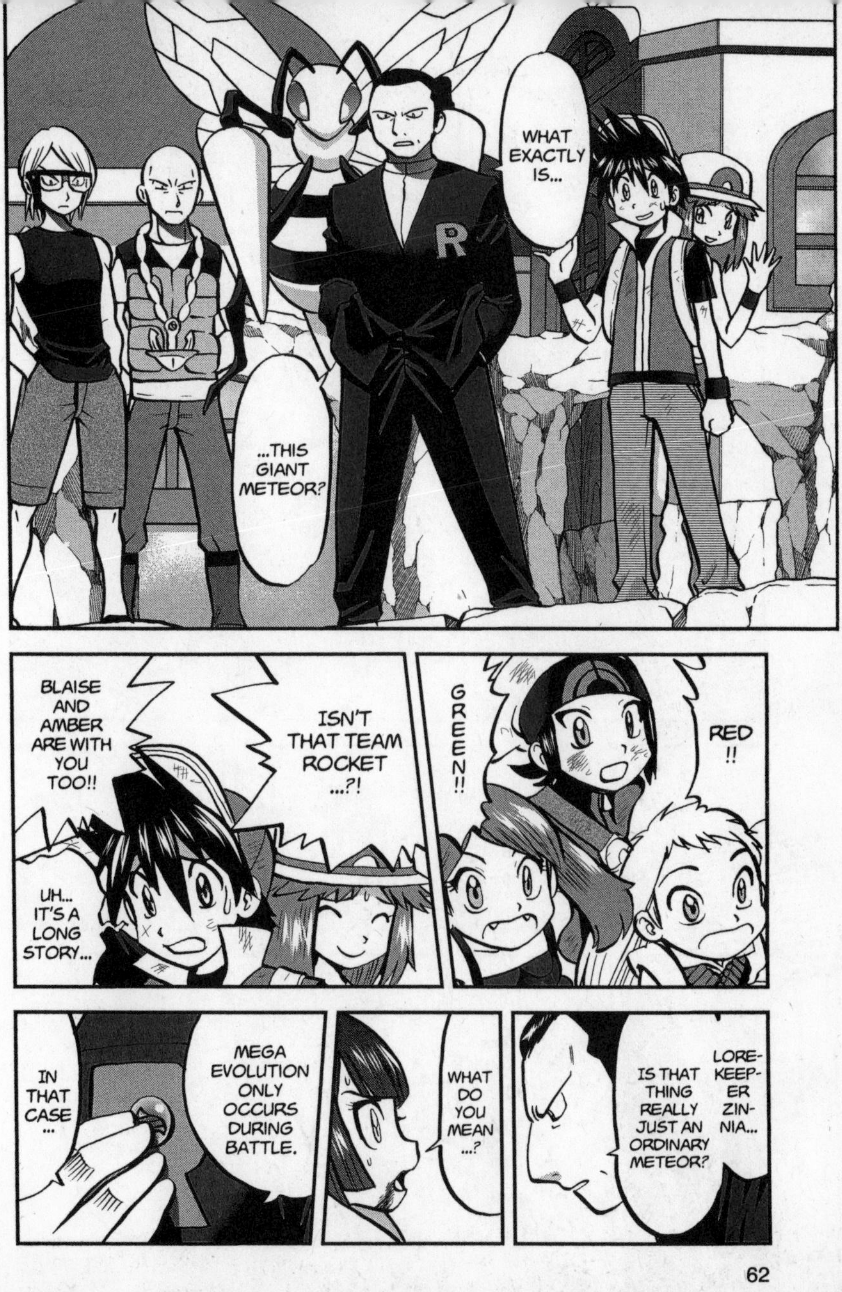
WHAT EXACTLY IS...
...THIS GIANT METEOR?
RED !!
GREEN!!
ISN'T THAT TEAM ROCKET ...?!
BLAISE AND AMBER ARE WITH YOU TOO!!
UH... IT'S A LONG STORY...
LOREKEEPER ZINNIA...
IS THAT THING REALLY JUST AN ORDINARY METEOR?
WHAT DO YOU MEAN ...?
MEGA EVOLUTION ONLY OCCURS DURING BATTLE.
IN THAT CASE ...

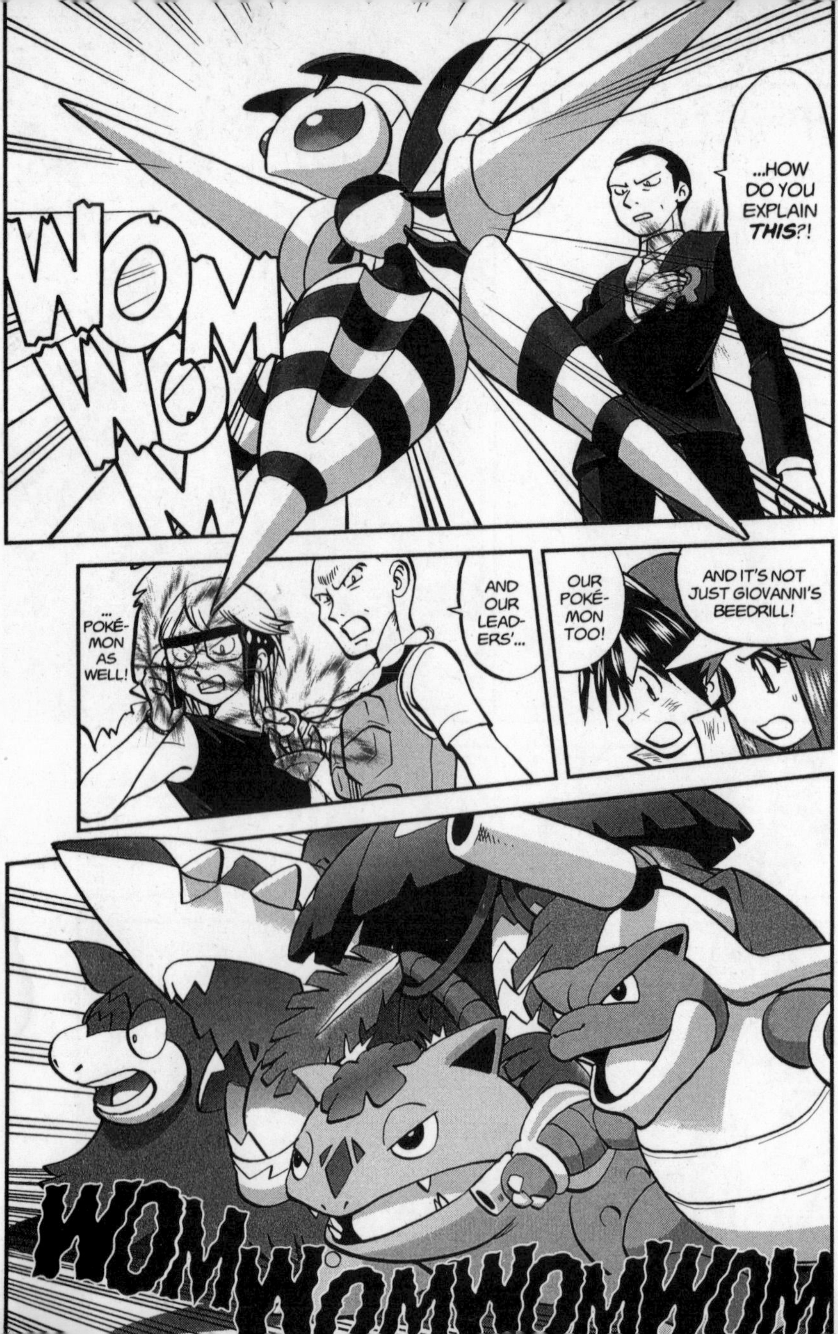
...HOW DO YOU EXPLAIN *THIS*?!
WOM WOM WOM
AND IT'S NOT JUST GIOVANNI'S BEEDRILL!
OUR POKÉMON TOO!
AND OUR LEADERS'...
...POKÉMON AS WELL!
WOMWOMWOMWOM

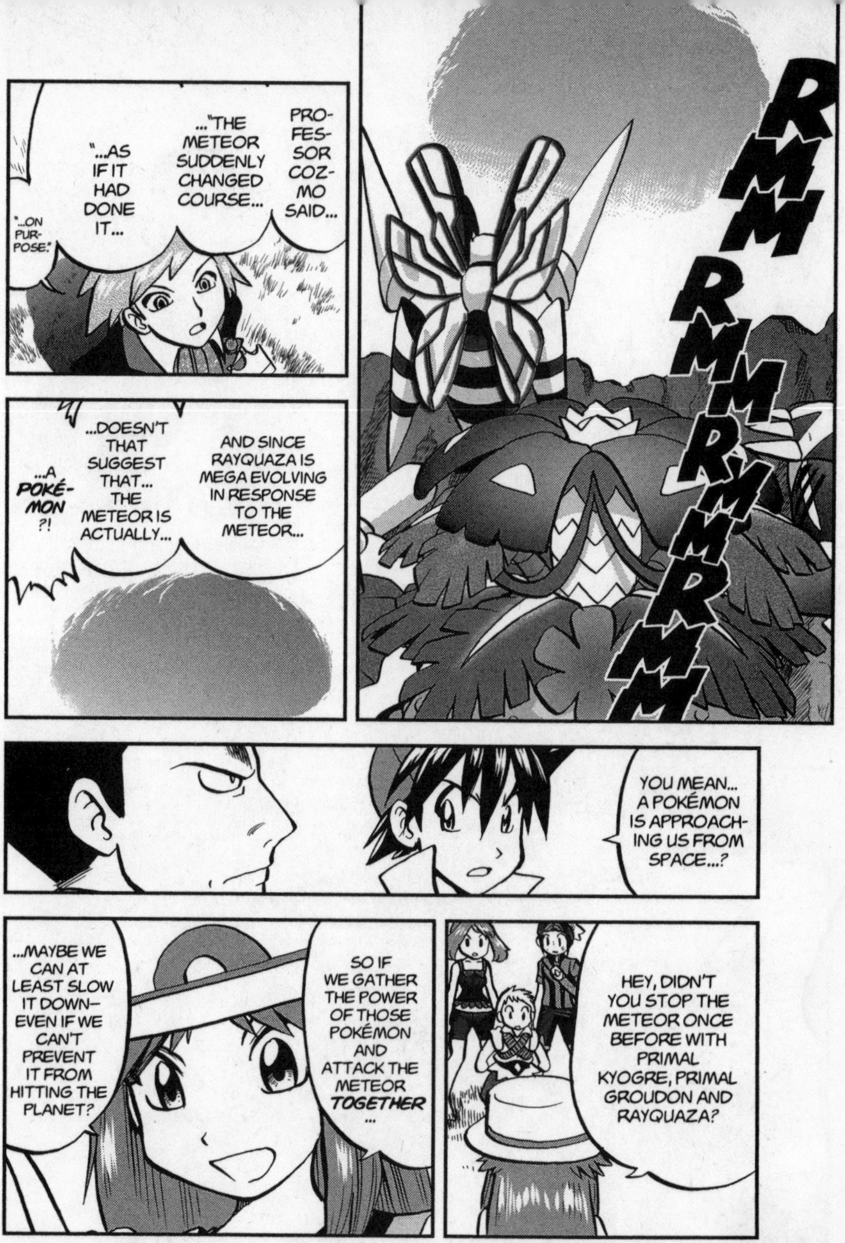
RMMMRMMMRMMMRMMM
PRO-FES-SOR COZ-MO SAID...
..."THE METEOR SUDDENLY CHANGED COURSE...
"...AS IF IT HAD DONE IT...
"...ON PUR-POSE."
AND SINCE RAYQUAZA IS MEGA EVOLVING IN RESPONSE TO THE METEOR...
...DOESN'T THAT SUGGEST THAT... THE METEOR IS ACTUALLY...
...A *POKÉ-MON* ?!
YOU MEAN... A POKÉMON IS APPROACH-ING US FROM SPACE...?
HEY, DIDN'T YOU STOP THE METEOR ONCE BEFORE WITH PRIMAL KYOGRE, PRIMAL GROUDON AND RAYQUAZA?
SO IF WE GATHER THE POWER OF THOSE POKÉMON AND ATTACK THE METEOR *TOGETHER* ...
...MAYBE WE CAN AT LEAST SLOW IT DOWN— EVEN IF WE CAN'T PREVENT IT FROM HITTING THE PLANET?

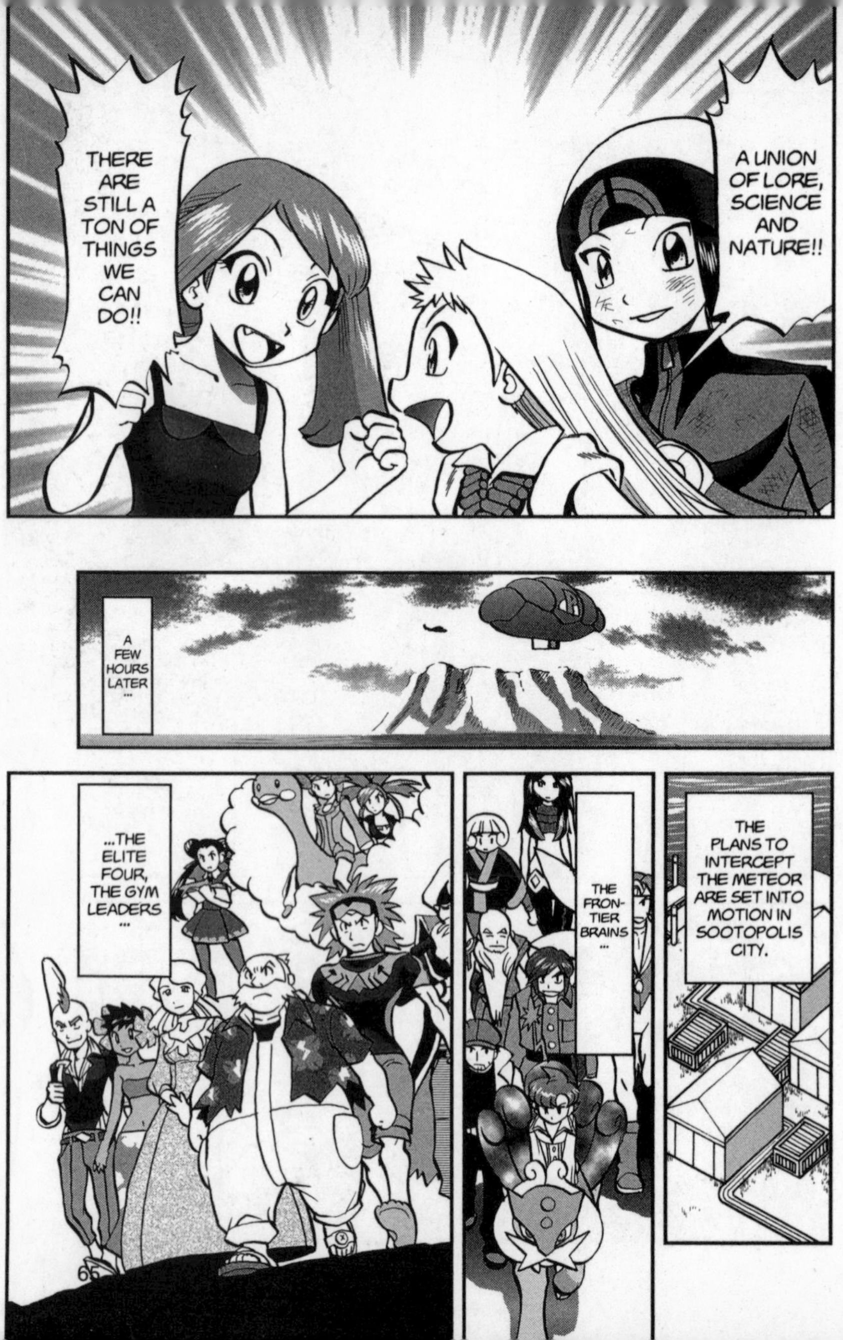
A UNION OF LORE, SCIENCE AND NATURE!!
THERE ARE STILL A TON OF THINGS WE CAN DO!!
A FEW HOURS LATER...
THE PLANS TO INTERCEPT THE METEOR ARE SET INTO MOTION IN SOOTOPOLIS CITY.
THE FRONTIER BRAINS...
...THE ELITE FOUR, THE GYM LEADERS...

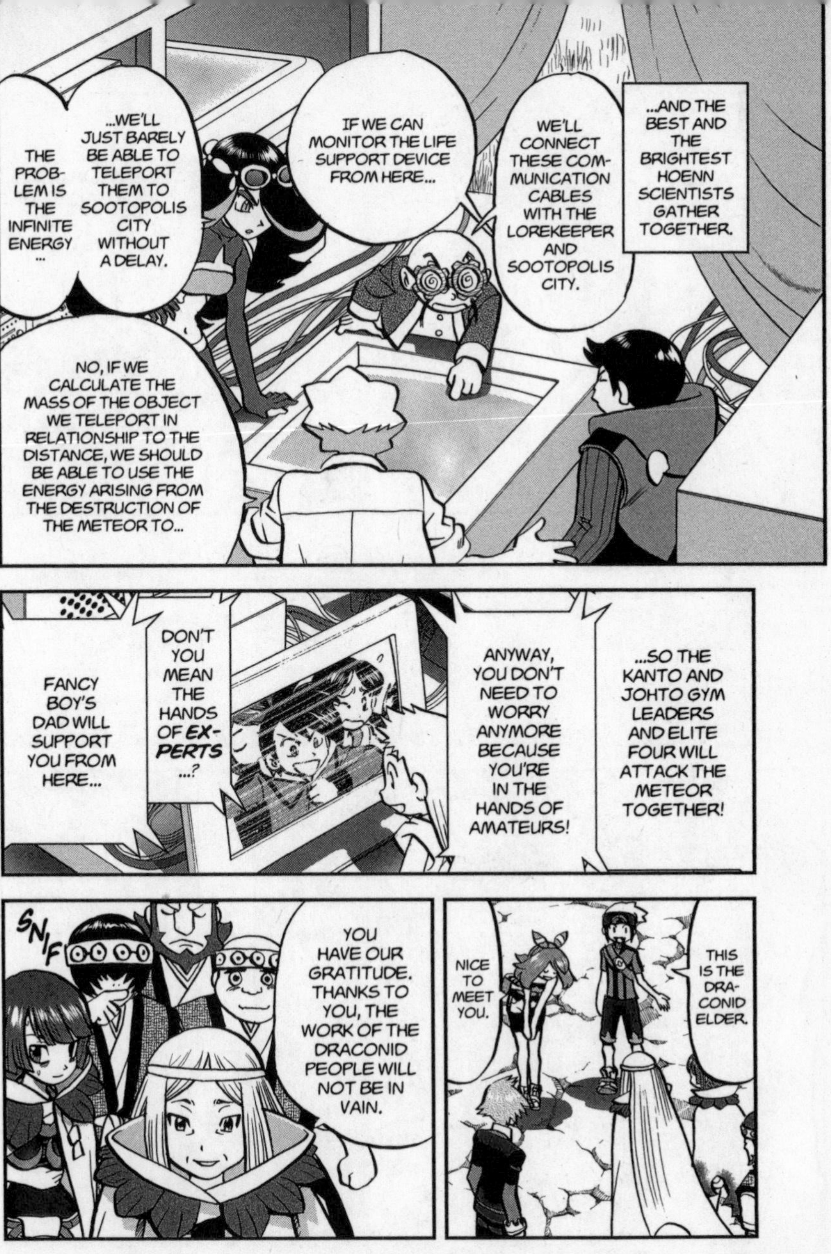
...AND THE BEST AND THE BRIGHTEST HOENN SCIENTISTS GATHER TOGETHER.
WE'LL CONNECT THESE COMMUNICATION CABLES WITH THE LOREKEEPER AND SOOTOPOLIS CITY.
IF WE CAN MONITOR THE LIFE SUPPORT DEVICE FROM HERE...
...WE'LL JUST BARELY BE ABLE TO TELEPORT THEM TO SOOTOPOLIS CITY WITHOUT A DELAY.
THE PROBLEM IS THE INFINITE ENERGY...
NO, IF WE CALCULATE THE MASS OF THE OBJECT WE TELEPORT IN RELATIONSHIP TO THE DISTANCE, WE SHOULD BE ABLE TO USE THE ENERGY ARISING FROM THE DESTRUCTION OF THE METEOR TO...
...SO THE KANTO AND JOHTO GYM LEADERS AND ELITE FOUR WILL ATTACK THE METEOR TOGETHER!
ANYWAY, YOU DON'T NEED TO WORRY ANYMORE BECAUSE YOU'RE IN THE HANDS OF AMATEURS!
DON'T YOU MEAN THE HANDS OF ***EXPERTS***...?
FANCY BOY'S DAD WILL SUPPORT YOU FROM HERE...
THIS IS THE DRACONID ELDER.
NICE TO MEET YOU.
YOU HAVE OUR GRATITUDE. THANKS TO YOU, THE WORK OF THE DRACONID PEOPLE WILL NOT BE IN VAIN.
SNIF

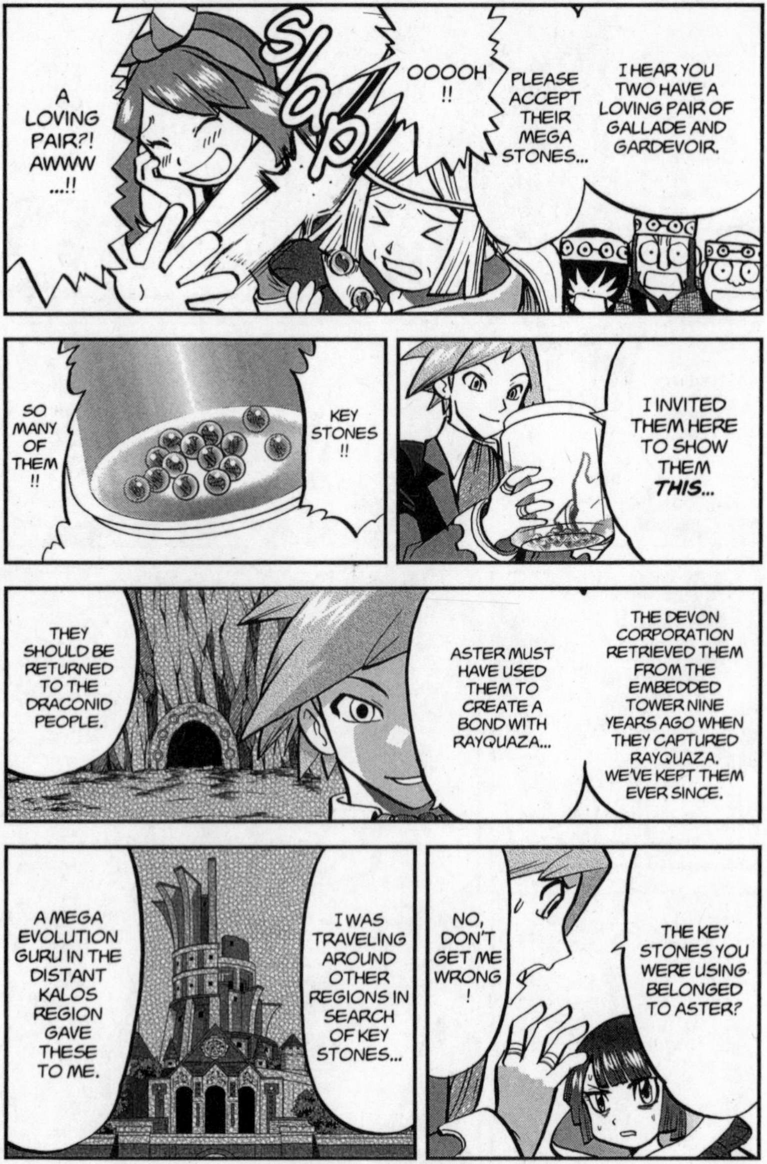
I HEAR YOU TWO HAVE A LOVING PAIR OF GALLADE AND GARDEVOIR.
PLEASE ACCEPT THEIR MEGA STONES...
OOOOH!!
SLAP
A LOVING PAIR?! AWWW...!!
I INVITED THEM HERE TO SHOW THEM ***THIS...***
KEY STONES!!
SO MANY OF THEM!!
THE DEVON CORPORATION RETRIEVED THEM FROM THE EMBEDDED TOWER NINE YEARS AGO WHEN THEY CAPTURED RAYQUAZA. WE'VE KEPT THEM EVER SINCE.
ASTER MUST HAVE USED THEM TO CREATE A BOND WITH RAYQUAZA...
THEY SHOULD BE RETURNED TO THE DRACONID PEOPLE.
THE KEY STONES YOU WERE USING BELONGED TO ASTER?
NO, DON'T GET ME WRONG!
I WAS TRAVELING AROUND OTHER REGIONS IN SEARCH OF KEY STONES...
A MEGA EVOLUTION GURU IN THE DISTANT KALOS REGION GAVE THESE TO ME.

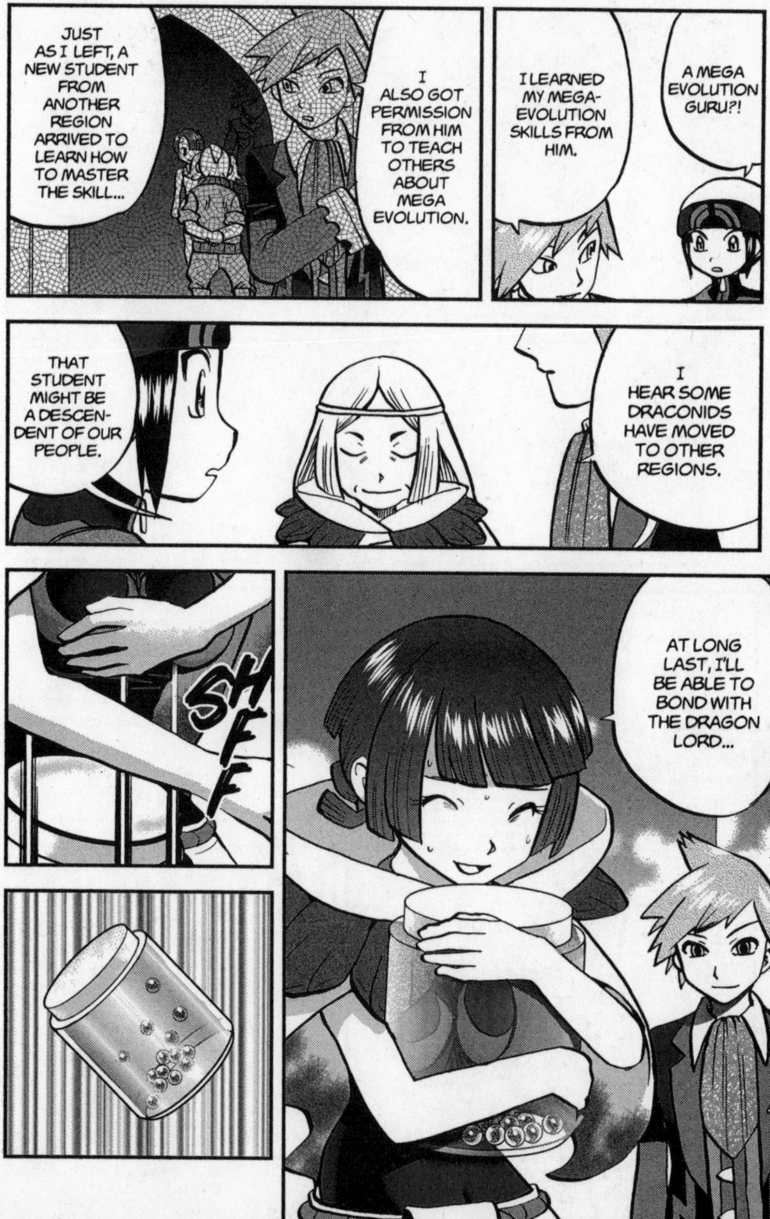
A MEGA EVOLUTION GURU?!
I LEARNED MY MEGA-EVOLUTION SKILLS FROM HIM.
I ALSO GOT PERMISSION FROM HIM TO TEACH OTHERS ABOUT MEGA EVOLUTION.
JUST AS I LEFT, A NEW STUDENT FROM ANOTHER REGION ARRIVED TO LEARN HOW TO MASTER THE SKILL...
I HEAR SOME DRACONIDS HAVE MOVED TO OTHER REGIONS.
THAT STUDENT MIGHT BE A DESCENDENT OF OUR PEOPLE.
AT LONG LAST, I'LL BE ABLE TO BOND WITH THE DRAGON LORD...
SHFF

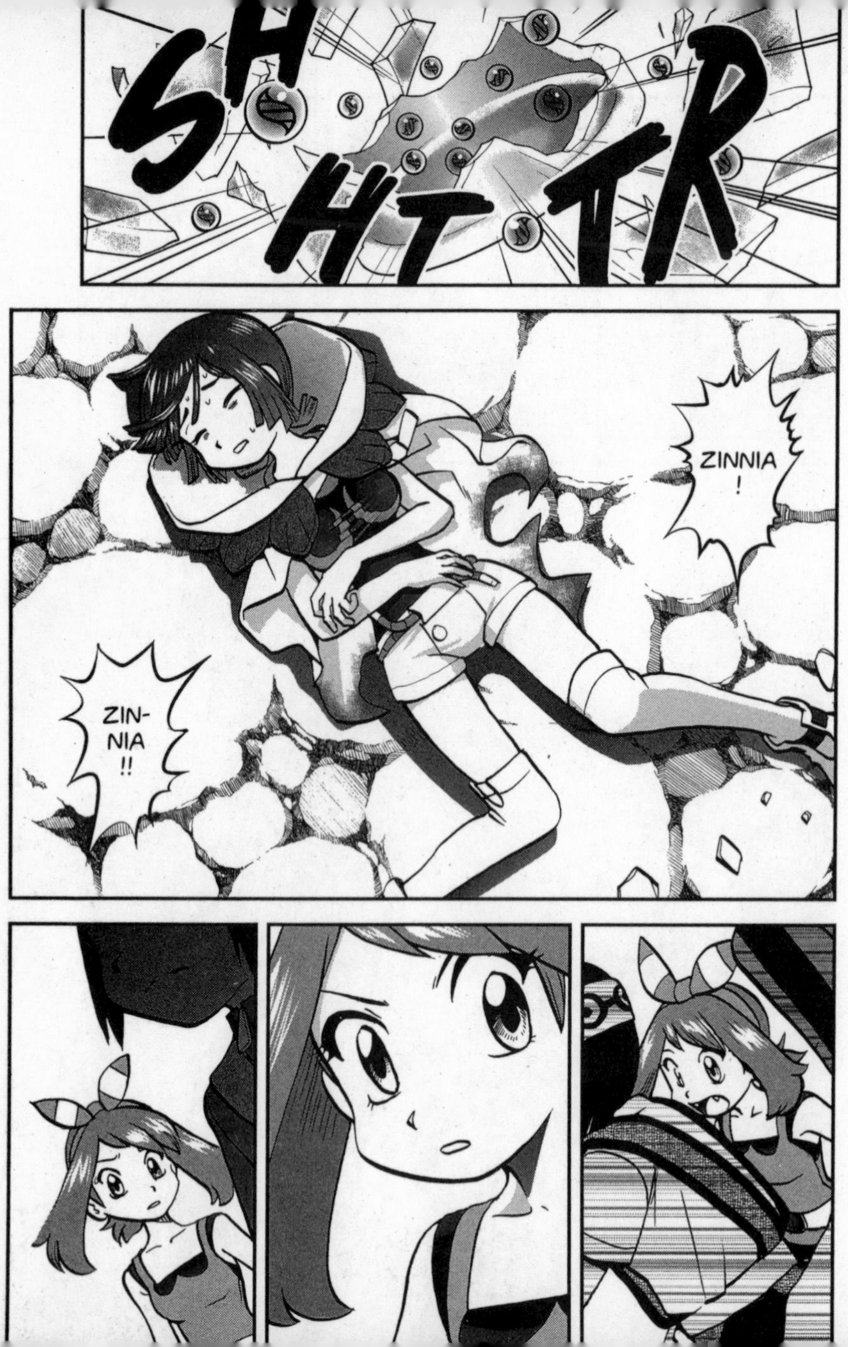
SHHTTR
ZINNIA !
ZIN- NIA !!

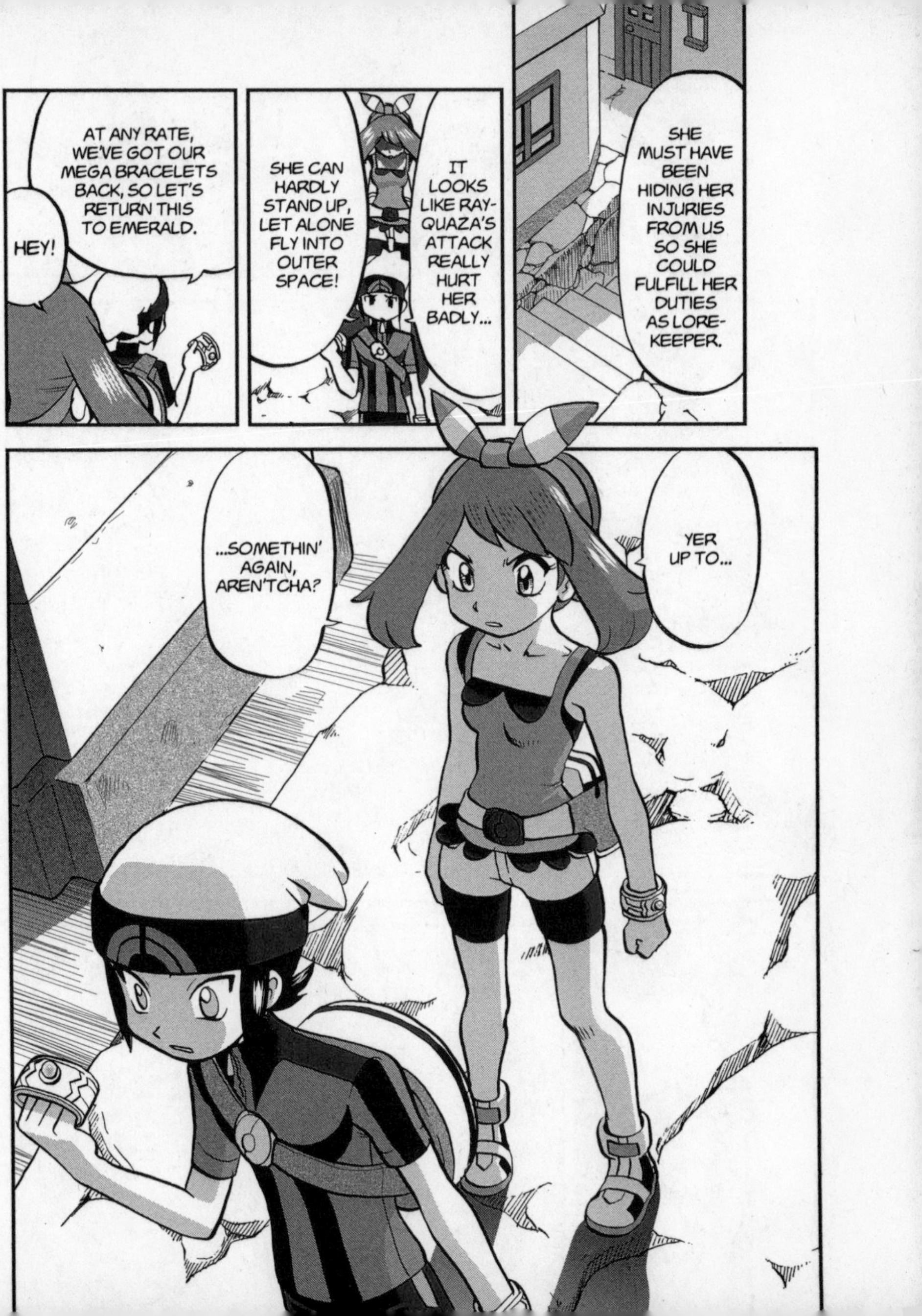
SHE MUST HAVE BEEN HIDING HER INJURIES FROM US SO SHE COULD FULFILL HER DUTIES AS LORE-KEEPER.
IT LOOKS LIKE RAY-QUAZA'S ATTACK REALLY HURT HER BADLY...
SHE CAN HARDLY STAND UP, LET ALONE FLY INTO OUTER SPACE!
AT ANY RATE, WE'VE GOT OUR MEGA BRACELETS BACK, SO LET'S RETURN THIS TO EMERALD.
HEY!
YER UP TO...
...SOMETHIN' AGAIN, AREN'TCHA?

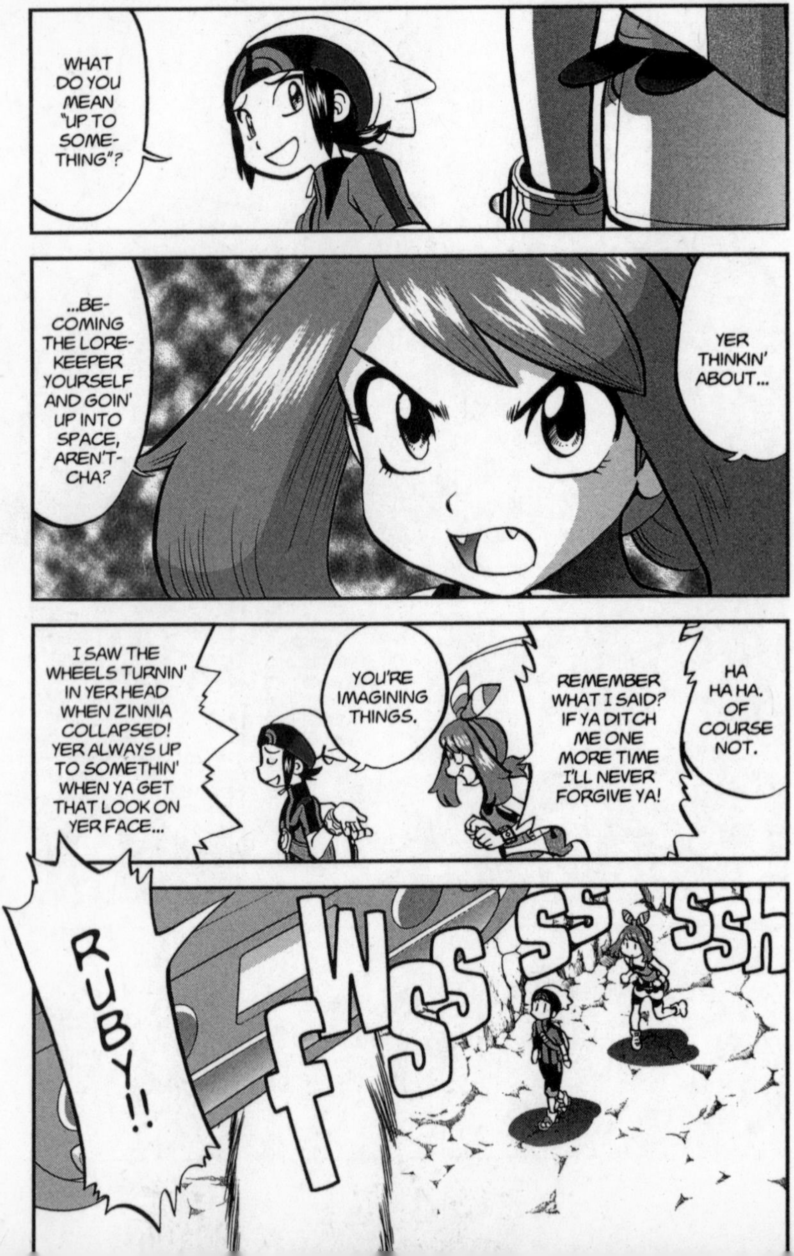
WHAT DO YOU MEAN "UP TO SOMETHING"?
YER THINKIN' ABOUT...
...BECOMING THE LOREKEEPER YOURSELF AND GOIN' UP INTO SPACE, AREN'T-CHA?
HA HA HA. OF COURSE NOT.
REMEMBER WHAT I SAID? IF YA DITCH ME ONE MORE TIME I'LL NEVER FORGIVE YA!
YOU'RE IMAGINING THINGS.
I SAW THE WHEELS TURNIN' IN YER HEAD WHEN ZINNIA COLLAPSED! YER ALWAYS UP TO SOMETHIN' WHEN YA GET THAT LOOK ON YER FACE...
FWSSSSSSH
RUBY!!

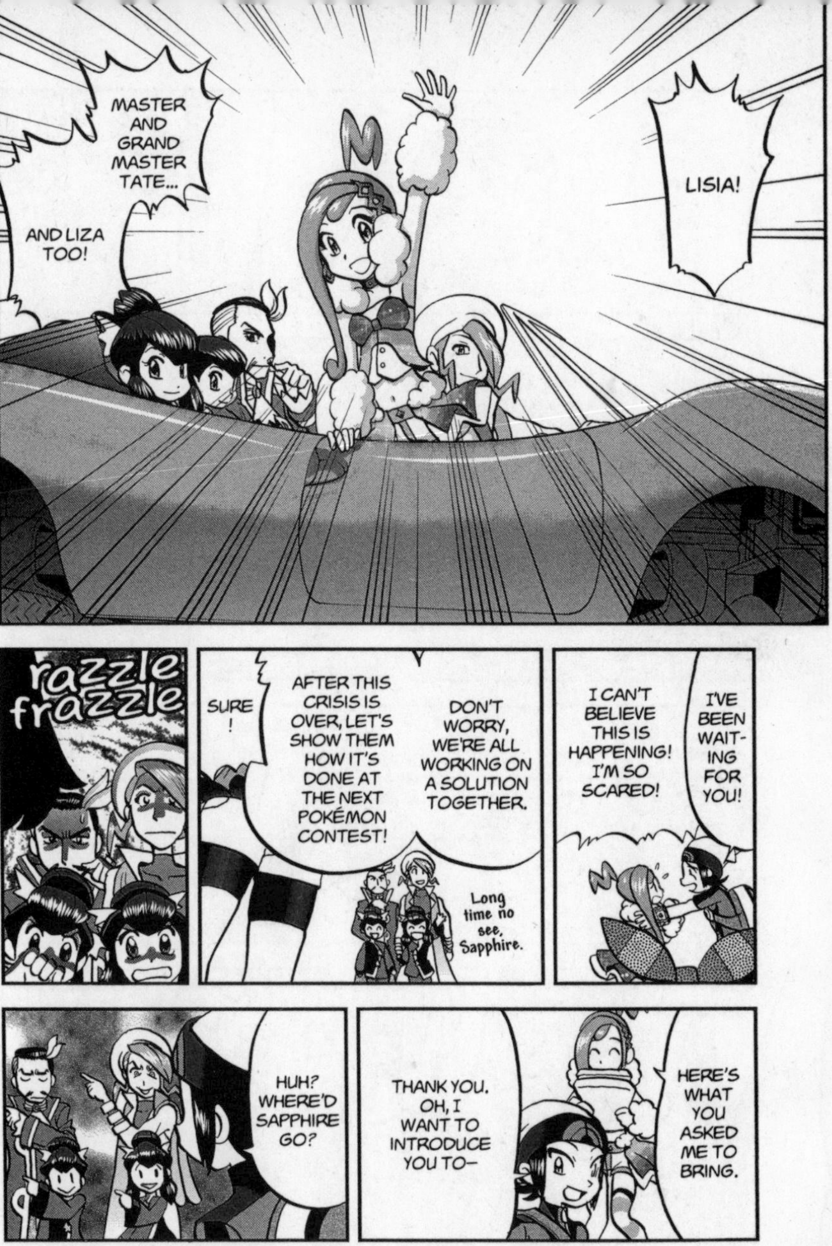
LISIA!
MASTER AND GRAND MASTER TATE...
AND LIZA TOO!
I'VE BEEN WAITING FOR YOU!
I CAN'T BELIEVE THIS IS HAPPENING! I'M SO SCARED!
DON'T WORRY, WE'RE ALL WORKING ON A SOLUTION TOGETHER.
AFTER THIS CRISIS IS OVER, LET'S SHOW THEM HOW IT'S DONE AT THE NEXT POKÉMON CONTEST!
SURE!
Long time no see, Sapphire.
razzle frazzle
HERE'S WHAT YOU ASKED ME TO BRING.
THANK YOU. OH, I WANT TO INTRODUCE YOU TO—
HUH? WHERE'D SAPPHIRE GO?

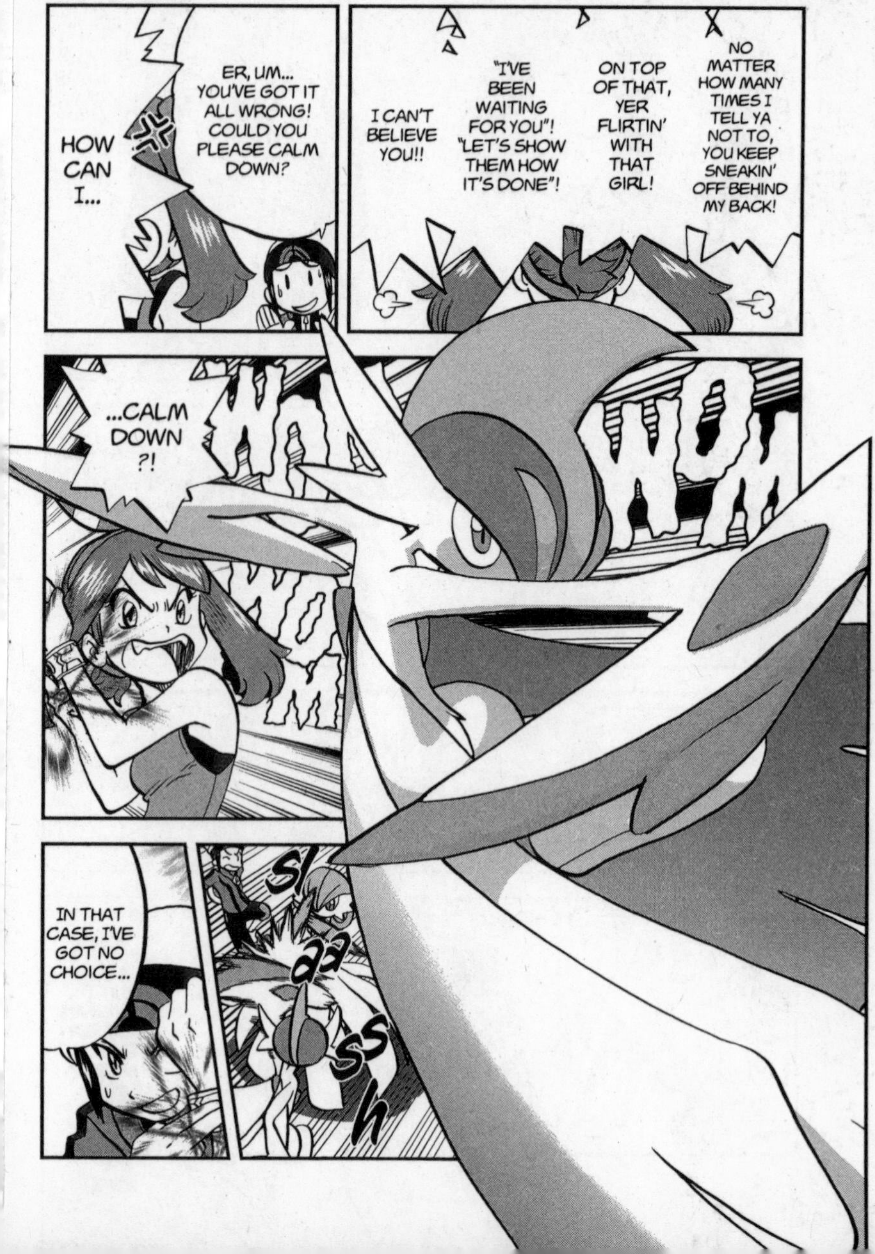
NO MATTER HOW MANY TIMES I TELL YA NOT TO, YOU KEEP SNEAKIN' OFF BEHIND MY BACK!
ON TOP OF THAT, YER FLIRTIN' WITH THAT GIRL!
"I'VE BEEN WAITING FOR YOU"! "LET'S SHOW THEM HOW IT'S DONE"!
I CAN'T BELIEVE YOU!!
ER, UM... YOU'VE GOT IT ALL WRONG! COULD YOU PLEASE CALM DOWN?
HOW CAN I...
...CALM DOWN ?!
IN THAT CASE, I'VE GOT NO CHOICE...

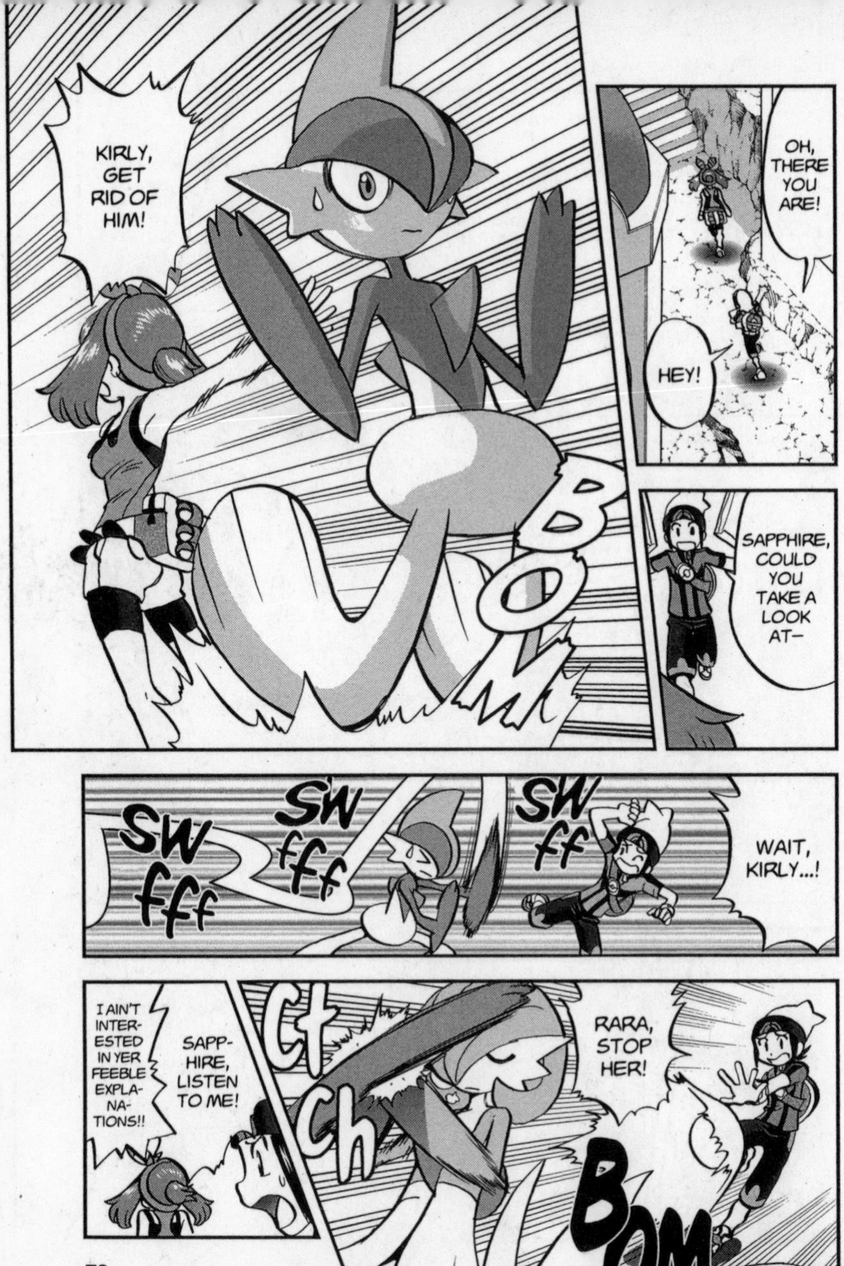
OH, THERE YOU ARE!
HEY!
SAPPHIRE, COULD YOU TAKE A LOOK AT—
KIRLY, GET RID OF HIM!
BOOM
WAIT, KIRLY...!
SWff
SWfff
SWfff
RARA, STOP HER!
BOM
Ct
Ch
SAPP-HIRE, LISTEN TO ME!
I AIN'T INTER-ESTED IN YER FEEBLE EXPLA-NA-TIONS!!

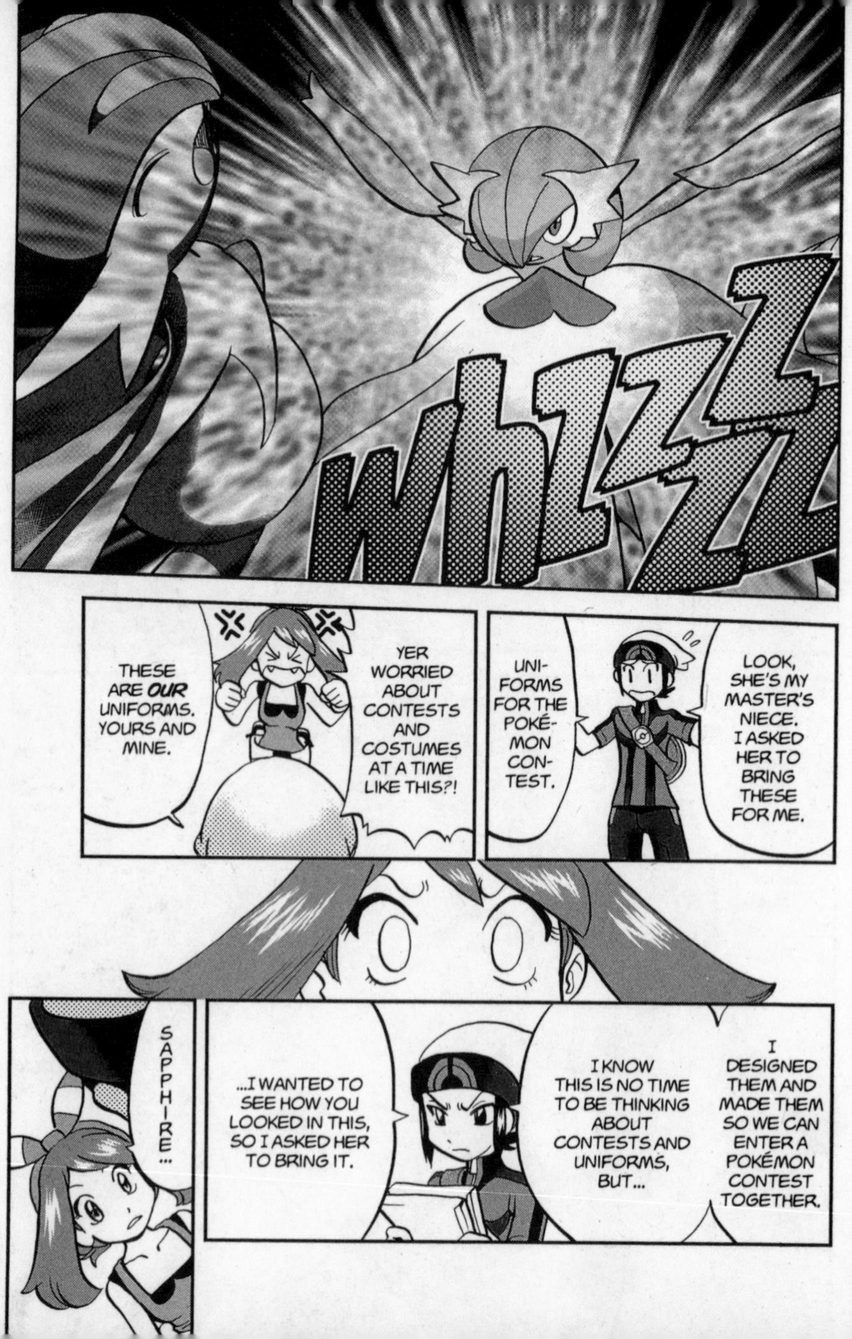
WHZZZZ
LOOK, SHE'S MY MASTER'S NIECE. I ASKED HER TO BRING THESE FOR ME.
UNIFORMS FOR THE POKÉMON CONTEST.
YER WORRIED ABOUT CONTESTS AND COSTUMES AT A TIME LIKE THIS?!
THESE ARE *OUR* UNIFORMS. YOURS AND MINE.
I DESIGNED THEM AND MADE THEM SO WE CAN ENTER A POKÉMON CONTEST TOGETHER.
I KNOW THIS IS NO TIME TO BE THINKING ABOUT CONTESTS AND UNIFORMS, BUT...
...I WANTED TO SEE HOW YOU LOOKED IN THIS, SO I ASKED HER TO BRING IT.
SAPPHIRE...

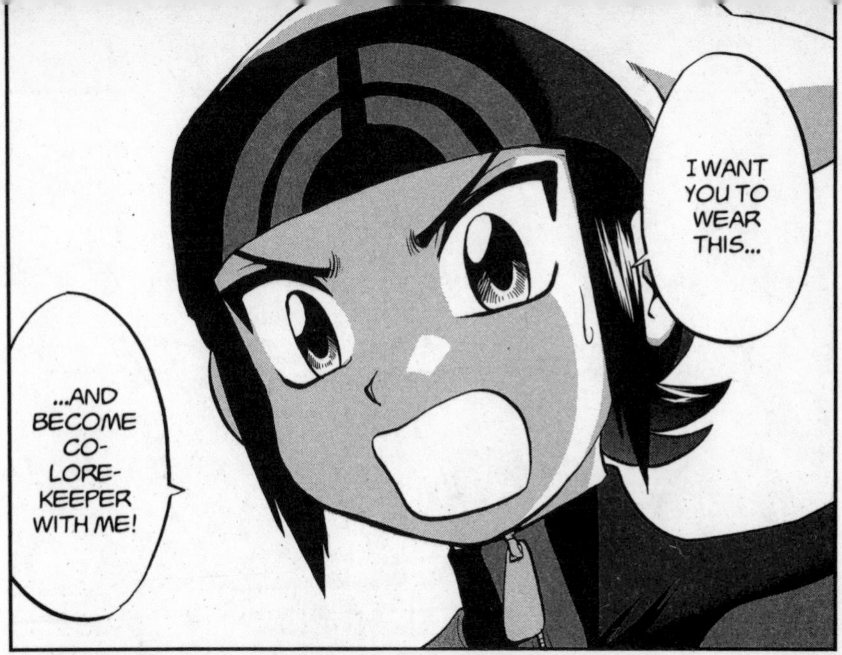
I WANT YOU TO WEAR THIS...
...AND BECOME CO-LORE-KEEPER WITH ME!
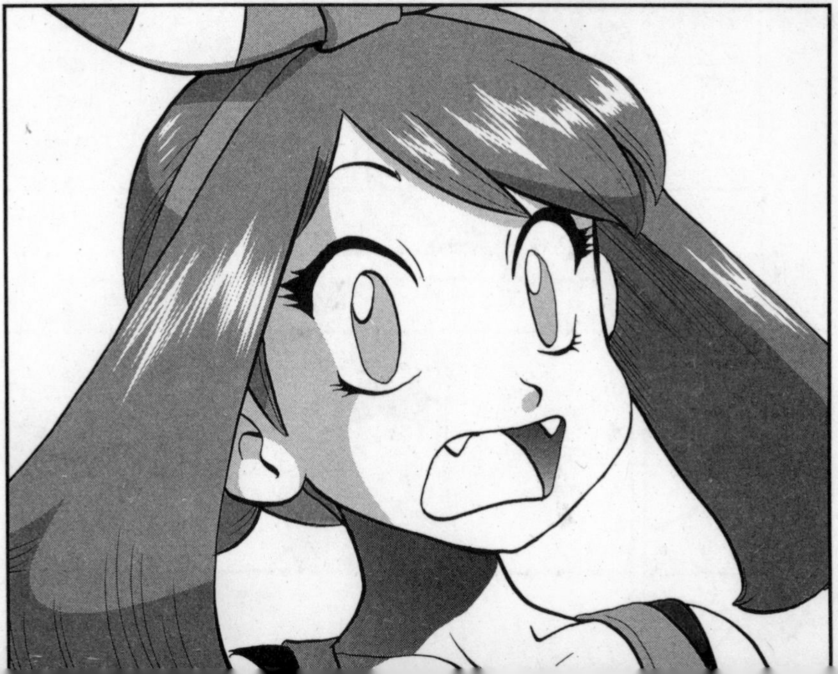

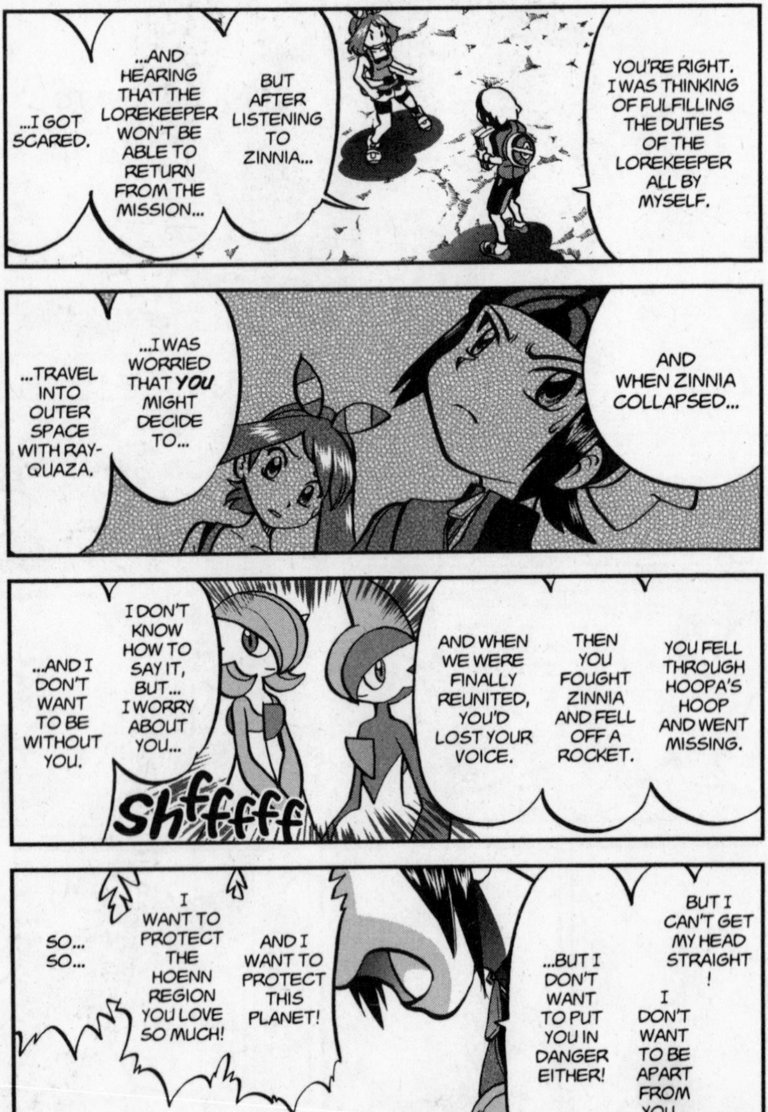
YOU'RE RIGHT. I WAS THINKING OF FULFILLING THE DUTIES OF THE LOREKEEPER ALL BY MYSELF.
BUT AFTER LISTENING TO ZINNIA...
...AND HEARING THAT THE LOREKEEPER WON'T BE ABLE TO RETURN FROM THE MISSION...
...I GOT SCARED.
AND WHEN ZINNIA COLLAPSED...
...I WAS WORRIED THAT ***YOU*** MIGHT DECIDE TO...
...TRAVEL INTO OUTER SPACE WITH RAY-QUAZA.
YOU FELL THROUGH HOOPA'S HOOP AND WENT MISSING.
THEN YOU FOUGHT ZINNIA AND FELL OFF A ROCKET.
AND WHEN WE WERE FINALLY REUNITED, YOU'D LOST YOUR VOICE.
I DON'T KNOW HOW TO SAY IT, BUT... I WORRY ABOUT YOU...
...AND I DON'T WANT TO BE WITHOUT YOU.
SHFFFFF
BUT I CAN'T GET MY HEAD STRAIGHT!
I DON'T WANT TO BE APART FROM YOU...
...BUT I DON'T WANT TO PUT YOU IN DANGER EITHER!
AND I WANT TO PROTECT THIS PLANET!
I WANT TO PROTECT THE HOENN REGION YOU LOVE SO MUCH!
SO... SO...

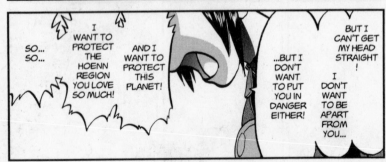

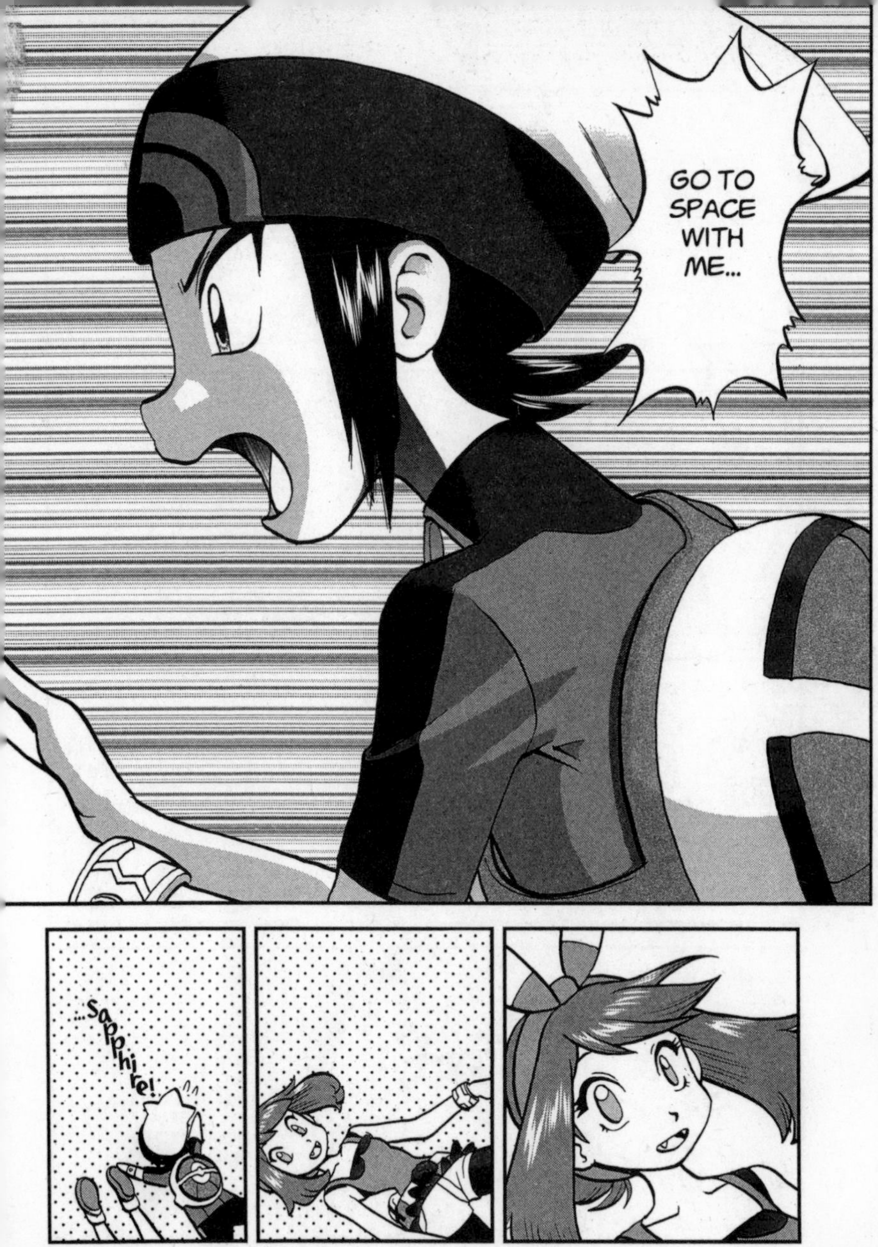
GO TO SPACE WITH ME...
...sapphire!

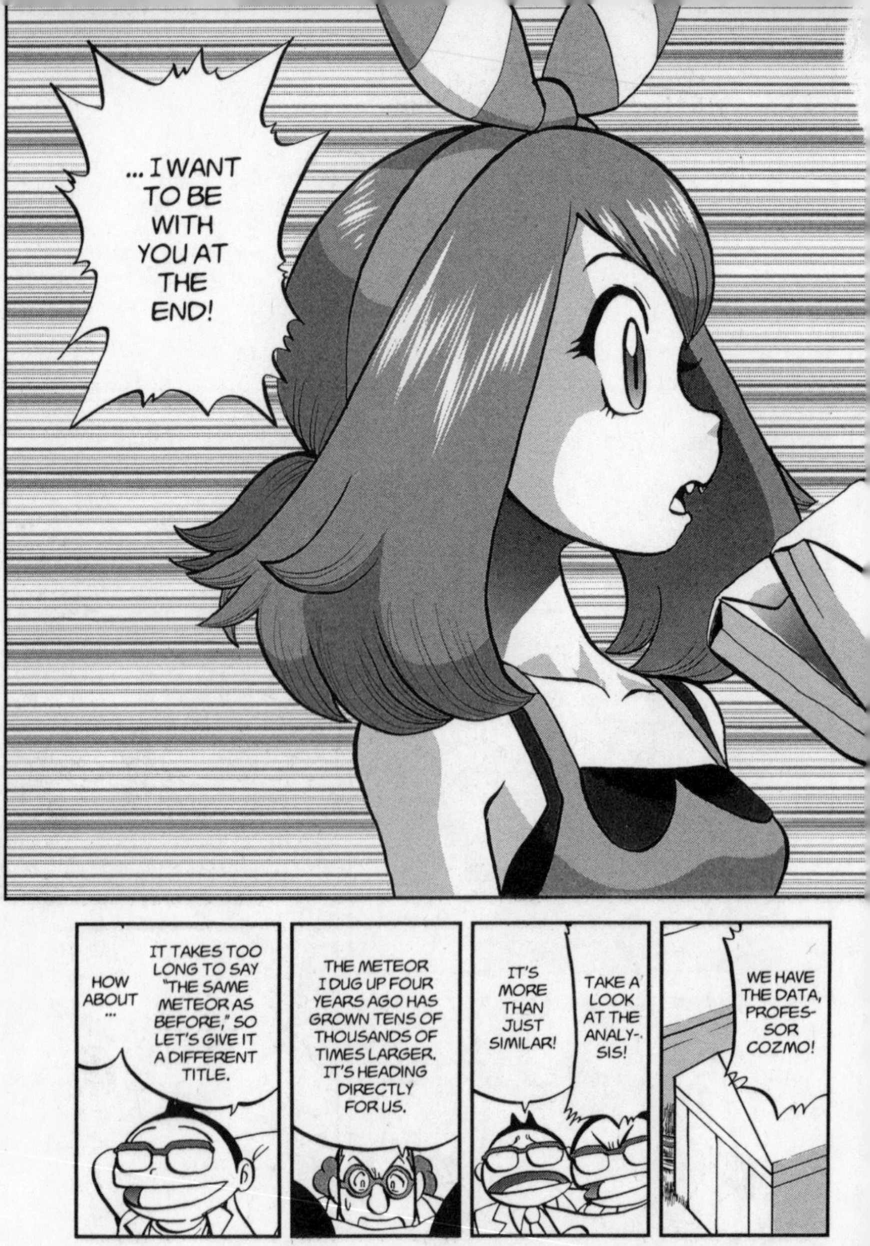
...I WANT TO BE WITH YOU AT THE END!
WE HAVE THE DATA, PROFES-SOR COZMO!
TAKE A LOOK AT THE ANALY-SIS!
IT'S MORE THAN JUST SIMILAR!
THE METEOR I DUG UP FOUR YEARS AGO HAS GROWN TENS OF THOUSANDS OF TIMES LARGER. IT'S HEADING DIRECTLY FOR US.
IT TAKES TOO LONG TO SAY "THE SAME METEOR AS BEFORE," SO LET'S GIVE IT A DIFFERENT TITLE.
HOW ABOUT ...

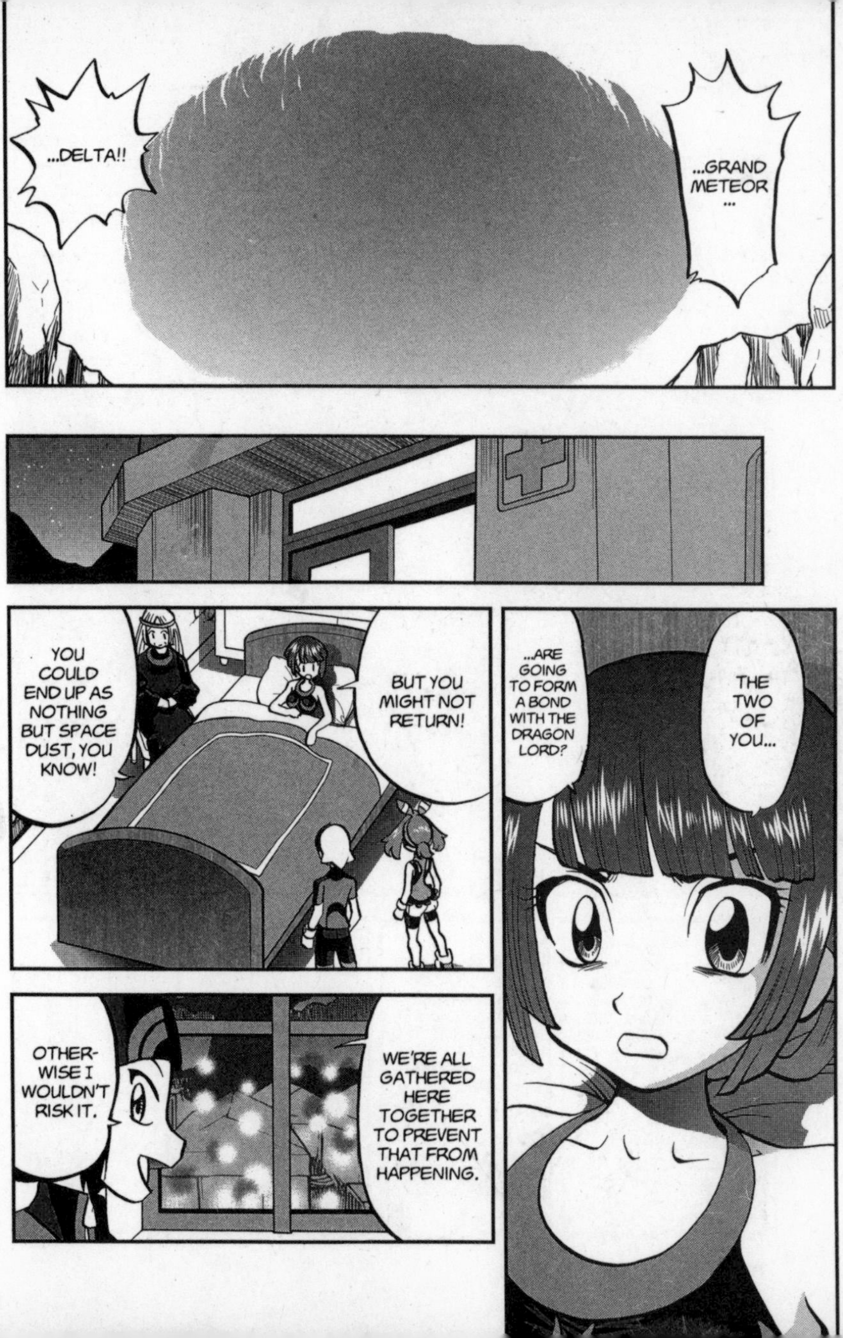
...GRAND METEOR ...
...DELTA!!
THE TWO OF YOU...
...ARE GOING TO FORM A BOND WITH THE DRAGON LORD?
BUT YOU MIGHT NOT RETURN!
YOU COULD END UP AS NOTHING BUT SPACE DUST, YOU KNOW!
WE'RE ALL GATHERED HERE TOGETHER TO PREVENT THAT FROM HAPPENING.
OTHER-WISE I WOULDN'T RISK IT.

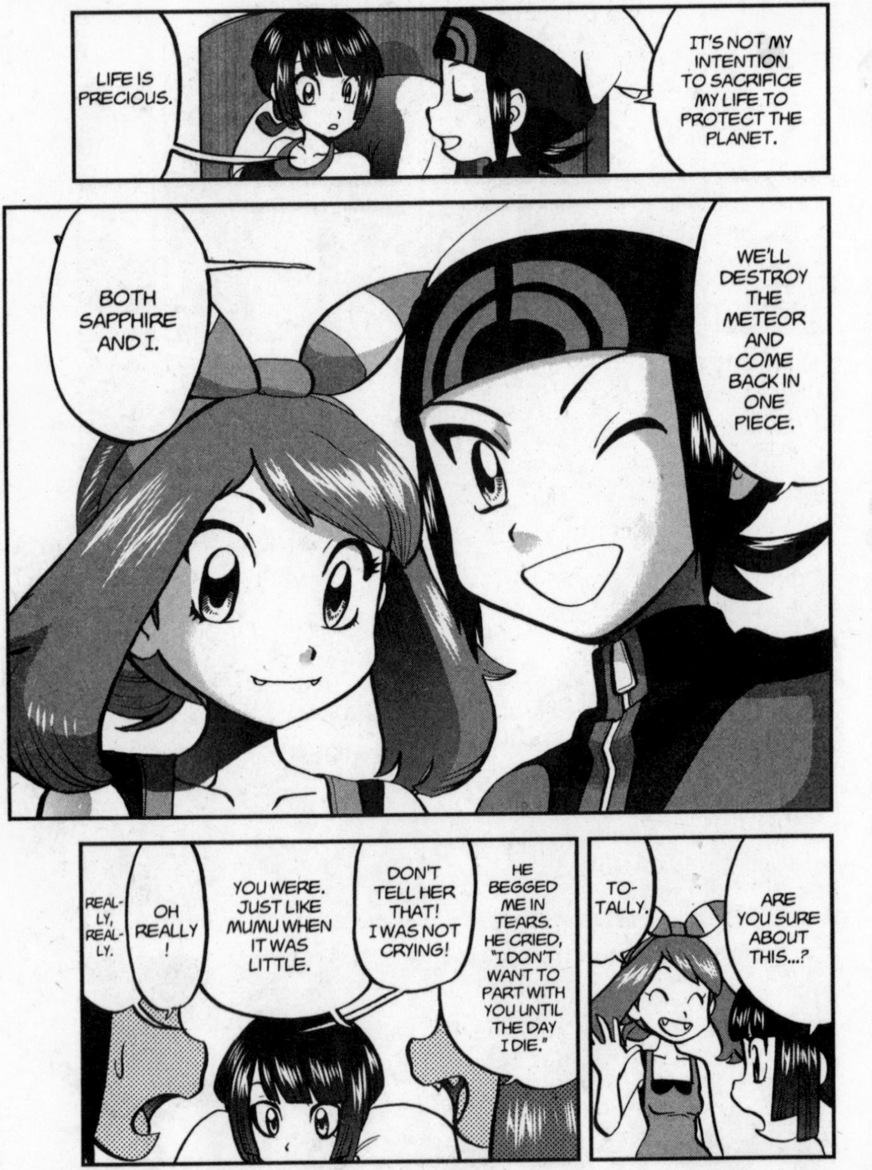
IT'S NOT MY INTENTION TO SACRIFICE MY LIFE TO PROTECT THE PLANET.
LIFE IS PRECIOUS.
WE'LL DESTROY THE METEOR AND COME BACK IN ONE PIECE.
BOTH SAPPHIRE AND I.
ARE YOU SURE ABOUT THIS...?
TO-TALLY.
HE BEGGED ME IN TEARS. HE CRIED, "I DON'T WANT TO PART WITH YOU UNTIL THE DAY I DIE."
DON'T TELL HER THAT! I WAS NOT CRYING!
YOU WERE. JUST LIKE MUMU WHEN IT WAS LITTLE.
OH REALLY!
REAL-LY, REAL-LY.

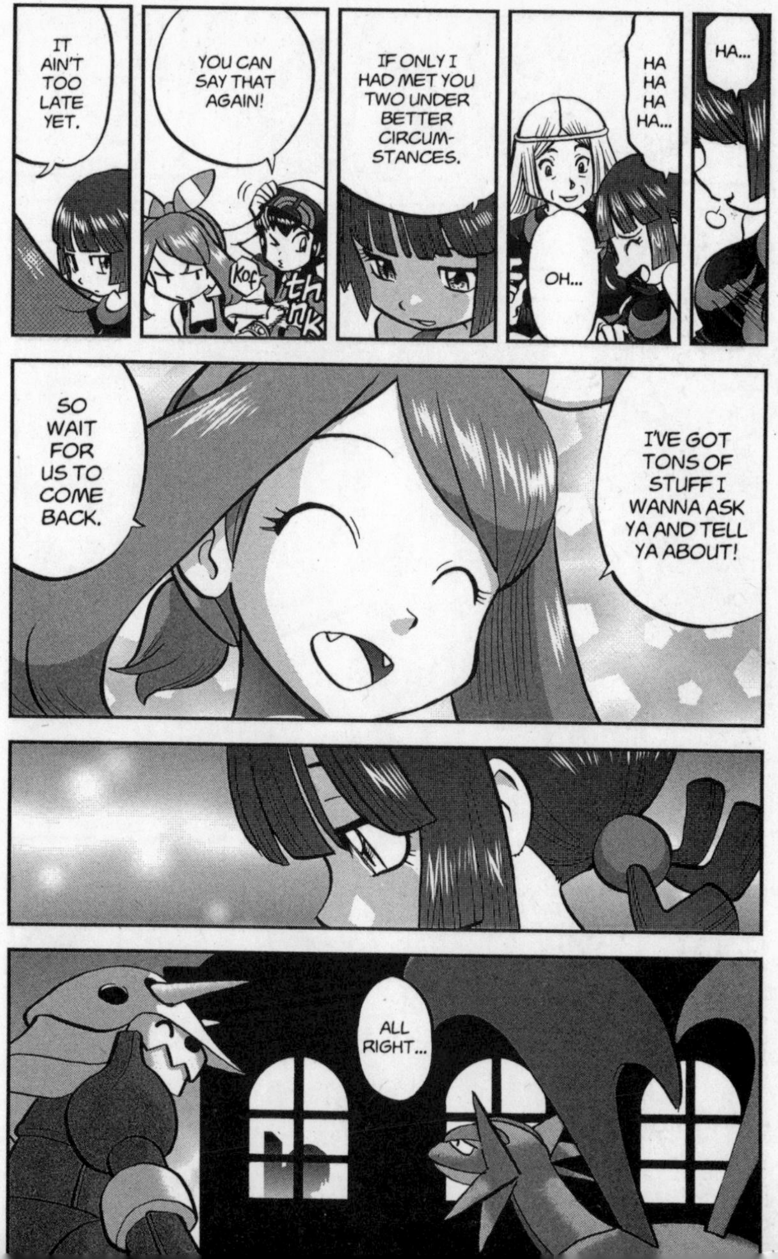
HA...
HA HA HA HA...
OH...
IF ONLY I HAD MET YOU TWO UNDER BETTER CIRCUM-STANCES.
thnk
Kof
YOU CAN SAY THAT AGAIN!
IT AIN'T TOO LATE YET.
I'VE GOT TONS OF STUFF I WANNA ASK YA AND TELL YA ABOUT!
SO WAIT FOR US TO COME BACK.
ALL RIGHT...

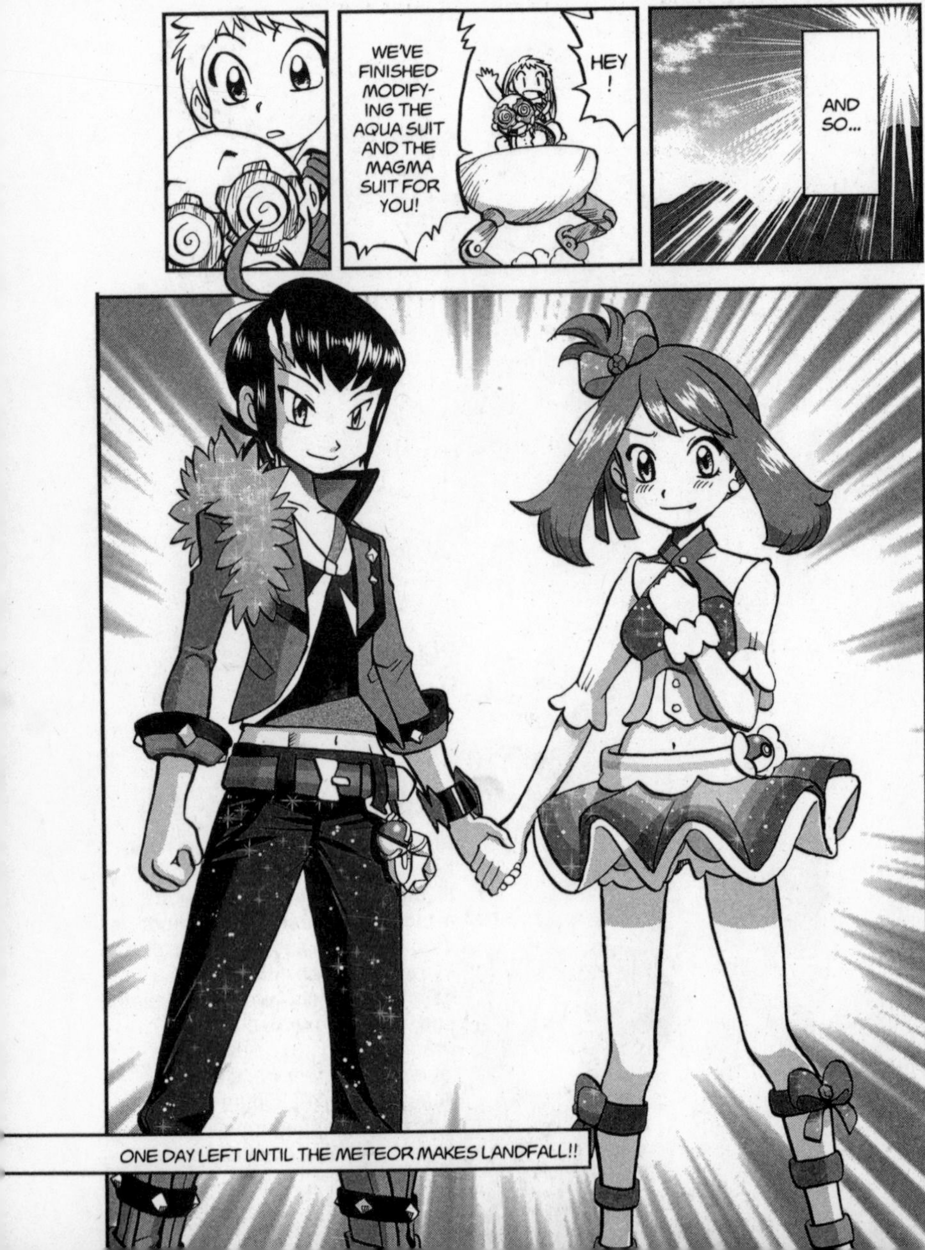
AND SO...
HEY!
WE'VE FINISHED MODIFYING THE AQUA SUIT AND THE MAGMA SUIT FOR YOU!
ONE DAY LEFT UNTIL THE METEOR MAKES LANDFALL!!

## DRAGON ASCENT

Attacks the opponent with a rapid boost in speed. It is a powerful Flying-type move in which you attack the opponent like a shooting star. The move has been recorded in a scroll which can otherwise be called an ancient Technical Machine and was safeguarded by the Draconids. The use of the move lowers the defense and special defense of the Pokémon that used it, but despite that drawback, it's an overwhelmingly powerful move.

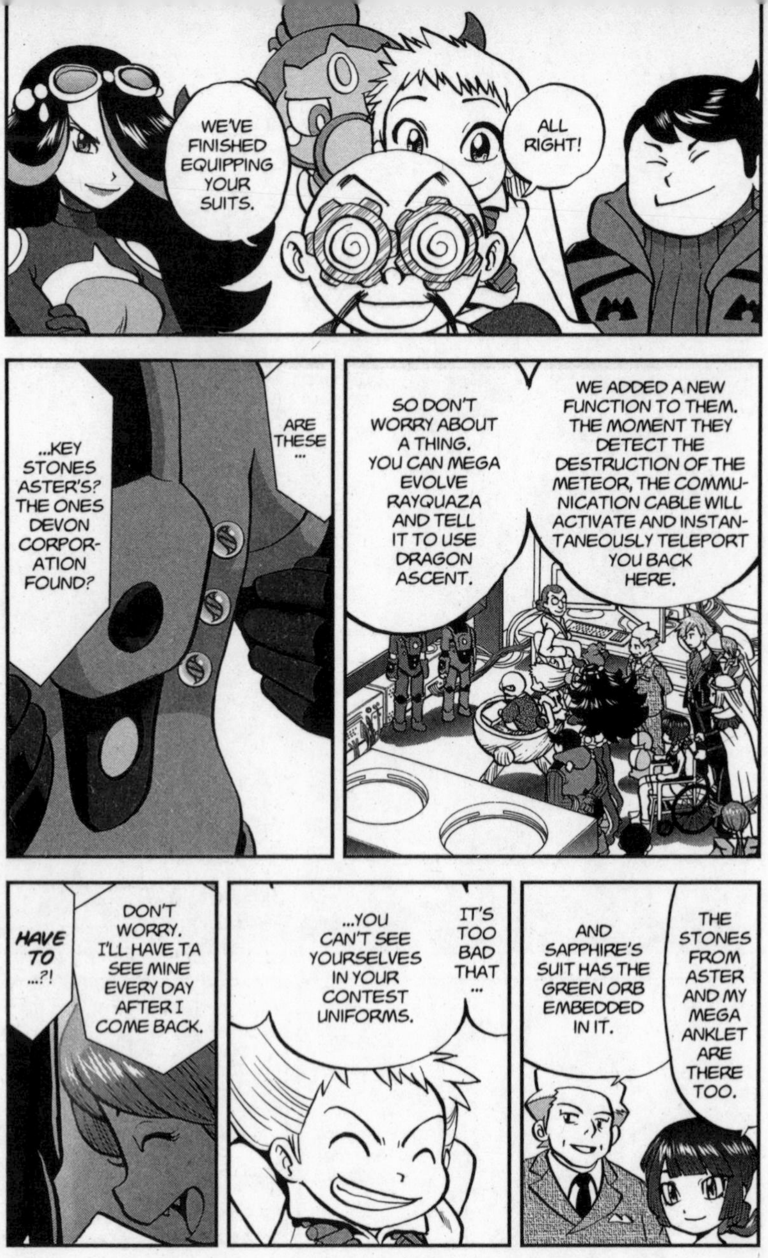
WE'VE FINISHED EQUIPPING YOUR SUITS.
ALL RIGHT!
WE ADDED A NEW FUNCTION TO THEM. THE MOMENT THEY DETECT THE DESTRUCTION OF THE METEOR, THE COMMUNICATION CABLE WILL ACTIVATE AND INSTANTANEOUSLY TELEPORT YOU BACK HERE.
SO DON'T WORRY ABOUT A THING. YOU CAN MEGA EVOLVE RAYQUAZA AND TELL IT TO USE DRAGON ASCENT.
ARE THESE ...
...KEY STONES ASTER'S? THE ONES DEVON CORPORATION FOUND?
THE STONES FROM ASTER AND MY MEGA ANKLET ARE THERE TOO.
AND SAPPHIRE'S SUIT HAS THE GREEN ORB EMBEDDED IN IT.
IT'S TOO BAD THAT ...
...YOU CAN'T SEE YOURSELVES IN YOUR CONTEST UNIFORMS.
DON'T WORRY. I'LL HAVE TA SEE MINE EVERY DAY AFTER I COME BACK.
HAVE TO ...?!

# Omega Alpha Adventure 21

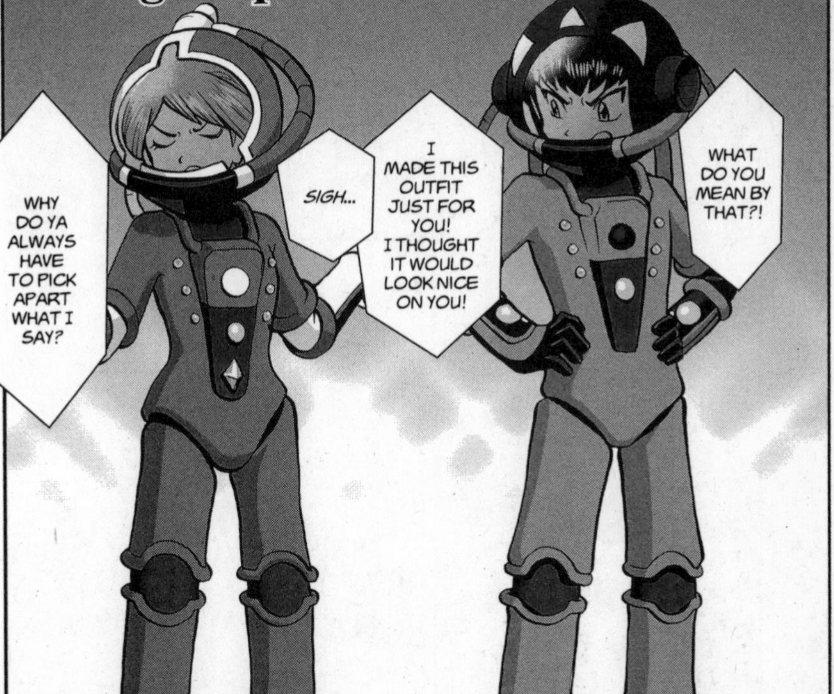
WHAT DO YOU MEAN BY THAT?!
I MADE THIS OUTFIT JUST FOR YOU! I THOUGHT IT WOULD LOOK NICE ON YOU!
SIGH...
WHY DO YA ALWAYS HAVE TO PICK APART WHAT I SAY?

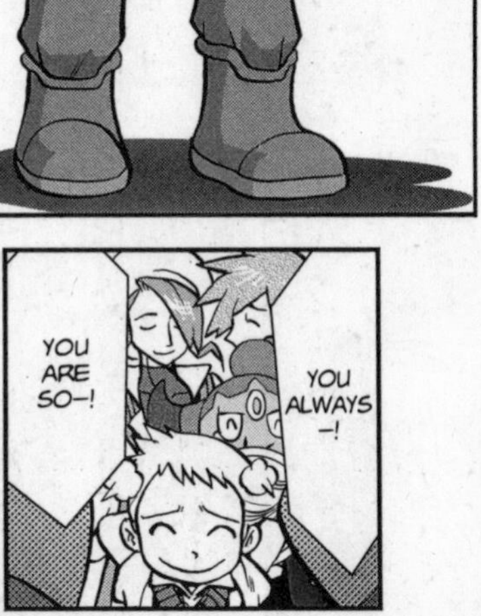
YOU ALWAYS —!
YOU ARE SO—!

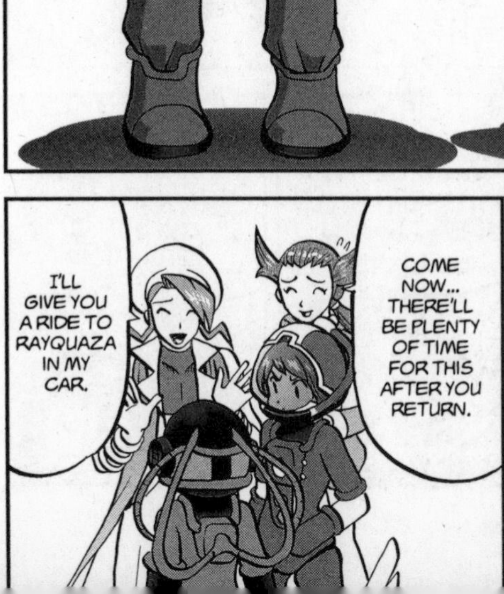
COME NOW... THERE'LL BE PLENTY OF TIME FOR THIS AFTER YOU RETURN.
I'LL GIVE YOU A RIDE TO RAYQUAZA IN MY CAR.

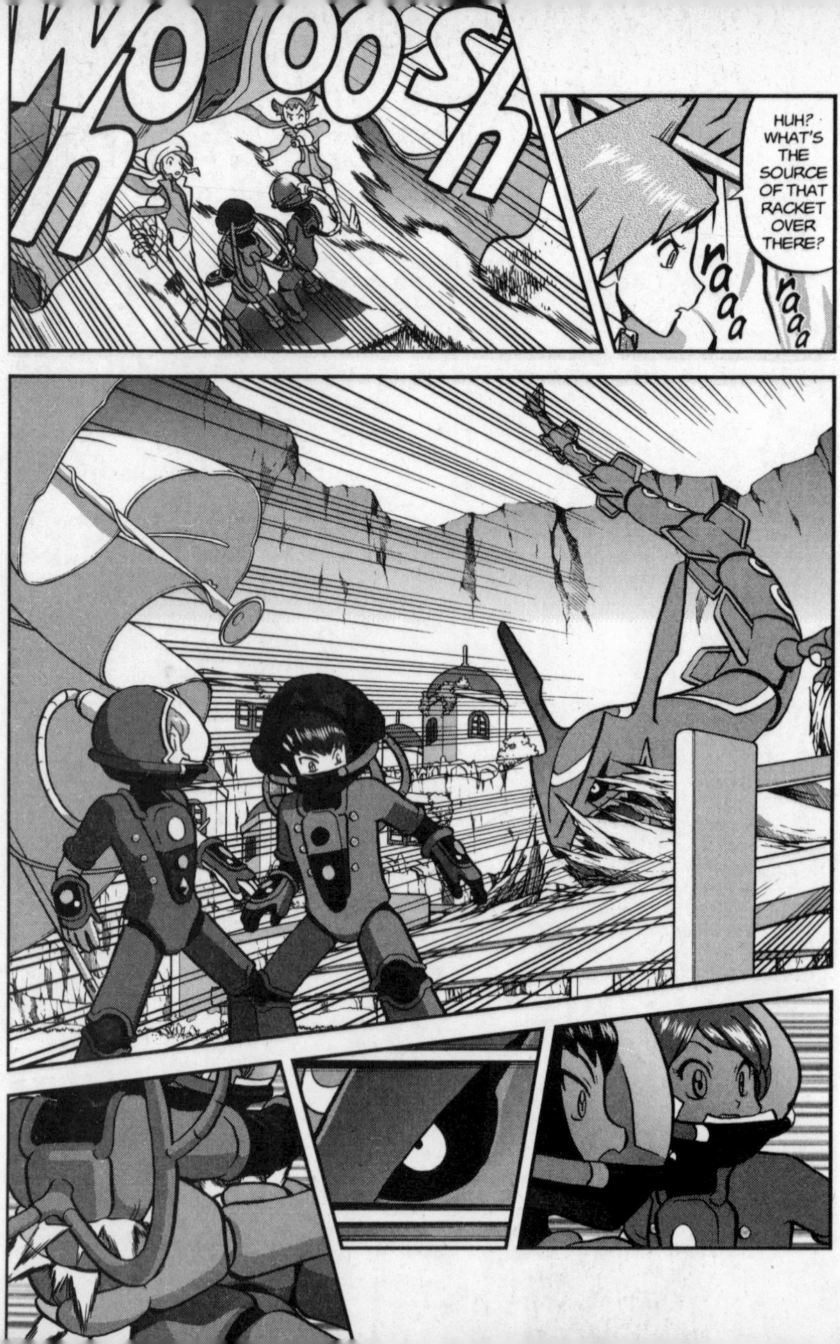
HUH? WHAT'S THE SOURCE OF THAT RACKET OVER THERE?
raaa raaa
WOOOOSH

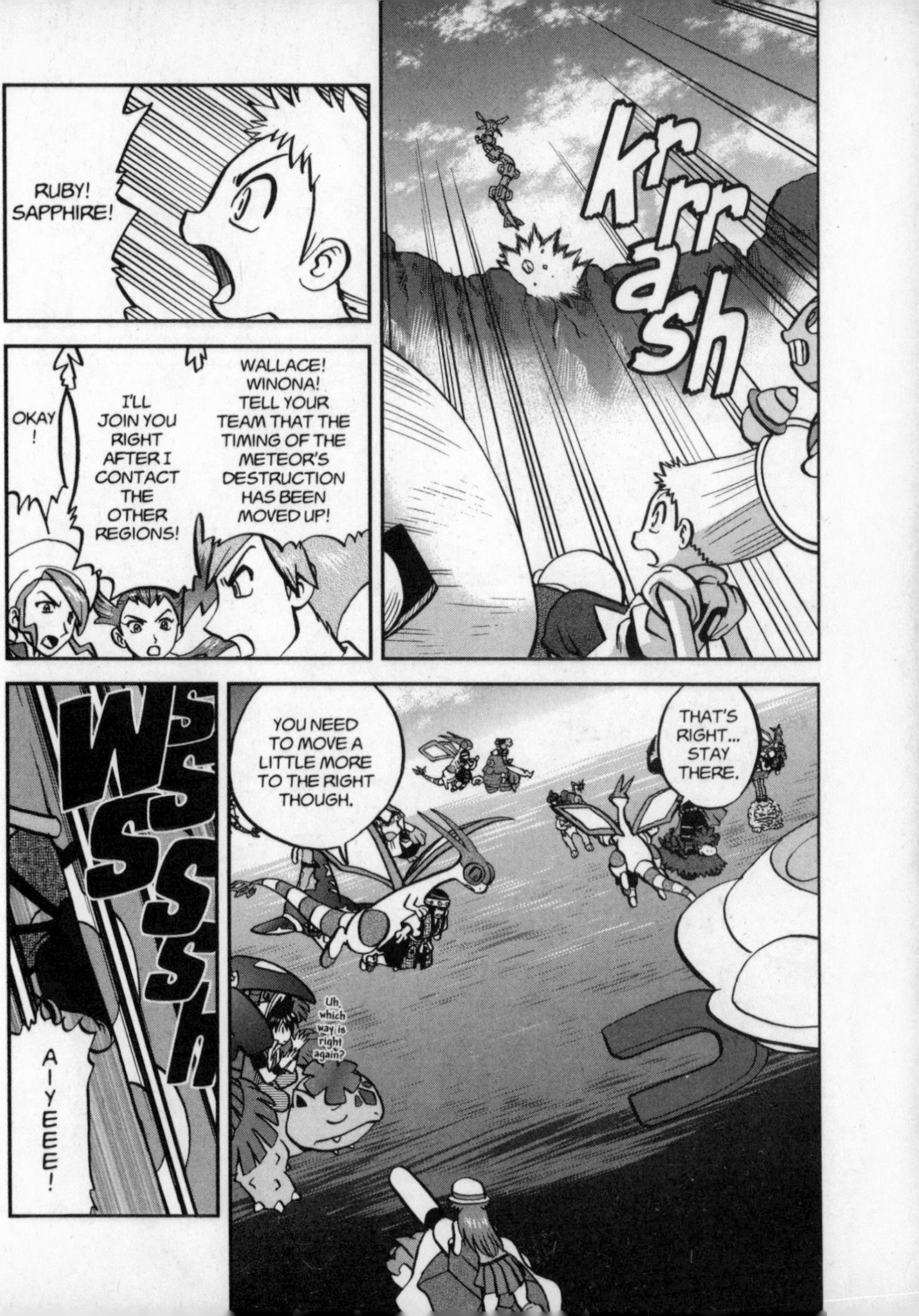
Krrrash
RUBY! SAPPHIRE!
WALLACE! WINONA! TELL YOUR TEAM THAT THE TIMING OF THE METEOR'S DESTRUCTION HAS BEEN MOVED UP!
I'LL JOIN YOU RIGHT AFTER I CONTACT THE OTHER REGIONS!
OKAY!
THAT'S RIGHT... STAY THERE.
YOU NEED TO MOVE A LITTLE MORE TO THE RIGHT THOUGH.
Uh, which way is right again?
WSSSh
AIYEEE!

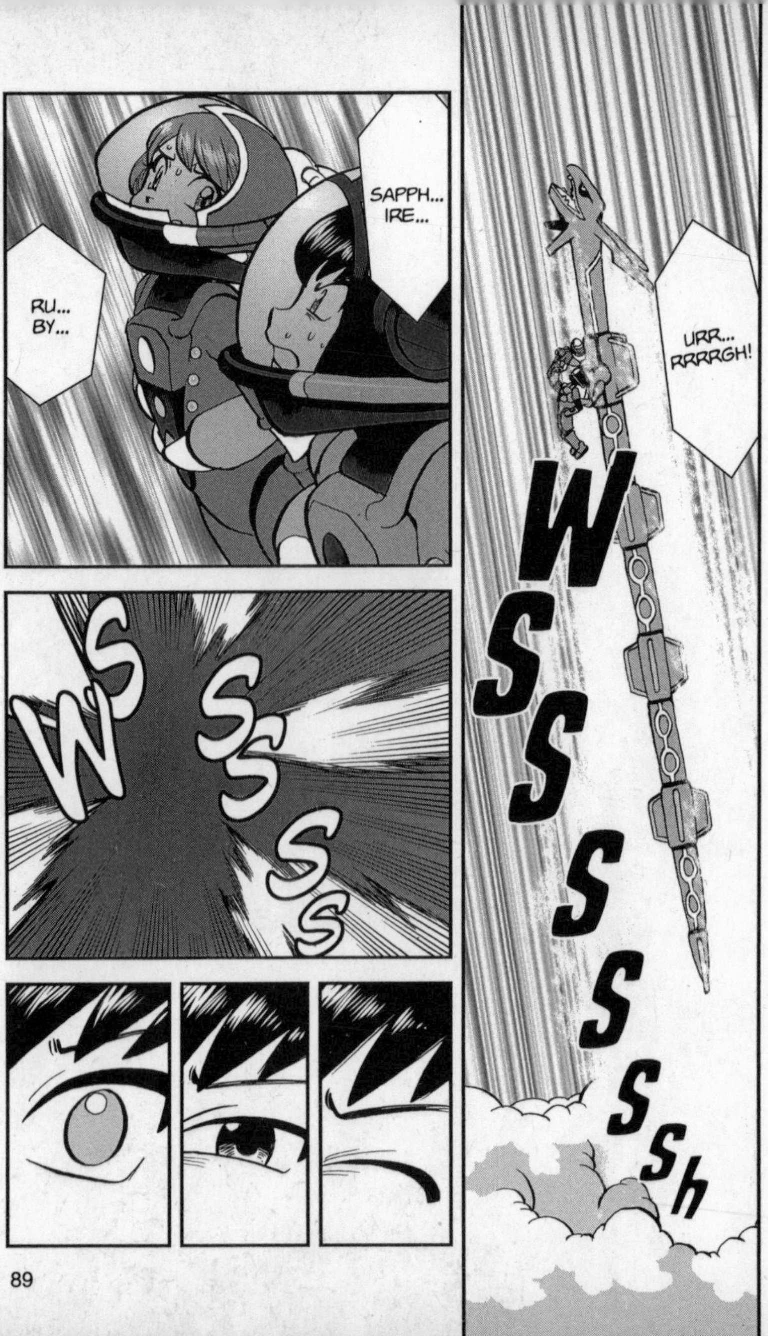
URR... RRRRGH!
WSSSSSSh
SAPPH... IRE...
RU... BY...
WSSSSS

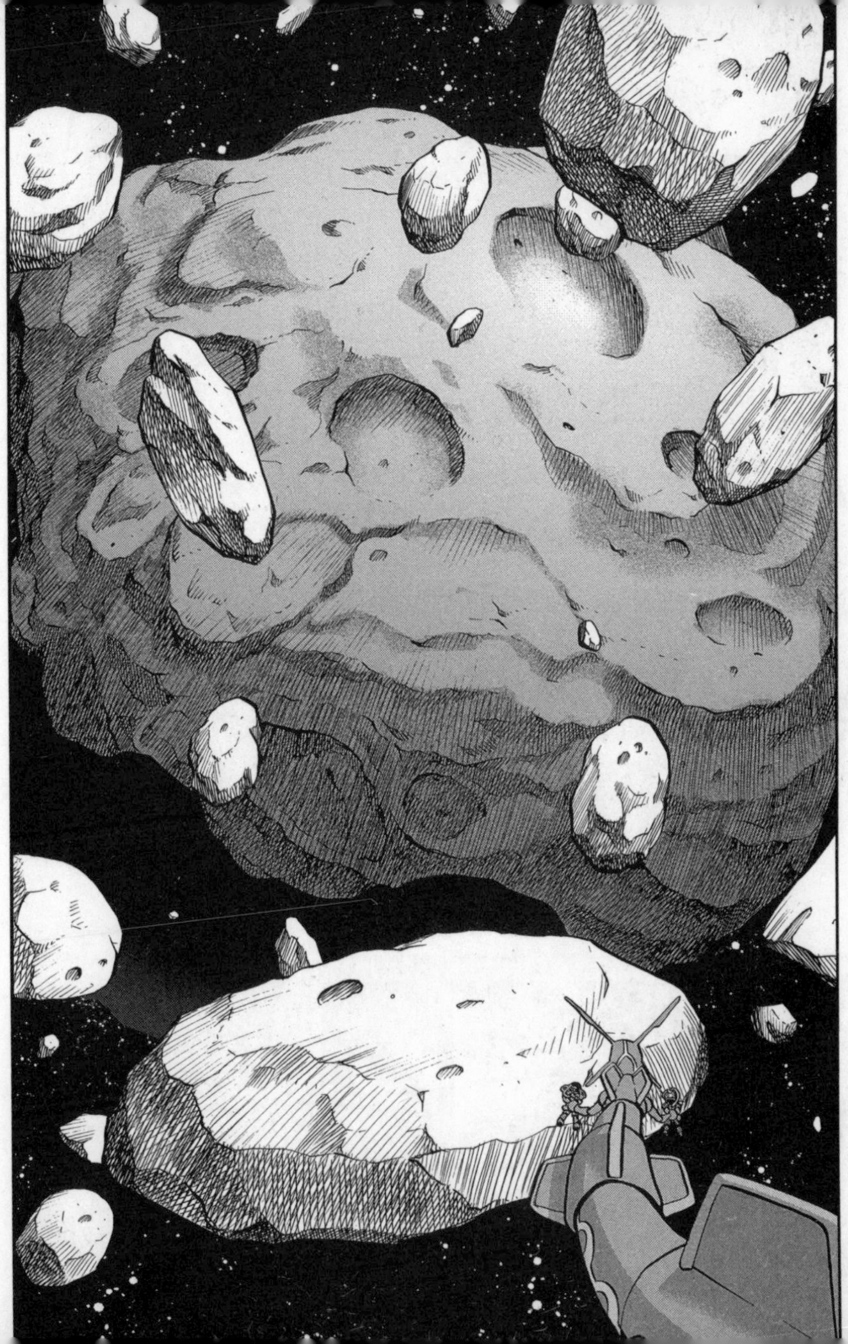

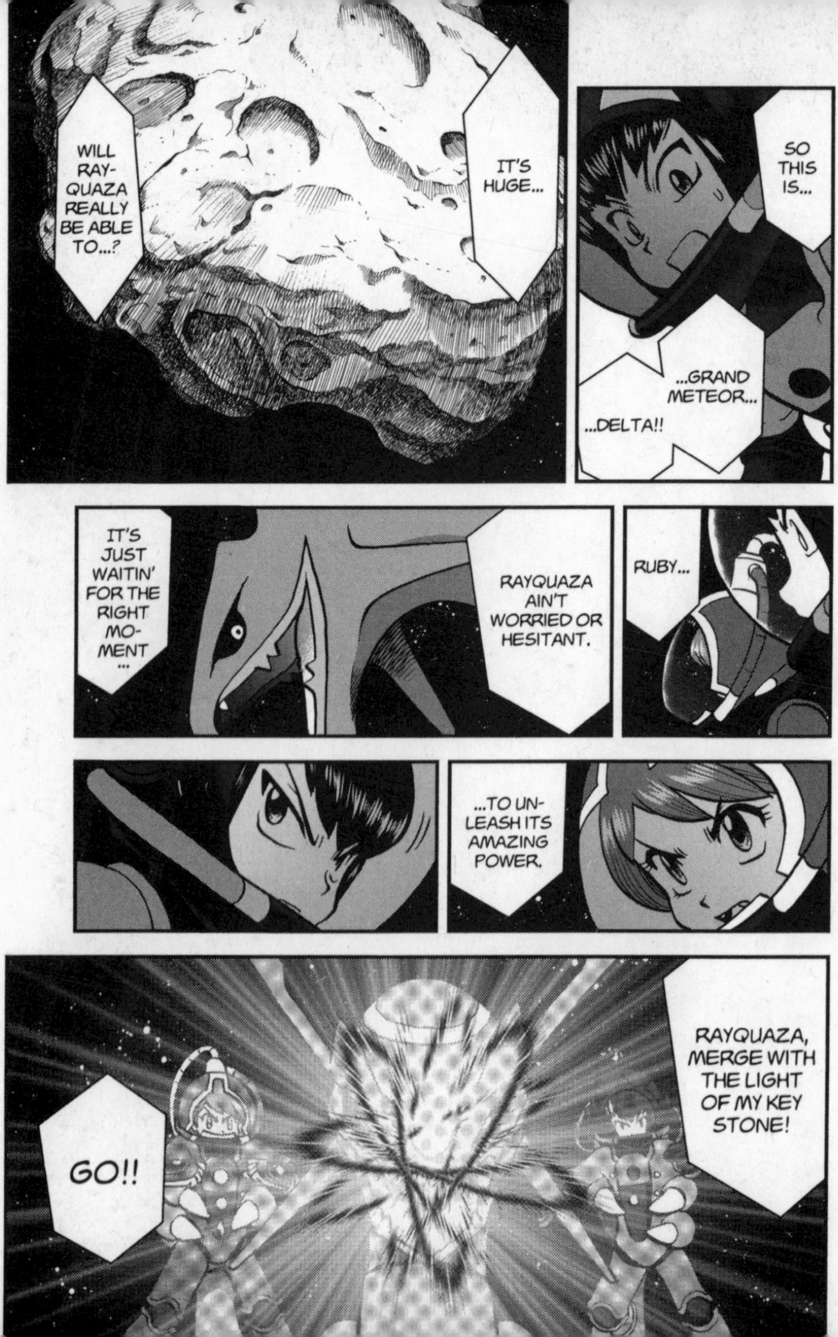
SO THIS IS...
...GRAND METEOR...
...DELTA!!
IT'S HUGE...
WILL RAY-QUAZA REALLY BE ABLE TO...?
RUBY...
RAYQUAZA AIN'T WORRIED OR HESITANT.
IT'S JUST WAITIN' FOR THE RIGHT MO-MENT...
...TO UN-LEASH ITS AMAZING POWER.
RAYQUAZA, MERGE WITH THE LIGHT OF MY KEY STONE!
GO!!

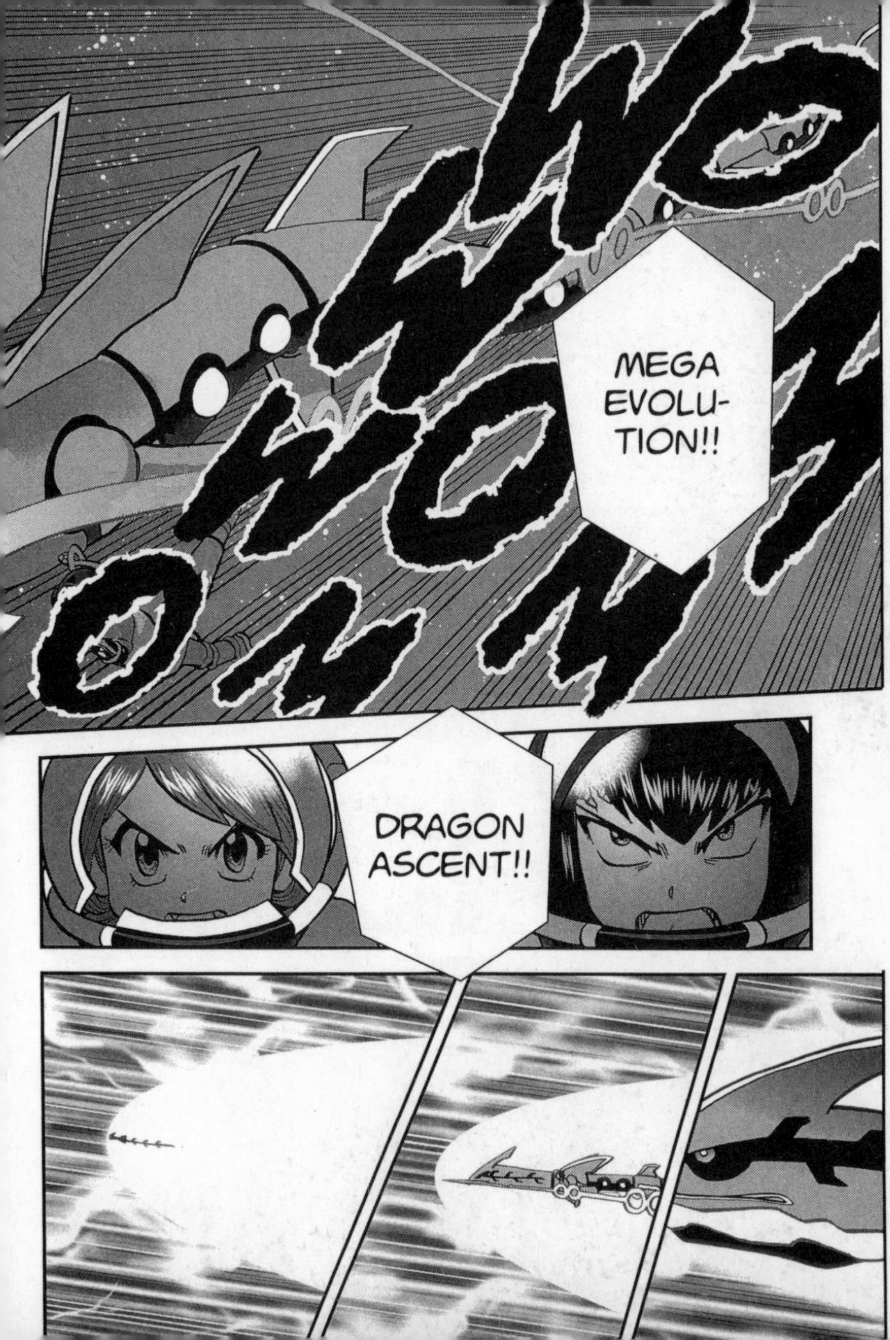
MEGA EVOLUTION!!
DRAGON ASCENT!!

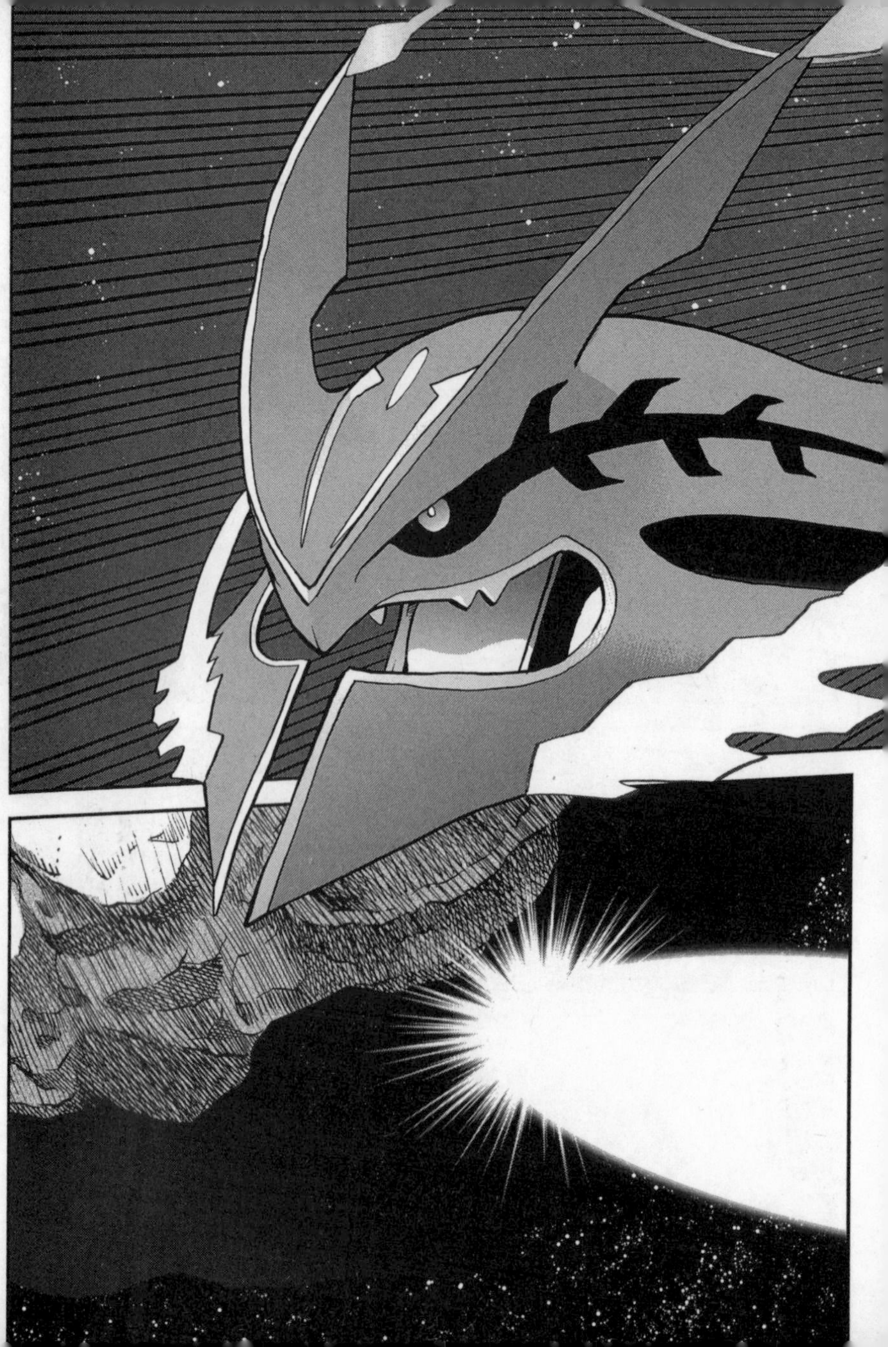

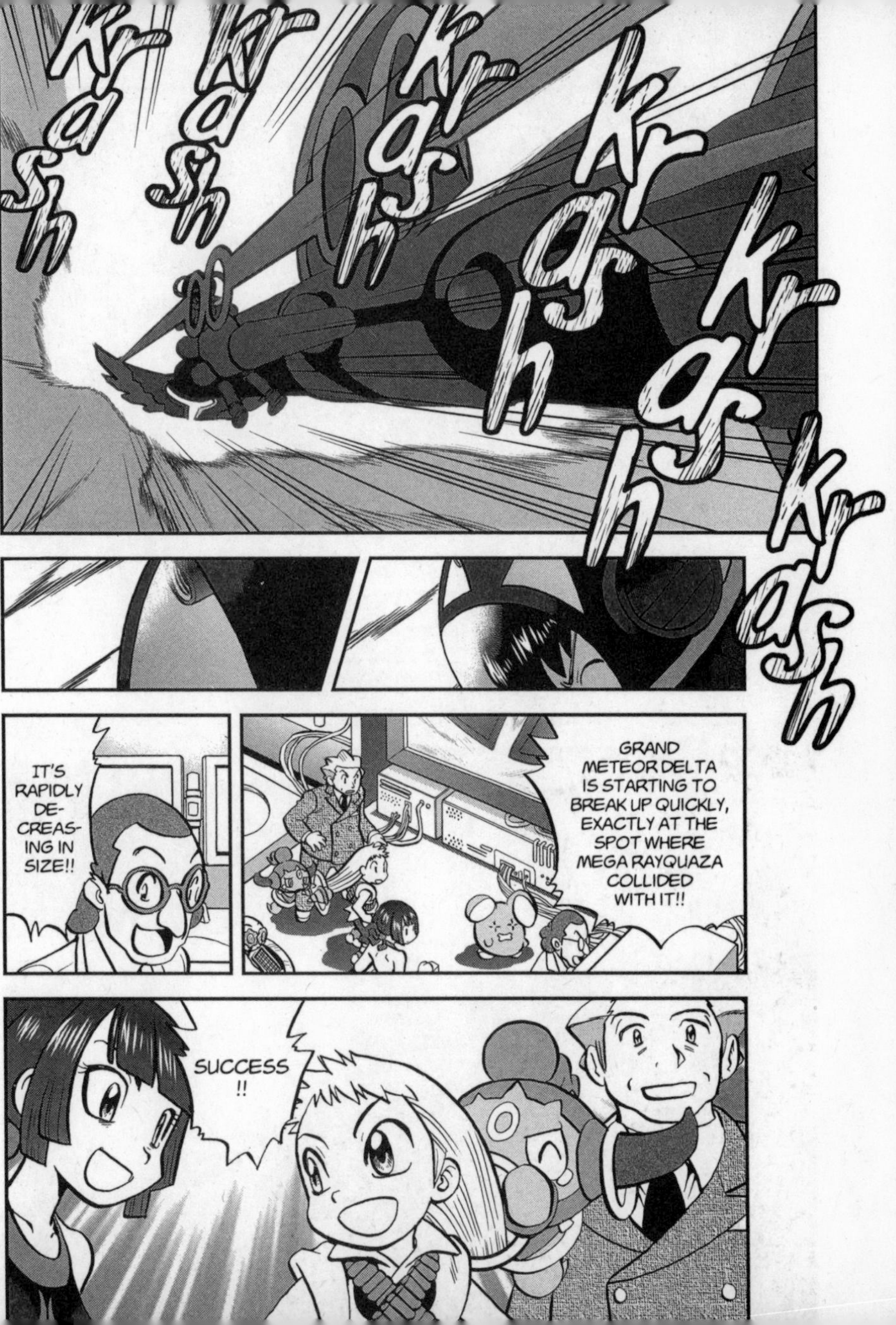
krash
krash
krash
krash
krash
krash
GRAND METEOR DELTA IS STARTING TO BREAK UP QUICKLY, EXACTLY AT THE SPOT WHERE MEGA RAYQUAZA COLLIDED WITH IT!!
IT'S RAPIDLY DE-CREAS-ING IN SIZE!!
SUCCESS!!

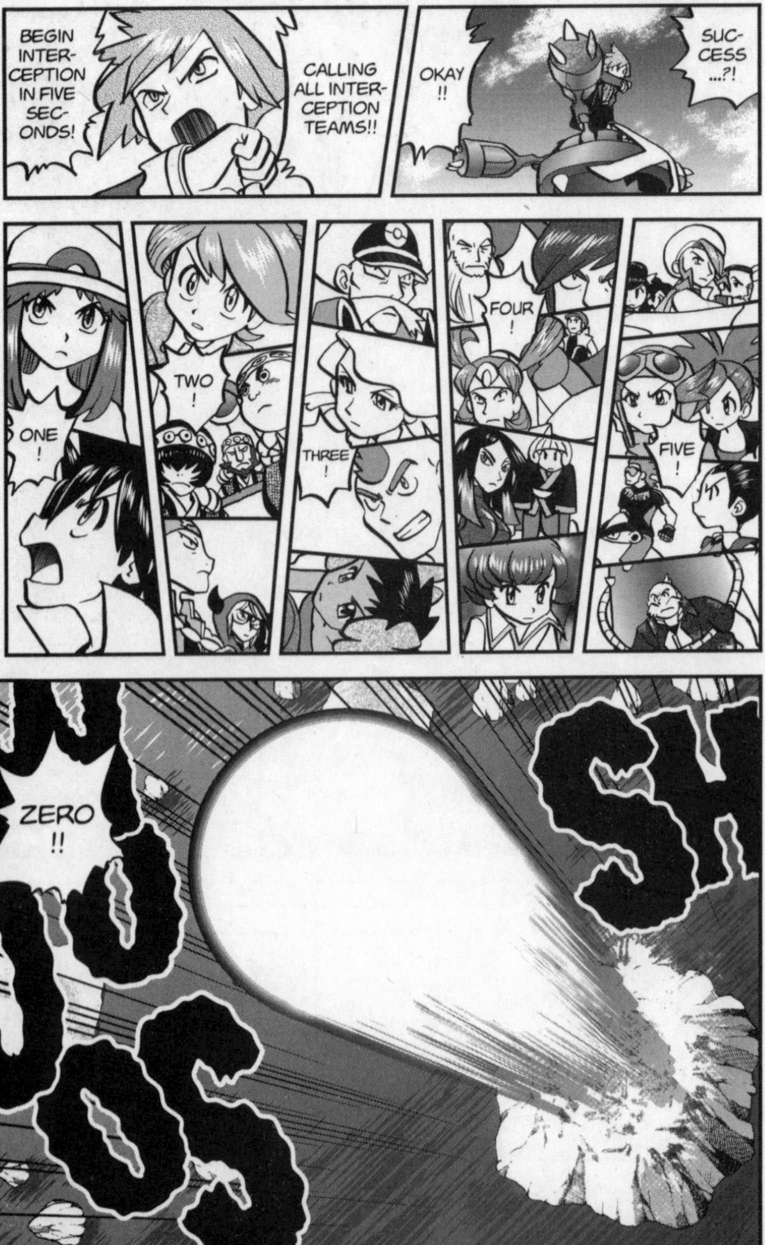
SUC-CESS ...?!
OKAY !!
CALLING ALL INTER-CEPTION TEAMS!!
BEGIN INTER-CEPTION IN FIVE SEC-ONDS!
FIVE !
FOUR !
THREE !
TWO !
ONE !
ZERO !!

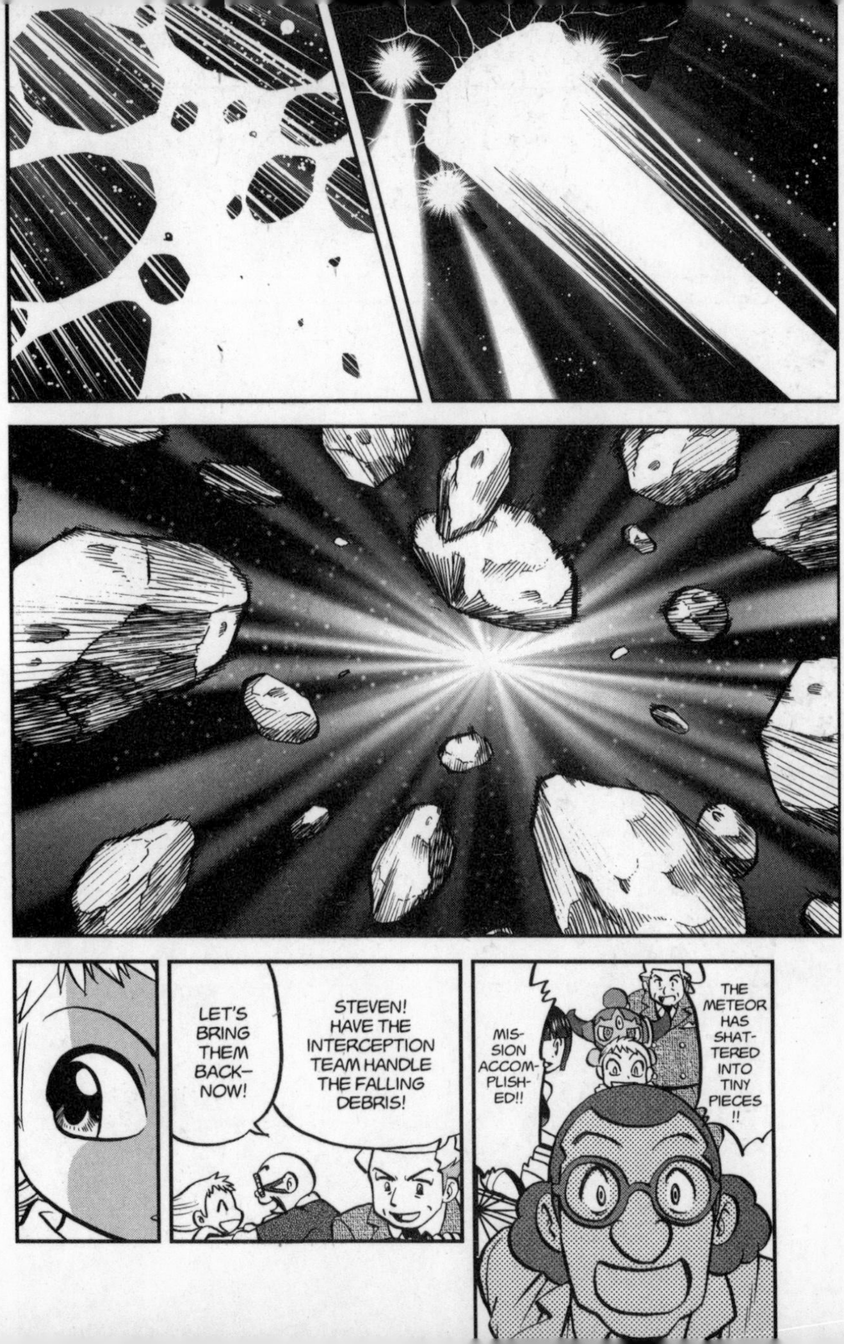
THE METEOR HAS SHATTERED INTO TINY PIECES!!
MISSION ACCOMPLISHED!!
STEVEN! HAVE THE INTERCEPTION TEAM HANDLE THE FALLING DEBRIS!
LET'S BRING THEM BACK—NOW!

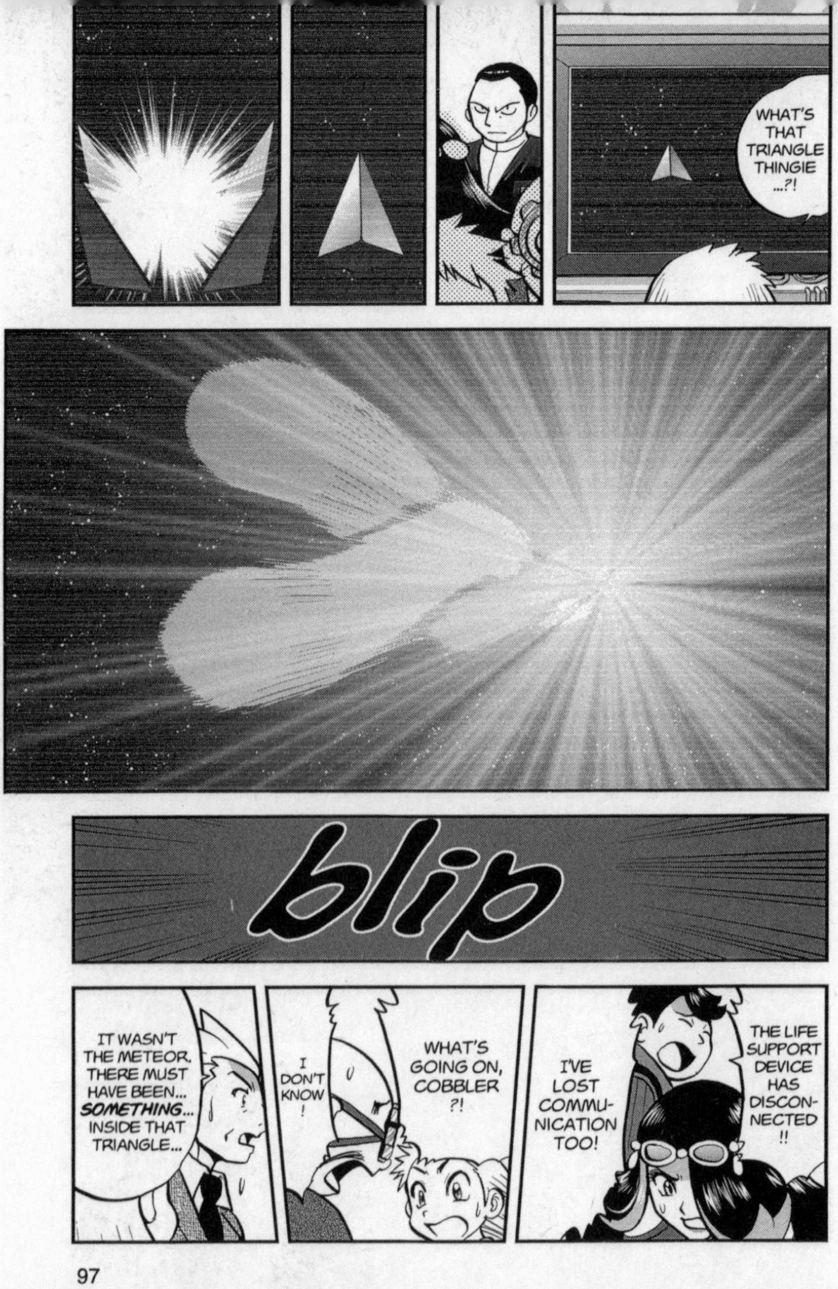
WHAT'S THAT TRIANGLE THINGIE ...?!
blip
THE LIFE SUPPORT DEVICE HAS DISCONNECTED!!
I'VE LOST COMMUNICATION TOO!
WHAT'S GOING ON, COBBLER?!
I DON'T KNOW!
IT WASN'T THE METEOR. THERE MUST HAVE BEEN... SOMETHING... INSIDE THAT TRIANGLE...

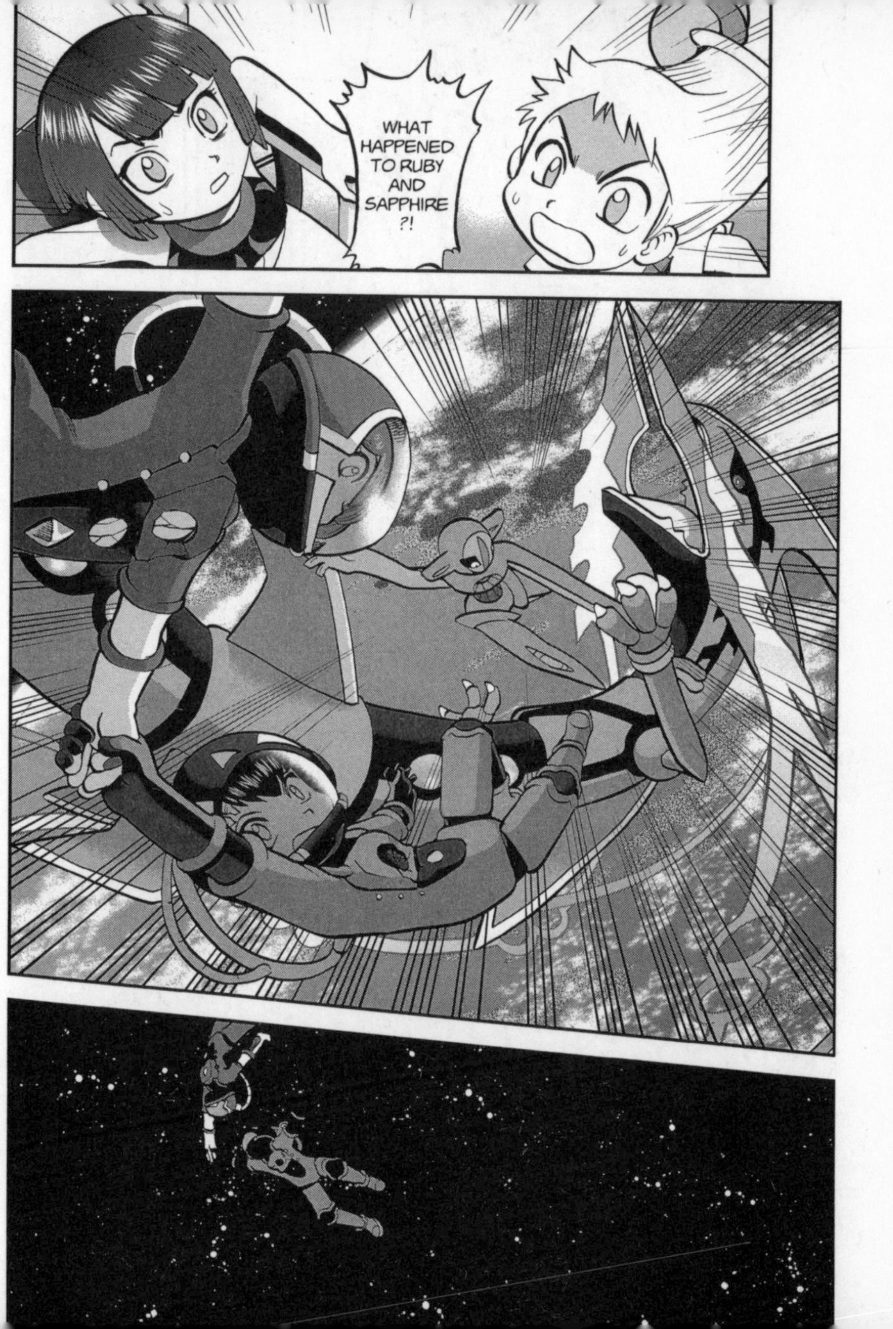
WHAT HAPPENED TO RUBY AND SAPPHIRE ?!

HOOPA, YOUR HOOP... BRING THEM BACK WITH YOUR HOOP!!

IT'S DEBRIS FROM THE METE-OR!!

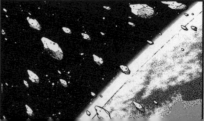

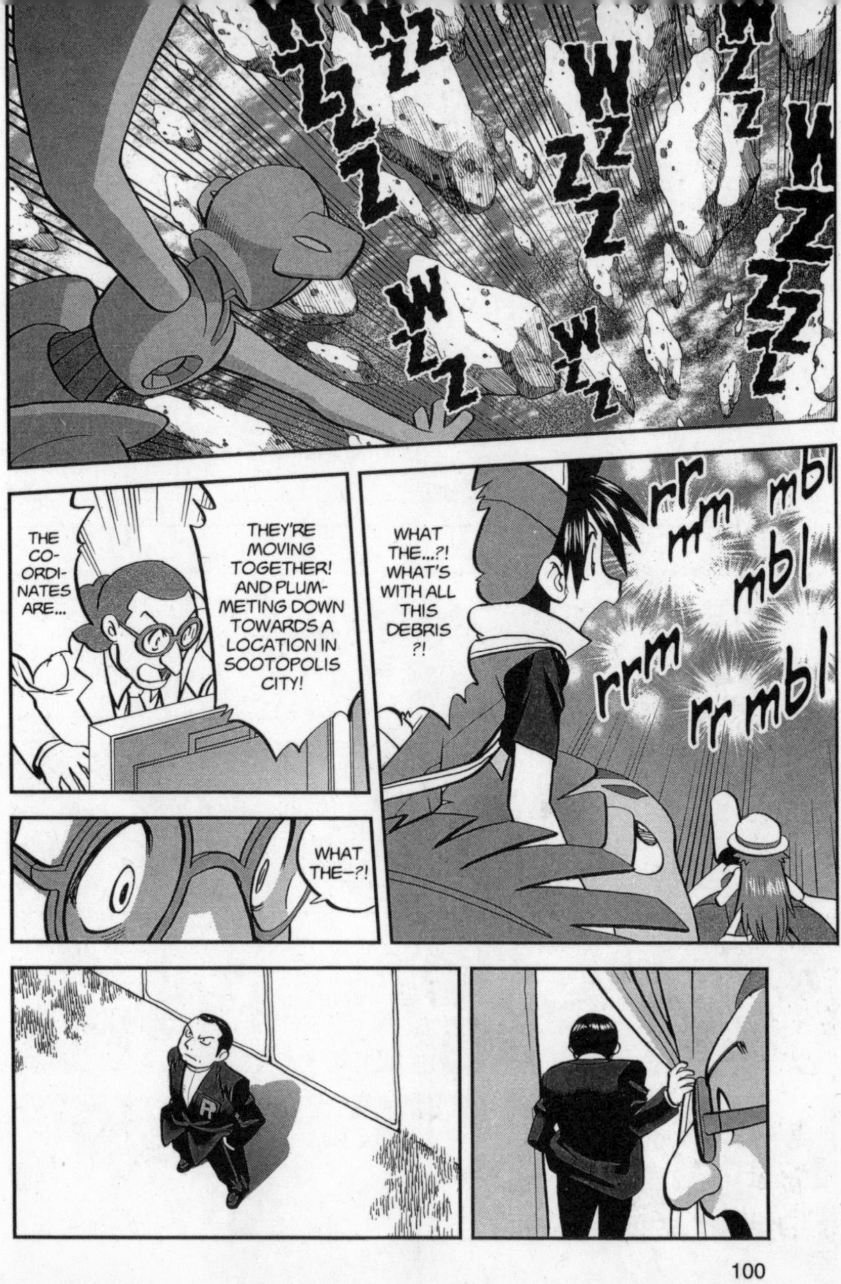
WZZZ
WZZZ
WZZ
WZZZ
WZZ
WZZ
rrmm mbl
mm mbl
rrm mbl
rr mbl
WHAT THE...?! WHAT'S WITH ALL THIS DEBRIS?!
THEY'RE MOVING TOGETHER! AND PLUMMETING DOWN TOWARDS A LOCATION IN SOOTOPOLIS CITY!
THE CO-ORDINATES ARE...
WHAT THE–?!

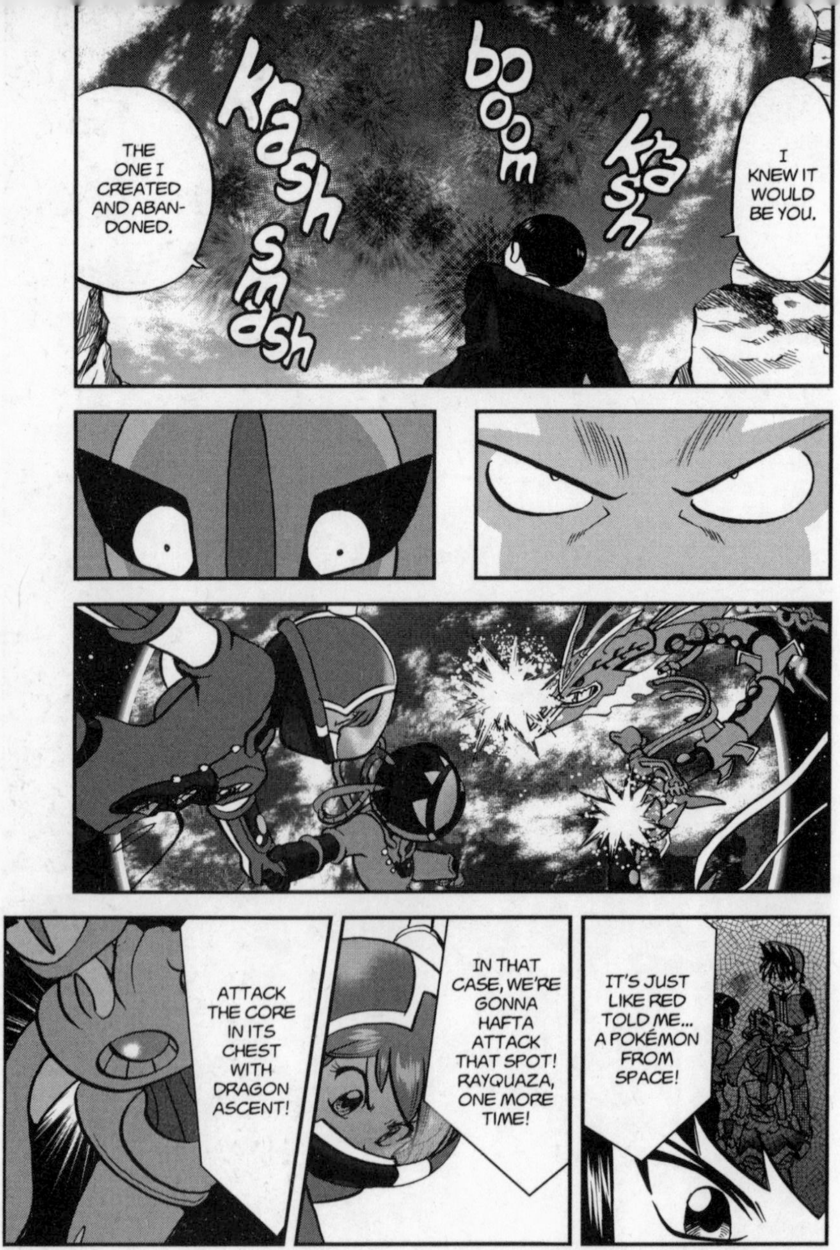
I KNEW IT WOULD BE YOU.
krash
boom
krash
smash
THE ONE I CREATED AND ABAN-DONED.
IT'S JUST LIKE RED TOLD ME... A POKÉMON FROM SPACE!
IN THAT CASE, WE'RE GONNA HAFTA ATTACK THAT SPOT! RAYQUAZA, ONE MORE TIME!
ATTACK THE CORE IN ITS CHEST WITH DRAGON ASCENT!

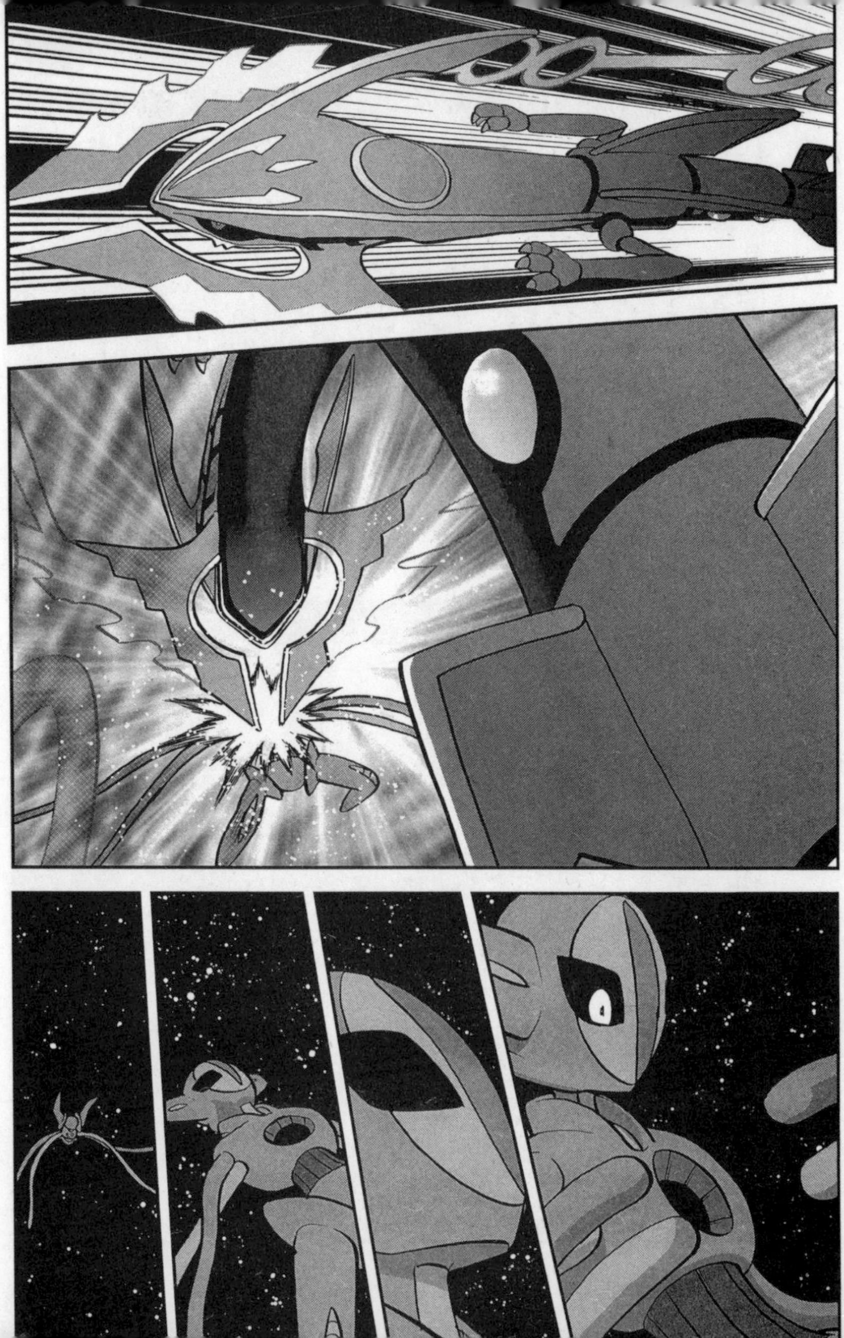

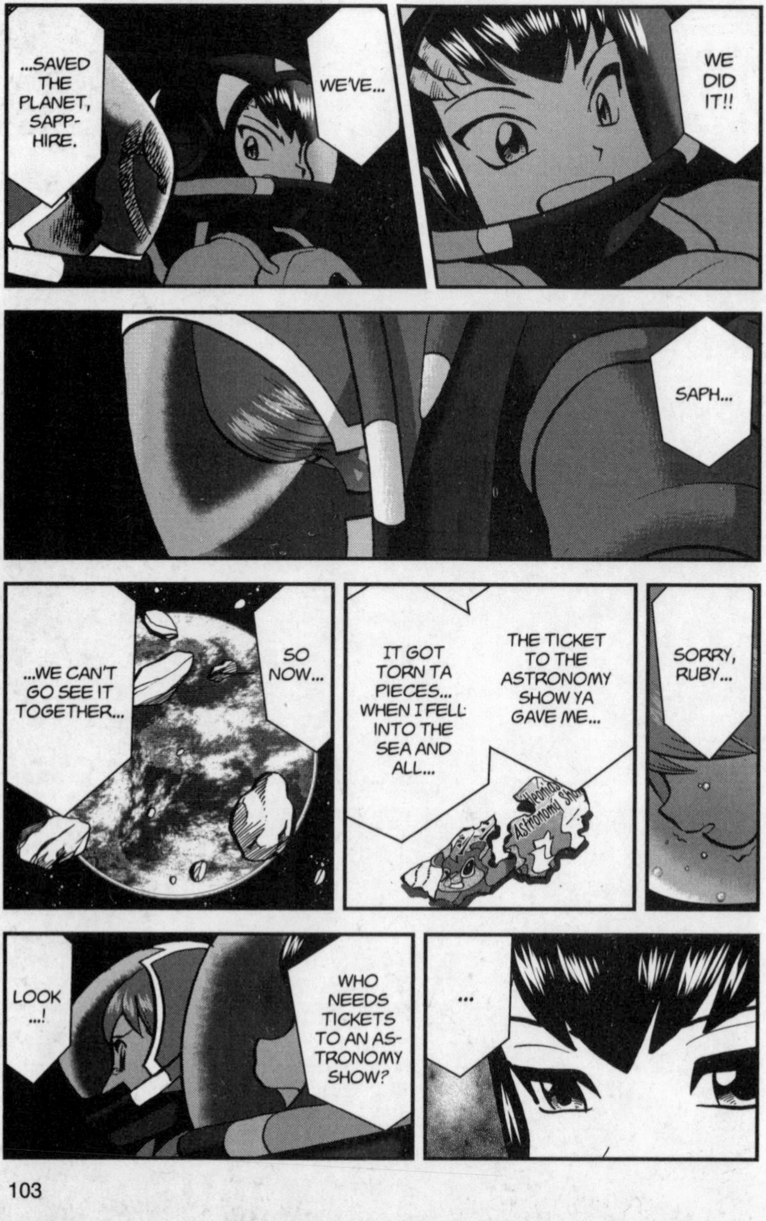
WE DID IT!!
WE'VE...
...SAVED THE PLANET, SAPP-HIRE.
SAPH...
SORRY, RUBY...
THE TICKET TO THE ASTRONOMY SHOW YA GAVE ME...
IT GOT TORN TA PIECES... WHEN I FELL INTO THE SEA AND ALL...
SO NOW...
...WE CAN'T GO SEE IT TOGETHER...
...
WHO NEEDS TICKETS TO AN AS-TRONOMY SHOW?
LOOK ...!

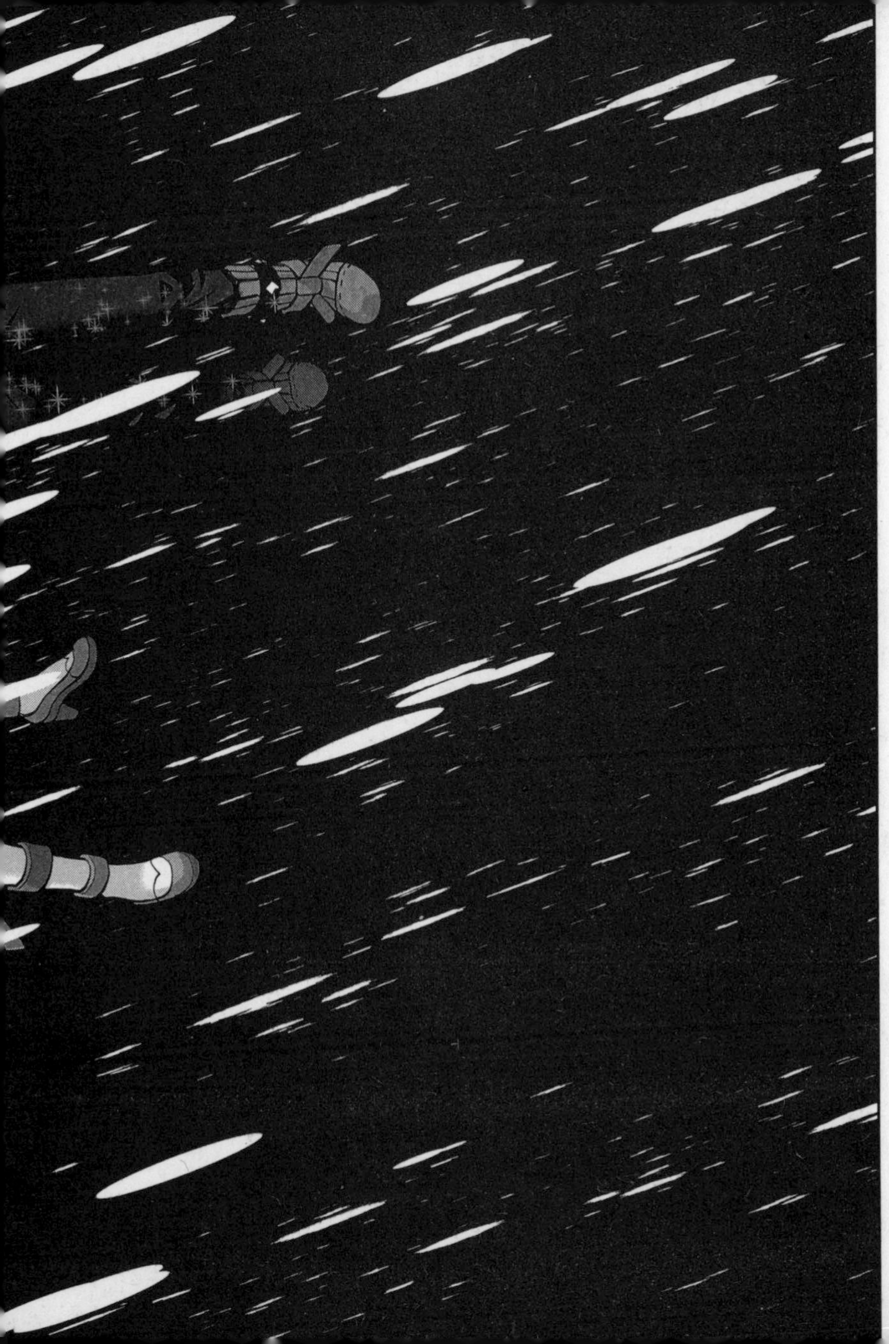

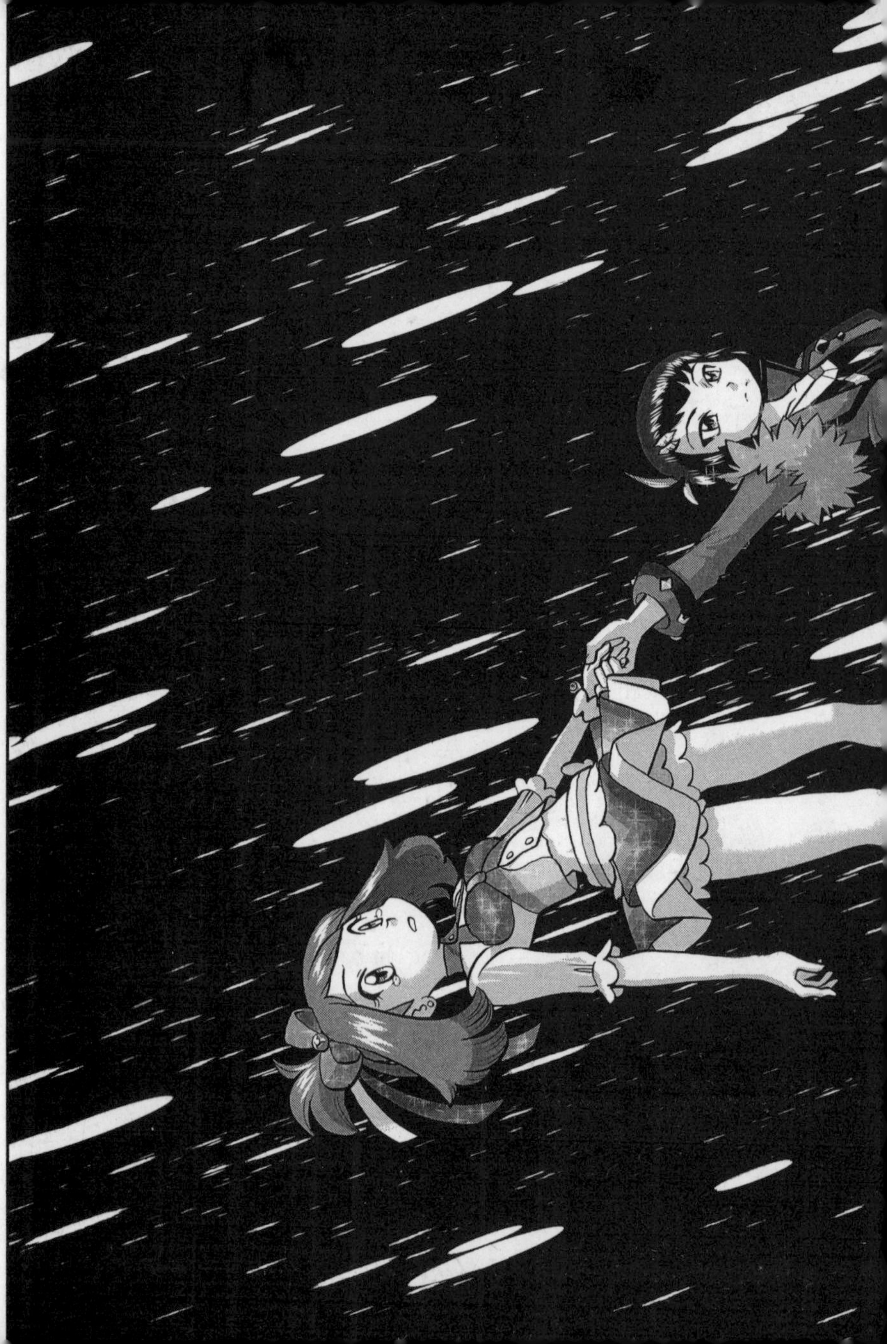

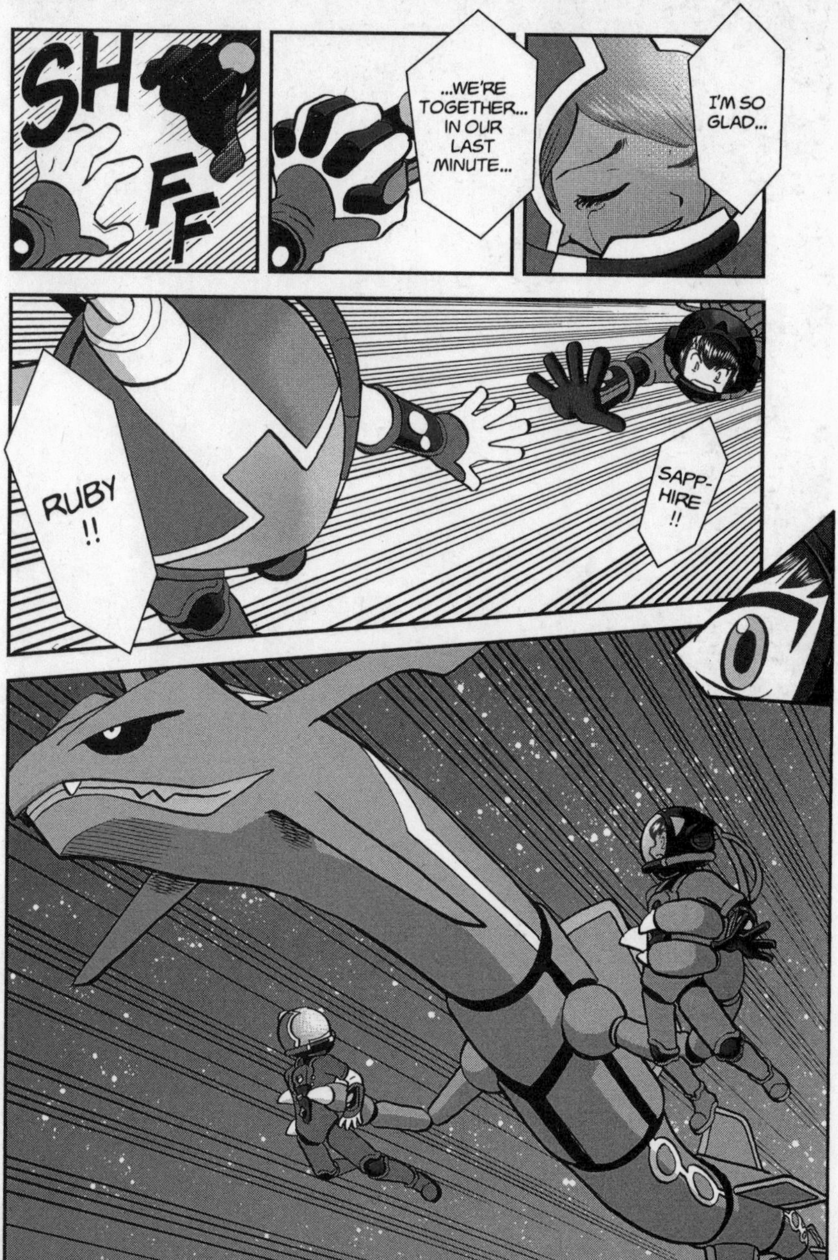
I'M SO GLAD...
...WE'RE TOGETHER... IN OUR LAST MINUTE...
SHFF
SAPP-HIRE !!
RUBY !!

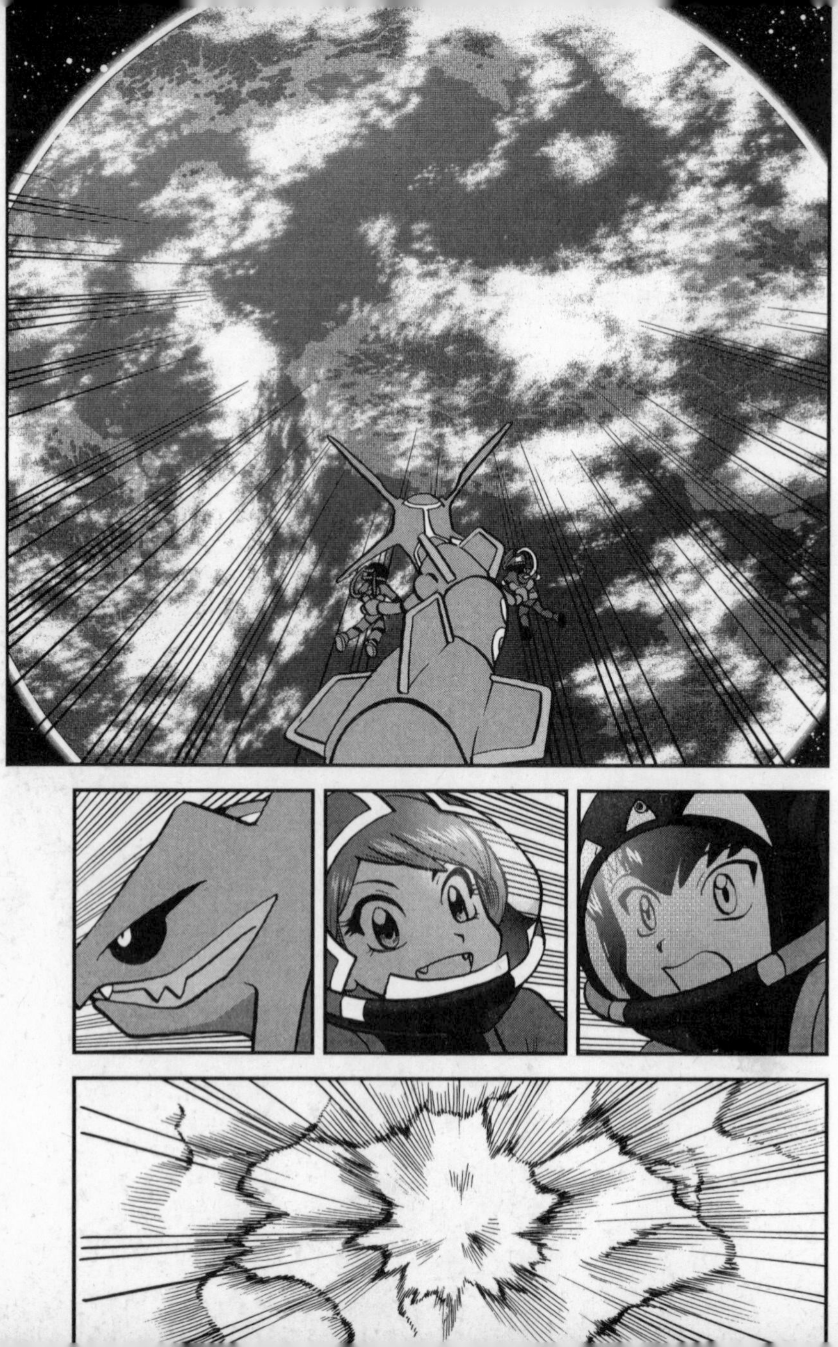

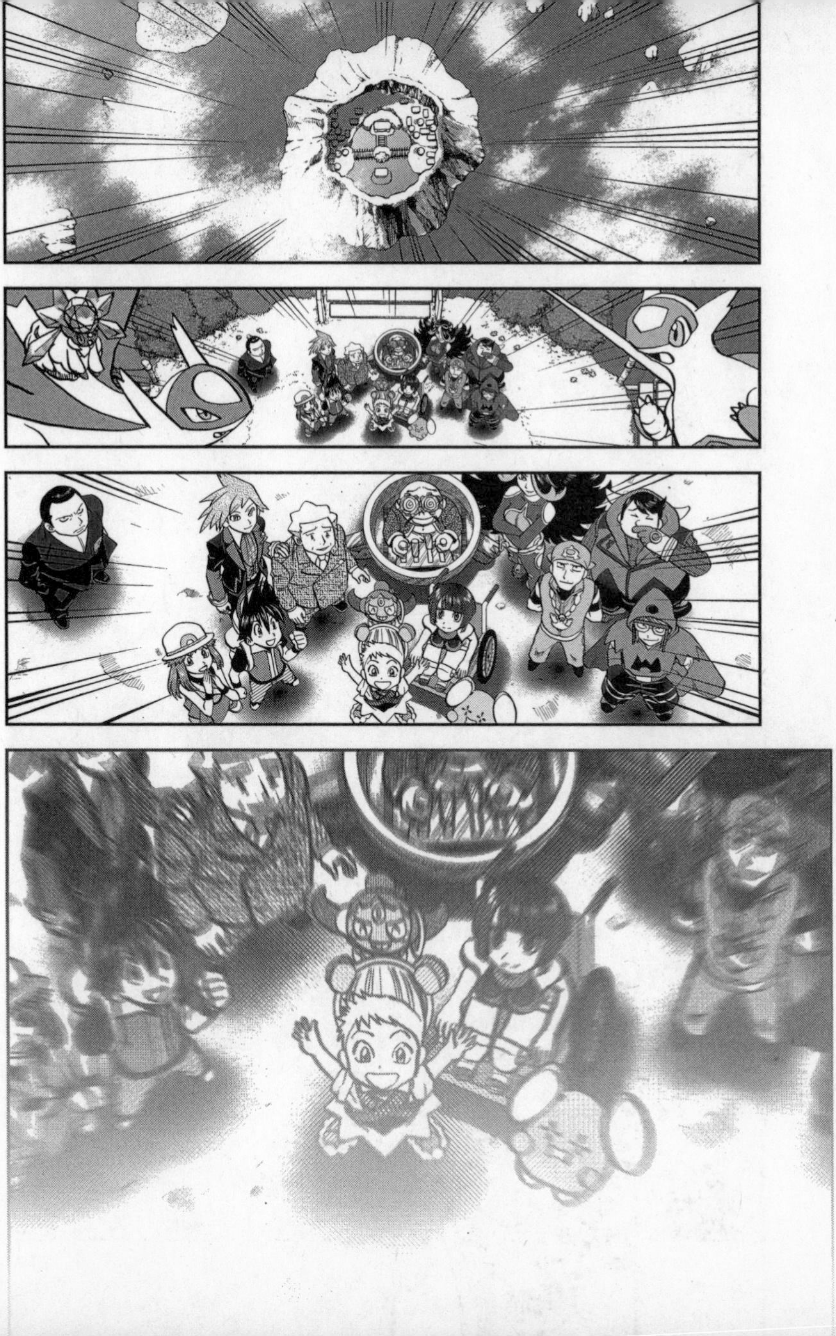

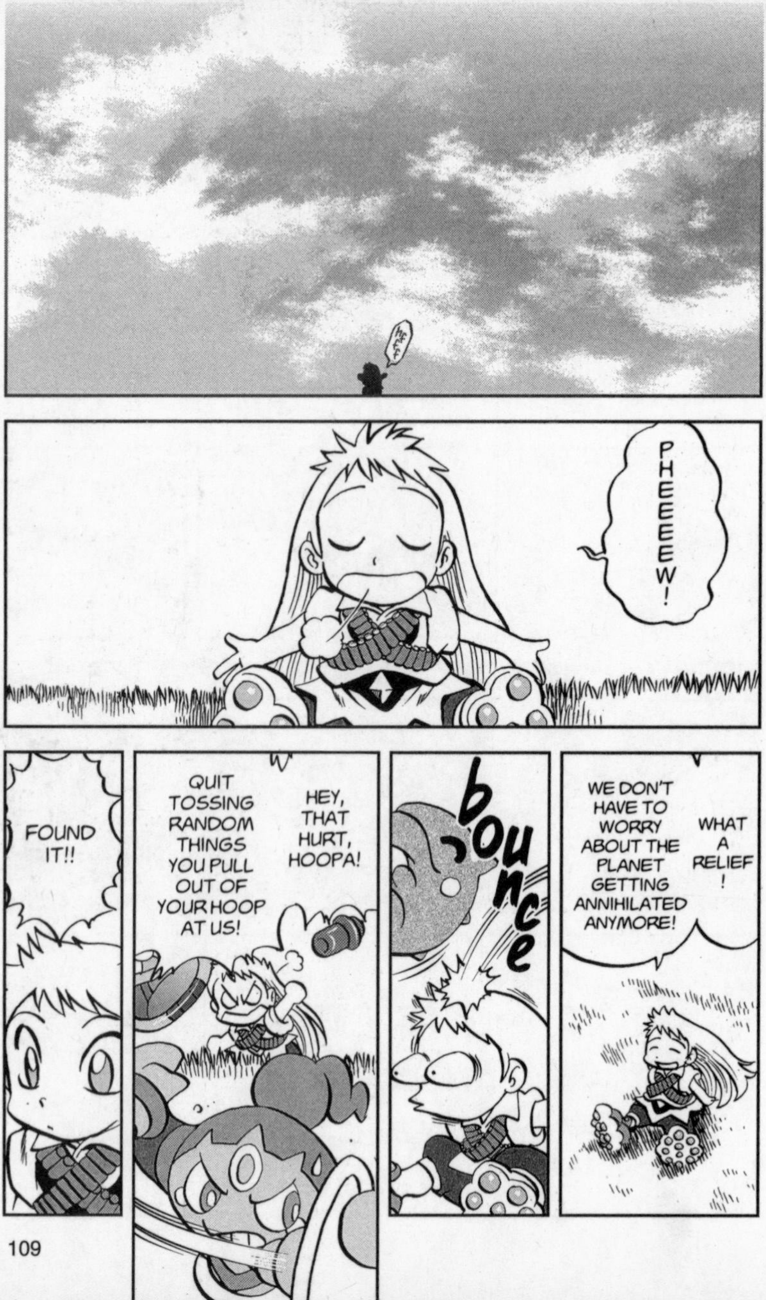
PHEEEEEW!
WHAT A RELIEF!
WE DON'T HAVE TO WORRY ABOUT THE PLANET GETTING ANNIHILATED ANYMORE!
bounce
HEY, THAT HURT, HOOPA!
QUIT TOSSING RANDOM THINGS YOU PULL OUT OF YOUR HOOP AT US!
FOUND IT!!

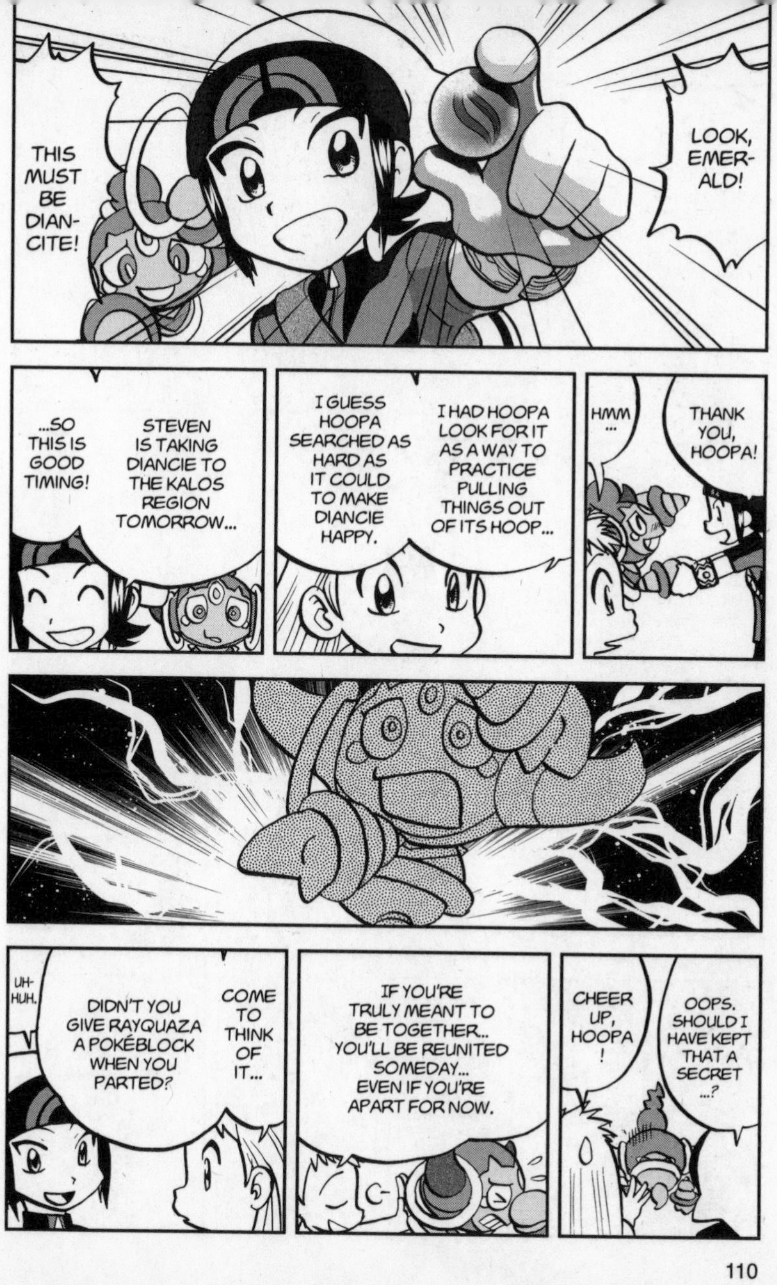
LOOK, EMERALD!
THIS MUST BE DIANCITE!
THANK YOU, HOOPA!
HMM ...
I HAD HOOPA LOOK FOR IT AS A WAY TO PRACTICE PULLING THINGS OUT OF ITS HOOP...
I GUESS HOOPA SEARCHED AS HARD AS IT COULD TO MAKE DIANCIE HAPPY.
STEVEN IS TAKING DIANCIE TO THE KALOS REGION TOMORROW...
...SO THIS IS GOOD TIMING!
OOPS. SHOULD I HAVE KEPT THAT A SECRET ...?
CHEER UP, HOOPA!
IF YOU'RE TRULY MEANT TO BE TOGETHER... YOU'LL BE REUNITED SOMEDAY... EVEN IF YOU'RE APART FOR NOW.
COME TO THINK OF IT...
DIDN'T YOU GIVE RAYQUAZA A POKÉBLOCK WHEN YOU PARTED?
UH-HUH.

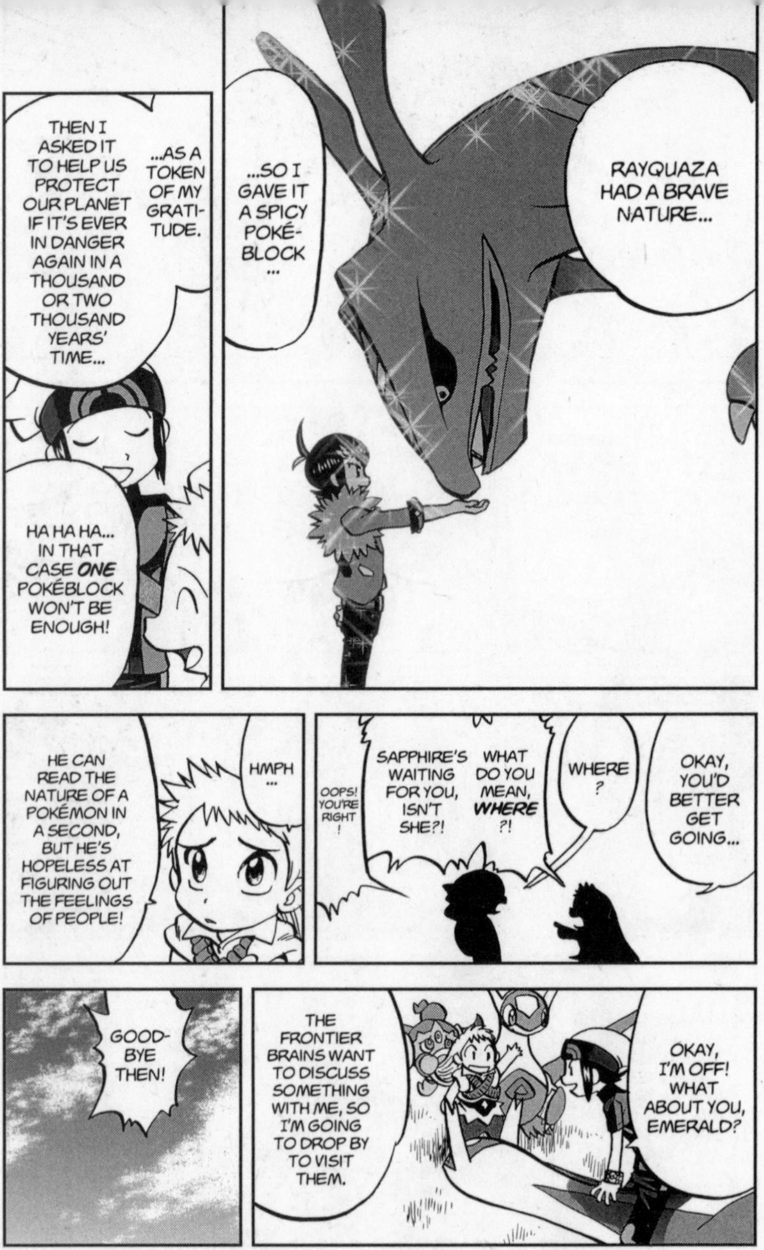
RAYQUAZA HAD A BRAVE NATURE...
...SO I GAVE IT A SPICY POKÉ-BLOCK ...
...AS A TOKEN OF MY GRATI-TUDE.
THEN I ASKED IT TO HELP US PROTECT OUR PLANET IF IT'S EVER IN DANGER AGAIN IN A THOUSAND OR TWO THOUSAND YEARS' TIME...
HA HA HA... IN THAT CASE ***ONE*** POKÉBLOCK WON'T BE ENOUGH!
OKAY, YOU'D BETTER GET GOING...
WHERE?
WHAT DO YOU MEAN, ***WHERE***?!
SAPPHIRE'S WAITING FOR YOU, ISN'T SHE?!
OOPS! YOU'RE RIGHT!
HMPH ...
HE CAN READ THE NATURE OF A POKÉMON IN A SECOND, BUT HE'S HOPELESS AT FIGURING OUT THE FEELINGS OF PEOPLE!
OKAY, I'M OFF! WHAT ABOUT YOU, EMERALD?
THE FRONTIER BRAINS WANT TO DISCUSS SOMETHING WITH ME, SO I'M GOING TO DROP BY TO VISIT THEM.
GOOD-BYE THEN!

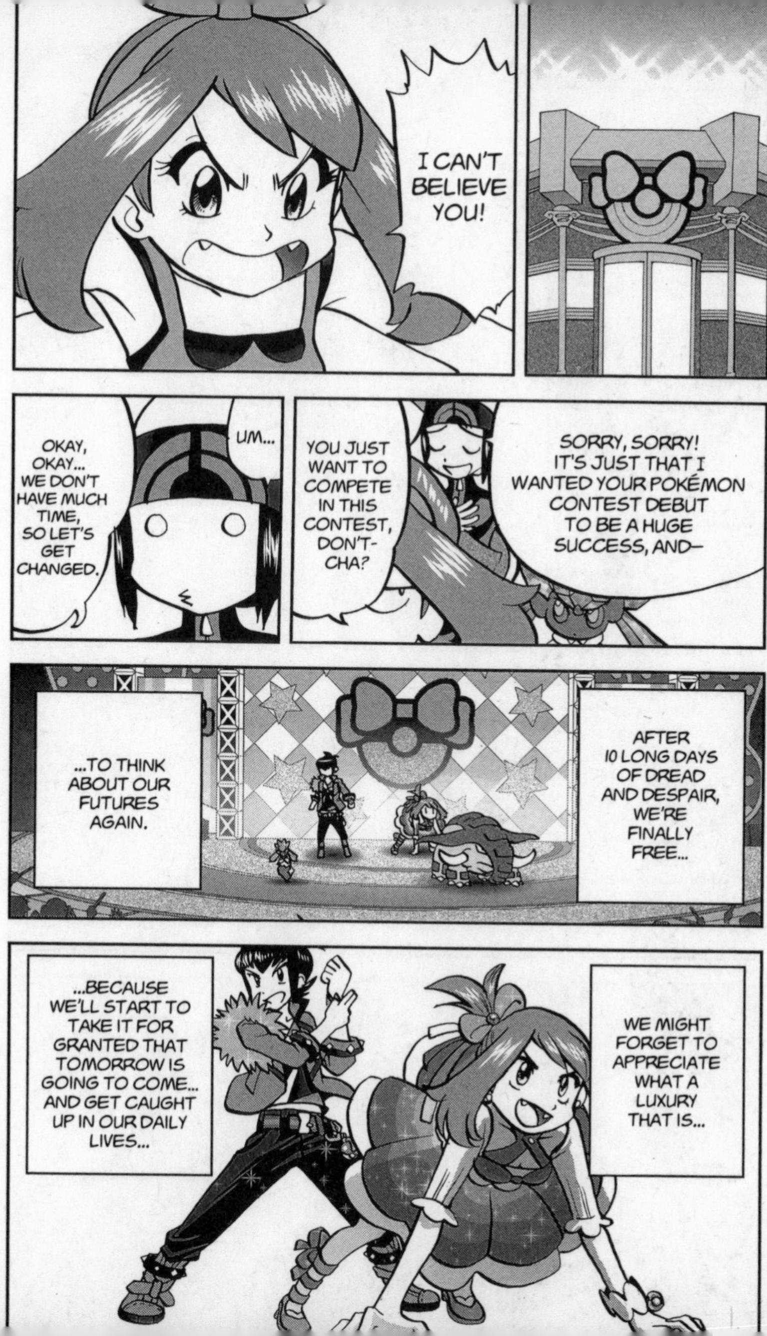
I CAN'T BELIEVE YOU!
SORRY, SORRY! IT'S JUST THAT I WANTED YOUR POKÉMON CONTEST DEBUT TO BE A HUGE SUCCESS, AND—
YOU JUST WANT TO COMPETE IN THIS CONTEST, DON'T-CHA?
UM...
OKAY, OKAY... WE DON'T HAVE MUCH TIME, SO LET'S GET CHANGED.
AFTER 10 LONG DAYS OF DREAD AND DESPAIR, WE'RE FINALLY FREE...
...TO THINK ABOUT OUR FUTURES AGAIN.
WE MIGHT FORGET TO APPRECIATE WHAT A LUXURY THAT IS...
...BECAUSE WE'LL START TO TAKE IT FOR GRANTED THAT TOMORROW IS GOING TO COME... AND GET CAUGHT UP IN OUR DAILY LIVES...

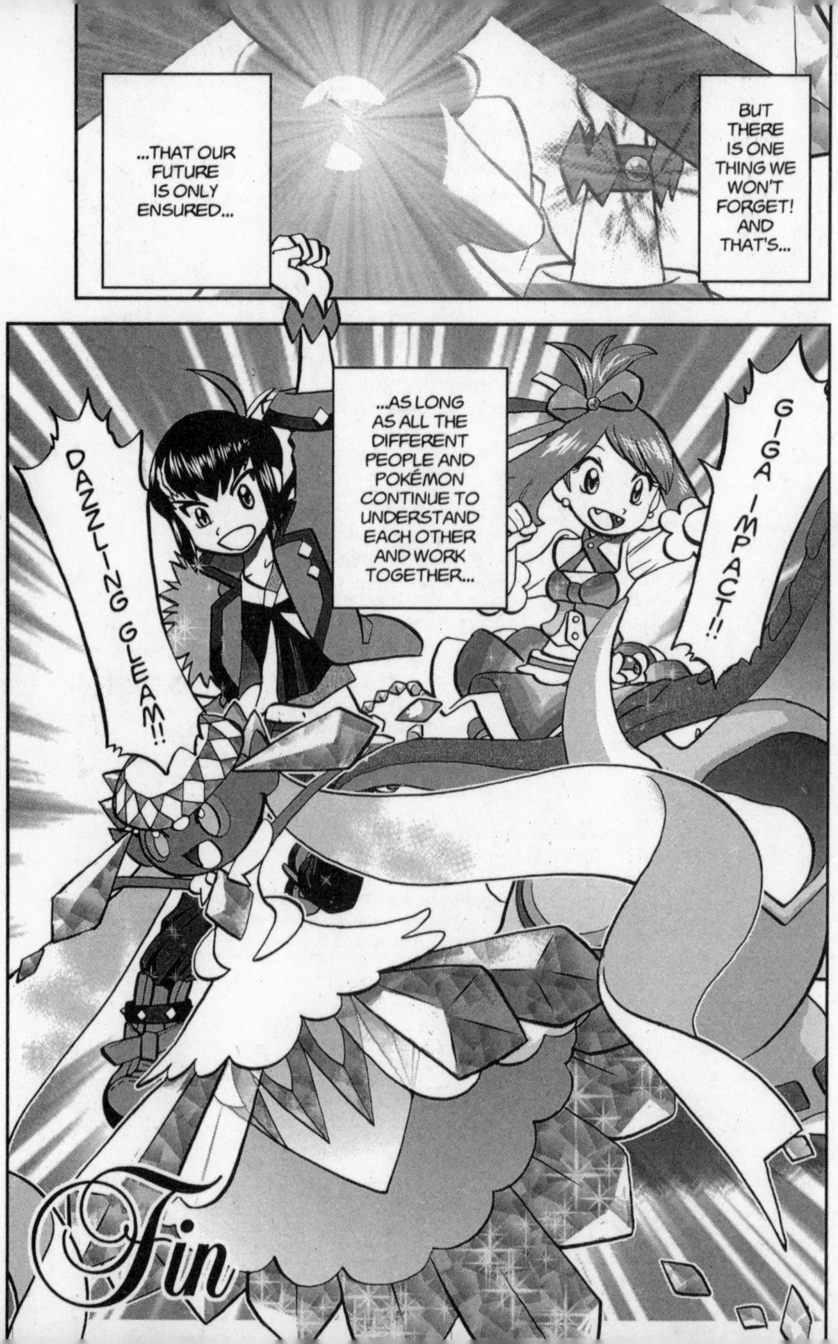
BUT THERE IS ONE THING WE WON'T FORGET! AND THAT'S...
...THAT OUR FUTURE IS ONLY ENSURED...
GIGA IMPACT!!
...AS LONG AS ALL THE DIFFERENT PEOPLE AND POKÉMON CONTINUE TO UNDERSTAND EACH OTHER AND WORK TOGETHER...
DAZZLING GLEAM!!
Fin

# Pokémon ΩRuby • αSapphire
## Volume 6
## VIZ Media Edition

Story by HIDENORI KUSAKA
Art by SATOSHI YAMAMOTO

©2017 The Pokémon Company International.
©1995–2016 Nintendo / Creatures Inc. / GAME FREAK inc.
TM, ®, and character names are trademarks of Nintendo.
POCKET MONSTERS SPECIAL ΩRUBY • αSAPPHIRE Vol. 3
by Hidenori KUSAKA, Satoshi YAMAMOTO
© 2015 Hidenori KUSAKA, Satoshi YAMAMOTO
All rights reserved.
Original Japanese edition published by SHOGAKUKAN.
English translation rights in the United States of America, Canada, the
United Kingdom, Ireland, Australia, New Zealand and India arranged with
SHOGAKUKAN.

**Translation**—Tetsuichiro Miyaki
**English Adaptation**—Bryant Turnage
**Touch-Up & Lettering**—Susan Daigle-Leach
**Design**—Julian [JR] Robinson
**Editor**—Annette Roman

Printed in the U.S.A.

Published by
VIZ Media, LLC
P.O. Box 77010
San Francisco, CA 94107

10 9 8 7 6 5 4 3 2 1
First printing, March 2018

www.viz.com

# Begin your Pokémon Adventure here in the Kanto region!

## ADVENTURES
### RED & BLUE BOX SET

Story by **HIDENORI KUSAKA**    Art by **MATO**

Includes
**POKÉMON
ADVENTURES**
Vols. 1-7
and a collectible
poster!

**All your favorite Pokémon game
characters jump out of the screen into
the pages of this action-packed manga!**

Red doesn't just want to train Pokémon, he wants
to be their friend too. Bulbasaur and Poliwhirl seem game.
But independent Pikachu won't be so easy to win over!

And watch out for Team Rocket, Red...
They only want to be your enemy!

### *Start the adventure today!*

www.viz.com

PERFECT
SQUARE

RATED
ALL AGES
ratings.viz.com

# The adventure continues in the Johto region!

**POKÉMON™ ADVENTURES**

## GOLD & SILVER BOX SET

Includes
**POKÉMON ADVENTURES**
Vols. 8-14
and a collectible poster!

Story by
### HIDENORI KUSAKA

Art by
### MATO,
### SATOSHI YAMAMOTO

More exciting Pokémon adventures starring Gold and his rival Silver! First someone steals Gold's backpack full of Poké Balls (and Pokémon!). Then someone steals Prof. Elm's Totodile. Can Gold catch the thief—or thieves?!

Keep an eye on Team Rocket, Gold... Could they be behind this crime wave?

**VIZ media**
www.viz.com

**PERFECT SQUARE**

RATED
**A**
ALL AGES
ratings.viz.com

STORY & ART BY **SANTA HARUKAZE**

**BLACK & WHITE**
$9.99 US / $10.99 CAN

**LEGENDARY POKÉMON**
$9.99 US / $10.99 CAN

**X•Y**
$12.99 US / $13.99 CAN

A Pokémon pocket-sized book chock-full of four-panel gags, Pokémon trivia and fun quizzes based on the characters you know and love!

**viz** media
www.viz.com

story by HIDENORI KUSAKA
art by SATOSHI YAMAMOTO

In this **two-volume** thriller, troublemaker Gold and feisty Silver must team up again to find their old enemy Lance and the Legendary Pokémon Arceus!

# Available now!

Pokémon
X•Y
1
Hidenori Kusaka
Satoshi Yamamoto

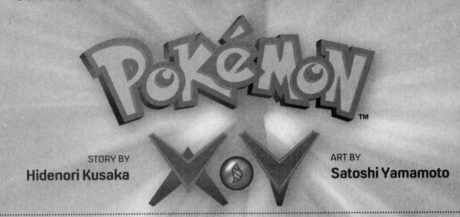

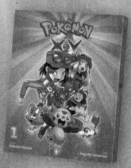

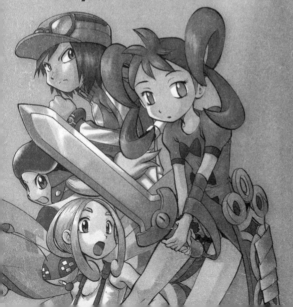

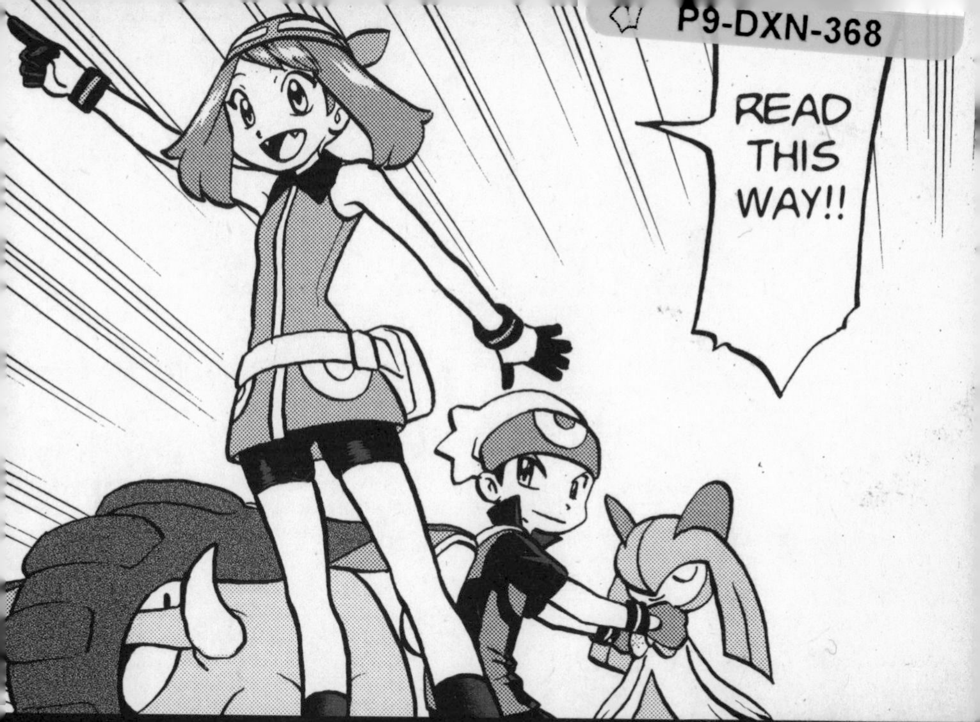
READ THIS WAY!!

## THIS IS THE END OF THIS GRAPHIC NOVEL!

To properly enjoy this VIZ Media graphic novel, please turn it around and begin reading from right to left.

This book has been printed in the original Japanese format in order to preserve the orientation of the original artwork. Have fun with it!

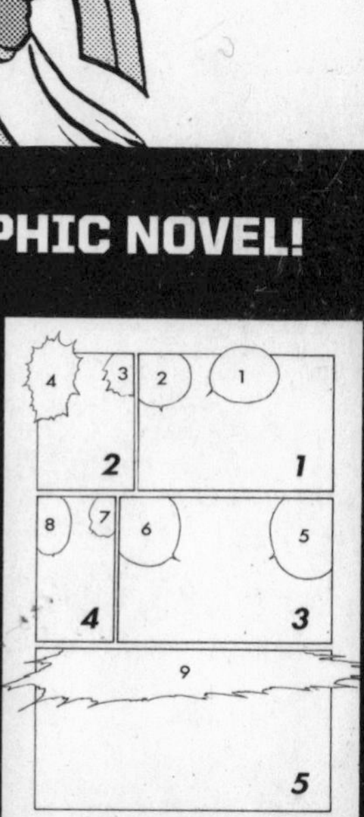
1
2
1
3
4
2
5
6
3
7
8
4
9
5
142

**Follow the action this way.**

# SURPRISE!

## You may be reading the wrong way!

It's true: In keeping with the original Japanese comic format, this book reads from right to left—so action, sound effects, and word balloons are completely reversed. This preserves the orientation of the original artwork—plus, it's fun! Check out the diagram shown here to get the hang of things, and then turn to the other side of the book to get started!

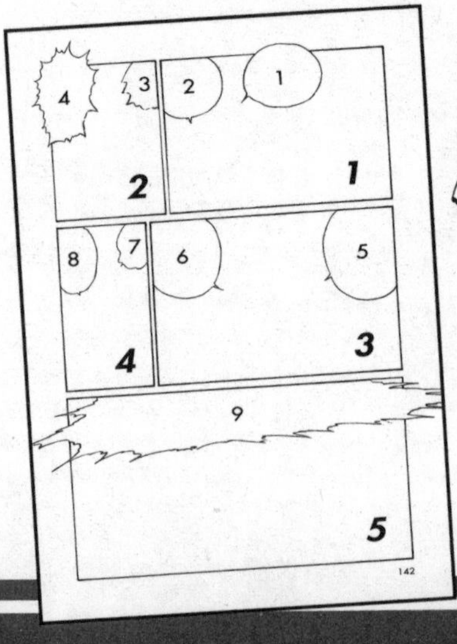
1
2
3
4
1
2
5
6
7
8
3
4
9
5
142

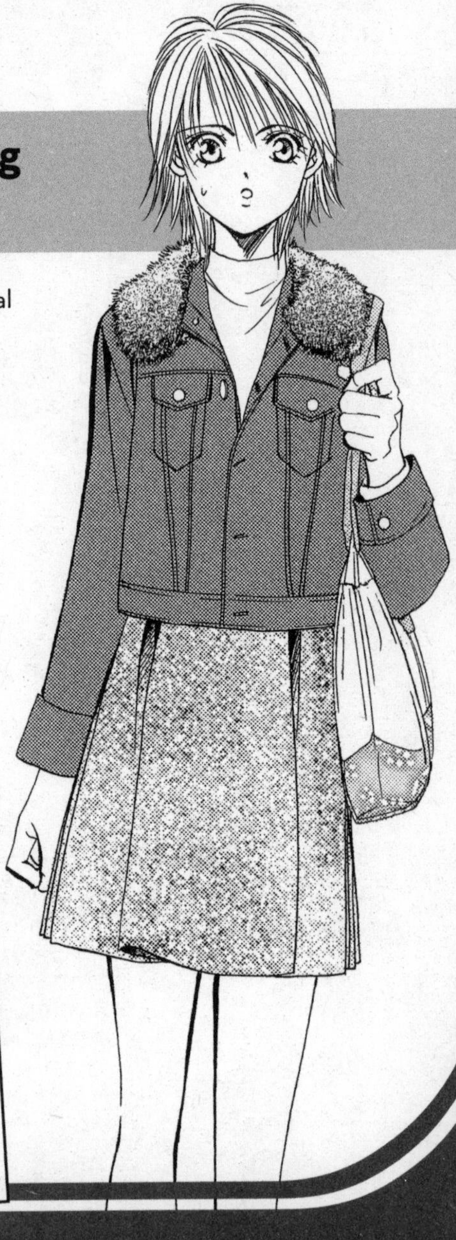

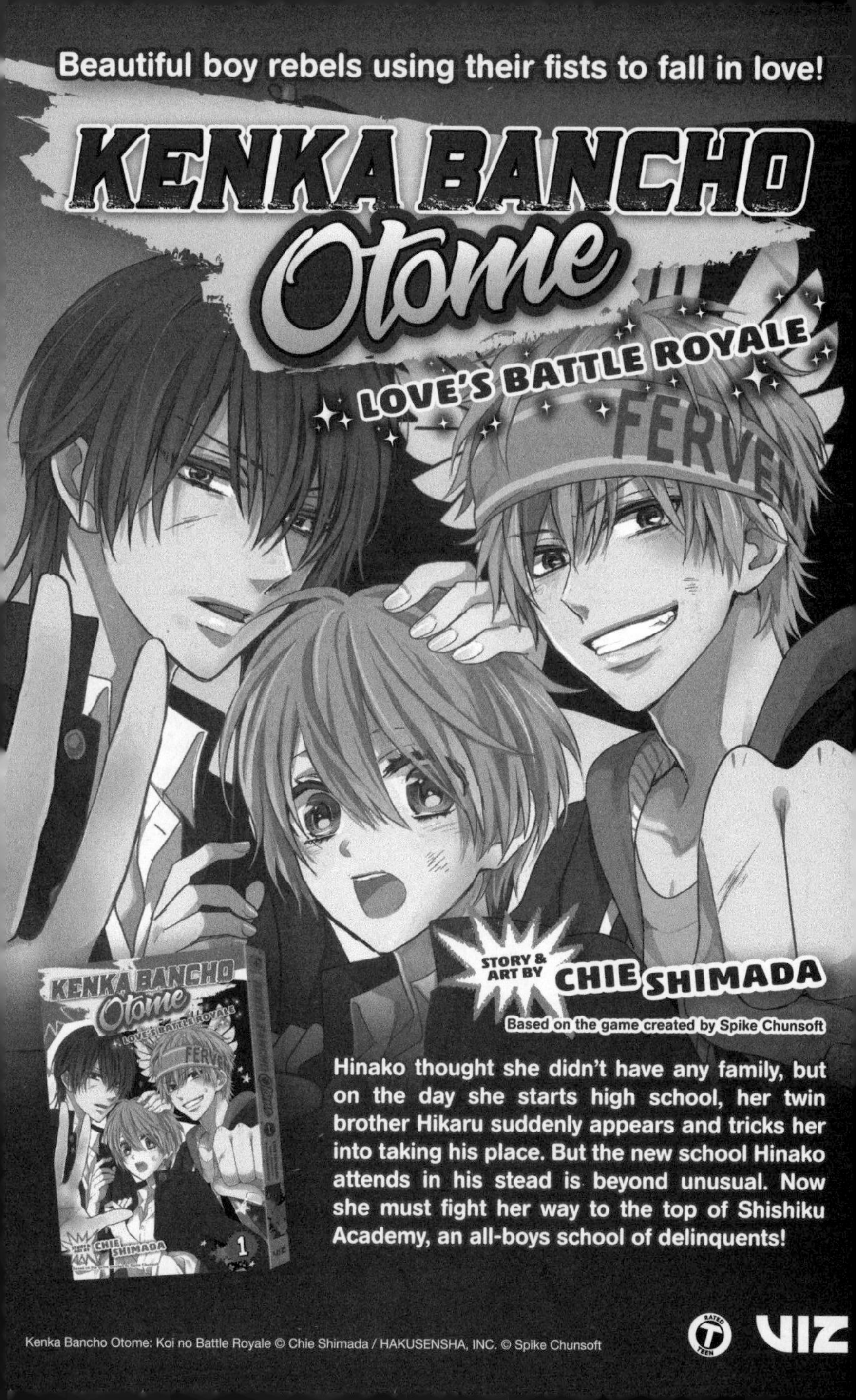
Beautiful boy rebels using their fists to fall in love!
KENKA BANCHO
Otome
LOVE'S BATTLE ROYALE
FERVEN
STORY & ART BY
CHIE SHIMADA
Based on the game created by Spike Chunsoft
Hinako thought she didn't have any family, but on the day she starts high school, her twin brother Hikaru suddenly appears and tricks her into taking his place. But the new school Hinako attends in his stead is beyond unusual. Now she must fight her way to the top of Shishiku Academy, an all-boys school of delinquents!
KENKA BANCHO
Otome
LOVE'S BATTLE ROYALE
CHIE SHIMADA
1
Kenka Bancho Otome: Koi no Battle Royale © Chie Shimada / HAKUSENSHA, INC. © Spike Chunsoft
RATED T TEEN
VIZ

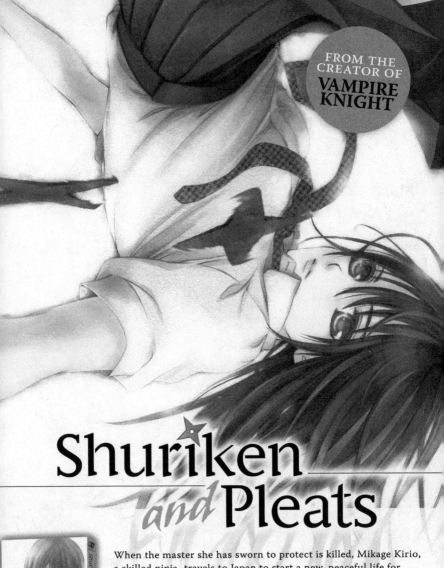

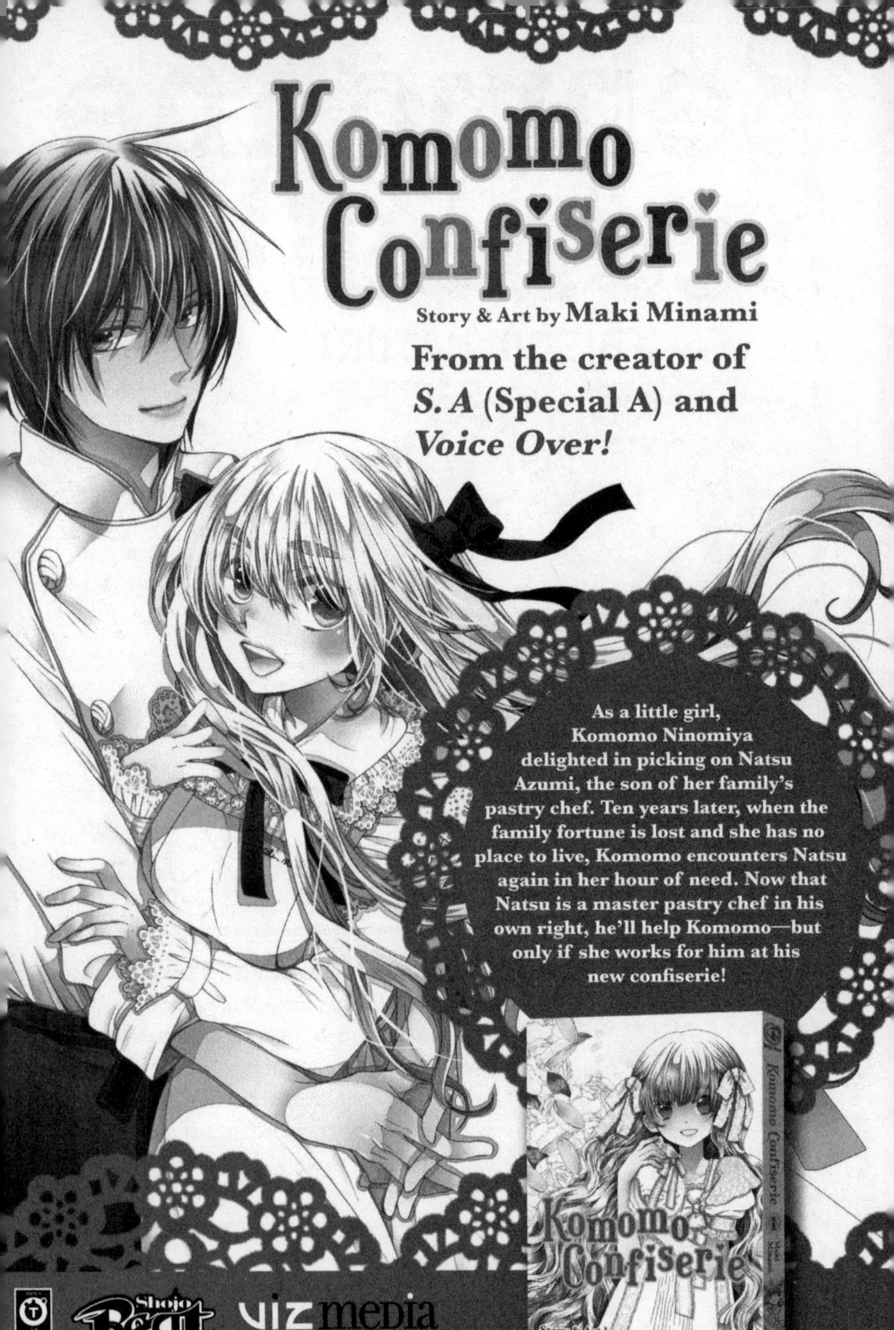
Komomo Confiserie
Story & Art by Maki Minami
From the creator of S. A (Special A) and Voice Over!
As a little girl, Komomo Ninomiya delighted in picking on Natsu Azumi, the son of her family's pastry chef. Ten years later, when the family fortune is lost and she has no place to live, Komomo encounters Natsu again in her hour of need. Now that Natsu is a master pastry chef in his own right, he'll help Komomo—but only if she works for him at his new confiserie!
Komomo Confiserie
Story & Art by
Maki Minami
Vol. 1
TEEN
ratings.viz.com
Shojo Beat
viz media
viz.com

# Behind the Scenes!!

STORY AND ART BY **BISCO HATORI**

From the creator of
Ouran High School
Host Club

Ranmaru Kurisu comes from a family of hardy, rough-and-tumble fisherfolk and he sticks out at home like a delicate, artistic sore thumb. It's given him a raging inferiority complex and a permanently pessimistic outlook. Now that he's in college, he's hoping to find a sense of belonging. But after a whole life of being left out, does he even know how to fit in?!

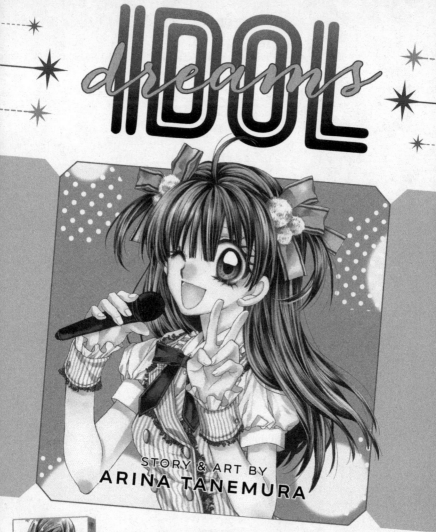

# IDOL dreams

## STORY & ART BY ARINA TANEMURA

At age 31, office worker Chikage Deguchi feels she missed her chances at love and success. When word gets out that she's a virgin, Chikage is humiliated and wishes she could turn back time to when she was still young and popular. She takes an experimental drug that changes her appearance back to when she was 15. Now Chikage is determined to pursue everything she missed out on all those years ago—including becoming a star!

www.viz.com

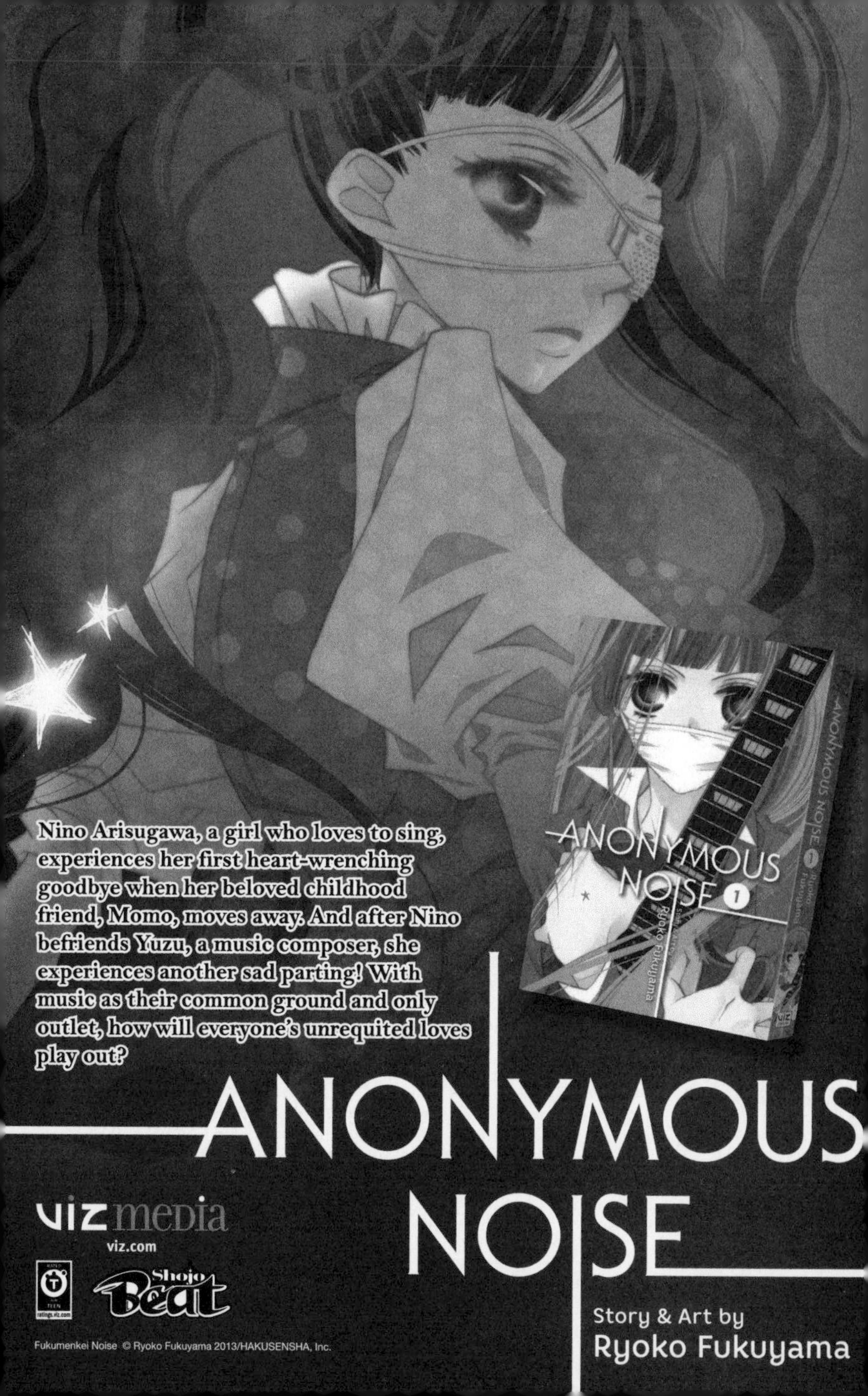
Nino Arisugawa, a girl who loves to sing, experiences her first heart-wrenching goodbye when her beloved childhood friend, Momo, moves away. And after Nino befriends Yuzu, a music composer, she experiences another sad parting! With music as their common ground and only outlet, how will everyone's unrequited loves play out?
ANONYMOUS NOISE 1
Ryoko Fukuyama
ANONYMOUS NOISE
Story & Art by
Ryoko Fukuyama
viz media
viz.com
Shojo Beat
Fukumenkei Noise © Ryoko Fukuyama 2013/HAKUSENSHA, Inc.

## SKIP-BEAT!

Vol. 42
Shojo Beat Edition

### STORY AND ART BY YOSHIKI NAKAMURA

English Translation & Adaptation/Tomo Kimura
Touch-up Art & Lettering/Sabrina Heep .
Design/Veronica Casson
Editor/Pancha Diaz

Skip-Beat! by Yoshiki Nakamura © Yoshiki Nakamura 2018
All rights reserved. First published in Japan in 2018 by HAKUSENSHA, Inc., Tokyo.
English language translation rights arranged with HAKUSENSHA, Inc., Tokyo.

Printed in the U.S.A.

Published by VIZ Media, LLC
P.O. Box 77010
San Francisco, CA 94107

10 9 8 7 6 5 4 3 2 1
First printing, March 2019

viz.com

shojobeat.com

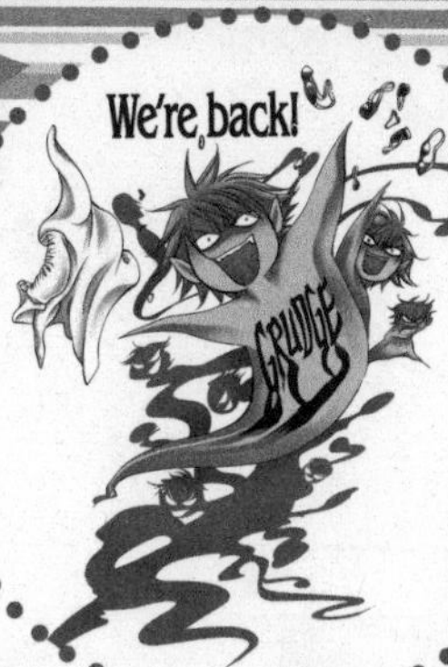
We're back!
GRUDGE

Yoshiki Nakamura is originally from Tokushima Prefecture. She started drawing manga in elementary school, which eventually led to her 1993 debut of *Yume de Au yori Suteki* (Better than Seeing in a Dream) in *Hana to Yume* magazine. Her other works include the basketball series *Saint Love*, *MVP wa Yuzurenai* (Can't Give Up MVP), *Blue Wars* and *Tokyo Crazy Paradise*, a series about a female bodyguard in 2020 Tokyo.

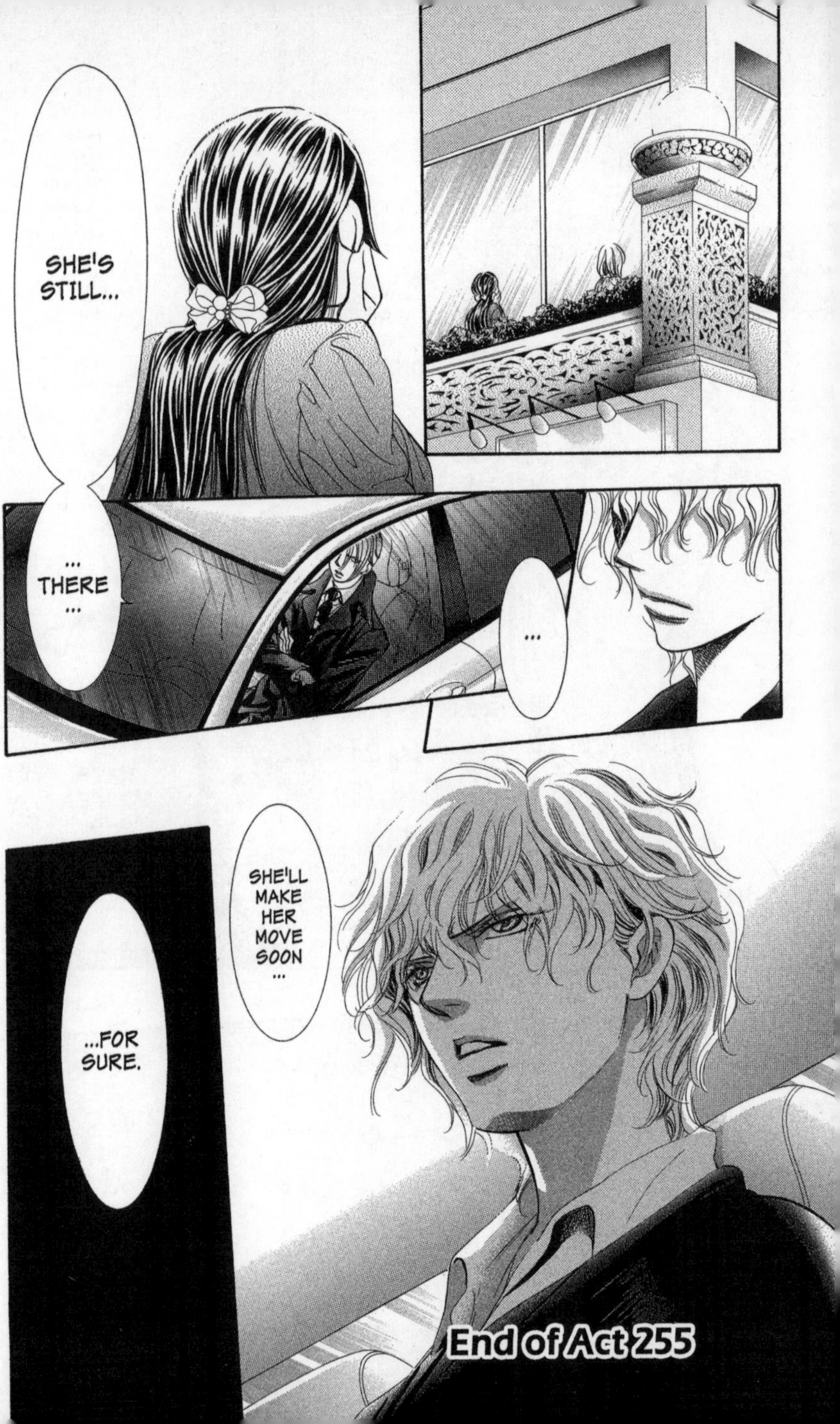
SHE'S STILL...
... THERE ...
...
SHE'LL MAKE HER MOVE SOON ...
...FOR SURE.
End of Act 255

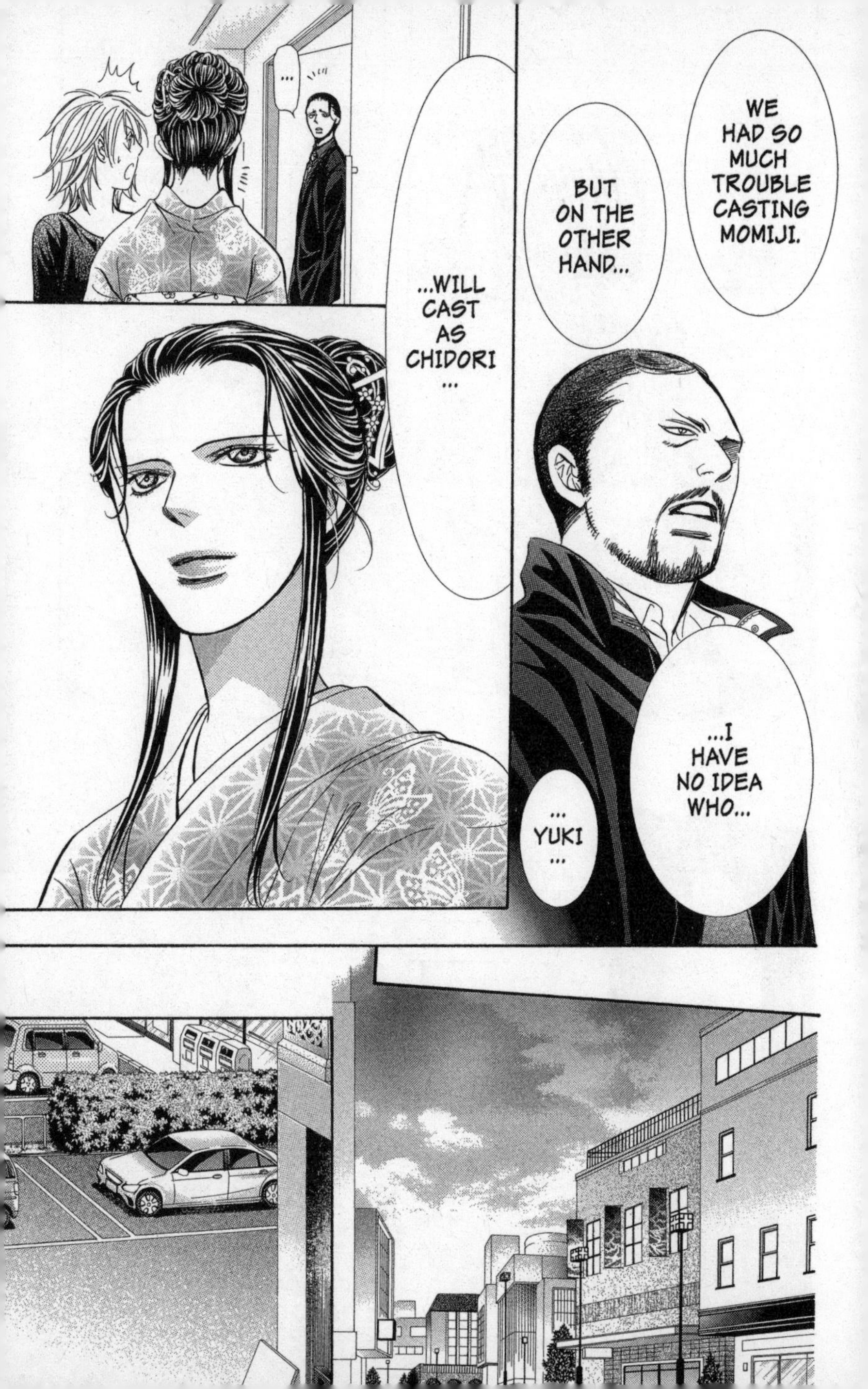
WE HAD SO MUCH TROUBLE CASTING MOMIJI.
BUT ON THE OTHER HAND...
...I HAVE NO IDEA WHO...
...YUKI...
...
...WILL CAST AS CHIDORI...

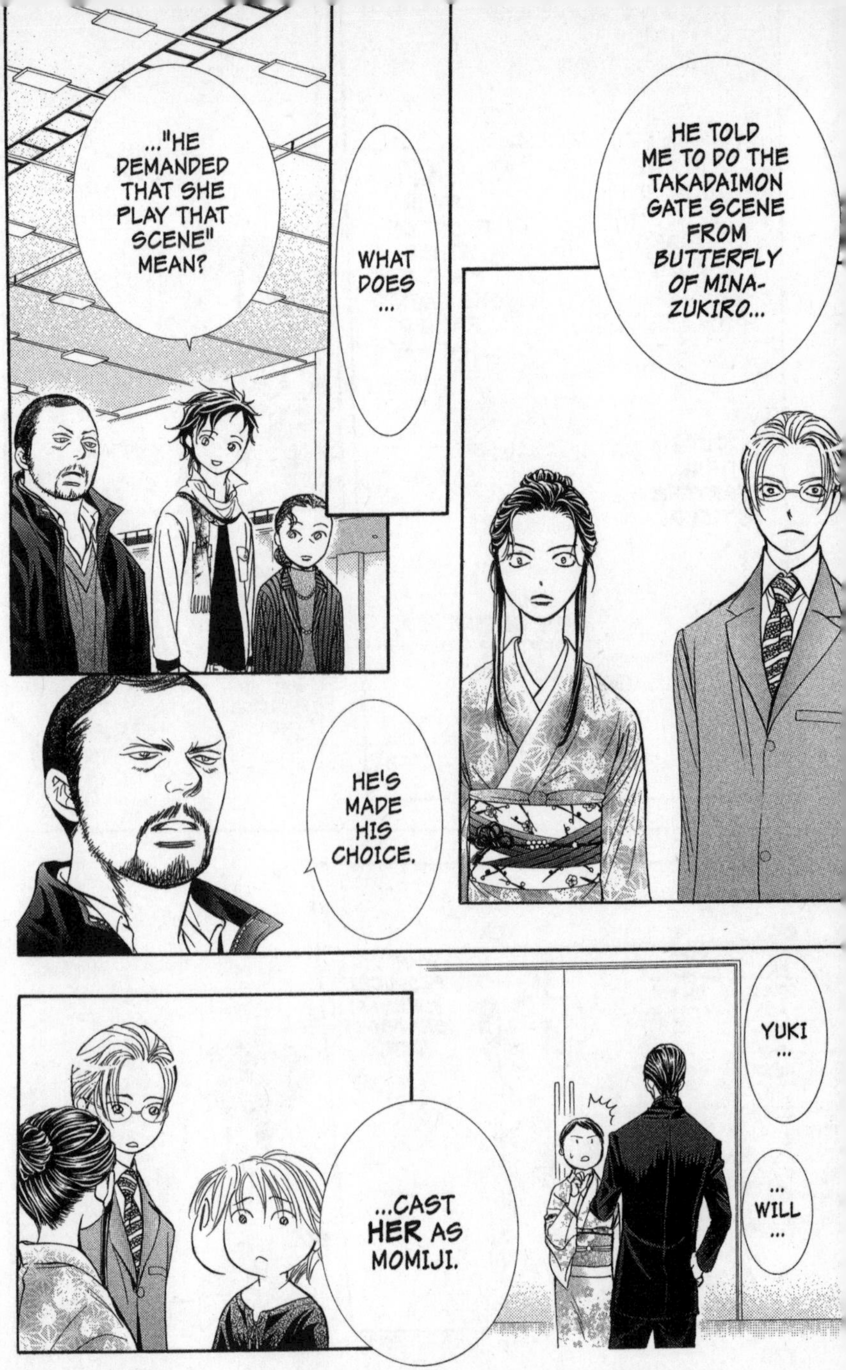
HE TOLD ME TO DO THE TAKADAIMON GATE SCENE FROM BUTTERFLY OF MINA-ZUKIRO...
WHAT DOES ...
..."HE DEMANDED THAT SHE PLAY THAT SCENE" MEAN?
HE'S MADE HIS CHOICE.
YUKI ...
... WILL ...
NU
...CAST HER AS MOMIJI.

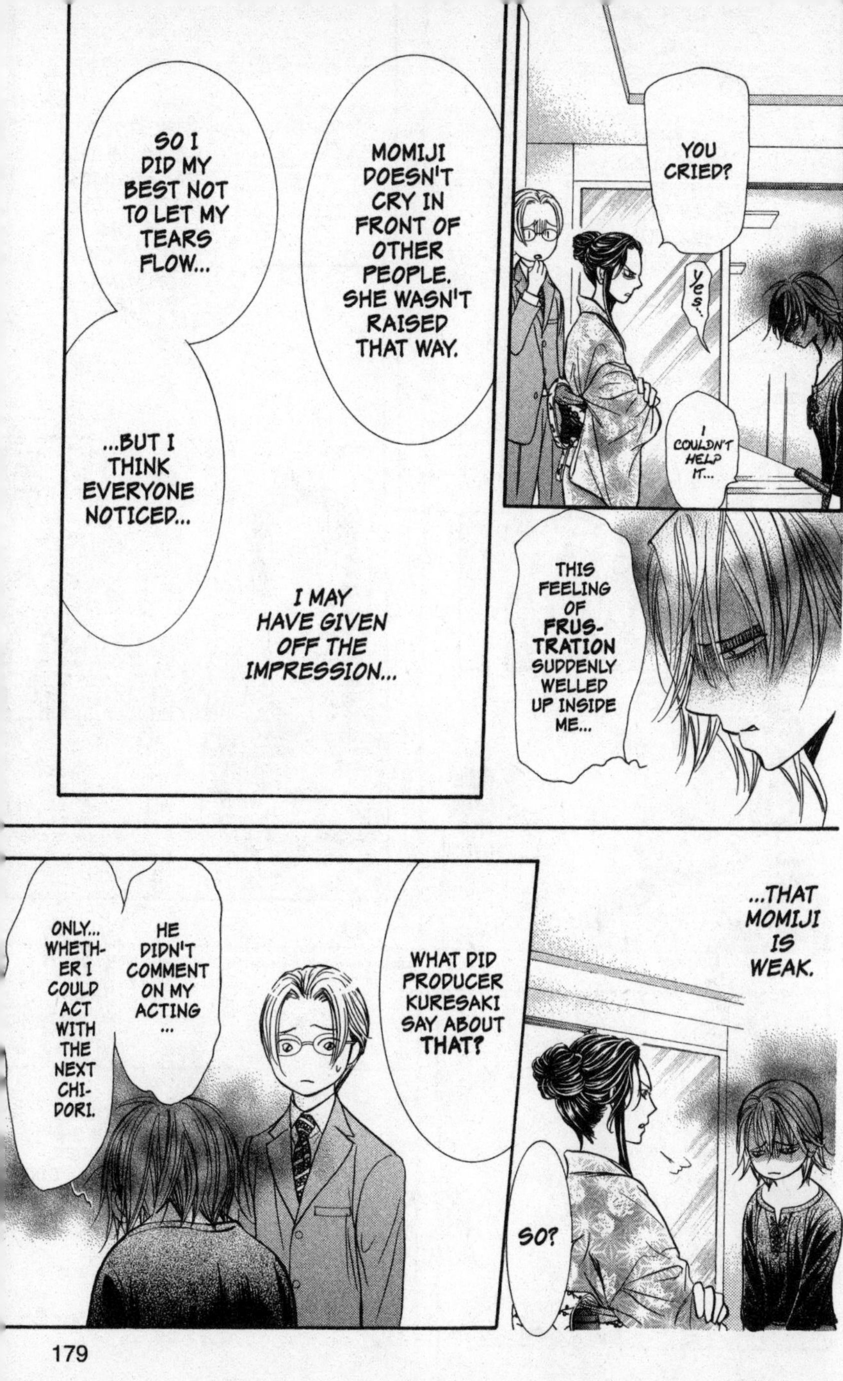
YOU CRIED?
Yes...
I COULDN'T HELP IT...
THIS FEELING OF FRUSTRATION SUDDENLY WELLED UP INSIDE ME...
MOMIJI DOESN'T CRY IN FRONT OF OTHER PEOPLE. SHE WASN'T RAISED THAT WAY.
SO I DID MY BEST NOT TO LET MY TEARS FLOW...
...BUT I THINK EVERYONE NOTICED...
I MAY HAVE GIVEN OFF THE IMPRESSION...
...THAT MOMIJI IS WEAK.
SO?
WHAT DID PRODUCER KURESAKI SAY ABOUT THAT?
HE DIDN'T COMMENT ON MY ACTING...
ONLY... WHETHER I COULD ACT WITH THE NEXT CHIDORI.

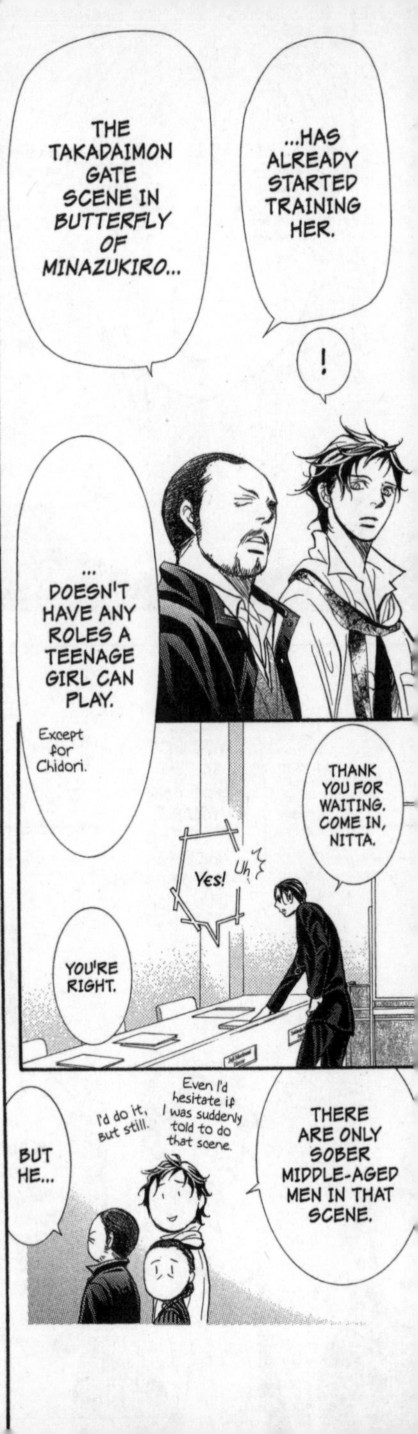
...HAS ALREADY STARTED TRAINING HER.
THE TAKADAIMON GATE SCENE IN BUTTERFLY OF MINAZUKIRO...
!
...DOESN'T HAVE ANY ROLES A TEENAGE GIRL CAN PLAY.
Except for Chidori.
THANK YOU FOR WAITING. COME IN, NITTA.
Uh
Yes!
YOU'RE RIGHT.
THERE ARE ONLY SOBER MIDDLE-AGED MEN IN THAT SCENE.
Even I'd hesitate if I was suddenly told to do that scene.
I'd do it, but still.
BUT HE...
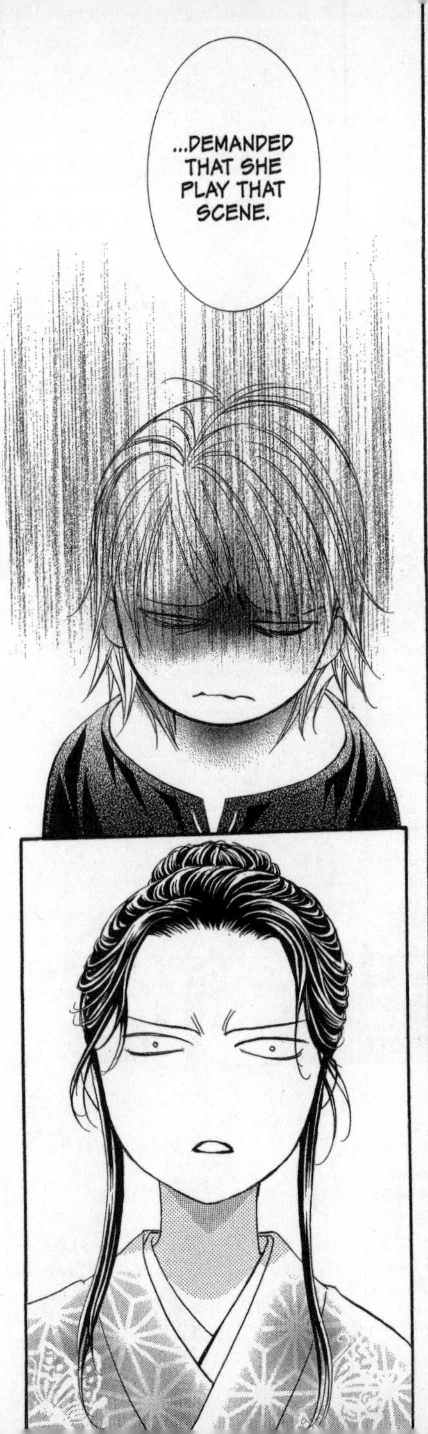
...DEMANDED THAT SHE PLAY THAT SCENE.

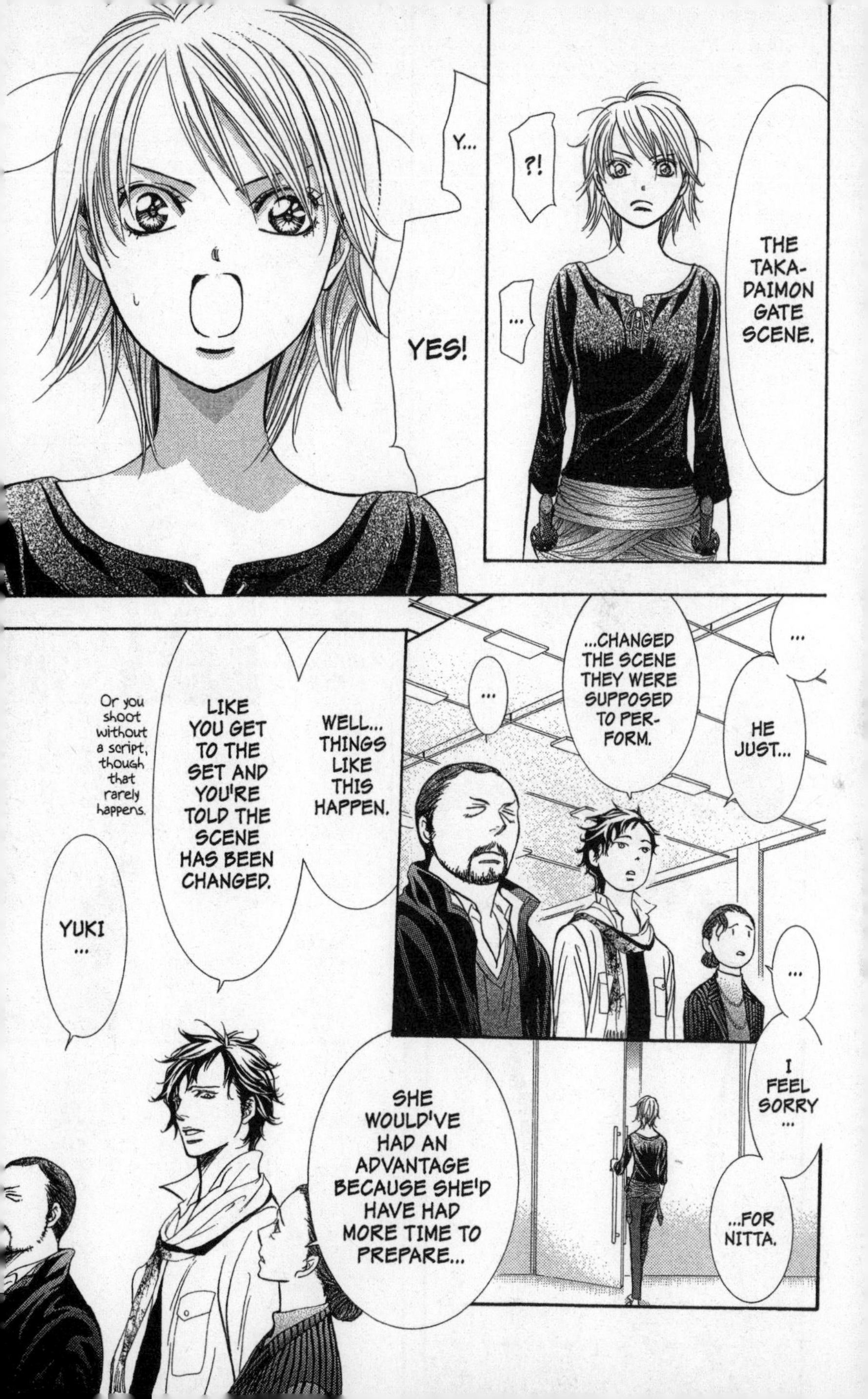
THE TAKA-DAIMON GATE SCENE.
?!
...
Y...
YES!
...
HE JUST...
...CHANGED THE SCENE THEY WERE SUPPOSED TO PER-FORM.
...
...
WELL... THINGS LIKE THIS HAPPEN.
LIKE YOU GET TO THE SET AND YOU'RE TOLD THE SCENE HAS BEEN CHANGED.
Or you shoot without a script, though that rarely happens.
YUKI...
I FEEL SORRY...
...FOR NITTA.
SHE WOULD'VE HAD AN ADVANTAGE BECAUSE SHE'D HAVE HAD MORE TIME TO PREPARE...

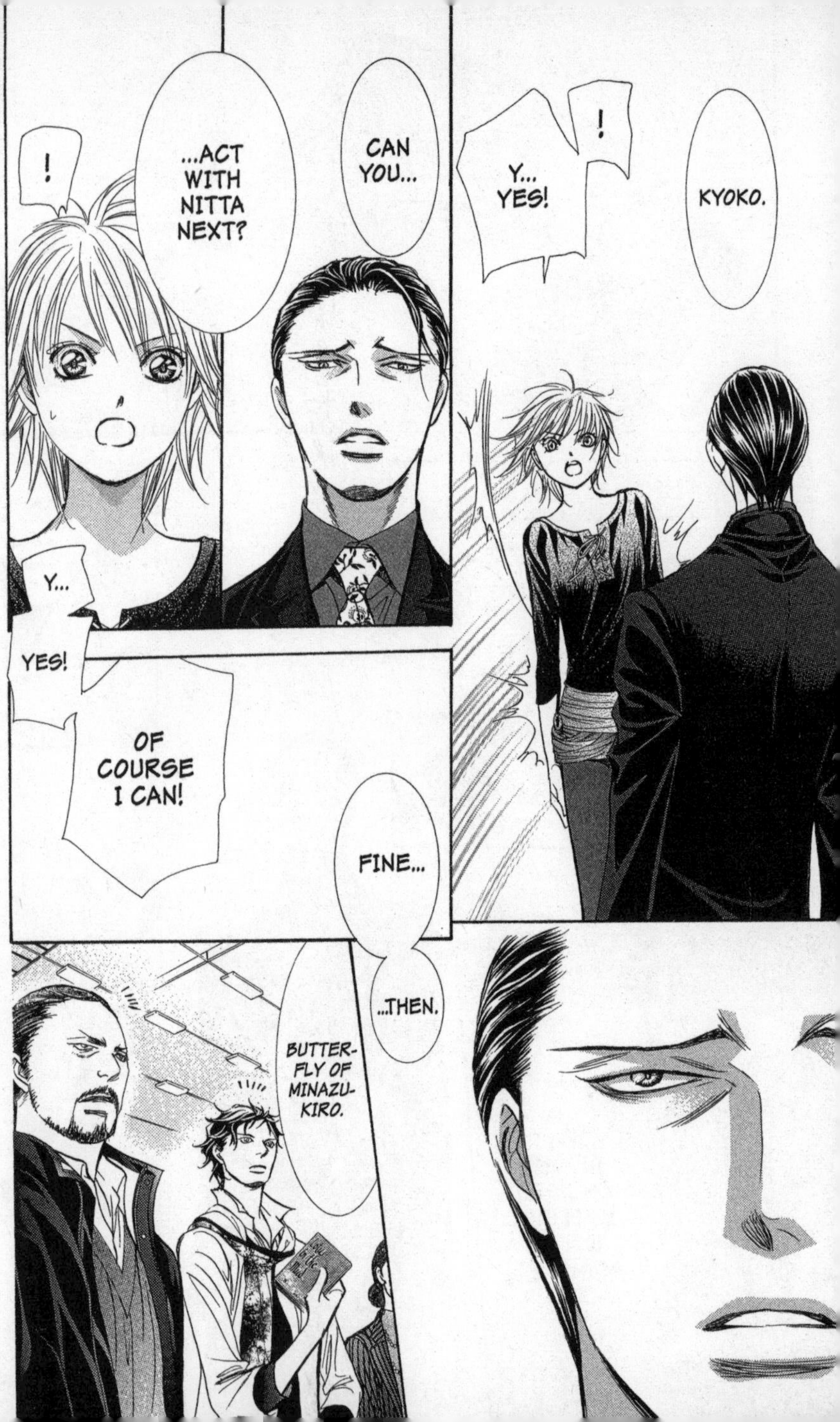
KYOKO.
!
Y... YES!
CAN YOU...
...ACT WITH NITTA NEXT?
!
Y...
YES!
OF COURSE I CAN!
FINE...
...THEN.
BUTTER-FLY OF MINAZU-KIRO.

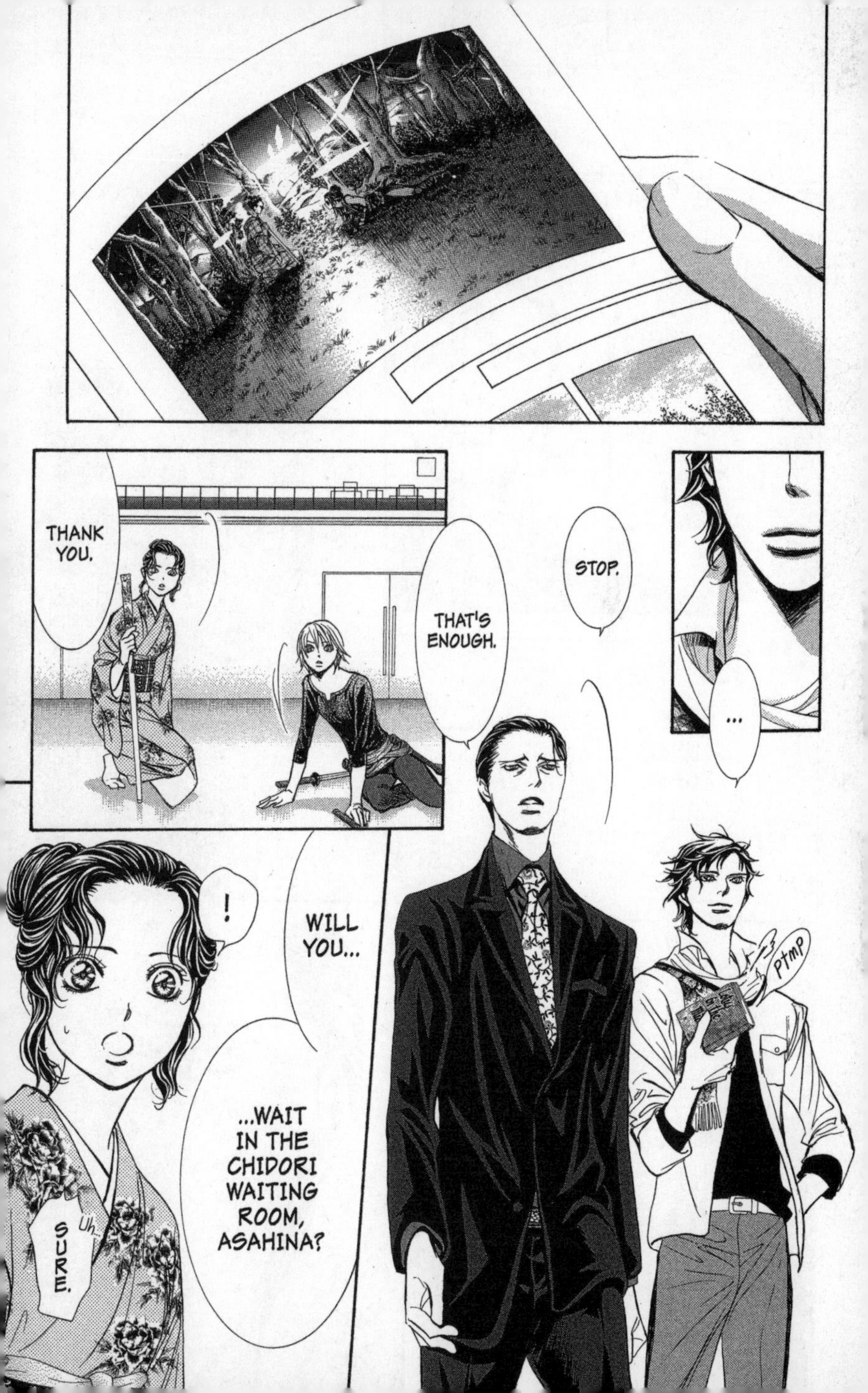
...
THANK YOU.
STOP.
THAT'S ENOUGH.
Ptmp
!
WILL YOU...
...WAIT IN THE CHIDORI WAITING ROOM, ASAHINA?
Uh...
SURE.

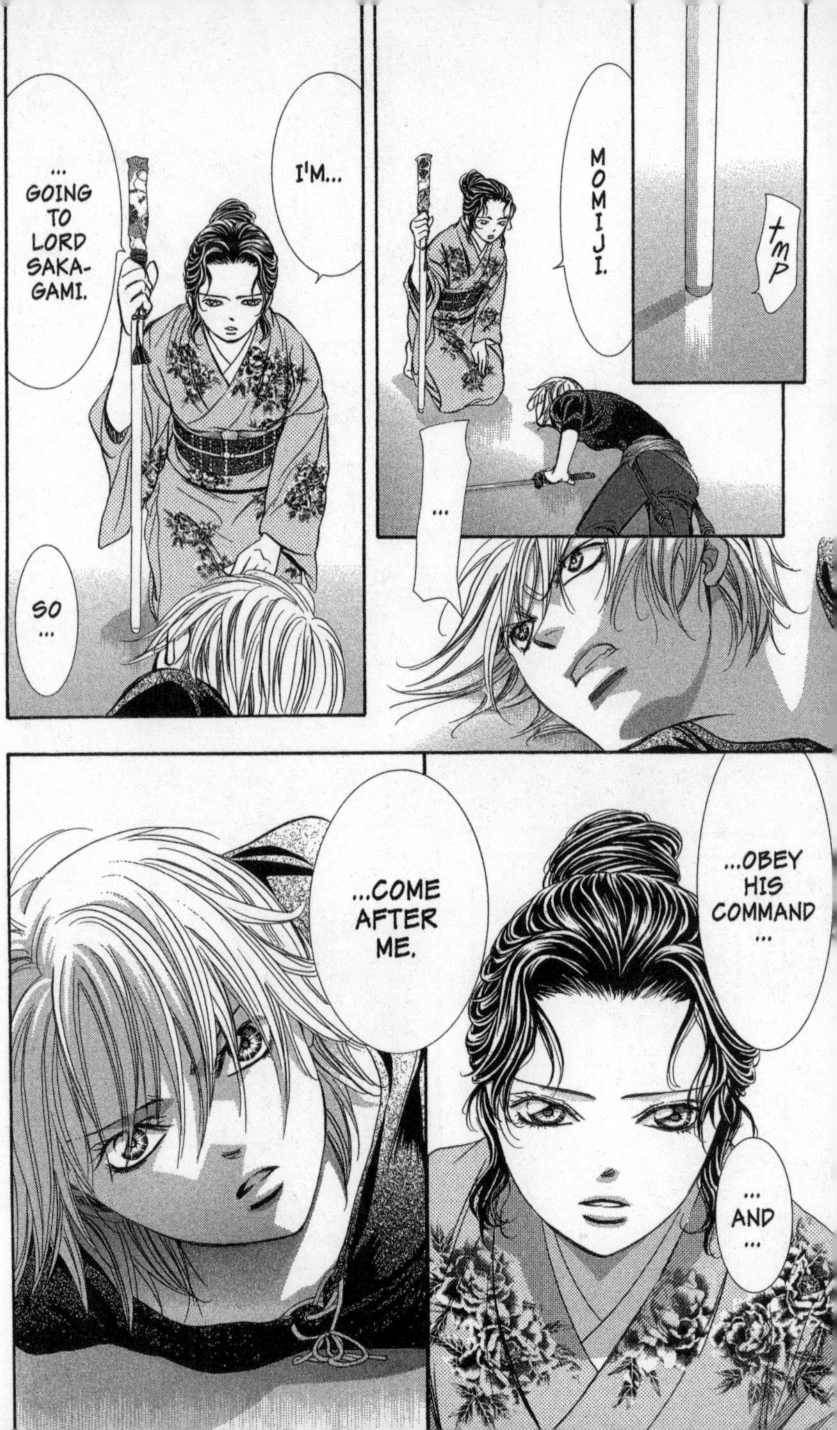
tmp
MOMIJI.
...
I'M...
...GOING TO LORD SAKA-GAMI.
SO...
...OBEY HIS COMMAND...
...AND...
...COME AFTER ME.

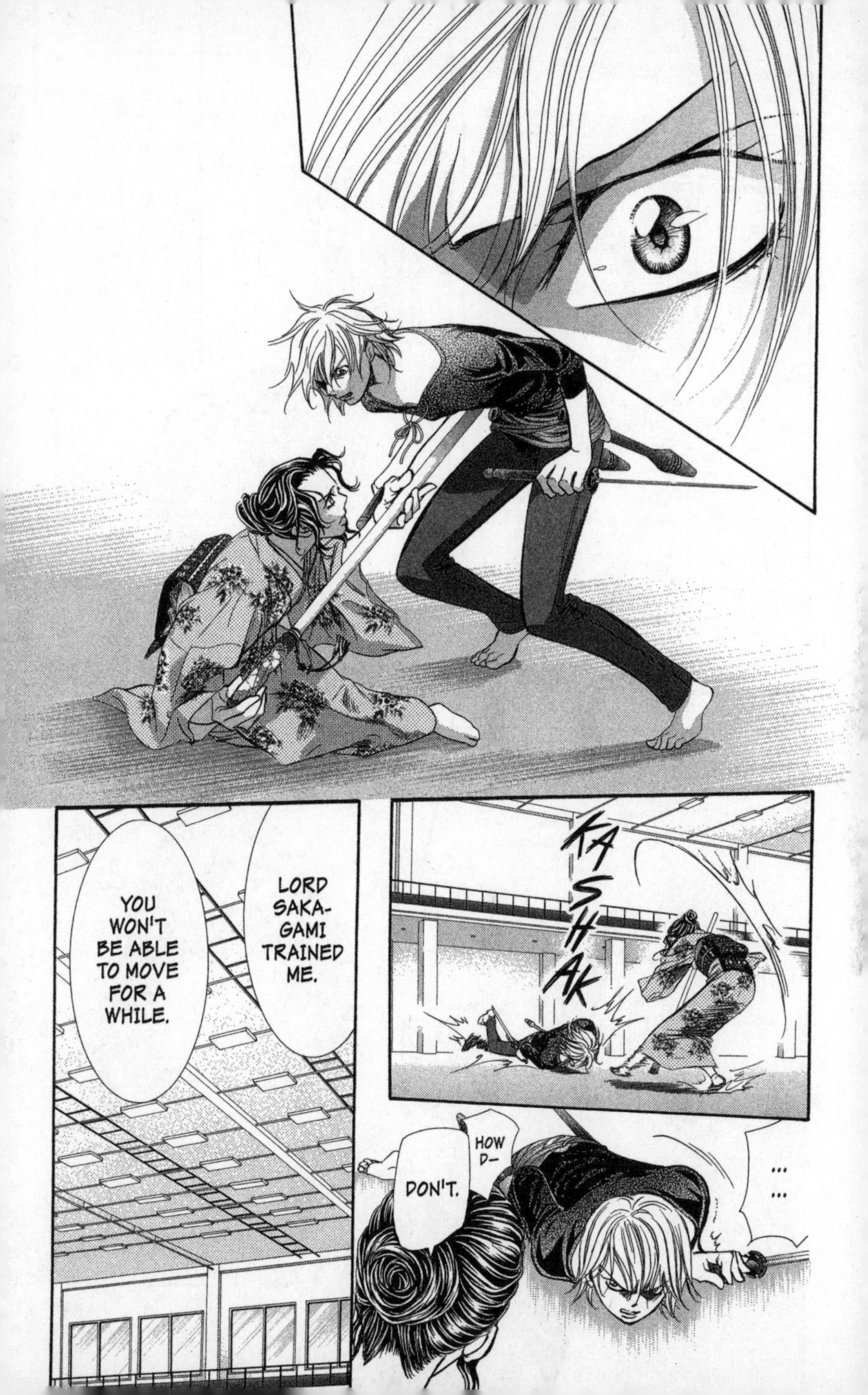
KASHAK
...
...
HOW D—
DON'T.
LORD SAKA-GAMI TRAINED ME.
YOU WON'T BE ABLE TO MOVE FOR A WHILE.

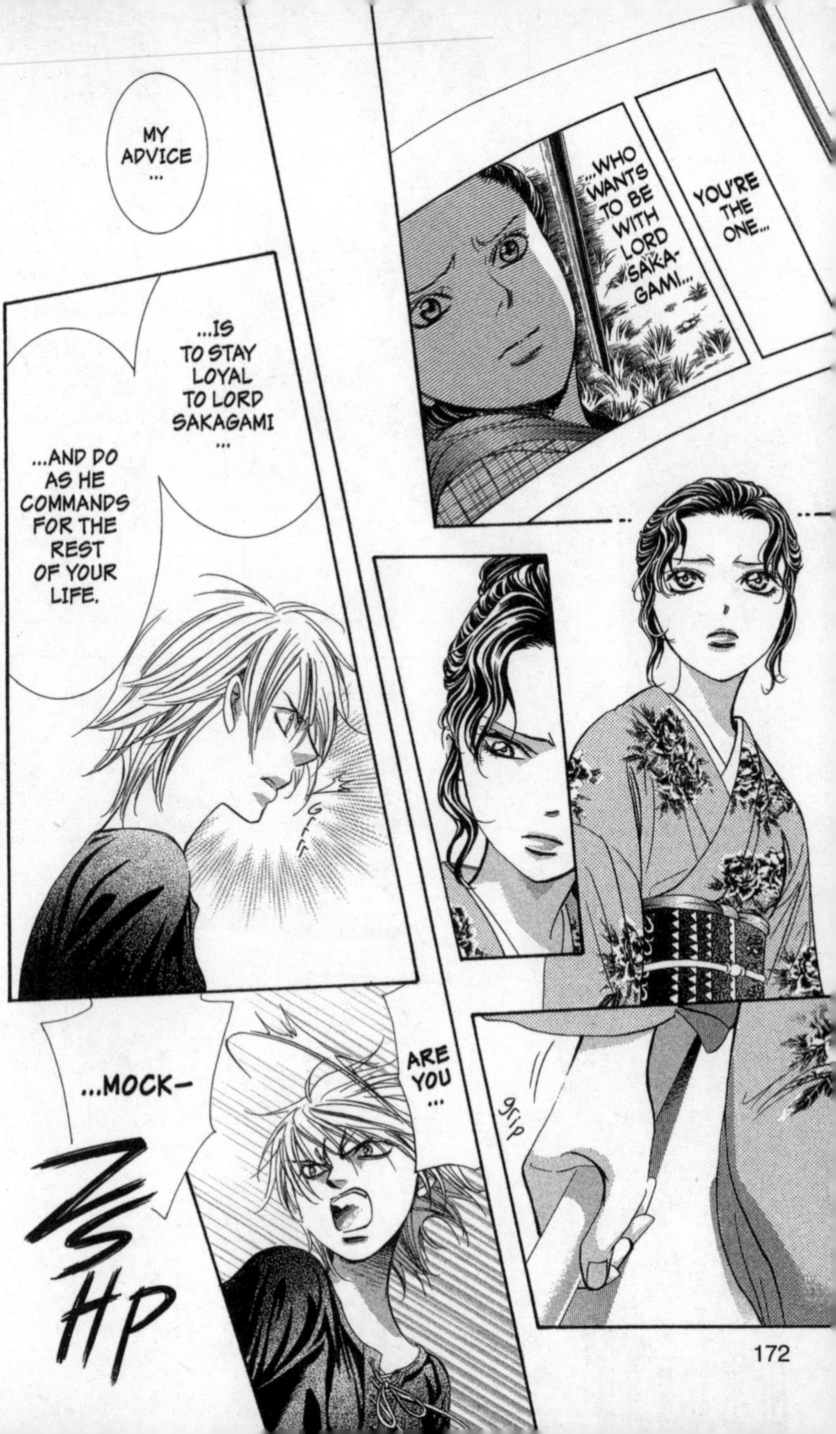
YOU'RE THE ONE...
...WHO WANTS TO BE WITH LORD SAKA-GAMI...
MY ADVICE ...
...IS TO STAY LOYAL TO LORD SAKAGAMI ...
...AND DO AS HE COMMANDS FOR THE REST OF YOUR LIFE.
ARE YOU ...
...MOCK-
ZSHP
grip

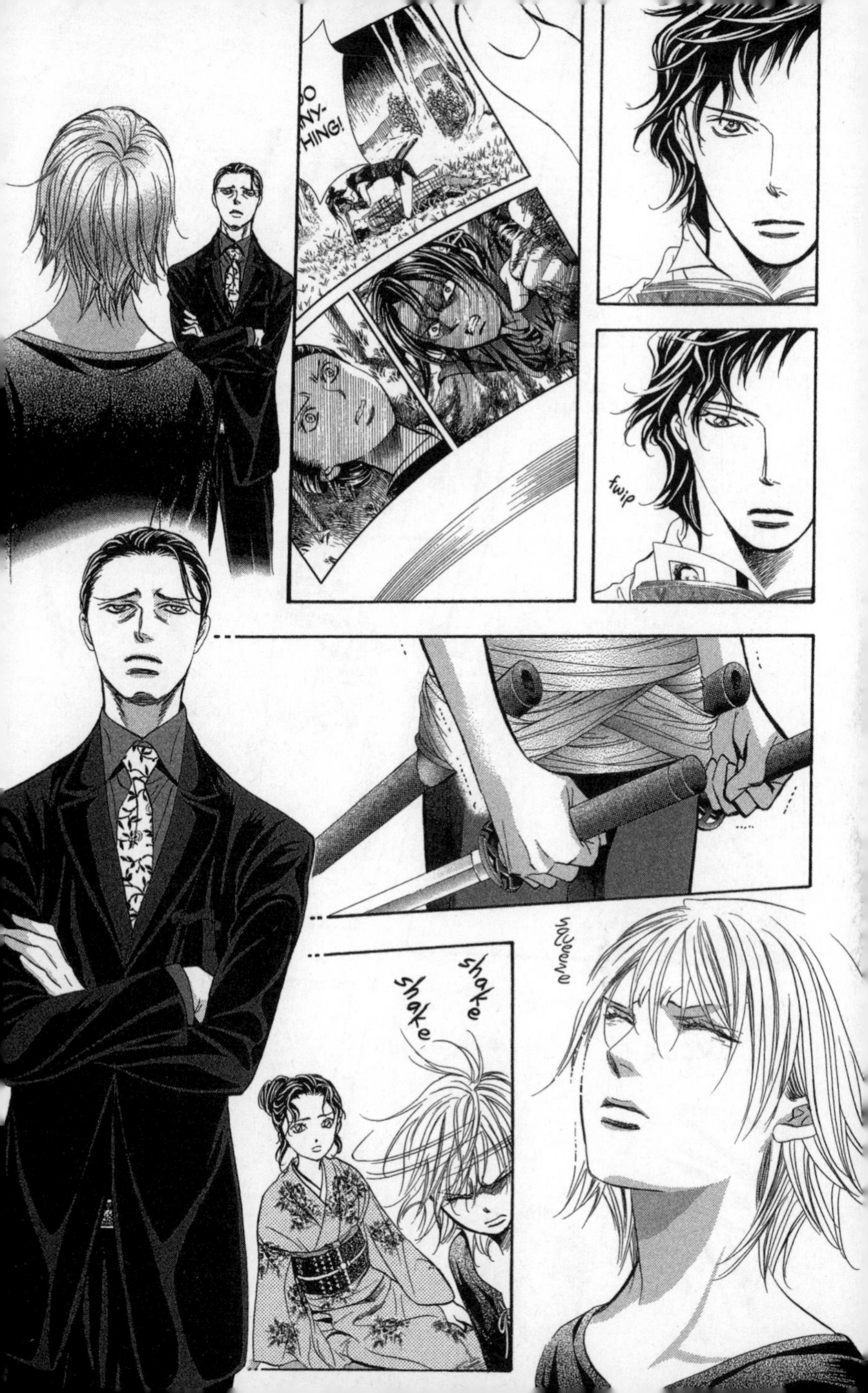
fwip
O NY- HING!
...
...
...
...
...
squeeze
shake shake

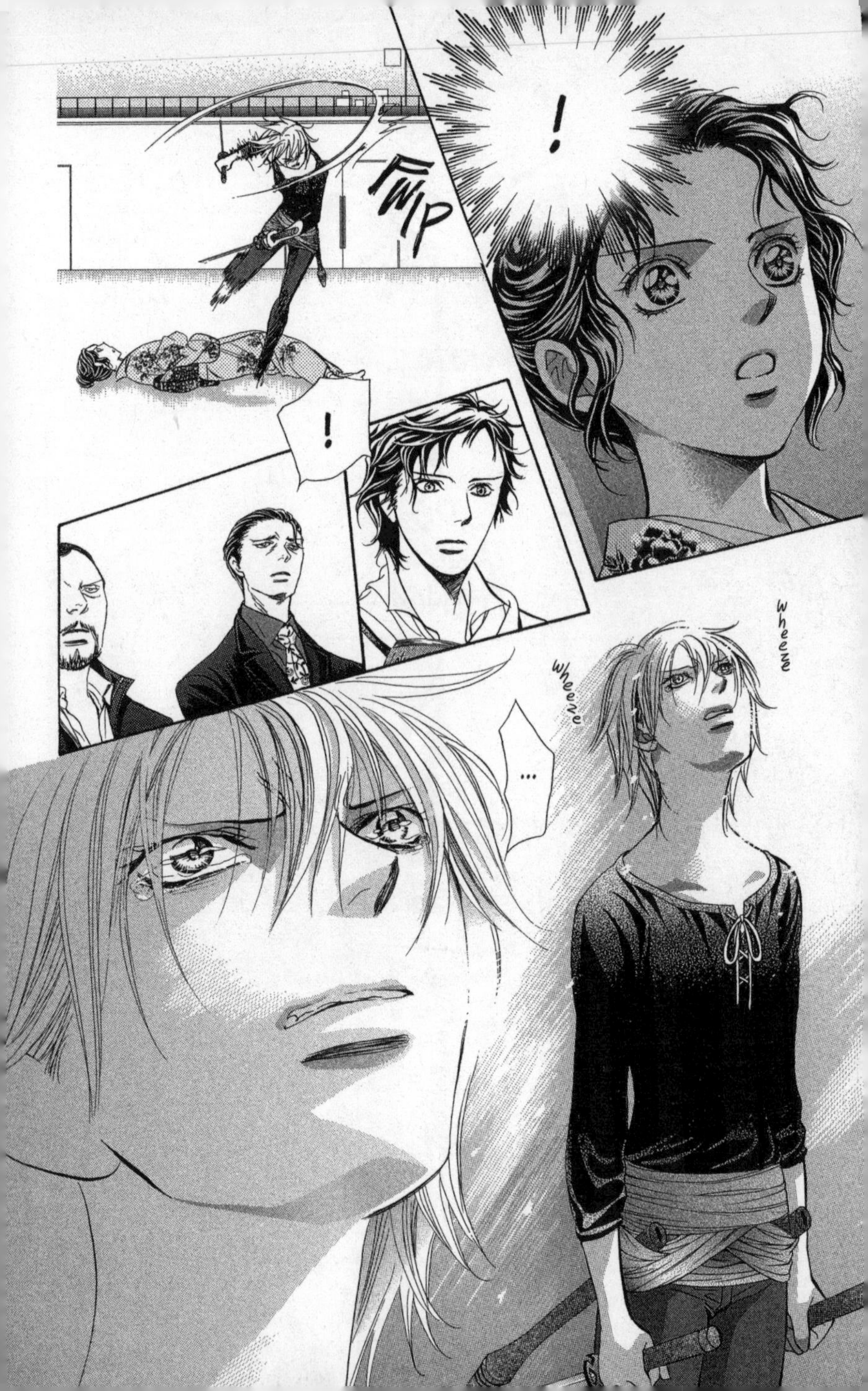
!
FWIP
!
wheeze
wheeze
...

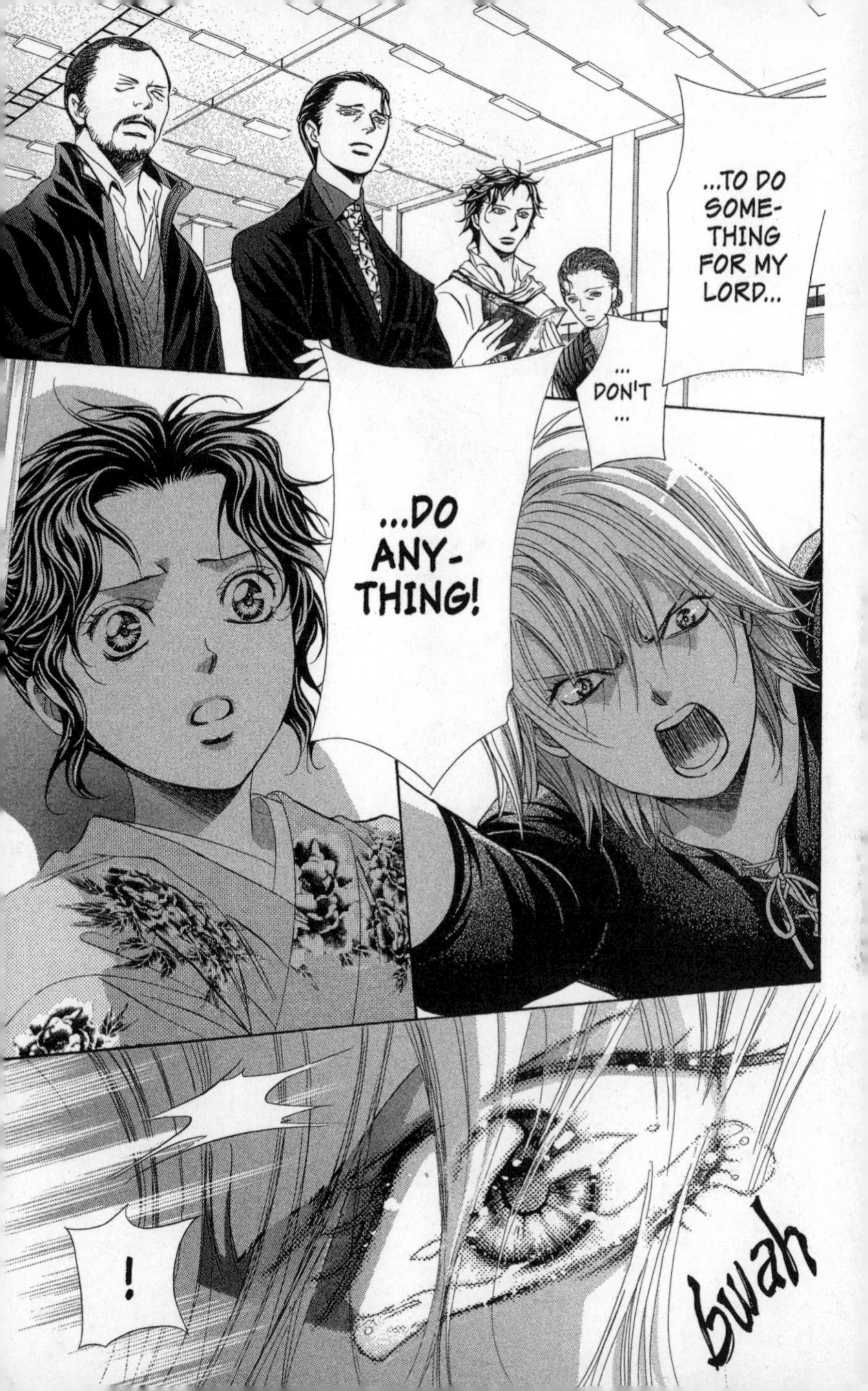
...TO DO SOMETHING FOR MY LORD...
... DON'T ...
...DO ANYTHING!
!
bwah

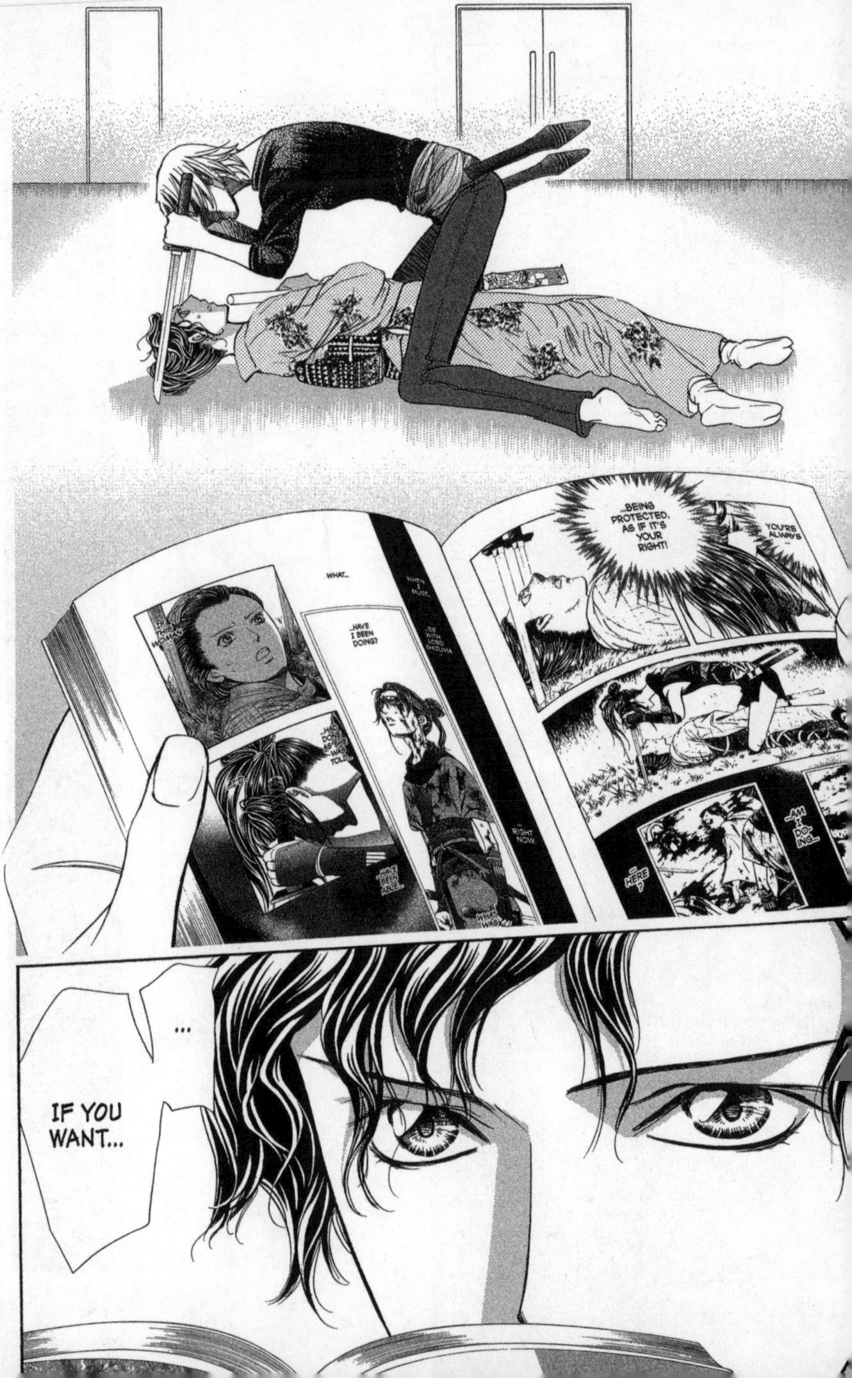

YOU'RE ALWAYS ...
...BEING PROTECTED, AS IF IT'S YOUR RIGHT!
...AM I DOING...
...HERE?
WHEN I MUST...
...BE WITH LORD SHIZUMA...
...RIGHT NOW.
WHAT...
...HAVE I BEEN DOING?
IF THIS WOMAN
...HAD DONE AS SHE WAS TOLD...
...HAVE BEEN ABLE...
WHAT WAS
...
IF YOU WANT...

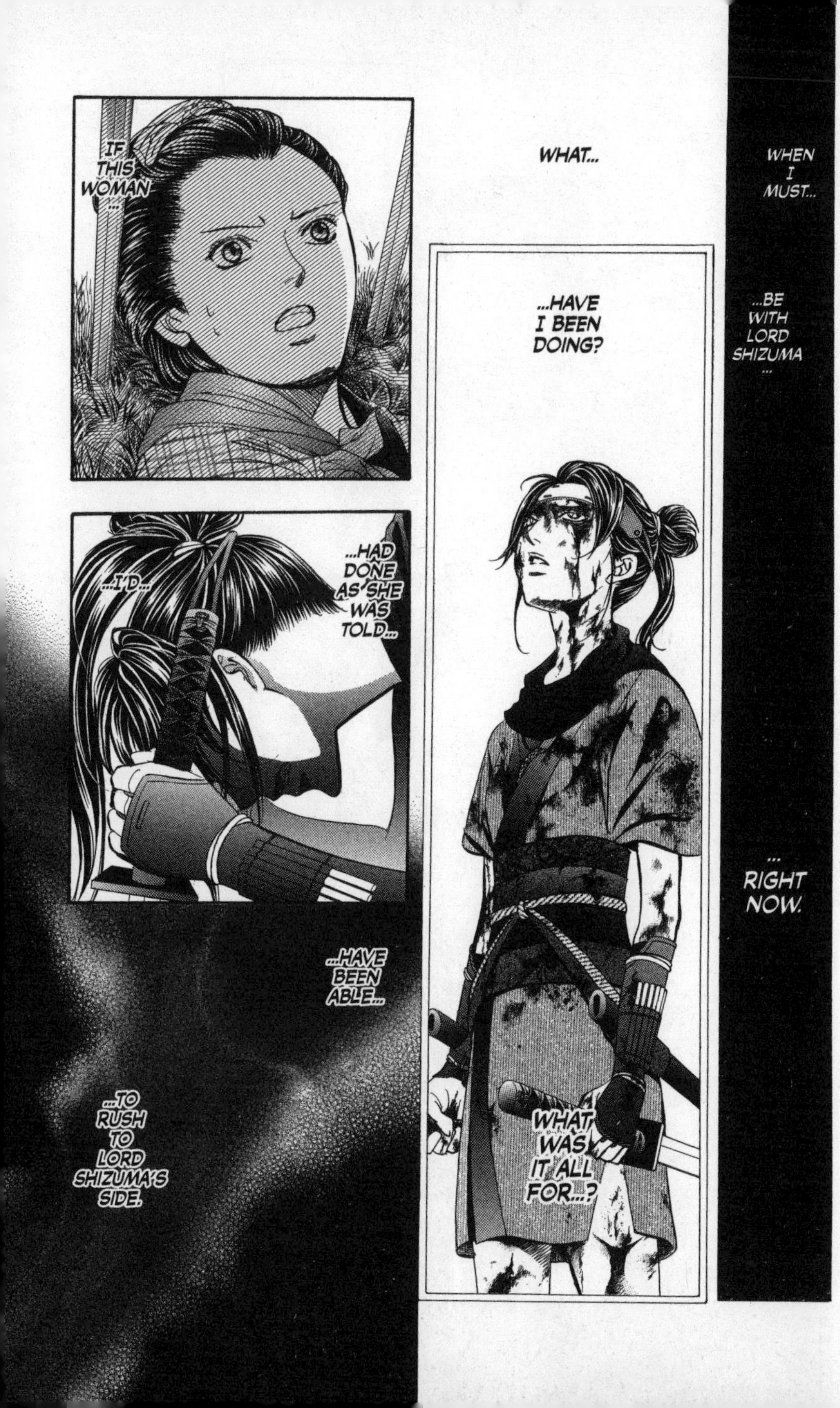
WHEN I MUST...
...BE WITH LORD SHIZUMA...
... RIGHT NOW.
WHAT...
...HAVE I BEEN DOING?
WHAT WAS IT ALL FOR...?
IF THIS WOMAN...
...HAD DONE AS SHE WAS TOLD...
...I'D...
...HAVE BEEN ABLE...
...TO RUSH TO LORD SHIZUMA'S SIDE.

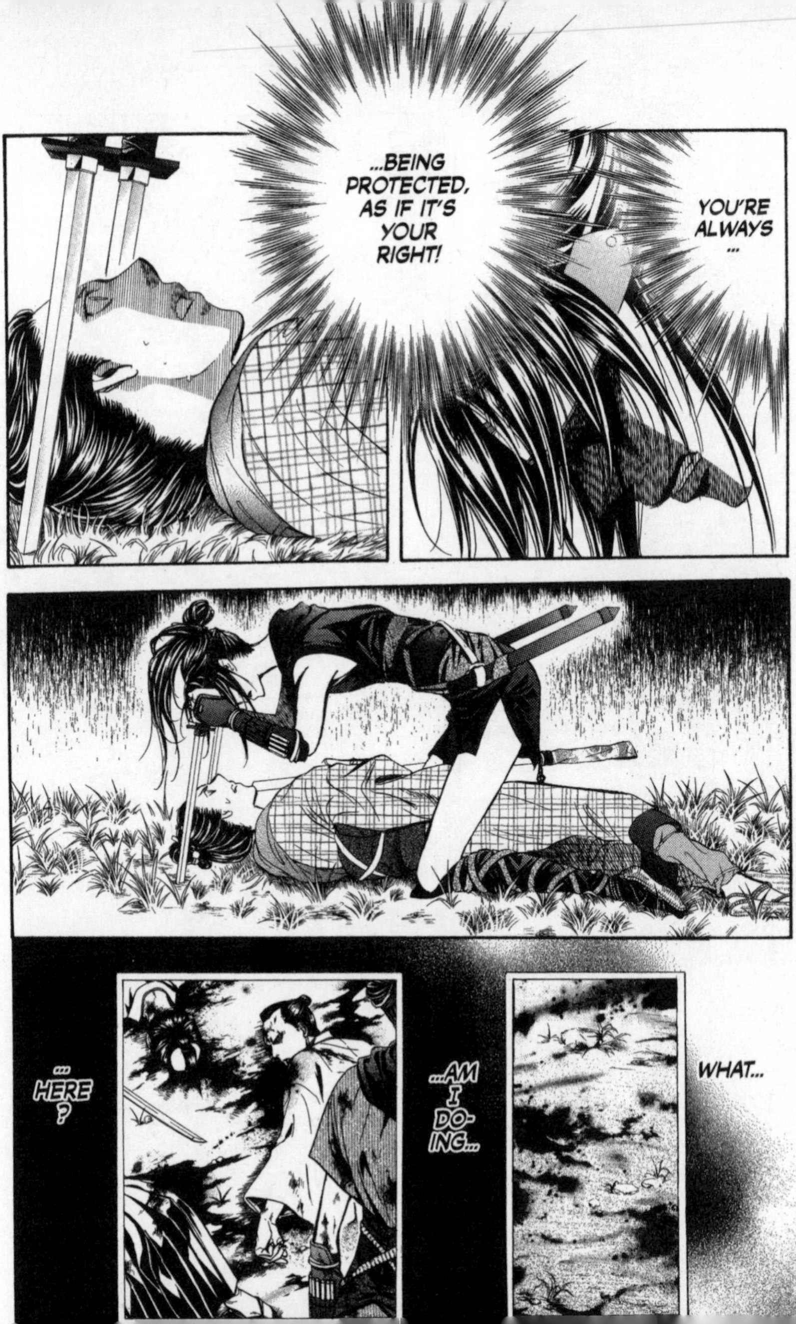
YOU'RE ALWAYS ...
...BEING PROTECTED, AS IF IT'S YOUR RIGHT!
WHAT...
...AM I DOING...
... HERE ?

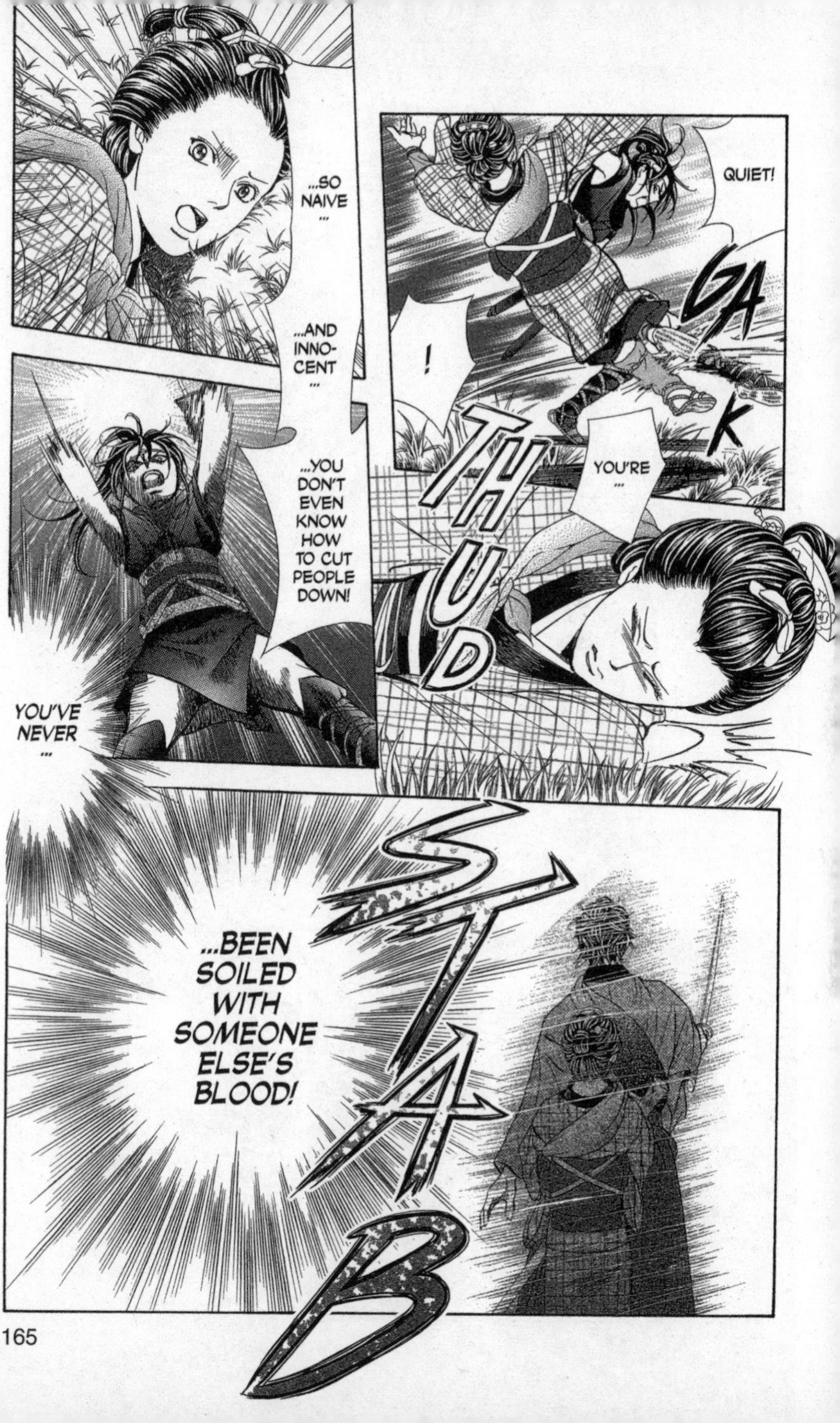
QUIET!
GAK
!
...SO NAIVE ...
YOU'RE ...
THUD
...AND INNO-CENT ...
...YOU DON'T EVEN KNOW HOW TO CUT PEOPLE DOWN!
YOU'VE NEVER ...
...BEEN SOILED WITH SOMEONE ELSE'S BLOOD!
STAB

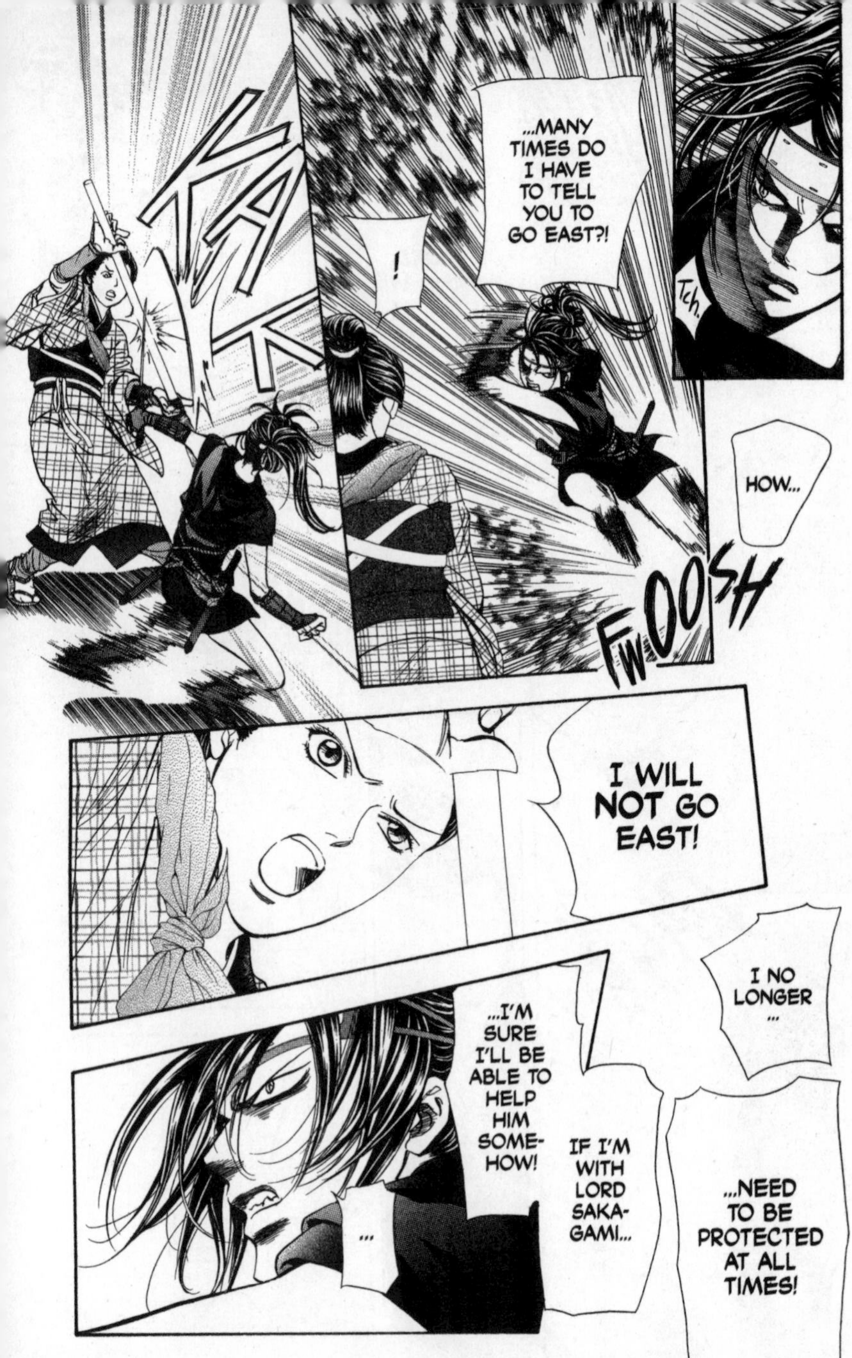
Tch.
...MANY TIMES DO I HAVE TO TELL YOU TO GO EAST?!
!
FWOOSH
KAKA
HOW...
I WILL NOT GO EAST!
I NO LONGER ...
...NEED TO BE PROTECTED AT ALL TIMES!
IF I'M WITH LORD SAKA-GAMI...
...I'M SURE I'LL BE ABLE TO HELP HIM SOME-HOW!
...

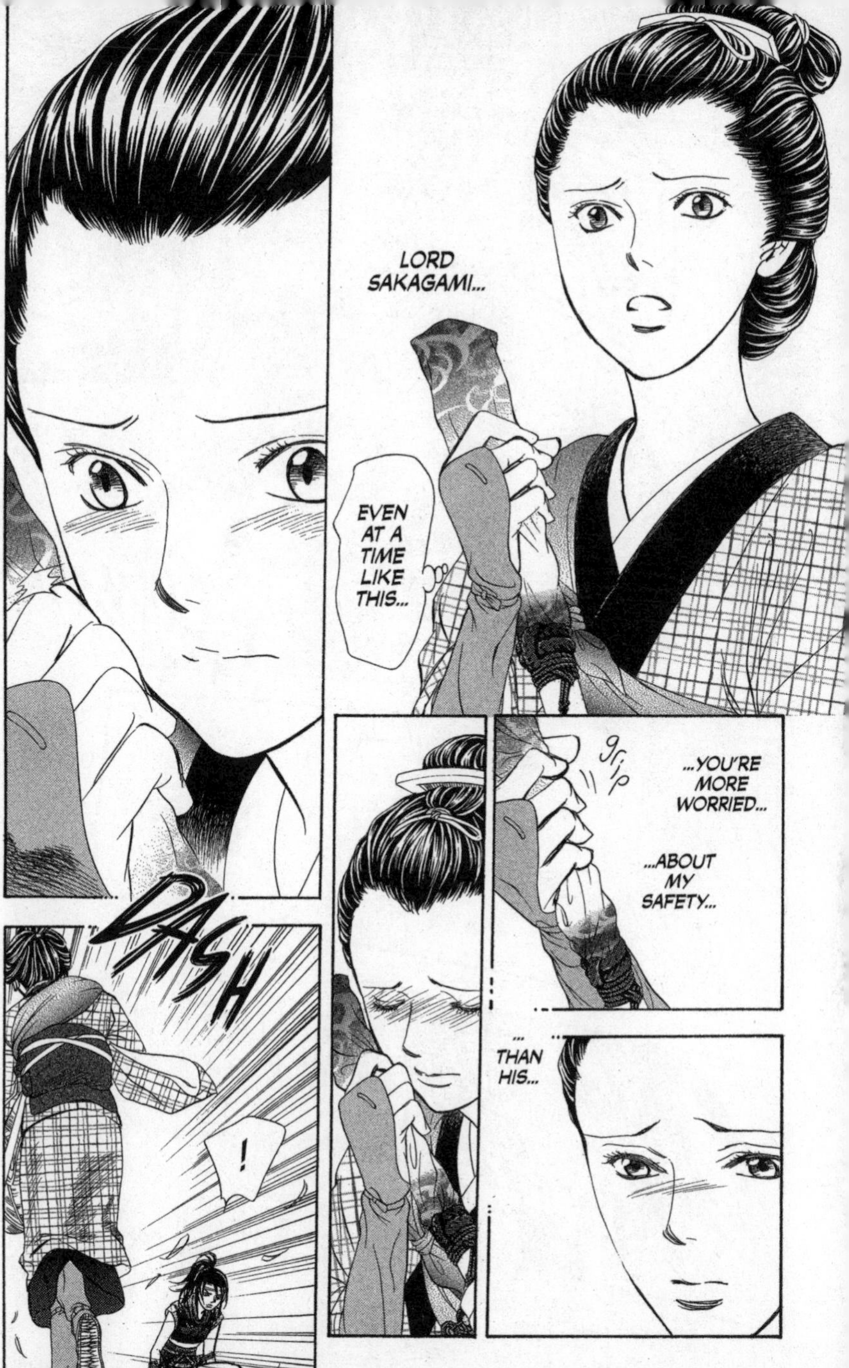
LORD SAKAGAMI...
EVEN AT A TIME LIKE THIS...
grip
...YOU'RE MORE WORRIED...
...ABOUT MY SAFETY...
... THAN HIS...
DASH
!

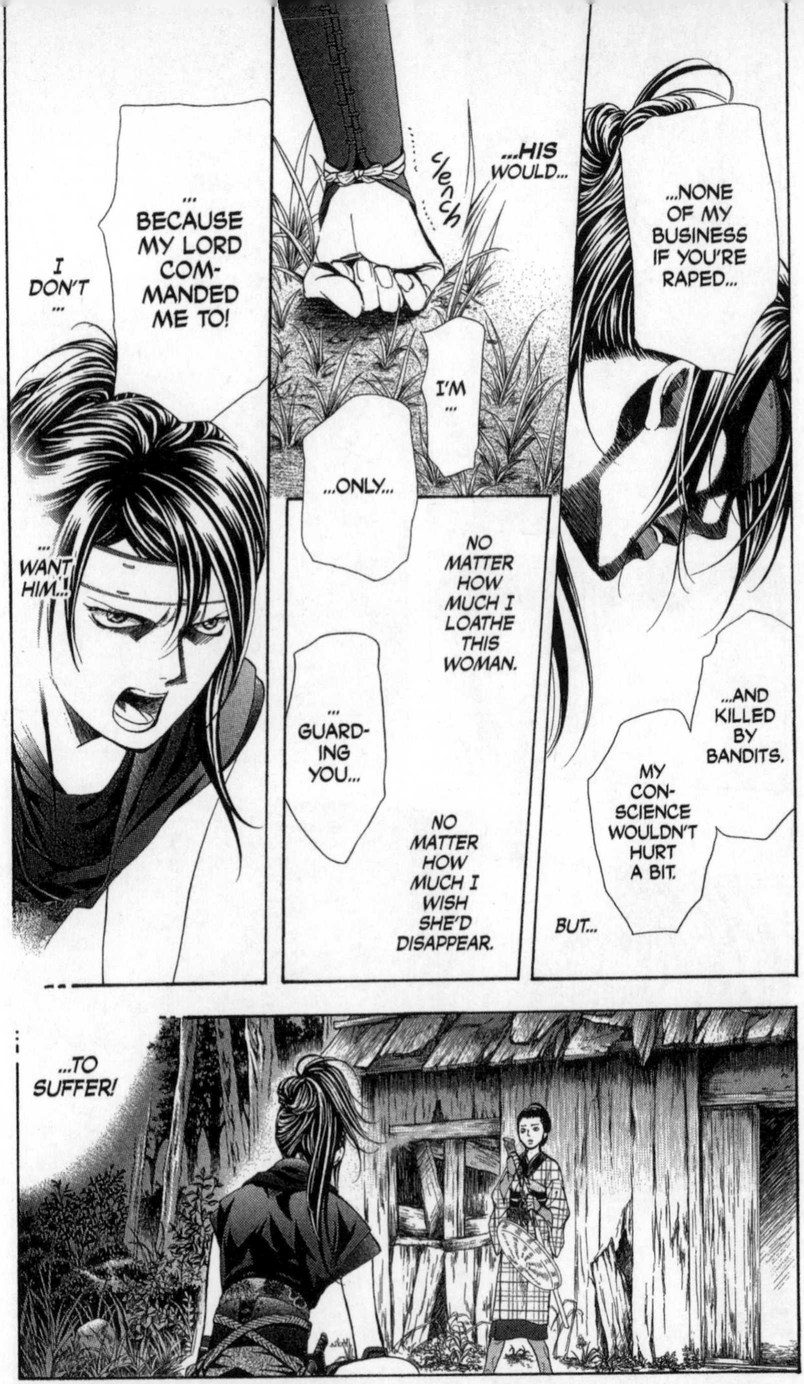
...NONE OF MY BUSINESS IF YOU'RE RAPED...
...AND KILLED BY BANDITS.
MY CONSCIENCE WOULDN'T HURT A BIT.
BUT...
...HIS WOULD...
clench
I'M ...
...ONLY...
NO MATTER HOW MUCH I LOATHE THIS WOMAN.
... GUARDING YOU...
NO MATTER HOW MUCH I WISH SHE'D DISAPPEAR.
... BECAUSE MY LORD COMMANDED ME TO!
I DON'T ...
... WANT HIM..!
...TO SUFFER!

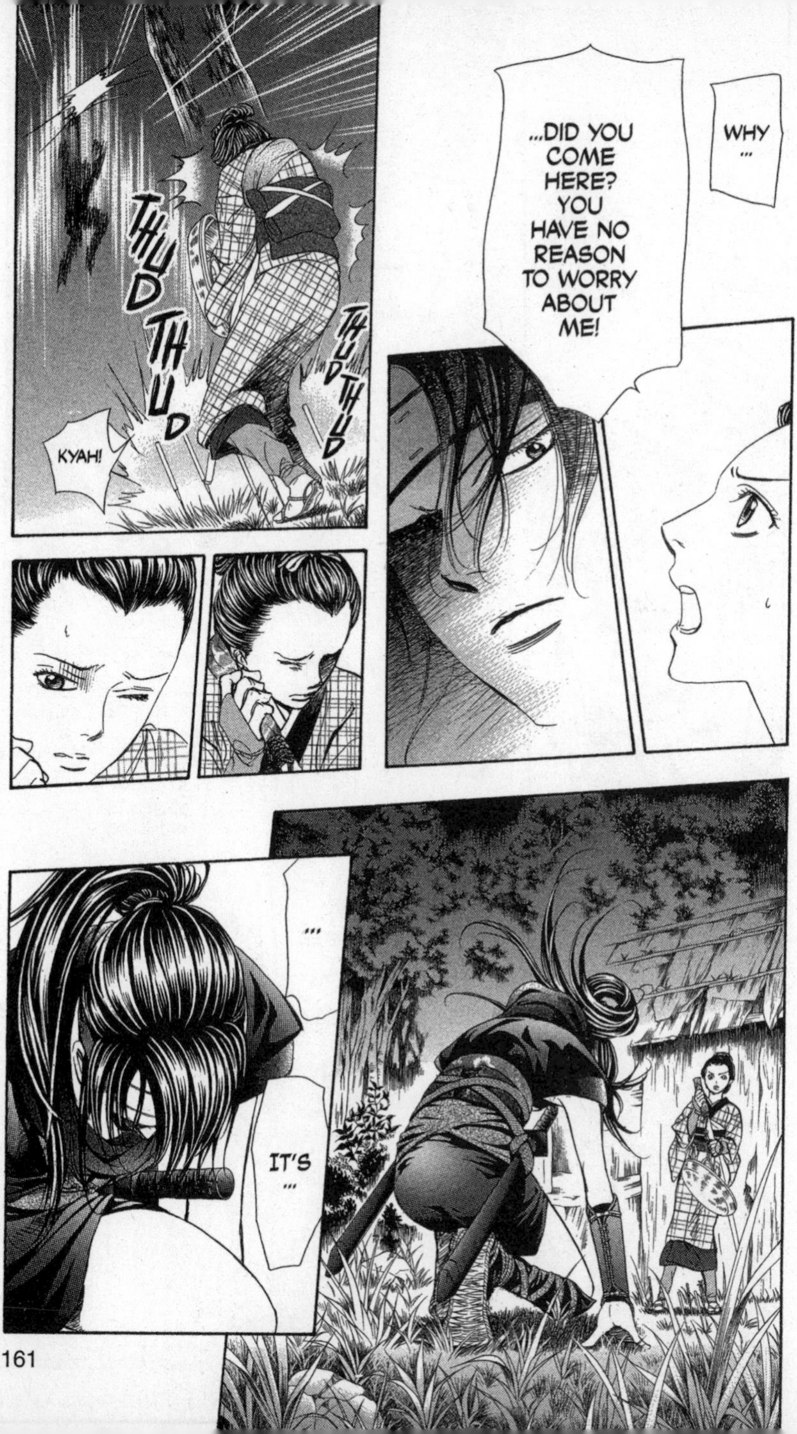
WHY ...
...DID YOU COME HERE? YOU HAVE NO REASON TO WORRY ABOUT ME!
THUD THUD
THUD THUD
KYAH!
...
IT'S ...

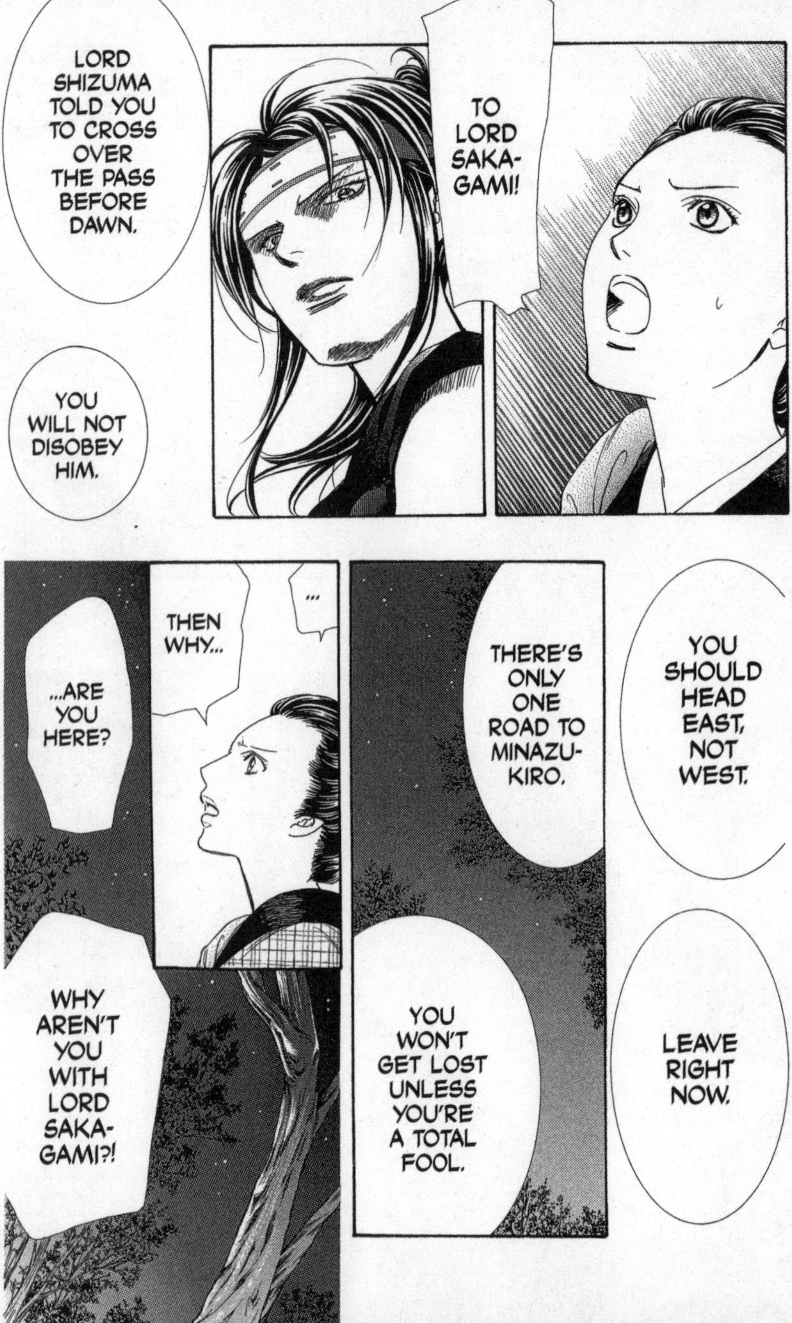
TO LORD SAKAGAMI!
LORD SHIZUMA TOLD YOU TO CROSS OVER THE PASS BEFORE DAWN.
YOU WILL NOT DISOBEY HIM.
YOU SHOULD HEAD EAST, NOT WEST.
THERE'S ONLY ONE ROAD TO MINAZUKIRO.
LEAVE RIGHT NOW.
YOU WON'T GET LOST UNLESS YOU'RE A TOTAL FOOL.
...
THEN WHY...
...ARE YOU HERE?
WHY AREN'T YOU WITH LORD SAKAGAMI?!

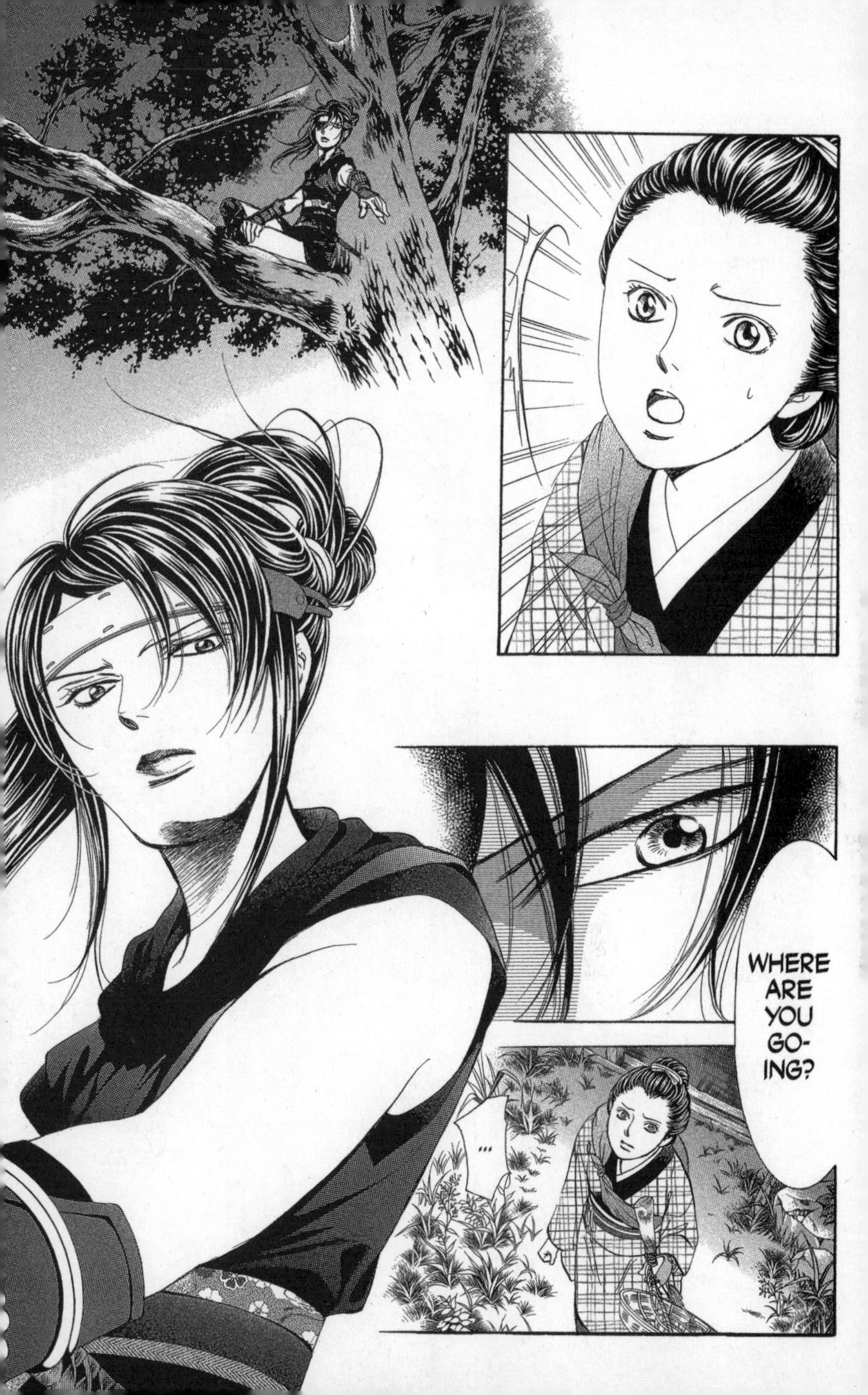
WHERE ARE YOU GO-ING?
...

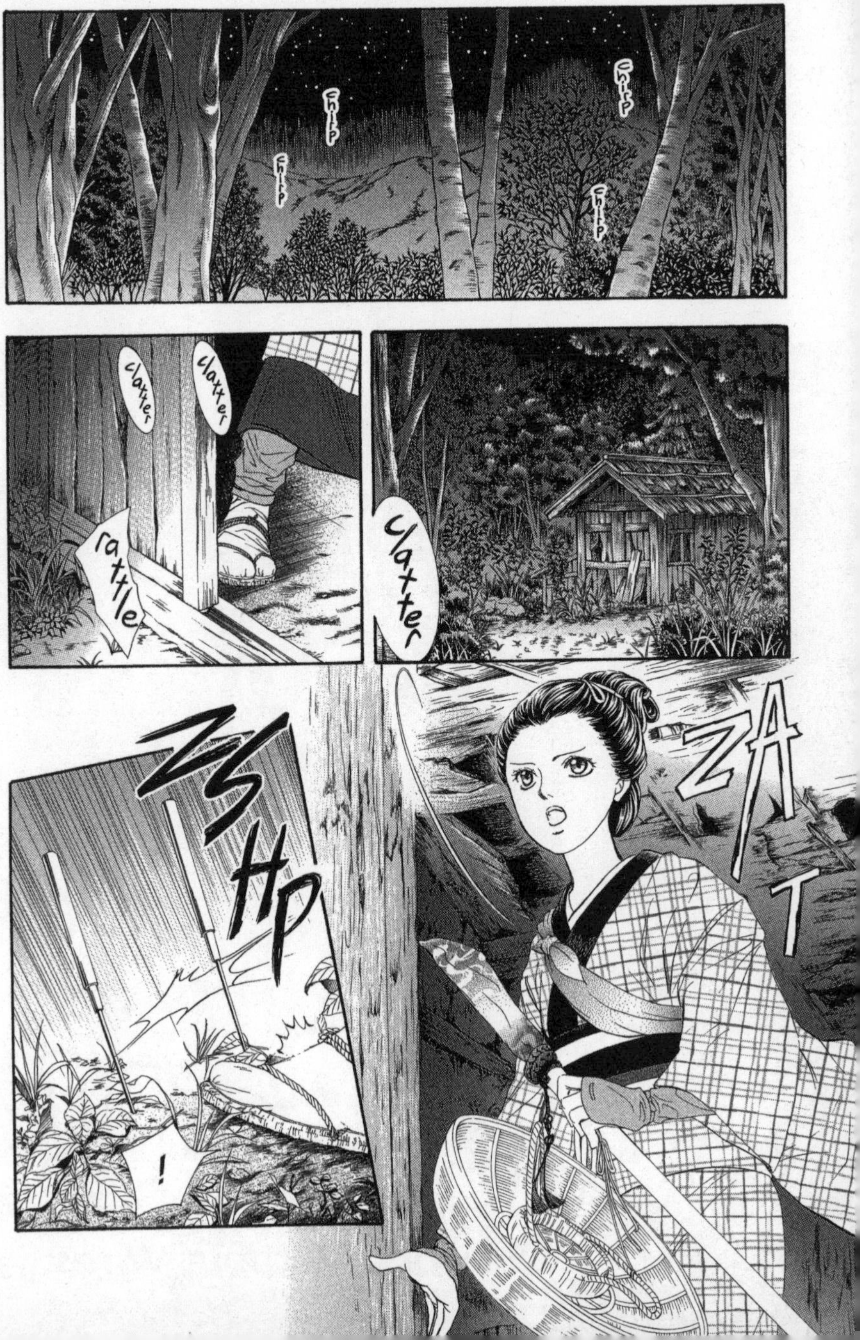
Chirp
Chirp
Chirp
Chirp
clatter
clatter
clatter
rattle
ZAT
ZSHP
!

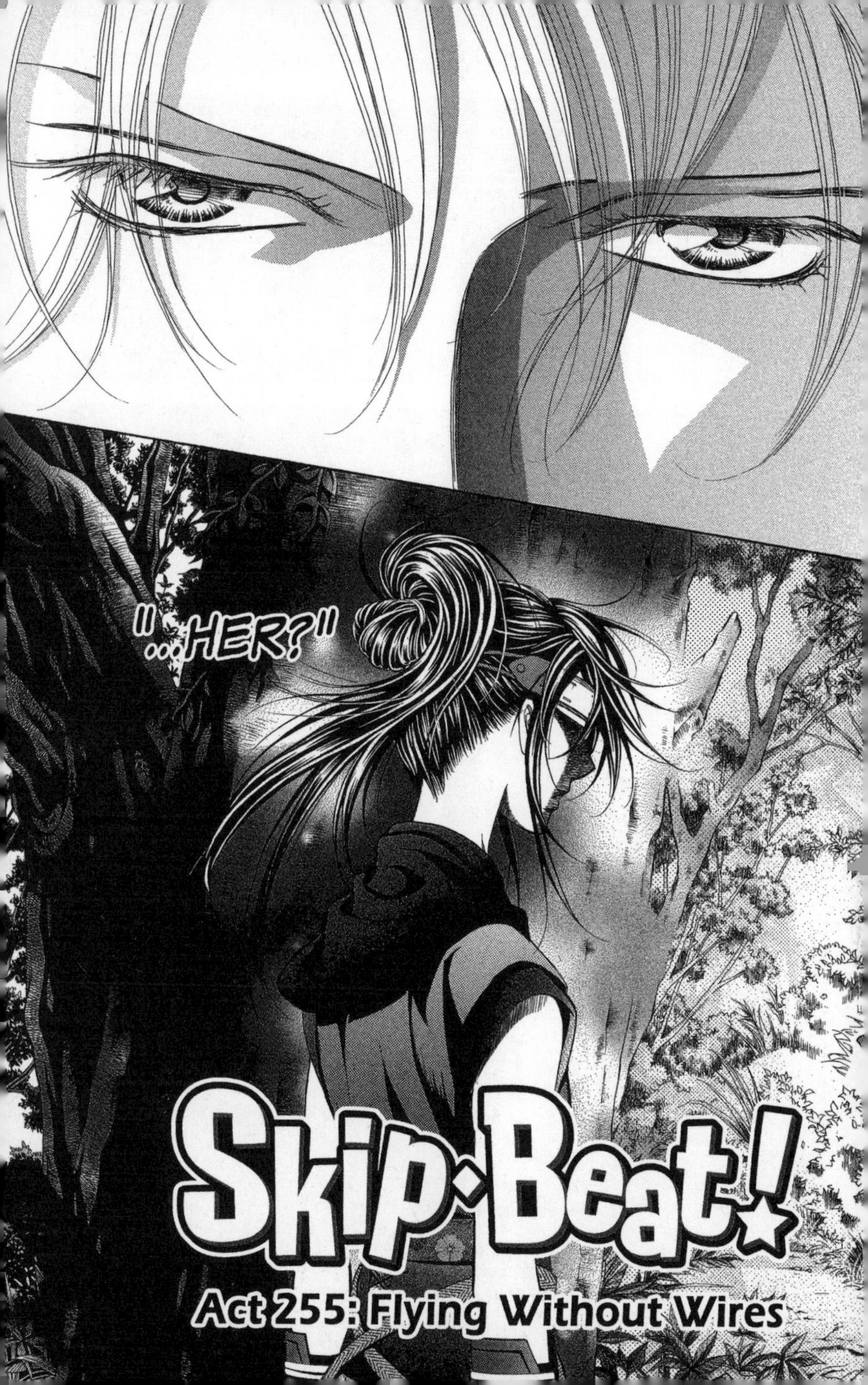
"...HER?"
Skip·Beat!
Act 255: Flying Without Wires

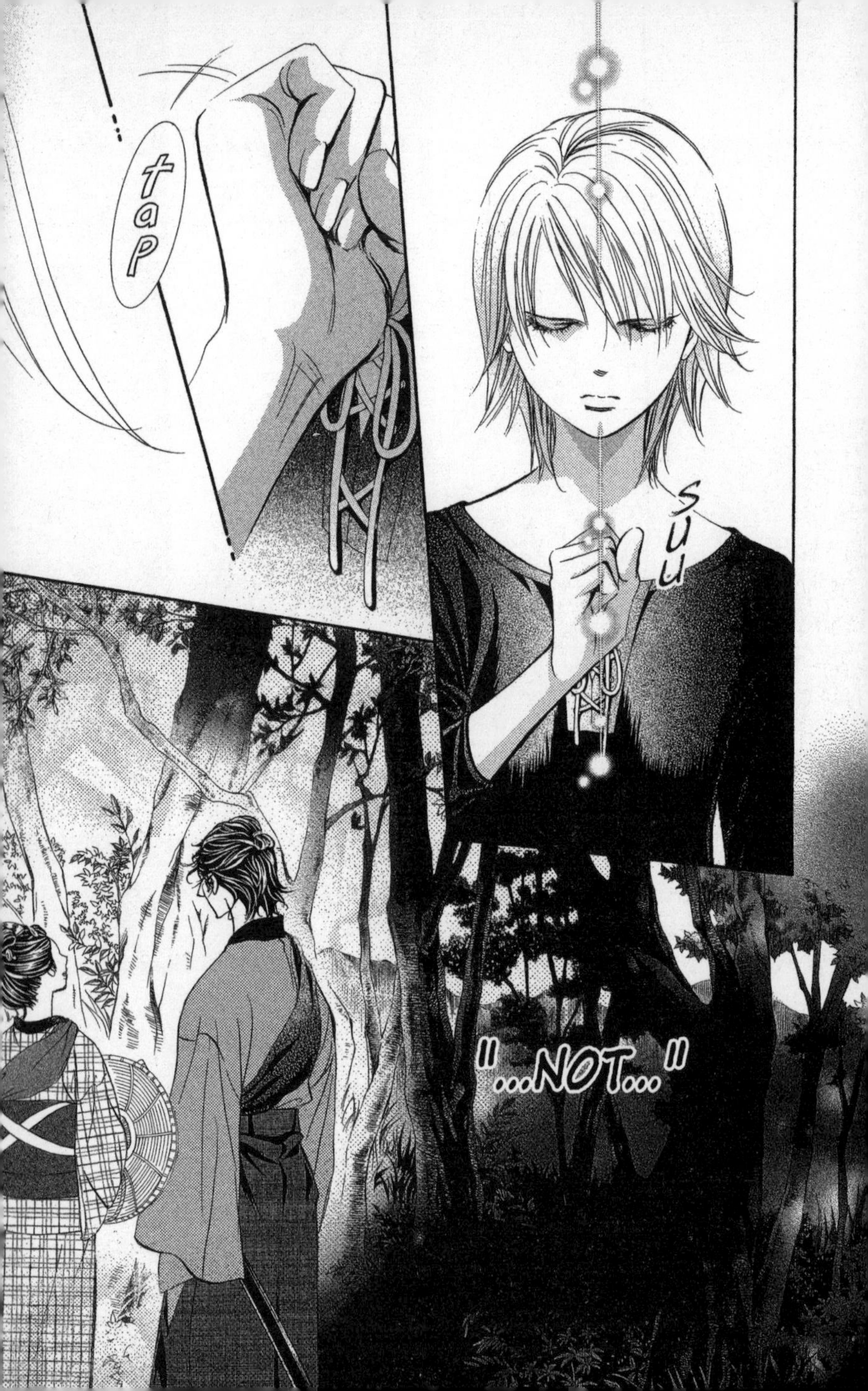
suu
tap
"...NOT..."

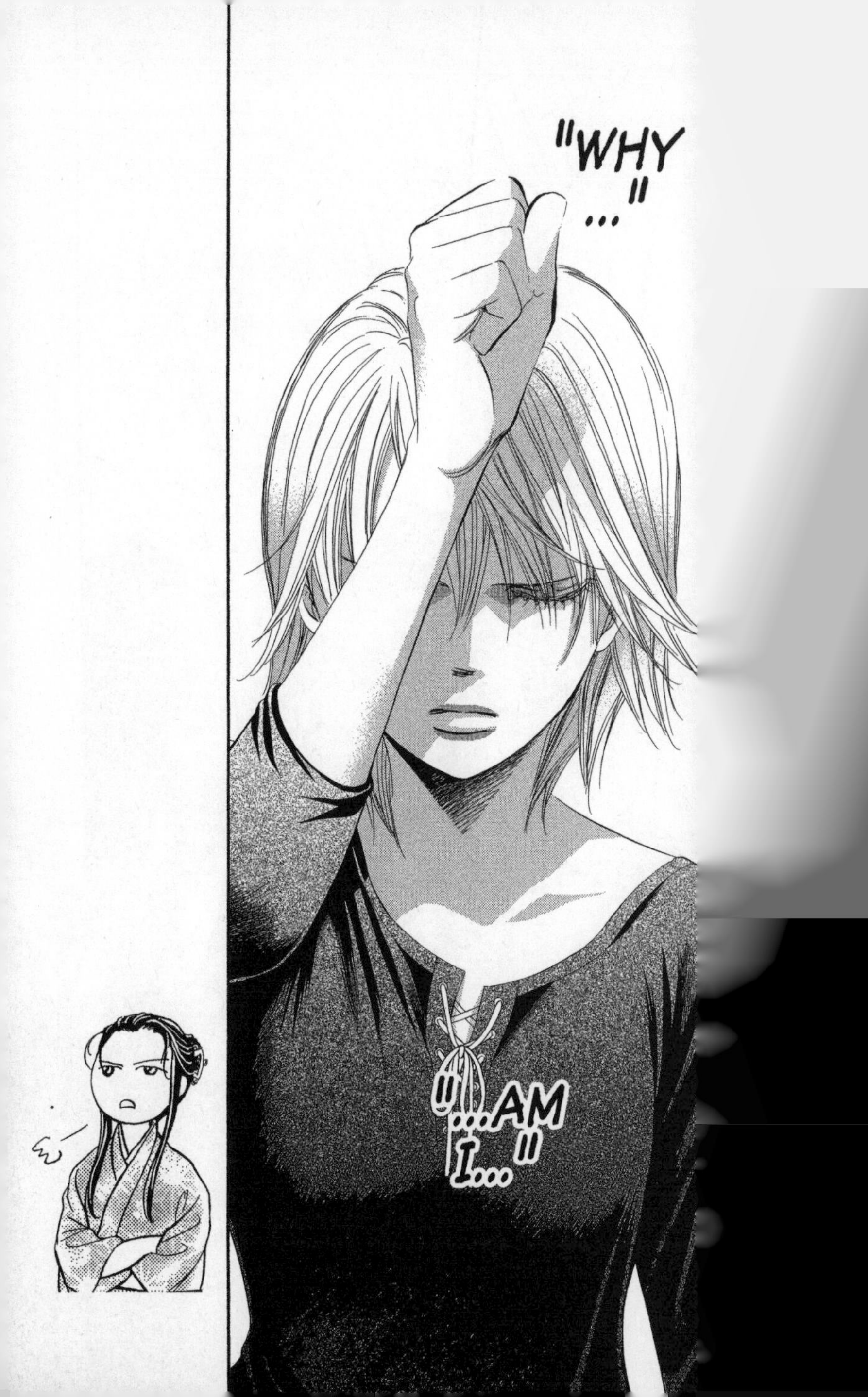
"WHY ..."
"...AM I..."

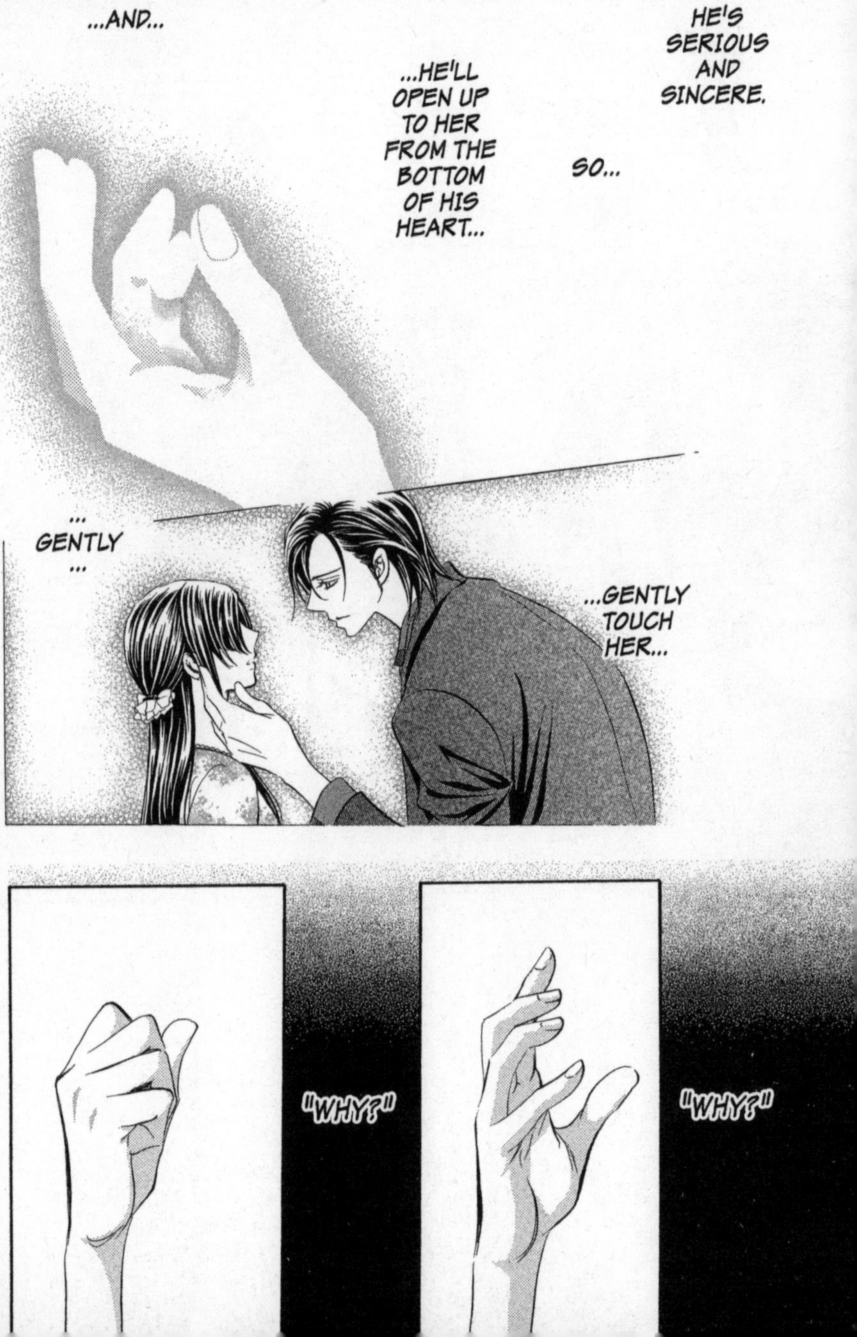
HE'S SERIOUS AND SINCERE.
SO...
...HE'LL OPEN UP TO HER FROM THE BOTTOM OF HIS HEART...
...AND...
...GENTLY TOUCH HER...
... GENTLY ...
"WHY?"
"WHY?"

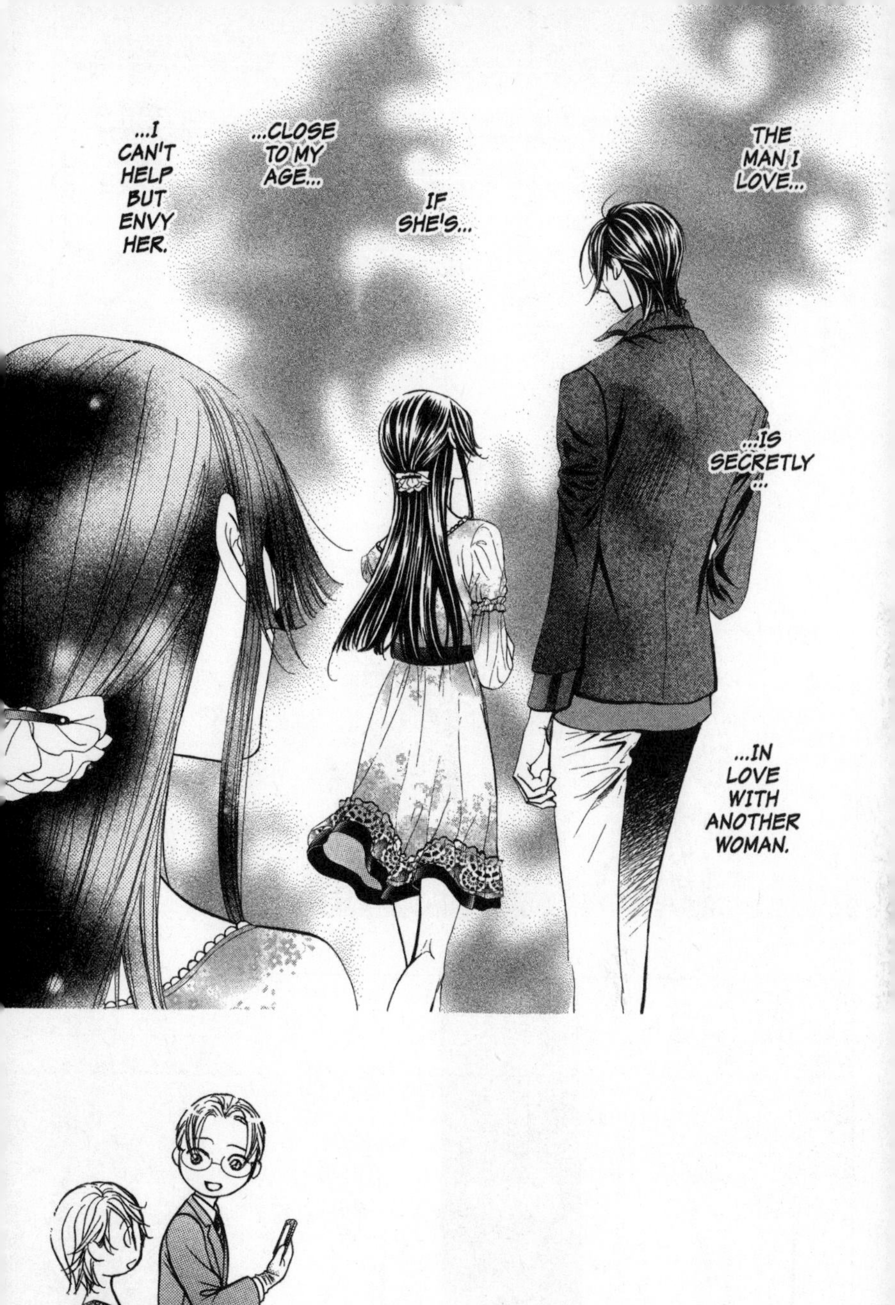
THE MAN I LOVE...
...IS SECRETLY...
...IN LOVE WITH ANOTHER WOMAN.
IF SHE'S...
...CLOSE TO MY AGE...
...I CAN'T HELP BUT ENVY HER.

I...

...WILL
BE...

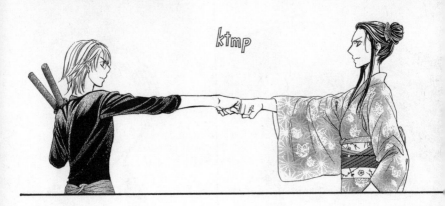

## ...MOMIJI.

**End of Act 254**

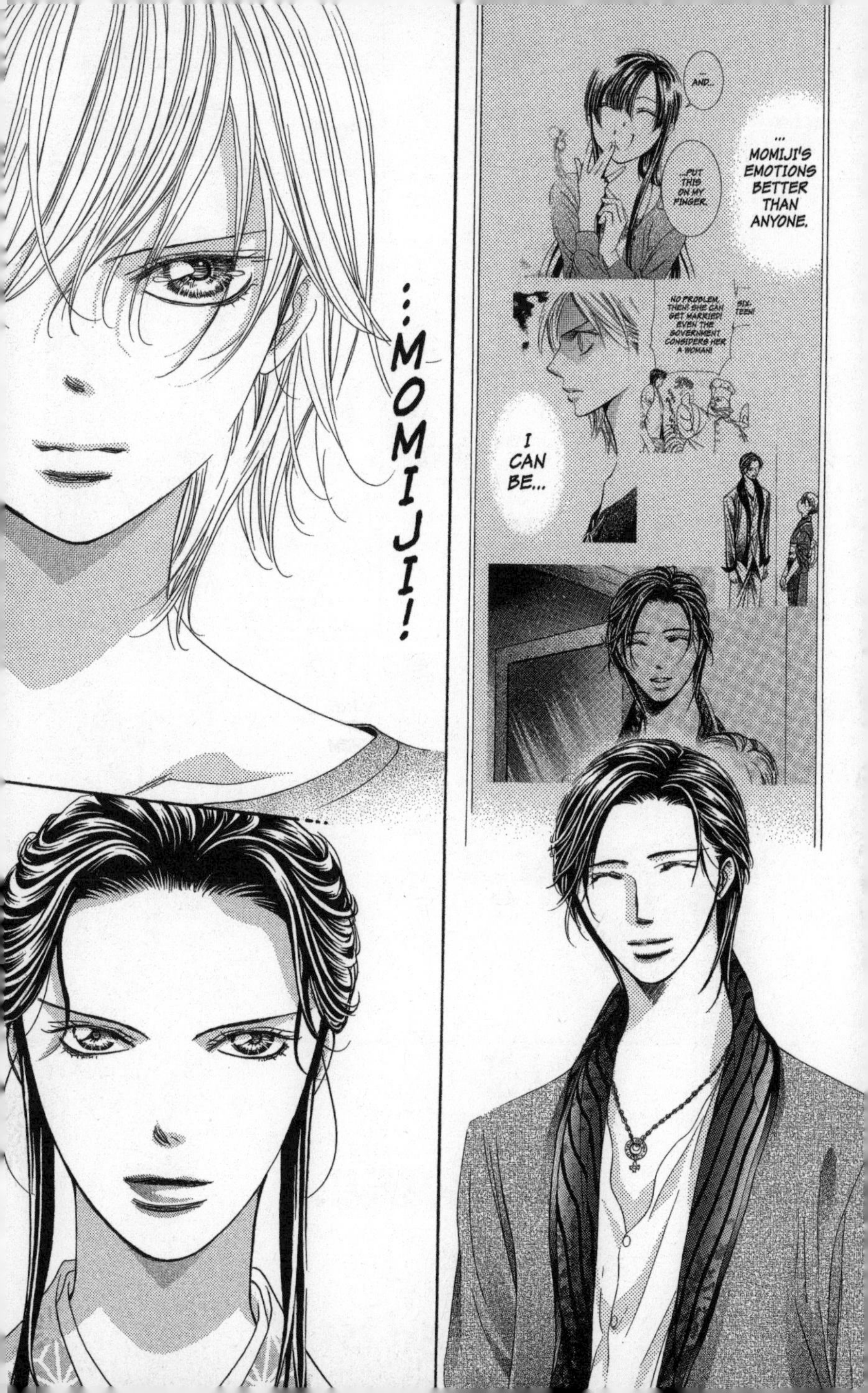
...AND...
...PUT THIS ON MY FINGER.
... MOMIJI'S EMOTIONS BETTER THAN ANYONE.
SIX-TEEN!
NO PROBLEM, THEN! SHE CAN GET MARRIED! EVEN THE GOVERNMENT CONSIDERS HER A WOMAN!
I CAN BE...
...MOMIJI!
...

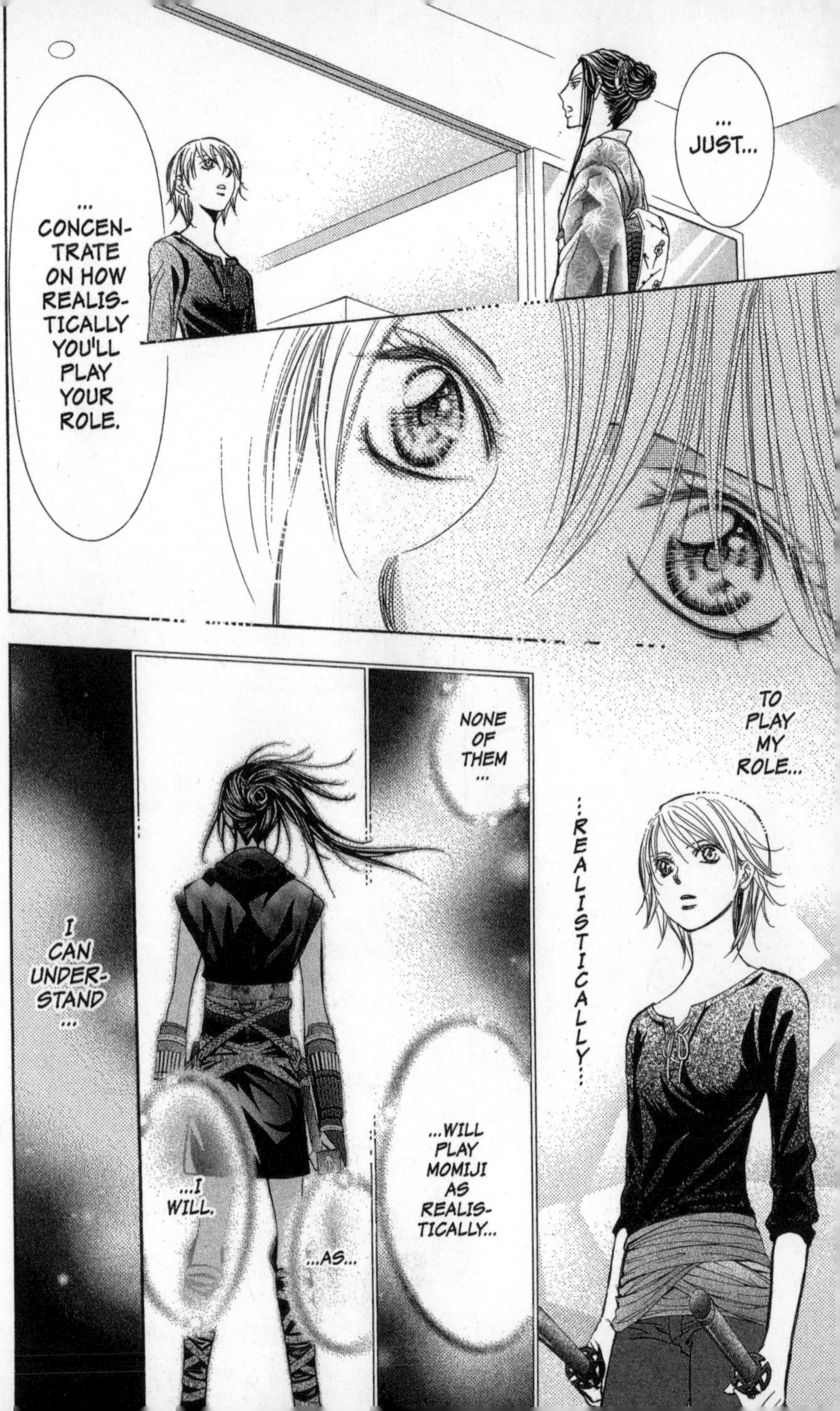
... JUST...
... CONCENTRATE ON HOW REALISTICALLY YOU'LL PLAY YOUR ROLE.
TO PLAY MY ROLE...
...REALISTICALLY...
NONE OF THEM...
...WILL PLAY MOMIJI AS REALISTICALLY...
...AS...
...I WILL.
I CAN UNDERSTAND...

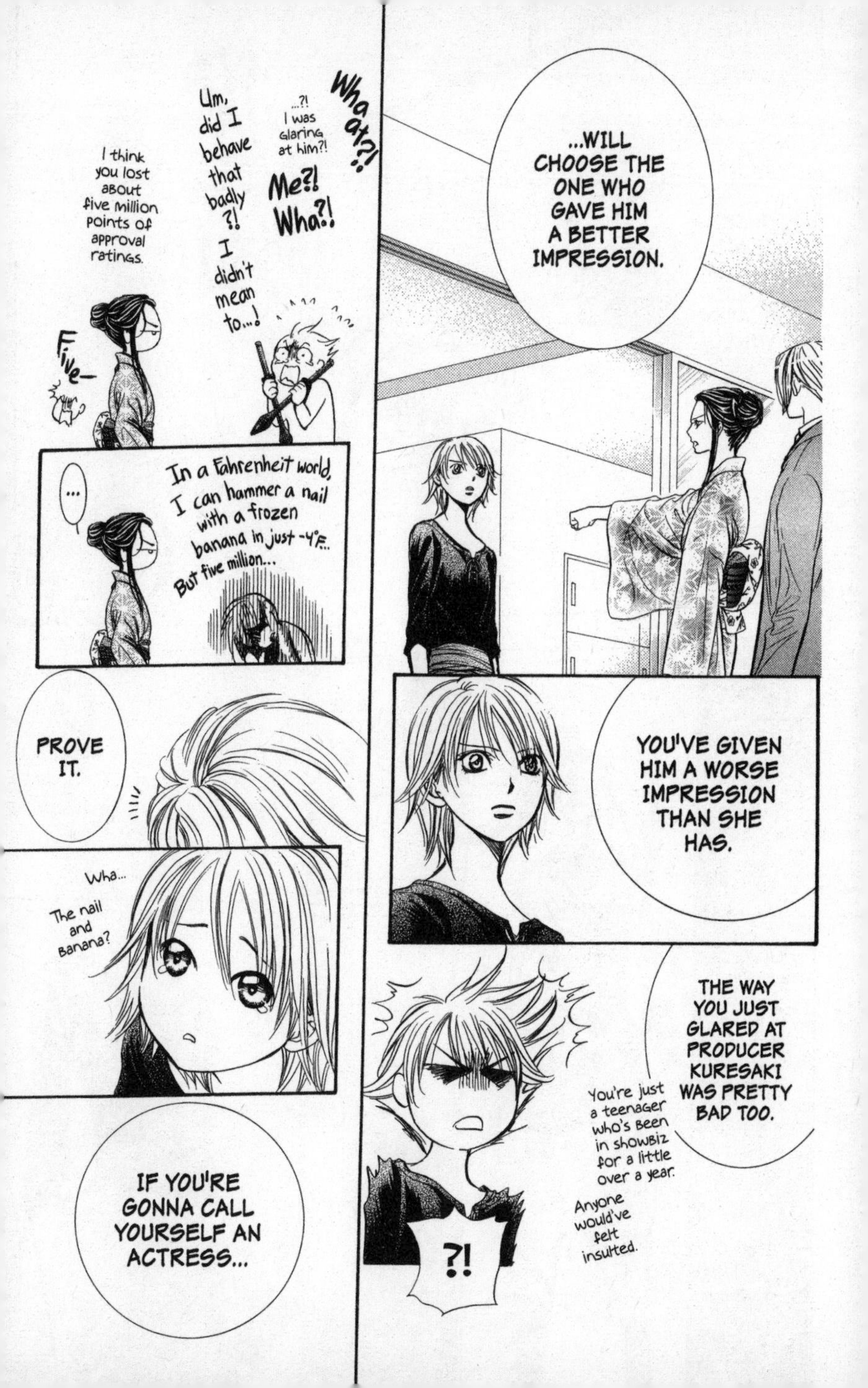
...WILL CHOOSE THE ONE WHO GAVE HIM A BETTER IMPRESSION.
YOU'VE GIVEN HIM A WORSE IMPRESSION THAN SHE HAS.
THE WAY YOU JUST GLARED AT PRODUCER KURESAKI WAS PRETTY BAD TOO.
You're just a teenager who's been in showbiz for a little over a year.
Anyone would've felt insulted.
?!
Whaat?!
...?! I was glaring at him?!
Me?! Wha?!
Um, did I behave that badly?! I didn't mean to...!
I think you lost about five million points of approval ratings.
Five—
In a Fahrenheit world, I can hammer a nail with a frozen banana in just -4°F... But five million...
...
PROVE IT.
Wha...
The nail and banana?
IF YOU'RE GONNA CALL YOURSELF AN ACTRESS...

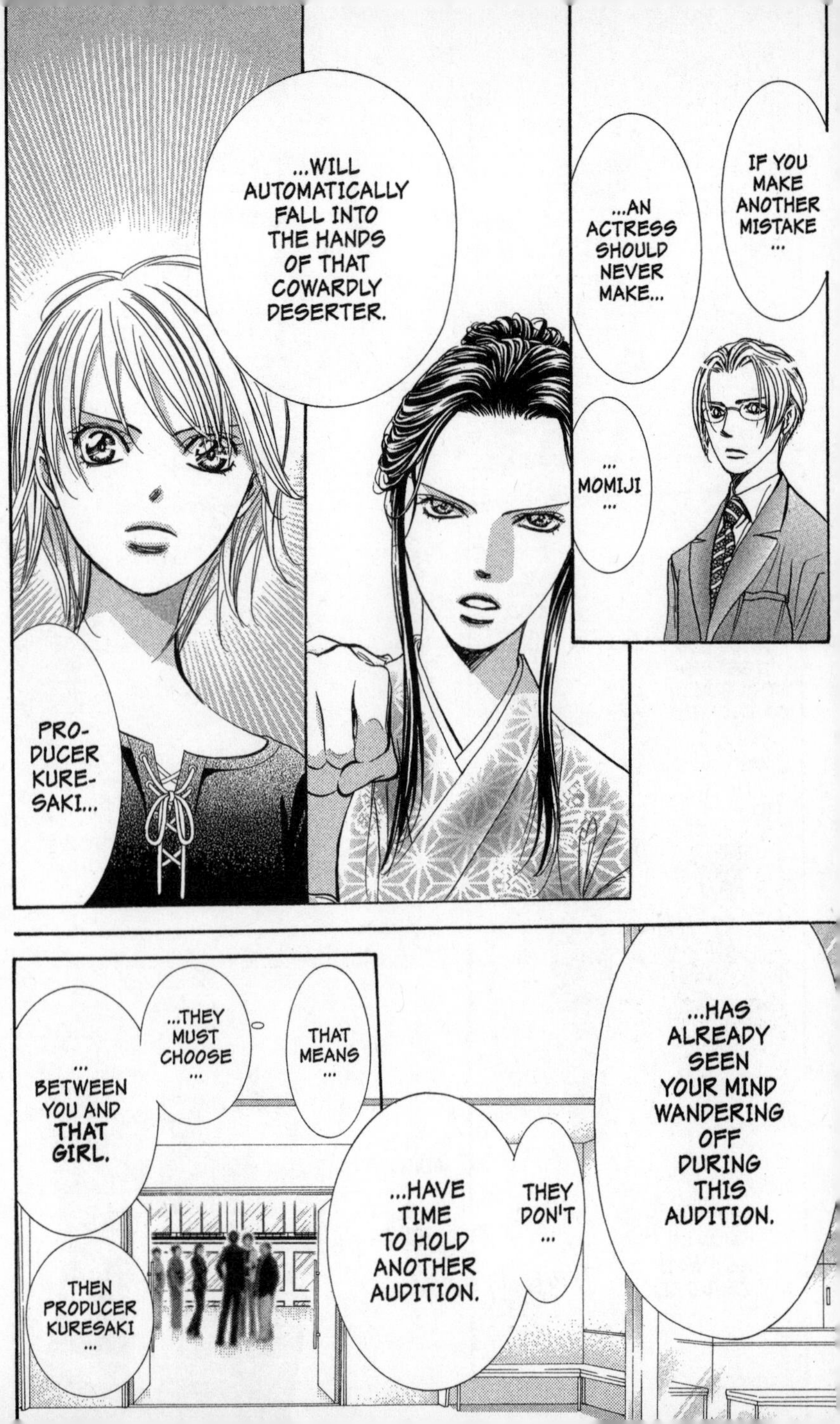
IF YOU MAKE ANOTHER MISTAKE ...
...AN ACTRESS SHOULD NEVER MAKE...
... MOMIJI ...
...WILL AUTOMATICALLY FALL INTO THE HANDS OF THAT COWARDLY DESERTER.
PRO-DUCER KURE-SAKI...
...HAS ALREADY SEEN YOUR MIND WANDERING OFF DURING THIS AUDITION.
THEY DON'T ...
...HAVE TIME TO HOLD ANOTHER AUDITION.
THAT MEANS ...
...THEY MUST CHOOSE ...
... BETWEEN YOU AND THAT GIRL.
THEN PRODUCER KURESAKI ...

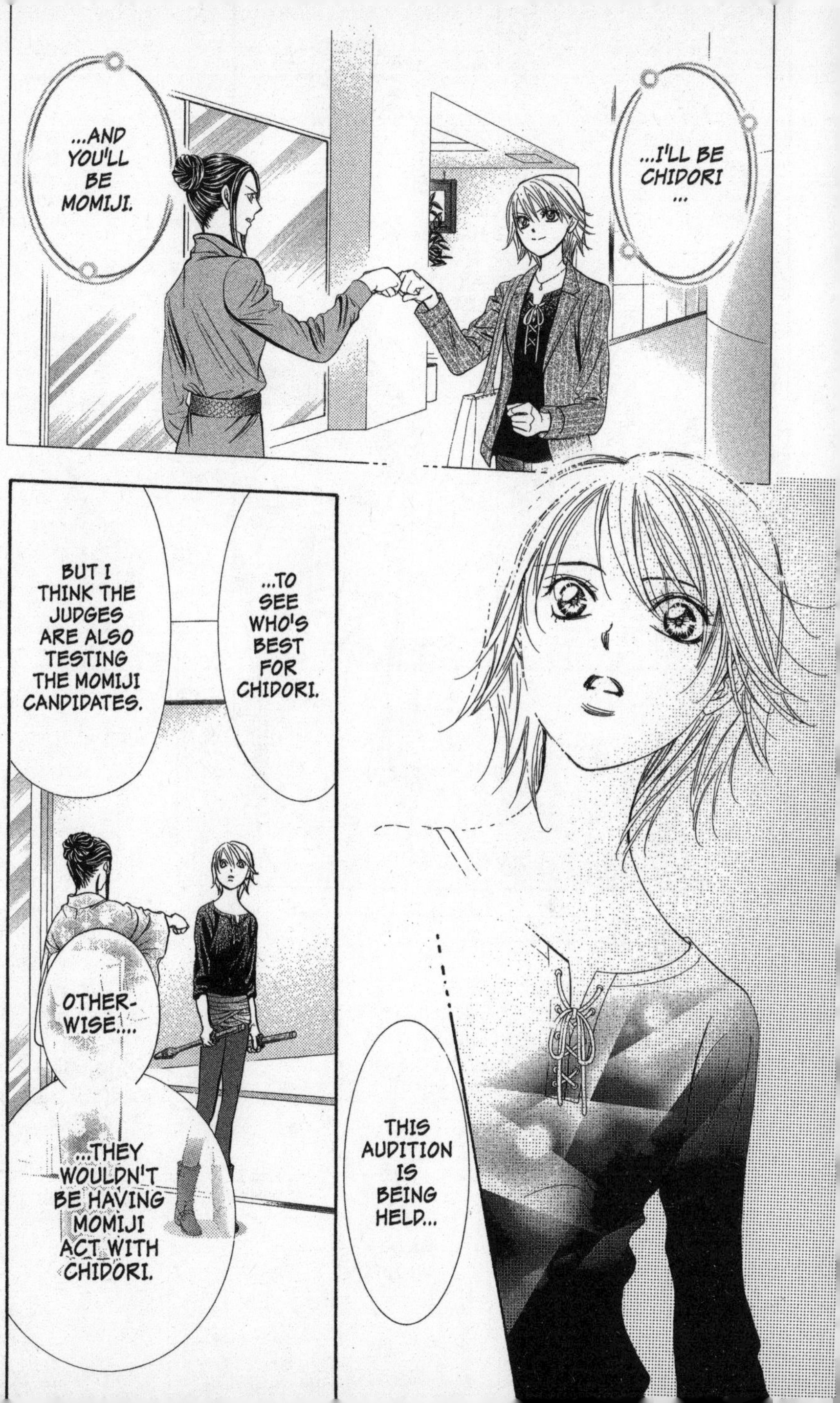
...I'LL BE CHIDORI ...
...AND YOU'LL BE MOMIJI.
THIS AUDITION IS BEING HELD...
...TO SEE WHO'S BEST FOR CHIDORI.
BUT I THINK THE JUDGES ARE ALSO TESTING THE MOMIJI CANDIDATES.
OTHER-WISE....
...THEY WOULDN'T BE HAVING MOMIJI ACT WITH CHIDORI.

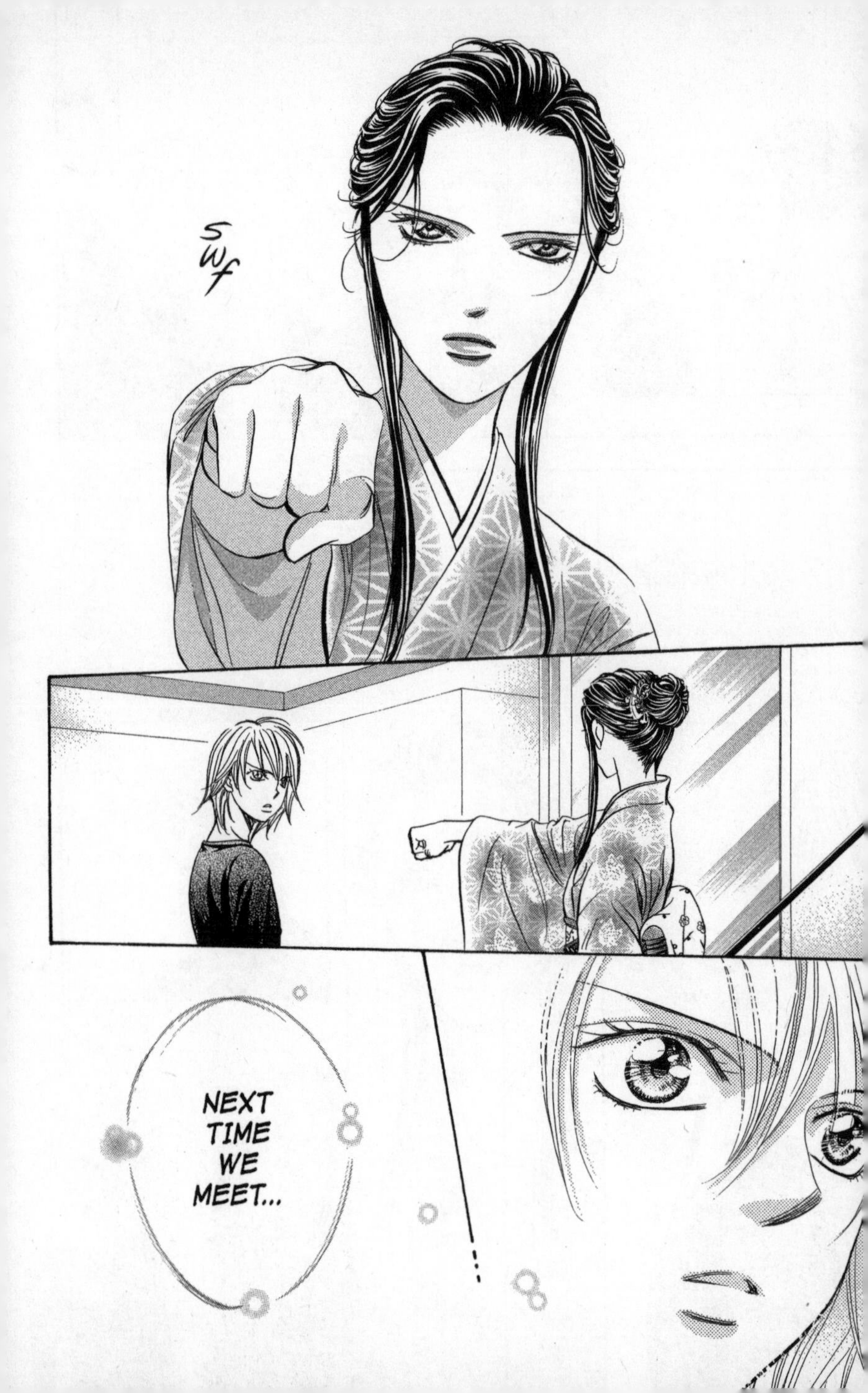
SWF
...
NEXT TIME WE MEET...

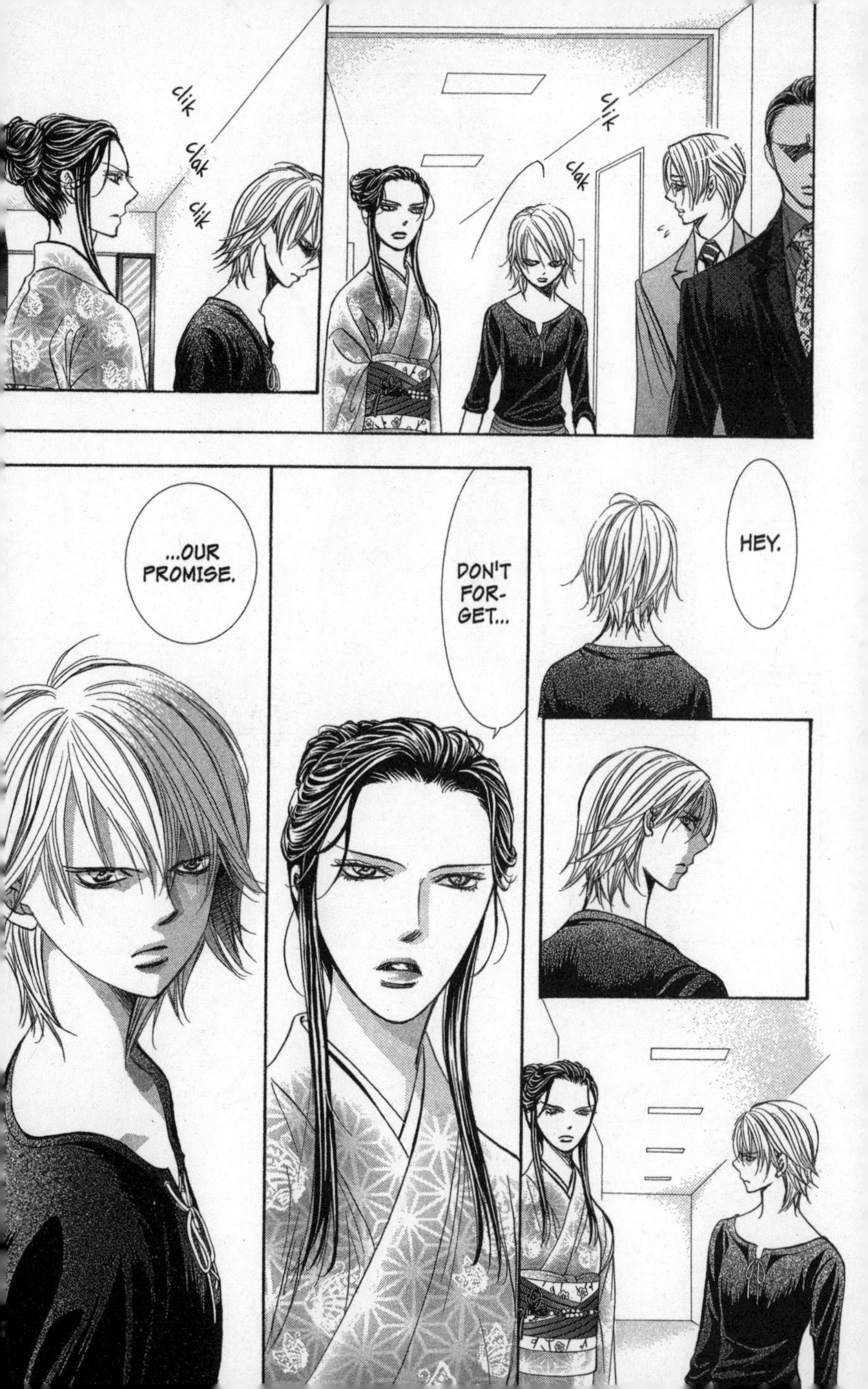
clik
clak
clik
clak
clik
HEY.
DON'T FOR-GET...
...OUR PROMISE.

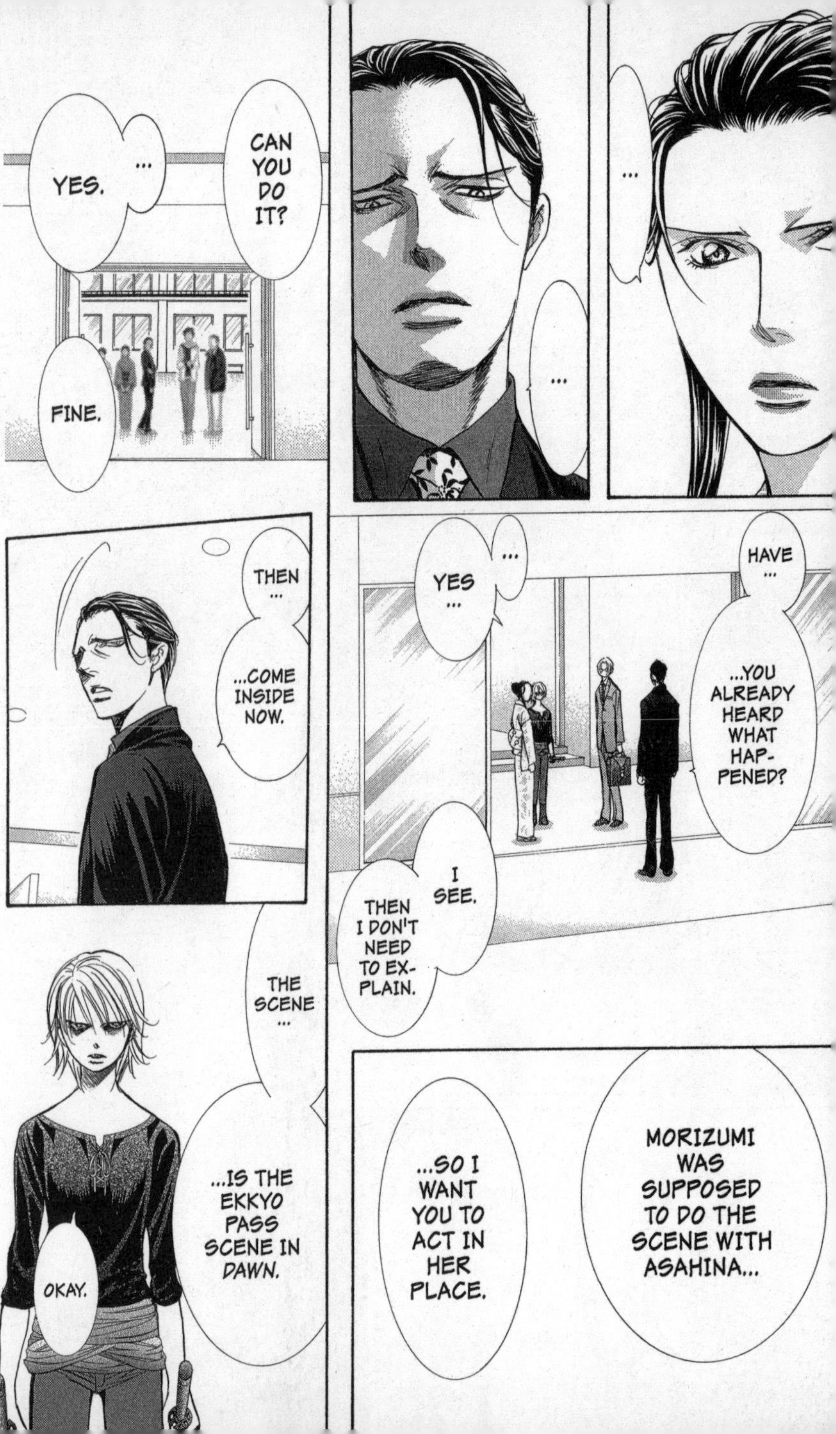
...
...
CAN YOU DO IT?
...
YES.
FINE.
HAVE ...
...YOU ALREADY HEARD WHAT HAPPENED?
...
YES ...
I SEE.
THEN I DON'T NEED TO EXPLAIN.
THEN ...
...COME INSIDE NOW.
MORIZUMI WAS SUPPOSED TO DO THE SCENE WITH ASAHINA...
...SO I WANT YOU TO ACT IN HER PLACE.
THE SCENE ...
...IS THE EKKYO PASS SCENE IN DAWN.
OKAY.

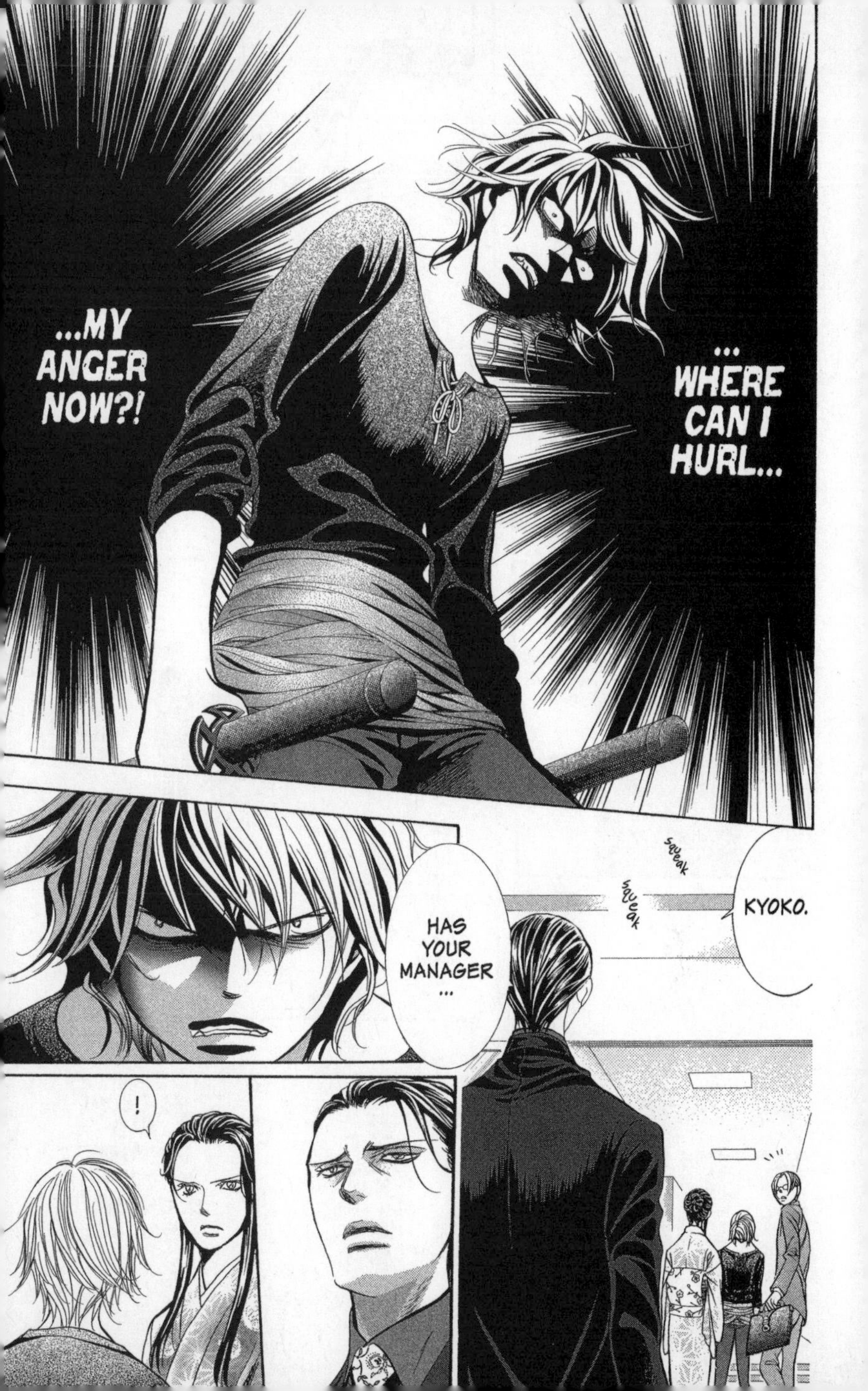
... WHERE CAN I HURL...
...MY ANGER NOW?!
squeak
squeak
KYOKO.
HAS YOUR MANAGER ...
!

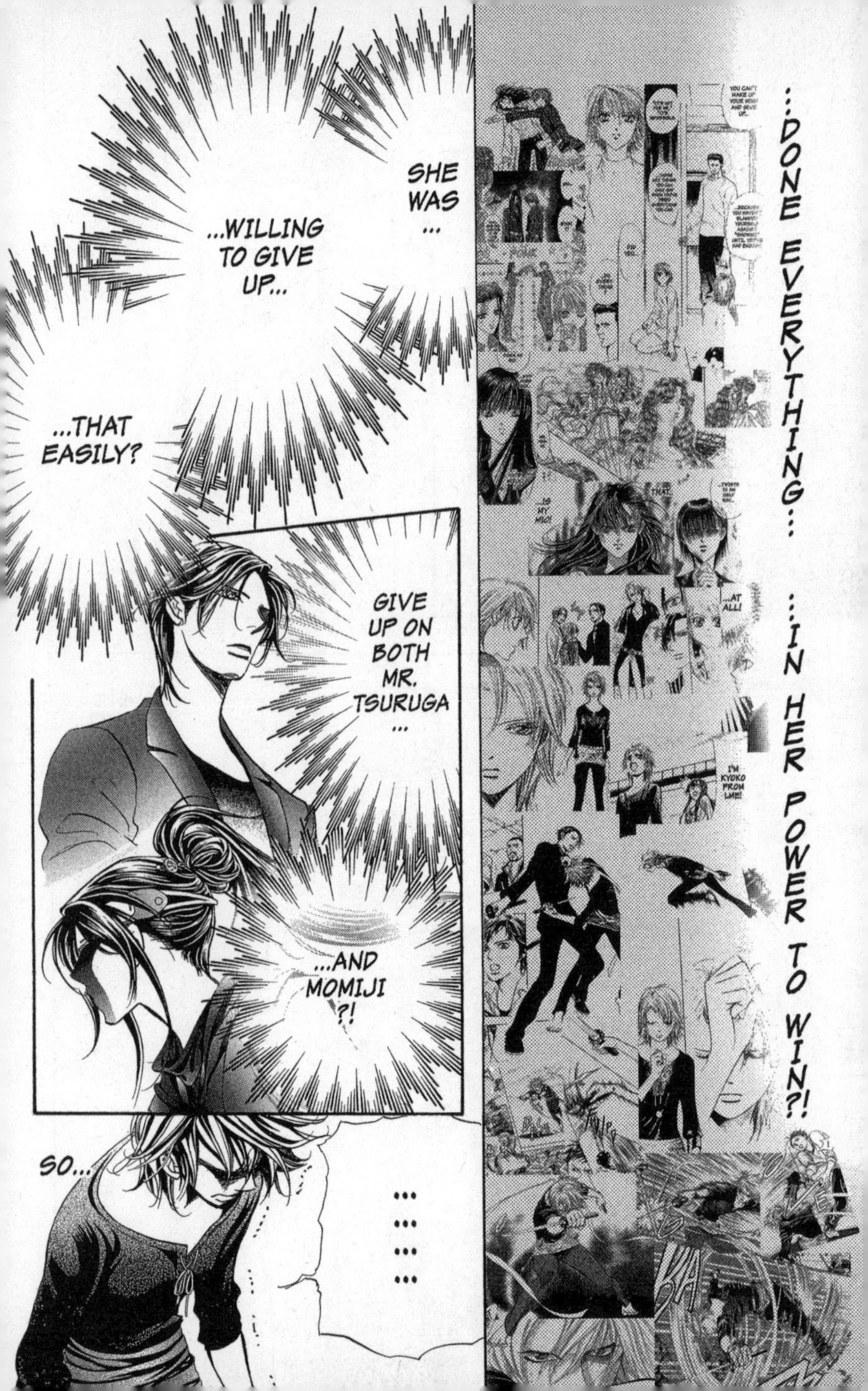
...DONE EVERYTHING...
...IS MY MIO!
...AT ALL!
I'M KYOKO FROM LME!
...IN HER POWER TO WIN?!
SHE WAS...
...WILLING TO GIVE UP...
...THAT EASILY?
GIVE UP ON BOTH MR. TSURUGA...
...AND MOMIJI?!
...
...
SO...

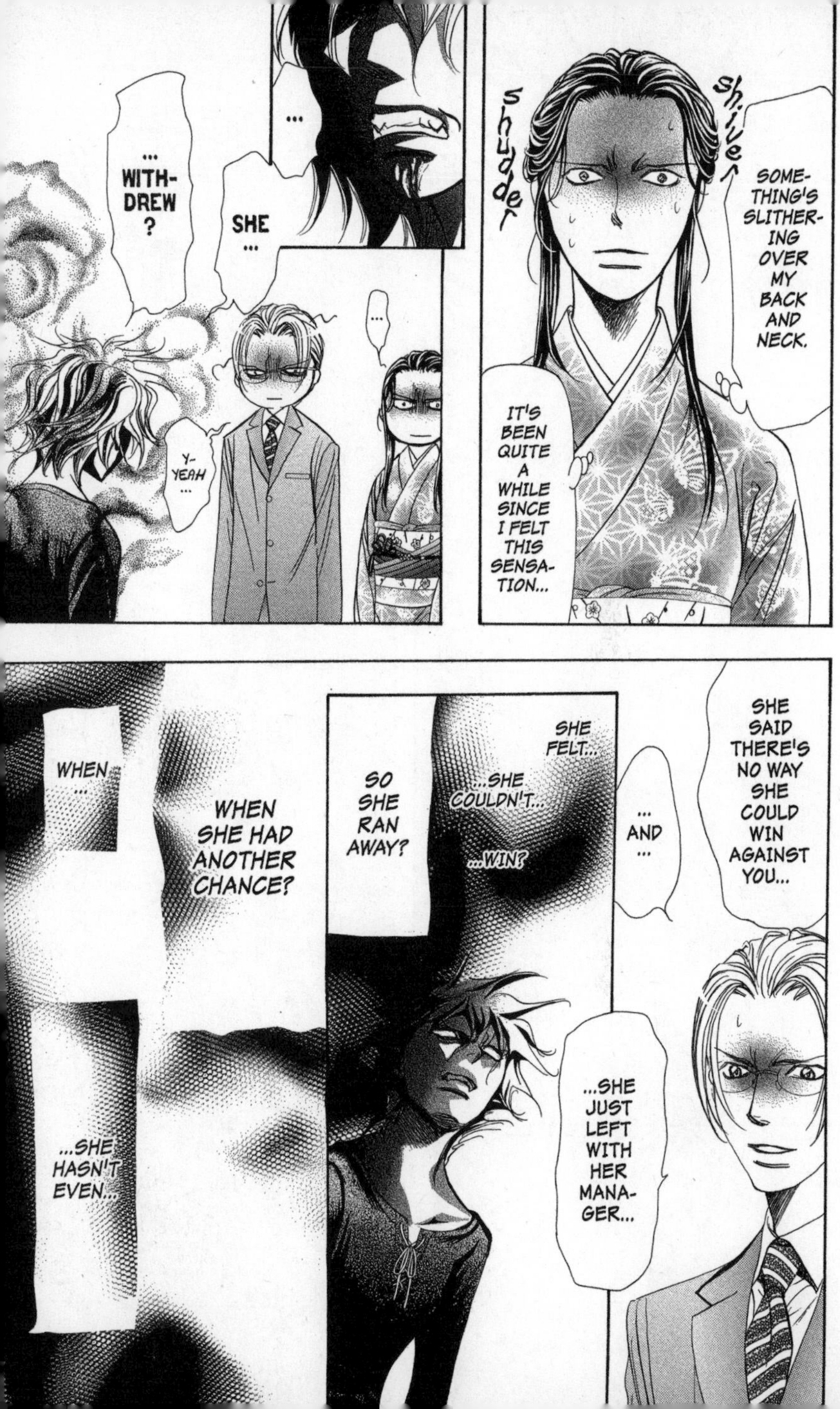
shiver
SOME-THING'S SLITHER-ING OVER MY BACK AND NECK.
shudder
IT'S BEEN QUITE A WHILE SINCE I FELT THIS SENSA-TION...
...
SHE ...
... WITH-DREW ?
....
Y-YEAH ...
SHE SAID THERE'S NO WAY SHE COULD WIN AGAINST YOU...
... AND ...
...SHE JUST LEFT WITH HER MANA-GER...
SHE FELT...
...SHE COULDN'T...
...WIN?
SO SHE RAN AWAY?
WHEN SHE HAD ANOTHER CHANCE?
WHEN ...
...SHE HASN'T EVEN...

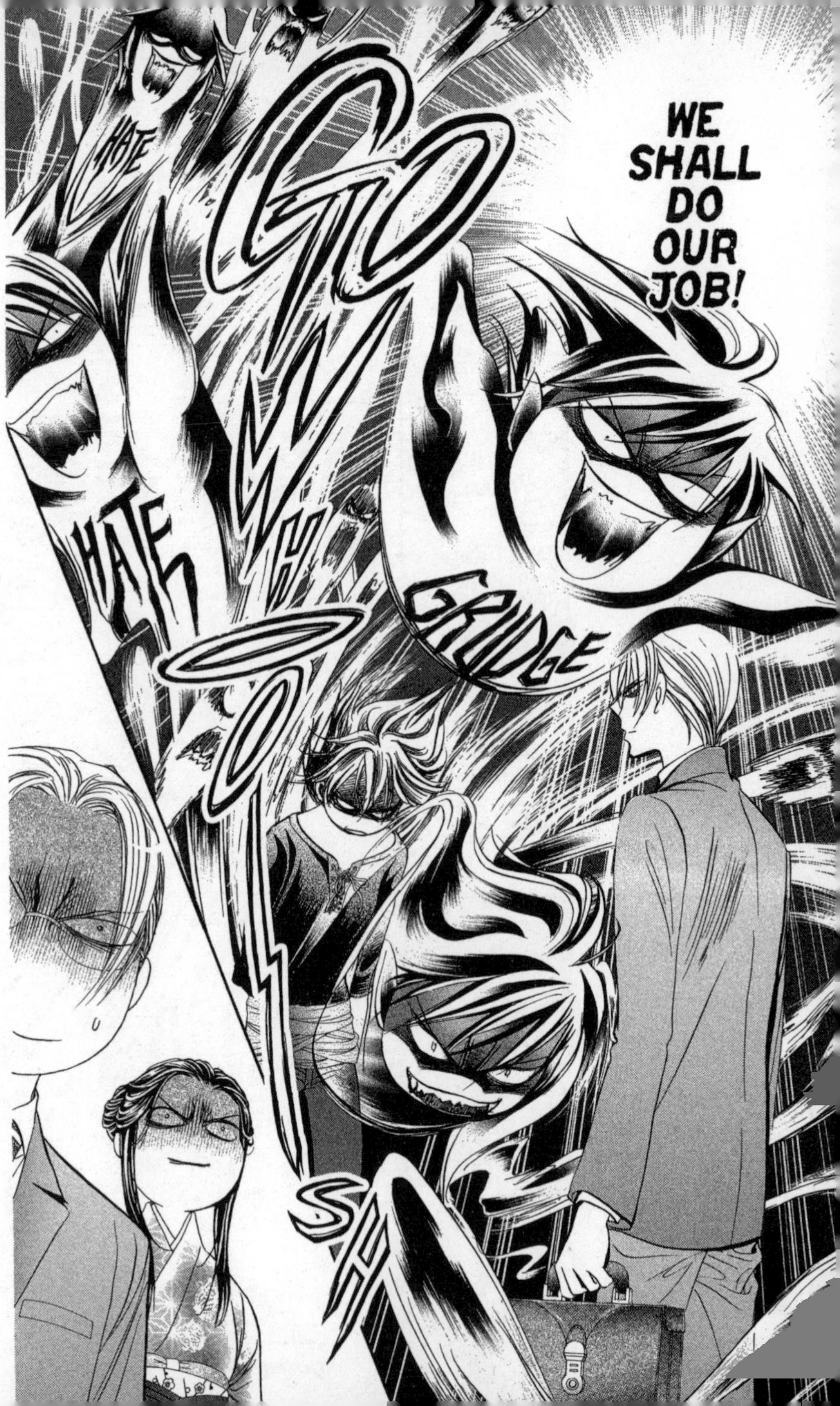
WE SHALL DO OUR JOB!
HATE
HATE
GRUDGE

...

YES.

READY, EVERY-ONE.

*tug*

THIS DARK FLOW CAN DESTROY EVEN THE GATES OF HELL.

THIS TIME...

...

CAP-TAIN.

THIS IS...

*chak*

*chak chak chak*

*chak chak chak*

HATE HATE

ZIP

zip

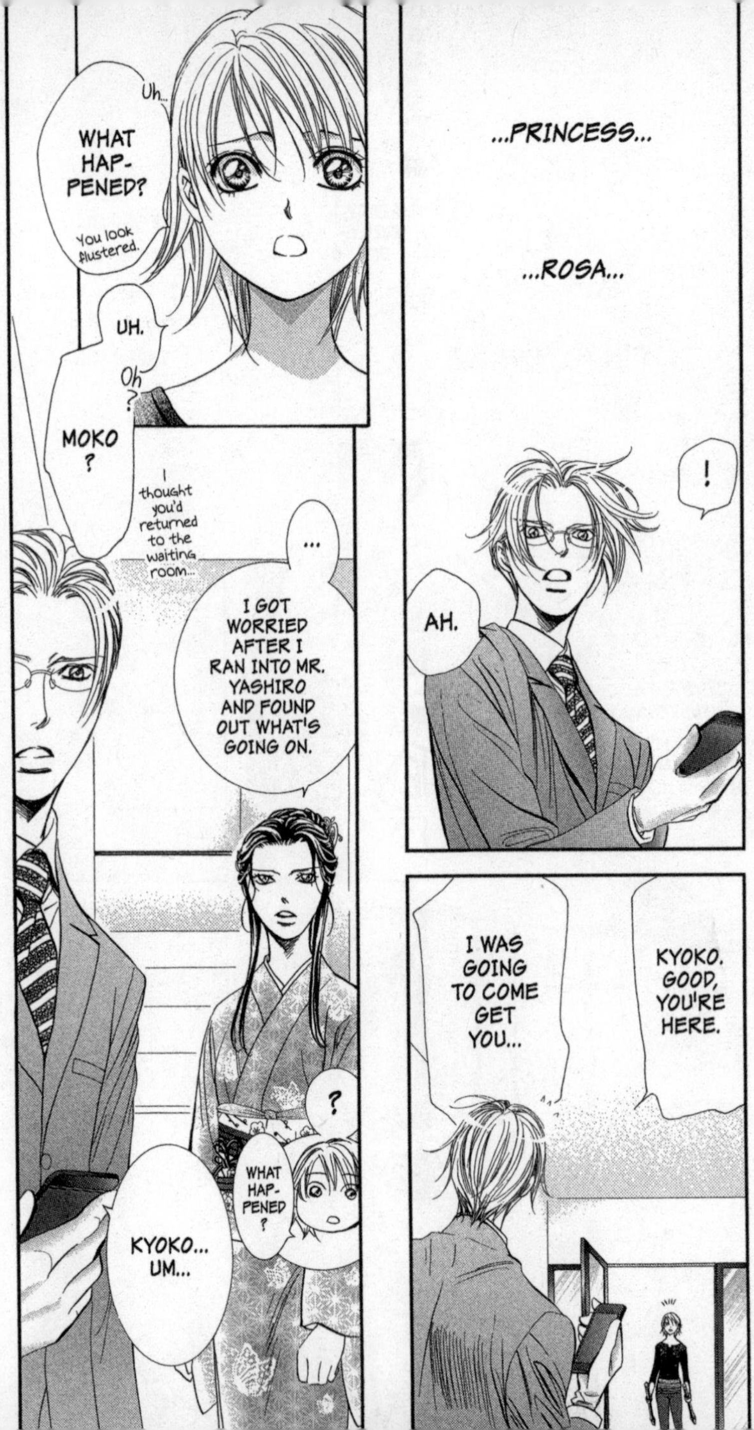
...PRINCESS...
...ROSA...
...RE-FUSES TO DISAP-PEAR...
!
AH.
...FROM ...
KYOKO. GOOD, YOU'RE HERE.
I WAS GOING TO COME GET YOU...
...MY HEART ...
Uh...
WHAT HAP-PENED?
You look flustered.
UH.
Oh?
MOKO?
I thought you'd returned to the waiting room...
...
I GOT WORRIED AFTER I RAN INTO MR. YASHIRO AND FOUND OUT WHAT'S GOING ON.
?
WHAT HAP-PENED?
KYOKO... UM...

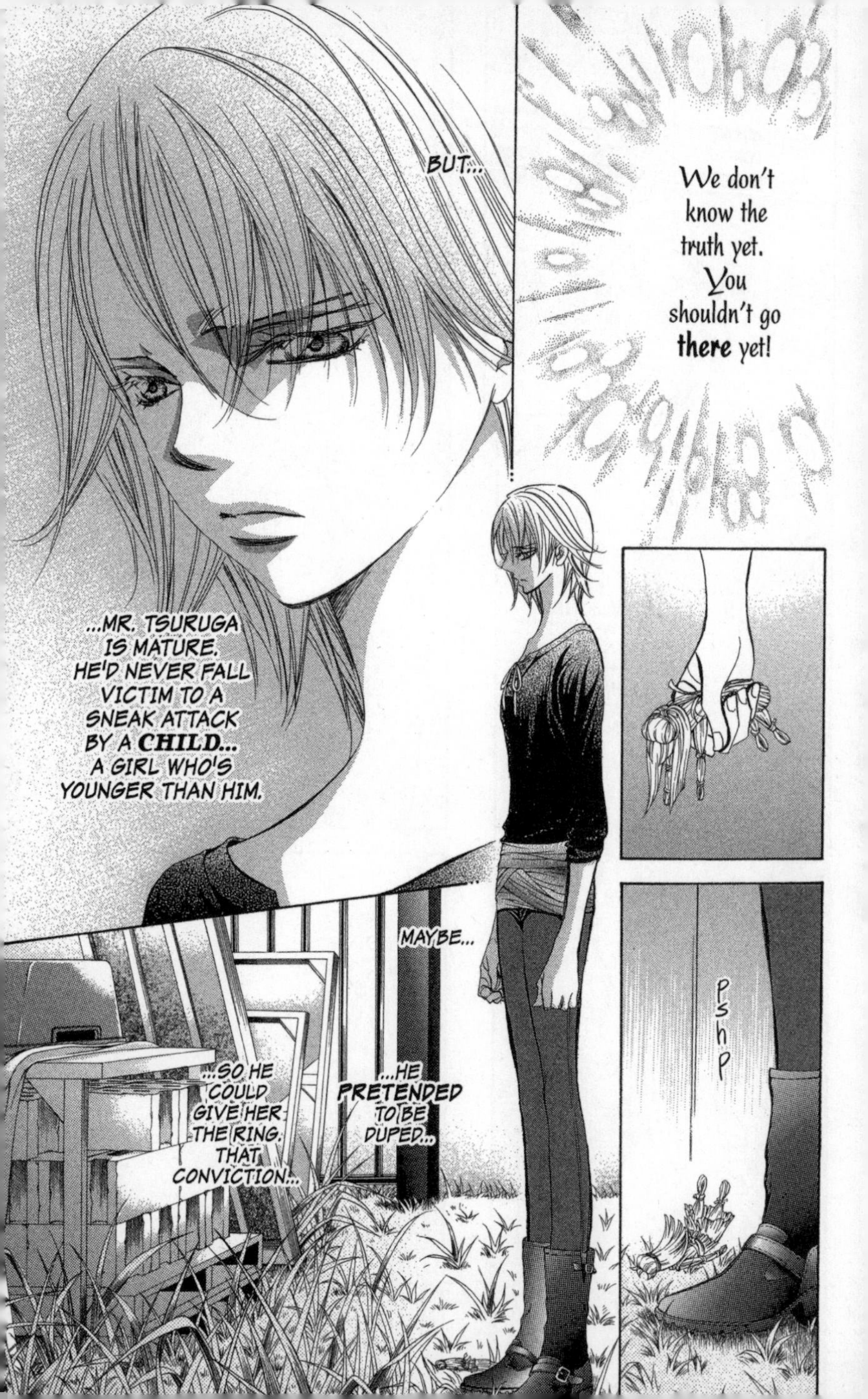
We don't know the truth yet. You shouldn't go there yet!
BUT...
...MR. TSURUGA IS MATURE. HE'D NEVER FALL VICTIM TO A SNEAK ATTACK BY A CHILD... A GIRL WHO'S YOUNGER THAN HIM.
PSHP
MAYBE...
...HE PRETENDED TO BE DUPED...
...SO HE COULD GIVE HER THE RING. THAT CONVICTION...

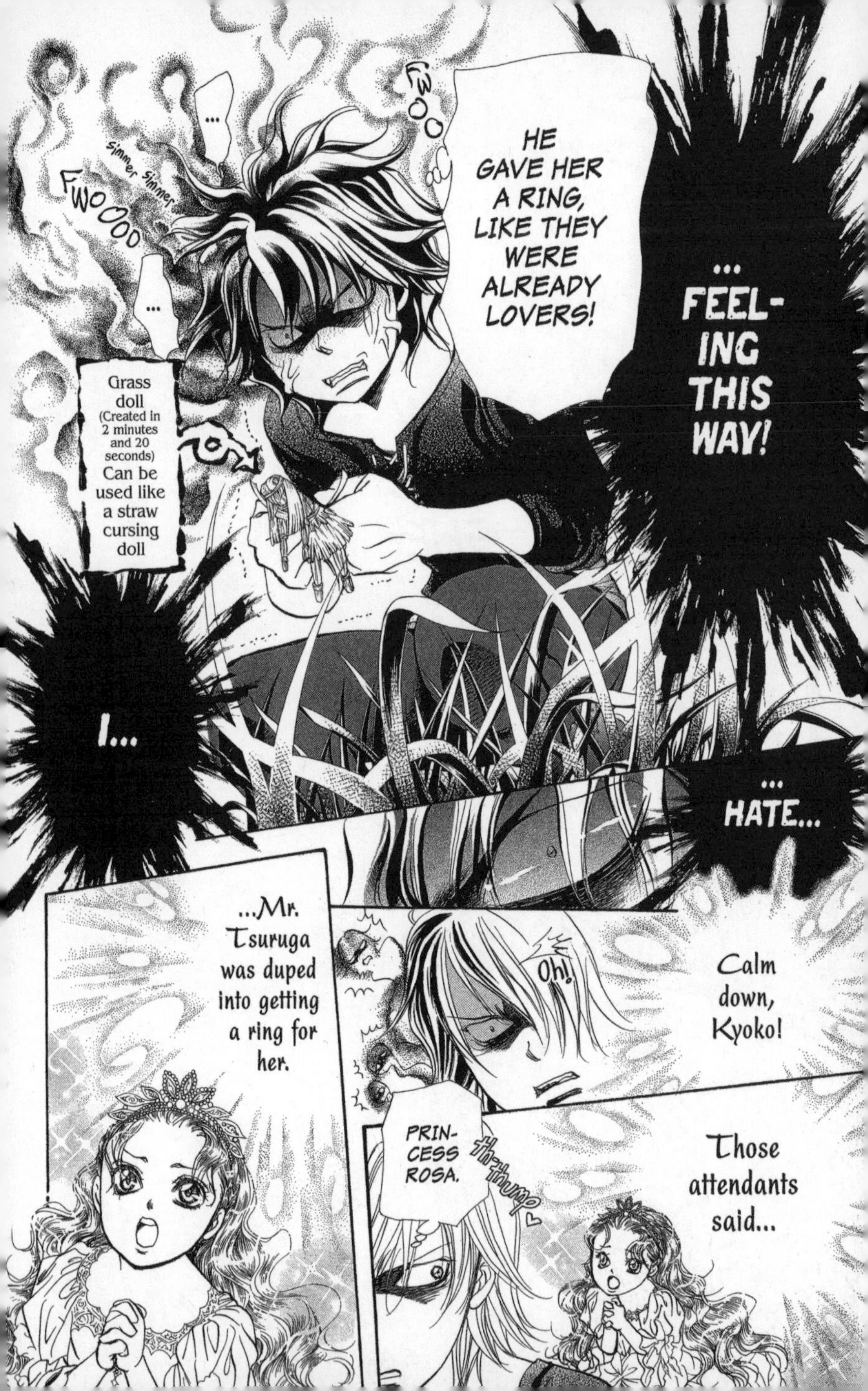
FWOOO
HE GAVE HER A RING, LIKE THEY WERE ALREADY LOVERS!
... FEEL-ING THIS WAY!
...
Simmer simmer
FWOOOO
...
Grass doll (Created in 2 minutes and 20 seconds) Can be used like a straw cursing doll
... HATE...
I...
Calm down, Kyoko!
Oh!
Those attendants said...
PRIN-CESS ROSA.
th-thump
...Mr. Tsuruga was duped into getting a ring for her.

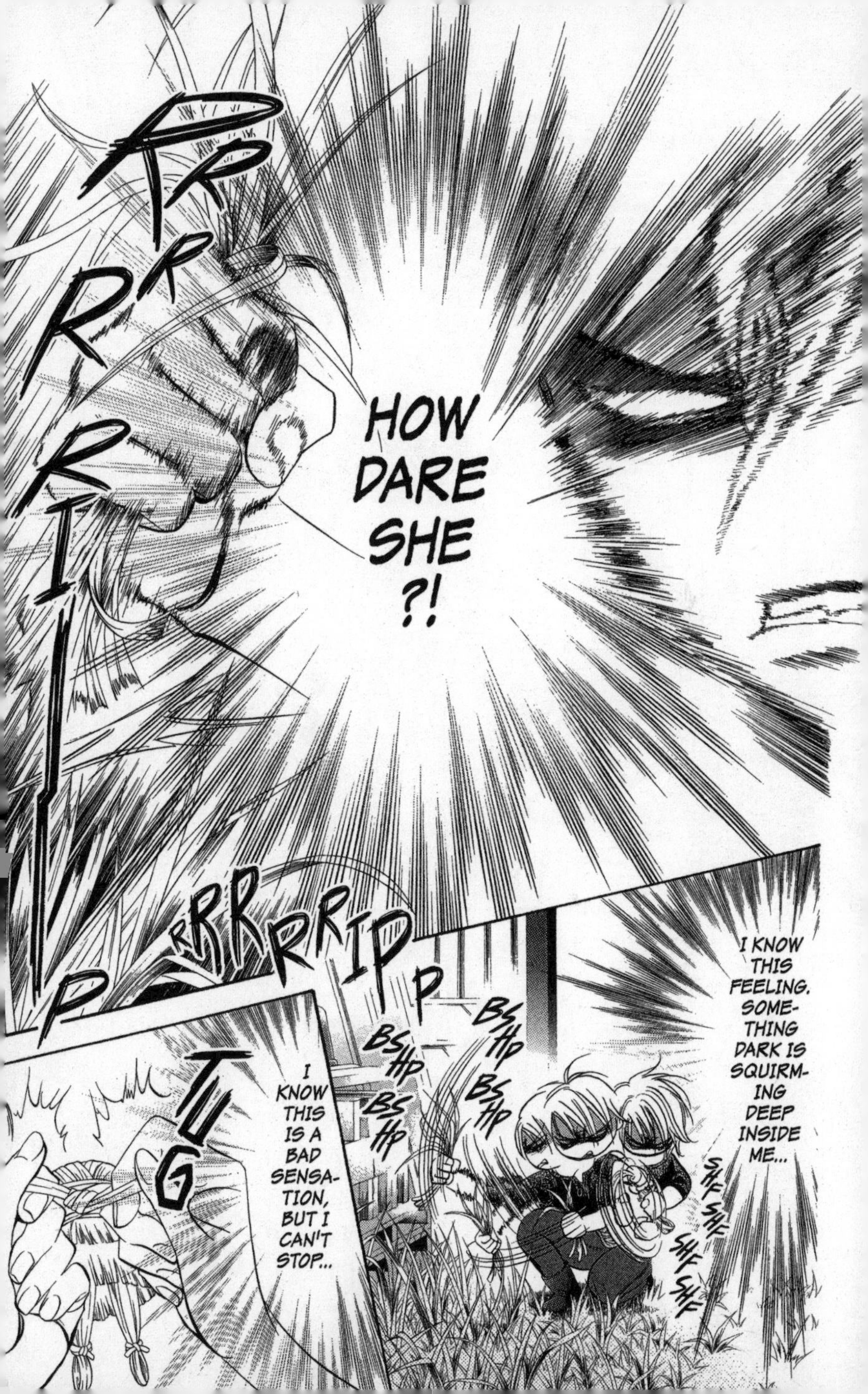
HOW DARE SHE?!
RRRRIIP
I KNOW THIS FEELING. SOMETHING DARK IS SQUIRMING DEEP INSIDE ME...
SHF SHF SHF SHF
BSHP BSHP BSHP BSHP
I KNOW THIS IS A BAD SENSATION, BUT I CAN'T STOP...
RRRRRIPP
TUG

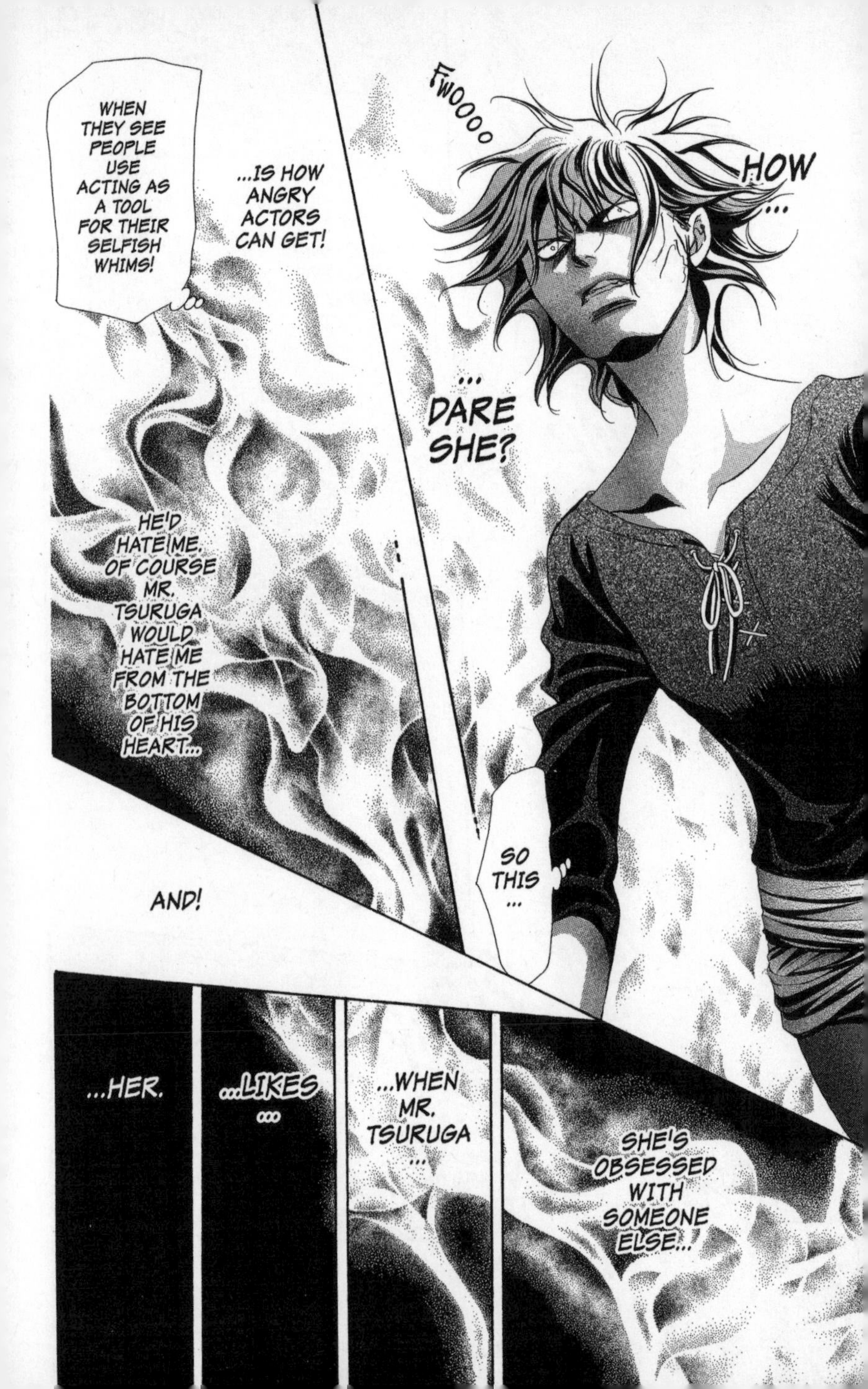
FWOOOO
HOW...
...DARE SHE?
SO THIS...
...IS HOW ANGRY ACTORS CAN GET!
WHEN THEY SEE PEOPLE USE ACTING AS A TOOL FOR THEIR SELFISH WHIMS!
HE'D HATE ME. OF COURSE MR. TSURUGA WOULD HATE ME FROM THE BOTTOM OF HIS HEART...
AND!
SHE'S OBSESSED WITH SOMEONE ELSE...
...WHEN MR. TSURUGA...
...LIKES...
...HER.

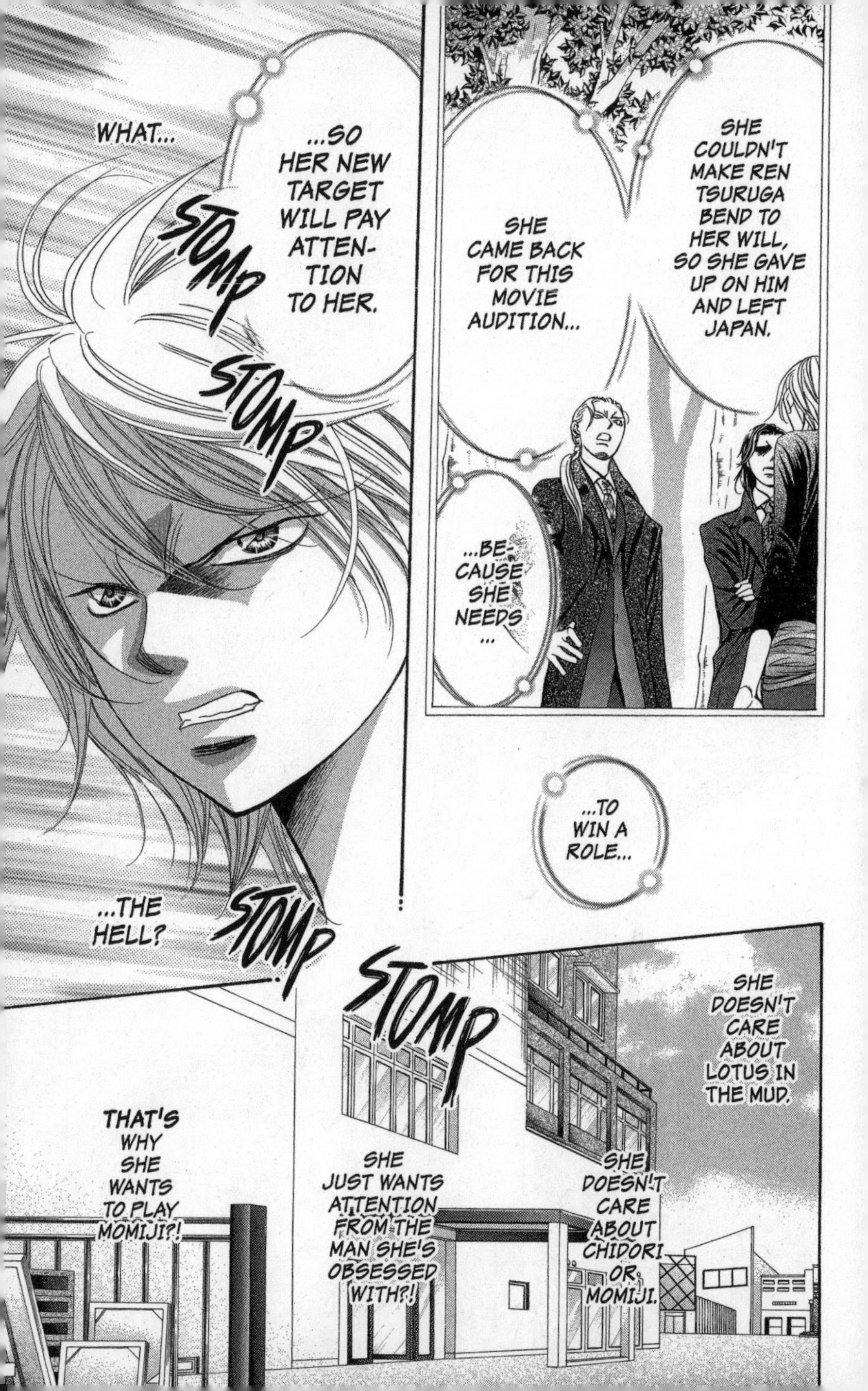
SHE COULDN'T MAKE REN TSURUGA BEND TO HER WILL, SO SHE GAVE UP ON HIM AND LEFT JAPAN.
SHE CAME BACK FOR THIS MOVIE AUDITION...
...BE-CAUSE SHE NEEDS...
...TO WIN A ROLE...
...SO HER NEW TARGET WILL PAY ATTEN-TION TO HER.
WHAT...
STOMP
STOMP
...THE HELL?
STOMP
STOMP
SHE DOESN'T CARE ABOUT LOTUS IN THE MUD.
SHE DOESN'T CARE ABOUT CHIDORI OR MOMIJI.
SHE JUST WANTS ATTENTION FROM THE MAN SHE'S OBSESSED WITH?!
THAT'S WHY SHE WANTS TO PLAY MOMIJI?!

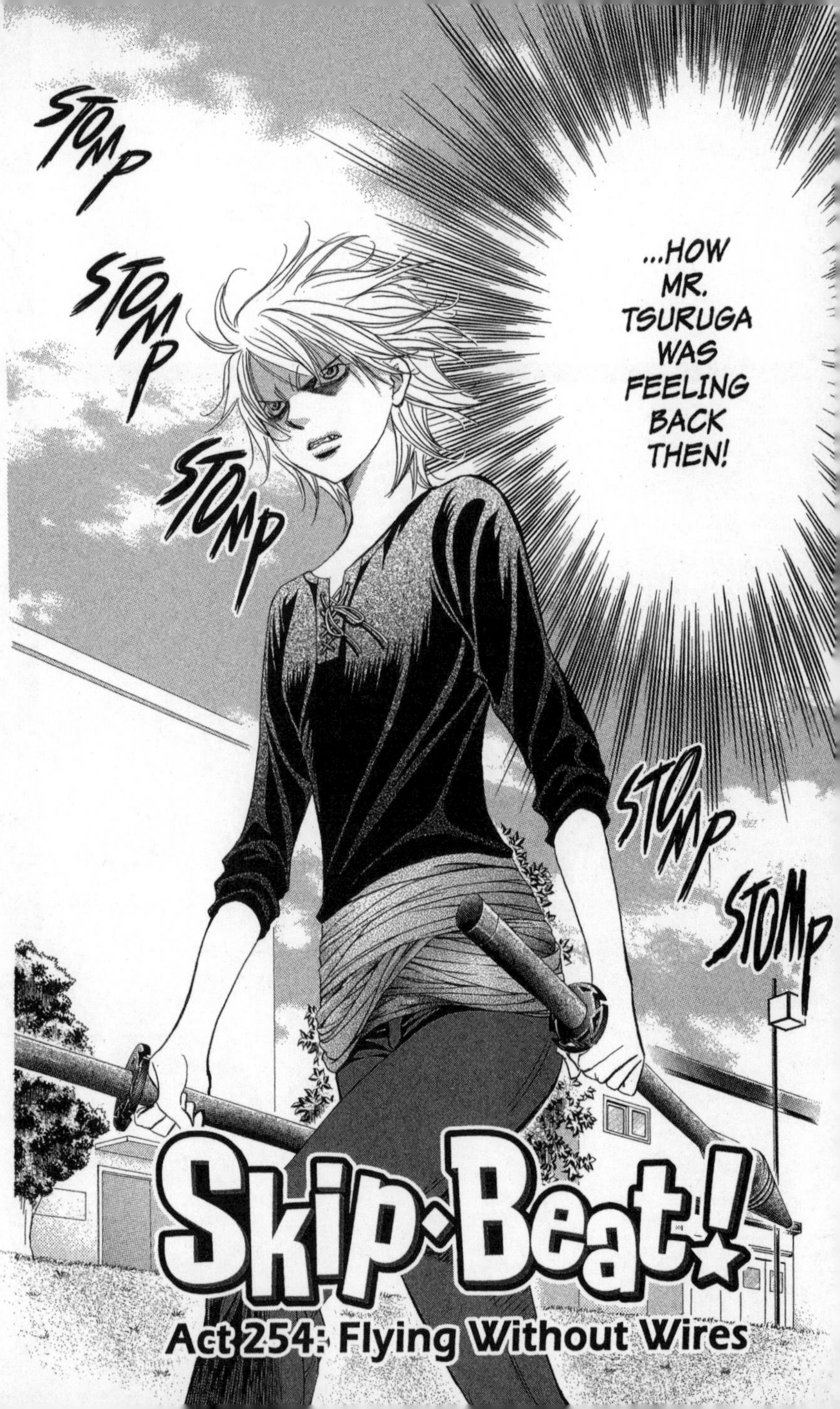
...HOW MR. TSURUGA WAS FEELING BACK THEN!
STOMP
STOMP
STOMP
STOMP
STOMP
Skip·Beat!
Act 254: Flying Without Wires

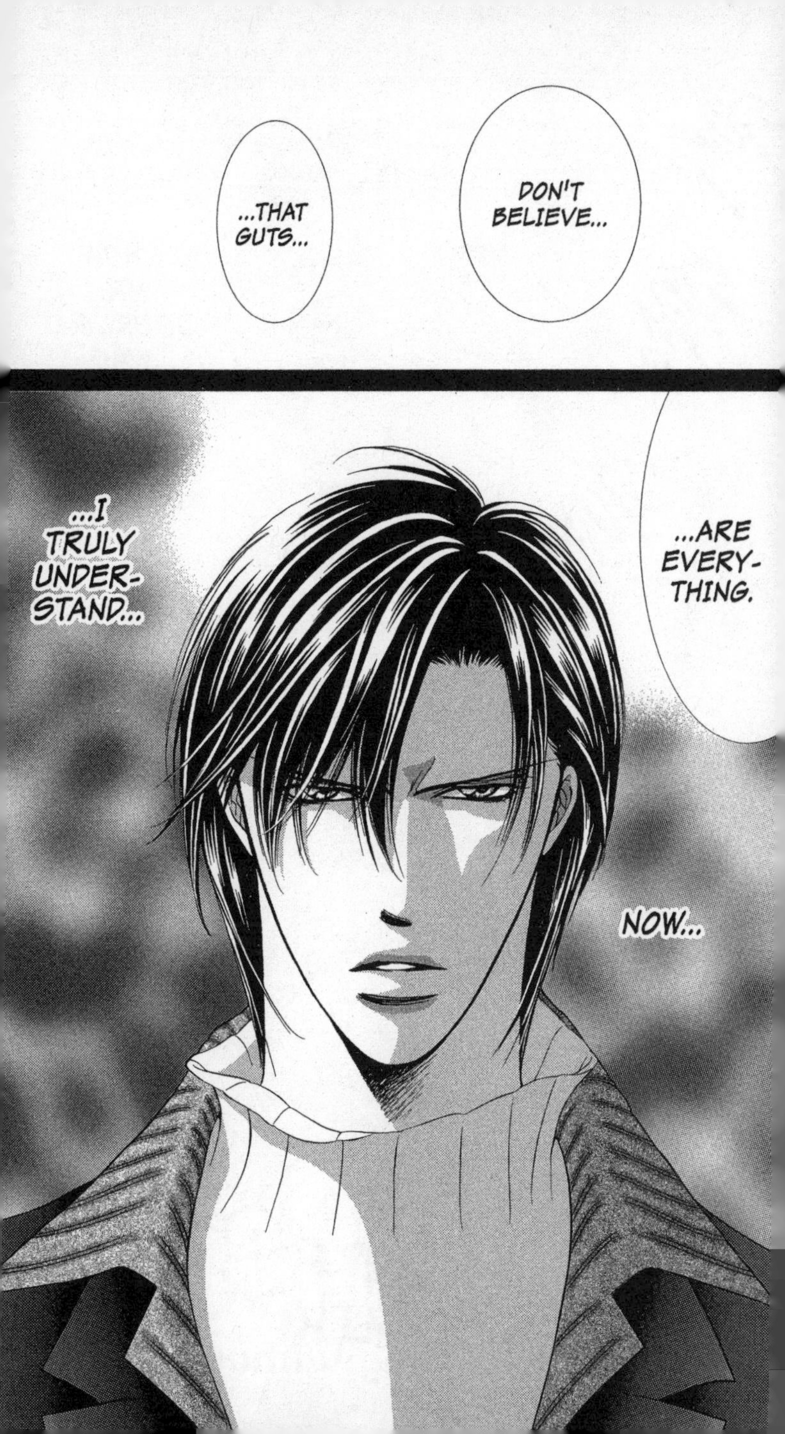
DON'T BELIEVE...
...THAT GUTS...
...ARE EVERY-THING.
...I TRULY UNDER-STAND...
NOW...

Skip·Beat!

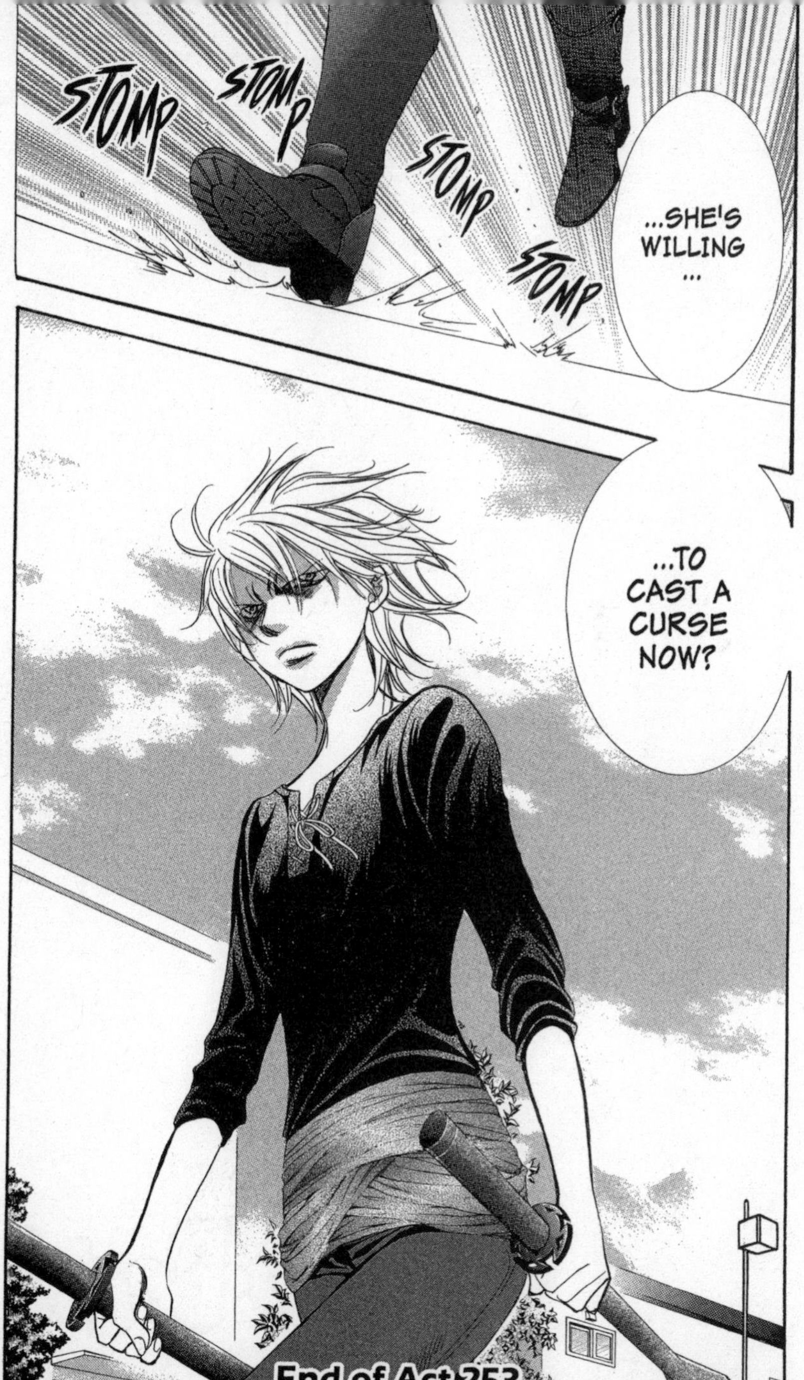
...SHE'S WILLING ...
STOMP
STOMP
STOMP
STOMP
...TO CAST A CURSE NOW?

End of Act 253

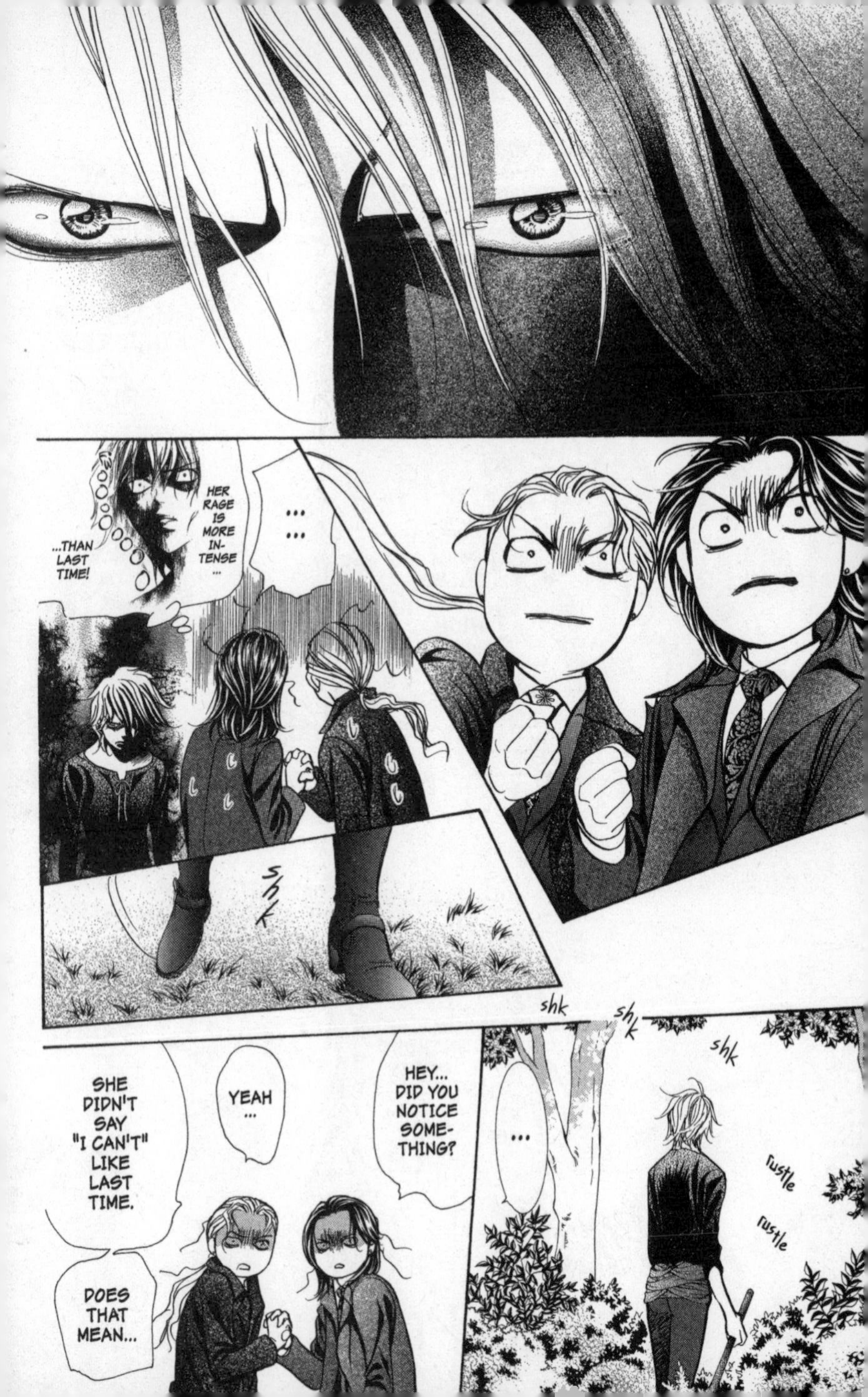

...
...
HER RAGE IS MORE IN-TENSE ...
...THAN LAST TIME!
shk
shk
shk
shk
...
rustle
rustle
HEY... DID YOU NOTICE SOME-THING?
YEAH ...
SHE DIDN'T SAY "I CAN'T" LIKE LAST TIME.
DOES THAT MEAN...

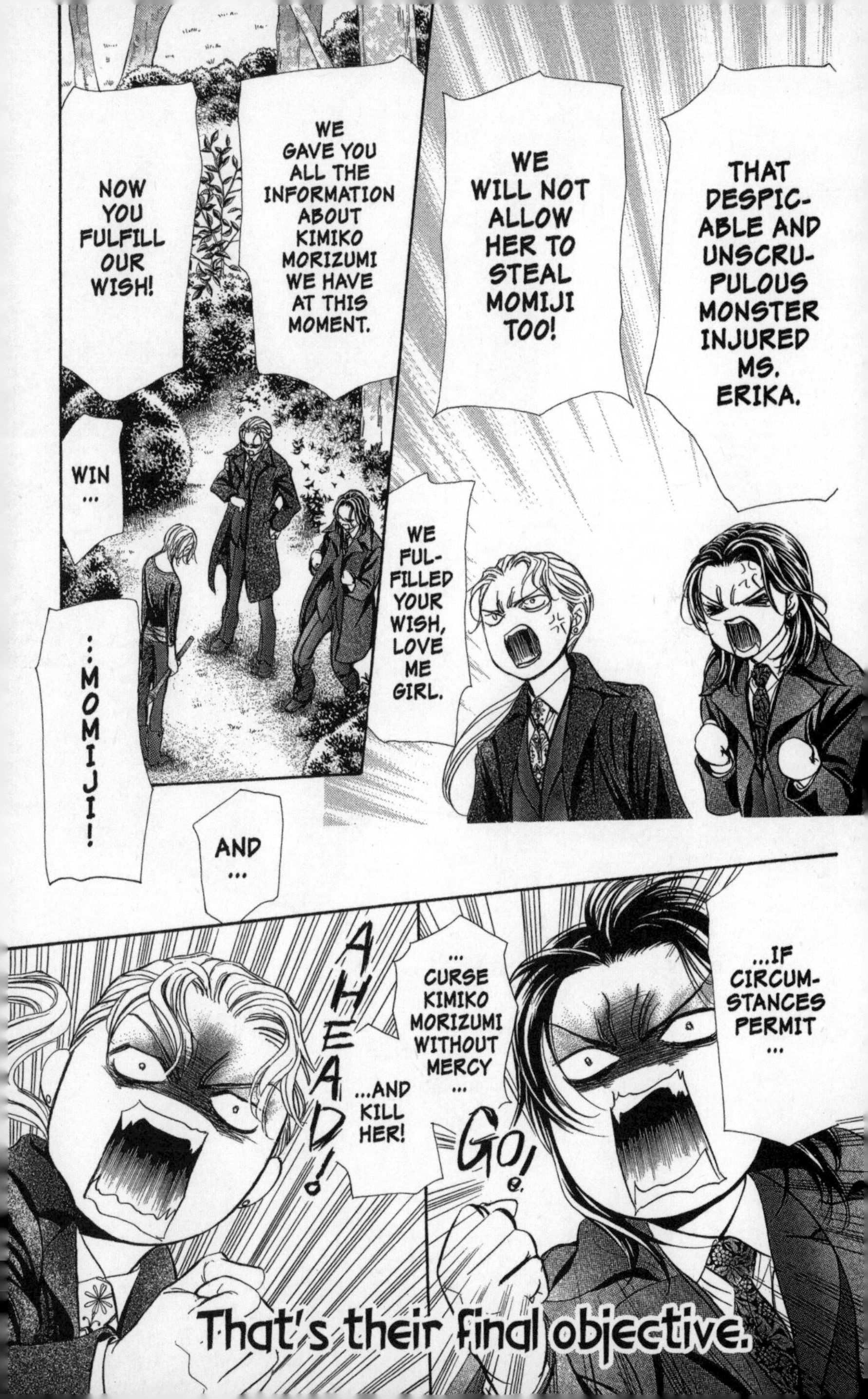
THAT DESPICABLE AND UNSCRUPULOUS MONSTER INJURED MS. ERIKA.
WE WILL NOT ALLOW HER TO STEAL MOMIJI TOO!
WE FULFILLED YOUR WISH, LOVE ME GIRL.
WE GAVE YOU ALL THE INFORMATION ABOUT KIMIKO MORIZUMI WE HAVE AT THIS MOMENT.
NOW YOU FULFILL OUR WISH!
WIN...
...MOMIJI!
AND...
...IF CIRCUMSTANCES PERMIT...
GO!
...CURSE KIMIKO MORIZUMI WITHOUT MERCY...
...AND KILL HER!
AHEAD!
That's their final objective.

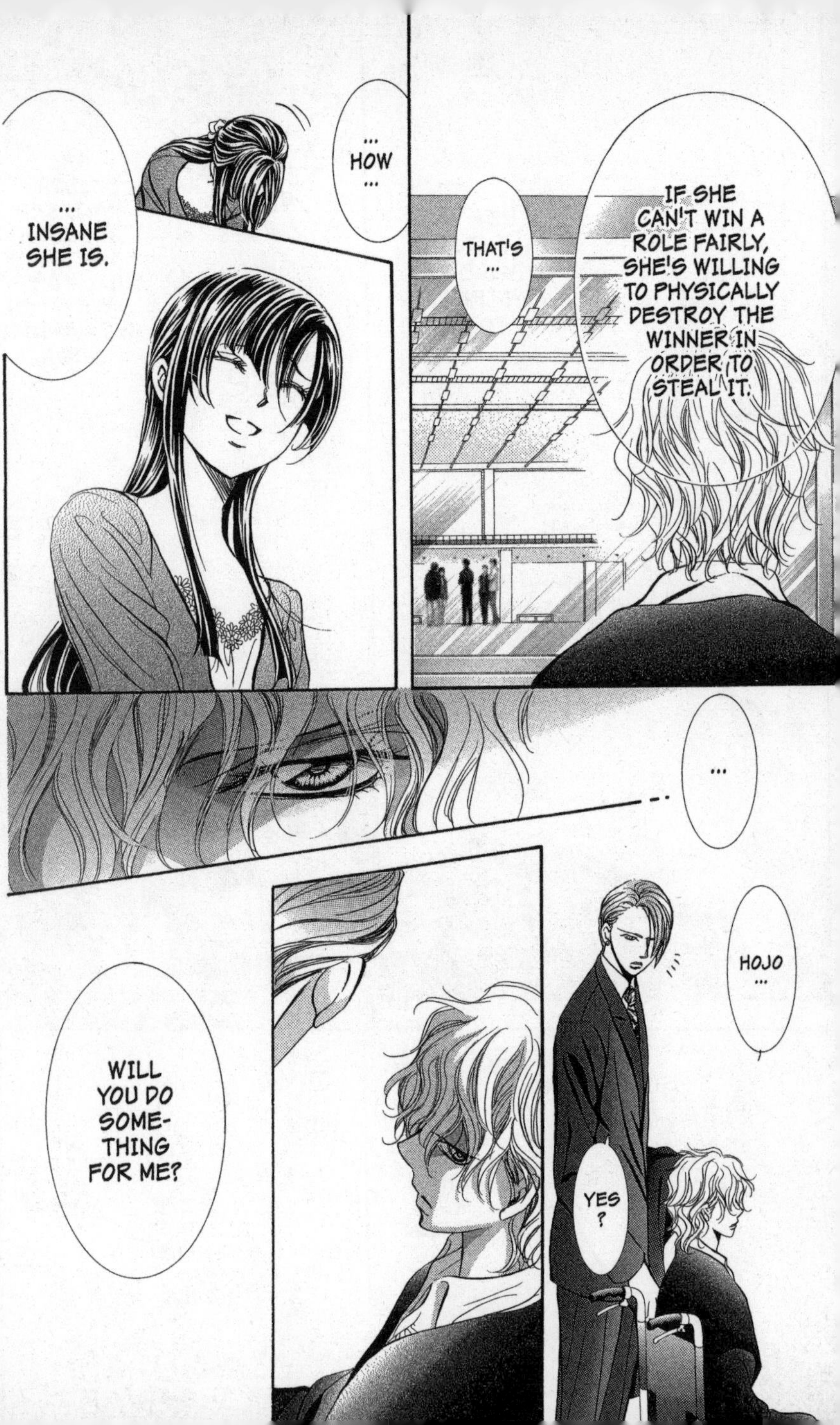
IF SHE CAN'T WIN A ROLE FAIRLY, SHE'S WILLING TO PHYSICALLY DESTROY THE WINNER IN ORDER TO STEAL IT.
THAT'S ...
... HOW ...
... INSANE SHE IS.
...
HOJO ...
YES ?
WILL YOU DO SOME-THING FOR ME?

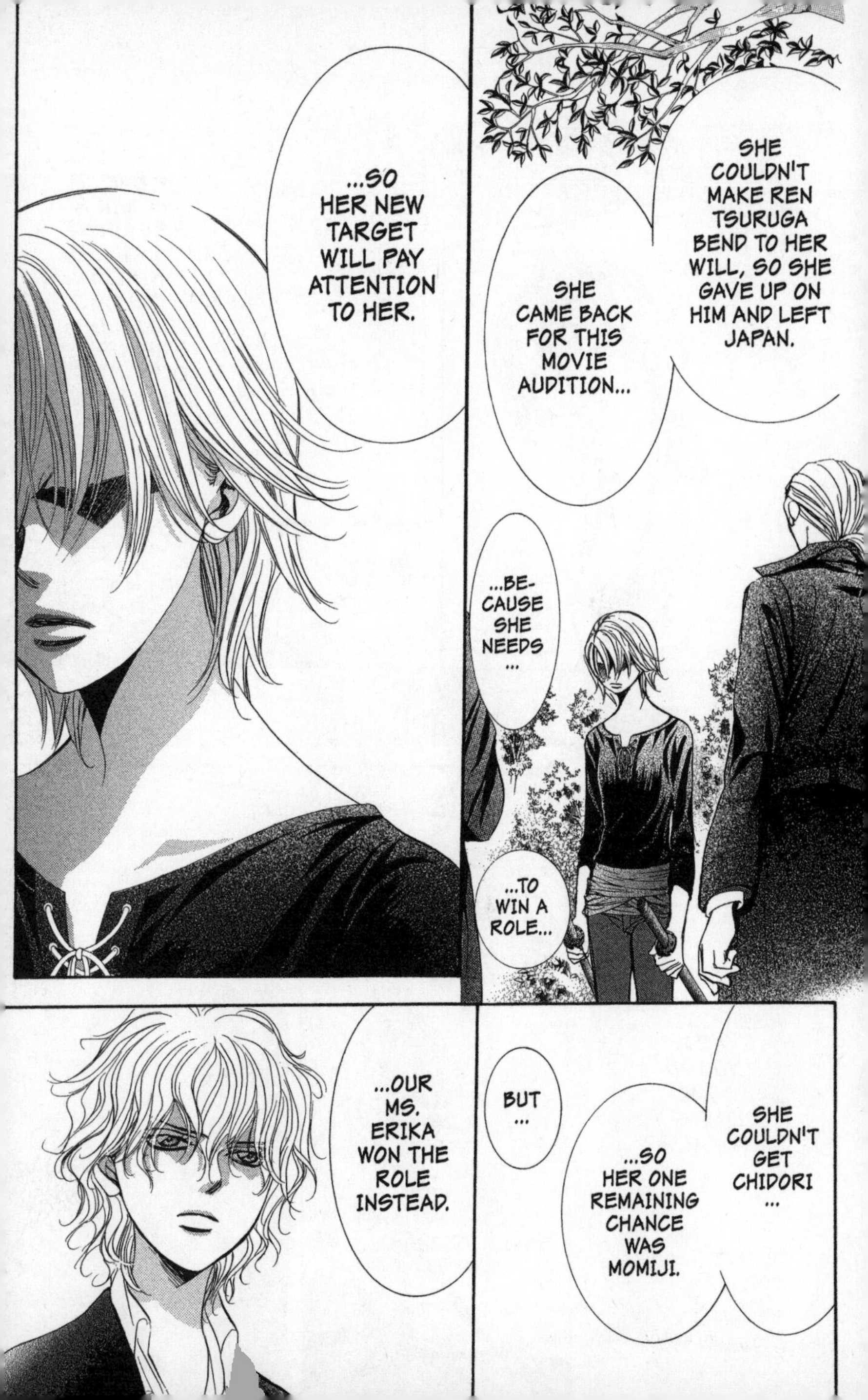
SHE COULDN'T MAKE REN TSURUGA BEND TO HER WILL, SO SHE GAVE UP ON HIM AND LEFT JAPAN.
SHE CAME BACK FOR THIS MOVIE AUDITION...
...BE-CAUSE SHE NEEDS...
...TO WIN A ROLE...
...SO HER NEW TARGET WILL PAY ATTENTION TO HER.
SHE COULDN'T GET CHIDORI...
...SO HER ONE REMAINING CHANCE WAS MOMIJI.
BUT...
...OUR MS. ERIKA WON THE ROLE INSTEAD.

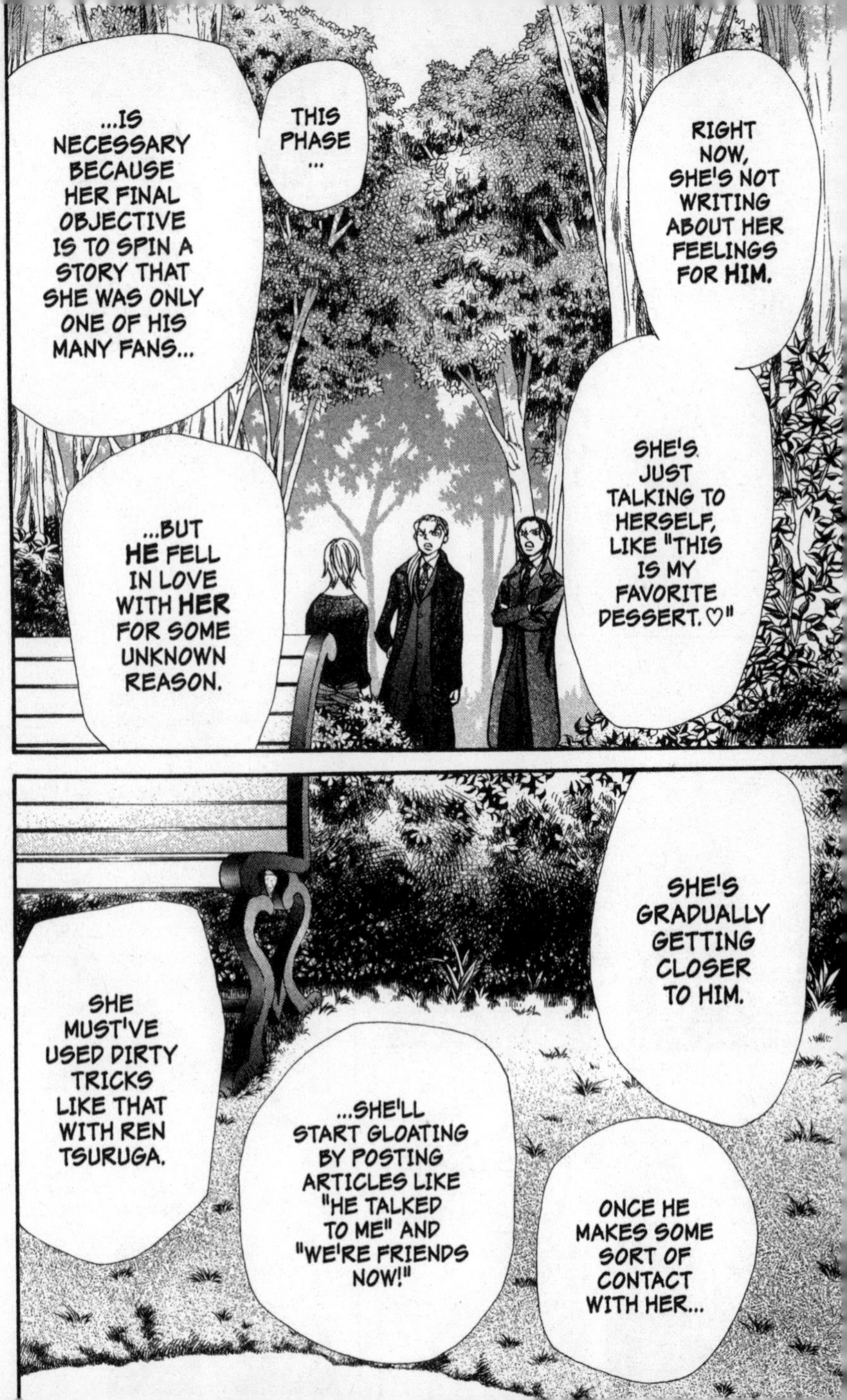
RIGHT NOW, SHE'S NOT WRITING ABOUT HER FEELINGS FOR HIM.
SHE'S JUST TALKING TO HERSELF, LIKE "THIS IS MY FAVORITE DESSERT. ♡"
THIS PHASE...
...IS NECESSARY BECAUSE HER FINAL OBJECTIVE IS TO SPIN A STORY THAT SHE WAS ONLY ONE OF HIS MANY FANS...
...BUT HE FELL IN LOVE WITH HER FOR SOME UNKNOWN REASON.
SHE'S GRADUALLY GETTING CLOSER TO HIM.
ONCE HE MAKES SOME SORT OF CONTACT WITH HER...
...SHE'LL START GLOATING BY POSTING ARTICLES LIKE "HE TALKED TO ME" AND "WE'RE FRIENDS NOW!"
SHE MUST'VE USED DIRTY TRICKS LIKE THAT WITH REN TSURUGA.

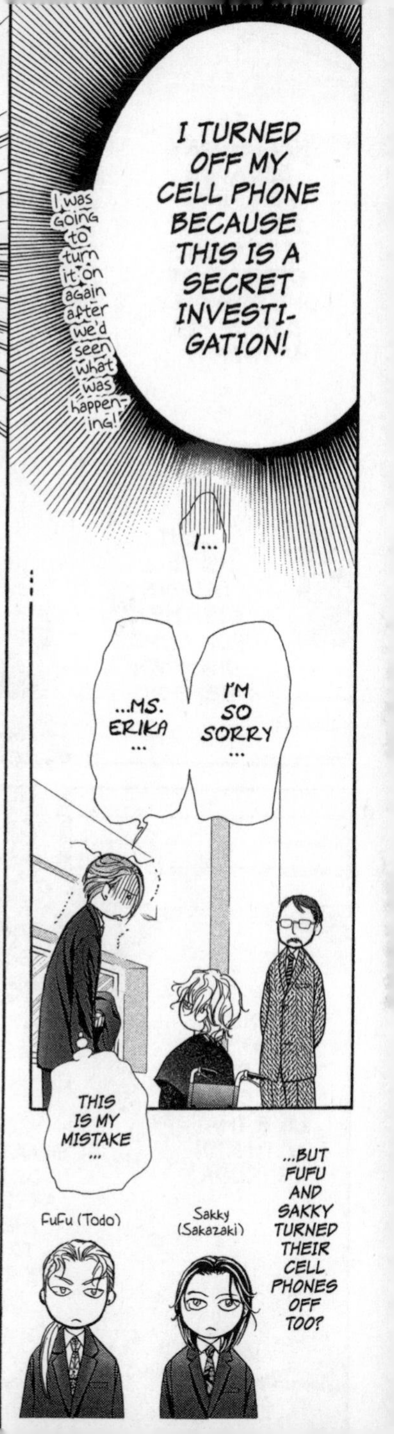
I TURNED OFF MY CELL PHONE BECAUSE THIS IS A SECRET INVESTIGATION!
I was going to turn it on again after we'd seen what was happening!
I...
I'M SO SORRY...
...MS. ERIKA...
THIS IS MY MISTAKE...
...BUT FUFU AND SAKKY TURNED THEIR CELL PHONES OFF TOO?
Sakky (Sakazaki)
FuFu (Todo)
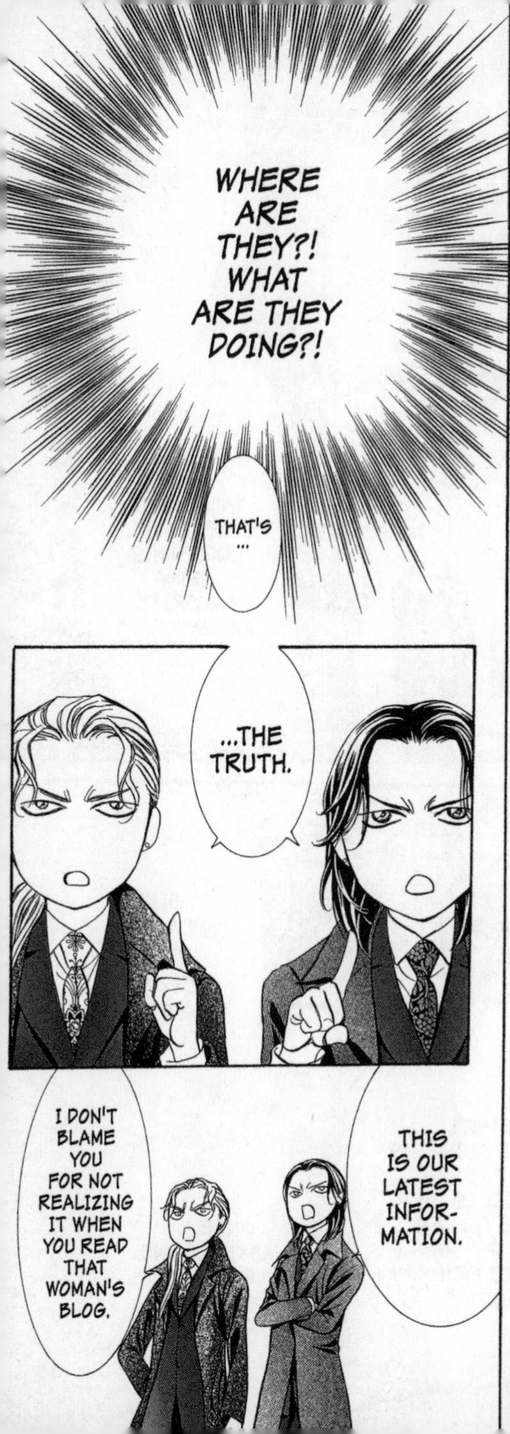
WHERE ARE THEY?! WHAT ARE THEY DOING?!
THAT'S...
...THE TRUTH.
THIS IS OUR LATEST INFORMATION.
I DON'T BLAME YOU FOR NOT REALIZING IT WHEN YOU READ THAT WOMAN'S BLOG.

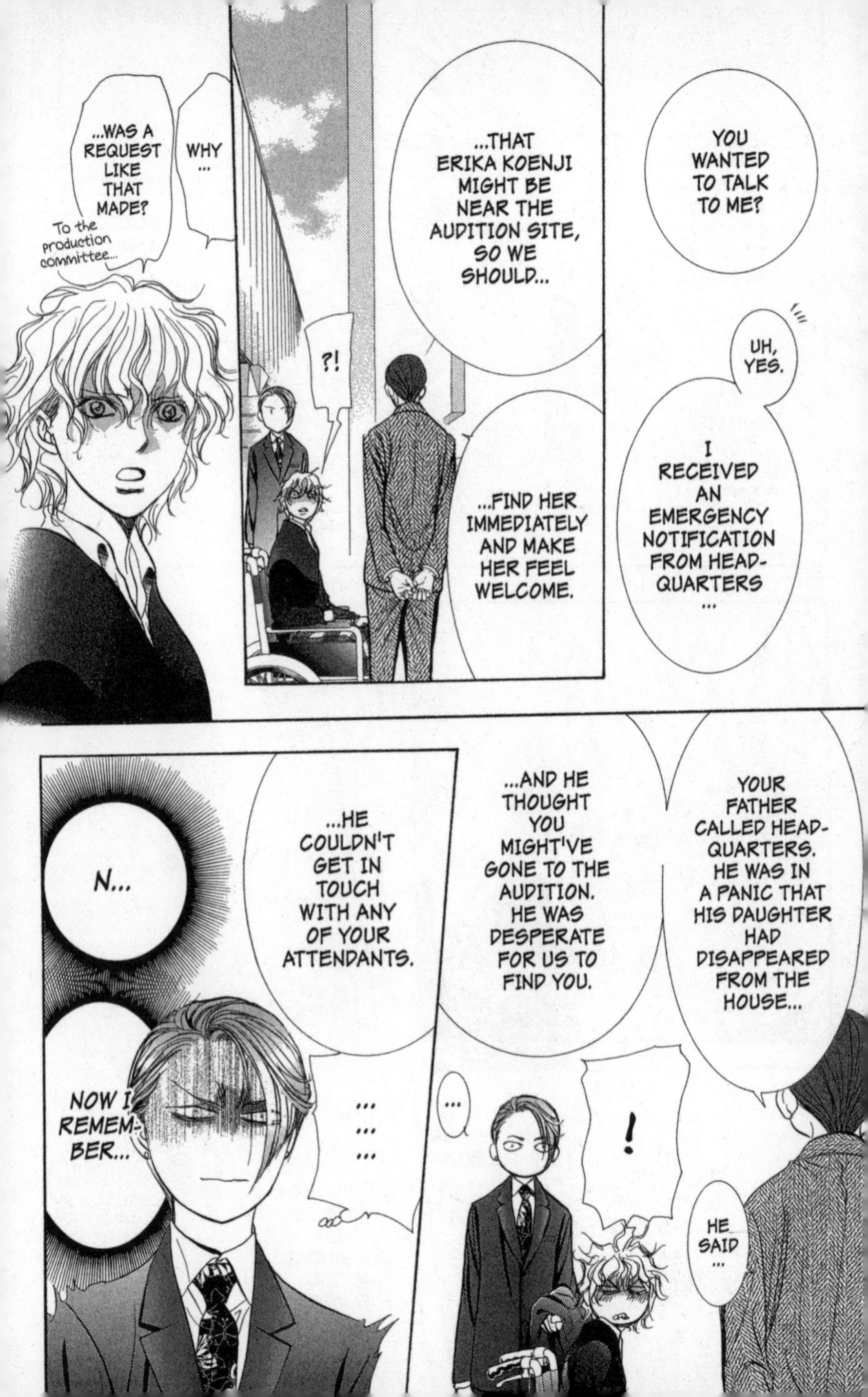
YOU WANTED TO TALK TO ME?
UH, YES.
I RECEIVED AN EMERGENCY NOTIFICATION FROM HEADQUARTERS...
...THAT ERIKA KOENJI MIGHT BE NEAR THE AUDITION SITE, SO WE SHOULD...
...FIND HER IMMEDIATELY AND MAKE HER FEEL WELCOME.
?!
WHY...
...WAS A REQUEST LIKE THAT MADE?
To the production committee...
YOUR FATHER CALLED HEADQUARTERS. HE WAS IN A PANIC THAT HIS DAUGHTER HAD DISAPPEARED FROM THE HOUSE...
...AND HE THOUGHT YOU MIGHT'VE GONE TO THE AUDITION. HE WAS DESPERATE FOR US TO FIND YOU.
...HE COULDN'T GET IN TOUCH WITH ANY OF YOUR ATTENDANTS.
HE SAID...
!
...
.........
N...
NOW I REMEMBER...

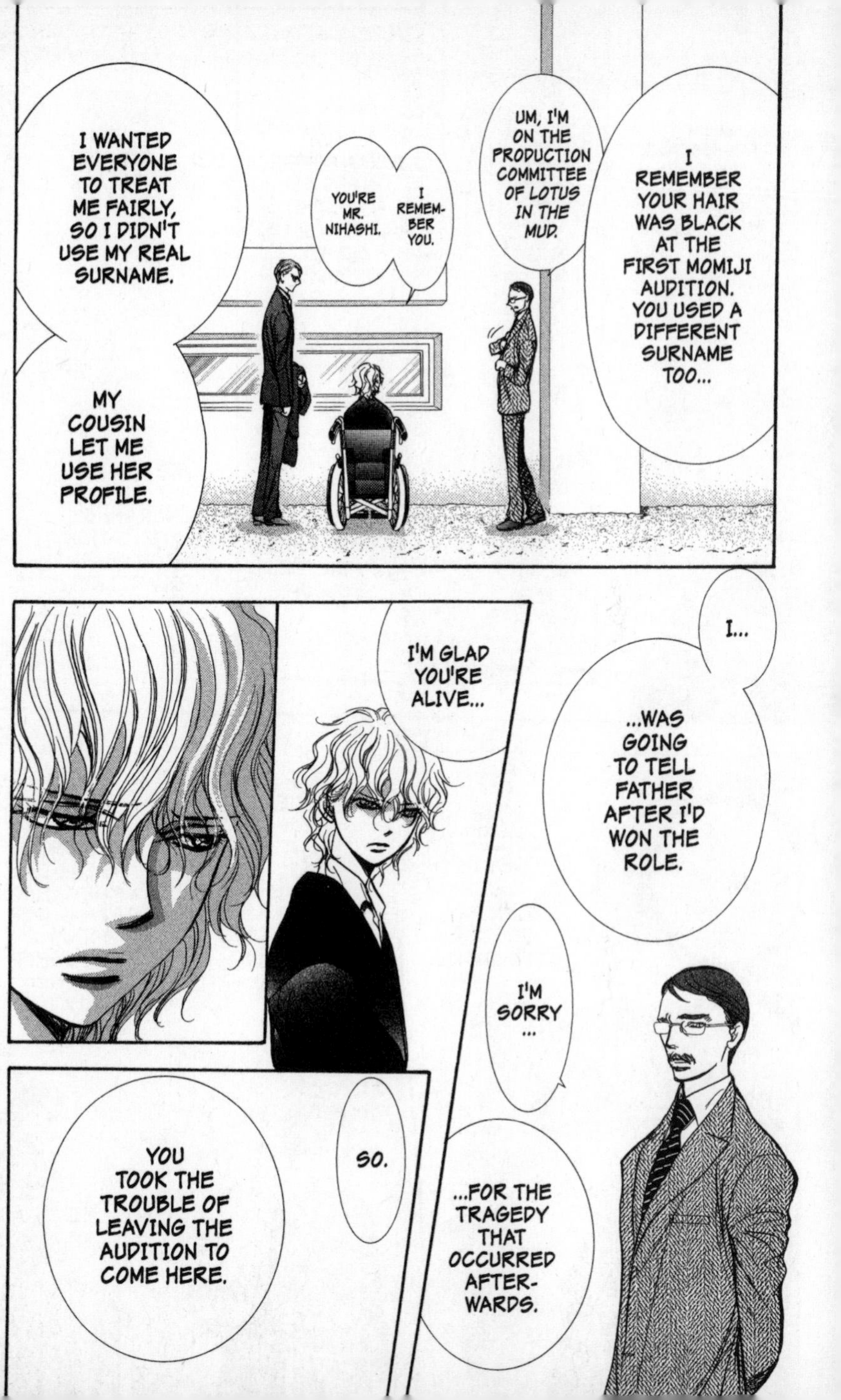
I REMEMBER YOUR HAIR WAS BLACK AT THE FIRST MOMIJI AUDITION. YOU USED A DIFFERENT SURNAME TOO...
UM, I'M ON THE PRODUCTION COMMITTEE OF LOTUS IN THE MUD.
I REMEMBER YOU.
YOU'RE MR. NIHASHI.
I WANTED EVERYONE TO TREAT ME FAIRLY, SO I DIDN'T USE MY REAL SURNAME.
MY COUSIN LET ME USE HER PROFILE.
I'M GLAD YOU'RE ALIVE...
I...
...WAS GOING TO TELL FATHER AFTER I'D WON THE ROLE.
I'M SORRY...
...FOR THE TRAGEDY THAT OCCURRED AFTER-WARDS.
SO.
YOU TOOK THE TROUBLE OF LEAVING THE AUDITION TO COME HERE.

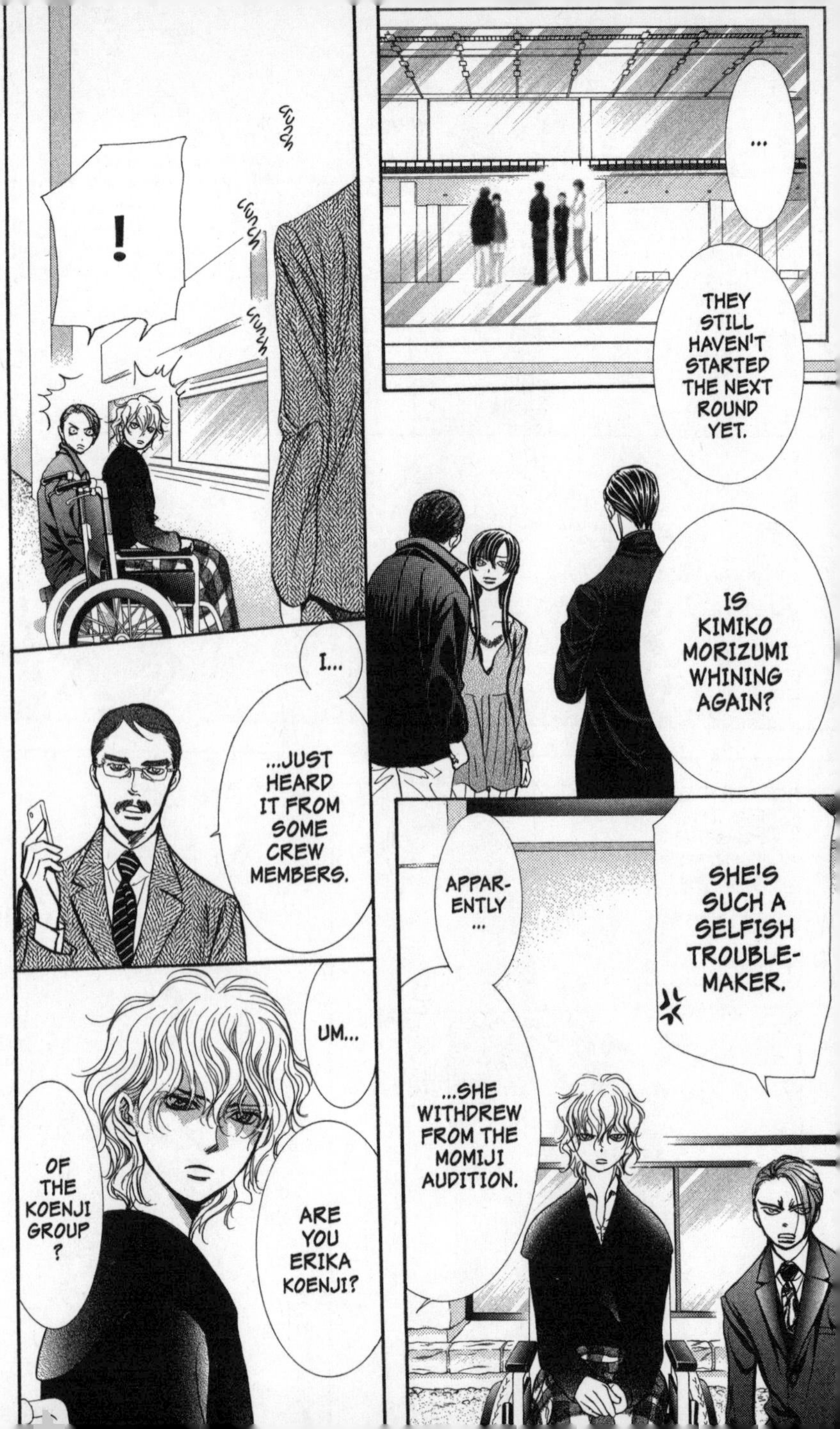
...
THEY STILL HAVEN'T STARTED THE NEXT ROUND YET.
IS KIMIKO MORIZUMI WHINING AGAIN?
SHE'S SUCH A SELFISH TROUBLE-MAKER.
APPAR-ENTLY ...
...SHE WITHDREW FROM THE MOMIJI AUDITION.
crunch
crunch
crunch
!
I...
...JUST HEARD IT FROM SOME CREW MEMBERS.
UM...
ARE YOU ERIKA KOENJI?
OF THE KOENJI GROUP?

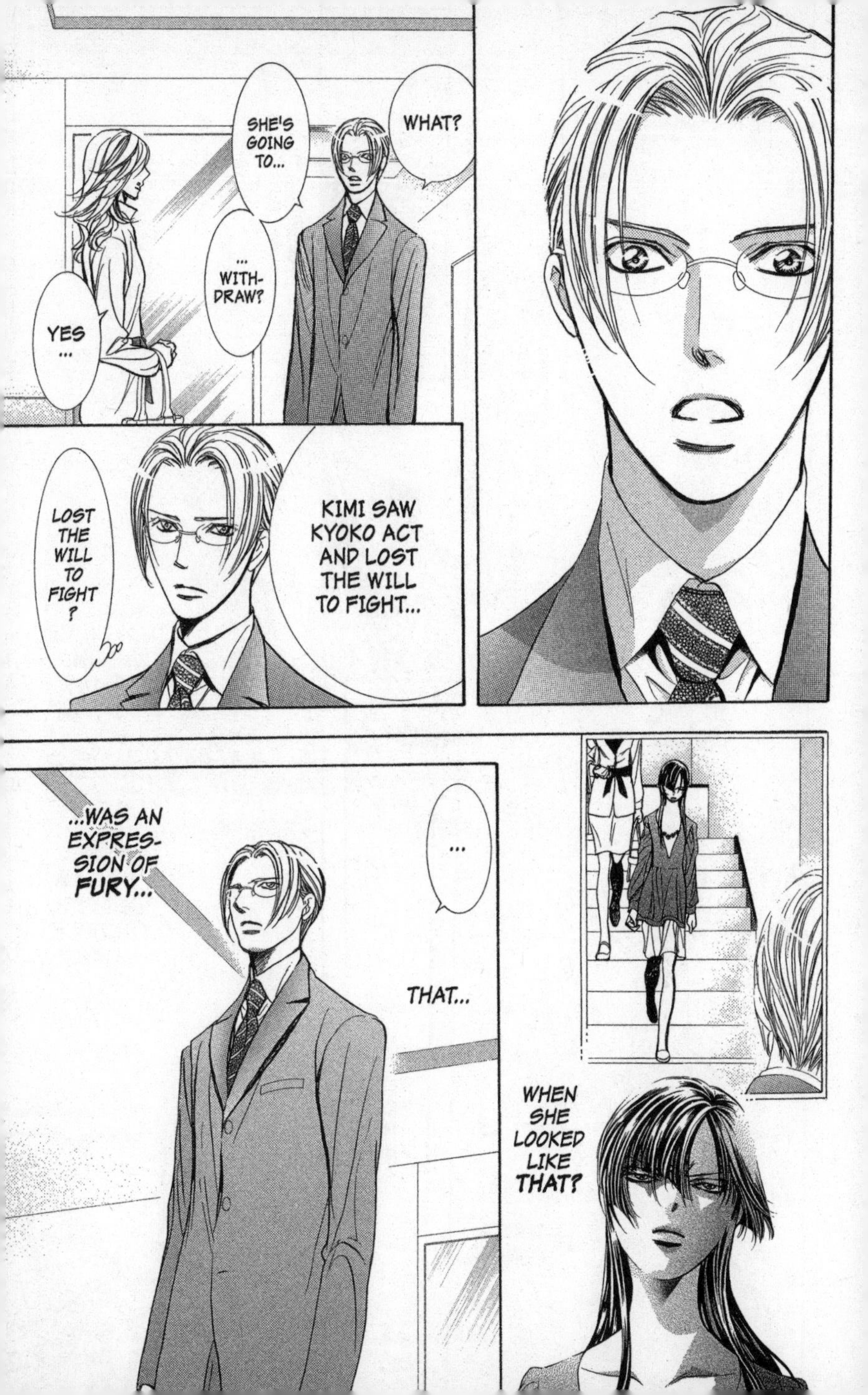
WHAT?
SHE'S GOING TO...
...WITHDRAW?
YES...
KIMI SAW KYOKO ACT AND LOST THE WILL TO FIGHT...
LOST THE WILL TO FIGHT?
WHEN SHE LOOKED LIKE THAT?
...
THAT...
...WAS AN EXPRESSION OF FURY...

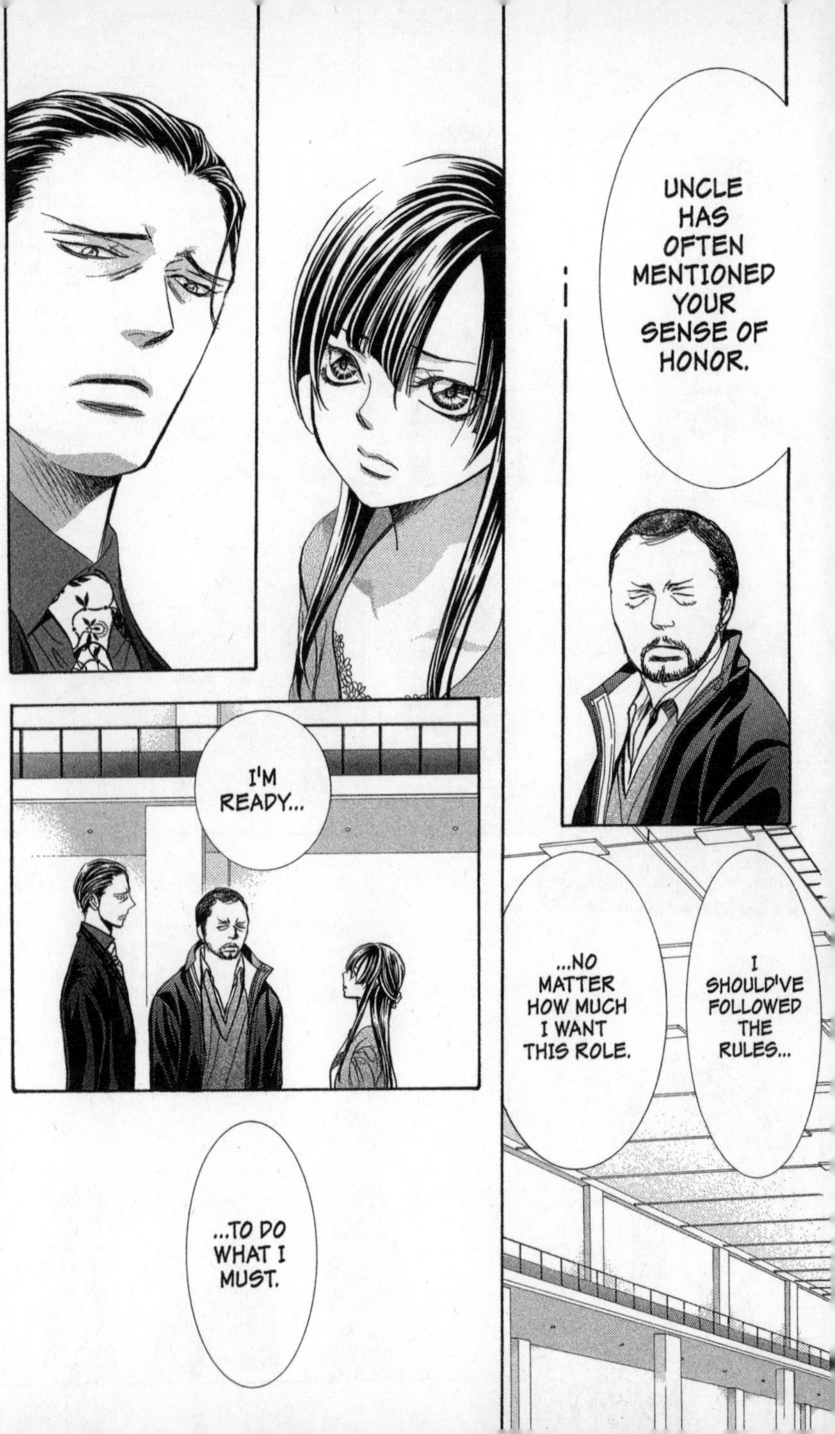
UNCLE HAS OFTEN MENTIONED YOUR SENSE OF HONOR.
I SHOULD'VE FOLLOWED THE RULES...
...NO MATTER HOW MUCH I WANT THIS ROLE.
I'M READY...
...TO DO WHAT I MUST.

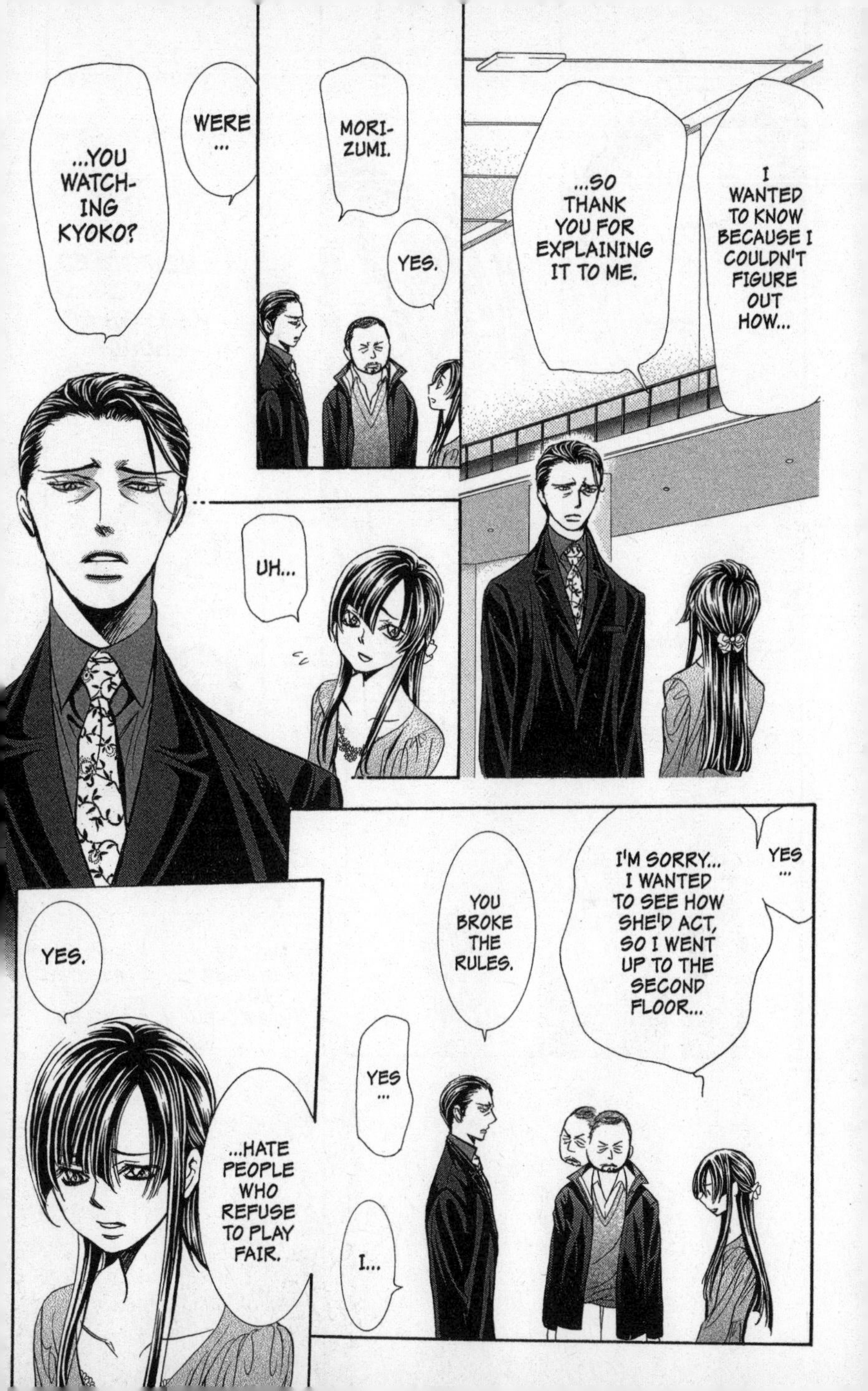
I WANTED TO KNOW BECAUSE I COULDN'T FIGURE OUT HOW...
...SO THANK YOU FOR EXPLAINING IT TO ME.
MORI-ZUMI.
YES.
WERE...
...YOU WATCHING-ING KYOKO?
UH...
YES...
I'M SORRY... I WANTED TO SEE HOW SHE'D ACT, SO I WENT UP TO THE SECOND FLOOR...
YOU BROKE THE RULES.
YES...
I...
YES.
...HATE PEOPLE WHO REFUSE TO PLAY FAIR.

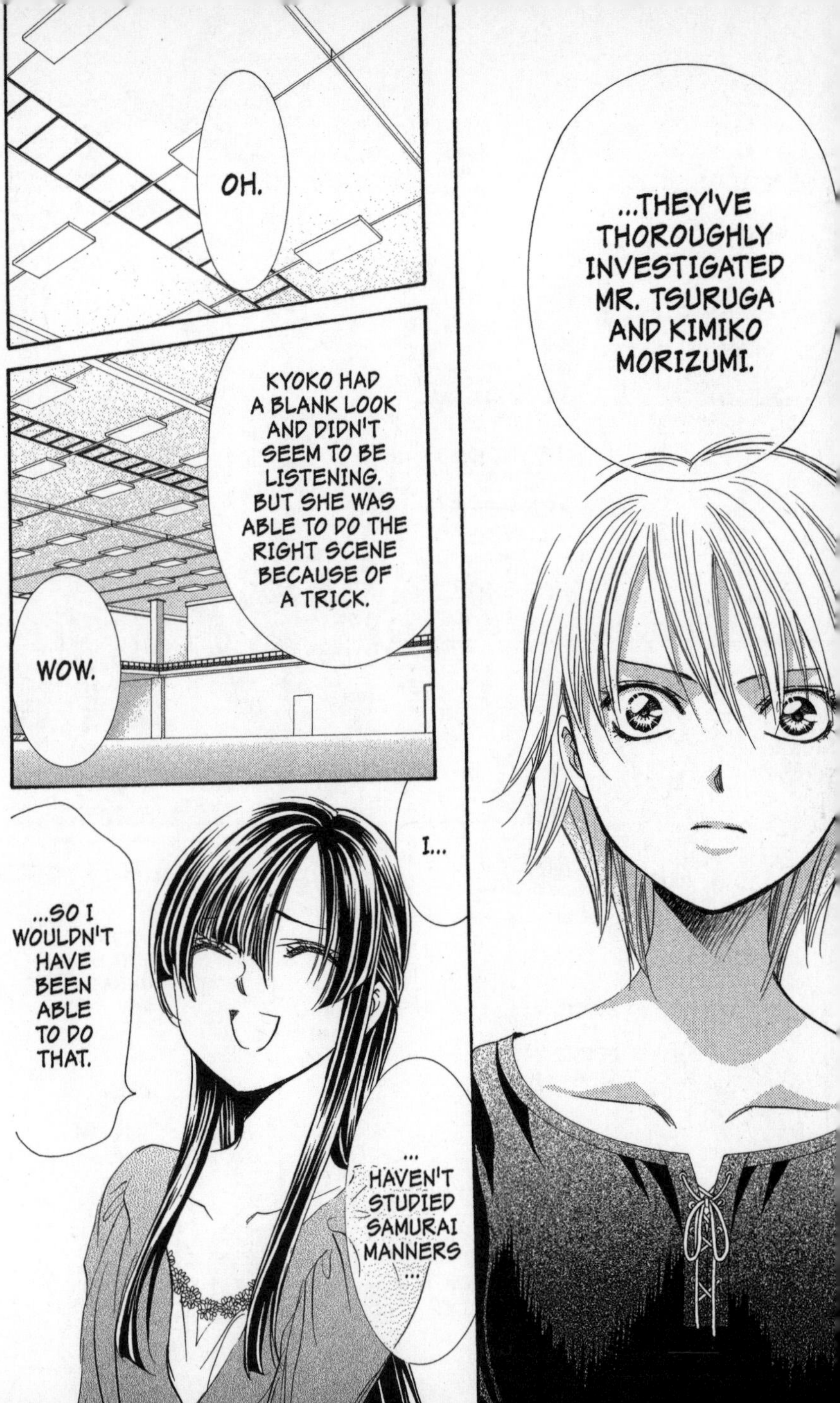
...THEY'VE THOROUGHLY INVESTIGATED MR. TSURUGA AND KIMIKO MORIZUMI.
OH.
KYOKO HAD A BLANK LOOK AND DIDN'T SEEM TO BE LISTENING. BUT SHE WAS ABLE TO DO THE RIGHT SCENE BECAUSE OF A TRICK.
WOW.
I...
...HAVEN'T STUDIED SAMURAI MANNERS...
...SO I WOULDN'T HAVE BEEN ABLE TO DO THAT.

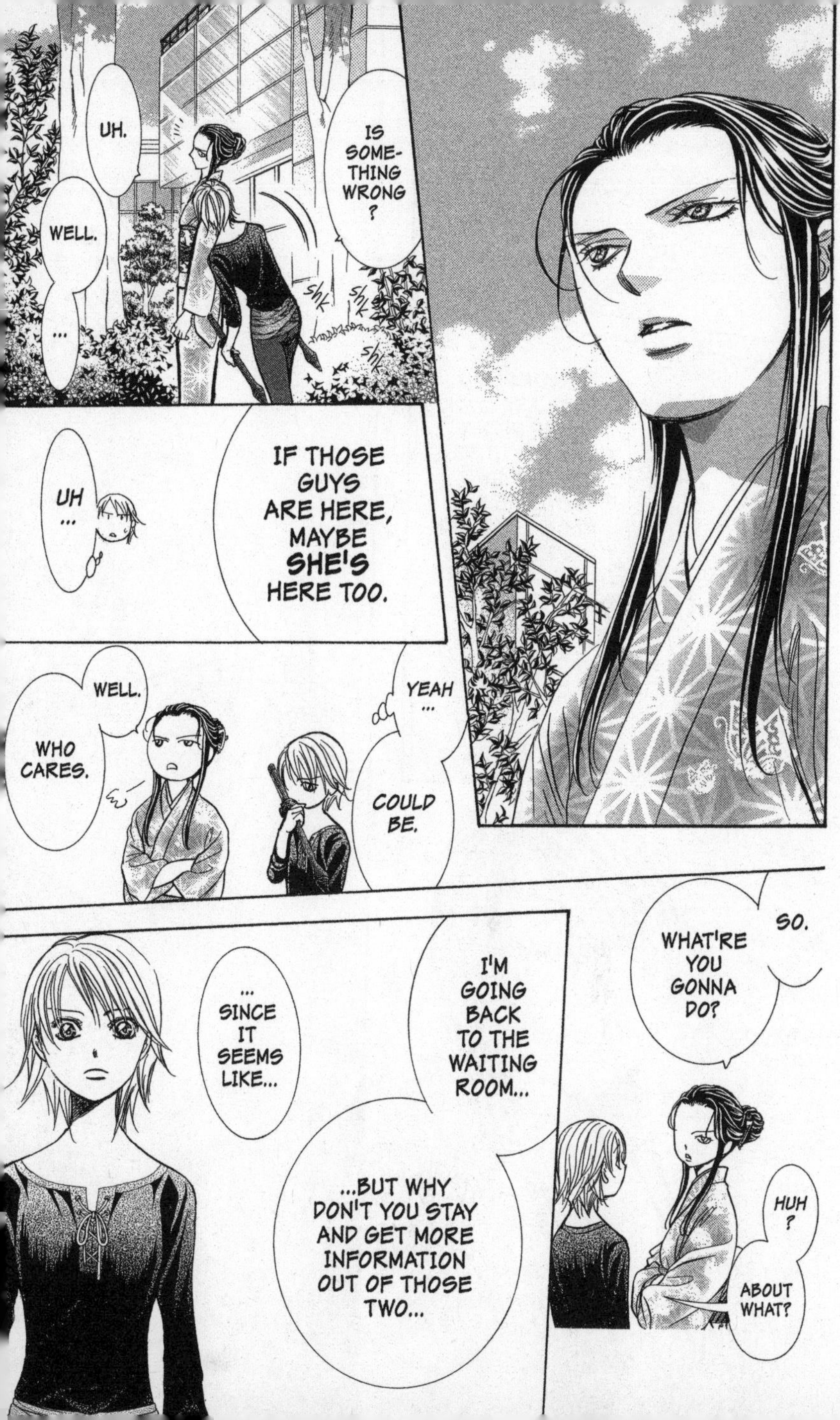

IS SOMETHING WRONG?
shk shk shk
UH.
WELL.
...
IF THOSE GUYS ARE HERE, MAYBE **SHE'S** HERE TOO.
UH ...
YEAH ...
COULD BE.
WELL.
WHO CARES.
SO.
WHAT'RE YOU GONNA DO?
HUH?
ABOUT WHAT?
I'M GOING BACK TO THE WAITING ROOM...
... SINCE IT SEEMS LIKE...
...BUT WHY DON'T YOU STAY AND GET MORE INFORMATION OUT OF THOSE TWO...

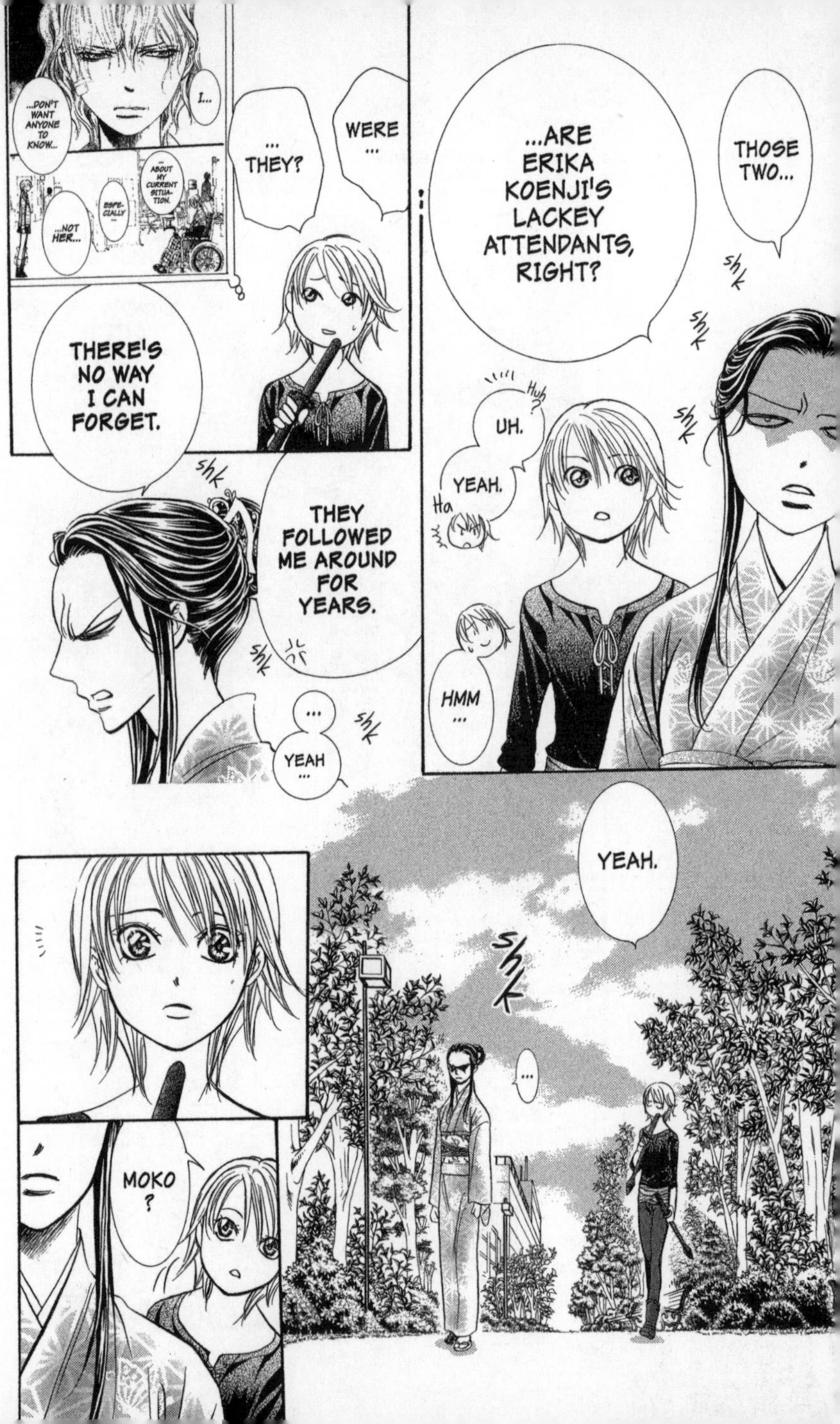
THOSE TWO...
...ARE ERIKA KOENJI'S LACKEY ATTENDANTS, RIGHT?
shk
shk
shk
Huh?
UH.
YEAH.
Ha
HMM...
WERE...
...THEY?
I...
...DON'T WANT ANYONE TO KNOW...
...ABOUT MY CURRENT SITUATION.
ESPECIALLY...
...NOT HER...
THERE'S NO WAY I CAN FORGET.
shk
THEY FOLLOWED ME AROUND FOR YEARS.
shk
...
YEAH...
shk
YEAH.
shk
...
MOKO?

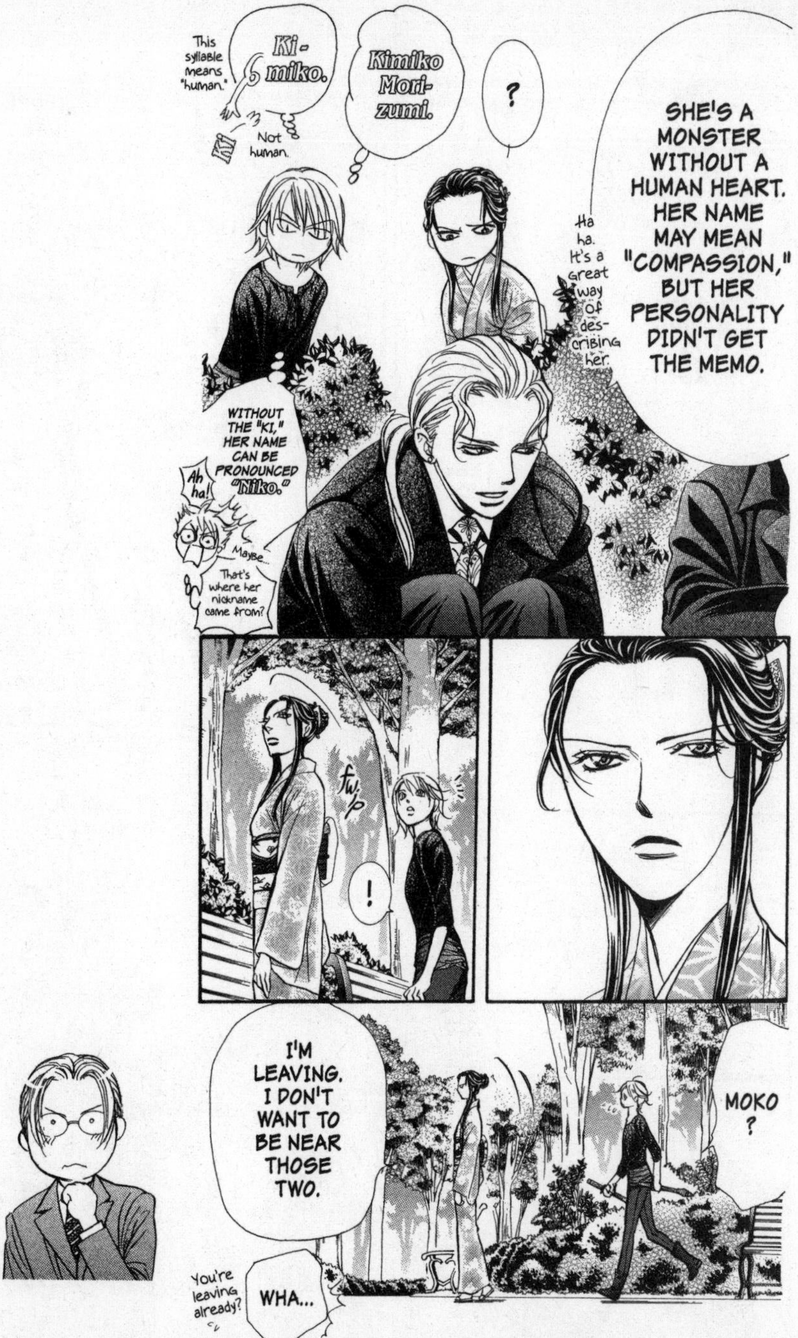
SHE'S A MONSTER WITHOUT A HUMAN HEART. HER NAME MAY MEAN "COMPASSION," BUT HER PERSONALITY DIDN'T GET THE MEMO.
Ha ha. It's a great way of des-cribing her.
?
Kimiko Mori-zumi.
Ki-miko.
This syllable means "human."
KI
Not human.
WITHOUT THE "KI," HER NAME CAN BE PRONOUNCED "Niko."
Ah ha!
Maybe...
That's where her nickname came from?
fwip
!
MOKO ?
I'M LEAVING. I DON'T WANT TO BE NEAR THOSE TWO.
WHA...
You're leaving already?

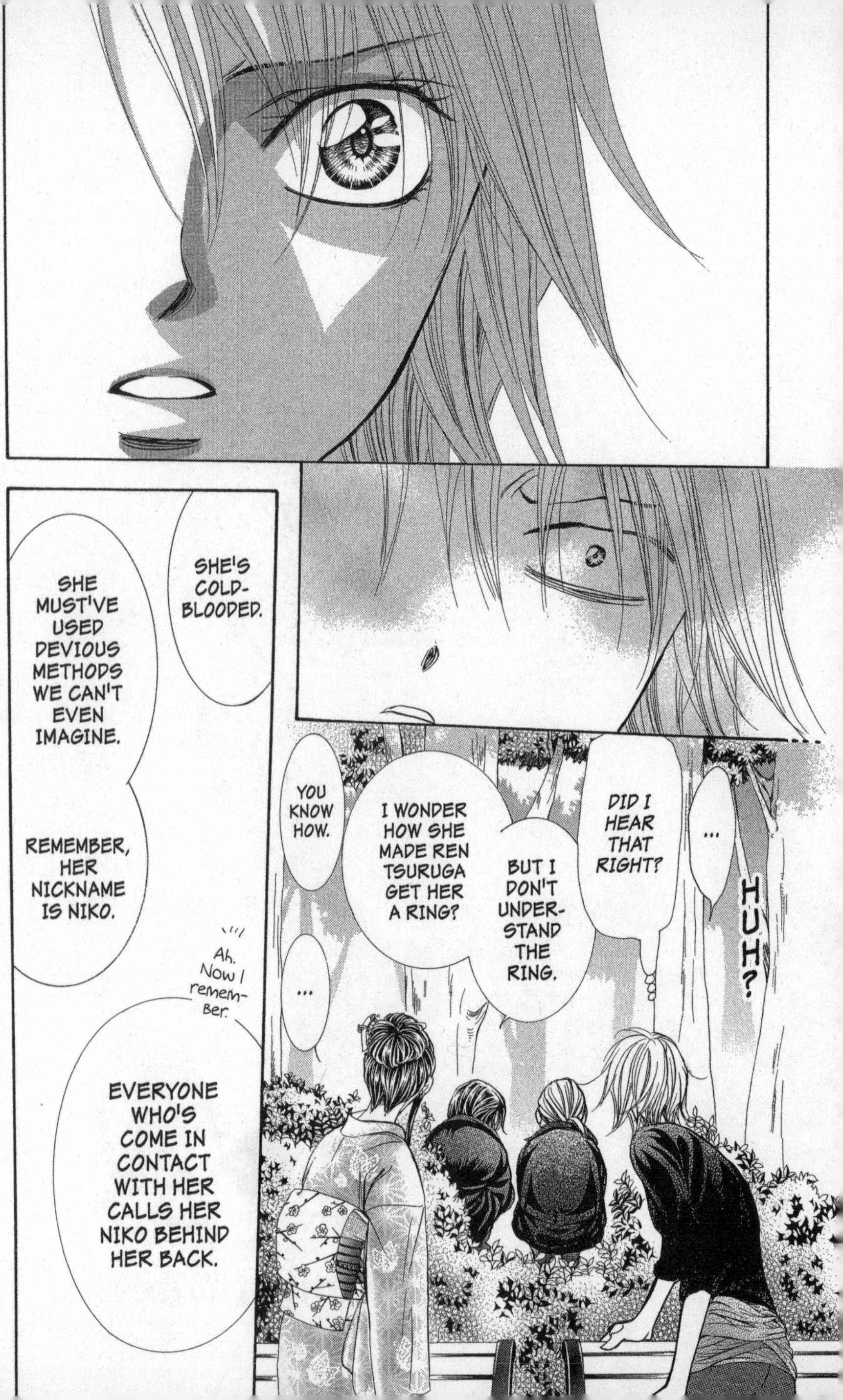
HUH?
...
DID I HEAR THAT RIGHT?
BUT I DON'T UNDERSTAND THE RING.
I WONDER HOW SHE MADE REN TSURUGA GET HER A RING?
YOU KNOW HOW.
...
SHE'S COLD-BLOODED.
SHE MUST'VE USED DEVIOUS METHODS WE CAN'T EVEN IMAGINE.
REMEMBER, HER NICKNAME IS NIKO.
Ah. Now I remember.
EVERYONE WHO'S COME IN CONTACT WITH HER CALLS HER NIKO BEHIND HER BACK.

"...AND SHOULD HAVE NO INTEREST IN REN TSURUGA."

"THAT GIRL IS OBSESSED WITH ANOTHER GUY RIGHT NOW..."

# Skip·Beat!

## Act 253: Flying Without Wires

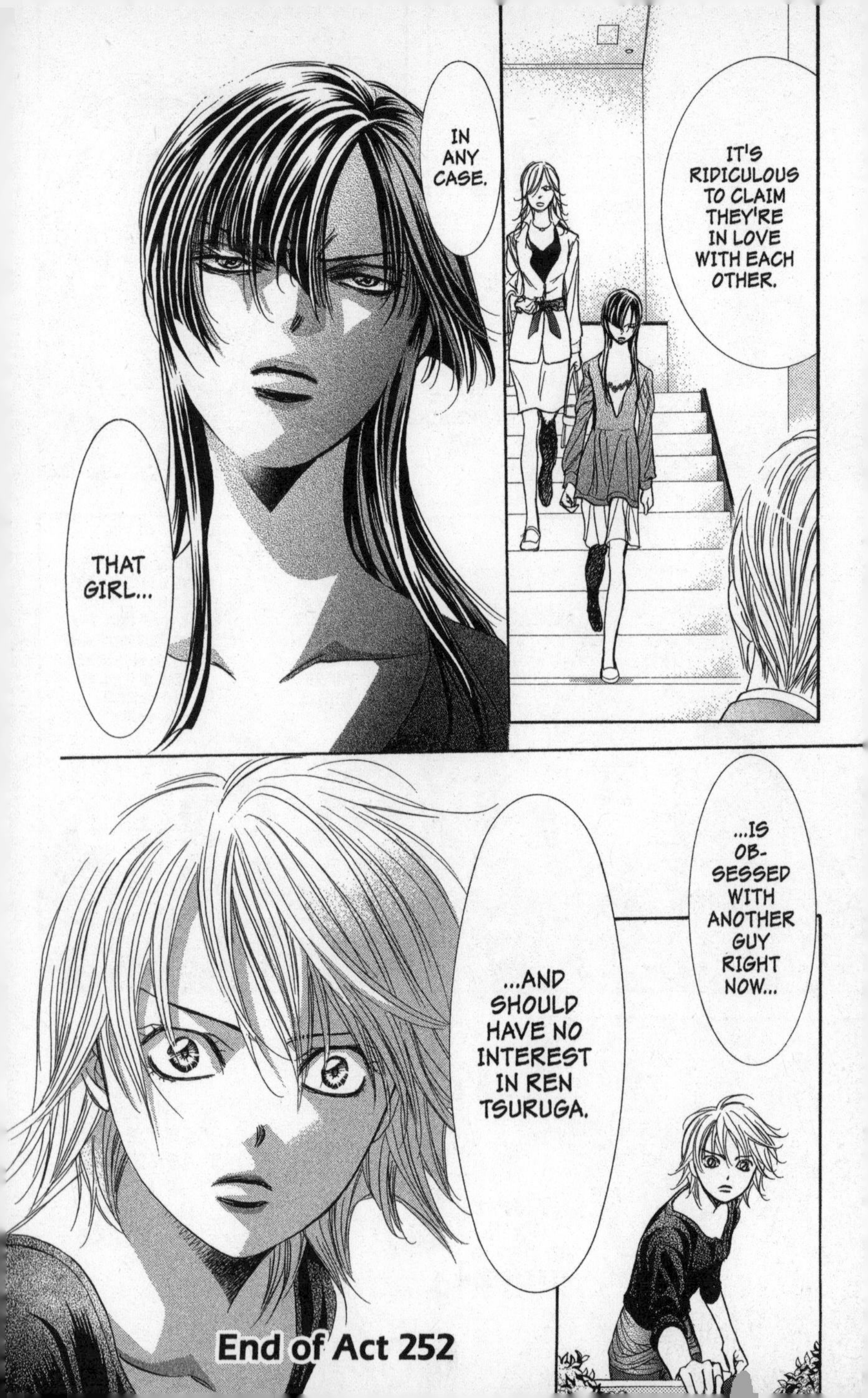
IT'S RIDICULOUS TO CLAIM THEY'RE IN LOVE WITH EACH OTHER.
IN ANY CASE.
THAT GIRL...
...IS OB-SESSED WITH ANOTHER GUY RIGHT NOW...
...AND SHOULD HAVE NO INTEREST IN REN TSURUGA.

End of Act 252

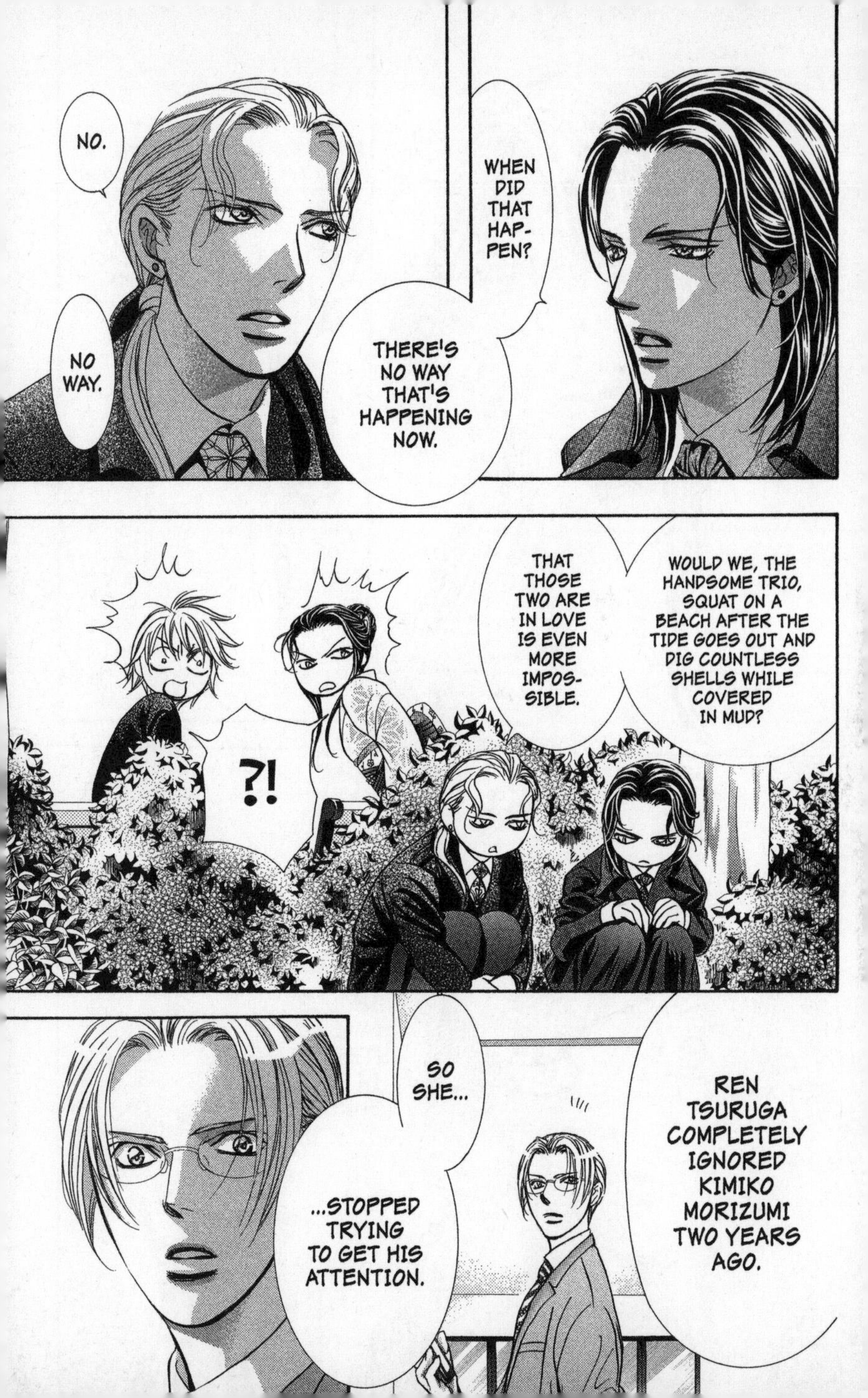
WHEN DID THAT HAP-PEN?
NO.
THERE'S NO WAY THAT'S HAPPENING NOW.
NO WAY.
WOULD WE, THE HANDSOME TRIO, SQUAT ON A BEACH AFTER THE TIDE GOES OUT AND DIG COUNTLESS SHELLS WHILE COVERED IN MUD?
THAT THOSE TWO ARE IN LOVE IS EVEN MORE IMPOS-SIBLE.
?!
REN TSURUGA COMPLETELY IGNORED KIMIKO MORIZUMI TWO YEARS AGO.
SO SHE...
...STOPPED TRYING TO GET HIS ATTENTION.

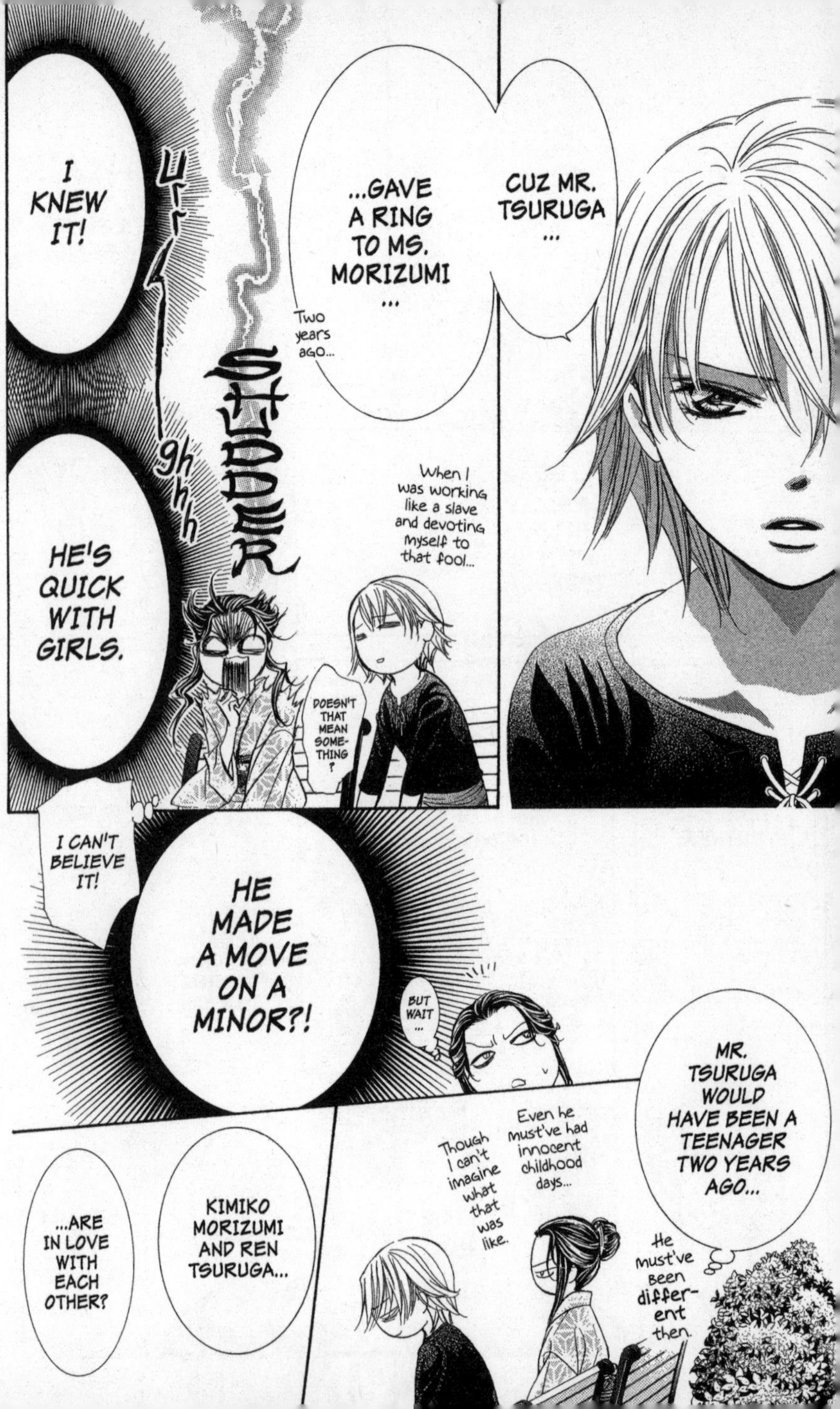
CUZ MR. TSURUGA ...
...GAVE A RING TO MS. MORIZUMI ...
Two years ago...
When I was working like a slave and devoting myself to that fool...
DOESN'T THAT MEAN SOME-THING?
SHUDDER
Urrrghhh
I KNEW IT!
HE'S QUICK WITH GIRLS.
MR. TSURUGA WOULD HAVE BEEN A TEENAGER TWO YEARS AGO...
BUT WAIT ...
HE MADE A MOVE ON A MINOR?!
I CAN'T BELIEVE IT!
He must've been differ-ent then.
Even he must've had innocent childhood days...
Though I can't imagine what that was like.
KIMIKO MORIZUMI AND REN TSURUGA...
...ARE IN LOVE WITH EACH OTHER?

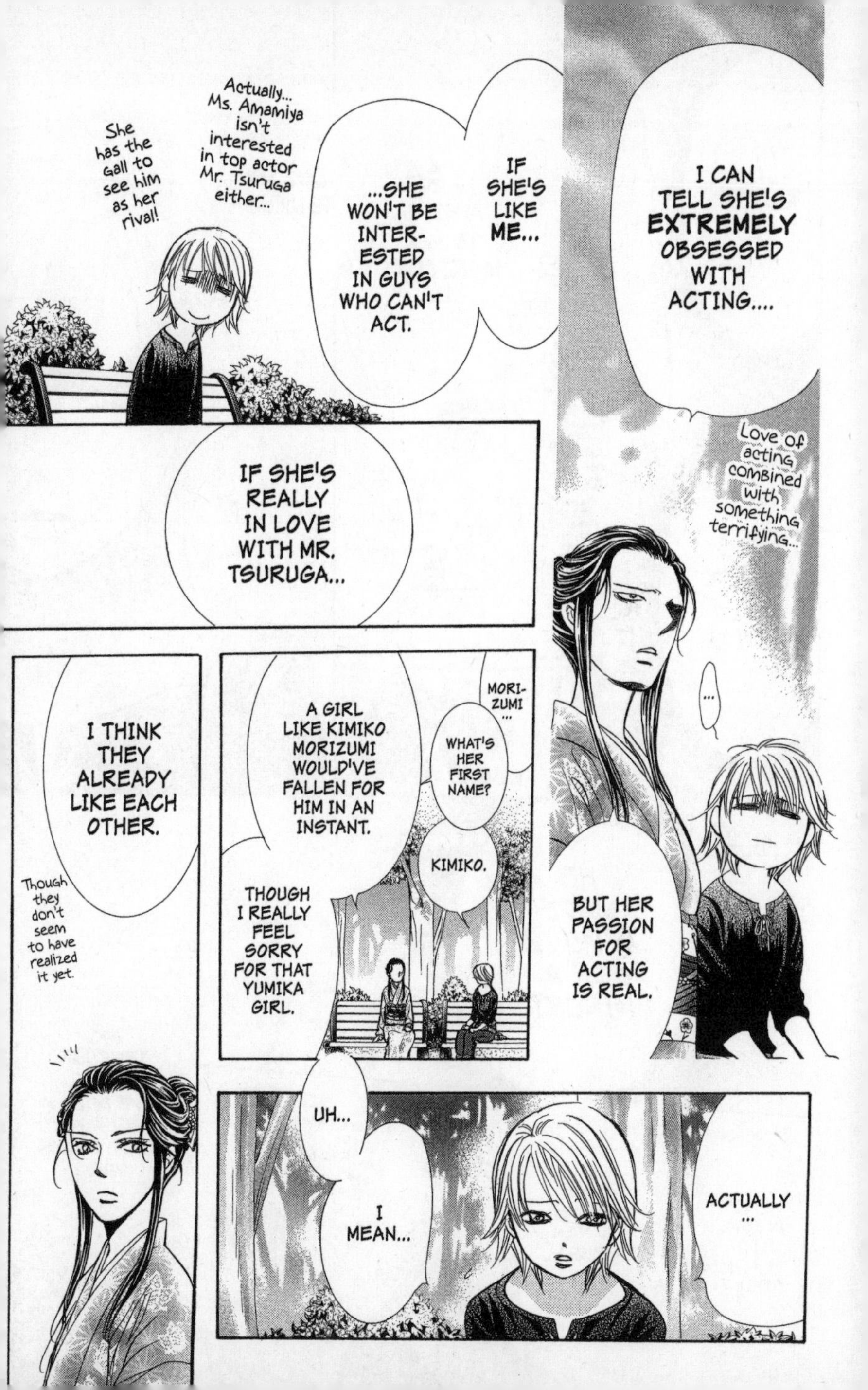

I CAN TELL SHE'S EXTREMELY OBSESSED WITH ACTING....
Love of acting combined with something terrifying...
...
BUT HER PASSION FOR ACTING IS REAL.
IF SHE'S LIKE ME...
...SHE WON'T BE INTER-ESTED IN GUYS WHO CAN'T ACT.
Actually... Ms. Amamiya isn't interested in top actor Mr. Tsuruga either...
She has the gall to see him as her rival!
IF SHE'S REALLY IN LOVE WITH MR. TSURUGA...
MORI-ZUMI...
WHAT'S HER FIRST NAME?
KIMIKO.
A GIRL LIKE KIMIKO MORIZUMI WOULD'VE FALLEN FOR HIM IN AN INSTANT.
THOUGH I REALLY FEEL SORRY FOR THAT YUMIKA GIRL.
I THINK THEY ALREADY LIKE EACH OTHER.
Though they don't seem to have realized it yet.
ACTUALLY...
UH...
I MEAN...

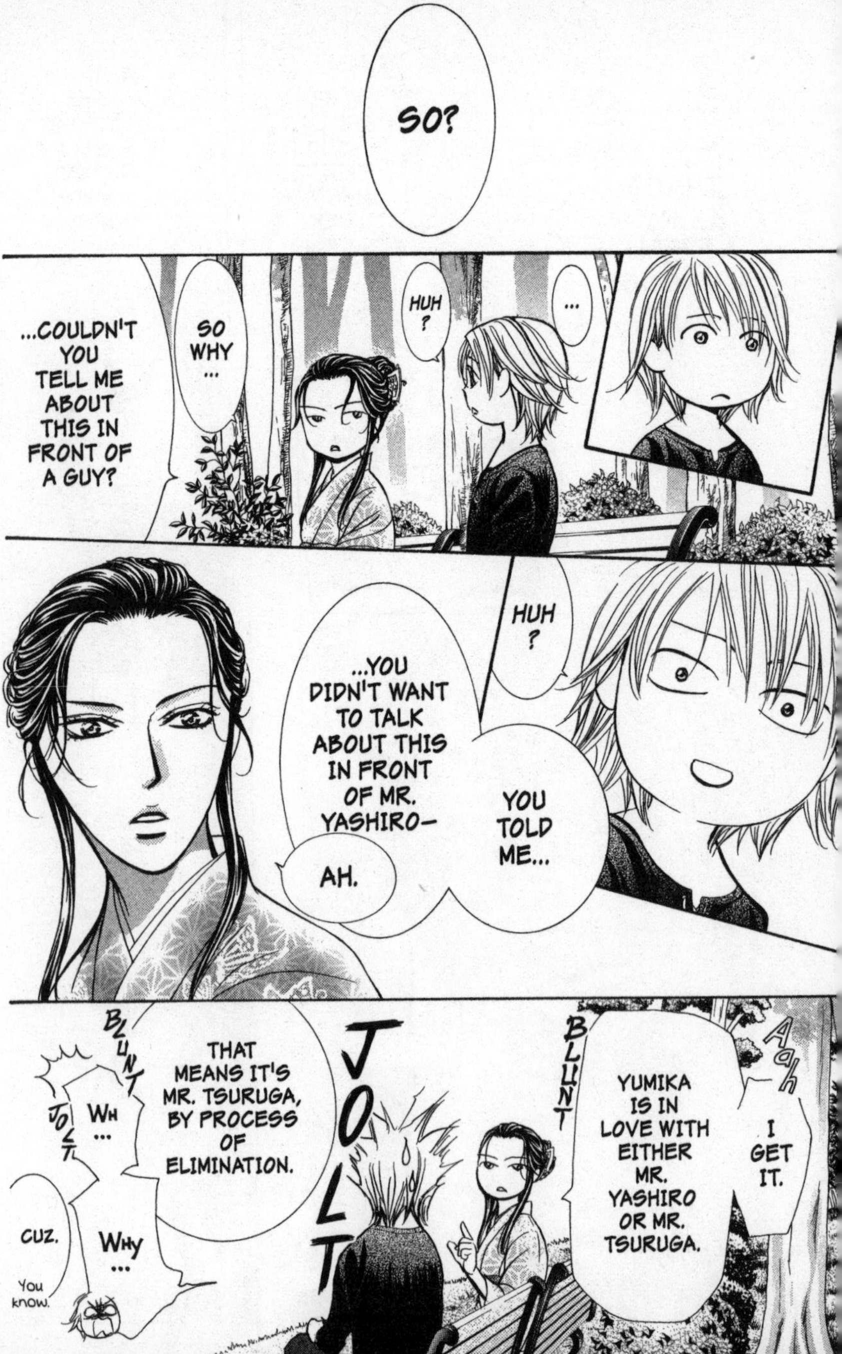
SO?
...
HUH?
SO WHY ...
...COULDN'T YOU TELL ME ABOUT THIS IN FRONT OF A GUY?
HUH?
YOU TOLD ME...
...YOU DIDN'T WANT TO TALK ABOUT THIS IN FRONT OF MR. YASHIRO—
AH.
Aah
I GET IT.
BLUNT
YUMIKA IS IN LOVE WITH EITHER MR. YASHIRO OR MR. TSURUGA.
JOLT
THAT MEANS IT'S MR. TSURUGA, BY PROCESS OF ELIMINATION.
BLUNT
Wh ...
JOLT
Why ...
CUZ.
You know.

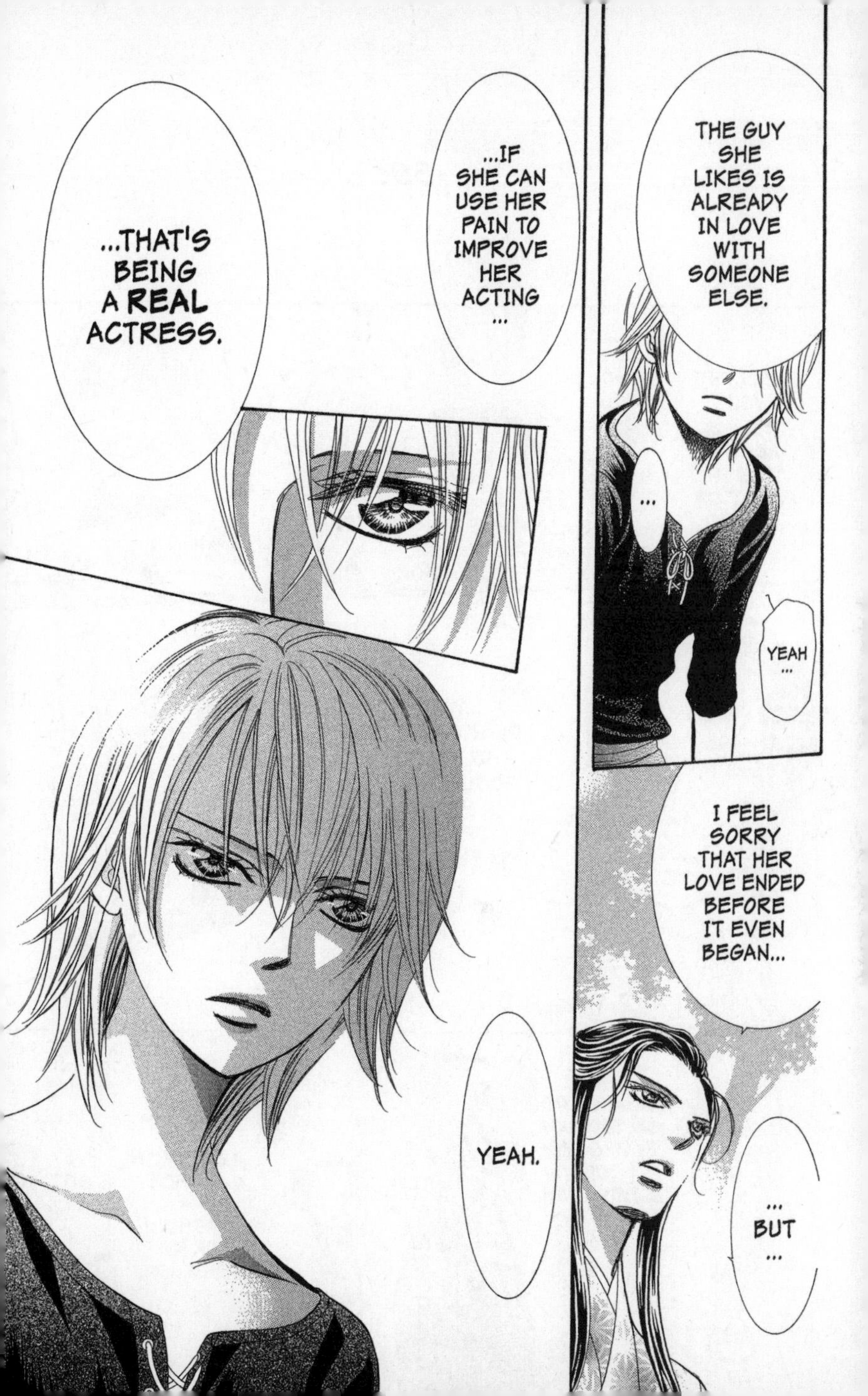
THE GUY SHE LIKES IS ALREADY IN LOVE WITH SOMEONE ELSE.
...
YEAH ...
...IF SHE CAN USE HER PAIN TO IMPROVE HER ACTING ...
...THAT'S BEING A REAL ACTRESS.
I FEEL SORRY THAT HER LOVE ENDED BEFORE IT EVEN BEGAN...
... BUT ...
YEAH.

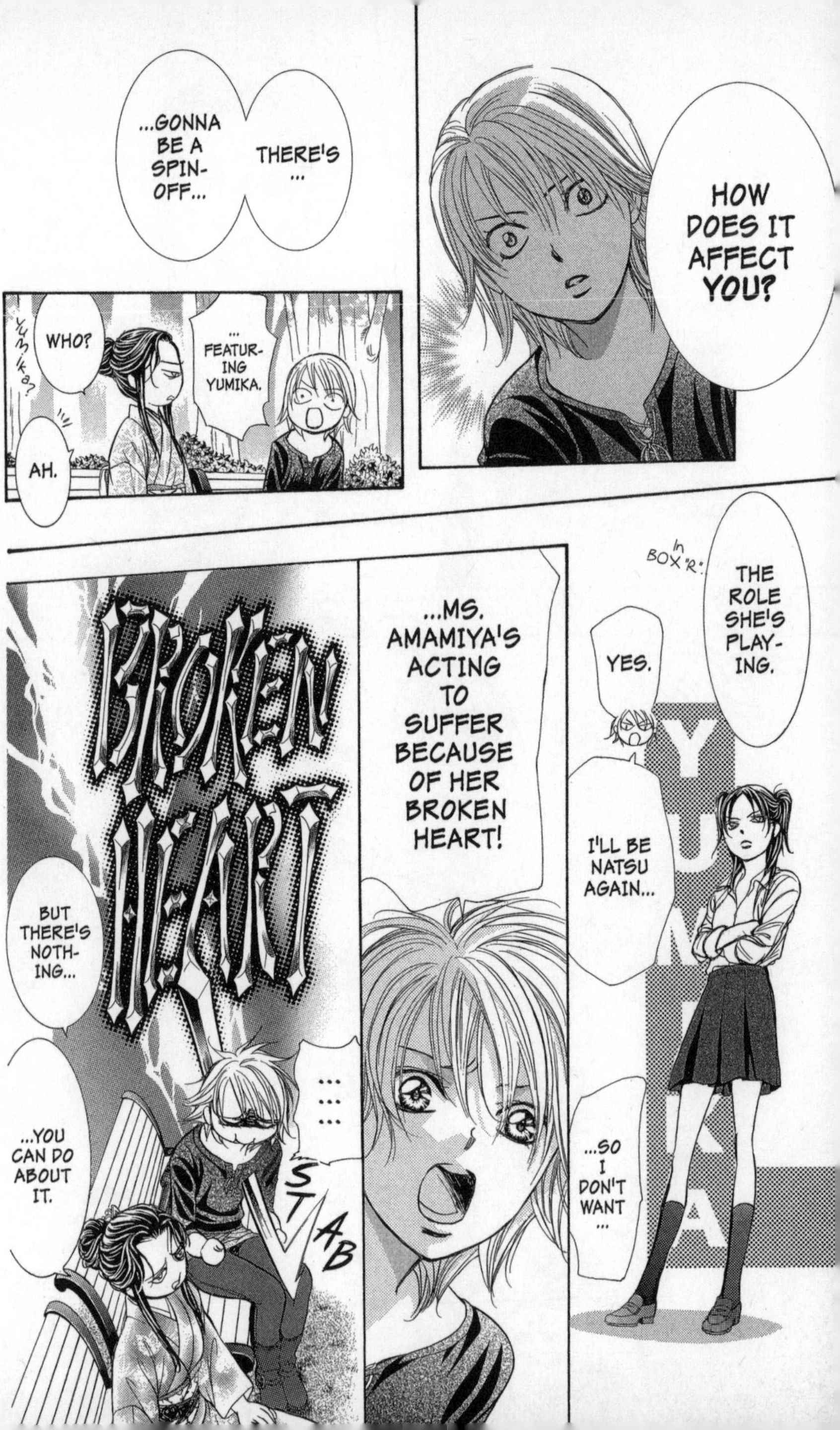
HOW DOES IT AFFECT YOU?
THERE'S ...
...GONNA BE A SPIN-OFF...
... FEATURING YUMIKA.
WHO?
Yumika?
AH.
In BOX "R".
THE ROLE SHE'S PLAYING.
YES.
YUMIKA
I'LL BE NATSU AGAIN...
...SO I DON'T WANT ...
...MS. AMAMIYA'S ACTING TO SUFFER BECAUSE OF HER BROKEN HEART!
BROKEN HEART
... ... ...
STAB
BUT THERE'S NOTHING...
...YOU CAN DO ABOUT IT.

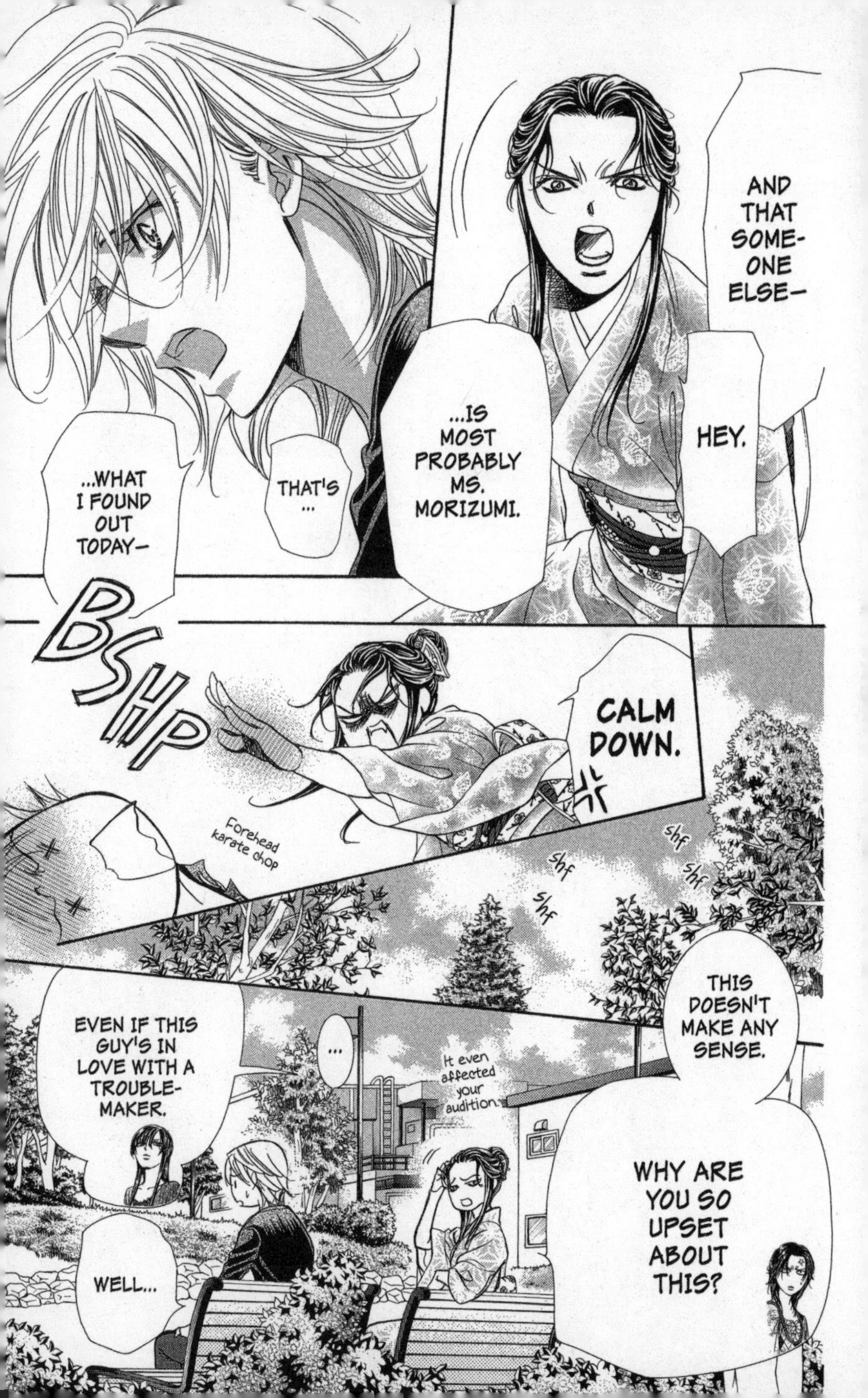
AND THAT SOME-ONE ELSE—
...IS MOST PROBABLY MS. MORIZUMI.
HEY.
THAT'S ...
...WHAT I FOUND OUT TODAY—
CALM DOWN.
BSHP
Forehead karate chop
shf
shf
shf
shf
THIS DOESN'T MAKE ANY SENSE.
WHY ARE YOU SO UPSET ABOUT THIS?
It even affected your audition.
...
EVEN IF THIS GUY'S IN LOVE WITH A TROUBLE-MAKER.
WELL...

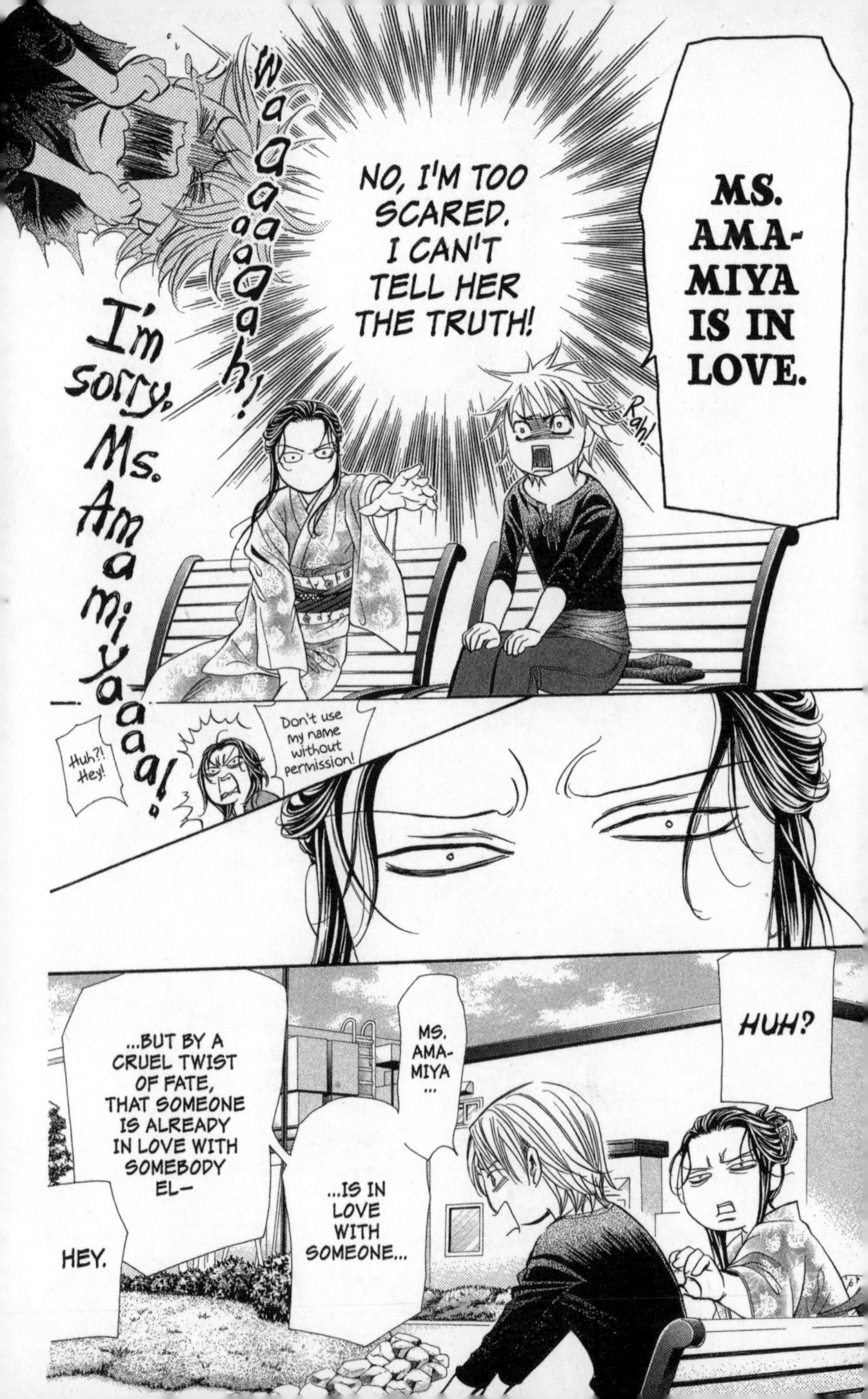
MS. AMA-MIYA IS IN LOVE.
Rah!
NO, I'M TOO SCARED. I CAN'T TELL HER THE TRUTH!
Waaaaaaaah!
I'm sorry. Ms. Amamiyaaaa!
Don't use my name without permission!
Huh?! Hey!
HUH?
MS. AMA-MIYA...
...IS IN LOVE WITH SOMEONE...
...BUT BY A CRUEL TWIST OF FATE, THAT SOMEONE IS ALREADY IN LOVE WITH SOMEBODY EL—
HEY.

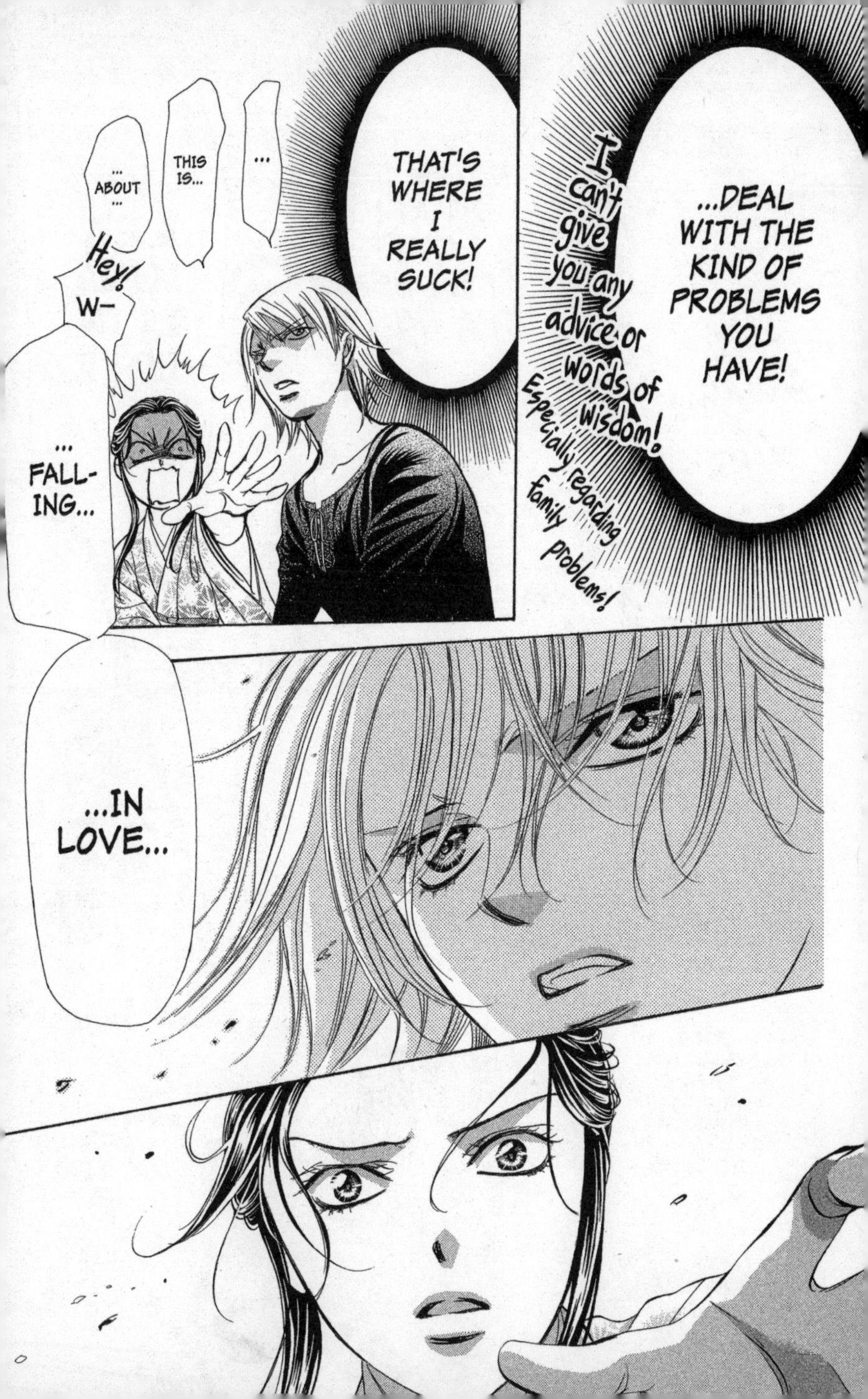
...DEAL WITH THE KIND OF PROBLEMS YOU HAVE!
I can't give you any advice or words of wisdom!
Especially regarding family problems!
THAT'S WHERE I REALLY SUCK!
...
THIS IS...
... ABOUT ...
Hey! W-
... FALLING...
...IN LOVE...

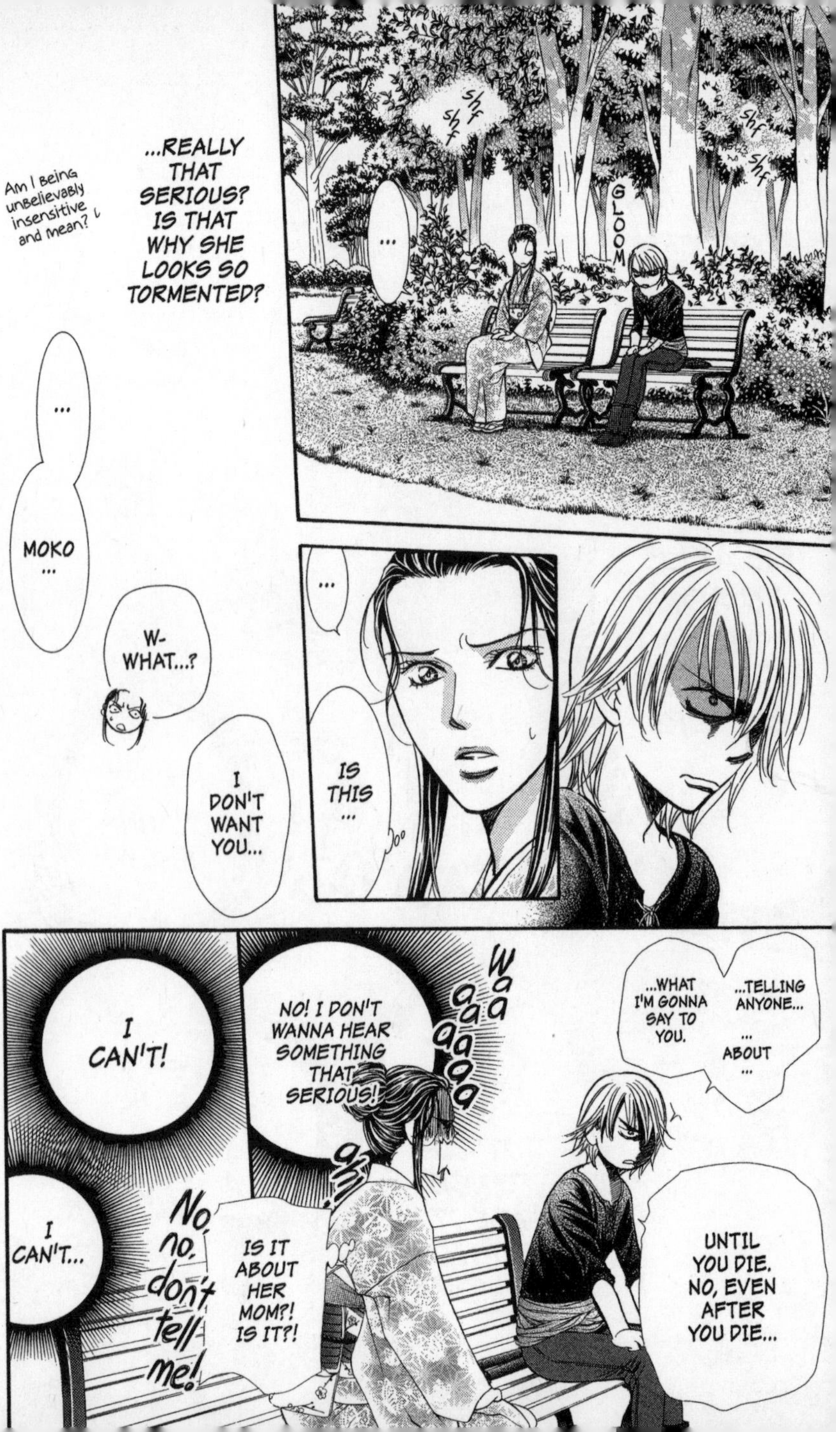
shf shf shf
shf shf
GLOOM
...
...REALLY THAT SERIOUS? IS THAT WHY SHE LOOKS SO TORMENTED?
Am I being unbelievably insensitive and mean?
...
MOKO ...
W-WHAT...?
...
IS THIS ...
I DON'T WANT YOU...
...TELLING ANYONE... ... ABOUT ...
...WHAT I'M GONNA SAY TO YOU.
UNTIL YOU DIE. NO, EVEN AFTER YOU DIE...
Waaaaaaaaaa
NO! I DON'T WANNA HEAR SOMETHING THAT SERIOUS!
IS IT ABOUT HER MOM?! IS IT?!
No, no, don't tell me!
I CAN'T!
I CAN'T...

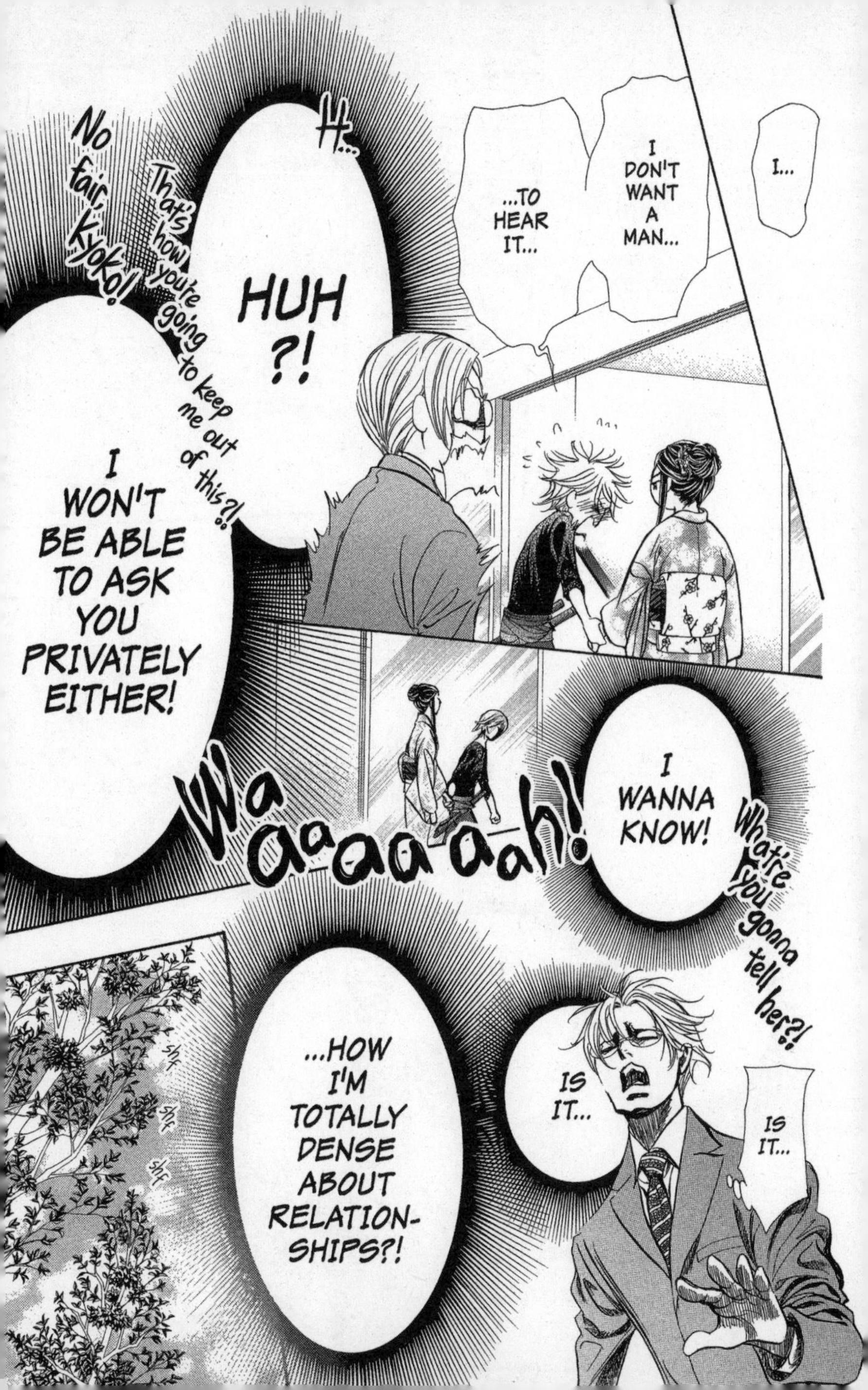
I...
I DON'T WANT A MAN...
...TO HEAR IT...
H...
HUH?!
That's how you're going to keep me out of this?!
No fair, Kyoko!
I WON'T BE ABLE TO ASK YOU PRIVATELY EITHER!
I WANNA KNOW!
What're you gonna tell her?!
Waaaaaah!
IS IT...
IS IT...
...HOW I'M TOTALLY DENSE ABOUT RELATION-SHIPS?!
shf
shf
shf

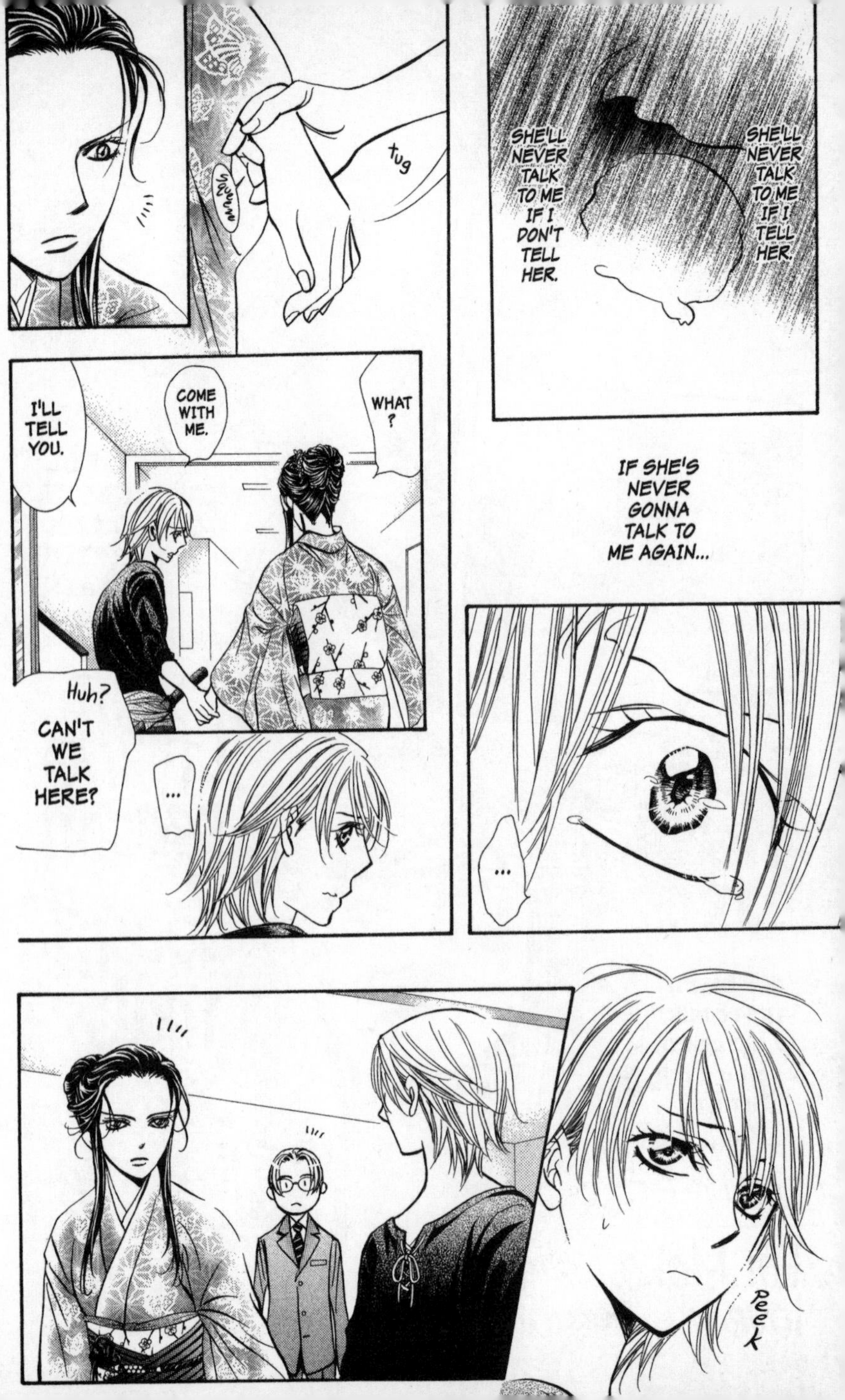

SHE'LL NEVER TALK TO ME IF I TELL HER.
SHE'LL NEVER TALK TO ME IF I DON'T TELL HER.
tug
IF SHE'S NEVER GONNA TALK TO ME AGAIN...
WHAT?
COME WITH ME.
I'LL TELL YOU.
...
Huh? CAN'T WE TALK HERE?
...
Peek

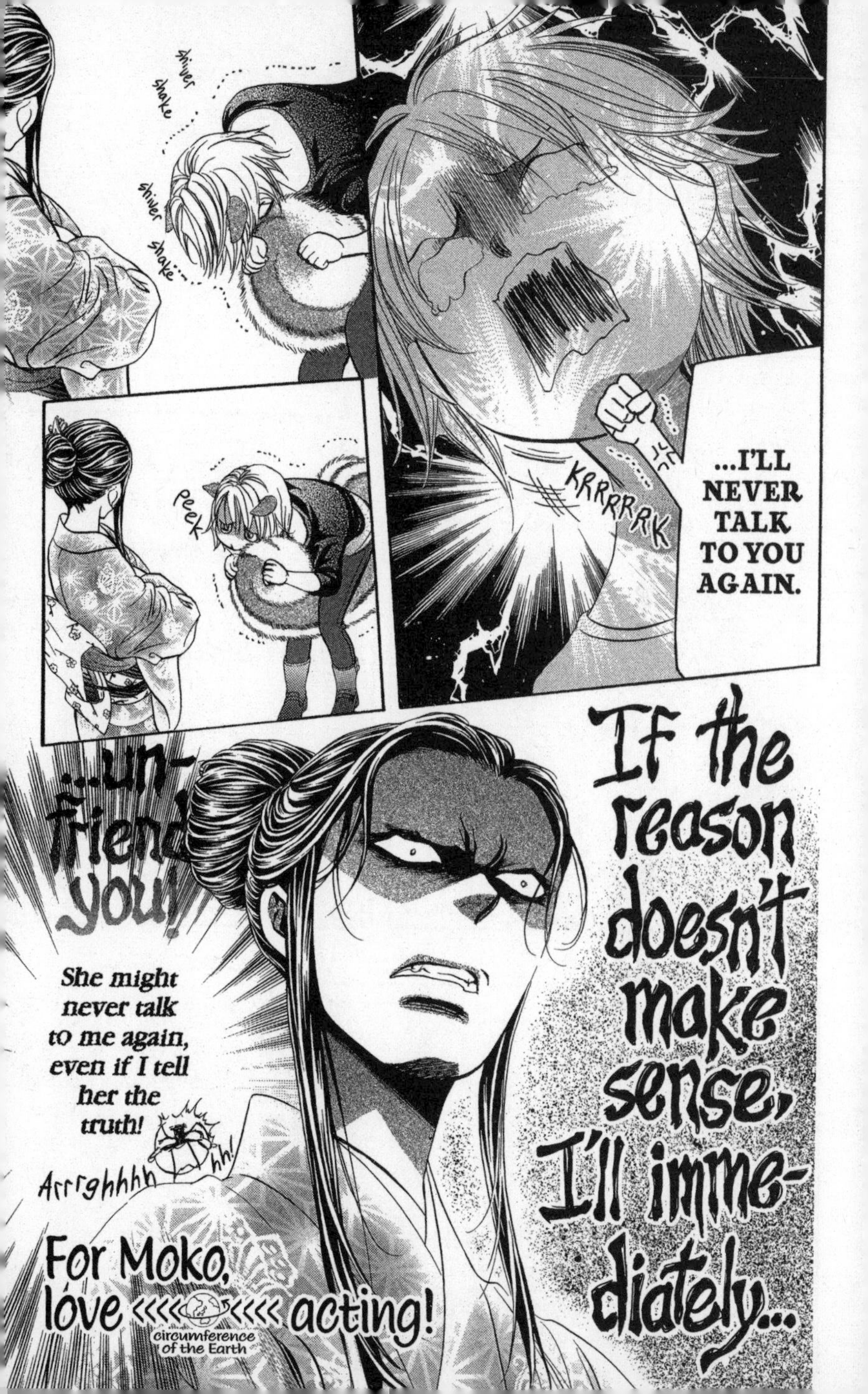
KRRRRRK
...I'LL NEVER TALK TO YOU AGAIN.
shiver shake
shiver shake
peek
If the reason doesn't make sense, I'll imme-diately...
...un-friend you!
She might never talk to me again, even if I tell her the truth!
Arrrghhhhhh!
For Moko, love <<<<< <<<<< acting!
circumference of the Earth

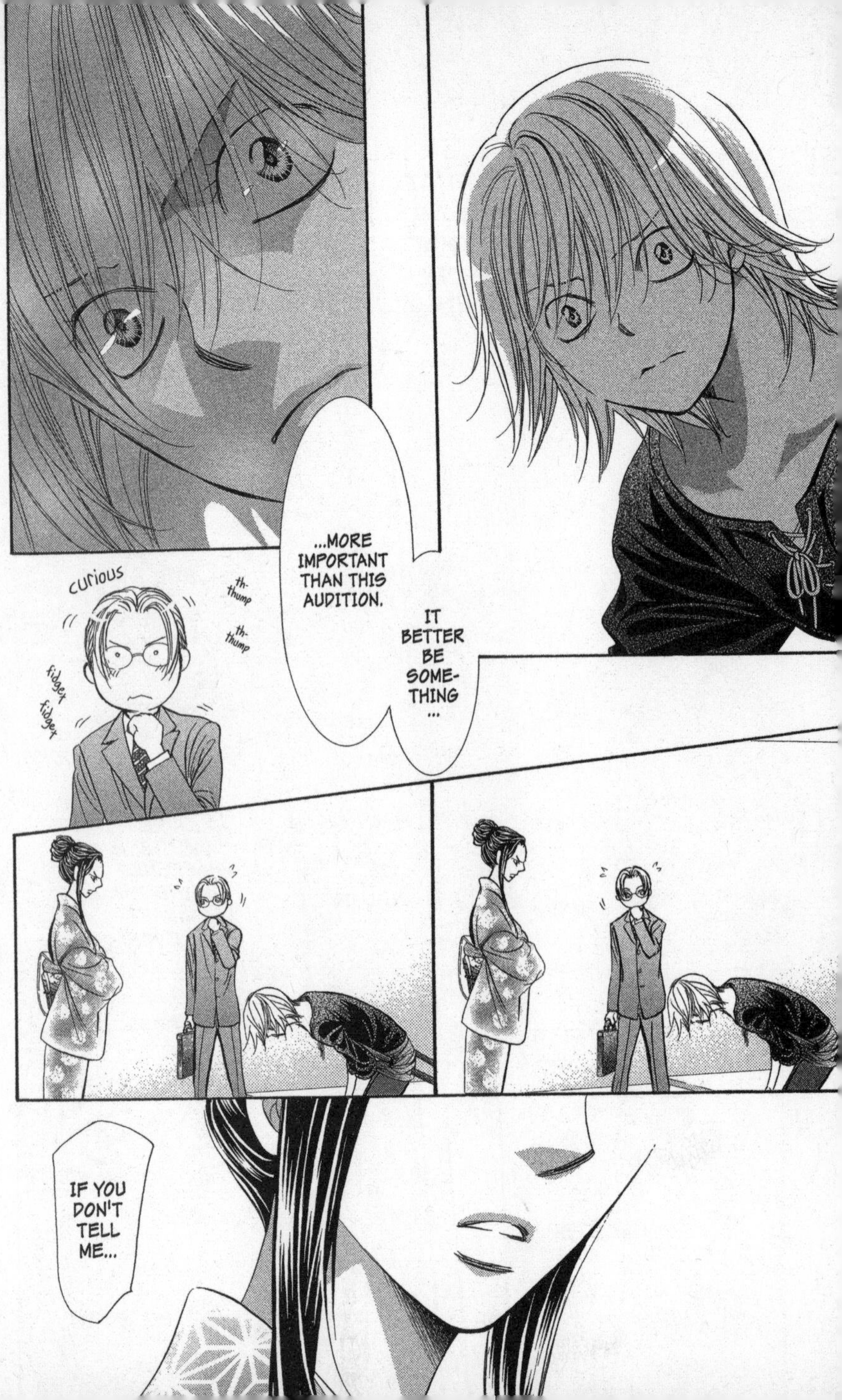
...MORE IMPORTANT THAN THIS AUDITION.
IT BETTER BE SOME-THING...
curious
th-thump
th-thump
fidget fidget
IF YOU DON'T TELL ME...

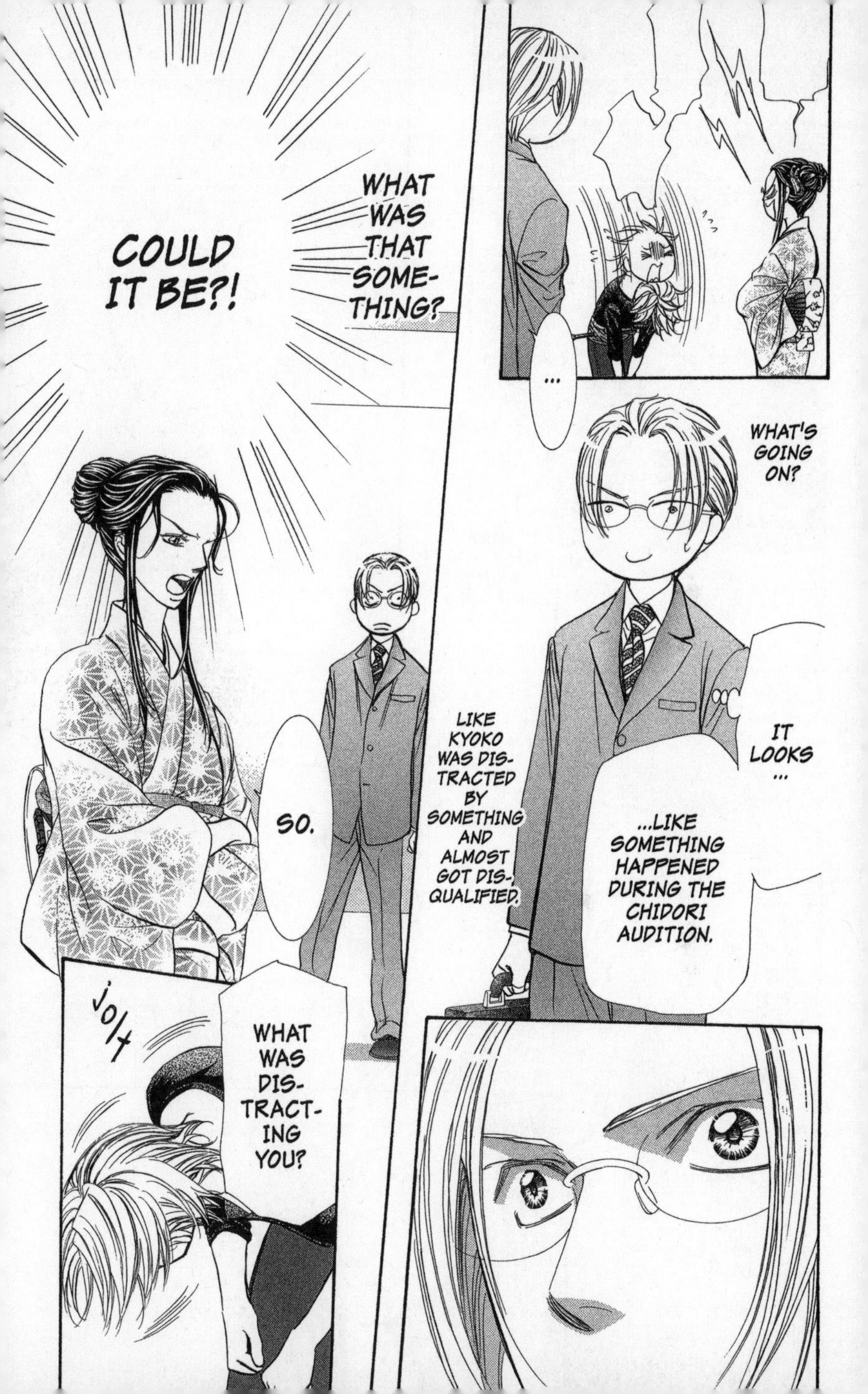
...
WHAT'S GOING ON?
IT LOOKS...
...LIKE SOMETHING HAPPENED DURING THE CHIDORI AUDITION.
LIKE KYOKO WAS DISTRACTED BY SOMETHING AND ALMOST GOT DISQUALIFIED.
WHAT WAS THAT SOMETHING?
COULD IT BE?!
SO.
jolt
WHAT WAS DISTRACTING YOU?

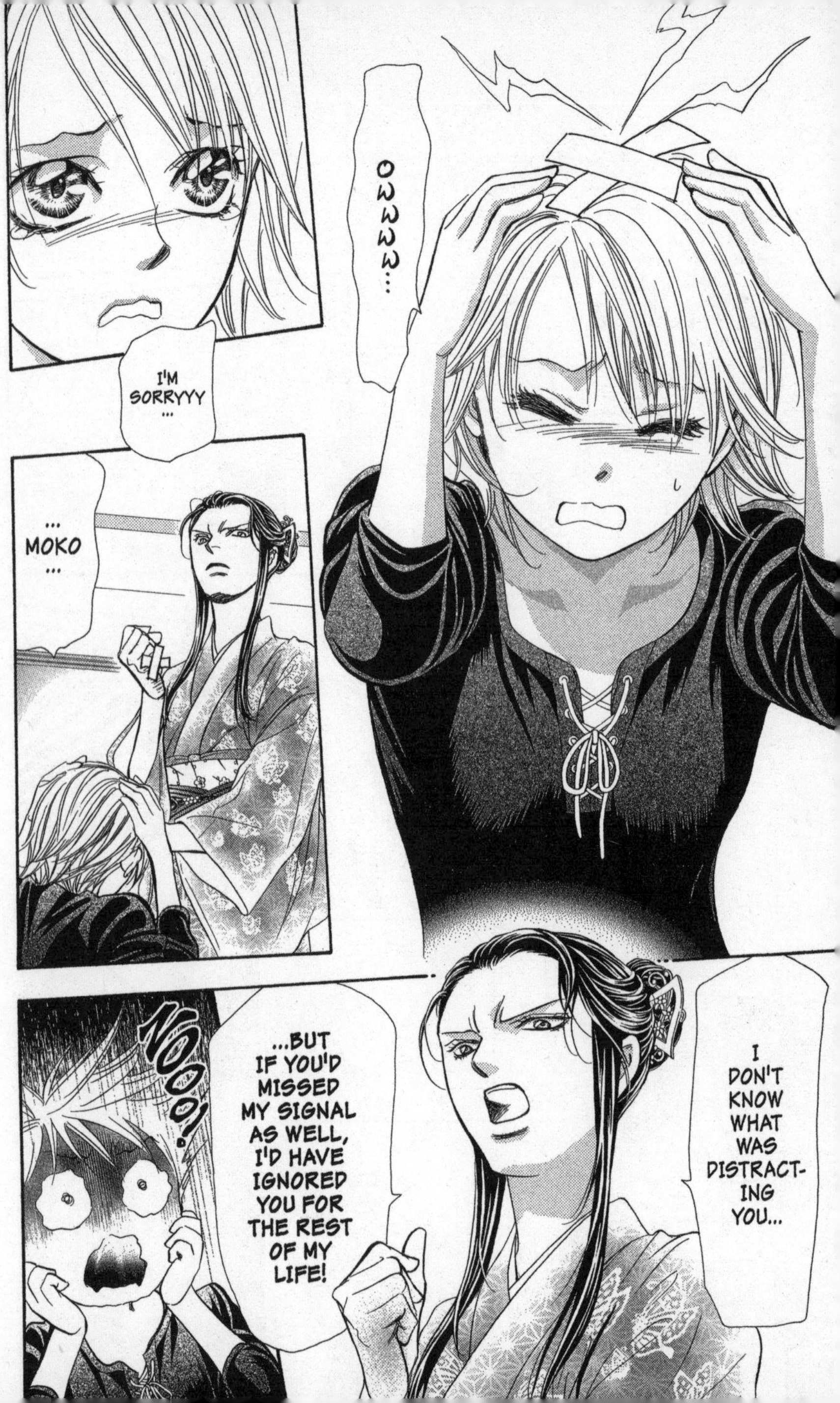
OWWWW...
I'M SORRYYY...
...MOKO...
I DON'T KNOW WHAT WAS DISTRACTING YOU...
...BUT IF YOU'D MISSED MY SIGNAL AS WELL, I'D HAVE IGNORED YOU FOR THE REST OF MY LIFE!
NOOO!

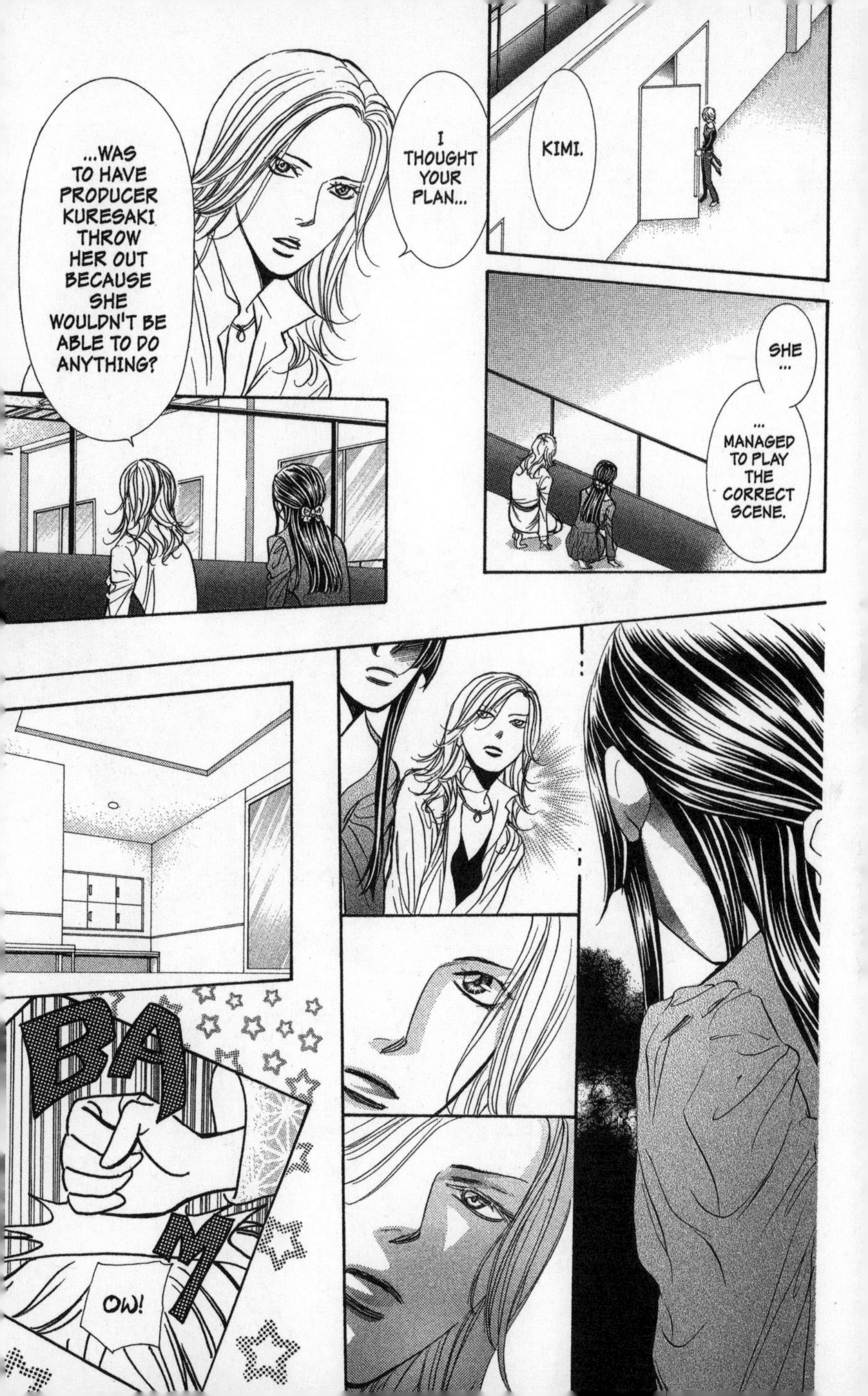
KIMI.
I THOUGHT YOUR PLAN...
...WAS TO HAVE PRODUCER KURESAKI THROW HER OUT BECAUSE SHE WOULDN'T BE ABLE TO DO ANYTHING?
SHE ...
... MANAGED TO PLAY THE CORRECT SCENE.
BAM
OW!

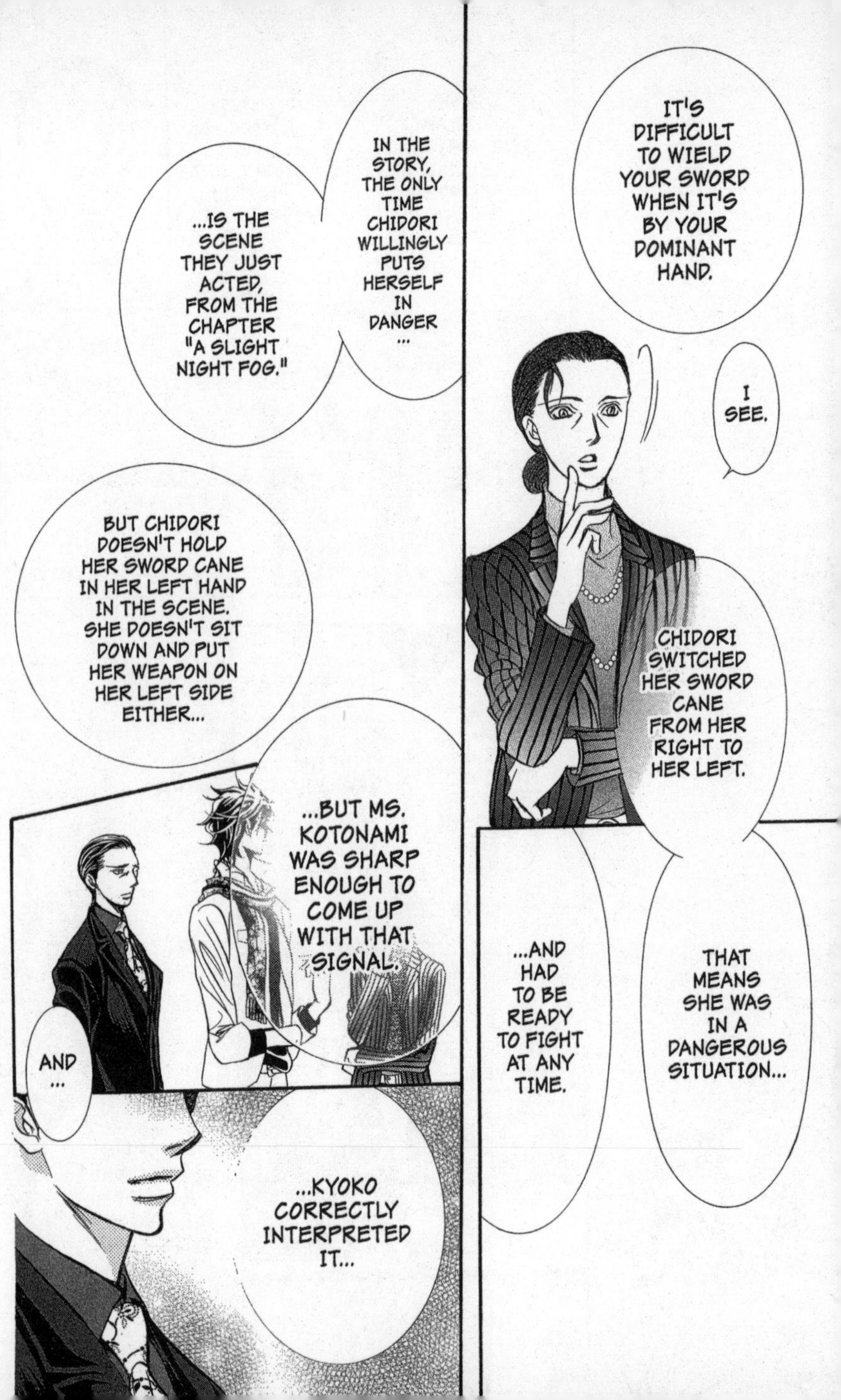
IT'S DIFFICULT TO WIELD YOUR SWORD WHEN IT'S BY YOUR DOMINANT HAND.
I SEE.
CHIDORI SWITCHED HER SWORD CANE FROM HER RIGHT TO HER LEFT.
THAT MEANS SHE WAS IN A DANGEROUS SITUATION...
...AND HAD TO BE READY TO FIGHT AT ANY TIME.
IN THE STORY, THE ONLY TIME CHIDORI WILLINGLY PUTS HERSELF IN DANGER...
...IS THE SCENE THEY JUST ACTED, FROM THE CHAPTER "A SLIGHT NIGHT FOG."
BUT CHIDORI DOESN'T HOLD HER SWORD CANE IN HER LEFT HAND IN THE SCENE. SHE DOESN'T SIT DOWN AND PUT HER WEAPON ON HER LEFT SIDE EITHER...
...BUT MS. KOTONAMI WAS SHARP ENOUGH TO COME UP WITH THAT SIGNAL.
AND...
...KYOKO CORRECTLY INTERPRETED IT...

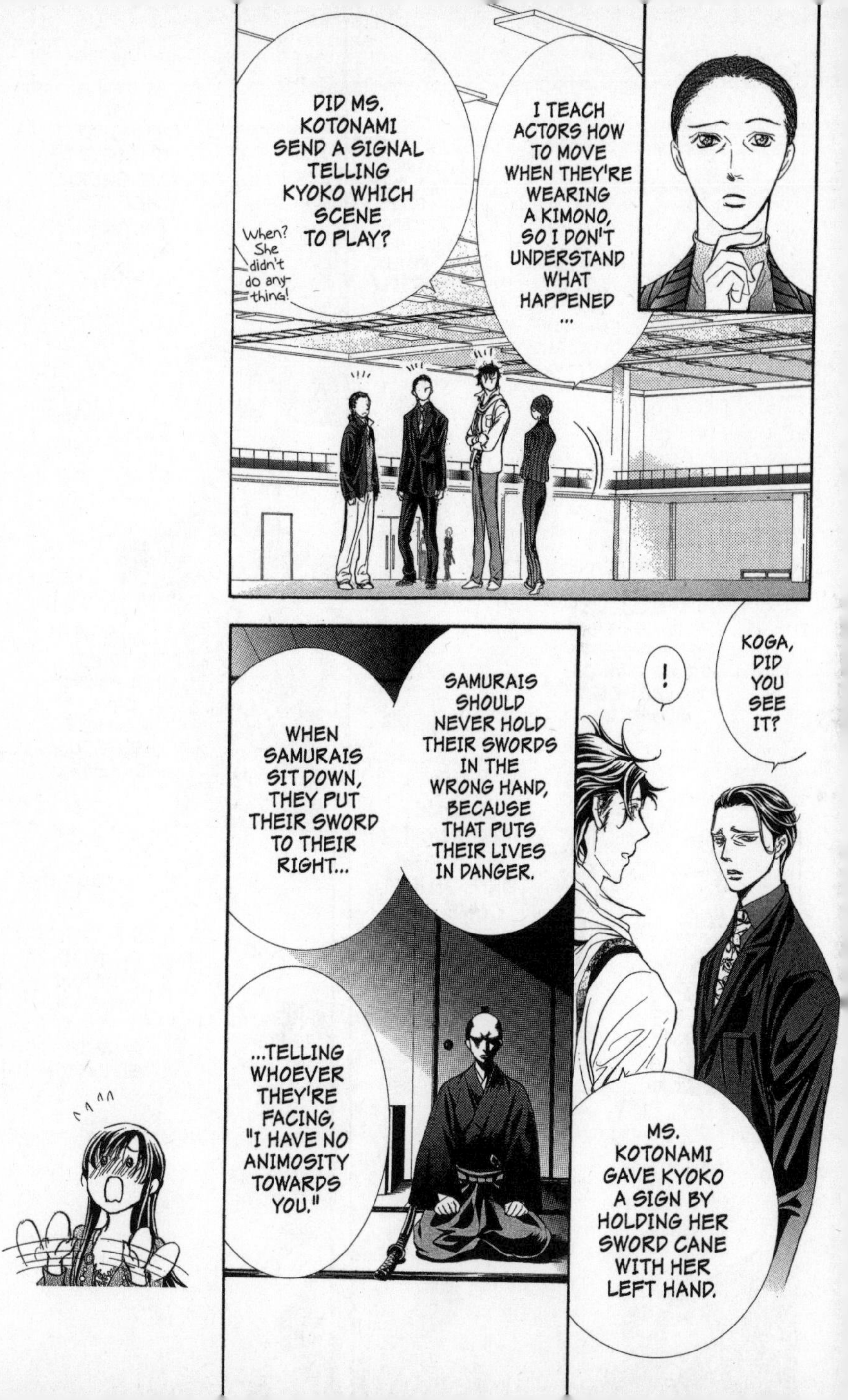
I TEACH ACTORS HOW TO MOVE WHEN THEY'RE WEARING A KIMONO, SO I DON'T UNDERSTAND WHAT HAPPENED ...
DID MS. KOTONAMI SEND A SIGNAL TELLING KYOKO WHICH SCENE TO PLAY?
When? She didn't do anything!
KOGA, DID YOU SEE IT?
!
MS. KOTONAMI GAVE KYOKO A SIGN BY HOLDING HER SWORD CANE WITH HER LEFT HAND.
SAMURAIS SHOULD NEVER HOLD THEIR SWORDS IN THE WRONG HAND, BECAUSE THAT PUTS THEIR LIVES IN DANGER.
WHEN SAMURAIS SIT DOWN, THEY PUT THEIR SWORD TO THEIR RIGHT...
...TELLING WHOEVER THEY'RE FACING, "I HAVE NO ANIMOSITY TOWARDS YOU."

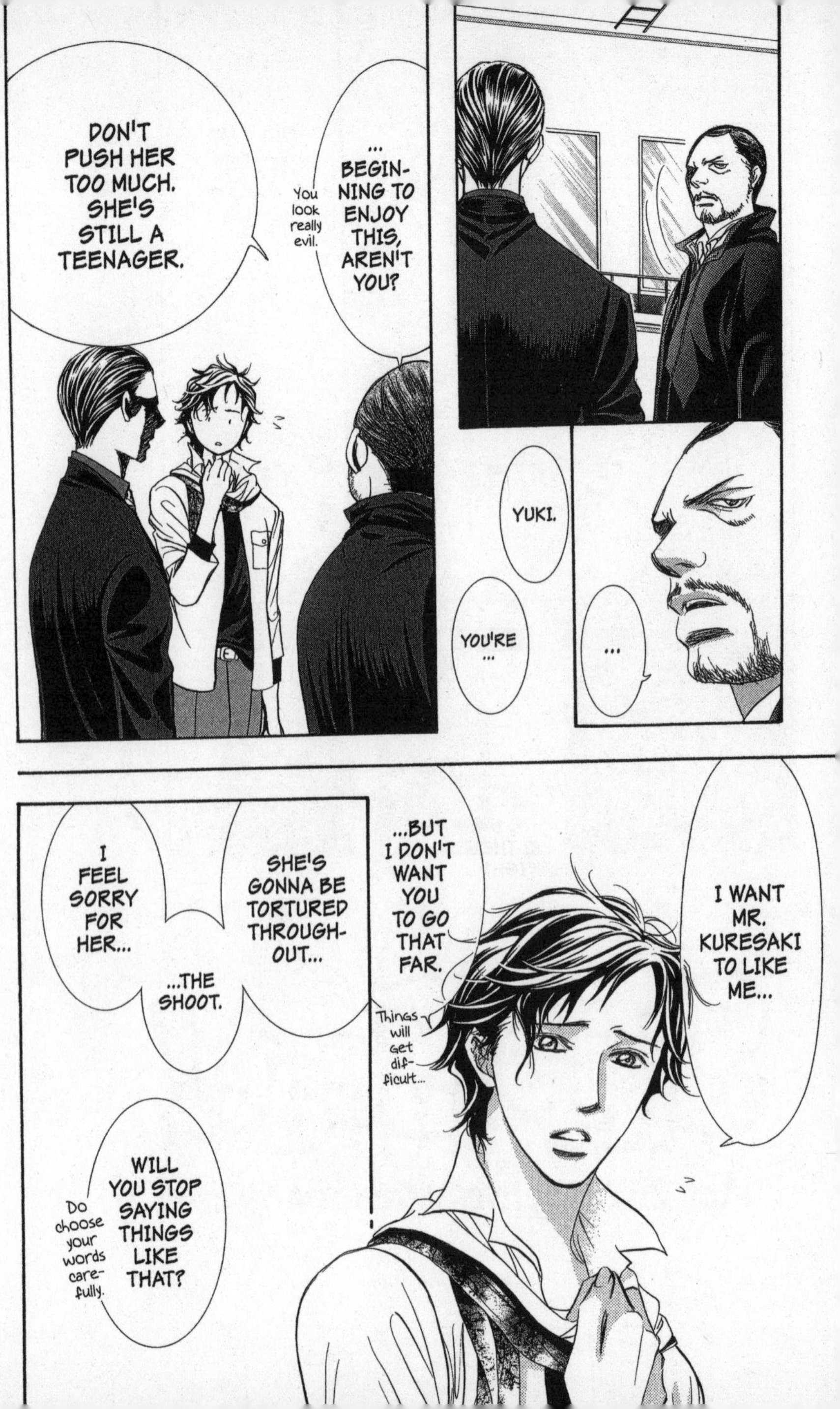
YUKI.
YOU'RE ...
...
... BEGINNING TO ENJOY THIS, AREN'T YOU?
You look really evil.
DON'T PUSH HER TOO MUCH. SHE'S STILL A TEENAGER.
I WANT MR. KURESAKI TO LIKE ME...
...BUT I DON'T WANT YOU TO GO THAT FAR.
Things will get difficult...
SHE'S GONNA BE TORTURED THROUGHOUT...
I FEEL SORRY FOR HER...
...THE SHOOT.
WILL YOU STOP SAYING THINGS LIKE THAT?
Do choose your words carefully.

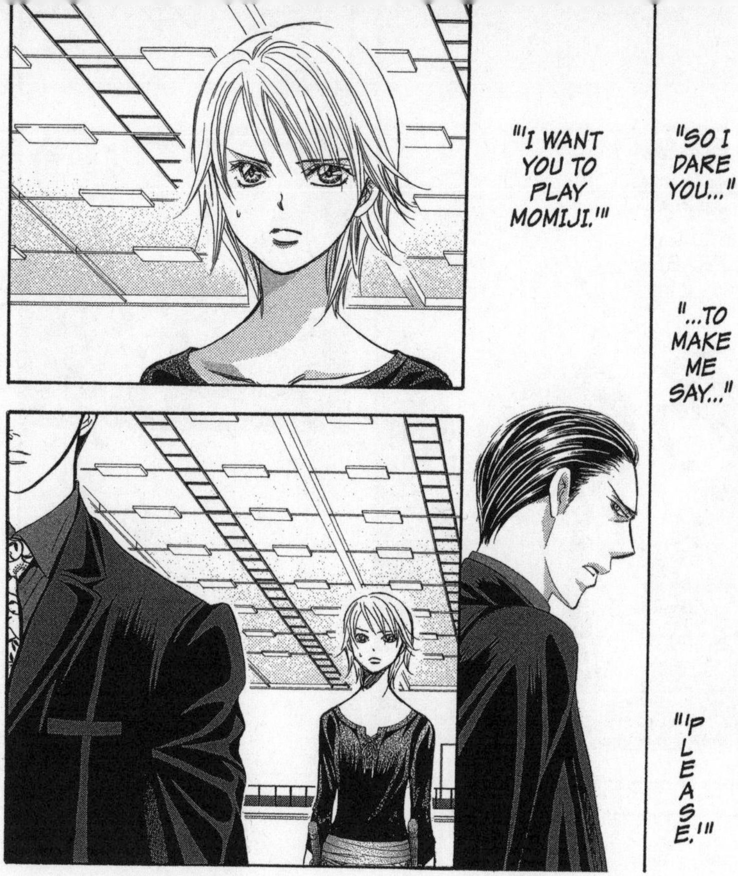
"SO I DARE YOU..."
"...TO MAKE ME SAY..."
"PLEASE."
"'I WANT YOU TO PLAY MOMIJI.'"

# Skip·Beat!

## Act 252: Flying Without Wires

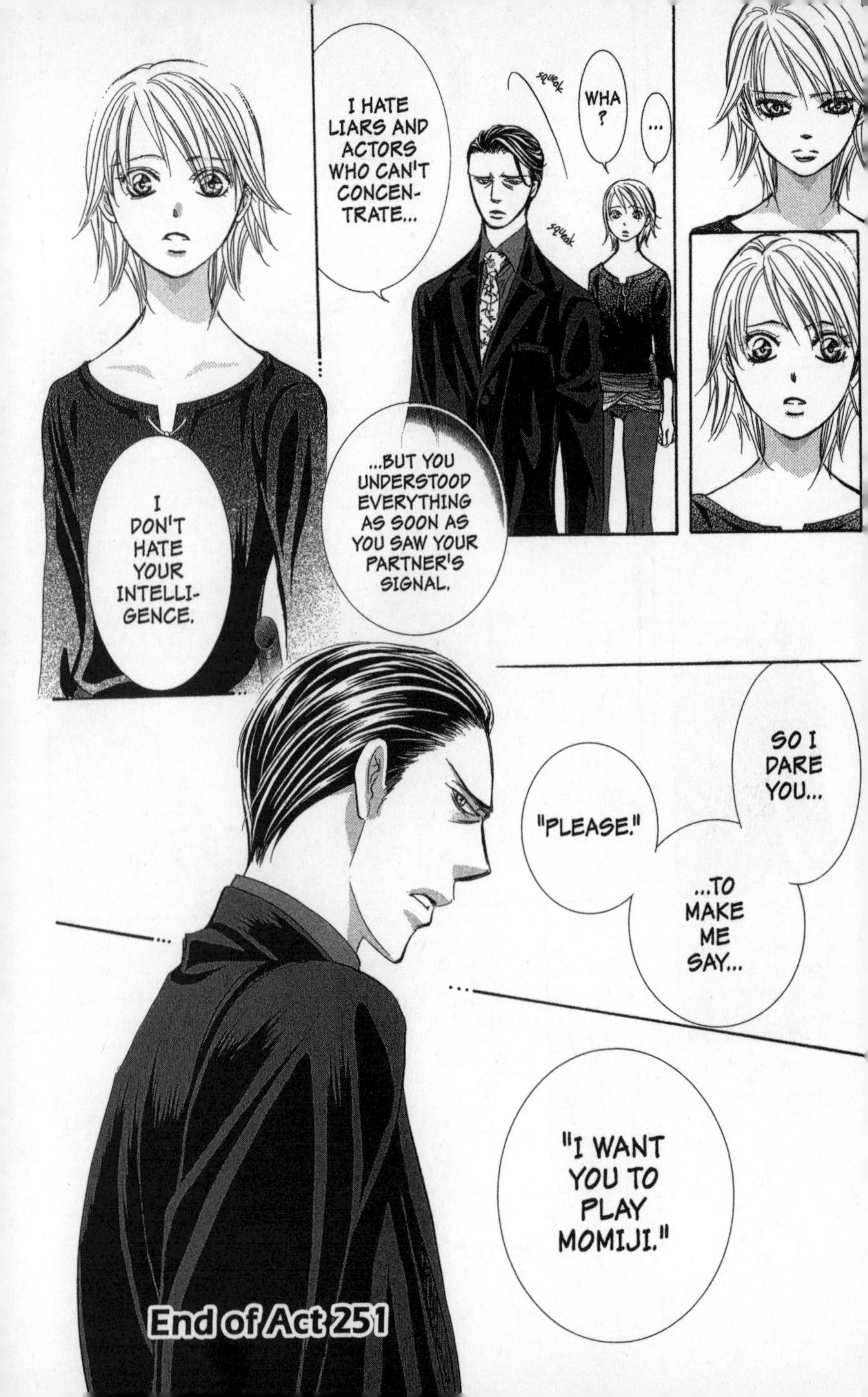

...
WHA?
squeak
I HATE LIARS AND ACTORS WHO CAN'T CONCENTRATE...
squeak
...BUT YOU UNDERSTOOD EVERYTHING AS SOON AS YOU SAW YOUR PARTNER'S SIGNAL.
I DON'T HATE YOUR INTELLIGENCE.
SO I DARE YOU...
...TO MAKE ME SAY...
"PLEASE."
"I WANT YOU TO PLAY MOMIJI."
End of Act 251

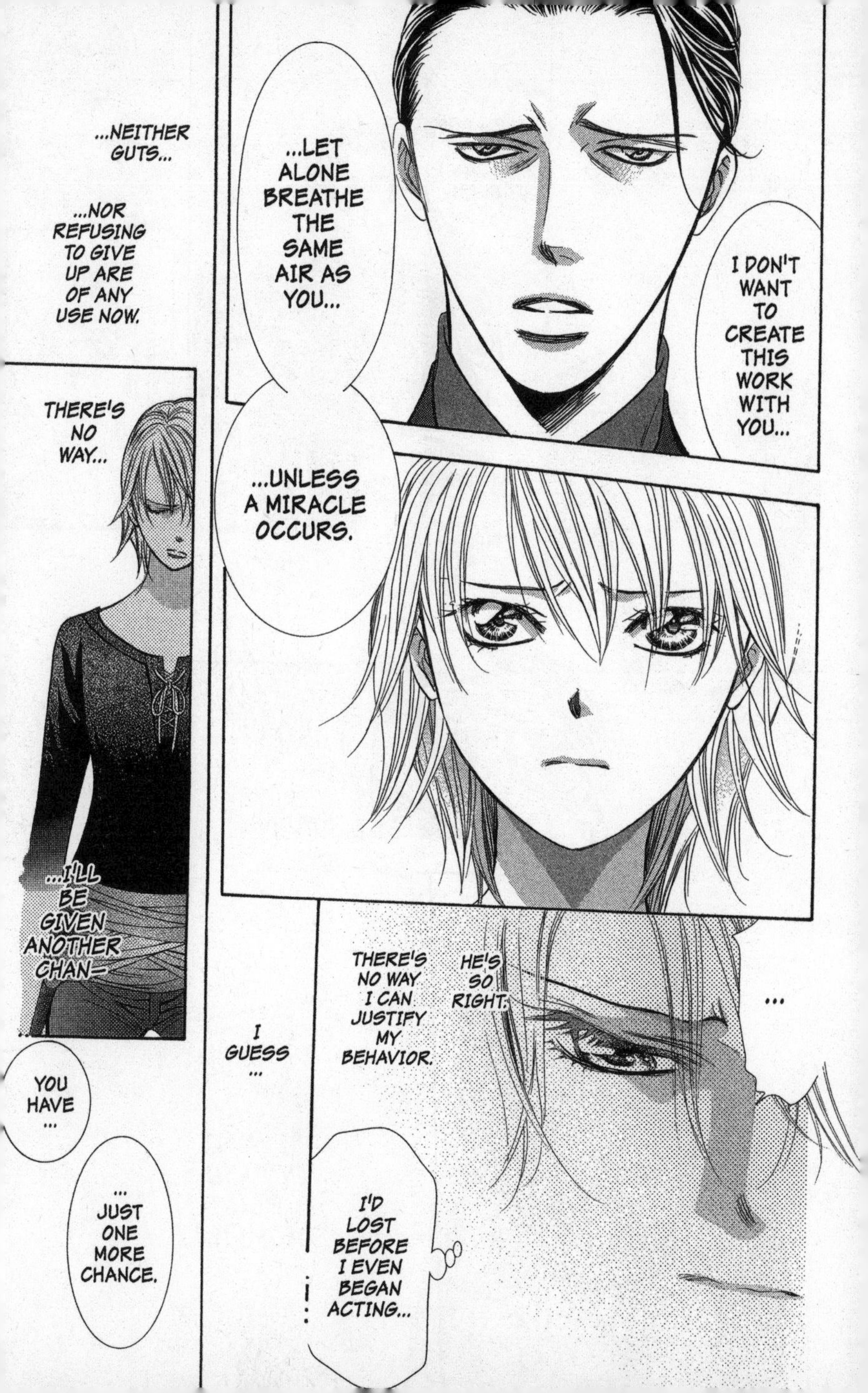
I DON'T WANT TO CREATE THIS WORK WITH YOU...
...LET ALONE BREATHE THE SAME AIR AS YOU...
...UNLESS A MIRACLE OCCURS.
...
HE'S SO RIGHT.
THERE'S NO WAY I CAN JUSTIFY MY BEHAVIOR.
I GUESS...
I'D LOST BEFORE I EVEN BEGAN ACTING...
...NEITHER GUTS...
...NOR REFUSING TO GIVE UP ARE OF ANY USE NOW.
THERE'S NO WAY...
...I'LL BE GIVEN ANOTHER CHAN—
YOU HAVE...
...JUST ONE MORE CHANCE.

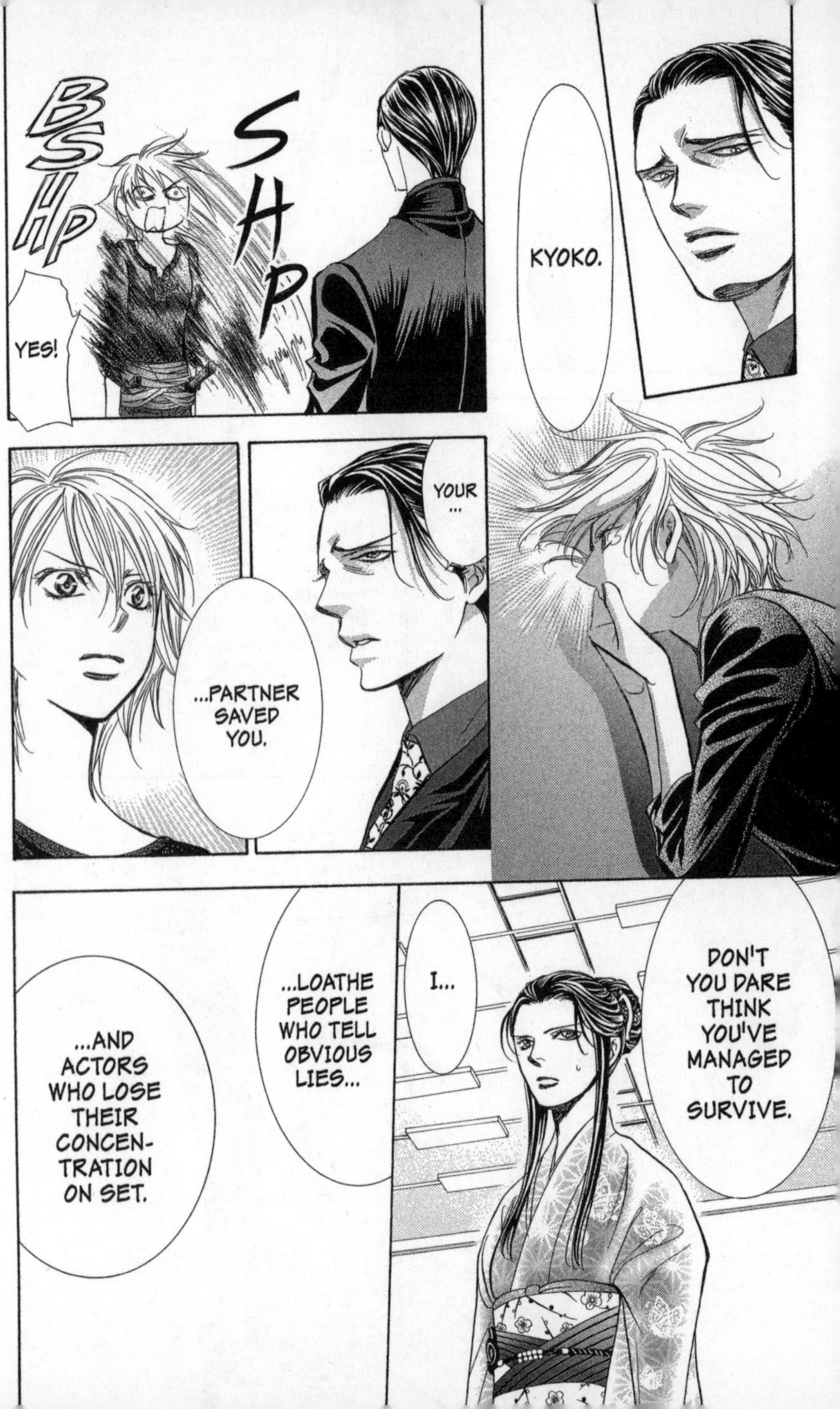
KYOKO.
SHP
BSHP
YES!
YOUR ...
...PARTNER SAVED YOU.
DON'T YOU DARE THINK YOU'VE MANAGED TO SURVIVE.
I...
...LOATHE PEOPLE WHO TELL OBVIOUS LIES...
...AND ACTORS WHO LOSE THEIR CONCEN-TRATION ON SET.

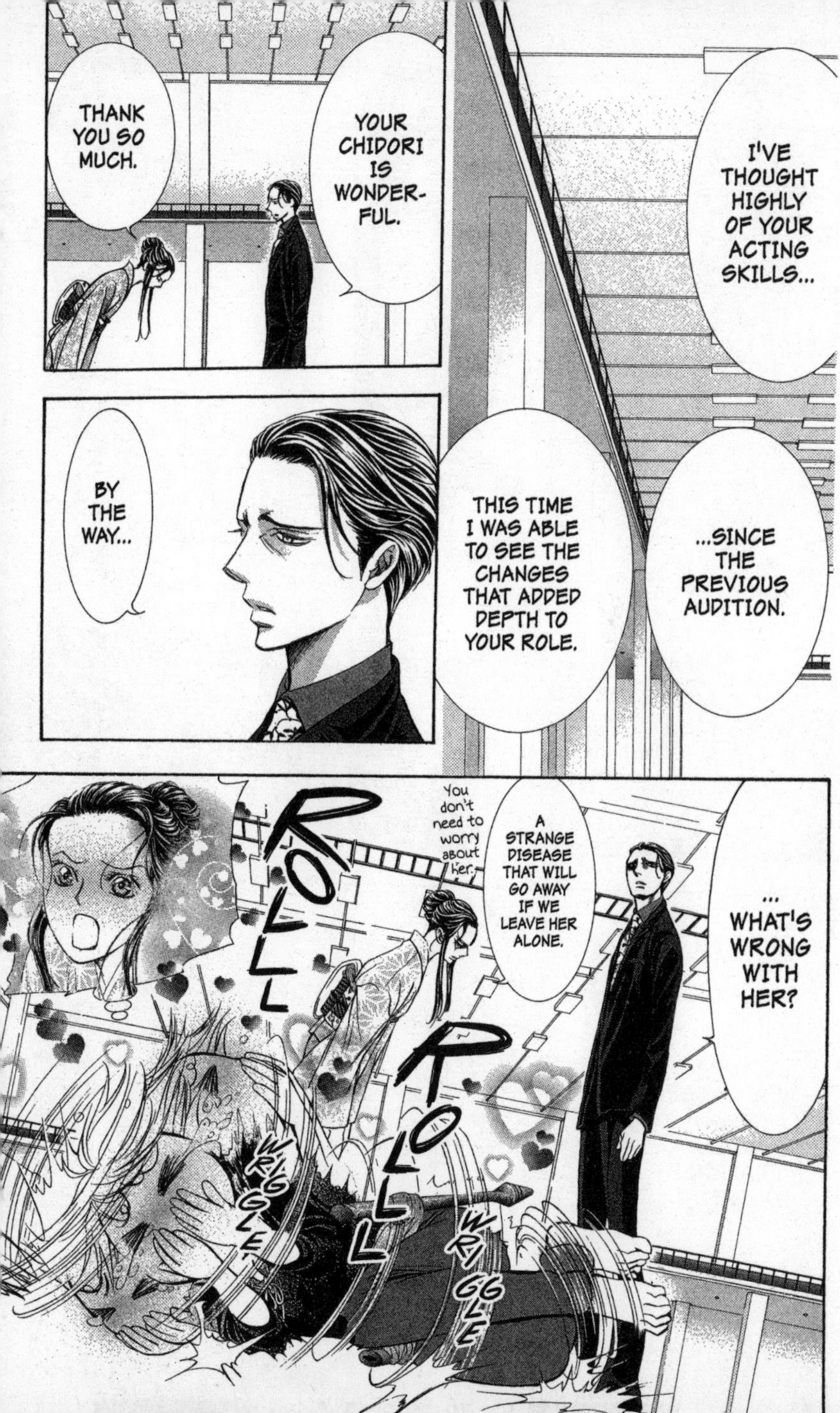
I'VE THOUGHT HIGHLY OF YOUR ACTING SKILLS...
...SINCE THE PREVIOUS AUDITION.
THIS TIME I WAS ABLE TO SEE THE CHANGES THAT ADDED DEPTH TO YOUR ROLE.
YOUR CHIDORI IS WONDERFUL.
THANK YOU SO MUCH.
BY THE WAY...
...WHAT'S WRONG WITH HER?
A STRANGE DISEASE THAT WILL GO AWAY IF WE LEAVE HER ALONE.
You don't need to worry about her.
ROLL
ROLL
WRIGGLE
WRIGGLE

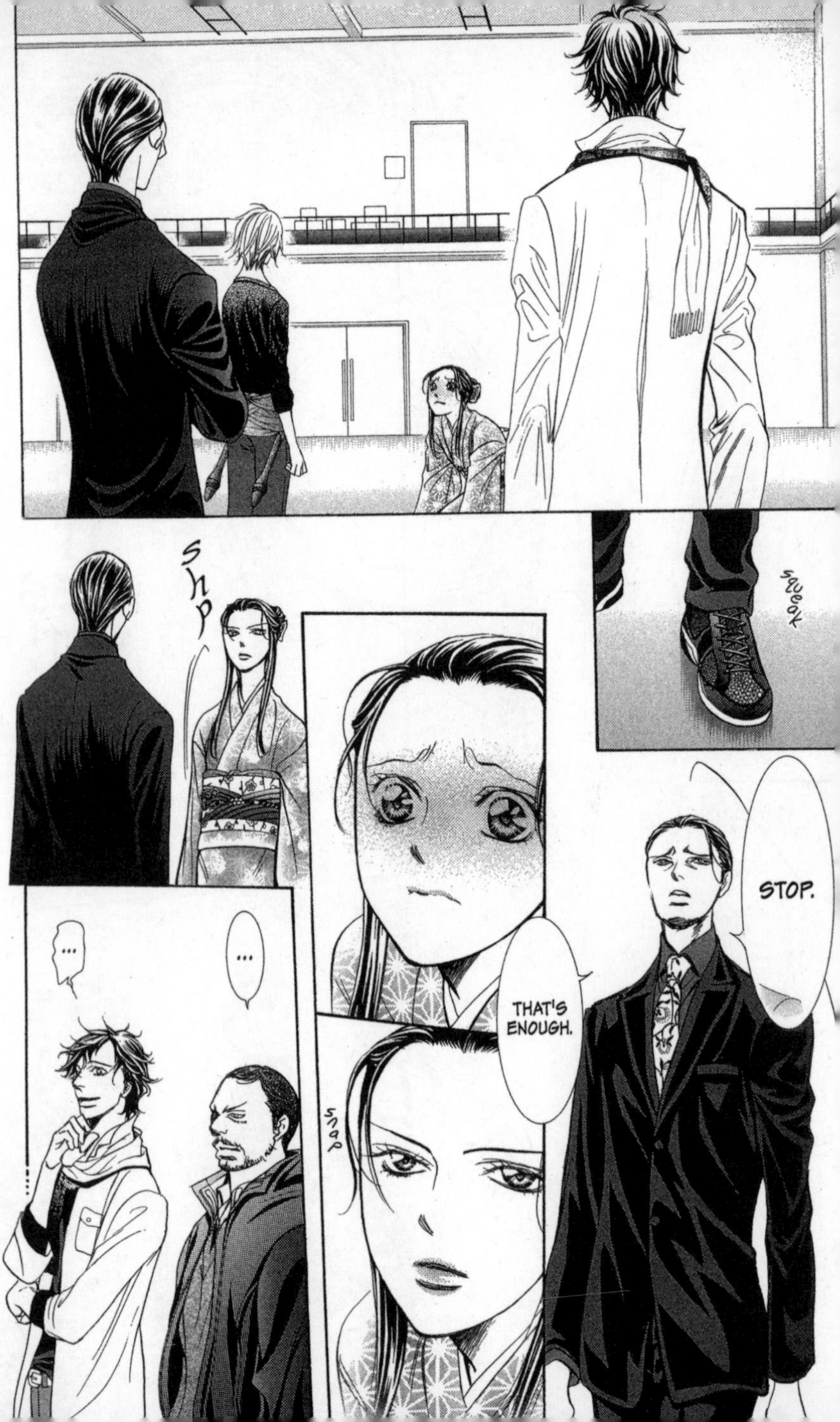
squeak
shp
STOP.
THAT'S ENOUGH.
snap
...
...

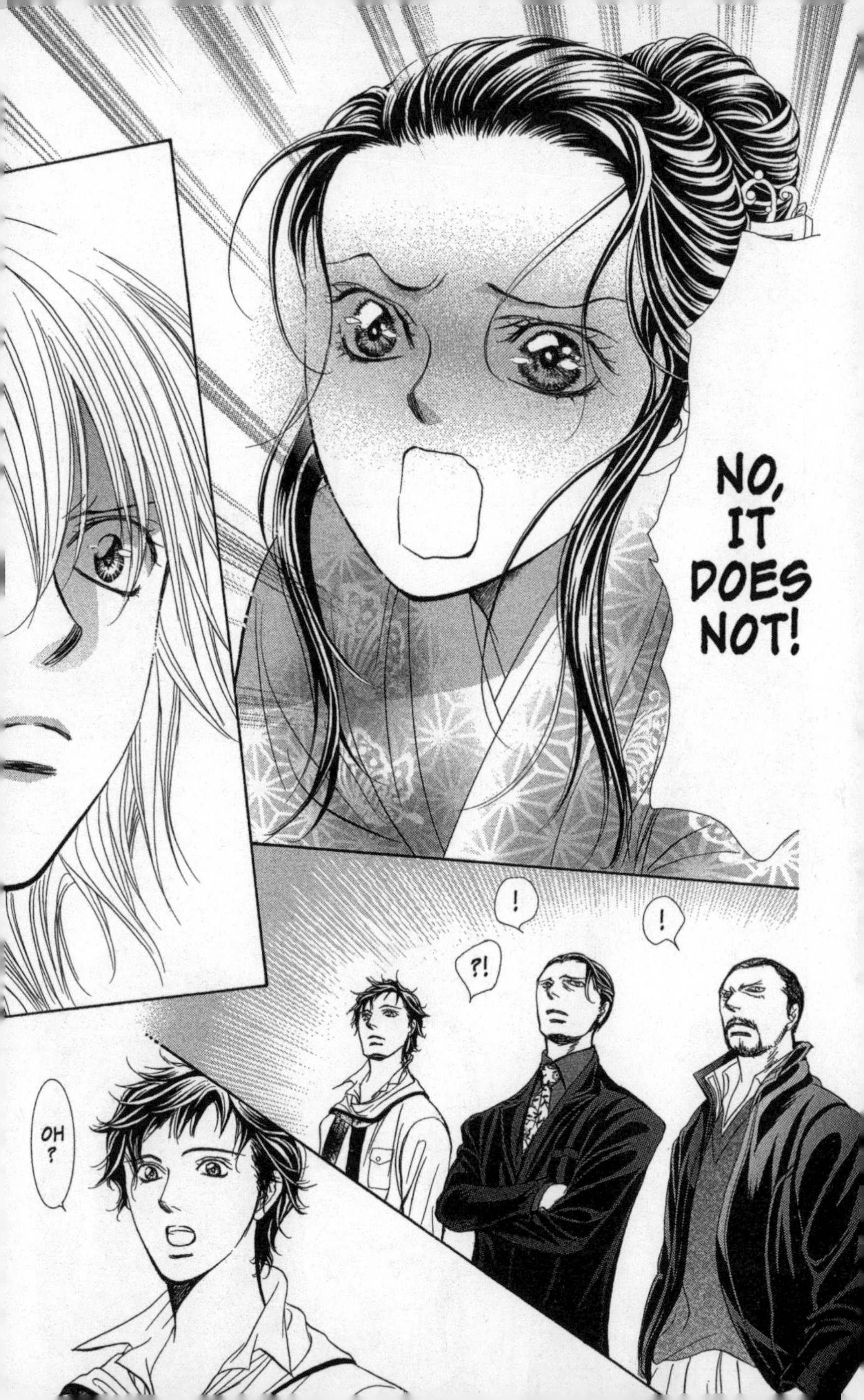
NO, IT DOES NOT!
!
!
?!
OH?

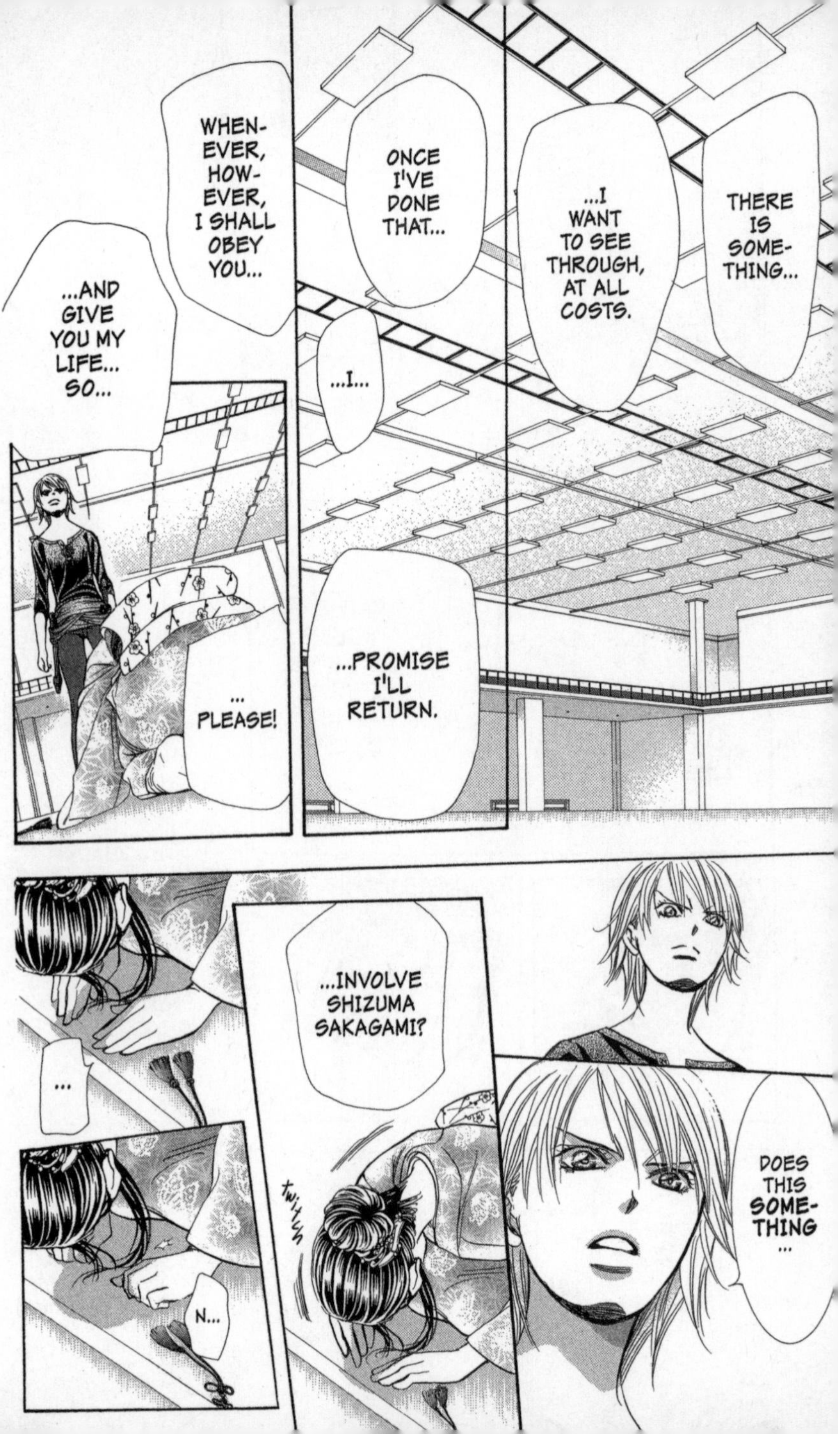
THERE IS SOME-THING...
...I WANT TO SEE THROUGH, AT ALL COSTS.
ONCE I'VE DONE THAT...
...I...
...PROMISE I'LL RETURN.
WHEN-EVER, HOW-EVER, I SHALL OBEY YOU...
...AND GIVE YOU MY LIFE... SO...
... PLEASE!
DOES THIS SOME-THING ...
...INVOLVE SHIZUMA SAKAGAMI?
...
twitch
N...

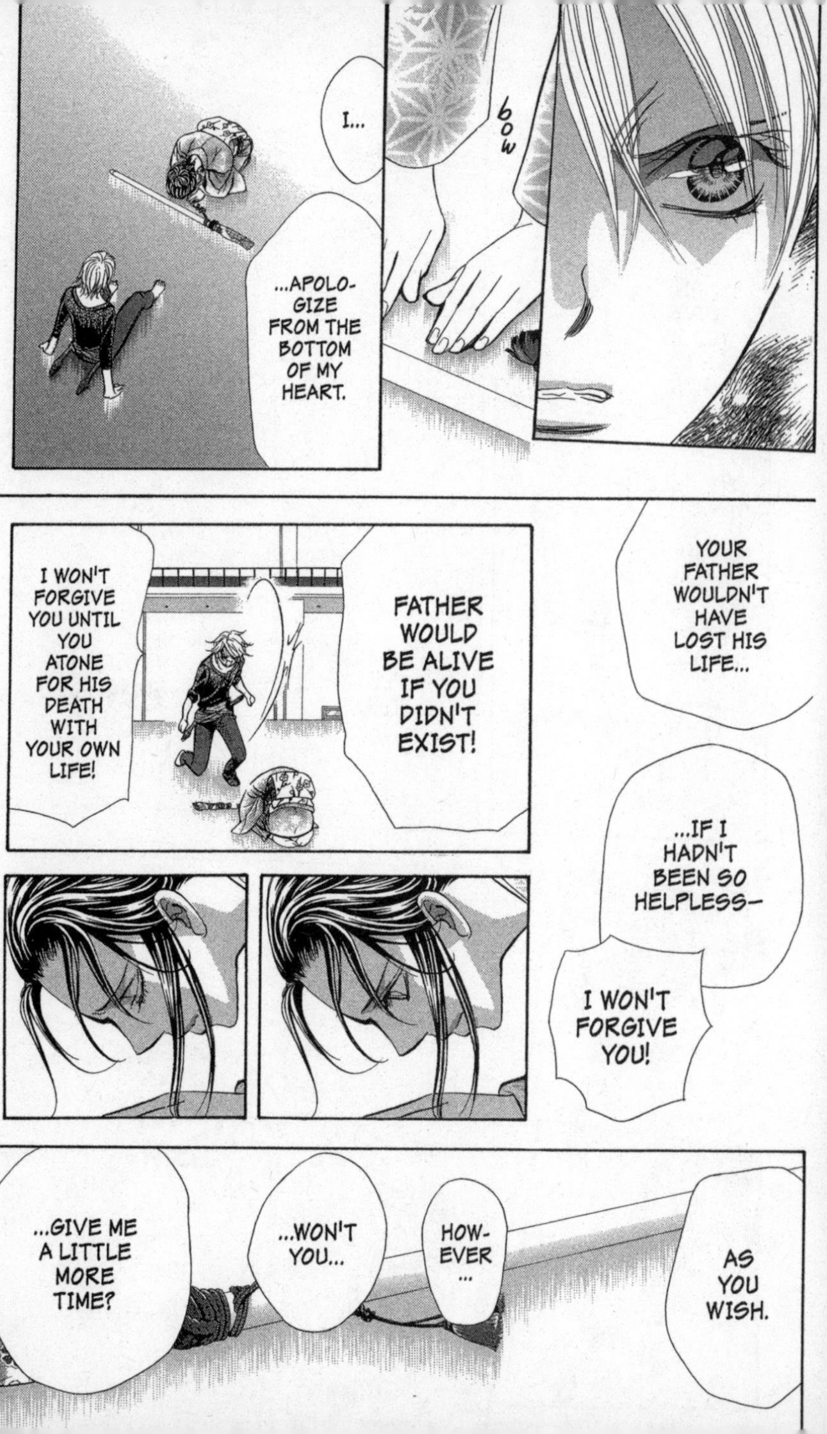
bow
I...
...APOLOGIZE FROM THE BOTTOM OF MY HEART.
YOUR FATHER WOULDN'T HAVE LOST HIS LIFE...
...IF I HADN'T BEEN SO HELPLESS—
I WON'T FORGIVE YOU!
FATHER WOULD BE ALIVE IF YOU DIDN'T EXIST!
I WON'T FORGIVE YOU UNTIL YOU ATONE FOR HIS DEATH WITH YOUR OWN LIFE!
AS YOU WISH.
HOWEVER...
...WON'T YOU...
...GIVE ME A LITTLE MORE TIME?

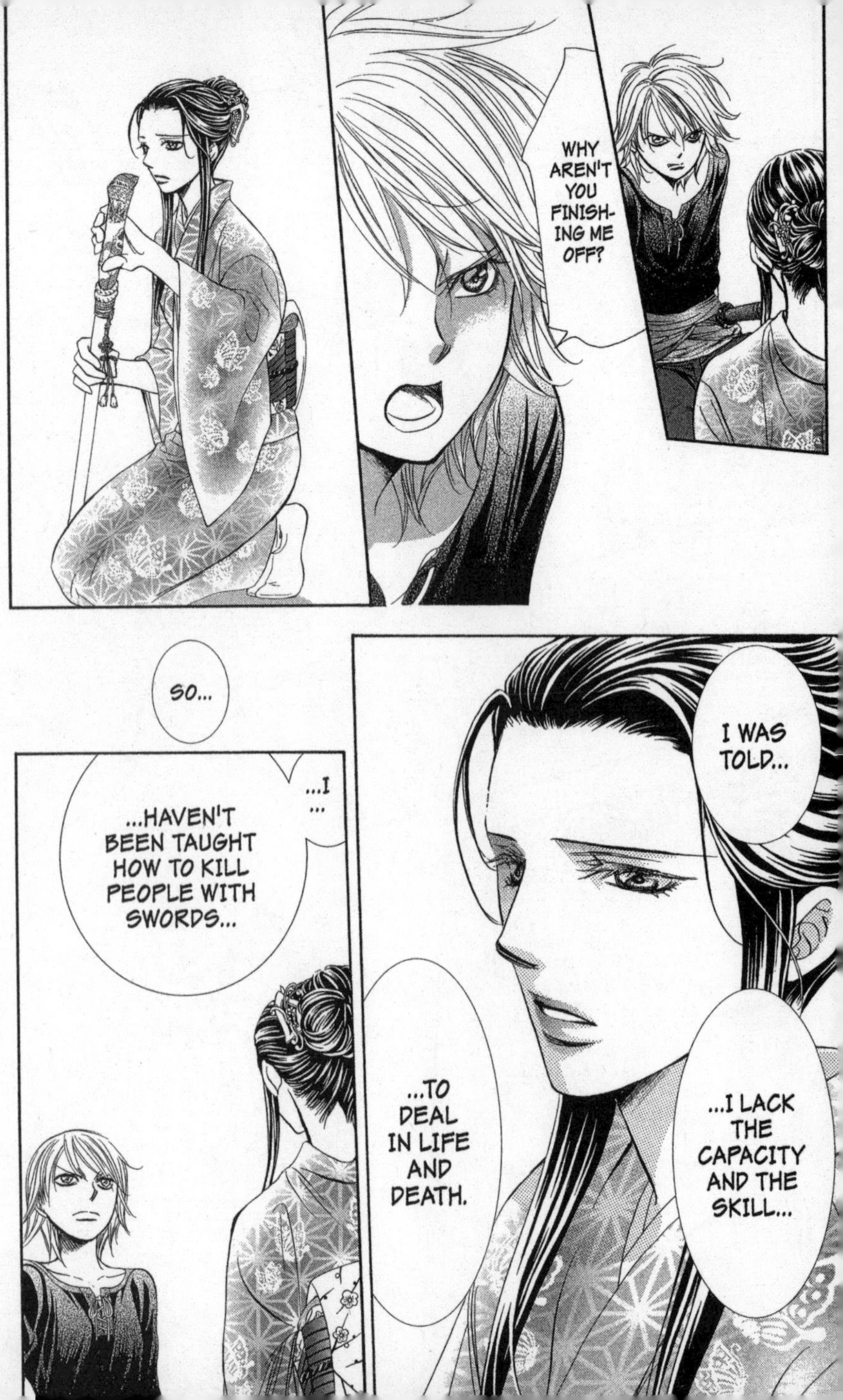
WHY AREN'T YOU FINISH-ING ME OFF?
I WAS TOLD...
...I LACK THE CAPACITY AND THE SKILL...
...TO DEAL IN LIFE AND DEATH.
SO...
...I ...
...HAVEN'T BEEN TAUGHT HOW TO KILL PEOPLE WITH SWORDS...

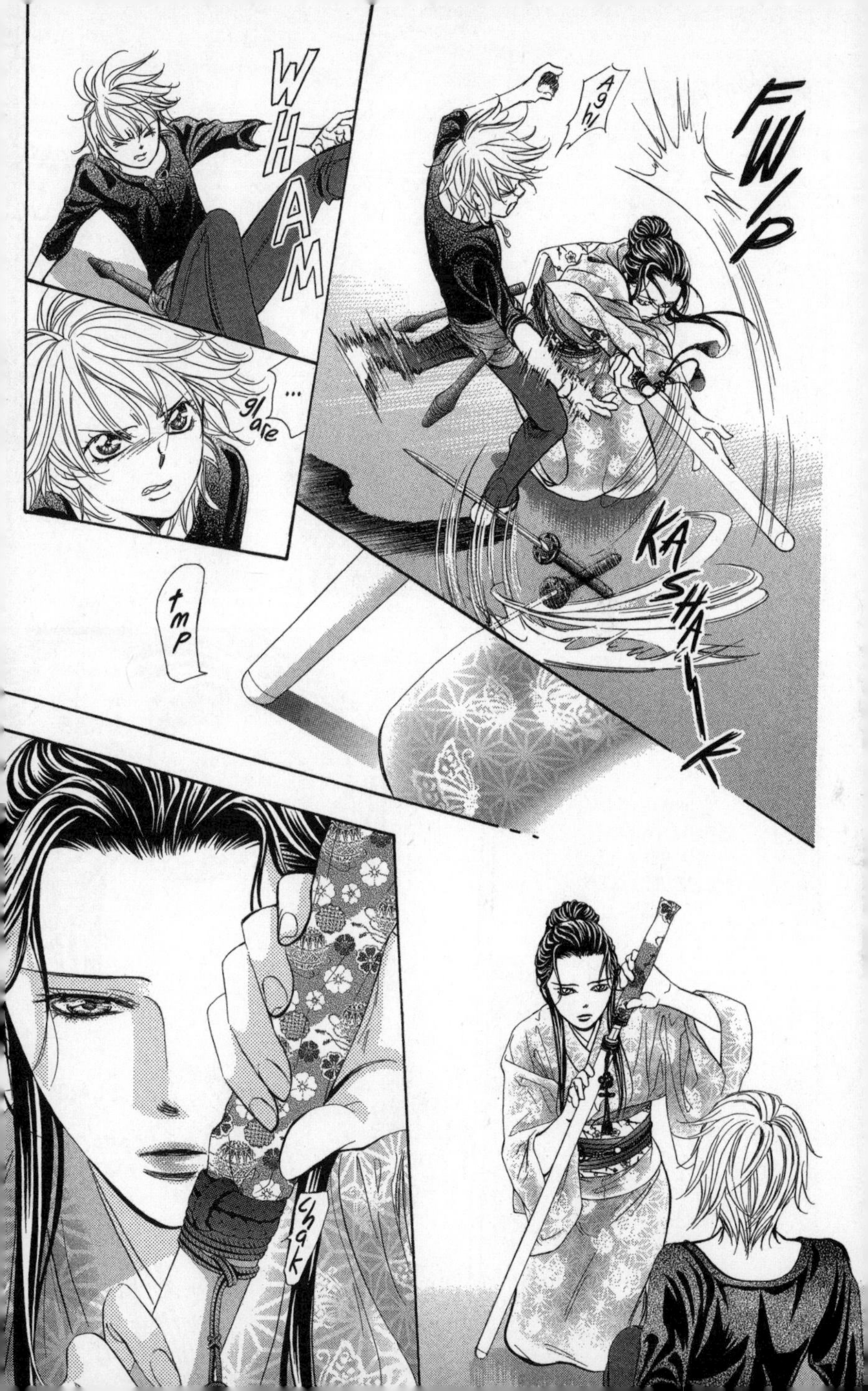
FWIP
Agh!
KASHAWK
WHAM
...
glare
tmp
chak

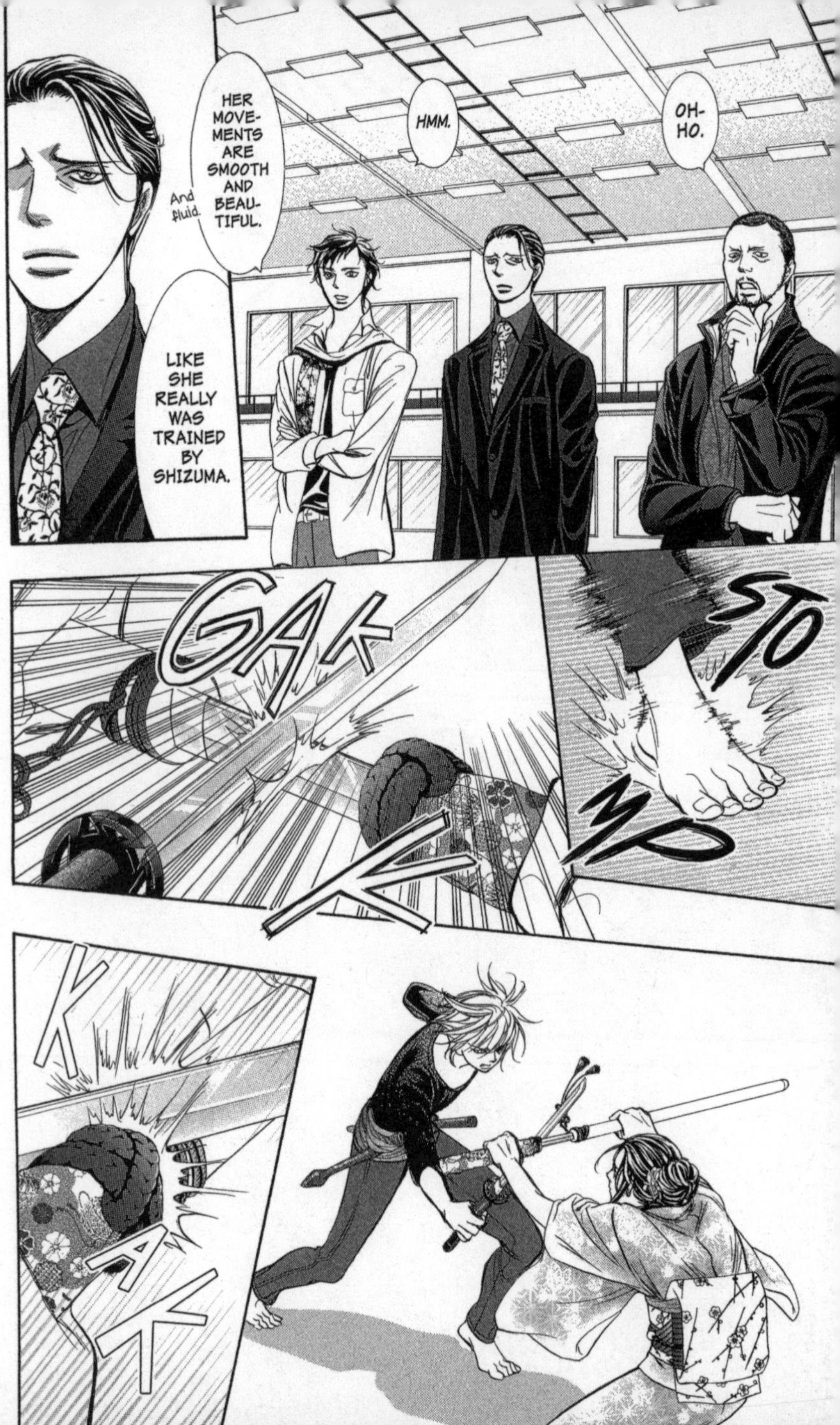
OH-HO.
HMM.
HER MOVEMENTS ARE SMOOTH AND BEAUTIFUL.
And fluid.
LIKE SHE REALLY WAS TRAINED BY SHIZUMA.
STOMP
GAKK
KAK

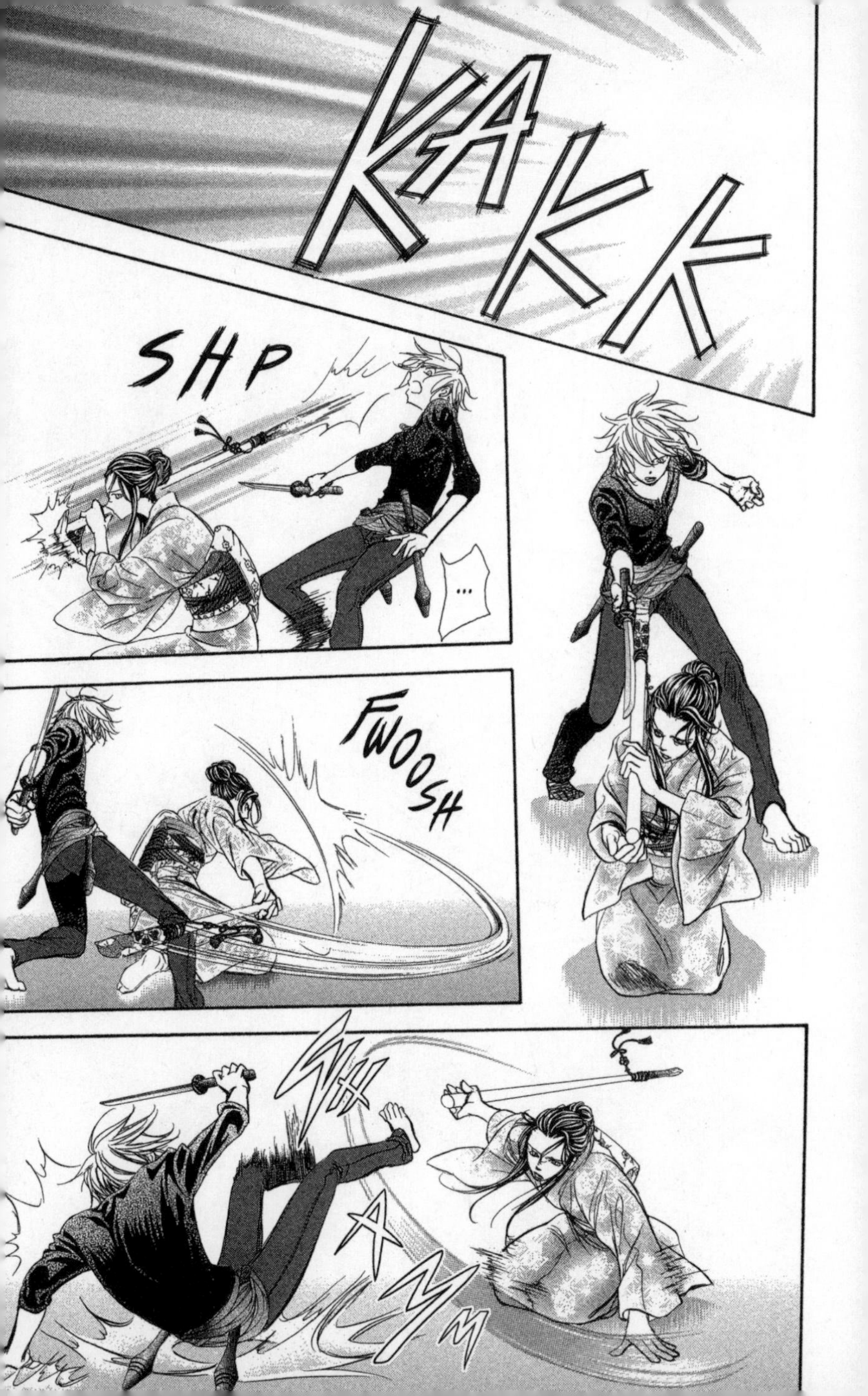
KAKKK
SHP
...
FWOOSH
SHAMM

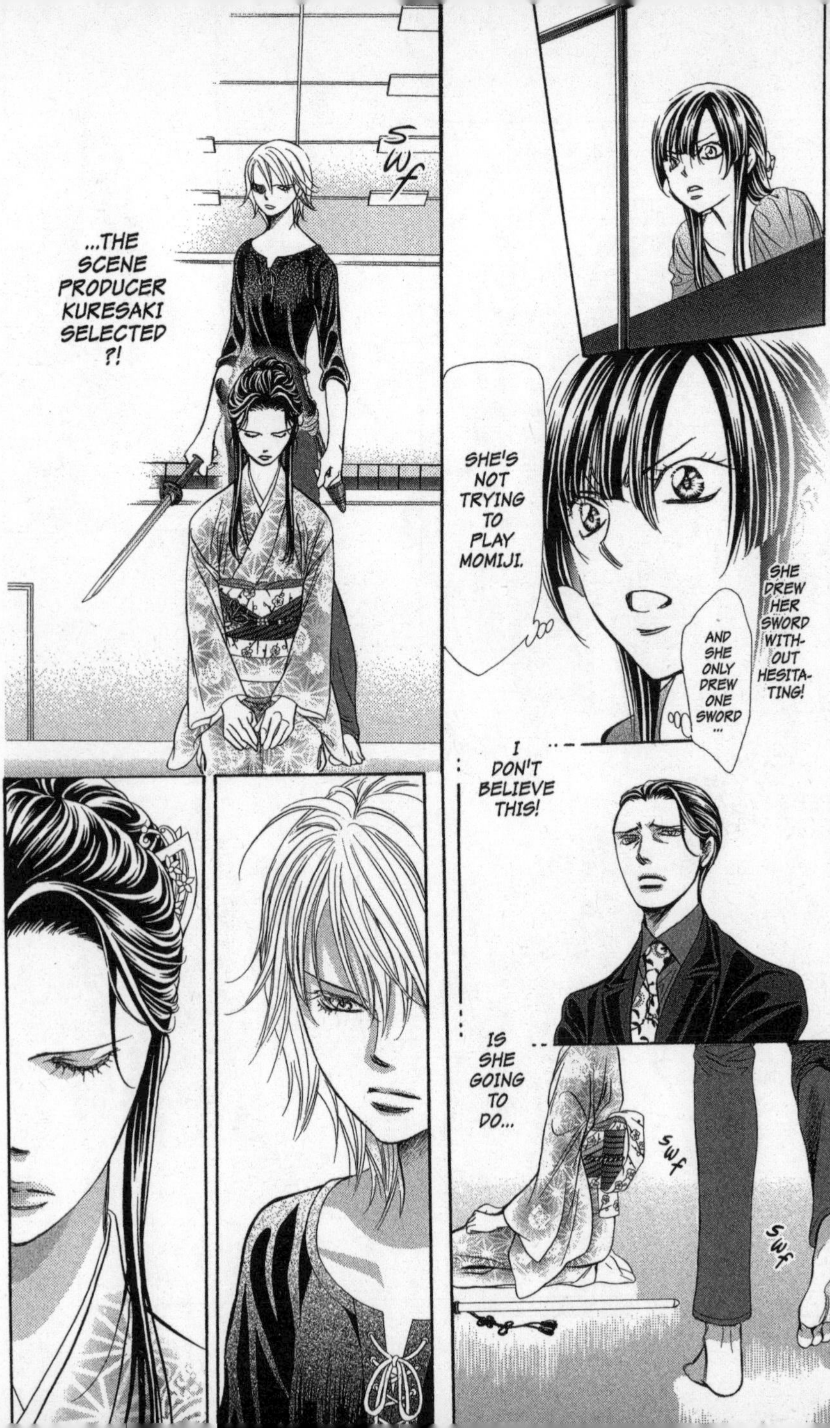

SHE DREW HER SWORD WITH-OUT HESITA-TING!
AND SHE ONLY DREW ONE SWORD...
SHE'S NOT TRYING TO PLAY MOMIJI.
I DON'T BELIEVE THIS!
IS SHE GOING TO DO...
SWF
SWF
SWF
...THE SCENE PRODUCER KURESAKI SELECTED?!

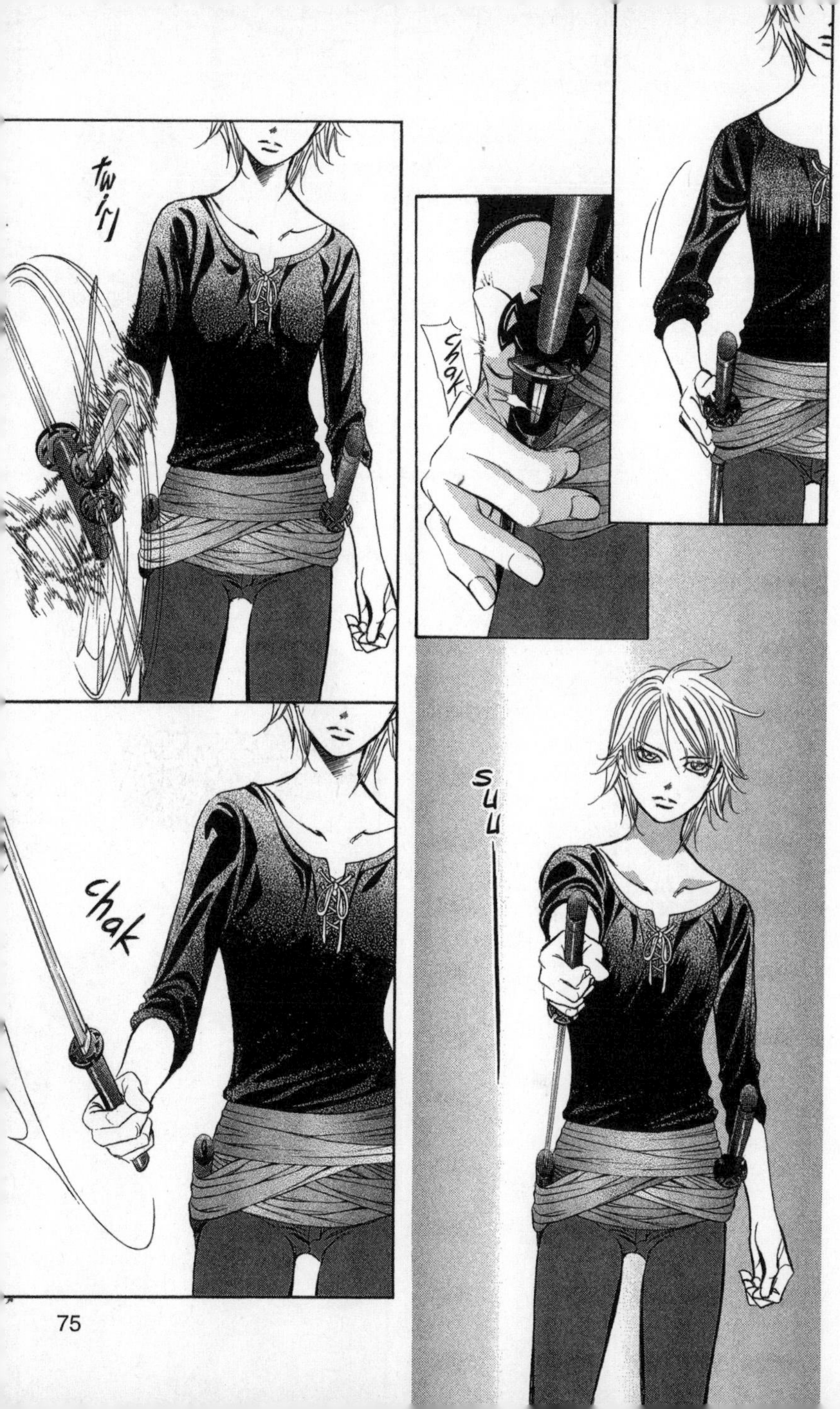
chak
suu
twirl
chak

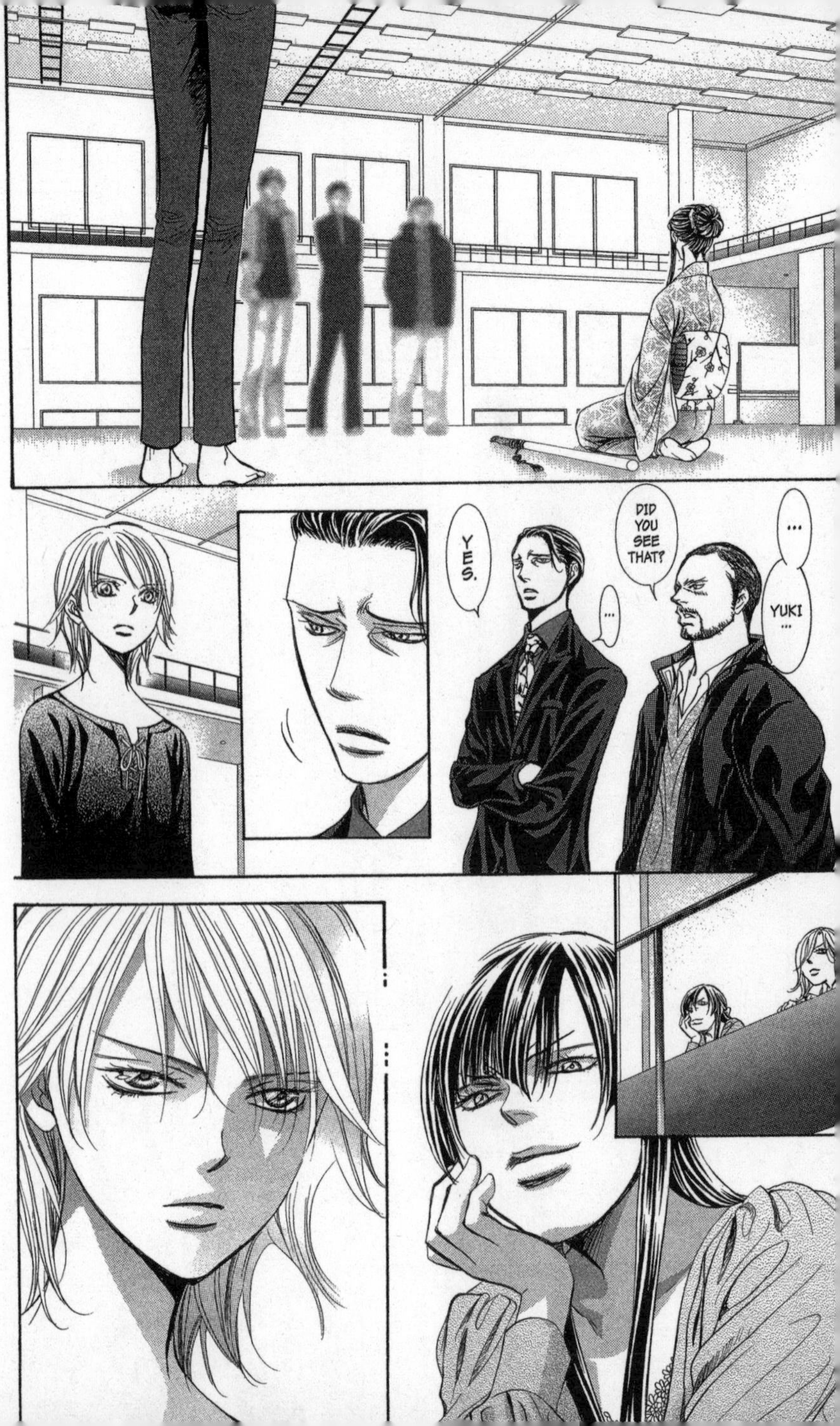
...
YUKI...
DID YOU SEE THAT?
YES.
...

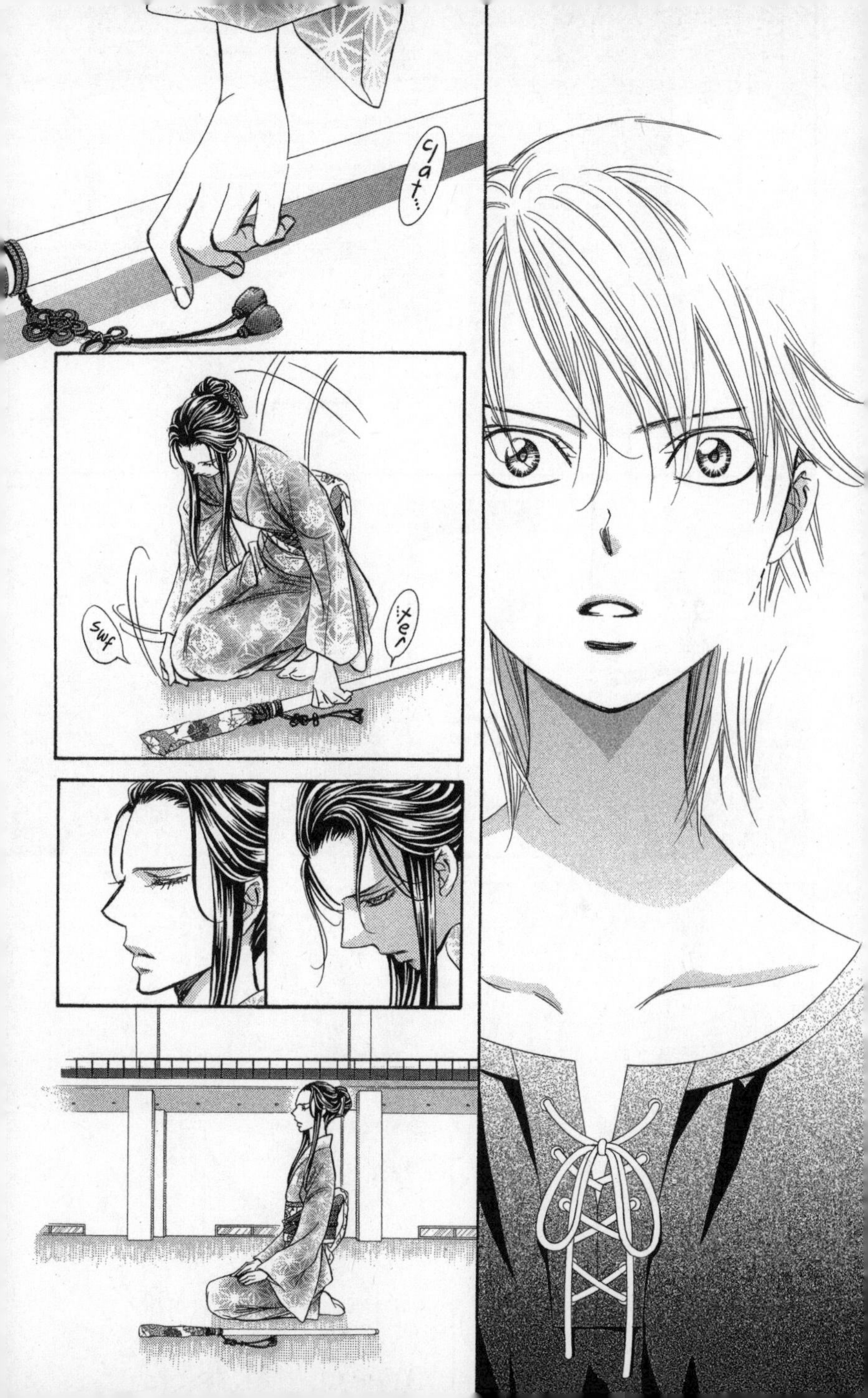
clat...
...ter
swf

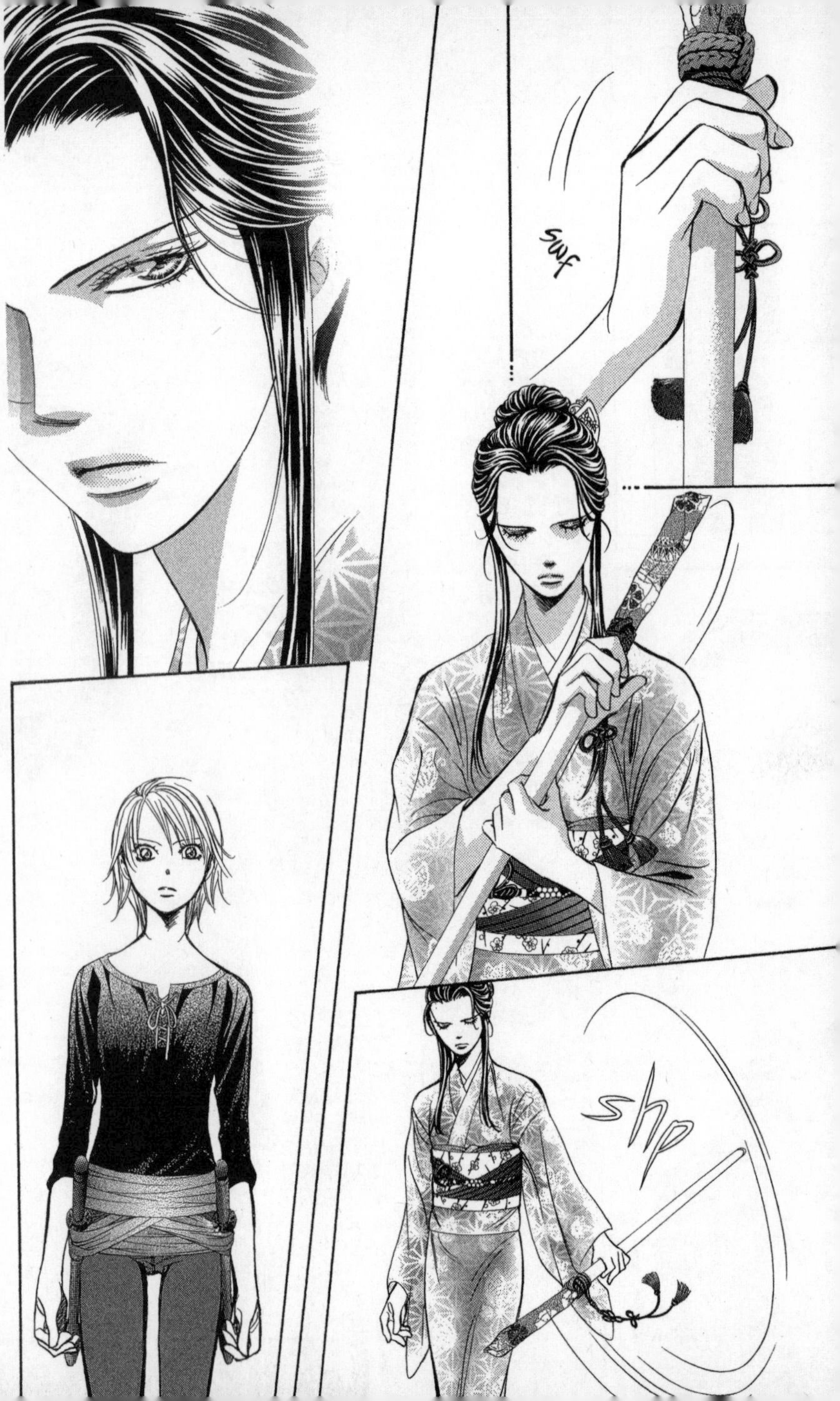
SWF
shp

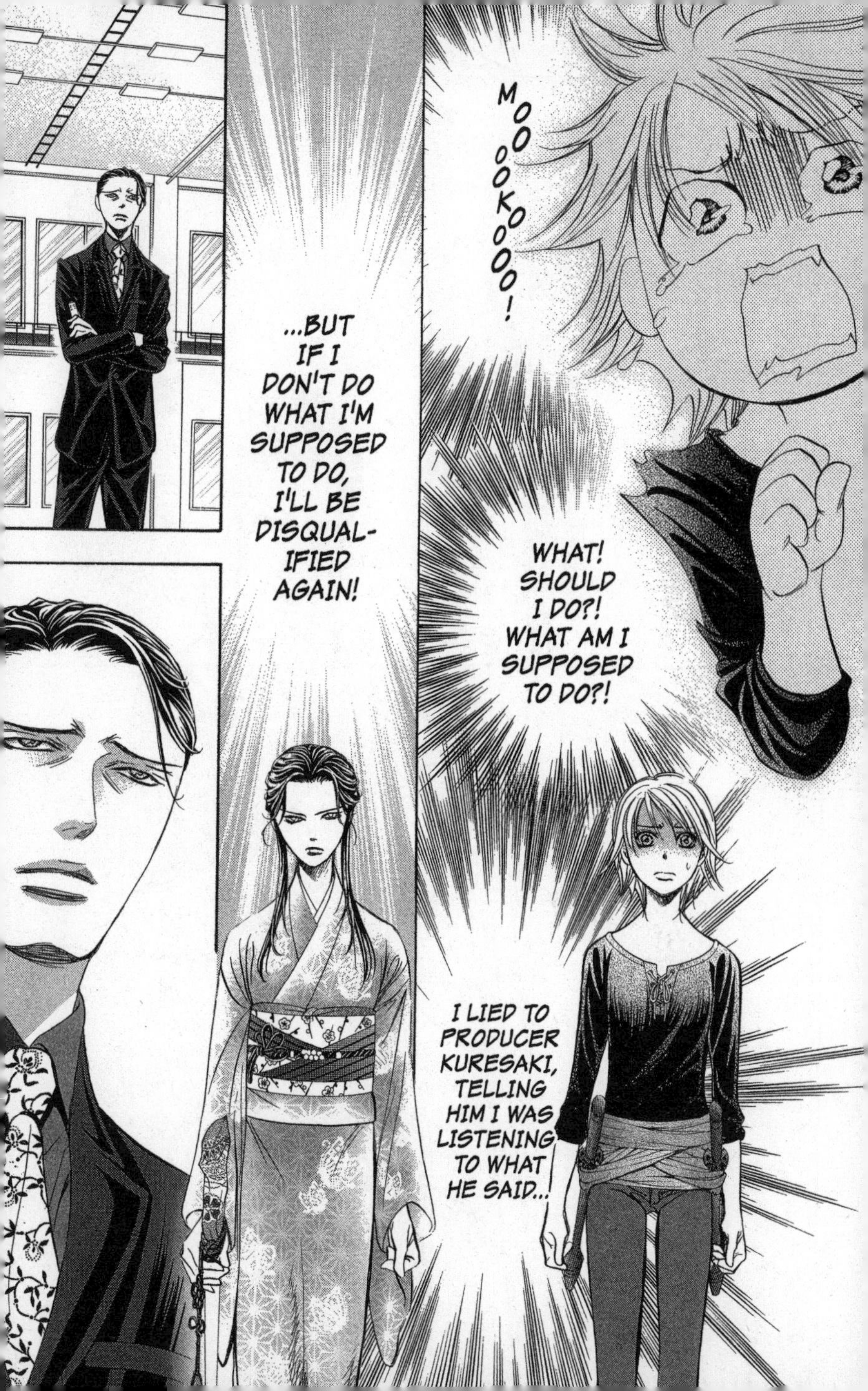

MOOOOKOOOOO!
WHAT! SHOULD I DO?! WHAT AM I SUPPOSED TO DO?!
I LIED TO PRODUCER KURESAKI, TELLING HIM I WAS LISTENING TO WHAT HE SAID...
...BUT IF I DON'T DO WHAT I'M SUPPOSED TO DO, I'LL BE DISQUAL-IFIED AGAIN!

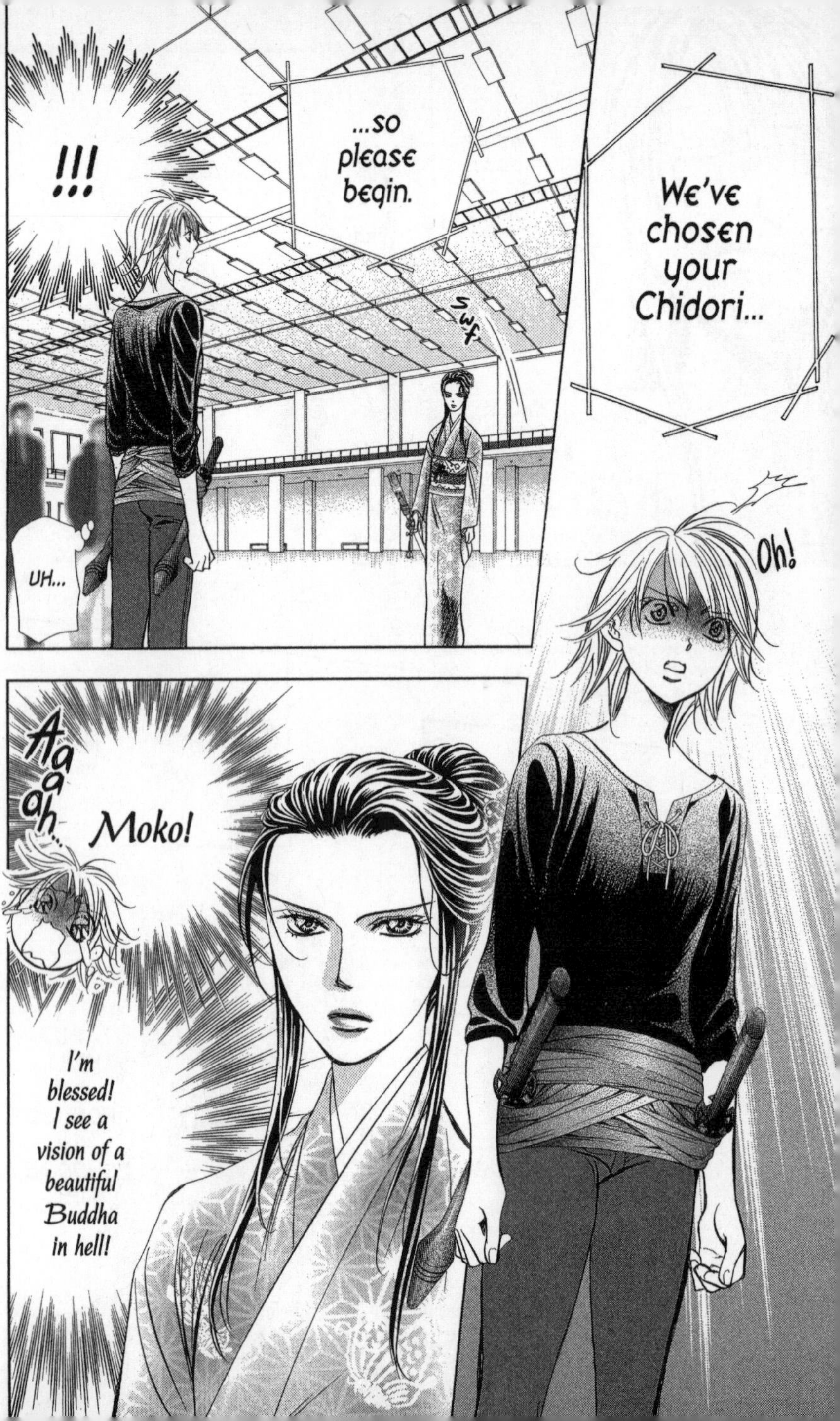
We've chosen your Chidori...
Oh!
...so please begin.
!!!
swf
UH...
Aaaah...
Moko!
I'm blessed! I see a vision of a beautiful Buddha in hell!

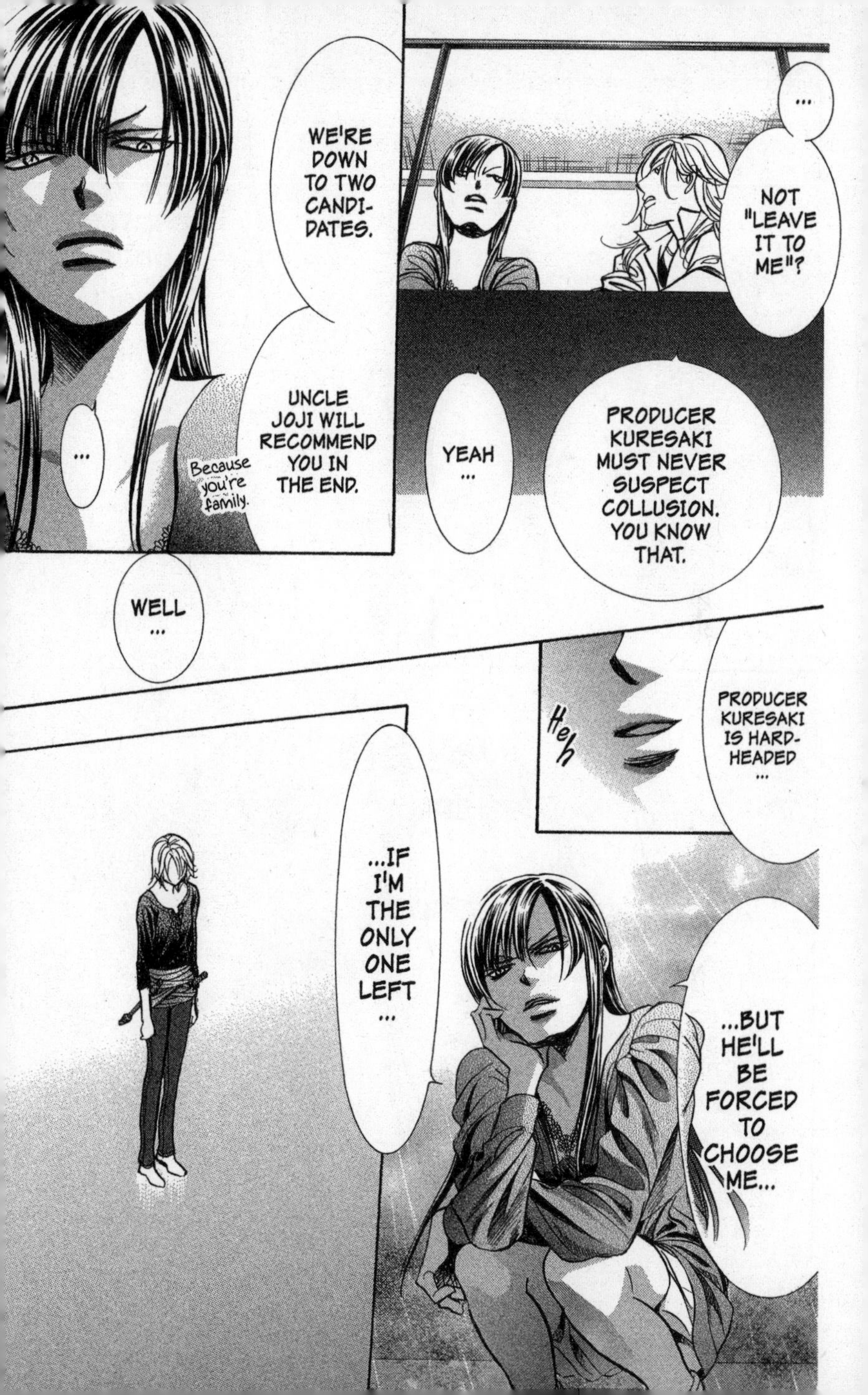
...
NOT "LEAVE IT TO ME"?
PRODUCER KURESAKI MUST NEVER SUSPECT COLLUSION. YOU KNOW THAT.
YEAH ...
WE'RE DOWN TO TWO CANDIDATES.
UNCLE JOJI WILL RECOMMEND YOU IN THE END.
Because you're family.
...
WELL ...
Heh
PRODUCER KURESAKI IS HARD-HEADED ...
...BUT HE'LL BE FORCED TO CHOOSE ME...
...IF I'M THE ONLY ONE LEFT ...

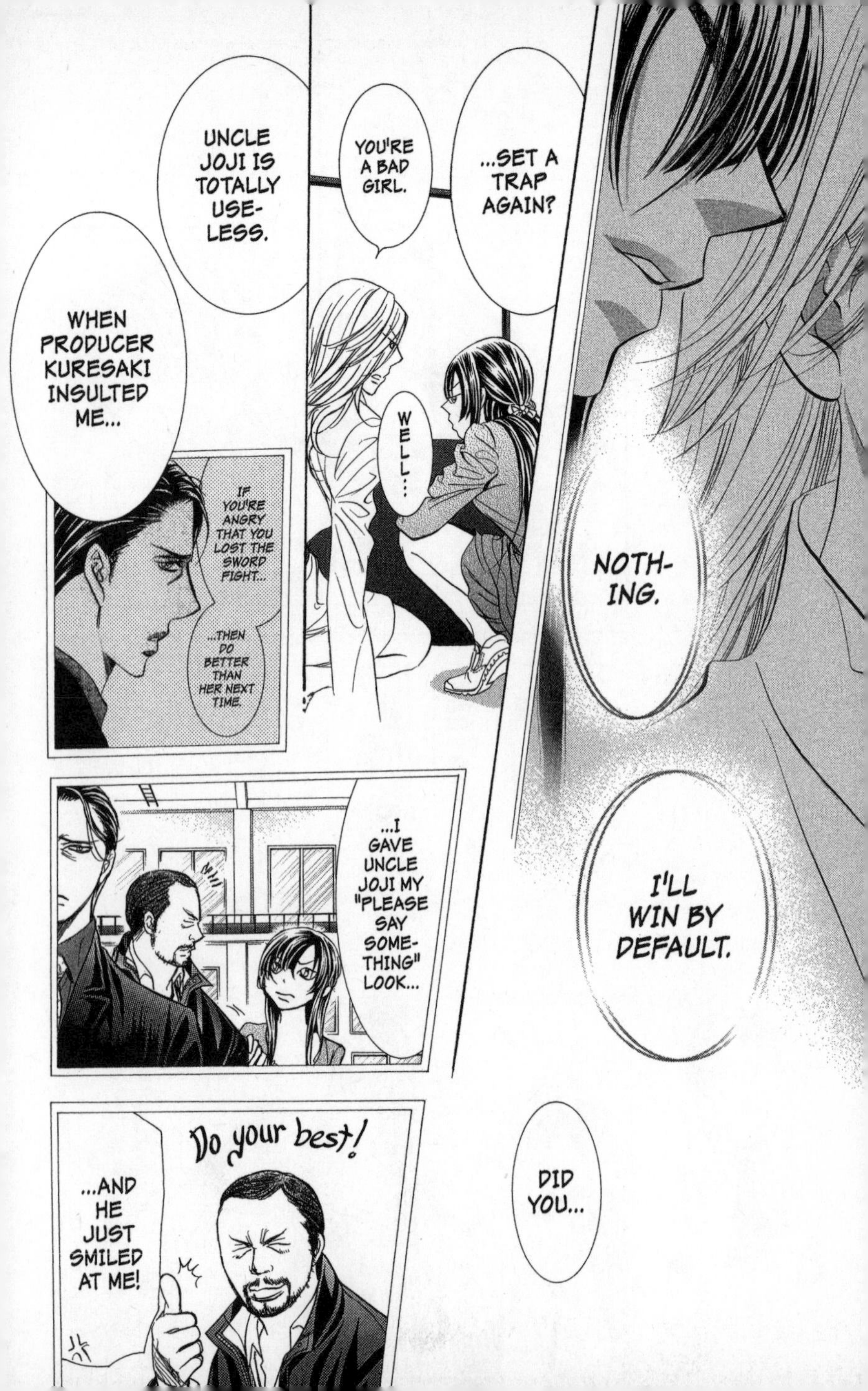
NOTH-ING.
I'LL WIN BY DEFAULT.
...SET A TRAP AGAIN?
YOU'RE A BAD GIRL.
WELL...
UNCLE JOJI IS TOTALLY USE-LESS.
WHEN PRODUCER KURESAKI INSULTED ME...
IF YOU'RE ANGRY THAT YOU LOST THE SWORD FIGHT...
...THEN DO BETTER THAN HER NEXT TIME.
...I GAVE UNCLE JOJI MY "PLEASE SAY SOME-THING" LOOK...
Do your best!
...AND HE JUST SMILED AT ME!
DID YOU...

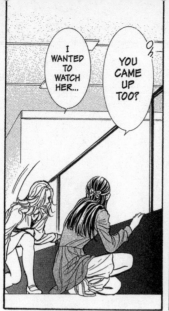

KIMI.
Oh,
YOU CAME UP TOO?
I WANTED TO WATCH HER...
... BECAUSE OF WHAT YOU SAID.
ka chak
WHAT ARE YOU GO-ING TO DO?
swf

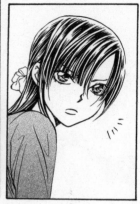

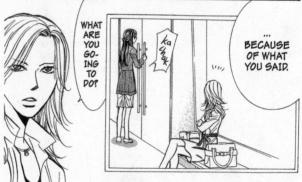

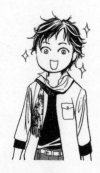

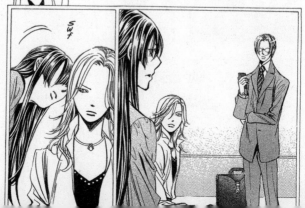

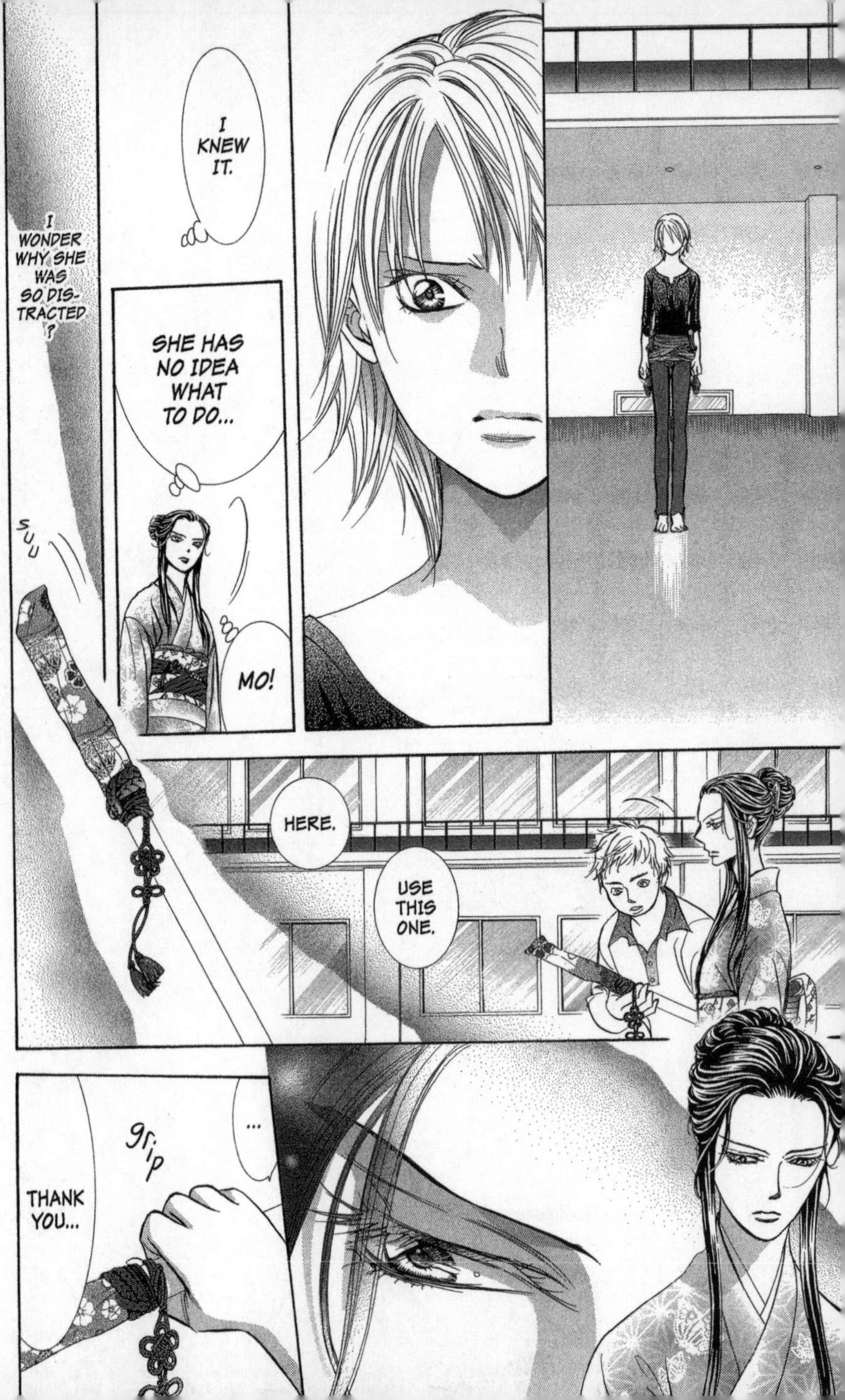
I KNEW IT.
SHE HAS NO IDEA WHAT TO DO...
MO!
I WONDER WHY SHE WAS SO DIS-TRACTED?
SUU
HERE.
USE THIS ONE.
...
grip
THANK YOU...

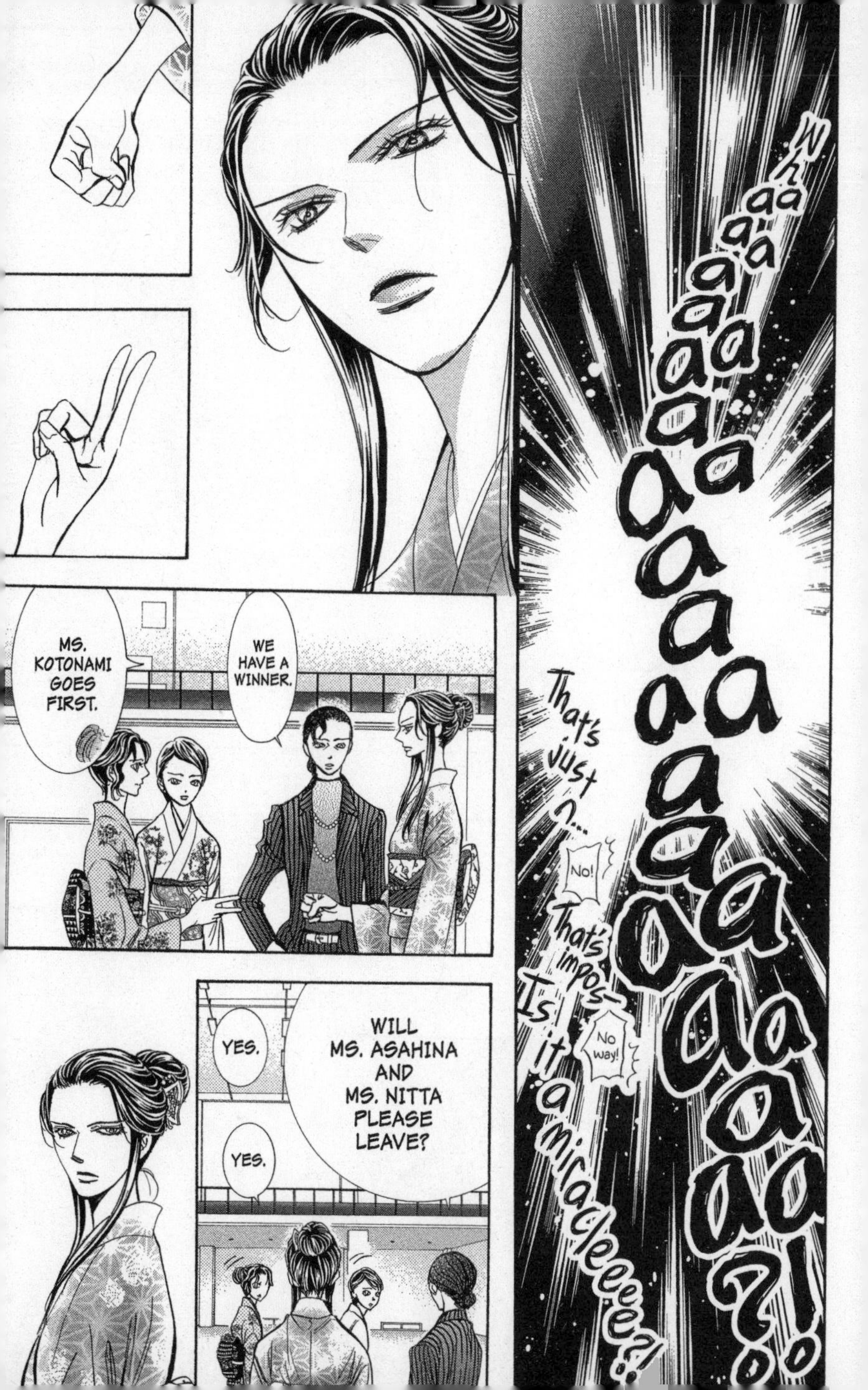
Whaaaaaaaaaaaaaaaaaaaaaaaaa?!
That's just a...
No!
That's impos—
No way!
Is it a miracleeee?!
WE HAVE A WINNER.
MS. KOTONAMI GOES FIRST.
WILL MS. ASAHINA AND MS. NITTA PLEASE LEAVE?
YES.
YES.

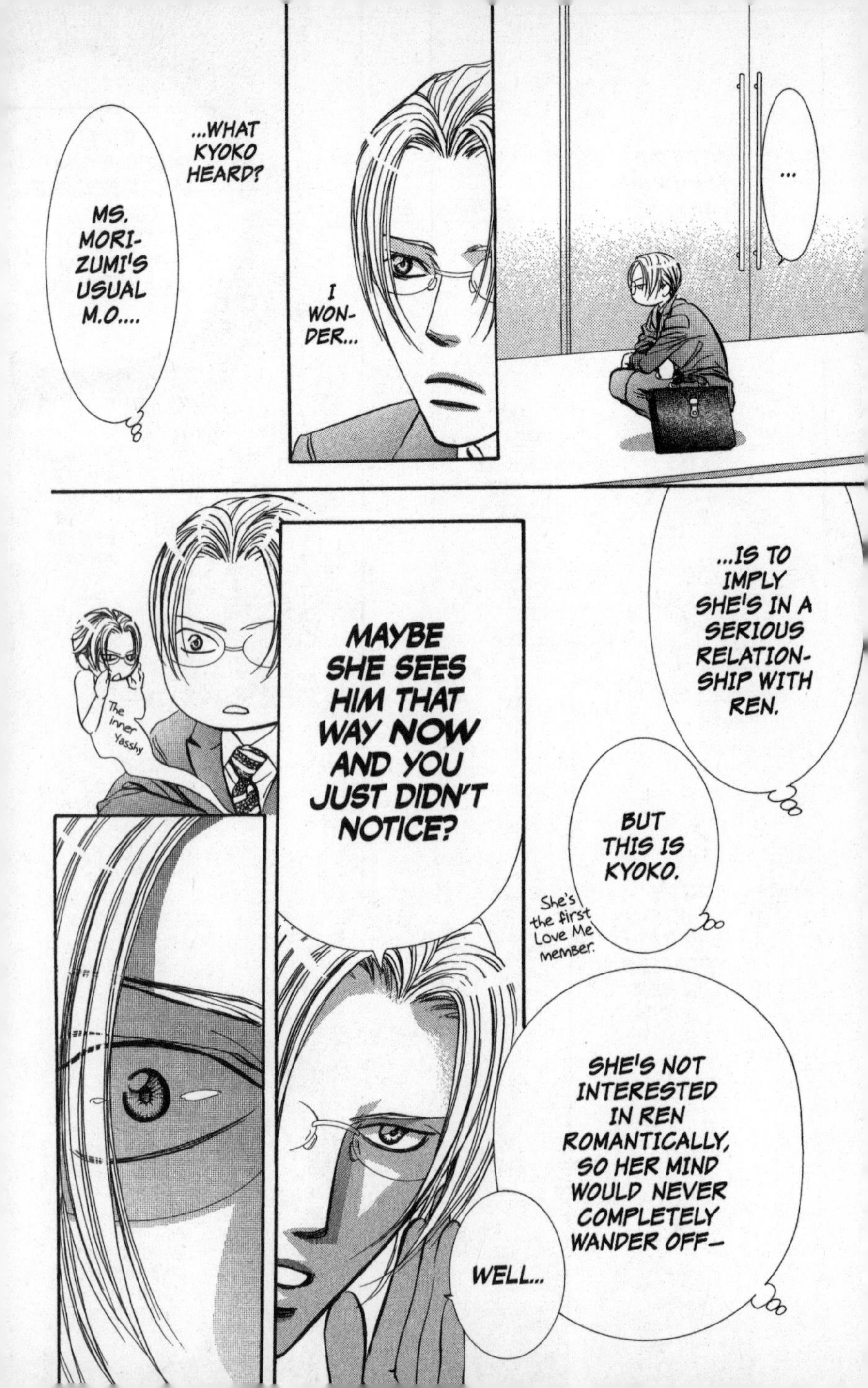
...
I WONDER...
...WHAT KYOKO HEARD?
MS. MORIZUMI'S USUAL M.O....
...IS TO IMPLY SHE'S IN A SERIOUS RELATIONSHIP WITH REN.
BUT THIS IS KYOKO.
She's the first Love Me member.
SHE'S NOT INTERESTED IN REN ROMANTICALLY, SO HER MIND WOULD NEVER COMPLETELY WANDER OFF—
WELL...
MAYBE SHE SEES HIM THAT WAY NOW AND YOU JUST DIDN'T NOTICE?
The inner Yasshy

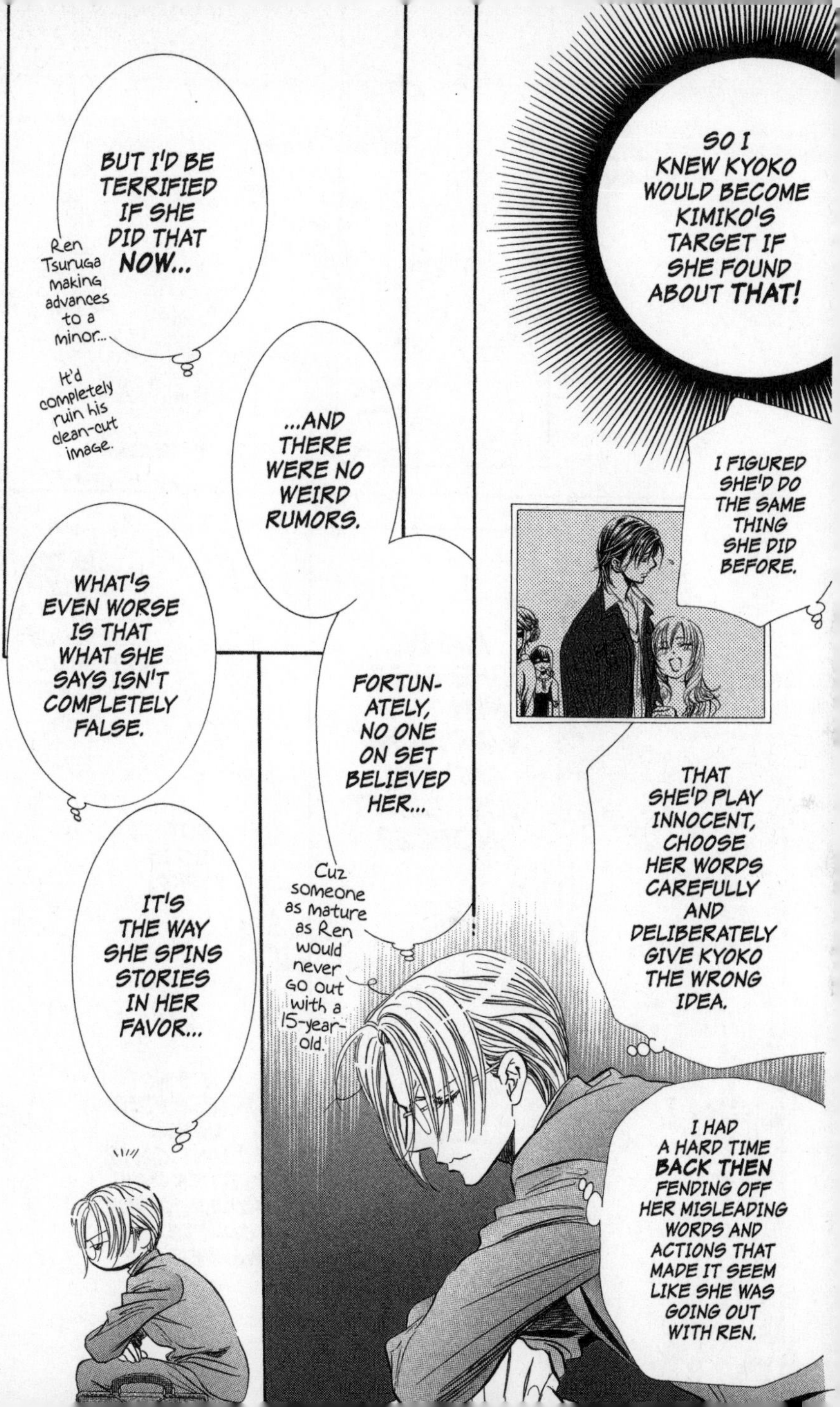
SO I KNEW KYOKO WOULD BECOME KIMIKO'S TARGET IF SHE FOUND ABOUT THAT!
I FIGURED SHE'D DO THE SAME THING SHE DID BEFORE.
THAT SHE'D PLAY INNOCENT, CHOOSE HER WORDS CAREFULLY AND DELIBERATELY GIVE KYOKO THE WRONG IDEA.
I HAD A HARD TIME BACK THEN FENDING OFF HER MISLEADING WORDS AND ACTIONS THAT MADE IT SEEM LIKE SHE WAS GOING OUT WITH REN.
FORTUN-ATELY, NO ONE ON SET BELIEVED HER...
Cuz someone as mature as Ren would never go out with a 15-year-old.
...AND THERE WERE NO WEIRD RUMORS.
BUT I'D BE TERRIFIED IF SHE DID THAT NOW...
Ren Tsuruga making advances to a minor...
It'd completely ruin his clean-cut image.
WHAT'S EVEN WORSE IS THAT WHAT SHE SAYS ISN'T COMPLETELY FALSE.
IT'S THE WAY SHE SPINS STORIES IN HER FAVOR...

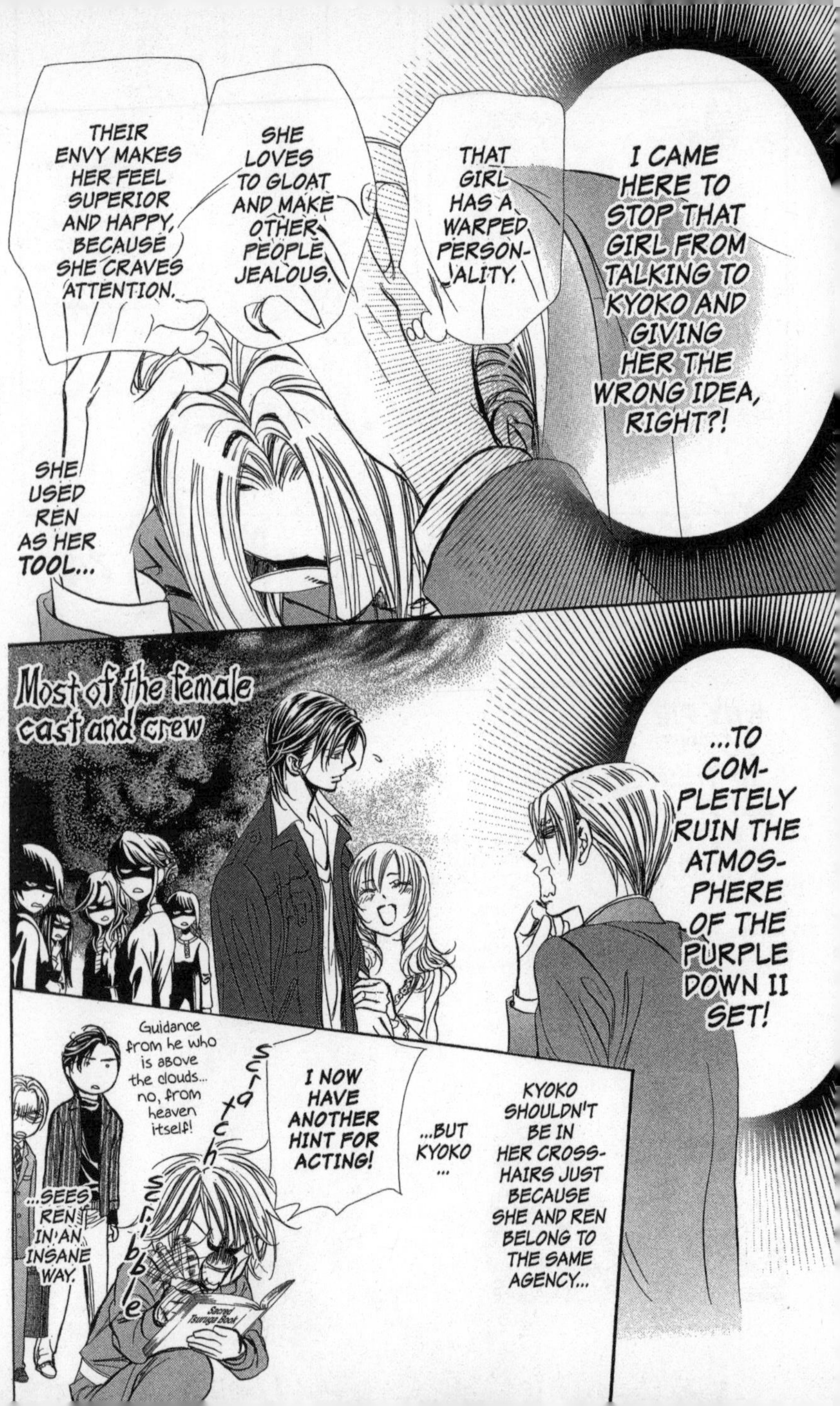
I CAME HERE TO STOP THAT GIRL FROM TALKING TO KYOKO AND GIVING HER THE WRONG IDEA, RIGHT?!
THAT GIRL HAS A WARPED PERSON-ALITY.
SHE LOVES TO GLOAT AND MAKE OTHER PEOPLE JEALOUS.
THEIR ENVY MAKES HER FEEL SUPERIOR AND HAPPY, BECAUSE SHE CRAVES ATTENTION.
SHE USED REN AS HER TOOL...
...TO COM-PLETELY RUIN THE ATMOS-PHERE OF THE PURPLE DOWN II SET!
Most of the female cast and crew
KYOKO SHOULDN'T BE IN HER CROSS-HAIRS JUST BECAUSE SHE AND REN BELONG TO THE SAME AGENCY...
...BUT KYOKO ...
I NOW HAVE ANOTHER HINT FOR ACTING!
scratch
scribble
Guidance from he who is above the clouds... no, from heaven itself!
...SEES REN IN AN INSANE WAY.
Sacred Tsuruga Book

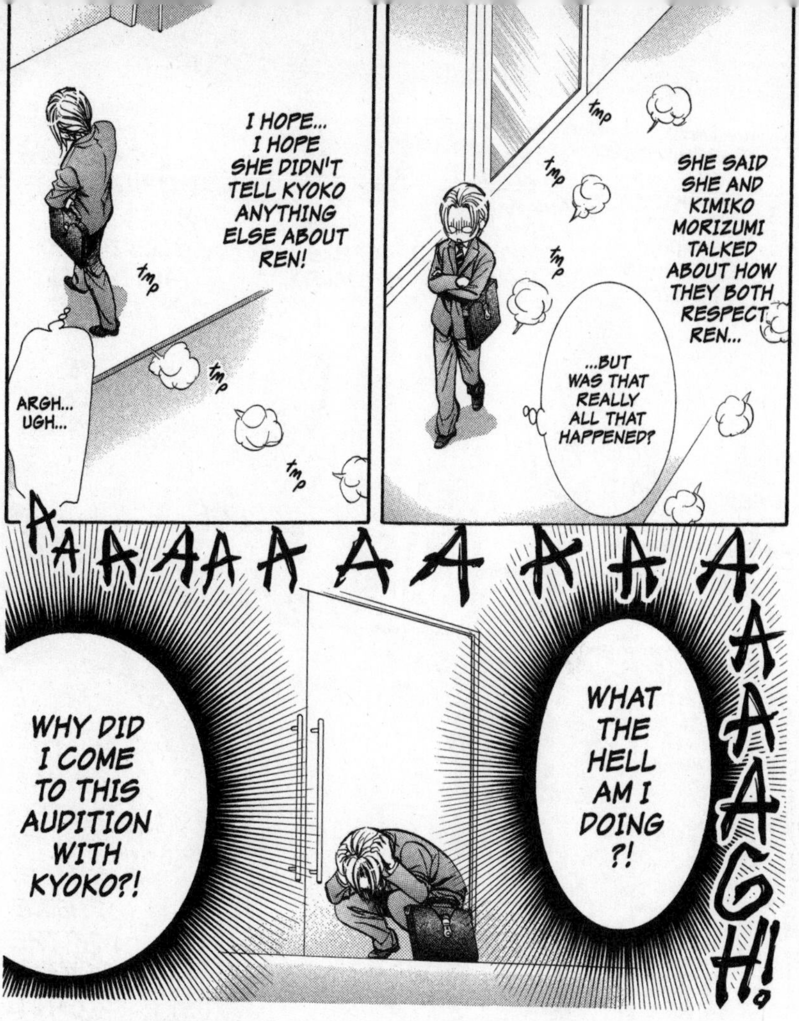
SHE SAID SHE AND KIMIKO MORIZUMI TALKED ABOUT HOW THEY BOTH RESPECT REN...
tmp
tmp
tmp
...BUT WAS THAT REALLY ALL THAT HAPPENED?
I HOPE... I HOPE SHE DIDN'T TELL KYOKO ANYTHING ELSE ABOUT REN!
tmp
tmp
tmp
ARGH... UGH...
AAAAAAAAAAAAAAGH!
WHAT THE HELL AM I DOING?!
WHY DID I COME TO THIS AUDITION WITH KYOKO?!

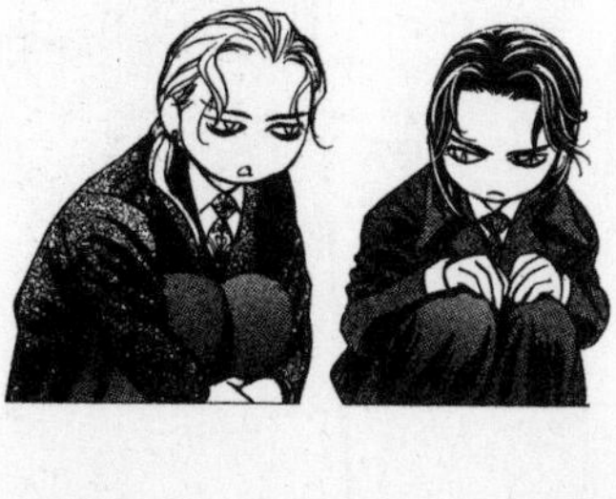

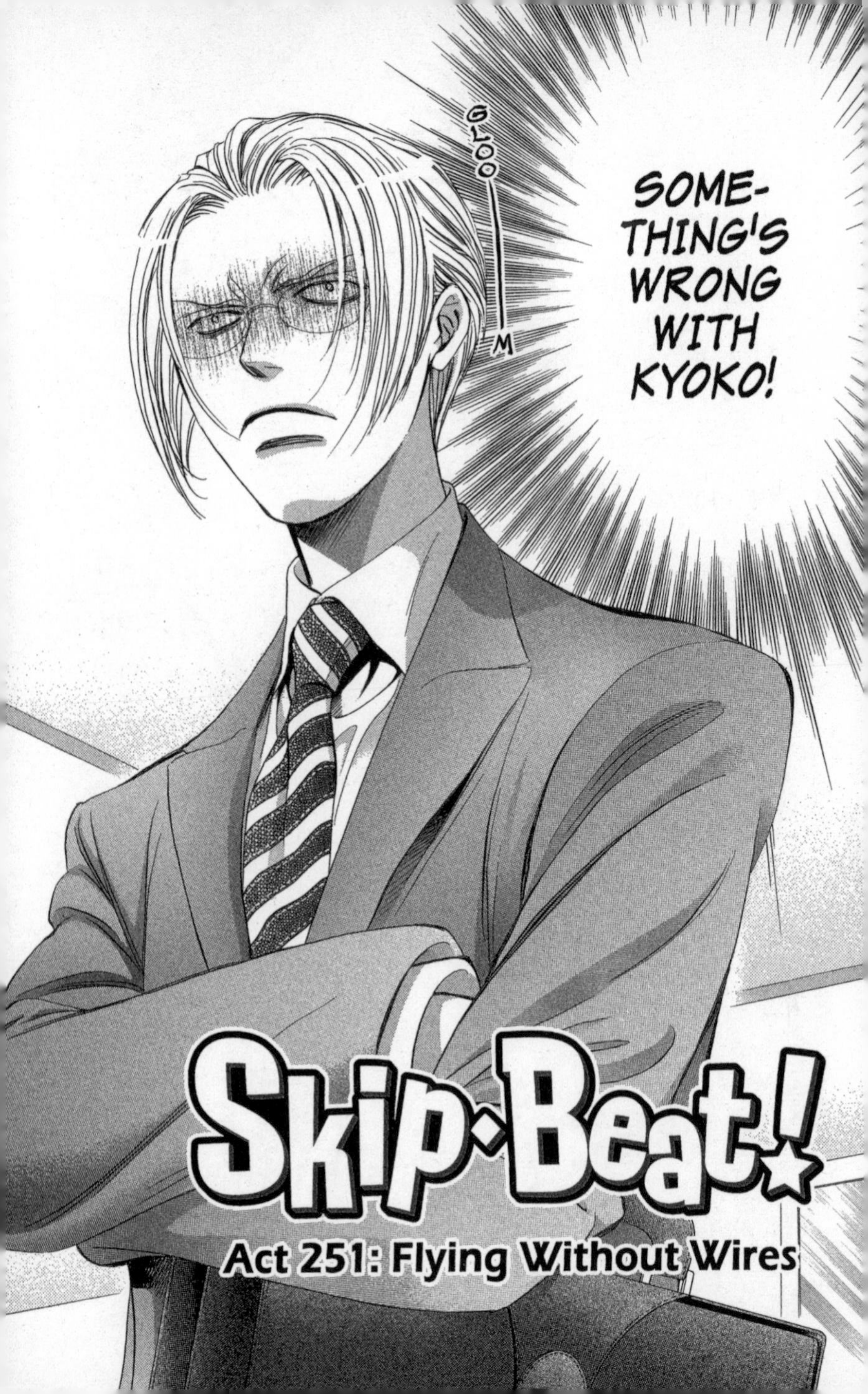
GLOOOM
SOME-THING'S WRONG WITH KYOKO!
Skip·Beat!
Act 251: Flying Without Wires

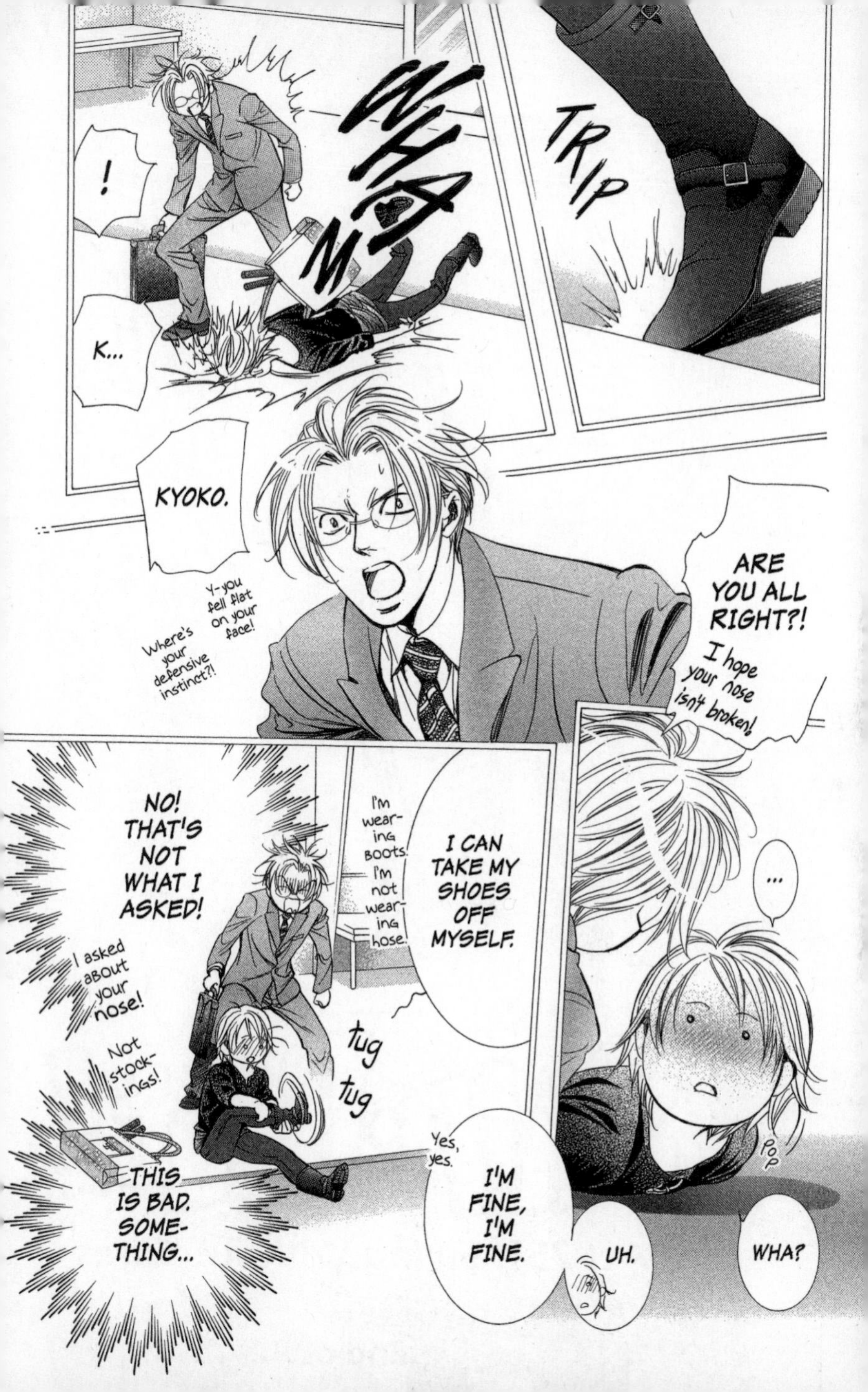
TRIP
WHAMM
!
K...
KYOKO.
ARE YOU ALL RIGHT?!
I hope your nose isn't broken!
Y-you fell flat on your face!
Where's your defensive instinct?!
...
POP
WHA?
UH.
I CAN TAKE MY SHOES OFF MYSELF.
I'm wear-ing boots. I'm not wear-ing hose.
tug tug
Yes, yes.
I'M FINE, I'M FINE.
NO! THAT'S NOT WHAT I ASKED!
I asked about your nose!
Not stock-ings!
THIS IS BAD. SOME-THING...

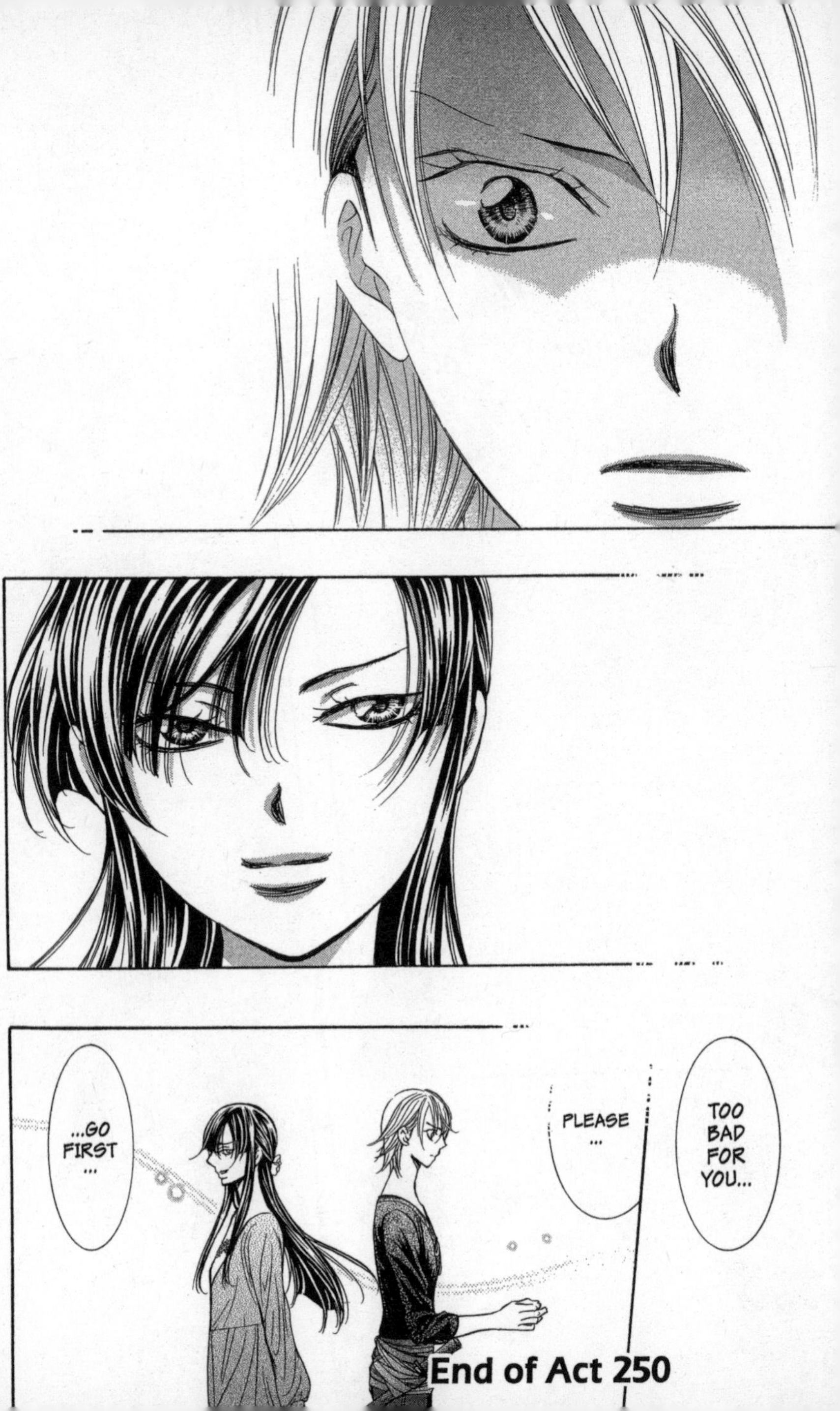
TOO BAD FOR YOU...
PLEASE ...
...GO FIRST ...
End of Act 250

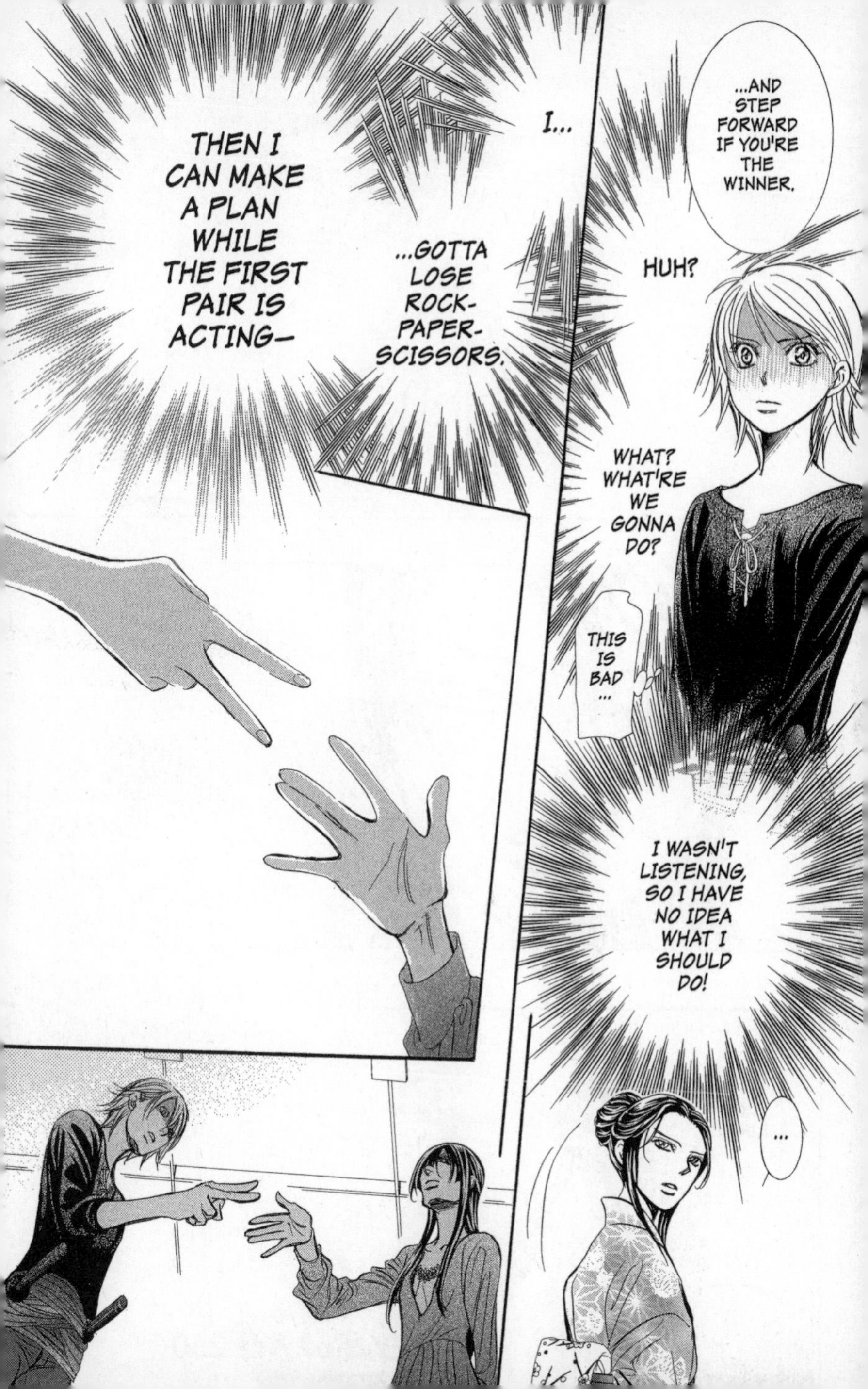
...AND STEP FORWARD IF YOU'RE THE WINNER.
HUH?
WHAT? WHAT'RE WE GONNA DO?
THIS IS BAD...
I WASN'T LISTENING, SO I HAVE NO IDEA WHAT I SHOULD DO!
...
I...
...GOTTA LOSE ROCK-PAPER-SCISSORS.
THEN I CAN MAKE A PLAN WHILE THE FIRST PAIR IS ACTING—

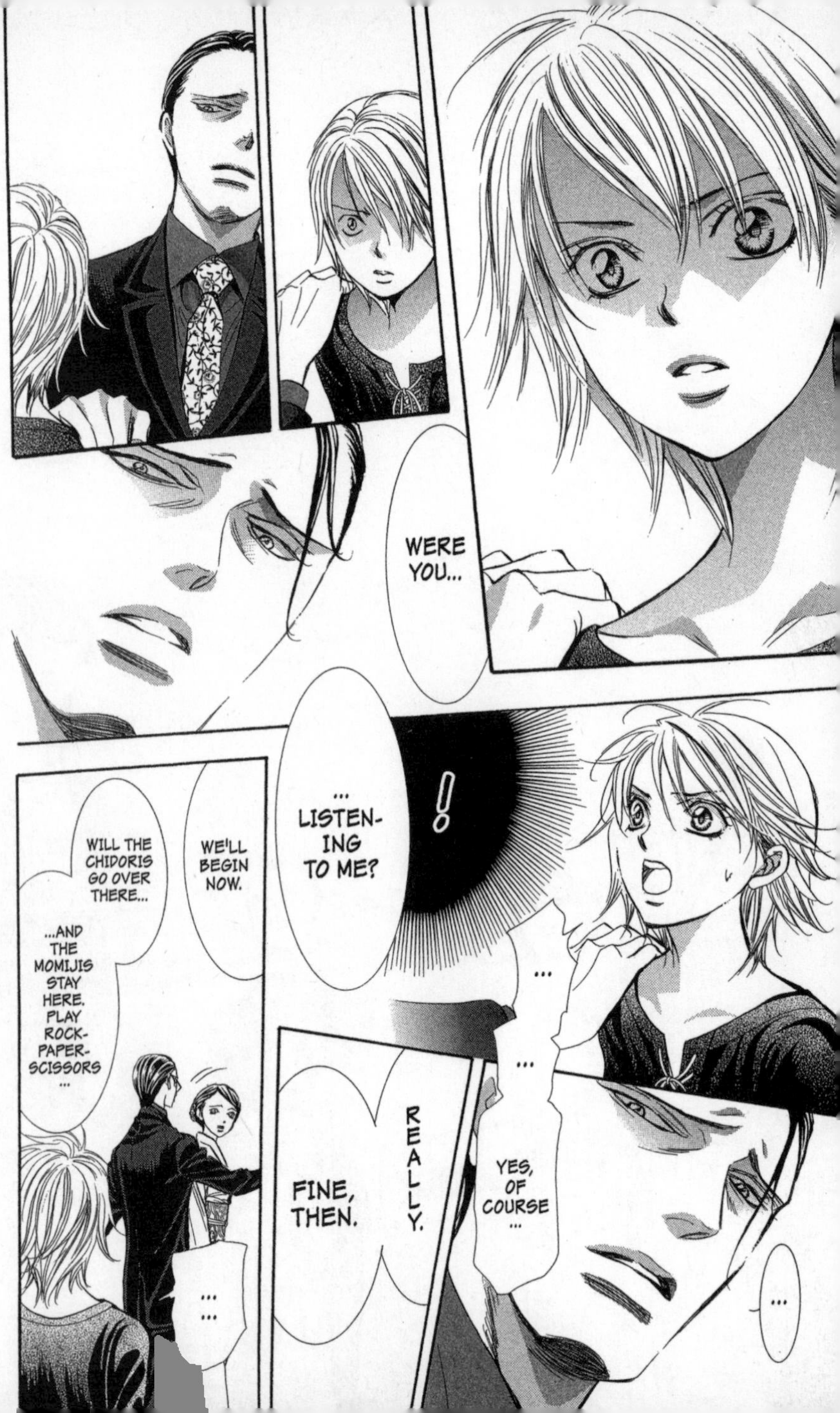
WERE YOU...
...LISTENING TO ME?
!
...
...
YES, OF COURSE...
...
REALLY.
FINE, THEN.
WE'LL BEGIN NOW.
WILL THE CHIDORIS GO OVER THERE...
...AND THE MOMIJIS STAY HERE. PLAY ROCK-PAPER-SCISSORS...
... ...

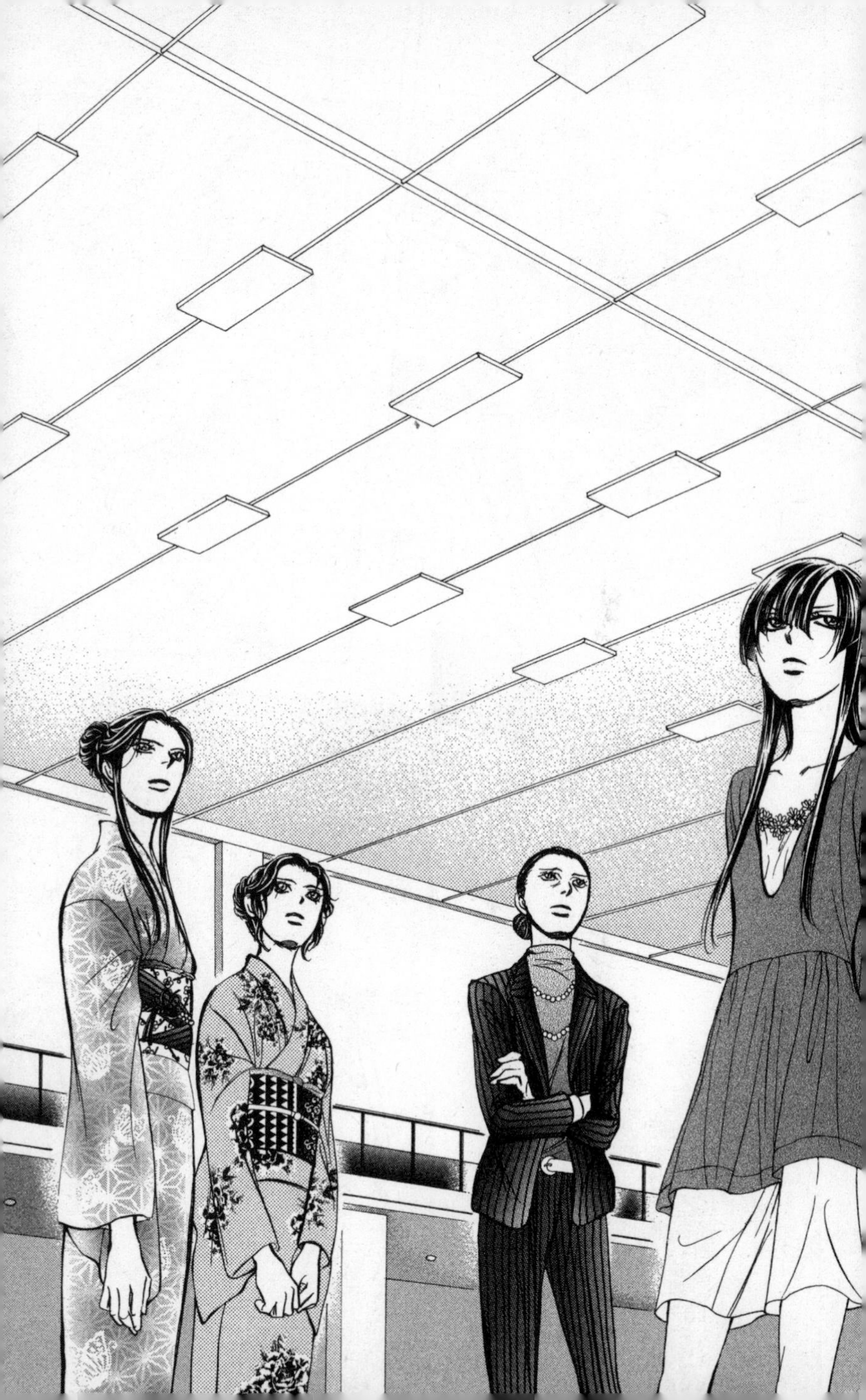

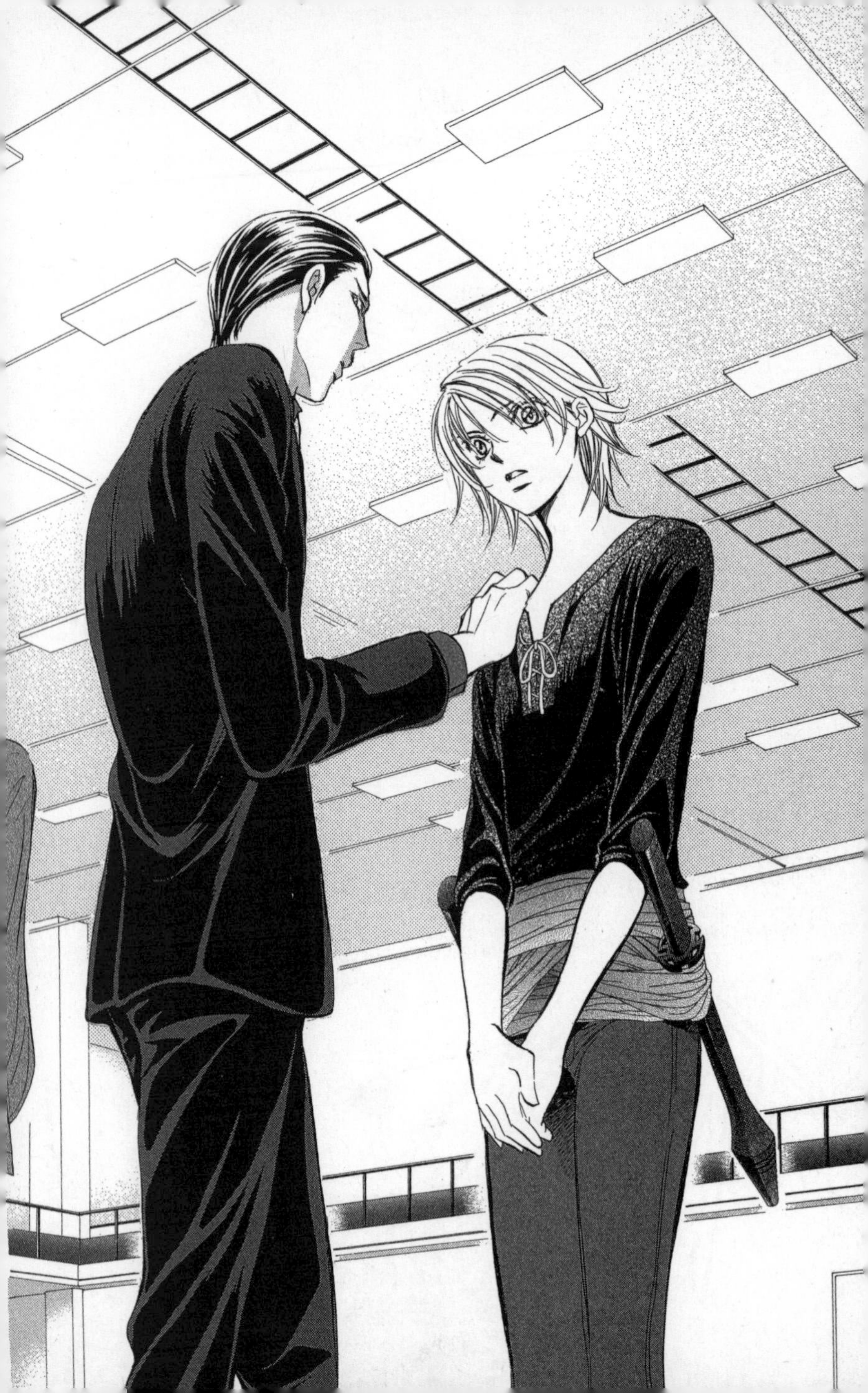

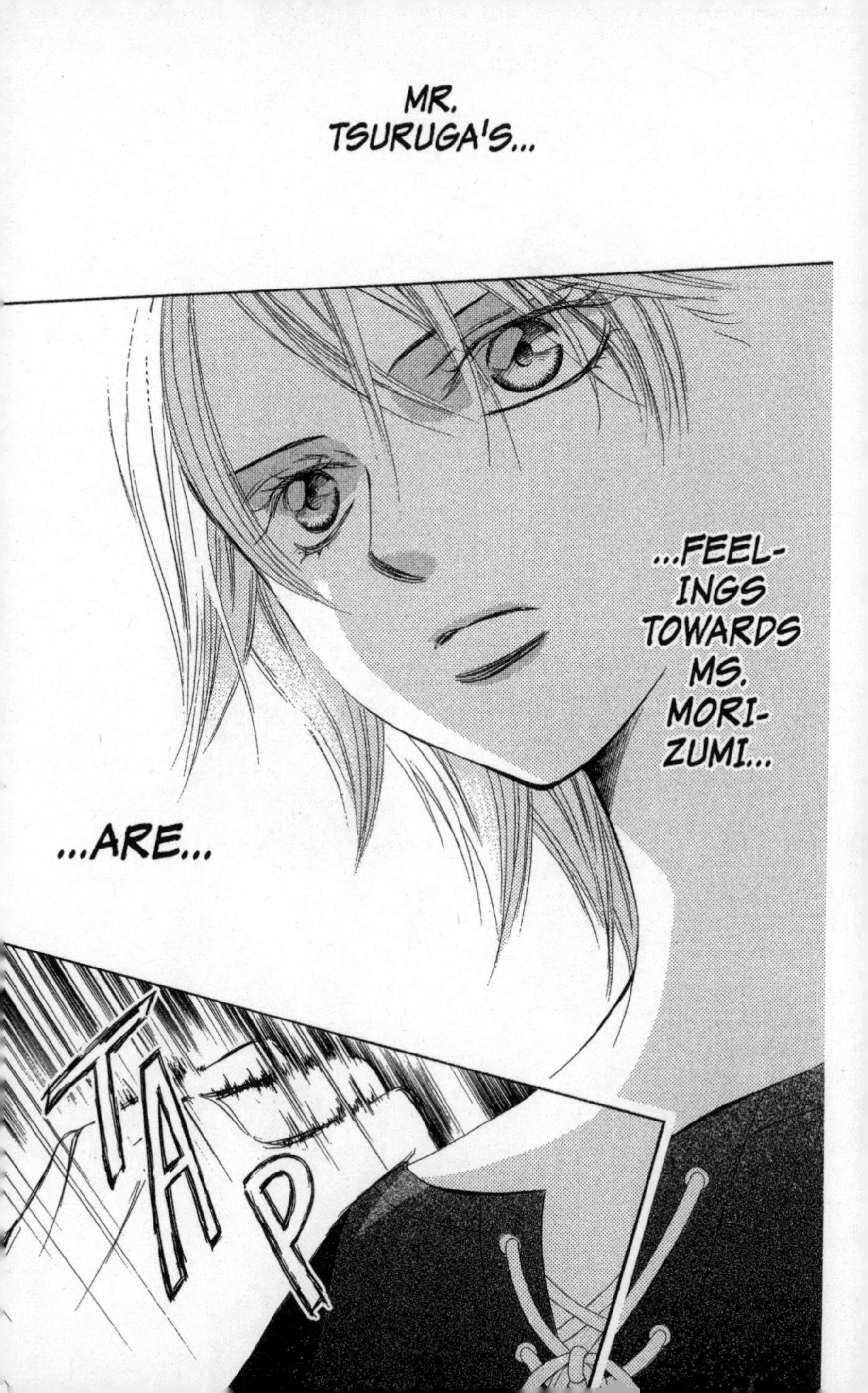
MR. TSURUGA'S...
...FEEL-INGS TOWARDS MS. MORI-ZUMI...
...ARE...
TAP

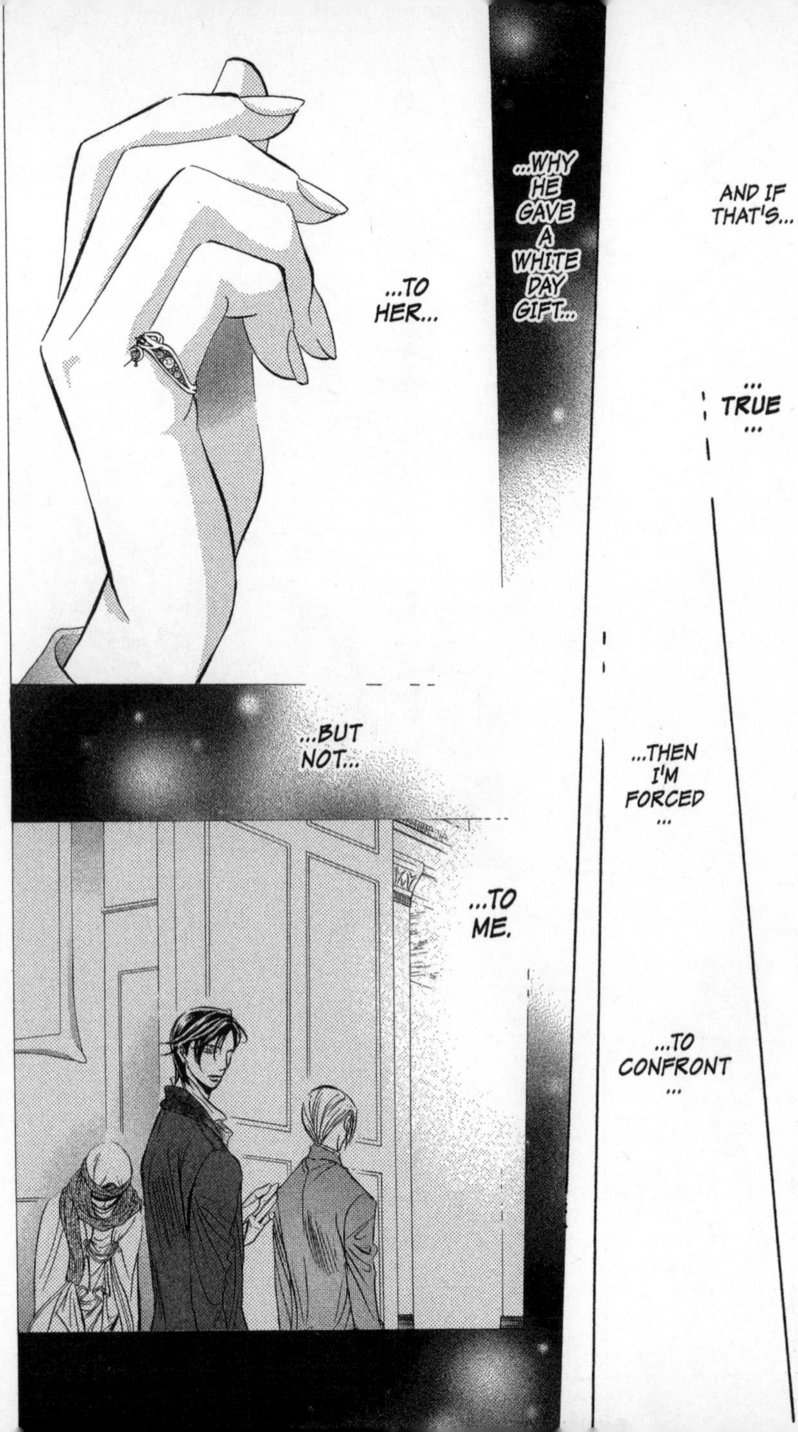
AND IF THAT'S...
...TRUE...
...THEN I'M FORCED...
...TO CONFRONT...
...WHY HE GAVE A WHITE DAY GIFT...
...TO HER...
...BUT NOT...
...TO ME.

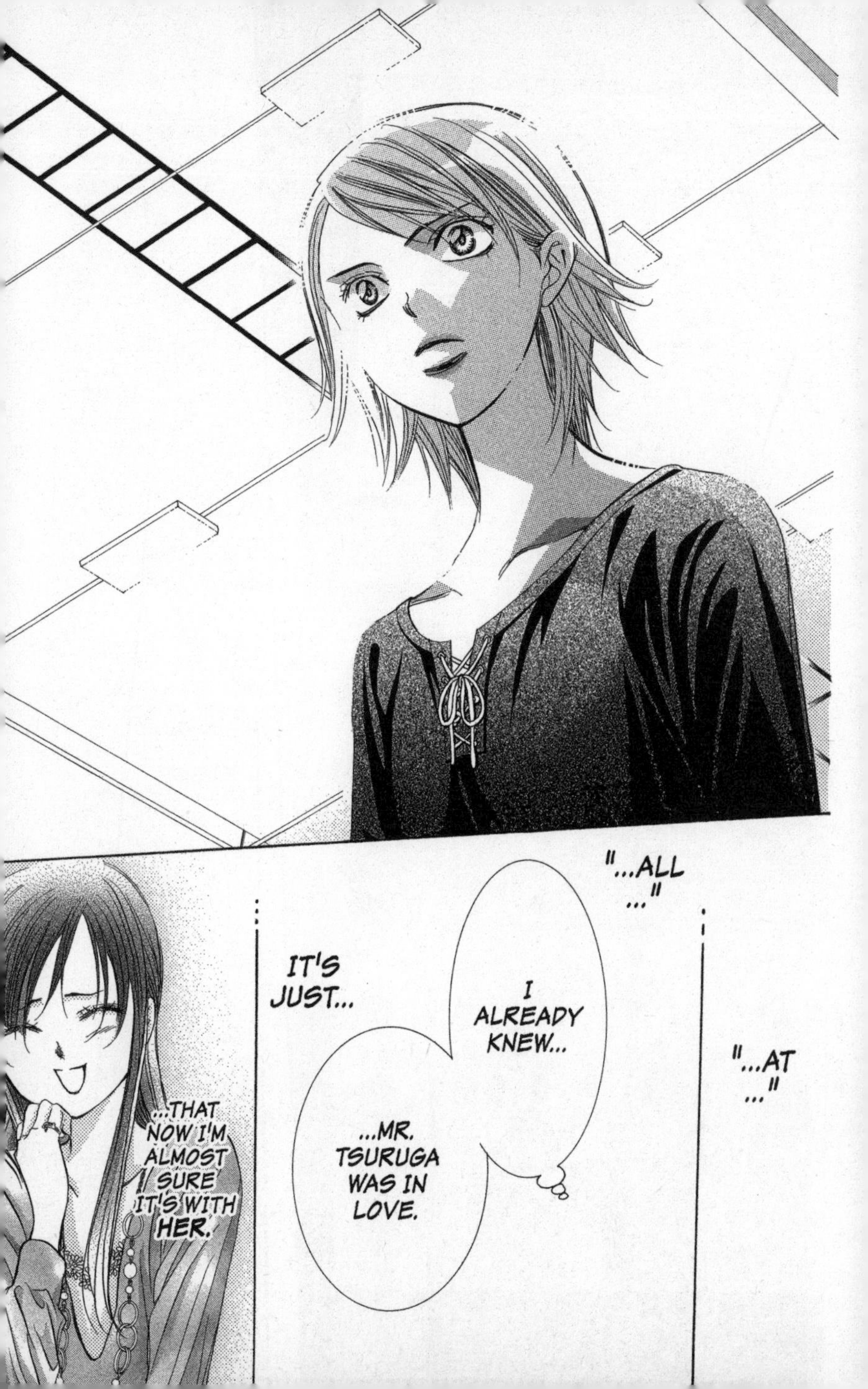
"...AT ..."
"...ALL ..."
IT'S JUST...
I ALREADY KNEW...
...MR. TSURUGA WAS IN LOVE.
...THAT NOW I'M ALMOST SURE IT'S WITH HER.

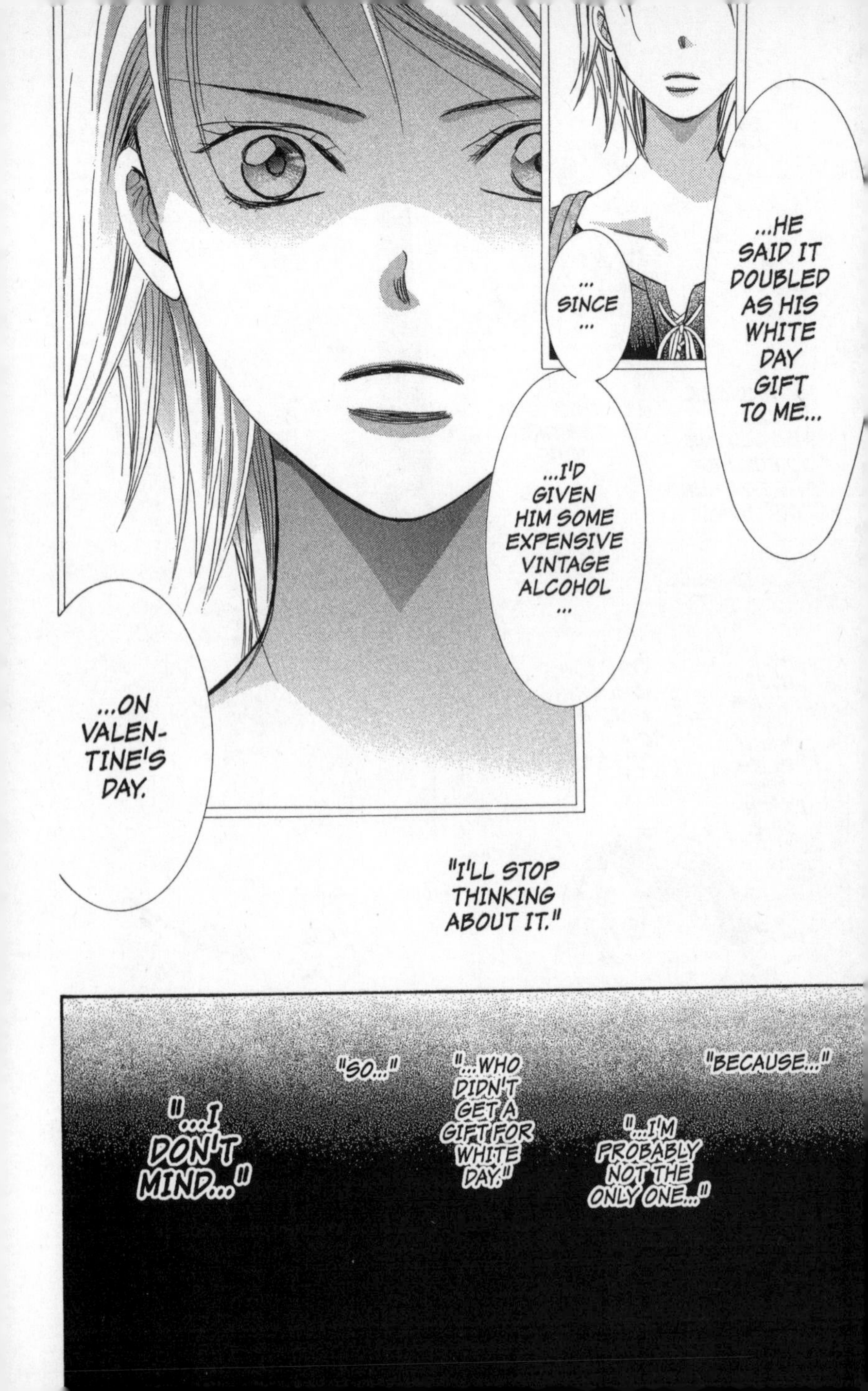
...HE SAID IT DOUBLED AS HIS WHITE DAY GIFT TO ME...
...SINCE...
...I'D GIVEN HIM SOME EXPENSIVE VINTAGE ALCOHOL...
...ON VALEN-TINE'S DAY.
"I'LL STOP THINKING ABOUT IT."
"BECAUSE..."
"...I'M PROBABLY NOT THE ONLY ONE..."
"...WHO DIDN'T GET A GIFT FOR WHITE DAY."
"SO..."
"...I DON'T MIND..."

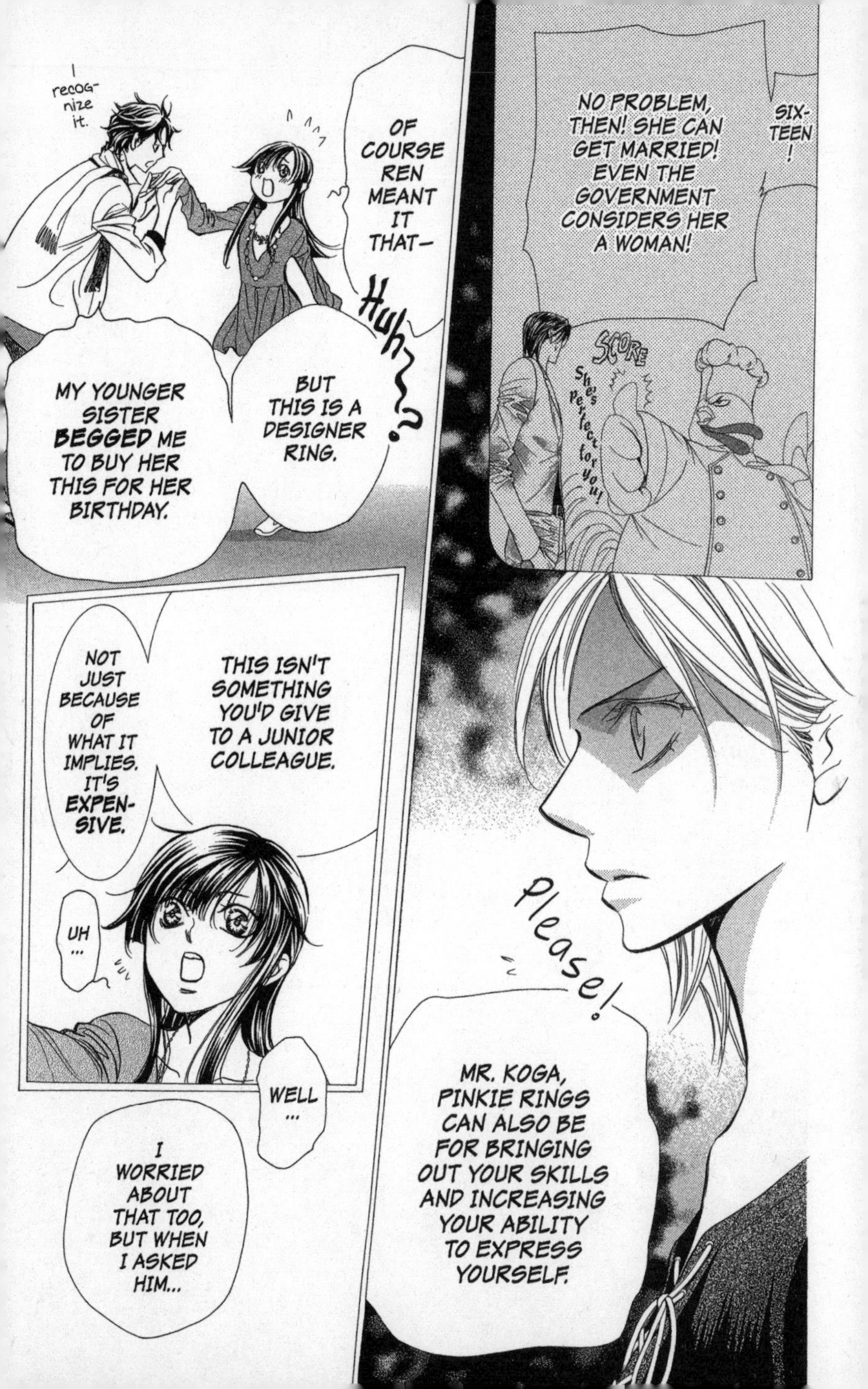
SIX-TEEN!
NO PROBLEM, THEN! SHE CAN GET MARRIED! EVEN THE GOVERNMENT CONSIDERS HER A WOMAN!
SCORE
She's perfect for you!
Please!
MR. KOGA, PINKIE RINGS CAN ALSO BE FOR BRINGING OUT YOUR SKILLS AND INCREASING YOUR ABILITY TO EXPRESS YOURSELF.
OF COURSE REN MEANT IT THAT—
Huh~~?
BUT THIS IS A DESIGNER RING.
MY YOUNGER SISTER BEGGED ME TO BUY HER THIS FOR HER BIRTHDAY.
I recog-nize it.
THIS ISN'T SOMETHING YOU'D GIVE TO A JUNIOR COLLEAGUE.
NOT JUST BECAUSE OF WHAT IT IMPLIES. IT'S EXPEN-SIVE.
UH...
WELL...
I WORRIED ABOUT THAT TOO, BUT WHEN I ASKED HIM...

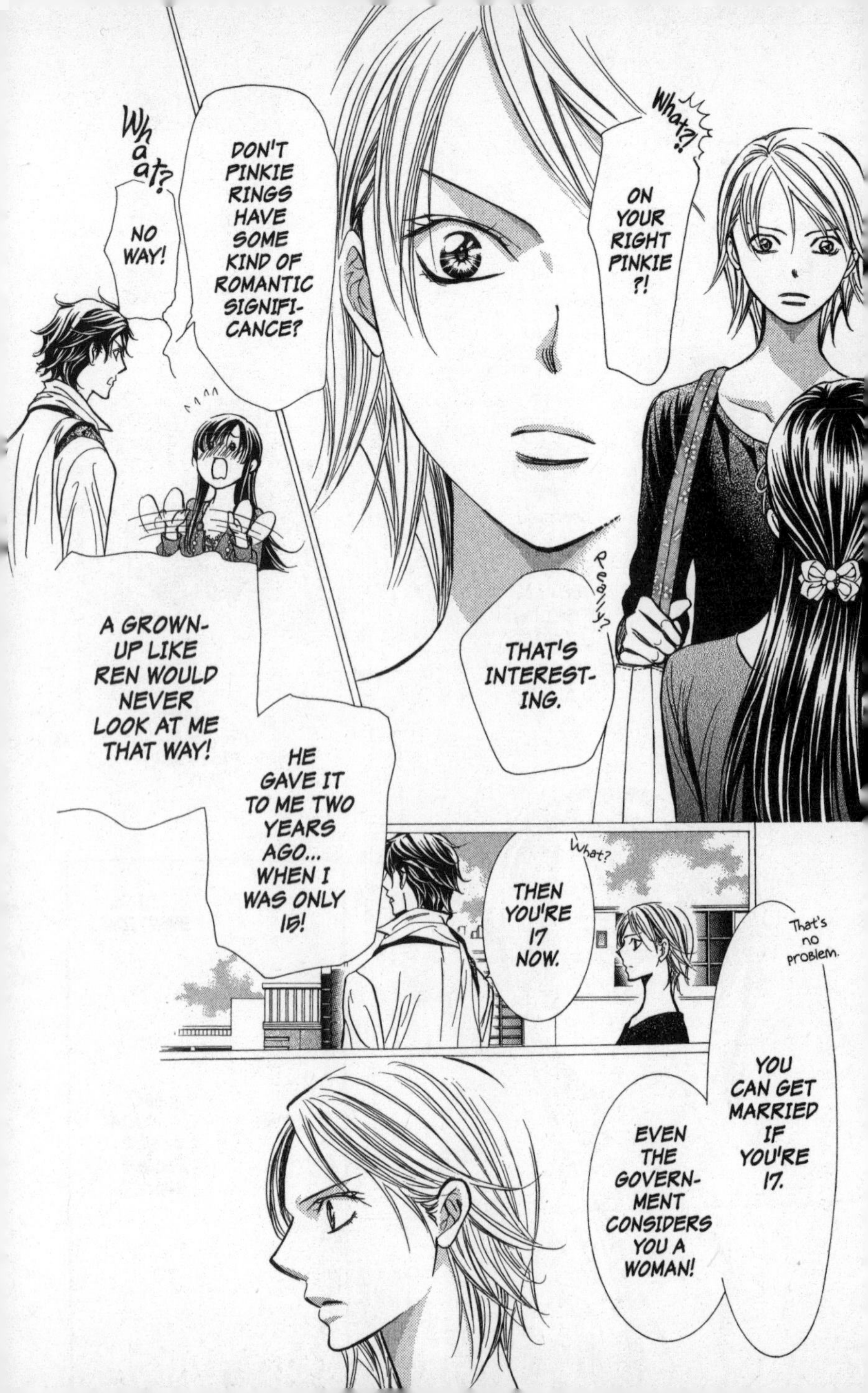
What?!
ON YOUR RIGHT PINKIE?!
DON'T PINKIE RINGS HAVE SOME KIND OF ROMANTIC SIGNIFICANCE?
Really?
THAT'S INTERESTING.
Whaat?
NO WAY!
A GROWN-UP LIKE REN WOULD NEVER LOOK AT ME THAT WAY!
HE GAVE IT TO ME TWO YEARS AGO... WHEN I WAS ONLY 15!
What?
THEN YOU'RE 17 NOW.
That's no problem.
YOU CAN GET MARRIED IF YOU'RE 17.
EVEN THE GOVERNMENT CONSIDERS YOU A WOMAN!

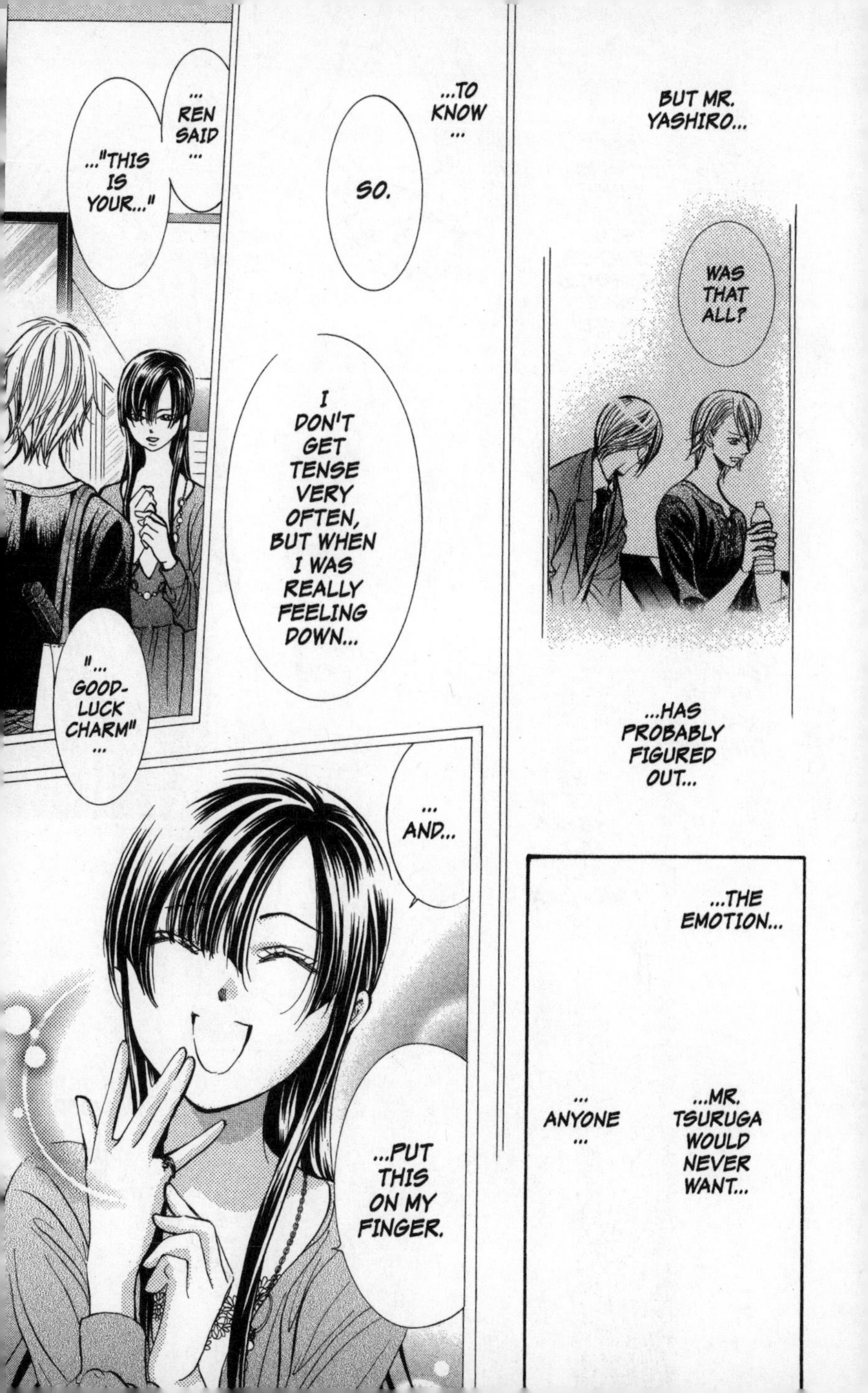
BUT MR. YASHIRO...
WAS THAT ALL?
...HAS PROBABLY FIGURED OUT...
...THE EMOTION...
...MR. TSURUGA WOULD NEVER WANT...
... ANYONE ...
...TO KNOW ...
SO.
I DON'T GET TENSE VERY OFTEN, BUT WHEN I WAS REALLY FEELING DOWN...
... REN SAID ...
..."THIS IS YOUR..."
"... GOOD-LUCK CHARM" ...
... AND...
...PUT THIS ON MY FINGER.

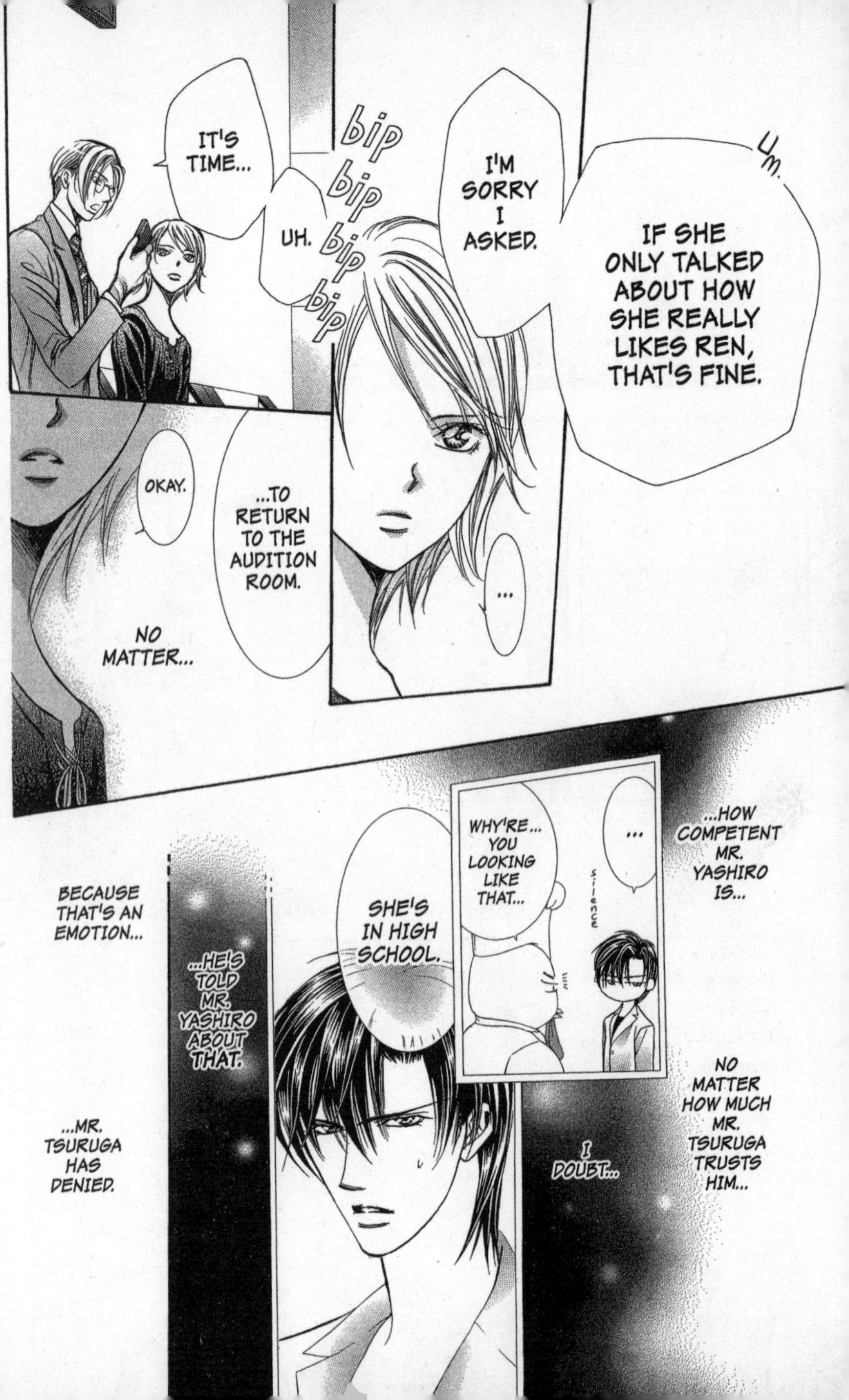
Um.
IF SHE ONLY TALKED ABOUT HOW SHE REALLY LIKES REN, THAT'S FINE.
I'M SORRY I ASKED.
...
bip bip bip bip
UH.
IT'S TIME...
...TO RETURN TO THE AUDITION ROOM.
OKAY.
NO MATTER...
...HOW COMPETENT MR. YASHIRO IS...
NO MATTER HOW MUCH MR. TSURUGA TRUSTS HIM...
...
silence
WHY'RE... YOU LOOKING LIKE THAT...
SHE'S IN HIGH SCHOOL.
I DOUBT...
...HE'S TOLD MR. YASHIRO ABOUT THAT.
BECAUSE THAT'S AN EMOTION...
...MR. TSURUGA HAS DENIED.

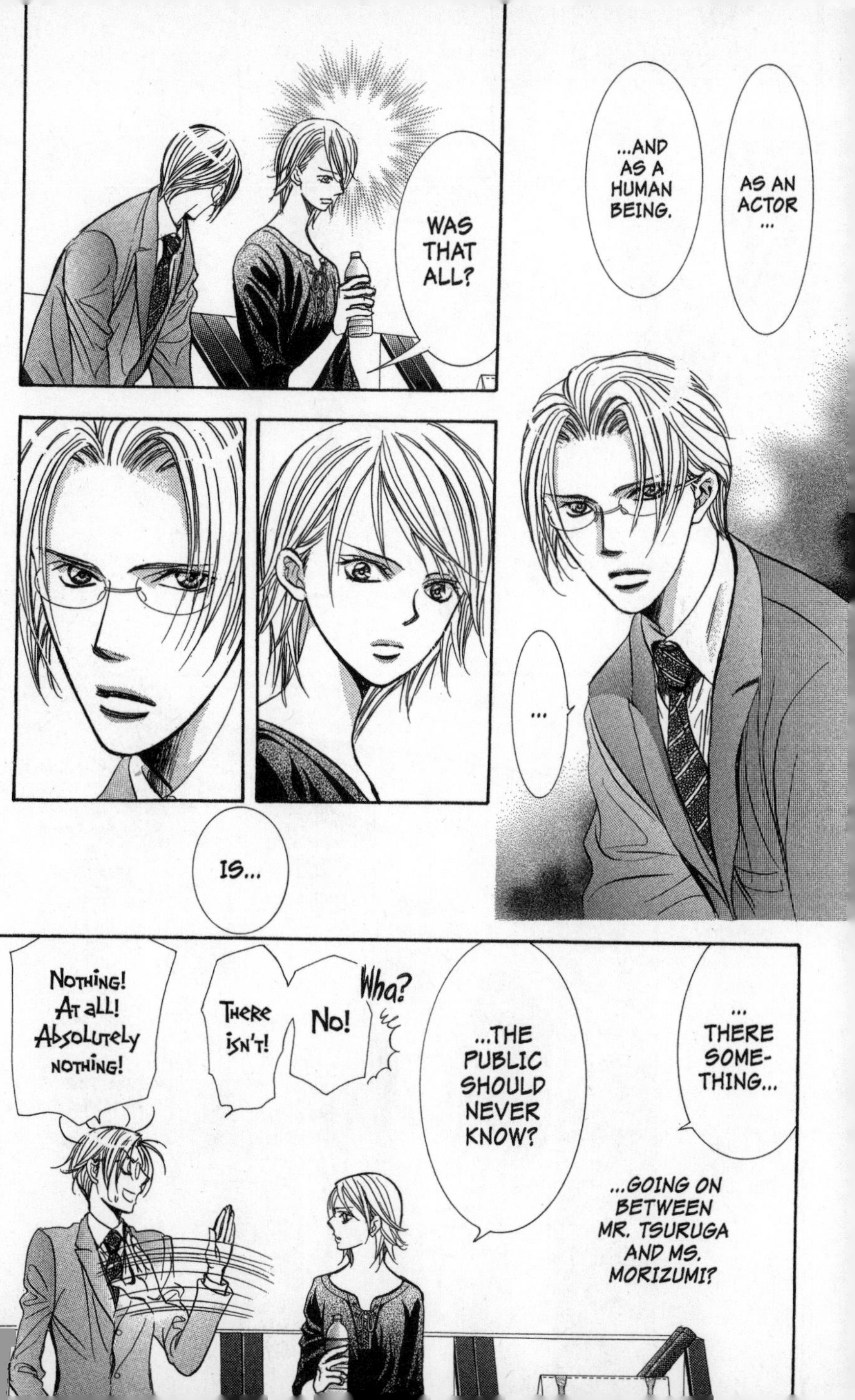
AS AN ACTOR ...
...AND AS A HUMAN BEING.
WAS THAT ALL?
...
IS...
... THERE SOMETHING...
...GOING ON BETWEEN MR. TSURUGA AND MS. MORIZUMI?
...THE PUBLIC SHOULD NEVER KNOW?
Wha?
No!
There isn't!
Nothing! At all! Absolutely nothing!

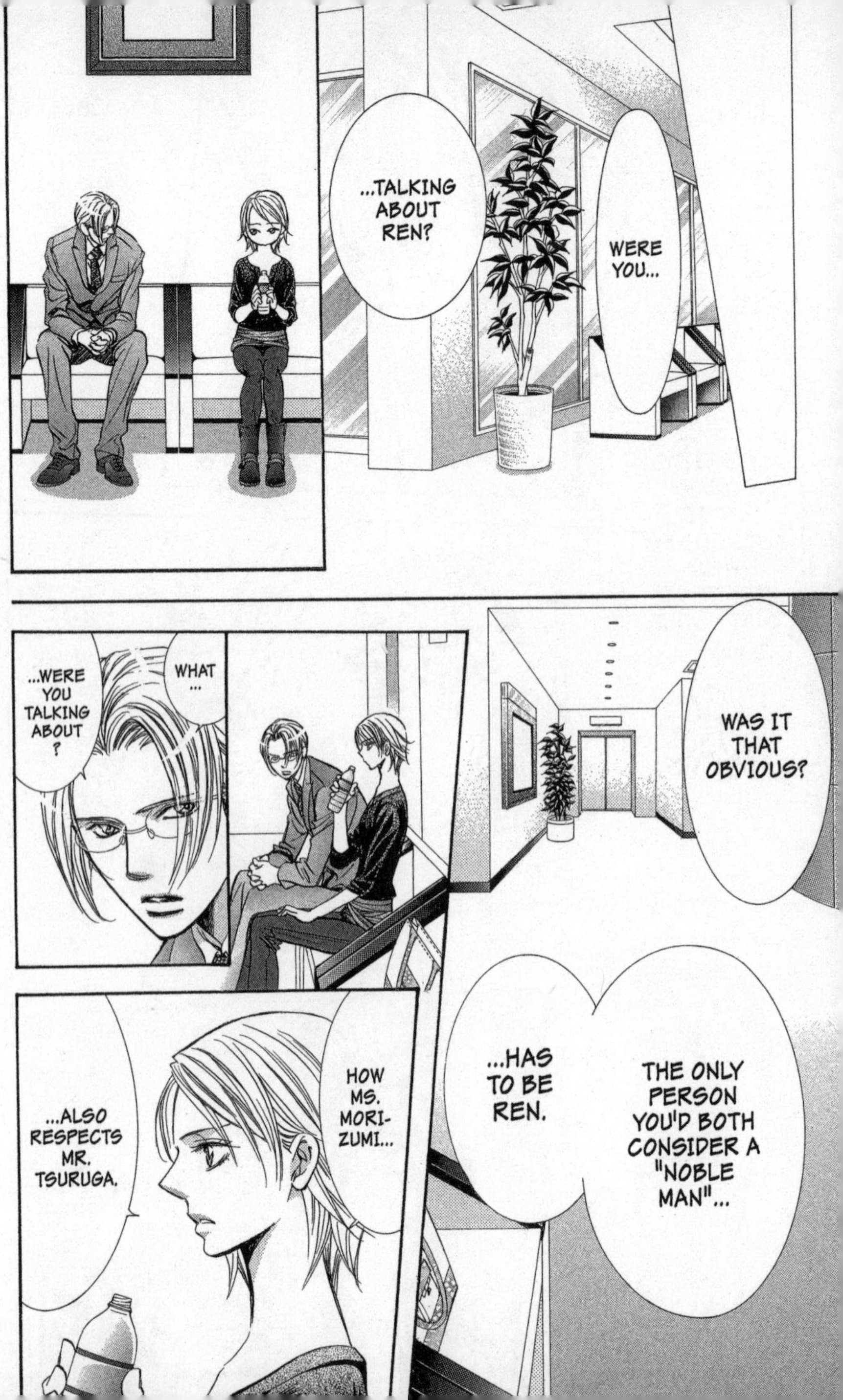
WERE YOU...
...TALKING ABOUT REN?
WAS IT THAT OBVIOUS?
WHAT ...
...WERE YOU TALKING ABOUT ?
THE ONLY PERSON YOU'D BOTH CONSIDER A "NOBLE MAN"...
...HAS TO BE REN.
HOW MS. MORI-ZUMI...
...ALSO RESPECTS MR. TSURUGA.

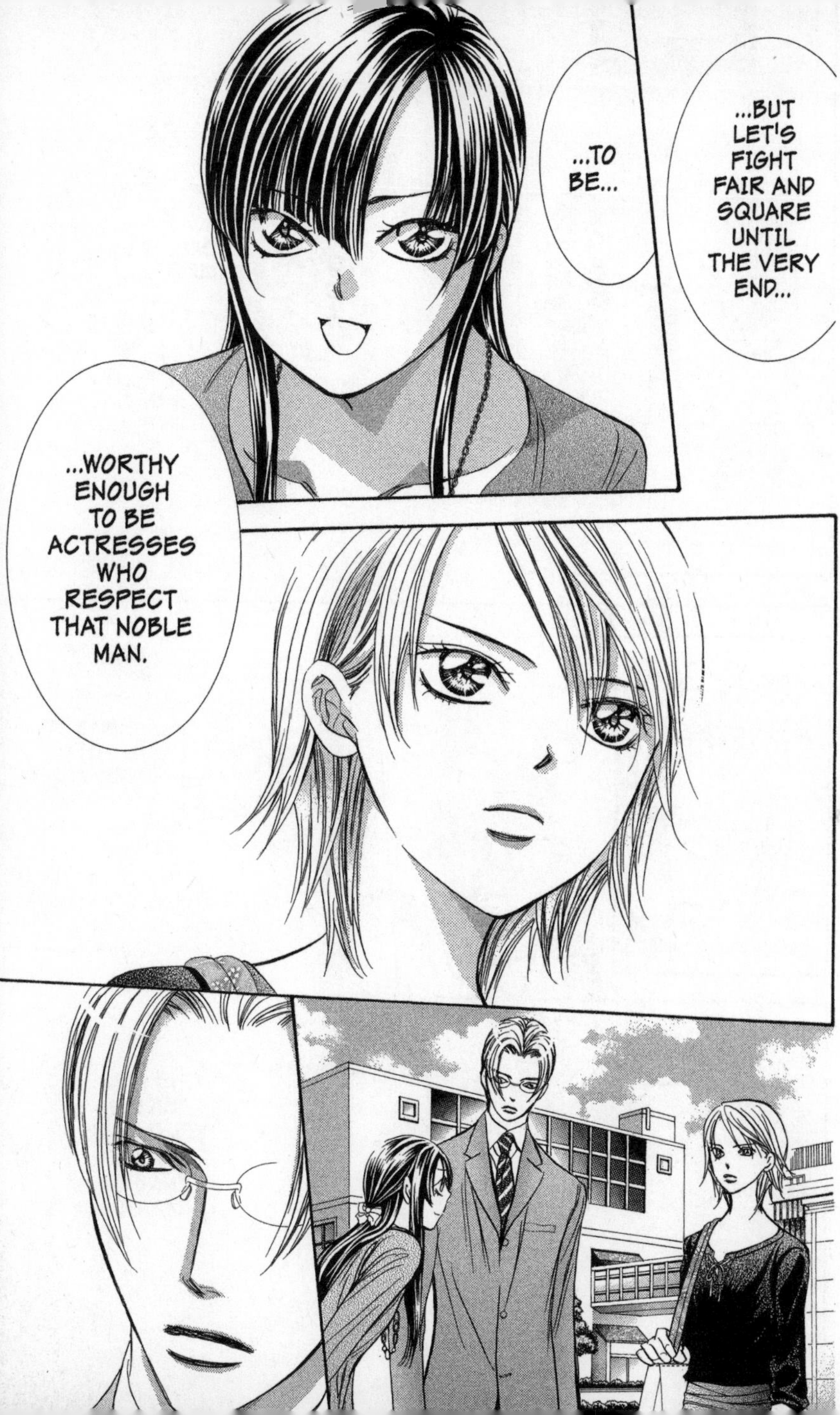
...BUT LET'S FIGHT FAIR AND SQUARE UNTIL THE VERY END...
...TO BE...
...WORTHY ENOUGH TO BE ACTRESSES WHO RESPECT THAT NOBLE MAN.

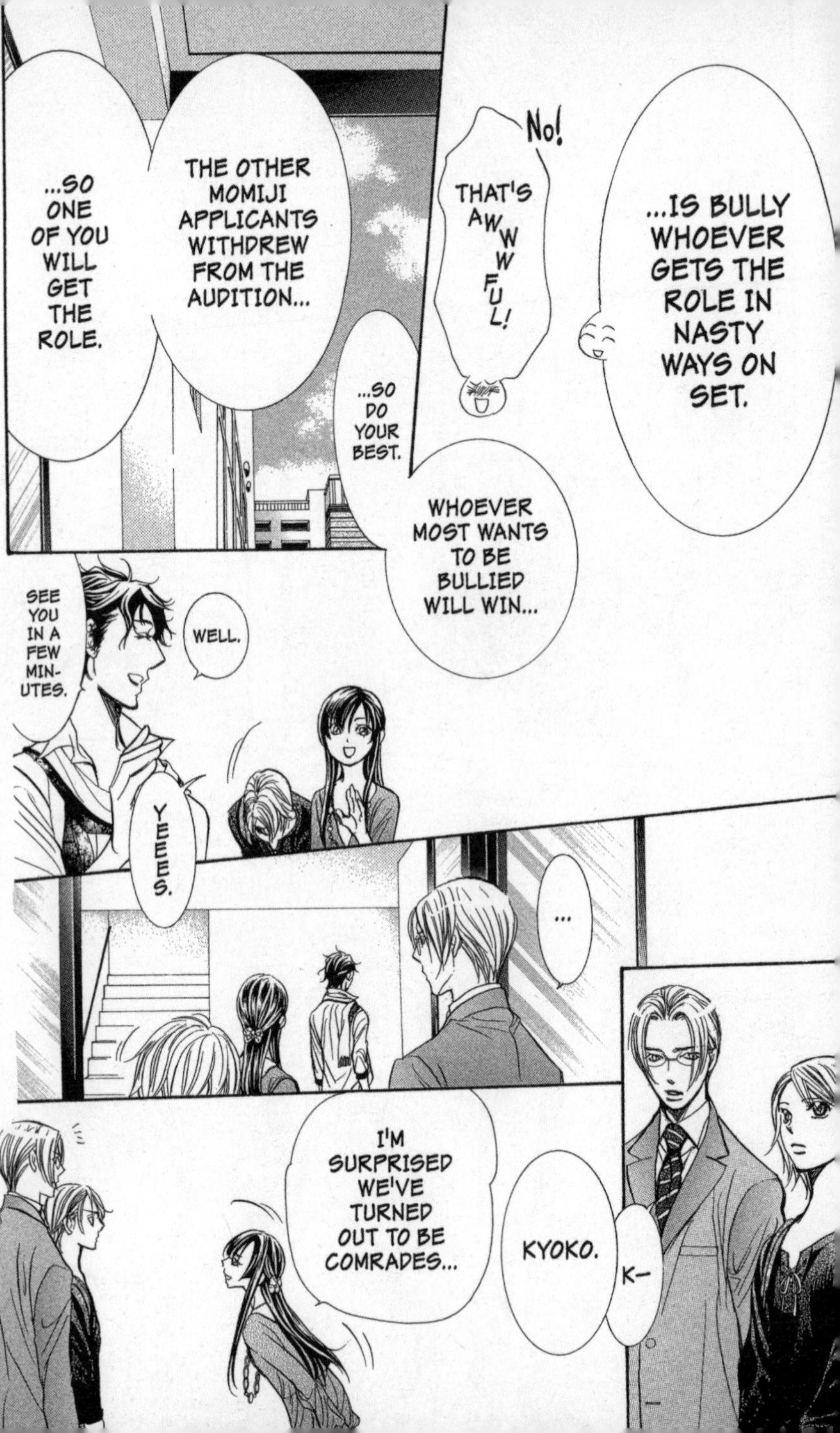
...IS BULLY WHOEVER GETS THE ROLE IN NASTY WAYS ON SET.
No! THAT'S AWWWFUL!
THE OTHER MOMIJI APPLICANTS WITHDREW FROM THE AUDITION...
...SO ONE OF YOU WILL GET THE ROLE.
...SO DO YOUR BEST.
WHOEVER MOST WANTS TO BE BULLIED WILL WIN...
WELL.
SEE YOU IN A FEW MIN-UTES.
YEEES.
...
K—
KYOKO.
I'M SURPRISED WE'VE TURNED OUT TO BE COMRADES...

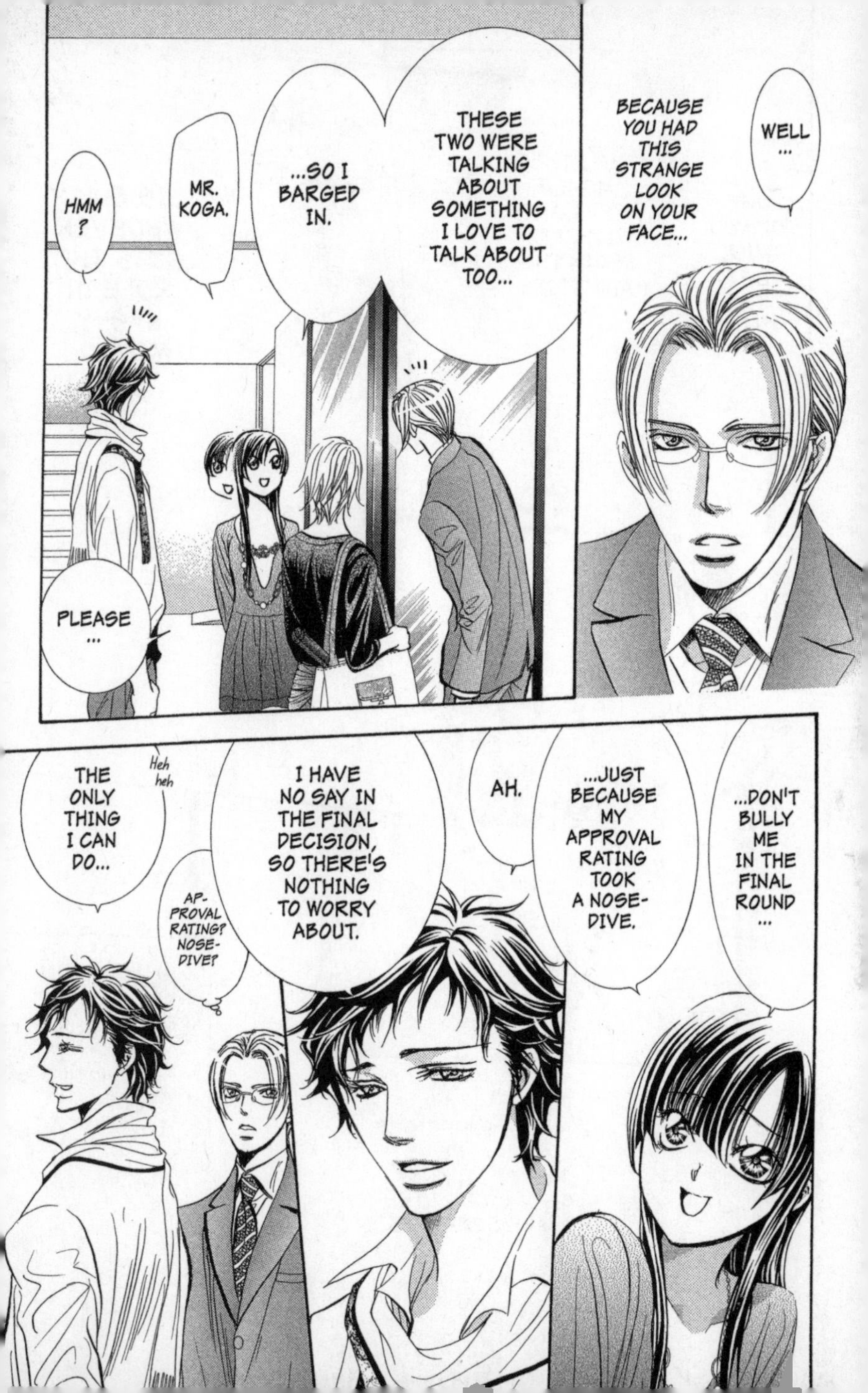
WELL ...
BECAUSE YOU HAD THIS STRANGE LOOK ON YOUR FACE...
THESE TWO WERE TALKING ABOUT SOMETHING I LOVE TO TALK ABOUT TOO...
...SO I BARGED IN.
MR. KOGA.
HMM ?
PLEASE ...
...DON'T BULLY ME IN THE FINAL ROUND ...
...JUST BECAUSE MY APPROVAL RATING TOOK A NOSE-DIVE.
AH.
I HAVE NO SAY IN THE FINAL DECISION, SO THERE'S NOTHING TO WORRY ABOUT.
AP-PROVAL RATING? NOSE-DIVE?
Heh heh
THE ONLY THING I CAN DO...

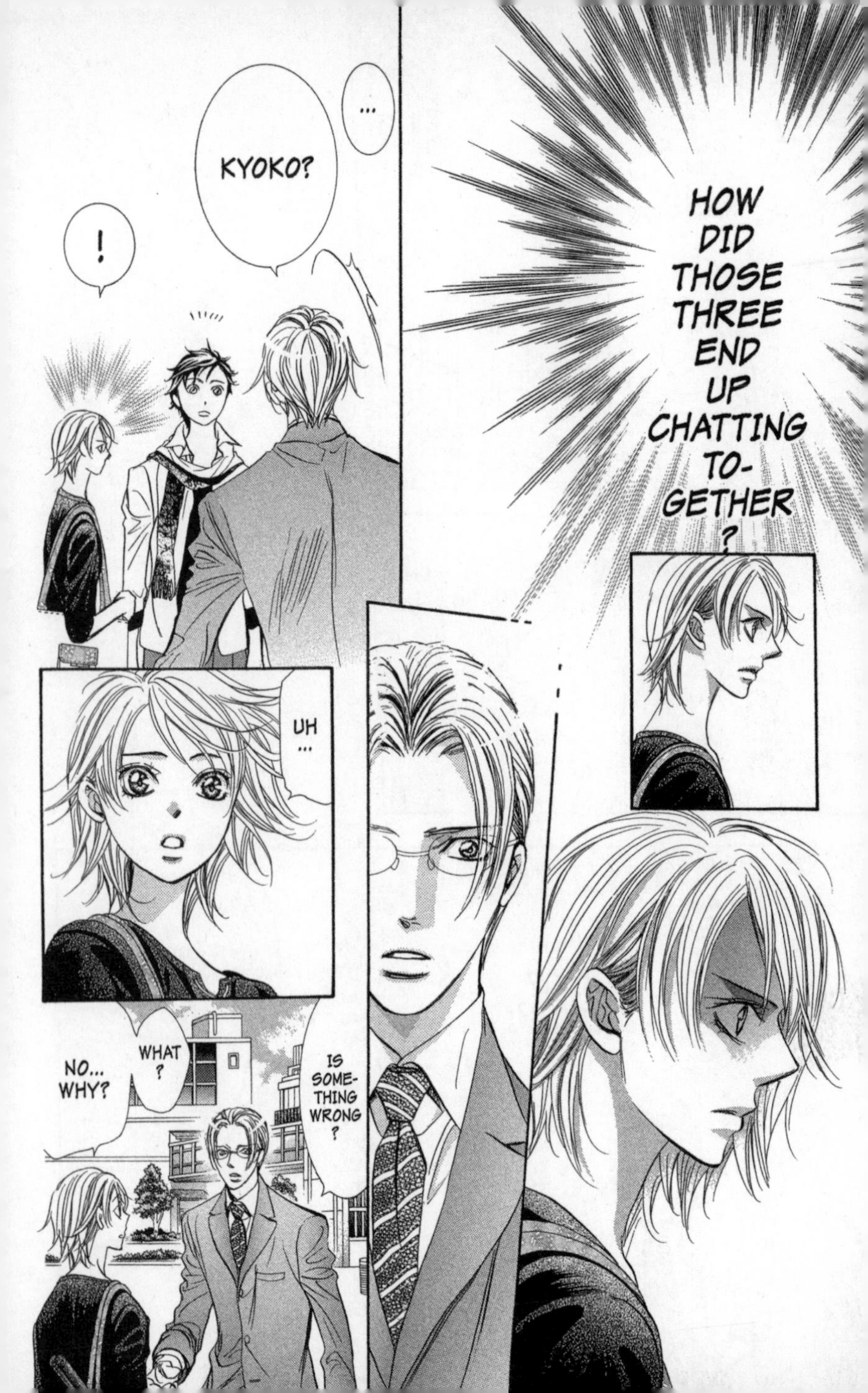
HOW DID THOSE THREE END UP CHATTING TO-GETHER?
...
KYOKO?
!
UH ...
IS SOME-THING WRONG?
WHAT?
NO... WHY?

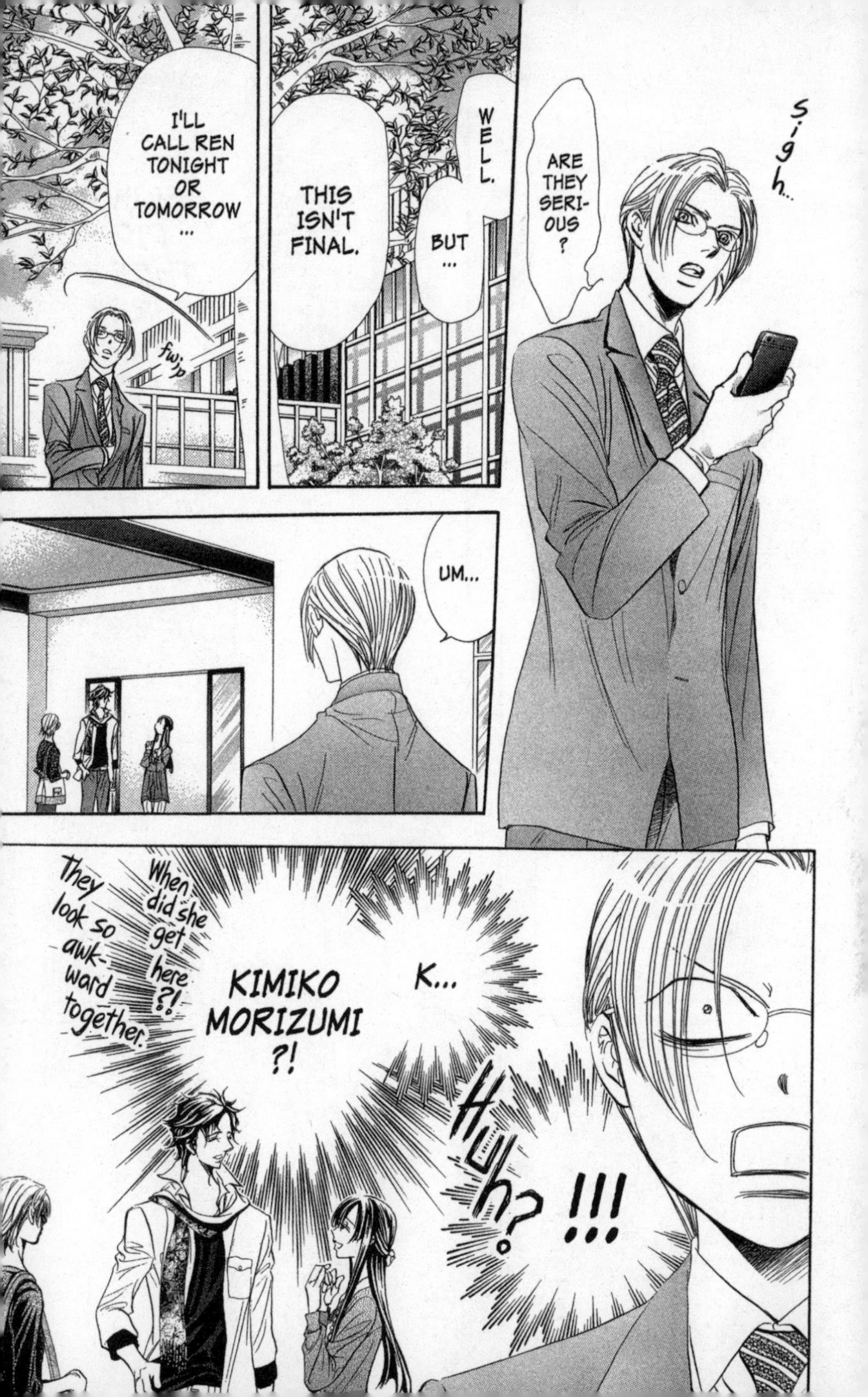
Sigh...
ARE THEY SERIOUS?
WELL.
BUT...
THIS ISN'T FINAL.
I'LL CALL REN TONIGHT OR TOMORROW...
fwip
UM...
HUh?!!!
K...
KIMIKO MORIZUMI?!
When did she get here?!
They look so awkward together.

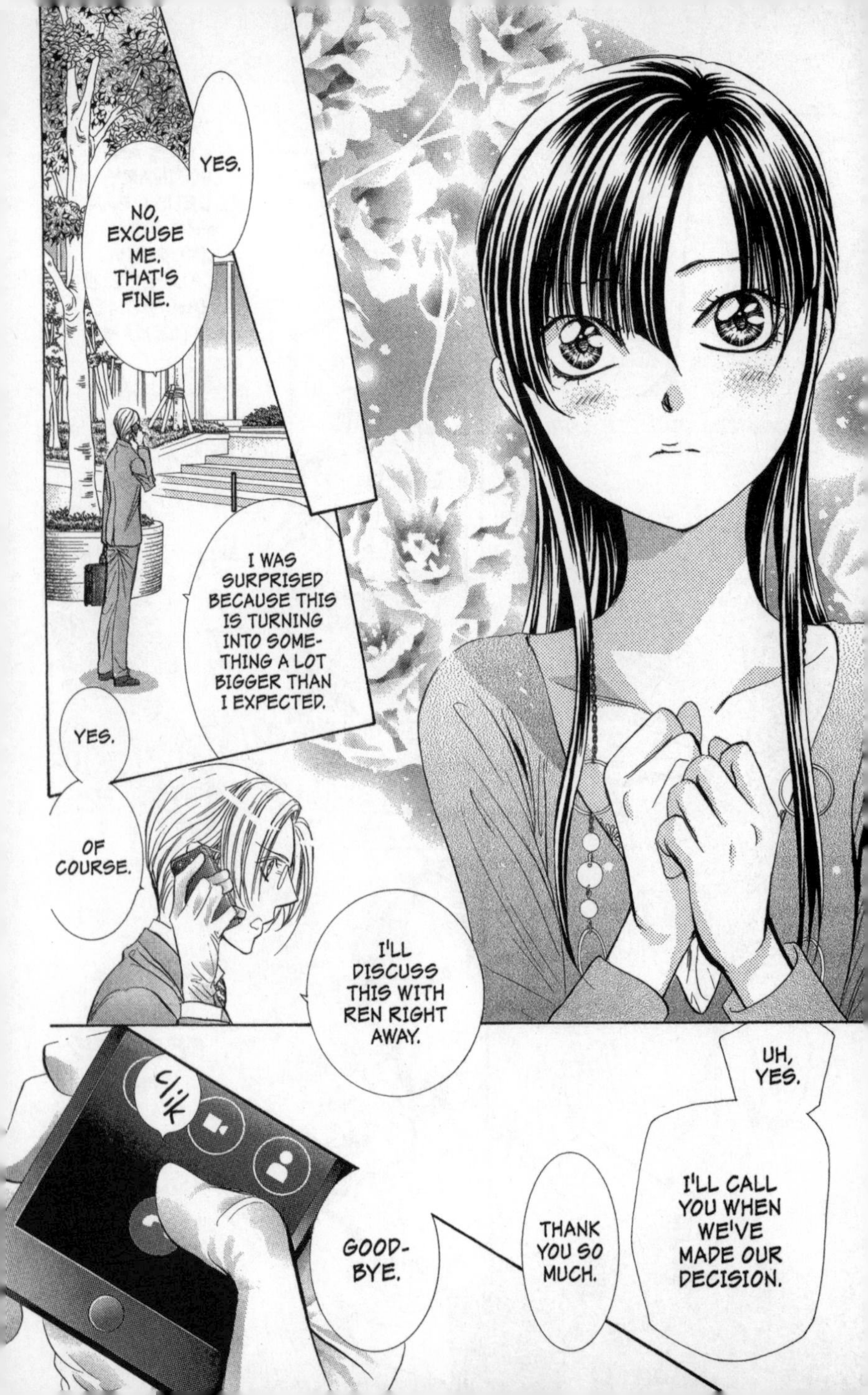
YES.
NO, EXCUSE ME. THAT'S FINE.
I WAS SURPRISED BECAUSE THIS IS TURNING INTO SOME-THING A LOT BIGGER THAN I EXPECTED.
YES.
OF COURSE.
I'LL DISCUSS THIS WITH REN RIGHT AWAY.
UH, YES.
I'LL CALL YOU WHEN WE'VE MADE OUR DECISION.
THANK YOU SO MUCH.
GOOD-BYE.
CLICK

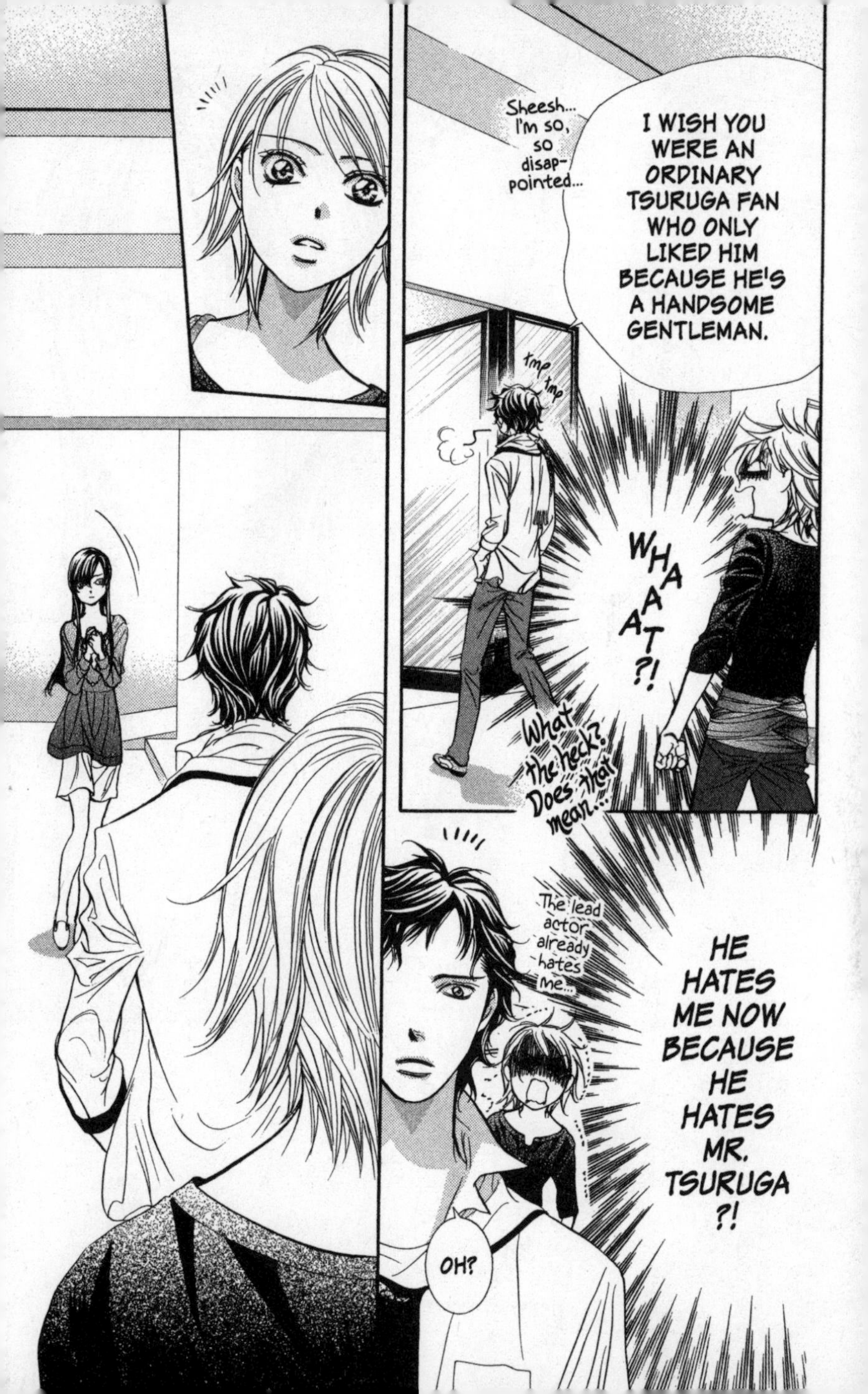
I WISH YOU WERE AN ORDINARY TSURUGA FAN WHO ONLY LIKED HIM BECAUSE HE'S A HANDSOME GENTLEMAN.
Sheesh... I'm so, so disappointed...
tmp tmp
WHAAAT?!
What the heck? Does that mean...
HE HATES ME NOW BECAUSE HE HATES MR. TSURUGA?!
The lead actor already hates me...
OH?

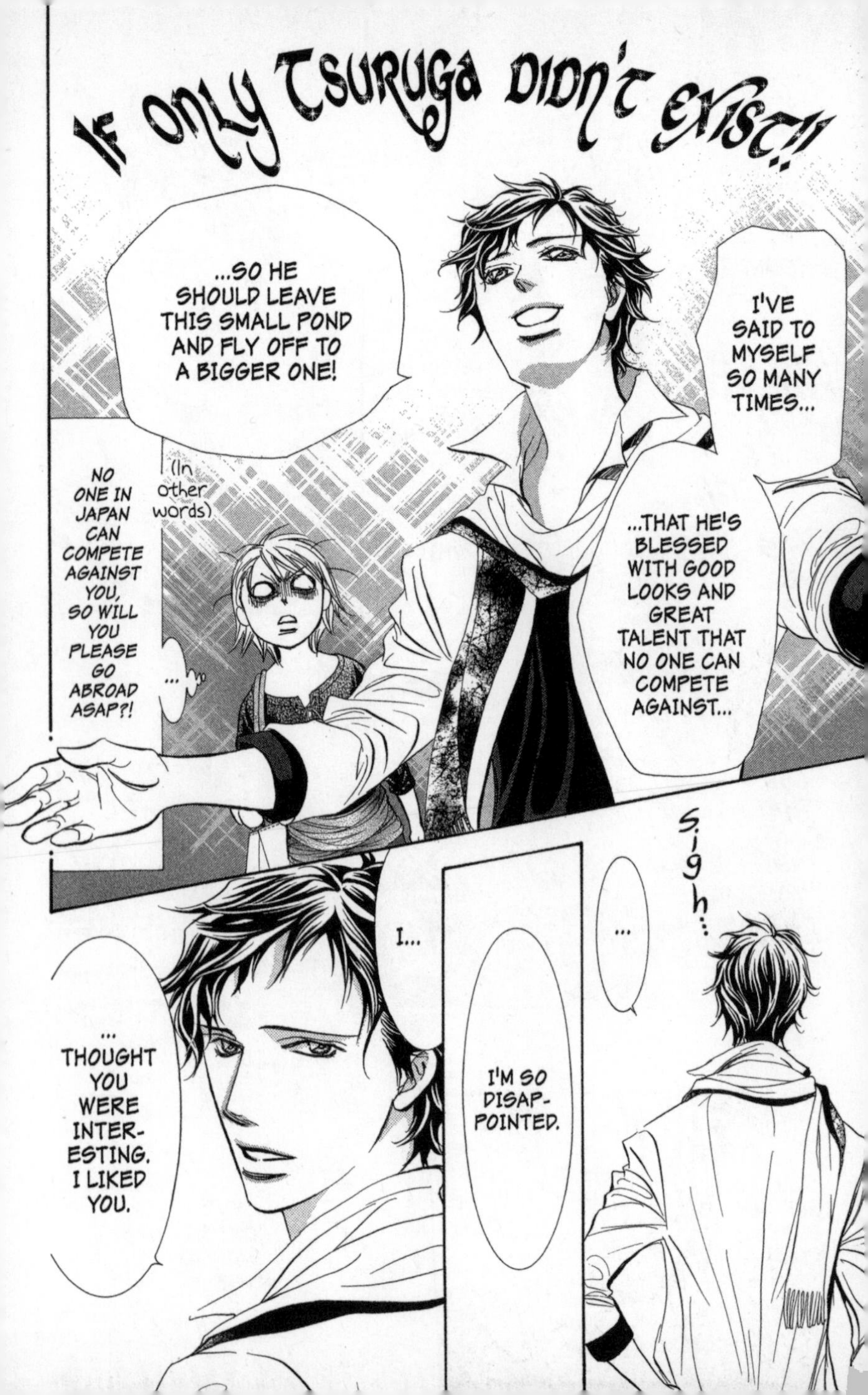
IF ONLY TSURUGA DIDN'T EXIST!!
I'VE SAID TO MYSELF SO MANY TIMES...
...THAT HE'S BLESSED WITH GOOD LOOKS AND GREAT TALENT THAT NO ONE CAN COMPETE AGAINST...
...SO HE SHOULD LEAVE THIS SMALL POND AND FLY OFF TO A BIGGER ONE!
(In other words)
NO ONE IN JAPAN CAN COMPETE AGAINST YOU, SO WILL YOU PLEASE GO ABROAD ASAP?!
...
Sigh...
...
I'M SO DISAP-POINTED.
I...
...THOUGHT YOU WERE INTER-ESTING. I LIKED YOU.

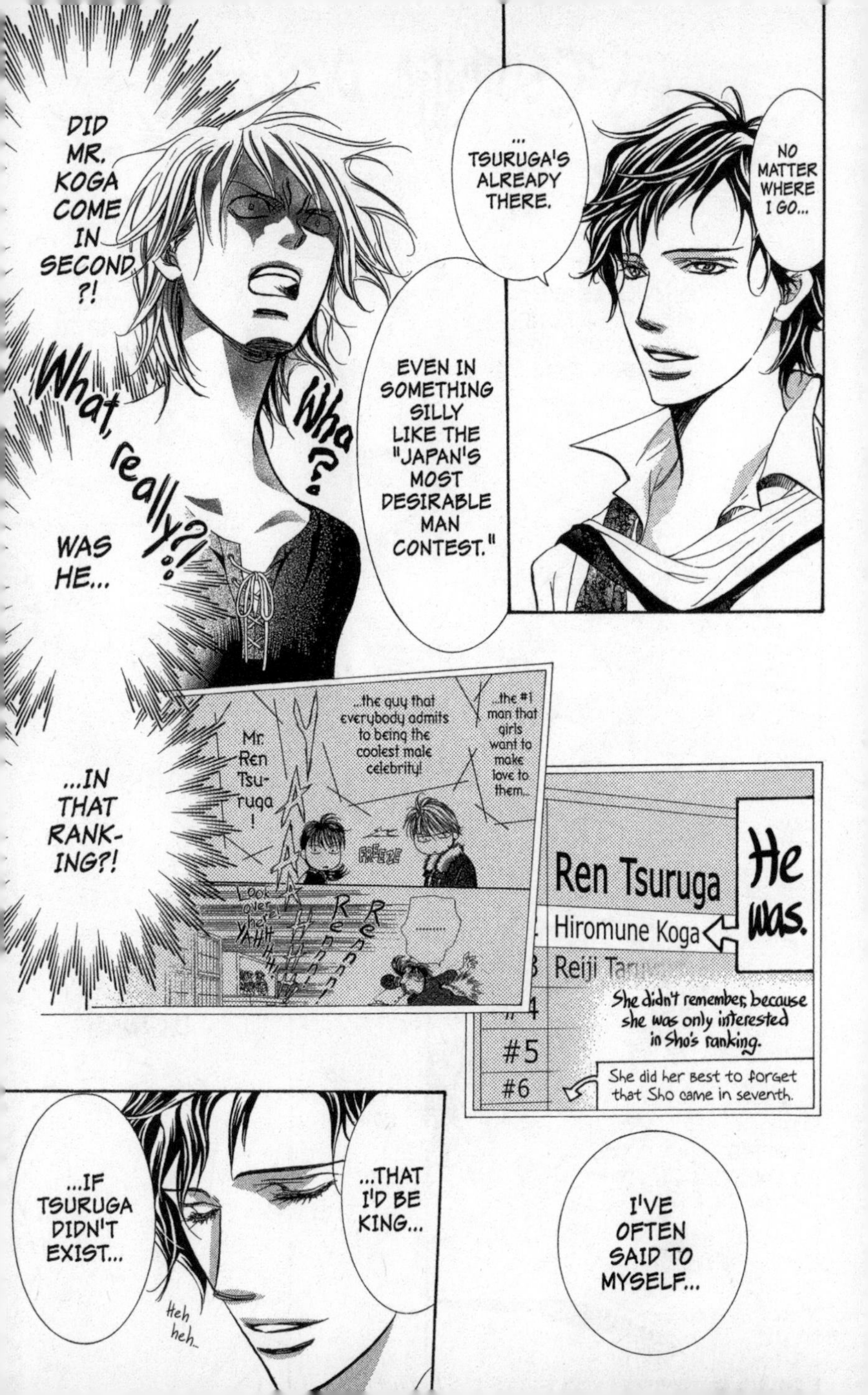
NO MATTER WHERE I GO...
...TSURUGA'S ALREADY THERE.
EVEN IN SOMETHING SILLY LIKE THE "JAPAN'S MOST DESIRABLE MAN CONTEST."
Wha?
What, really?!
DID MR. KOGA COME IN SECOND?!
WAS HE...
...IN THAT RANKING?!
He was.
Ren Tsuruga
Hiromune Koga
#5
#6
She didn't remember, because she was only interested in Sho's ranking.
She did her best to forget that Sho came in seventh.
...the #1 man that girls want to make love to them...
...the guy that everybody admits to being the coolest male celebrity!
Mr. Ren Tsuruga!
FREEZE
Rennnn!
Rennnn!
..........
I'VE OFTEN SAID TO MYSELF...
...THAT I'D BE KING...
...IF TSURUGA DIDN'T EXIST...
Heh heh...

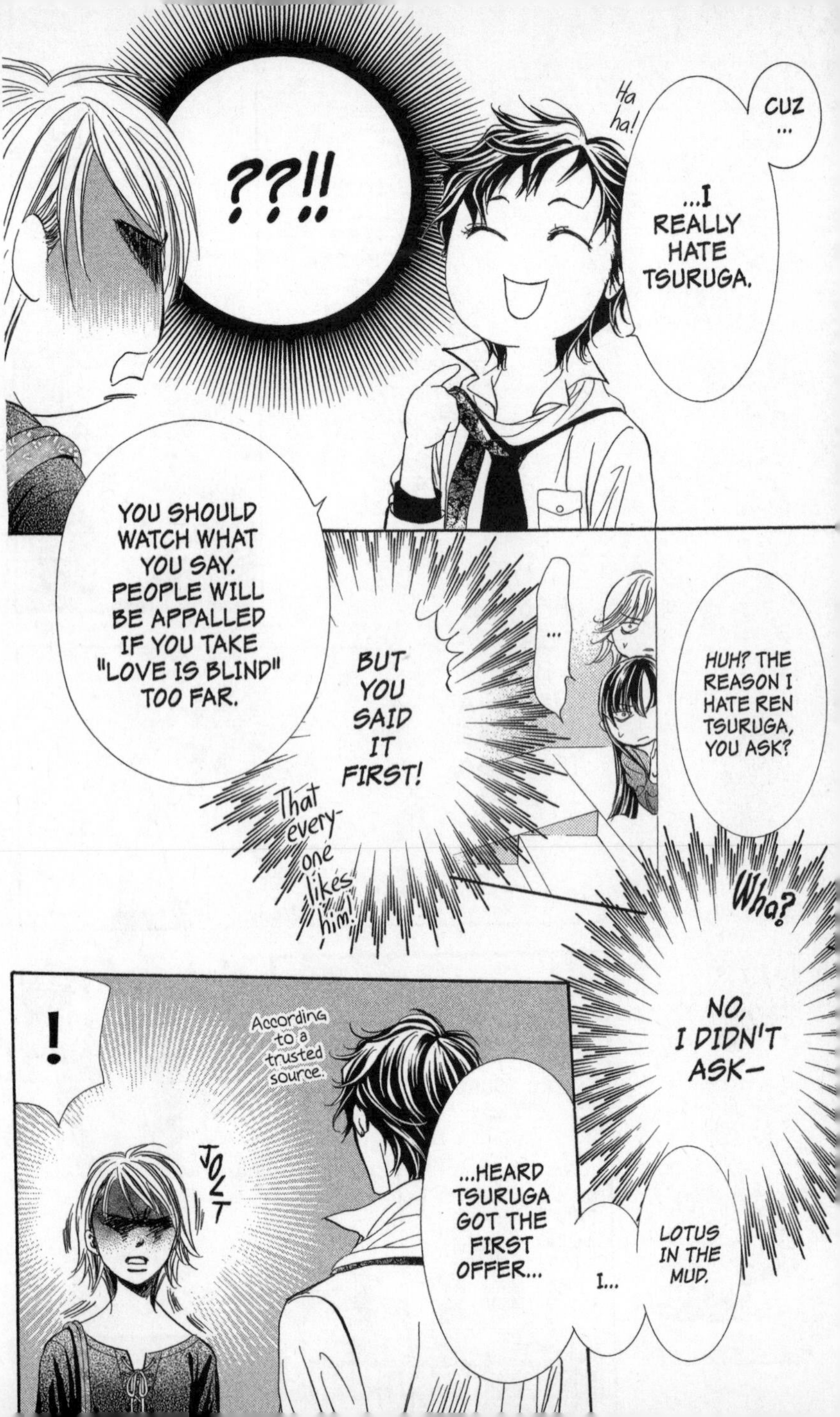
CUZ...
...I REALLY HATE TSURUGA.
Ha ha!
??!!
HUH? THE REASON I HATE REN TSURUGA, YOU ASK?
Wha?
...
YOU SHOULD WATCH WHAT YOU SAY. PEOPLE WILL BE APPALLED IF YOU TAKE "LOVE IS BLIND" TOO FAR.
BUT YOU SAID IT FIRST!
That every-one likes him!
NO, I DIDN'T ASK-
LOTUS IN THE MUD.
I...
...HEARD TSURUGA GOT THE FIRST OFFER...
According to a trusted source.
!
JOLT

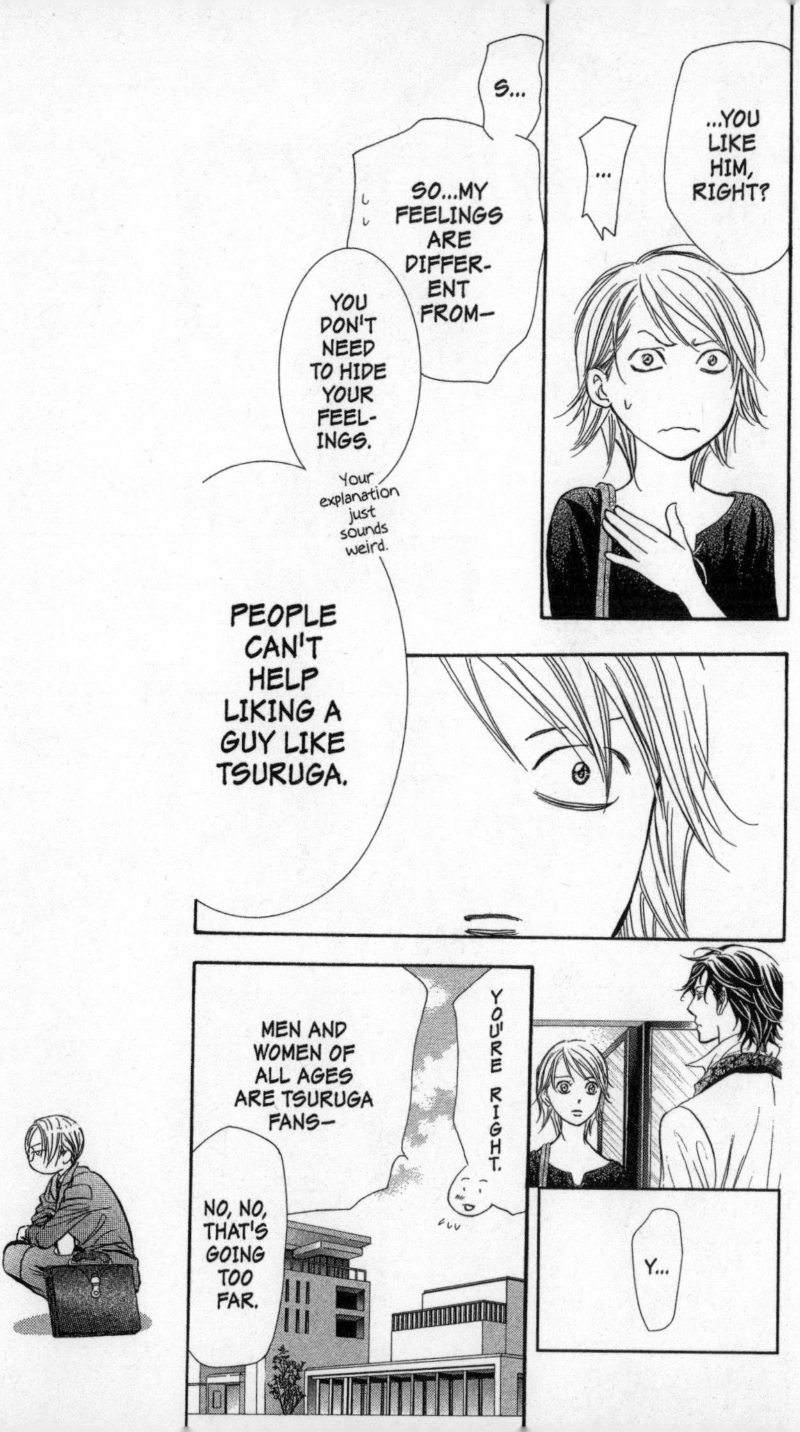
...YOU LIKE HIM, RIGHT?
...
S...
SO...MY FEELINGS ARE DIFFER-ENT FROM—
YOU DON'T NEED TO HIDE YOUR FEEL-INGS.
Your explanation just sounds weird.
PEOPLE CAN'T HELP LIKING A GUY LIKE TSURUGA.
Y...
YOU'RE RIGHT.
MEN AND WOMEN OF ALL AGES ARE TSURUGA FANS—
NO, NO, THAT'S GOING TOO FAR.

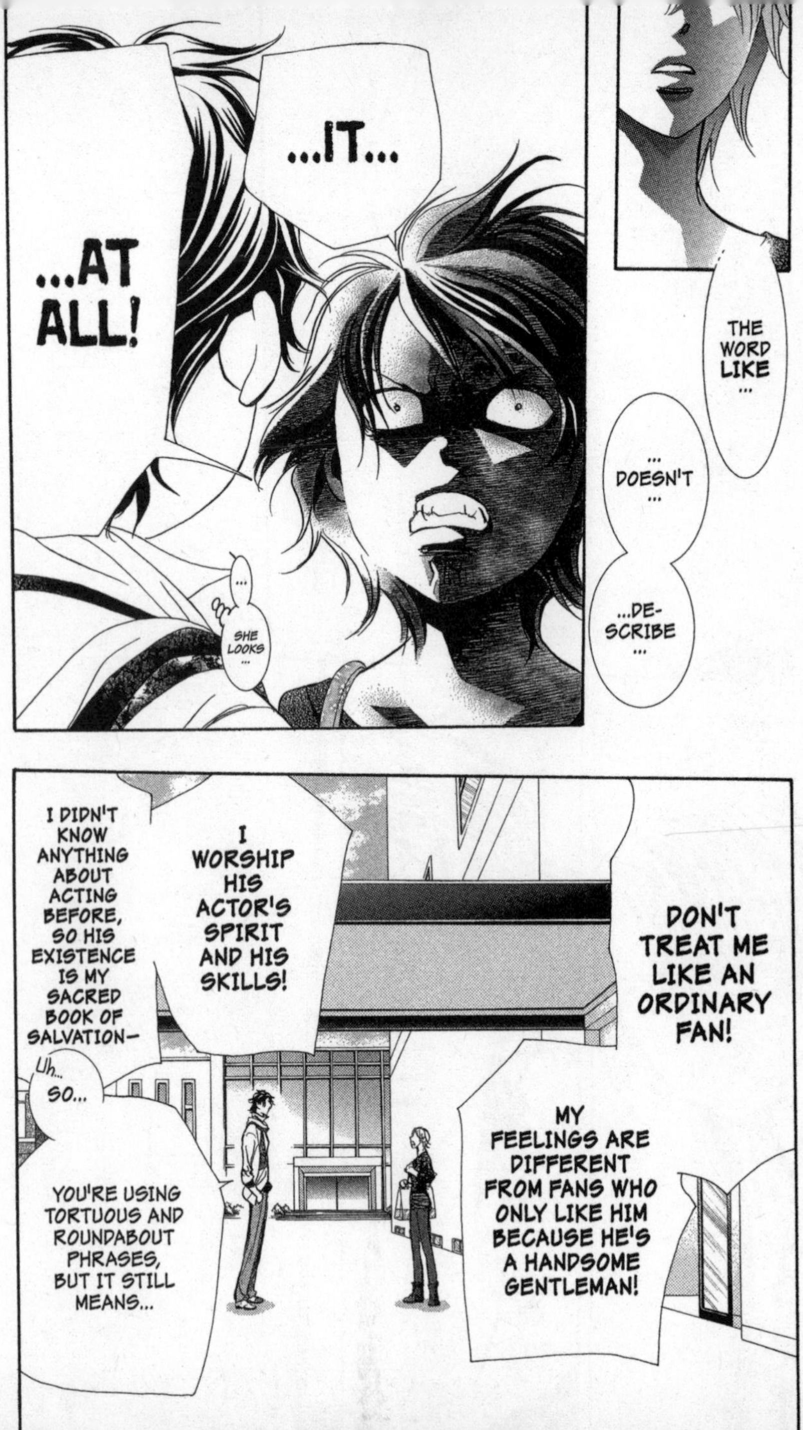
THE WORD LIKE...
...DOESN'T...
...DE-SCRIBE...
...IT...
...AT ALL!
... SHE LOOKS ...
DON'T TREAT ME LIKE AN ORDINARY FAN!
MY FEELINGS ARE DIFFERENT FROM FANS WHO ONLY LIKE HIM BECAUSE HE'S A HANDSOME GENTLEMAN!
I WORSHIP HIS ACTOR'S SPIRIT AND HIS SKILLS!
I DIDN'T KNOW ANYTHING ABOUT ACTING BEFORE, SO HIS EXISTENCE IS MY SACRED BOOK OF SALVATION—
Uh... SO...
YOU'RE USING TORTUOUS AND ROUNDABOUT PHRASES, BUT IT STILL MEANS...

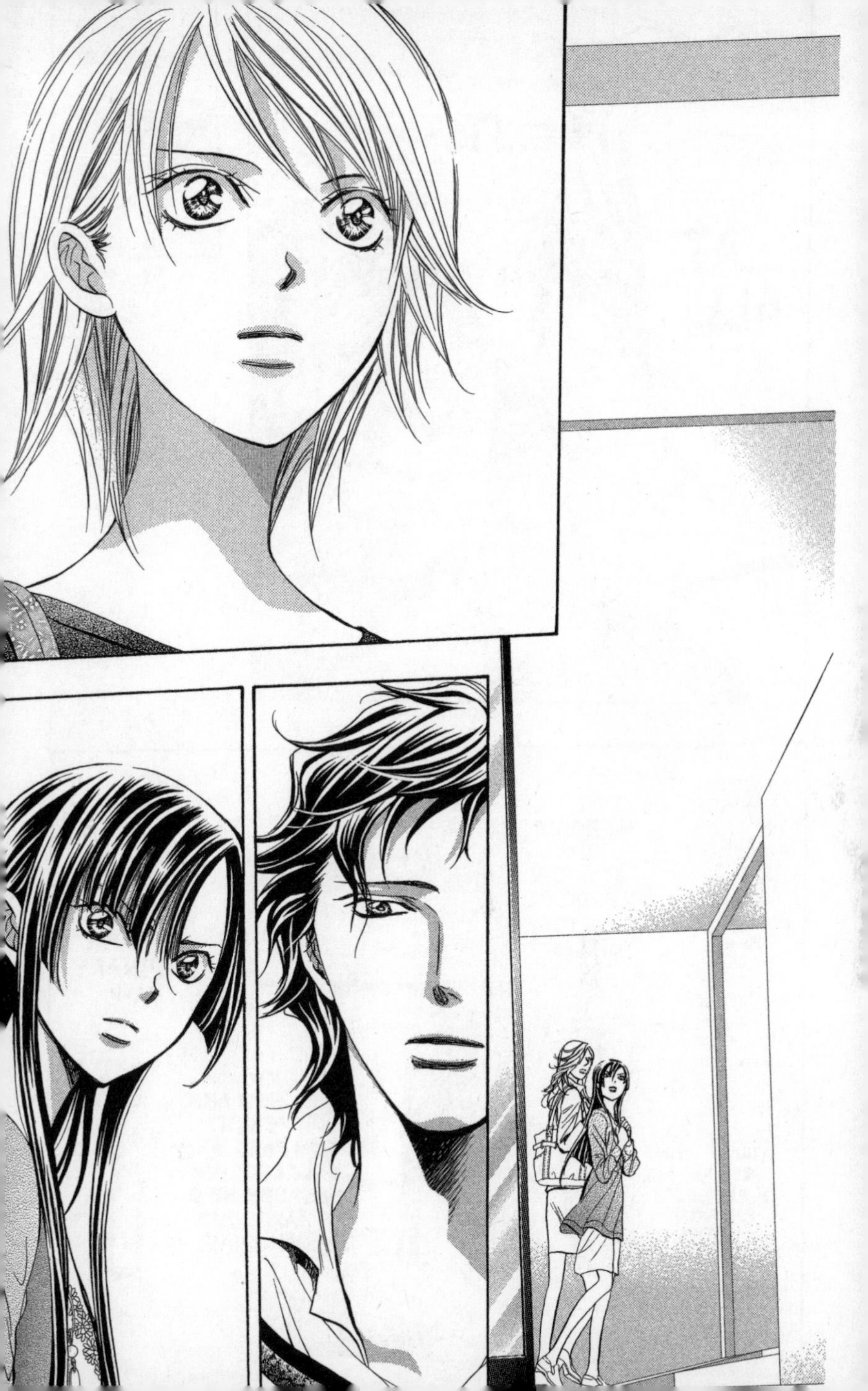

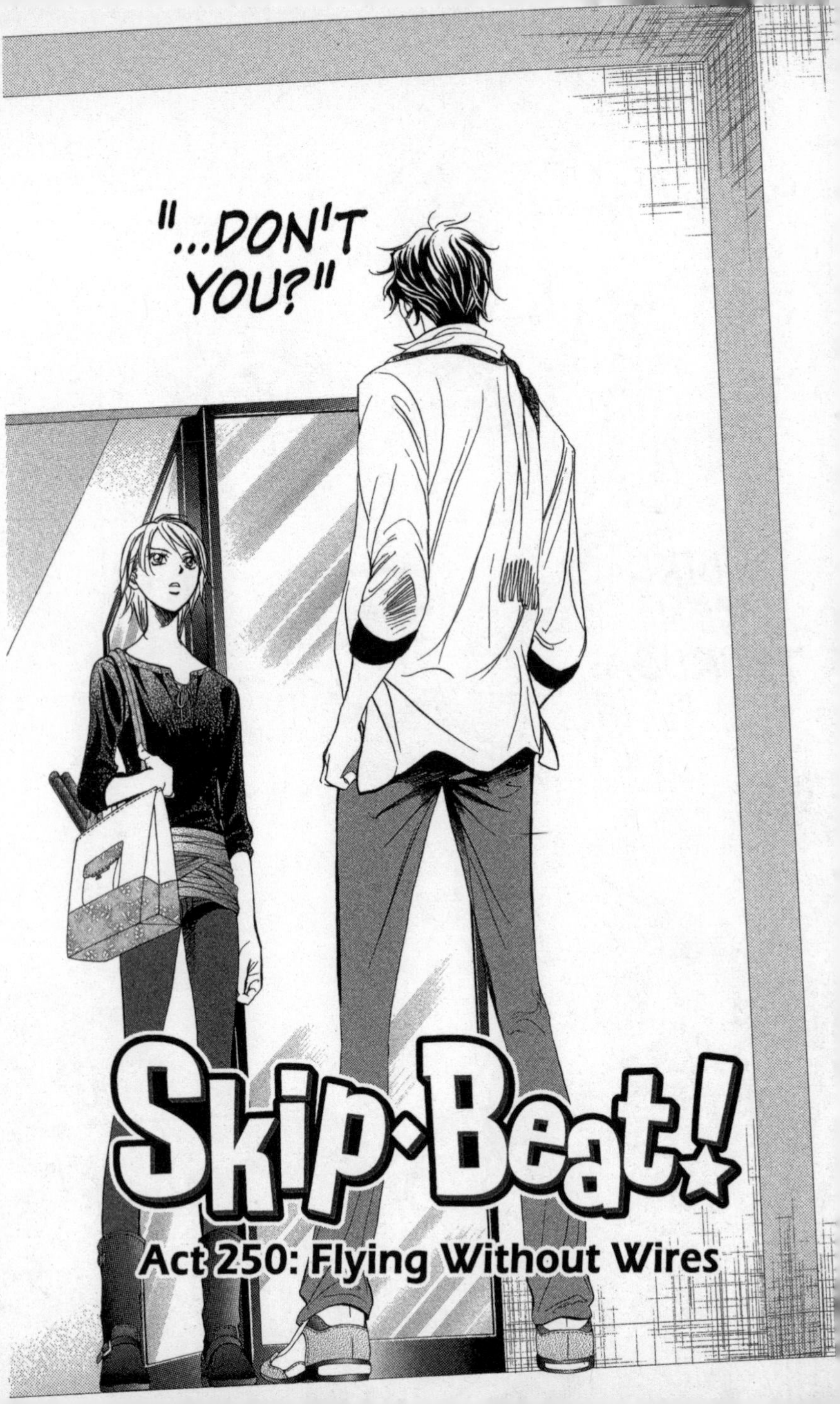
"...DON'T YOU?"
Skip·Beat!
Act 250: Flying Without Wires

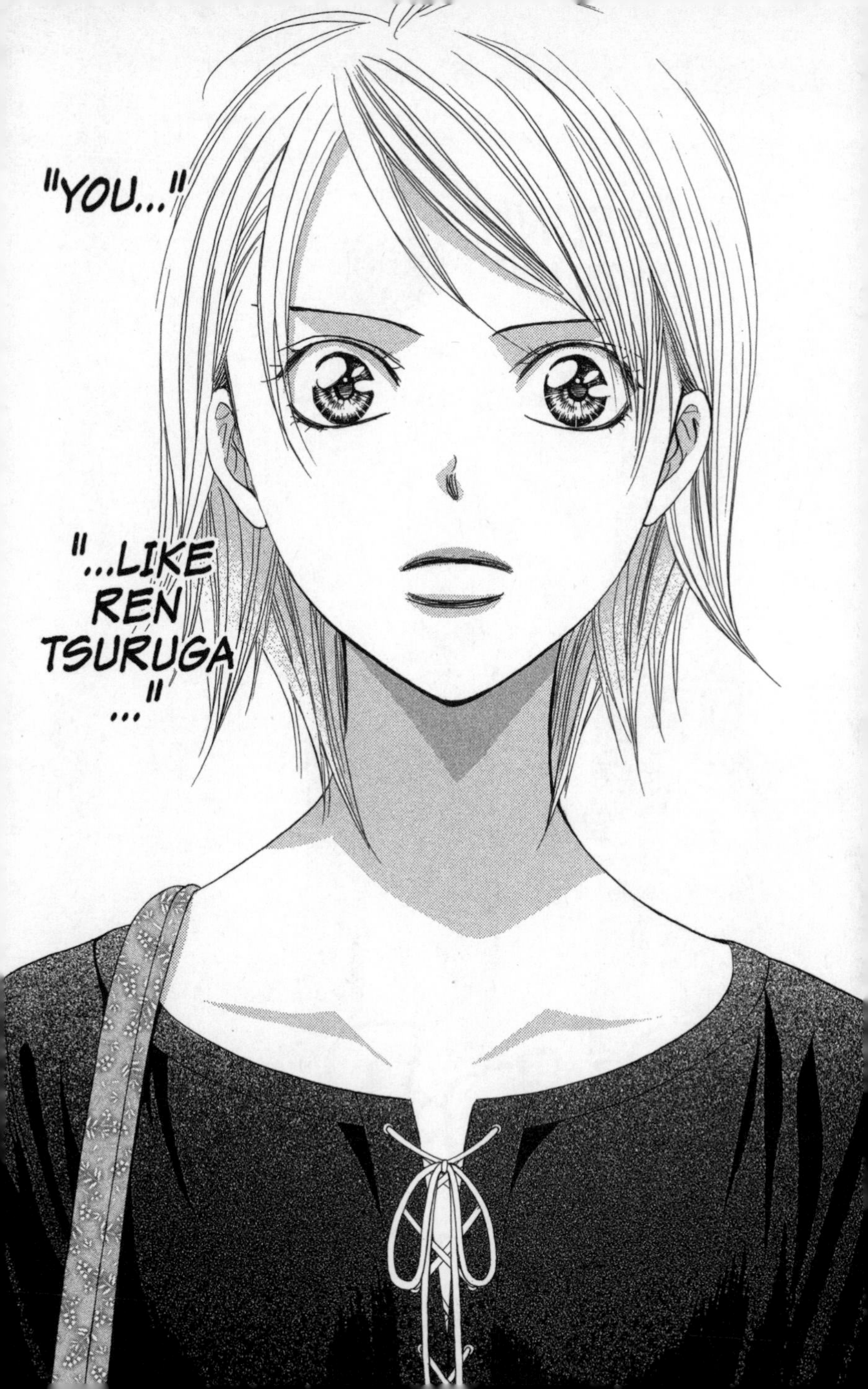
"YOU..."
"...LIKE REN TSURUGA..."

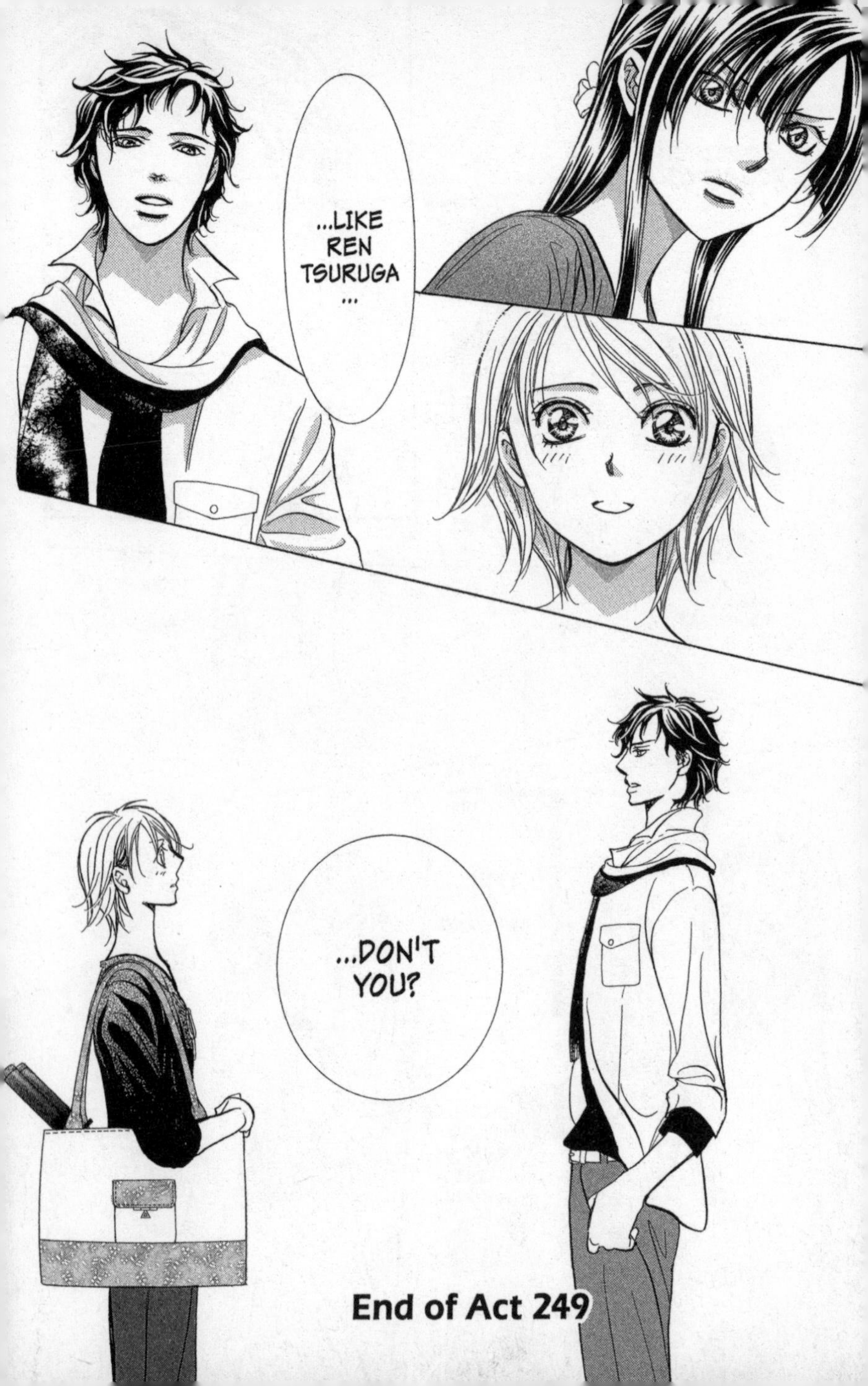
...LIKE REN TSURUGA ...
...DON'T YOU?

End of Act 249

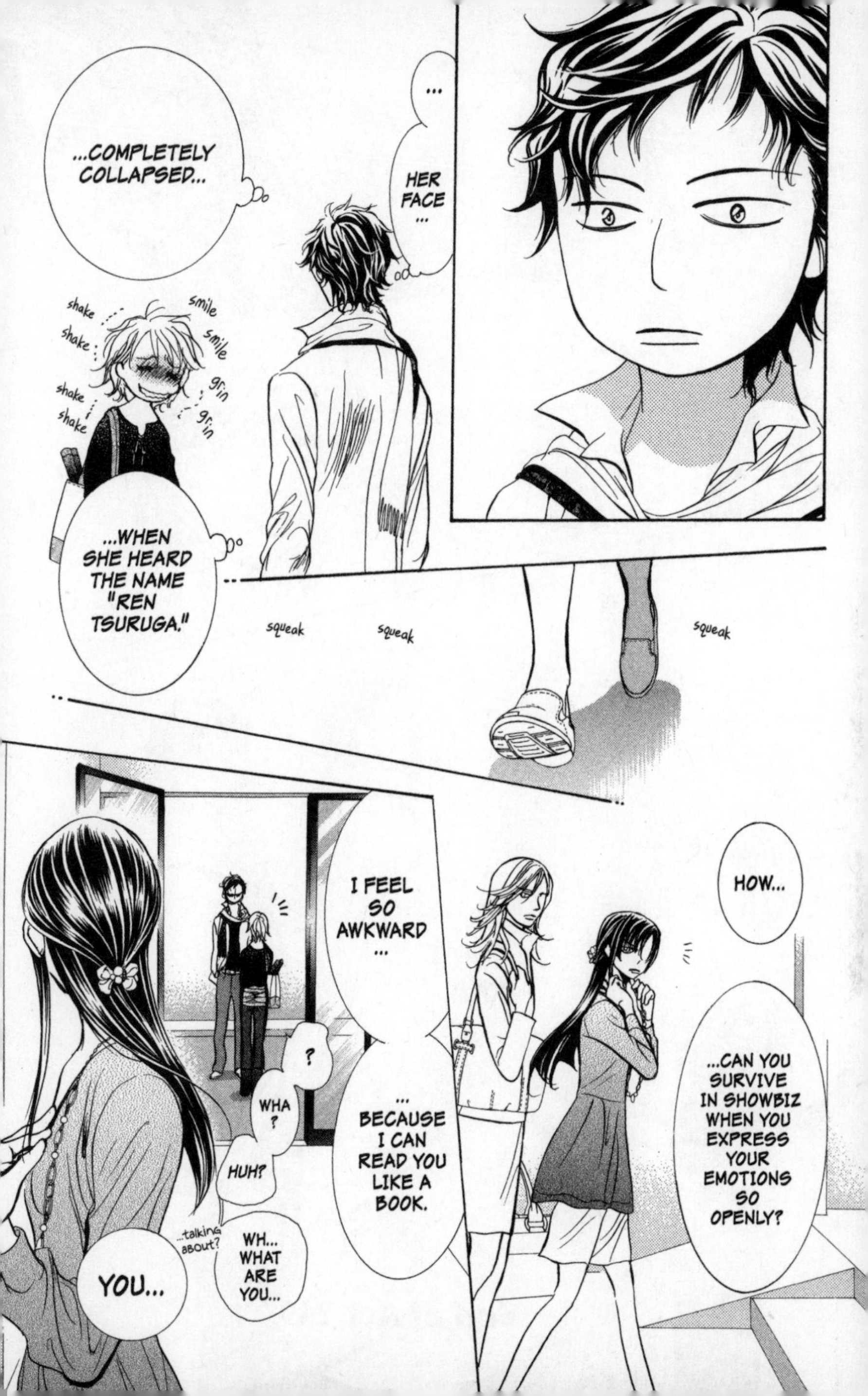
...
HER FACE ...
...COMPLETELY COLLAPSED...
smile smile
grin grin
shake shake shake shake
...WHEN SHE HEARD THE NAME "REN TSURUGA."
squeak
squeak
squeak
HOW...
...CAN YOU SURVIVE IN SHOWBIZ WHEN YOU EXPRESS YOUR EMOTIONS SO OPENLY?
I FEEL SO AWKWARD ...
... BECAUSE I CAN READ YOU LIKE A BOOK.
?
WHA ?
HUH?
WH... WHAT ARE YOU...
...talking about?
YOU...

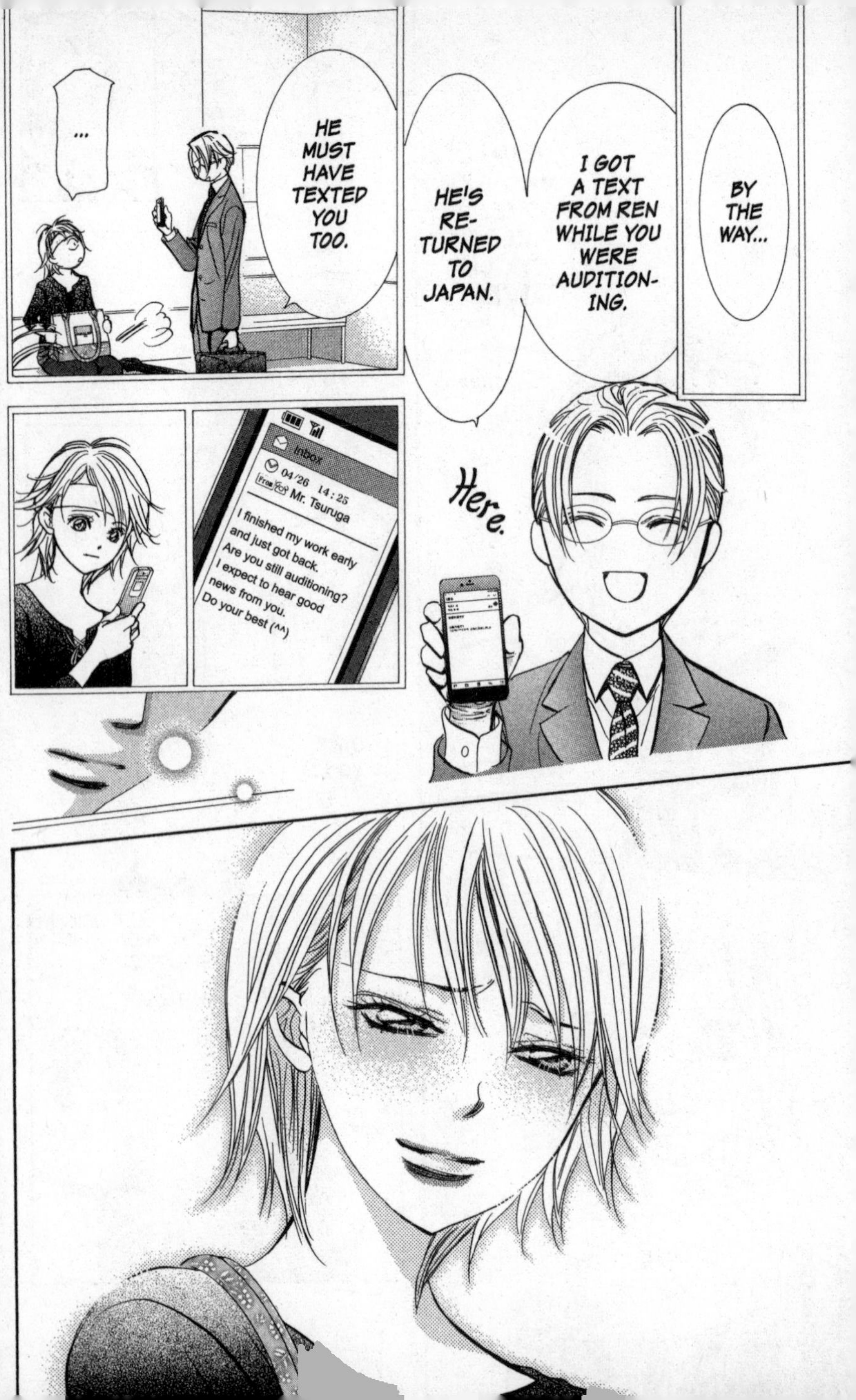
BY THE WAY...
I GOT A TEXT FROM REN WHILE YOU WERE AUDITION-ING.
HE'S RE-TURNED TO JAPAN.
HE MUST HAVE TEXTED YOU TOO.
...
Here.
Inbox
04/26 14:25
From Mr. Tsuruga
I finished my work early and just got back.
Are you still auditioning?
I expect to hear good news from you.
Do your best (^^)

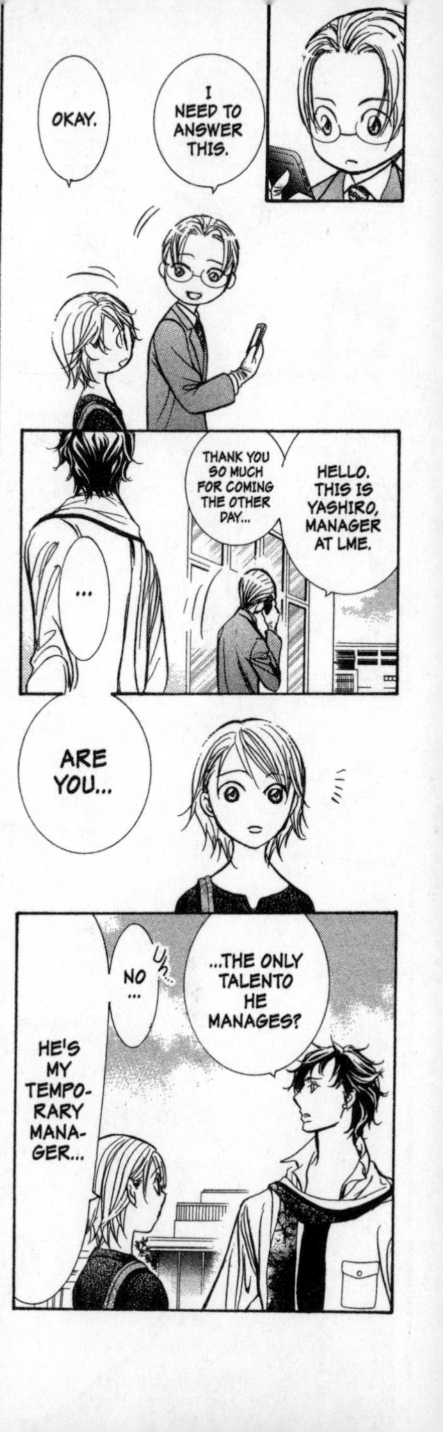
I NEED TO ANSWER THIS.
OKAY.
HELLO. THIS IS YASHIRO, MANAGER AT LME.
THANK YOU SO MUCH FOR COMING THE OTHER DAY...
...
ARE YOU...
...THE ONLY TALENTO HE MANAGES?
Uh...
NO...
HE'S MY TEMPORARY MANAGER...
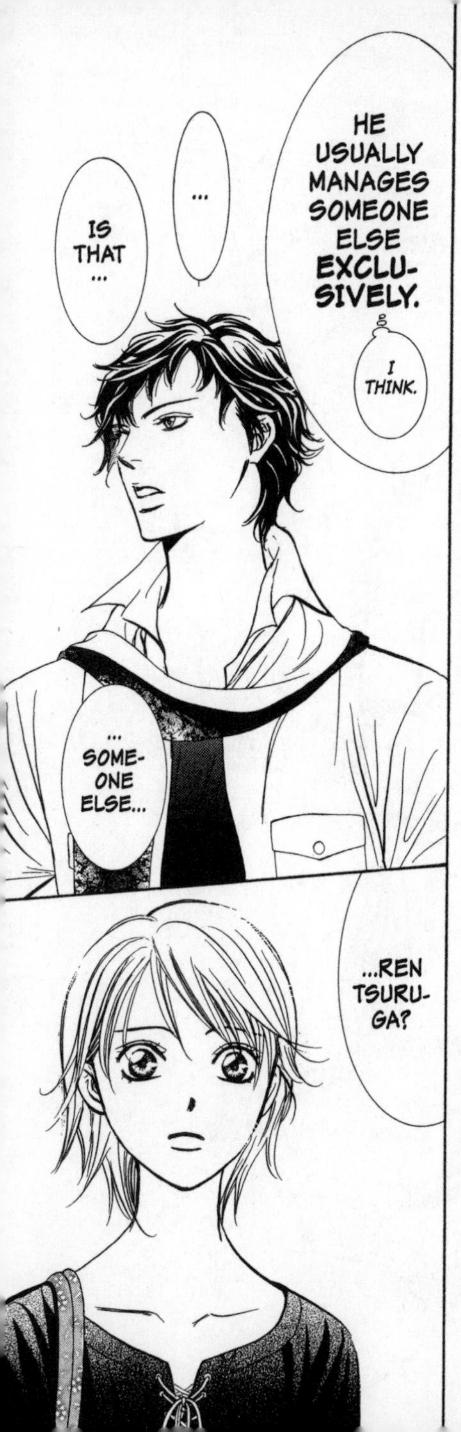
HE USUALLY MANAGES SOMEONE ELSE EXCLUSIVELY.
I THINK.
...
IS THAT...
...SOMEONE ELSE...
...REN TSURUGA?

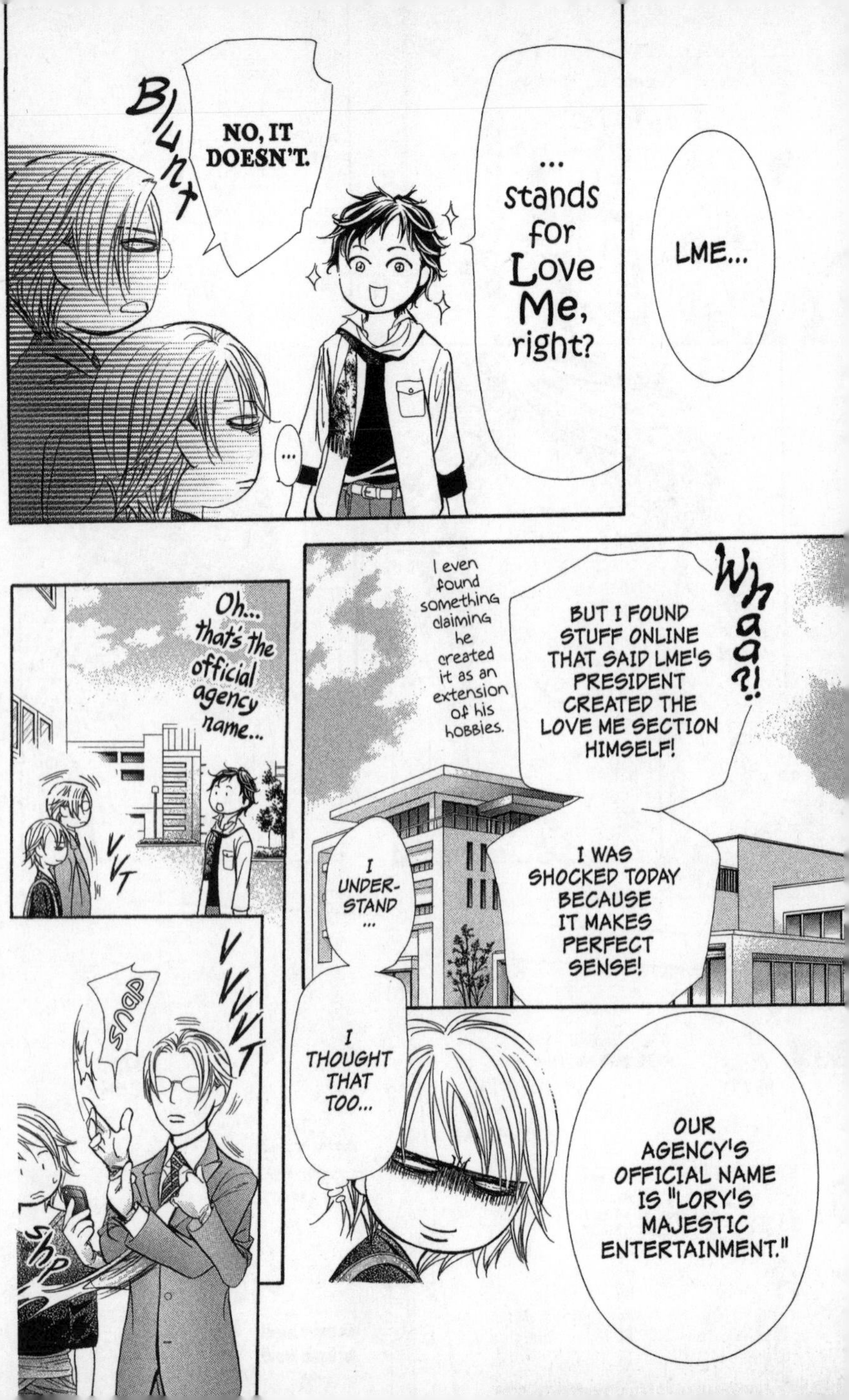
LME...
... stands for Love Me, right?
NO, IT DOESN'T.
Blunt
...
Whaa?!
BUT I FOUND STUFF ONLINE THAT SAID LME'S PRESIDENT CREATED THE LOVE ME SECTION HIMSELF!
I even found something claiming he created it as an extension of his hobbies.
I WAS SHOCKED TODAY BECAUSE IT MAKES PERFECT SENSE!
I UNDER-STAND...
Oh... that's the official agency name...
VVT
OUR AGENCY'S OFFICIAL NAME IS "LORY'S MAJESTIC ENTERTAINMENT."
I THOUGHT THAT TOO...
VVVVT
snap
shp

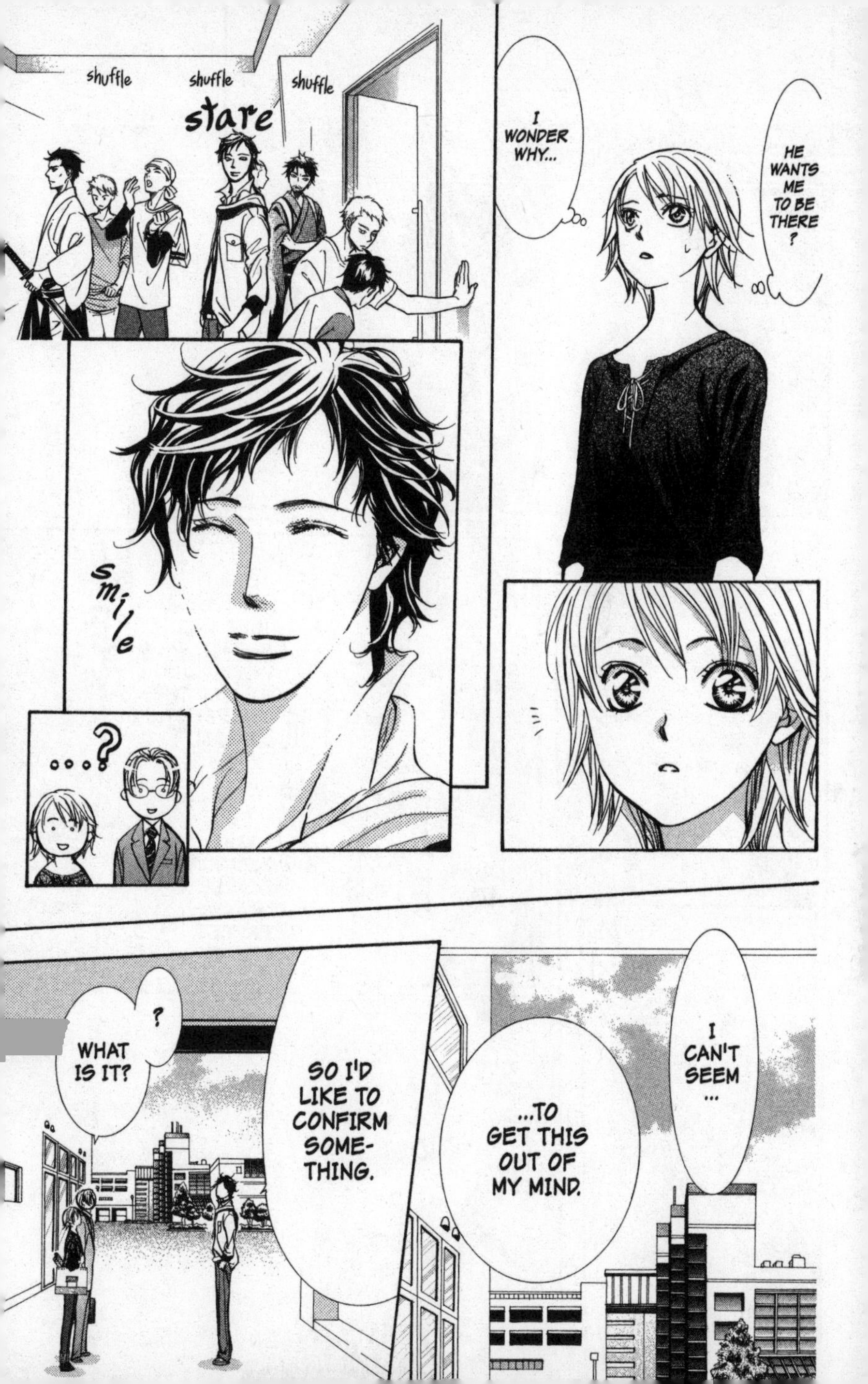
HE WANTS ME TO BE THERE?
I WONDER WHY...
shuffle
shuffle
shuffle
stare
smile
...?
I CAN'T SEEM...
...TO GET THIS OUT OF MY MIND.
SO I'D LIKE TO CONFIRM SOMETHING.
?
WHAT IS IT?

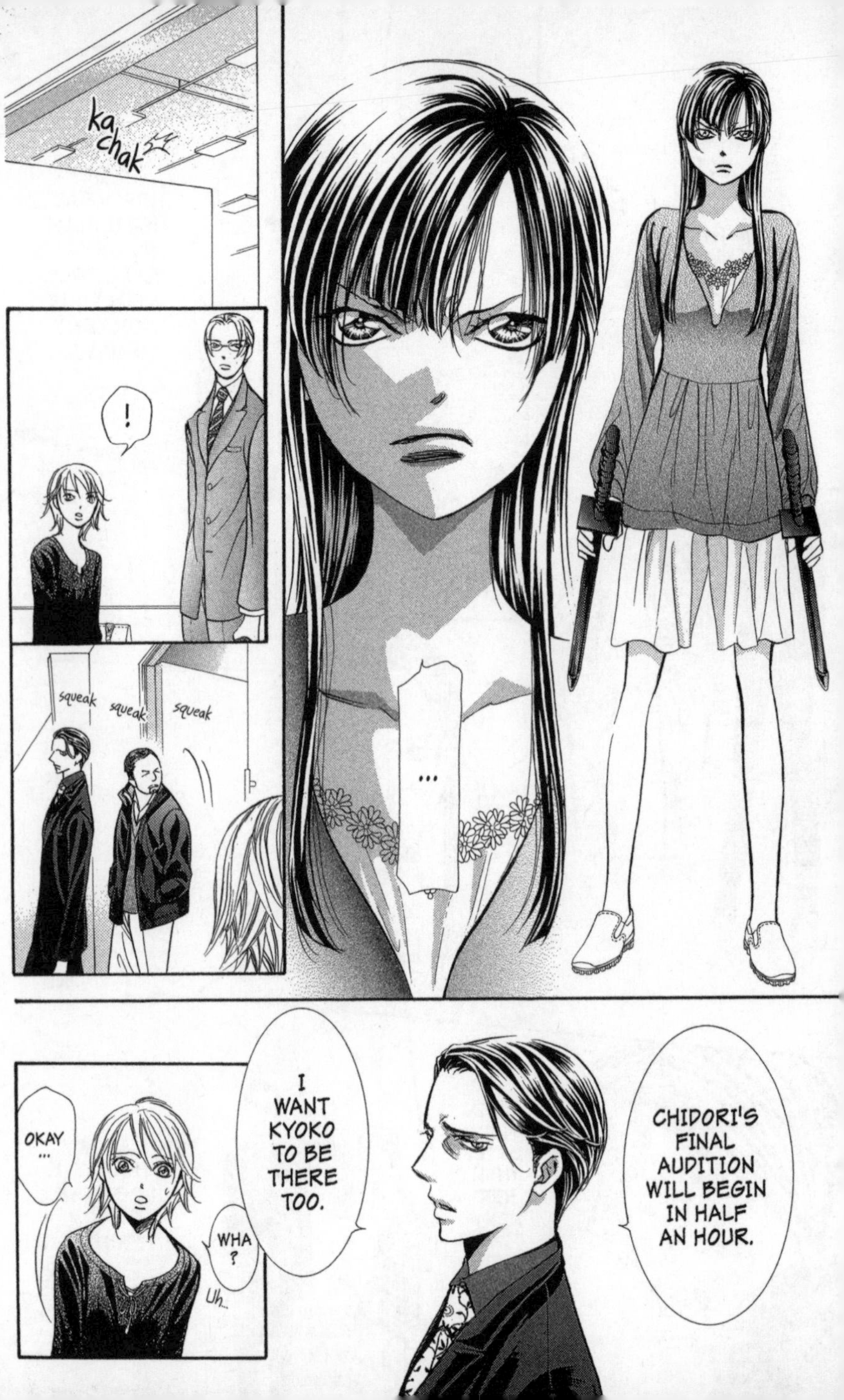
...
ka chak
!
squeak squeak squeak
CHIDORI'S FINAL AUDITION WILL BEGIN IN HALF AN HOUR.
I WANT KYOKO TO BE THERE TOO.
WHA?
Uh...
OKAY...

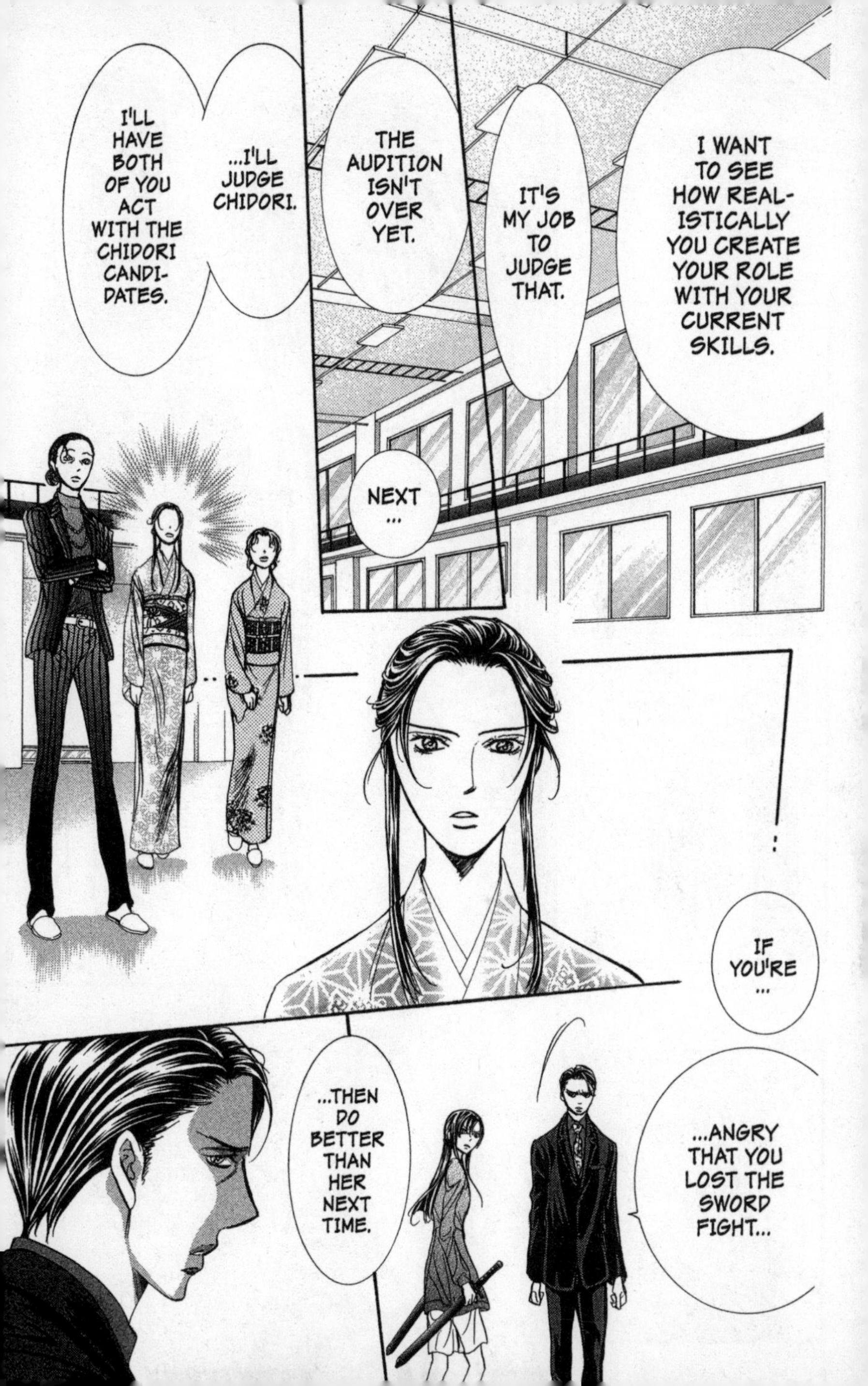
I WANT TO SEE HOW REALISTICALLY YOU CREATE YOUR ROLE WITH YOUR CURRENT SKILLS.
IT'S MY JOB TO JUDGE THAT.
THE AUDITION ISN'T OVER YET.
NEXT...
...I'LL JUDGE CHIDORI.
I'LL HAVE BOTH OF YOU ACT WITH THE CHIDORI CANDIDATES.
!
IF YOU'RE...
...ANGRY THAT YOU LOST THE SWORD FIGHT...
...THEN DO BETTER THAN HER NEXT TIME.

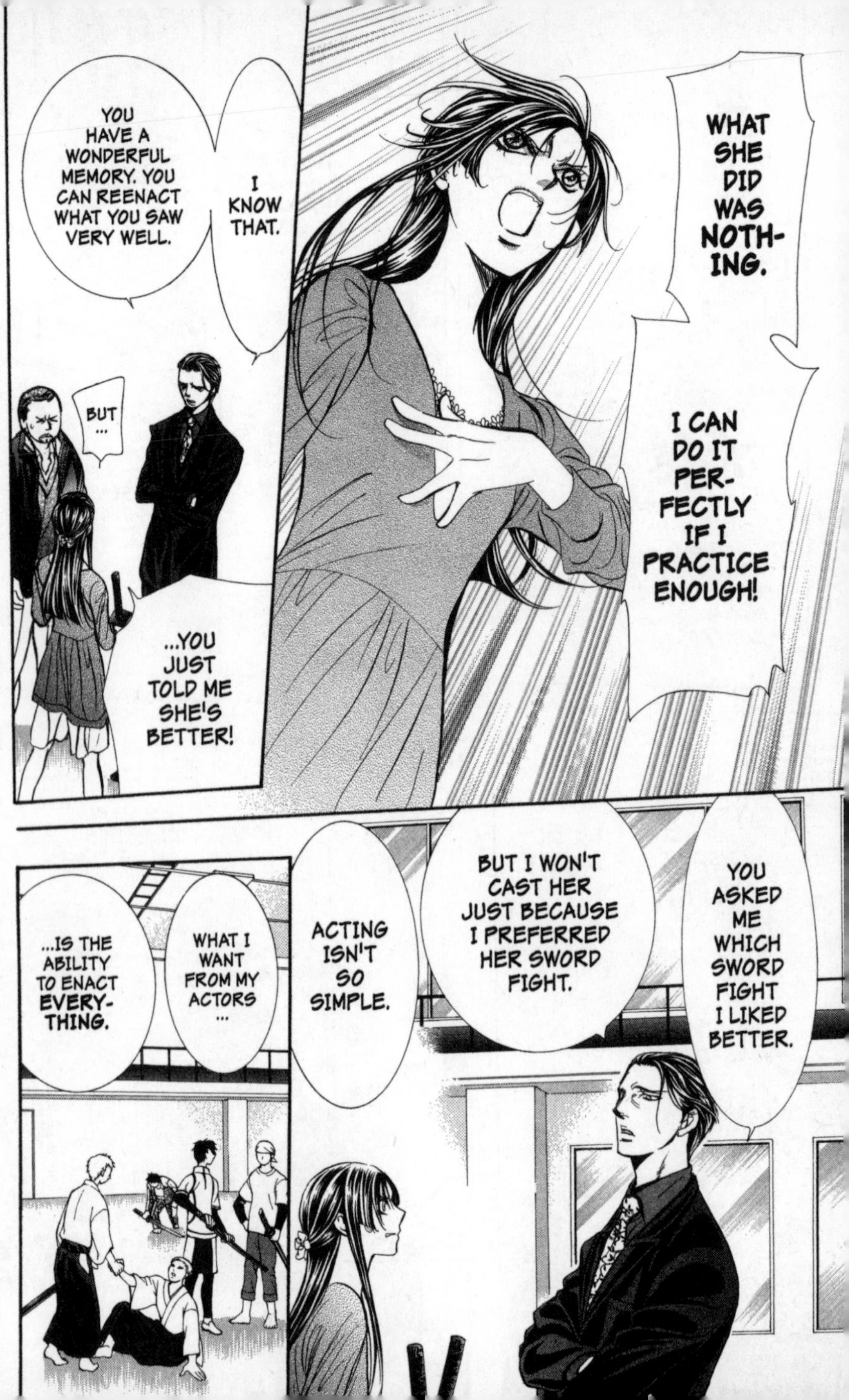
WHAT SHE DID WAS NOTHING.
I CAN DO IT PERFECTLY IF I PRACTICE ENOUGH!
I KNOW THAT.
YOU HAVE A WONDERFUL MEMORY. YOU CAN REENACT WHAT YOU SAW VERY WELL.
BUT ...
...YOU JUST TOLD ME SHE'S BETTER!
YOU ASKED ME WHICH SWORD FIGHT I LIKED BETTER.
BUT I WON'T CAST HER JUST BECAUSE I PREFERRED HER SWORD FIGHT.
ACTING ISN'T SO SIMPLE.
WHAT I WANT FROM MY ACTORS ...
...IS THE ABILITY TO ENACT EVERYTHING.

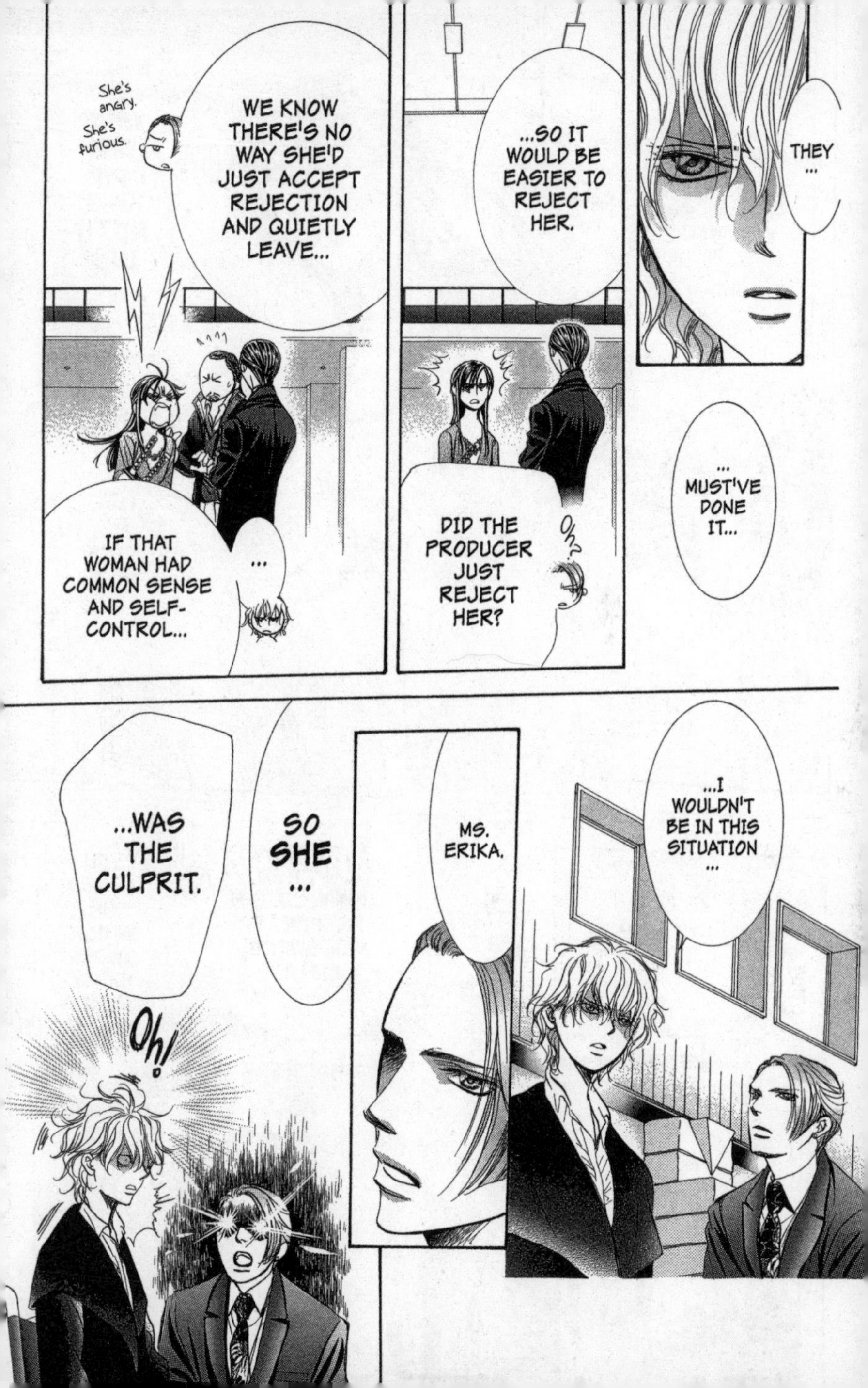
THEY ...
... MUST'VE DONE IT...
...SO IT WOULD BE EASIER TO REJECT HER.
DID THE PRODUCER JUST REJECT HER?
Oh?
WE KNOW THERE'S NO WAY SHE'D JUST ACCEPT REJECTION AND QUIETLY LEAVE...
She's angry.
She's furious.
IF THAT WOMAN HAD COMMON SENSE AND SELF-CONTROL...
...
...I WOULDN'T BE IN THIS SITUATION ...
MS. ERIKA.
SO SHE ...
...WAS THE CULPRIT.
Oh!

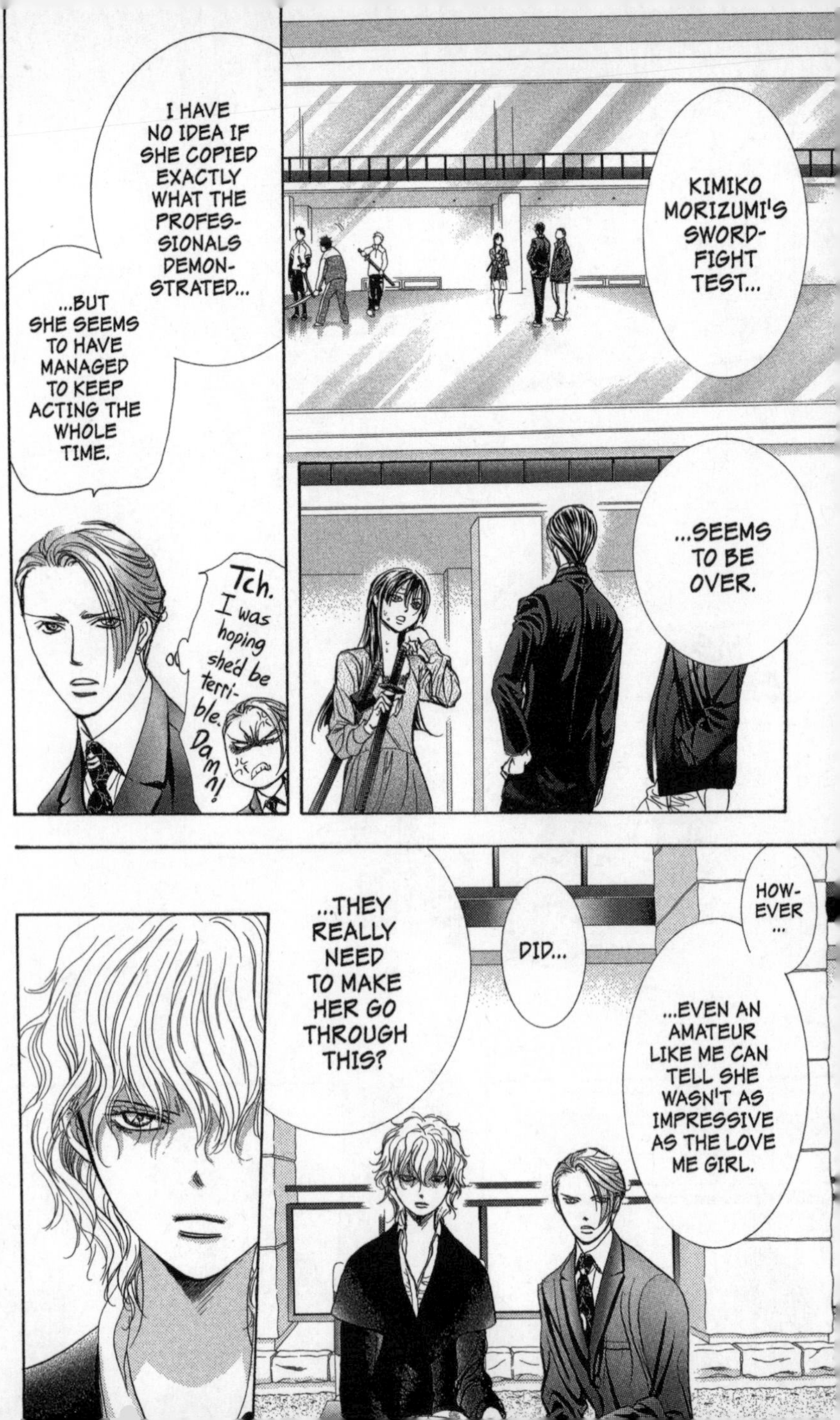
KIMIKO MORIZUMI'S SWORD-FIGHT TEST...
...SEEMS TO BE OVER.
I HAVE NO IDEA IF SHE COPIED EXACTLY WHAT THE PROFES-SIONALS DEMON-STRATED...
...BUT SHE SEEMS TO HAVE MANAGED TO KEEP ACTING THE WHOLE TIME.
Tch. I was hoping she'd be terri-ble. Damn!
HOW-EVER...
...EVEN AN AMATEUR LIKE ME CAN TELL SHE WASN'T AS IMPRESSIVE AS THE LOVE ME GIRL.
DID...
...THEY REALLY NEED TO MAKE HER GO THROUGH THIS?

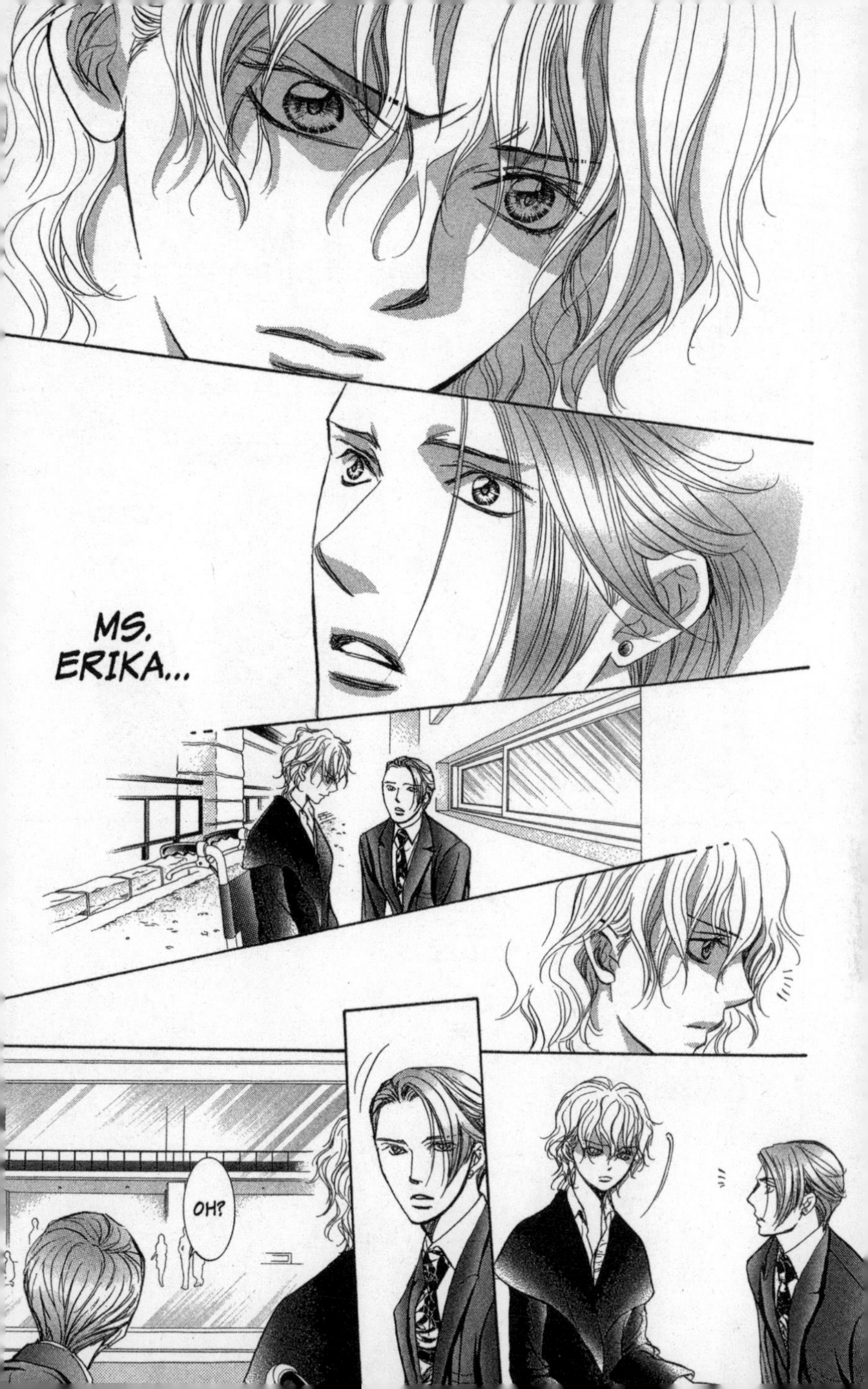
MS. ERIKA...
OH?

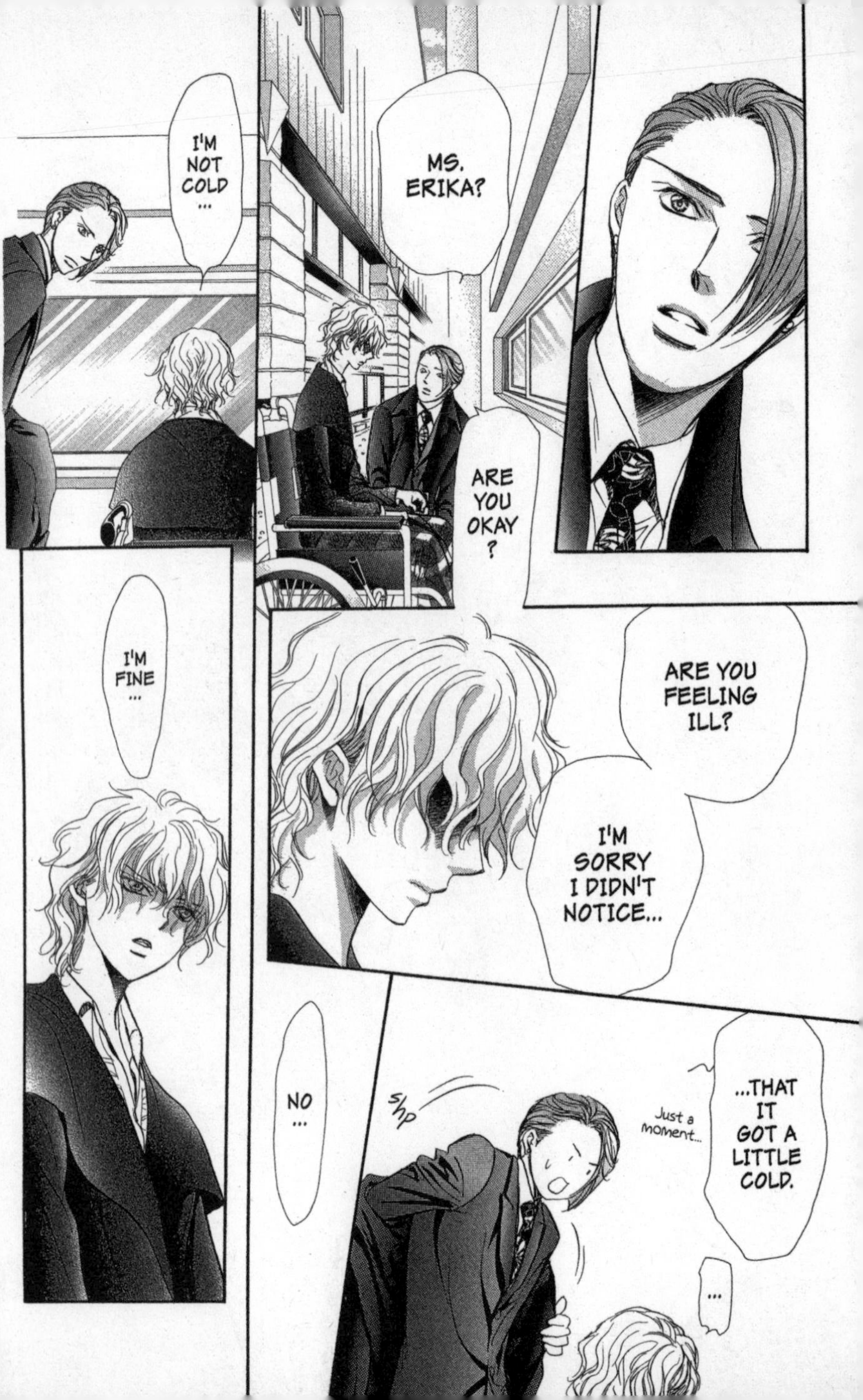
MS. ERIKA?
ARE YOU OKAY?
I'M NOT COLD...
ARE YOU FEELING ILL?
I'M SORRY I DIDN'T NOTICE...
...THAT IT GOT A LITTLE COLD.
Just a moment...
shp
NO...
...
I'M FINE...

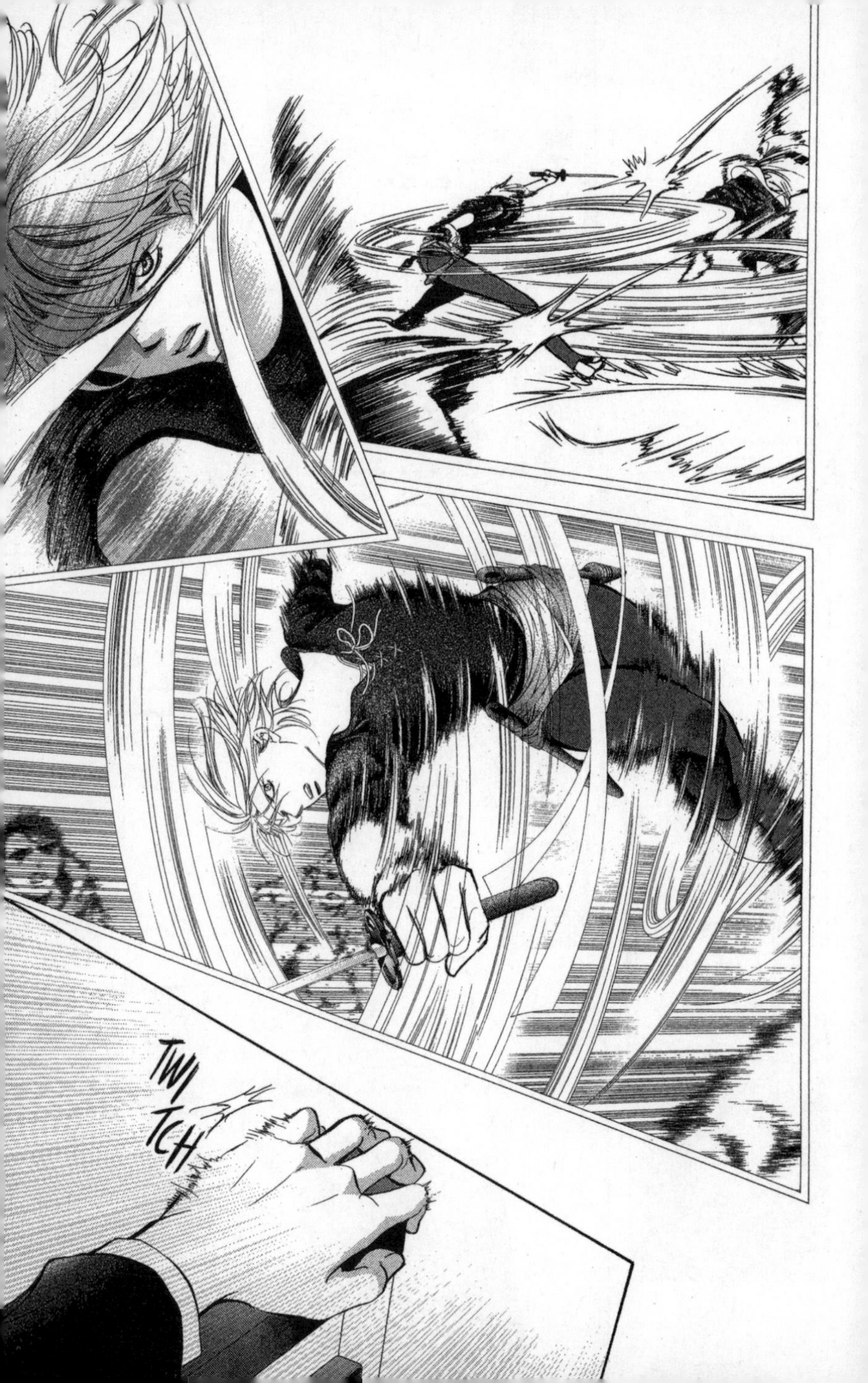
TWI
TCH

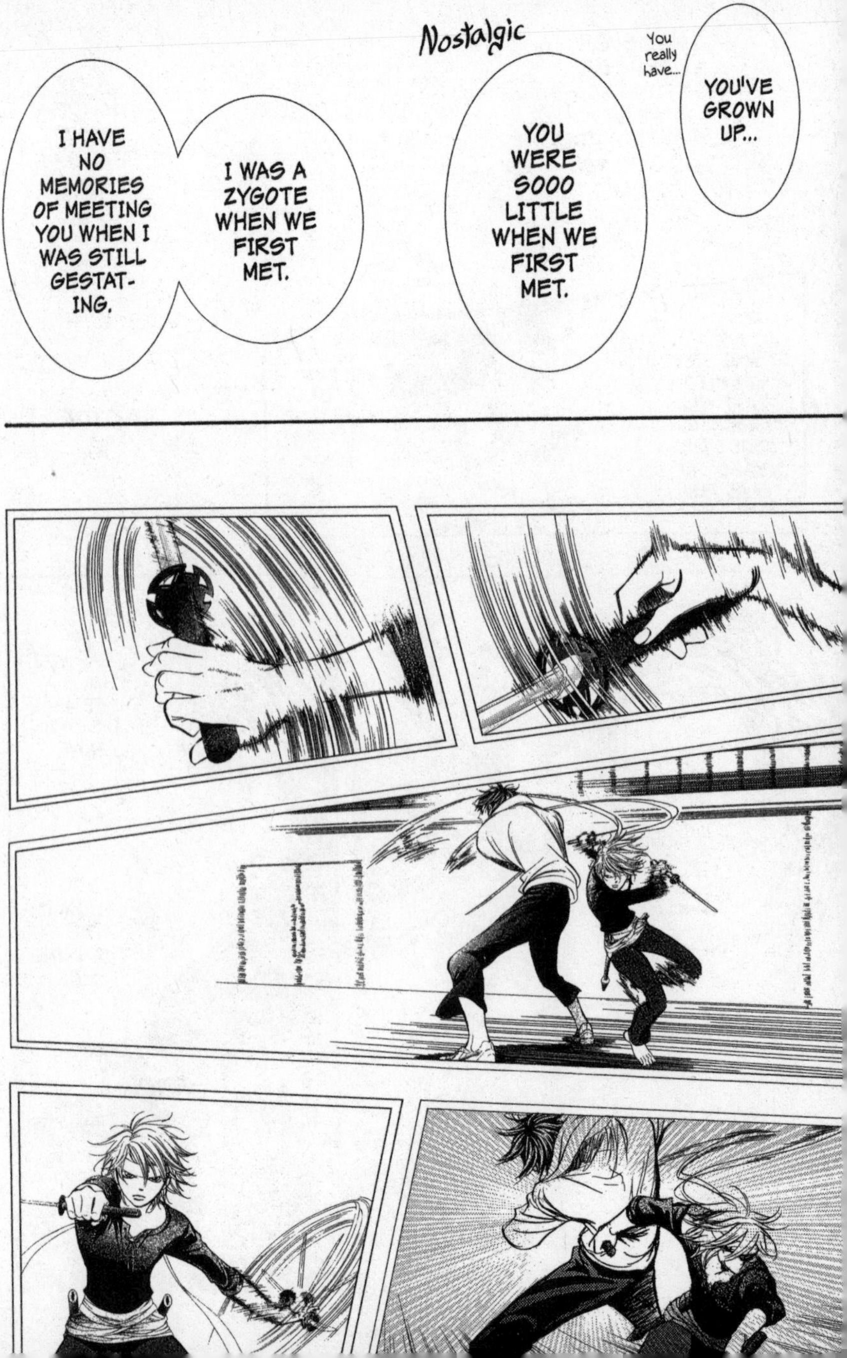
YOU'VE GROWN UP...
You really have...
Nostalgic
YOU WERE SOOO LITTLE WHEN WE FIRST MET.
I WAS A ZYGOTE WHEN WE FIRST MET.
I HAVE NO MEMORIES OF MEETING YOU WHEN I WAS STILL GESTAT-ING.

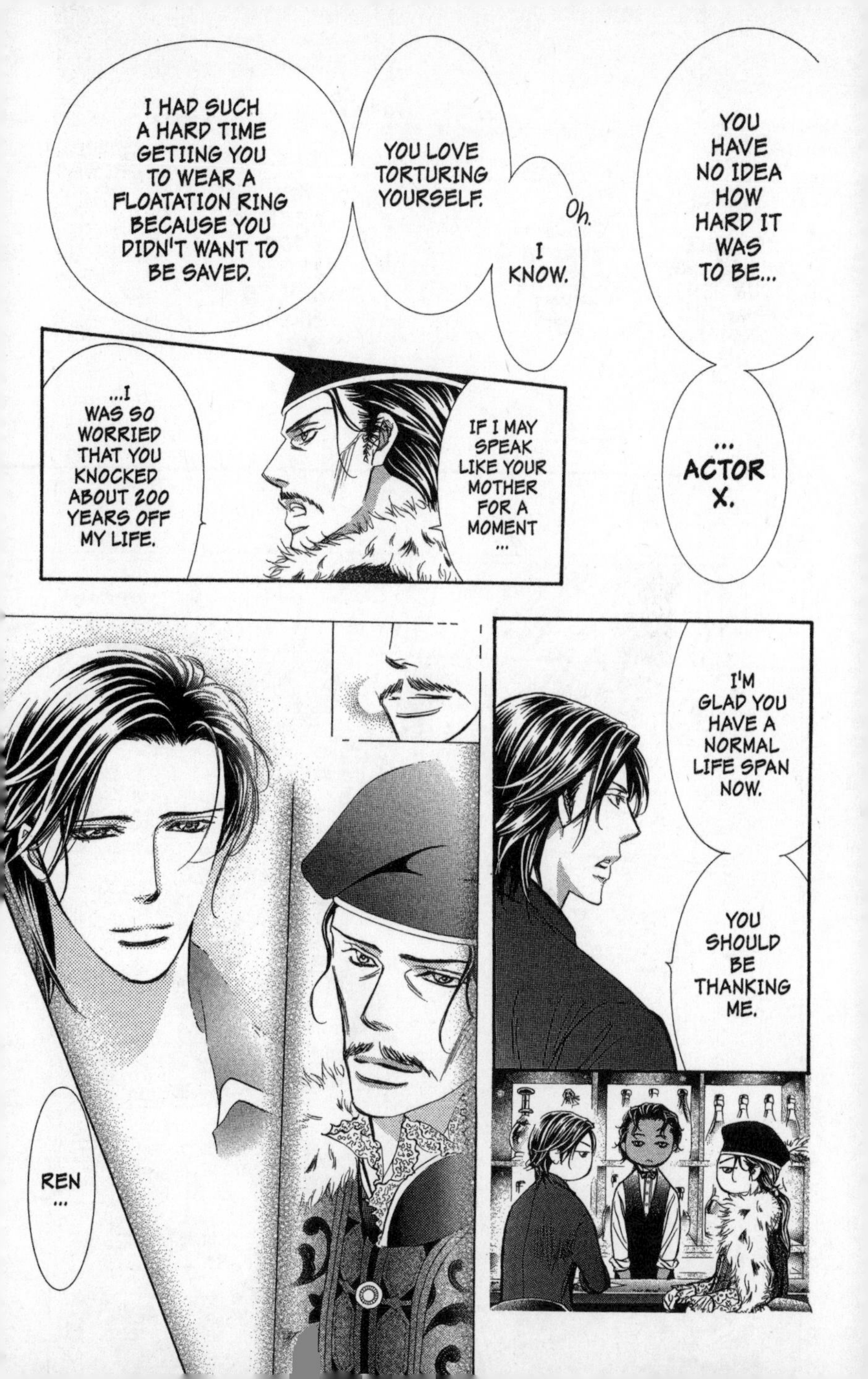
YOU HAVE NO IDEA HOW HARD IT WAS TO BE...
... ACTOR X.
Oh.
I KNOW.
YOU LOVE TORTURING YOURSELF.
I HAD SUCH A HARD TIME GETIING YOU TO WEAR A FLOATATION RING BECAUSE YOU DIDN'T WANT TO BE SAVED.
IF I MAY SPEAK LIKE YOUR MOTHER FOR A MOMENT ...
...I WAS SO WORRIED THAT YOU KNOCKED ABOUT 200 YEARS OFF MY LIFE.
I'M GLAD YOU HAVE A NORMAL LIFE SPAN NOW.
YOU SHOULD BE THANKING ME.
REN ...

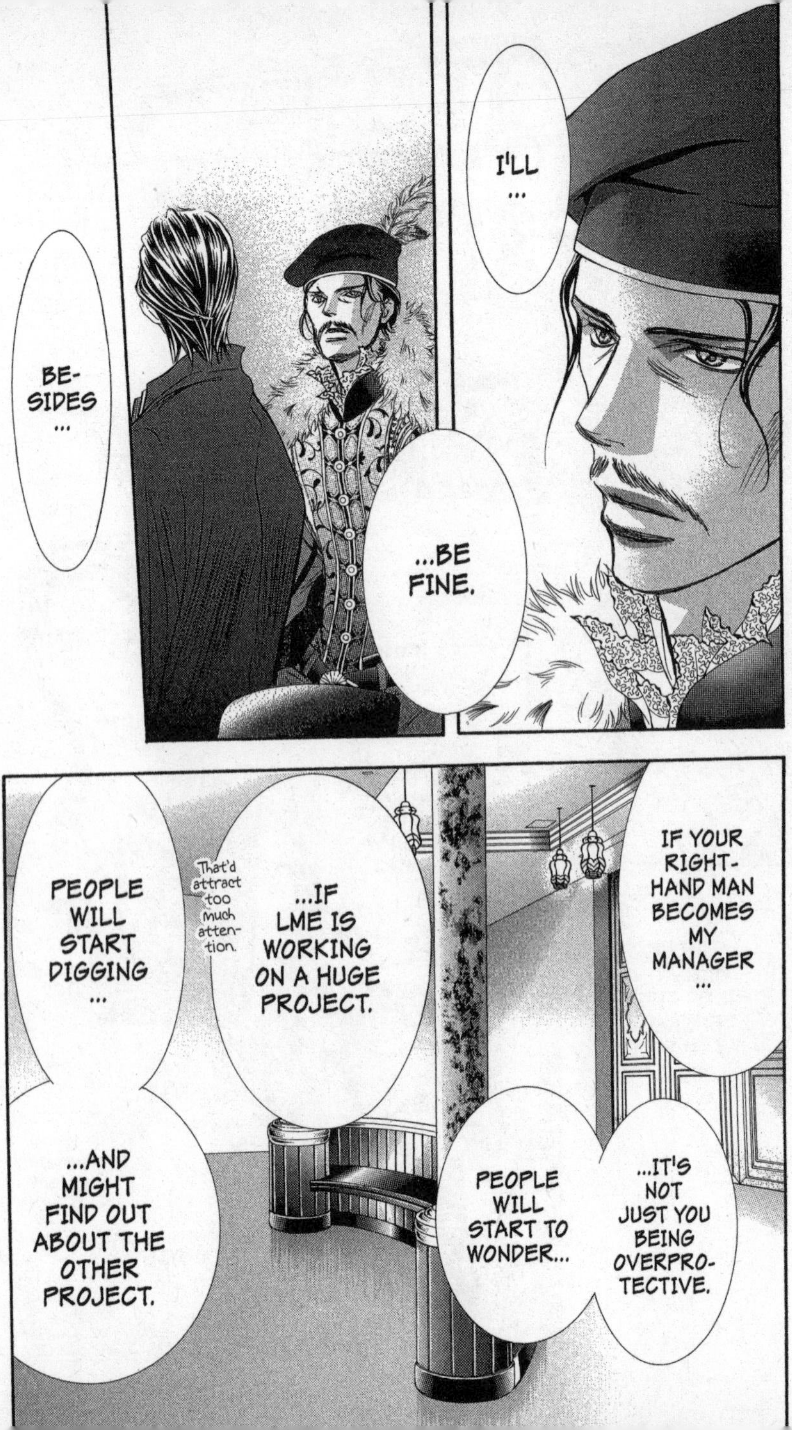
I'LL ...
...BE FINE.
BE-SIDES ...
IF YOUR RIGHT-HAND MAN BECOMES MY MANAGER ...
...IT'S NOT JUST YOU BEING OVERPROTECTIVE.
PEOPLE WILL START TO WONDER...
...IF LME IS WORKING ON A HUGE PROJECT.
That'd attract too much atten-tion.
PEOPLE WILL START DIGGING ...
...AND MIGHT FIND OUT ABOUT THE OTHER PROJECT.

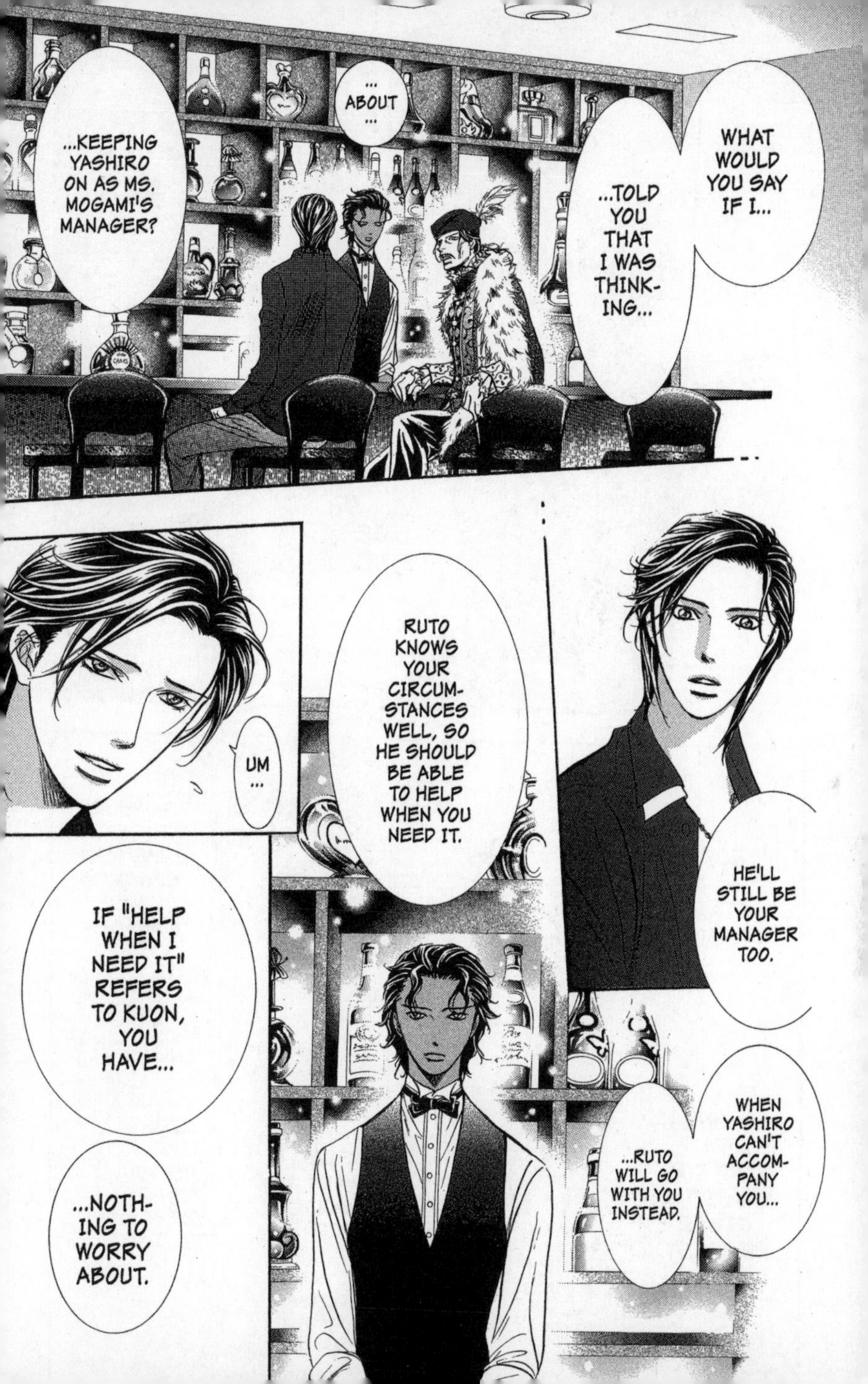
WHAT WOULD YOU SAY IF I...
...TOLD YOU THAT I WAS THINKING...
... ABOUT ...
...KEEPING YASHIRO ON AS MS. MOGAMI'S MANAGER?
HE'LL STILL BE YOUR MANAGER TOO.
WHEN YASHIRO CAN'T ACCOMPANY YOU...
...RUTO WILL GO WITH YOU INSTEAD.
RUTO KNOWS YOUR CIRCUMSTANCES WELL, SO HE SHOULD BE ABLE TO HELP WHEN YOU NEED IT.
UM ...
IF "HELP WHEN I NEED IT" REFERS TO KUON, YOU HAVE...
...NOTHING TO WORRY ABOUT.

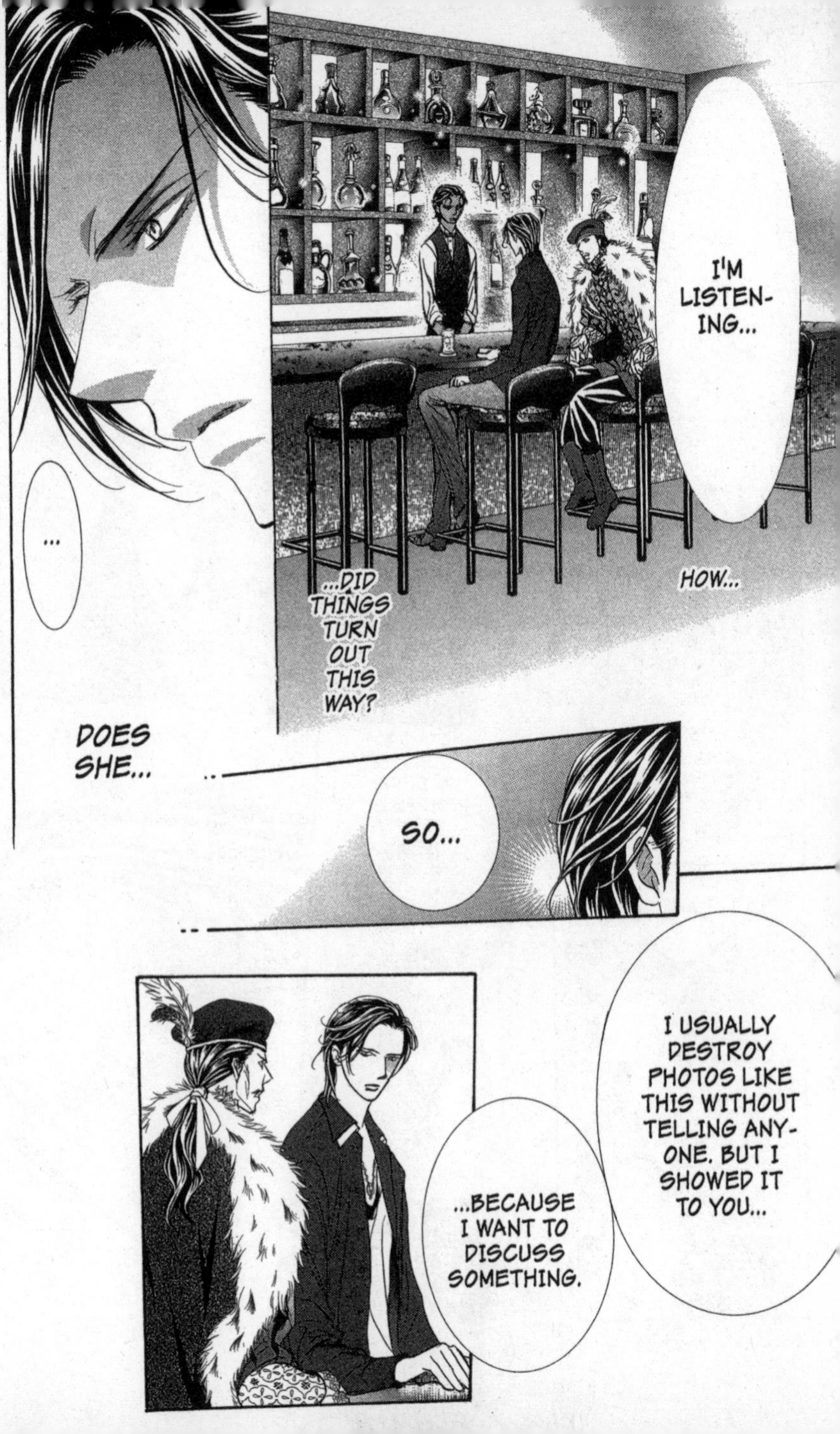
I'M LISTENING...
HOW...
...DID THINGS TURN OUT THIS WAY?
...
DOES SHE...
SO...
I USUALLY DESTROY PHOTOS LIKE THIS WITHOUT TELLING ANYONE. BUT I SHOWED IT TO YOU...
...BECAUSE I WANT TO DISCUSS SOMETHING.

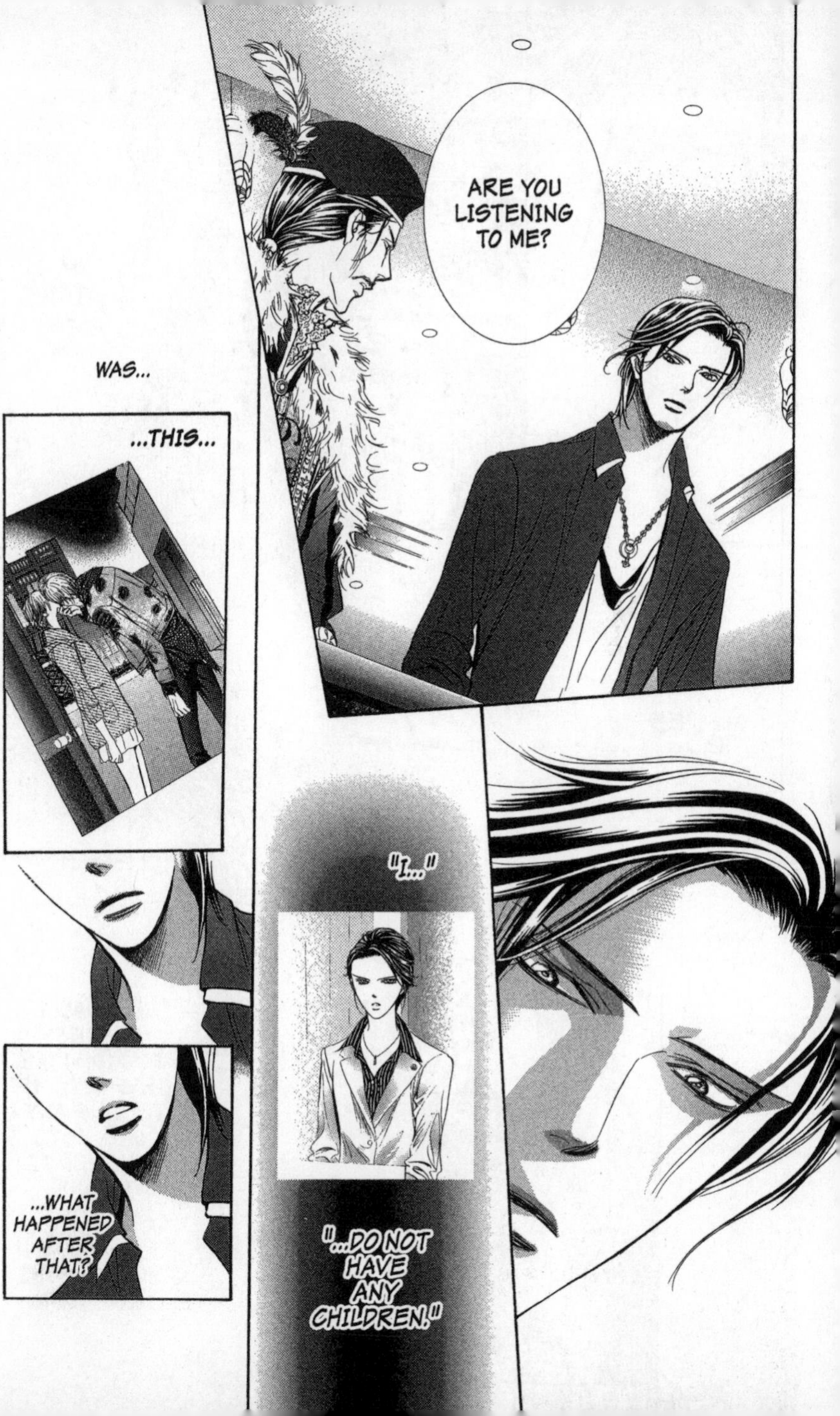
ARE YOU LISTENING TO ME?
WAS...
...THIS...
"I..."
"...DO NOT HAVE ANY CHILDREN."
...WHAT HAPPENED AFTER THAT?

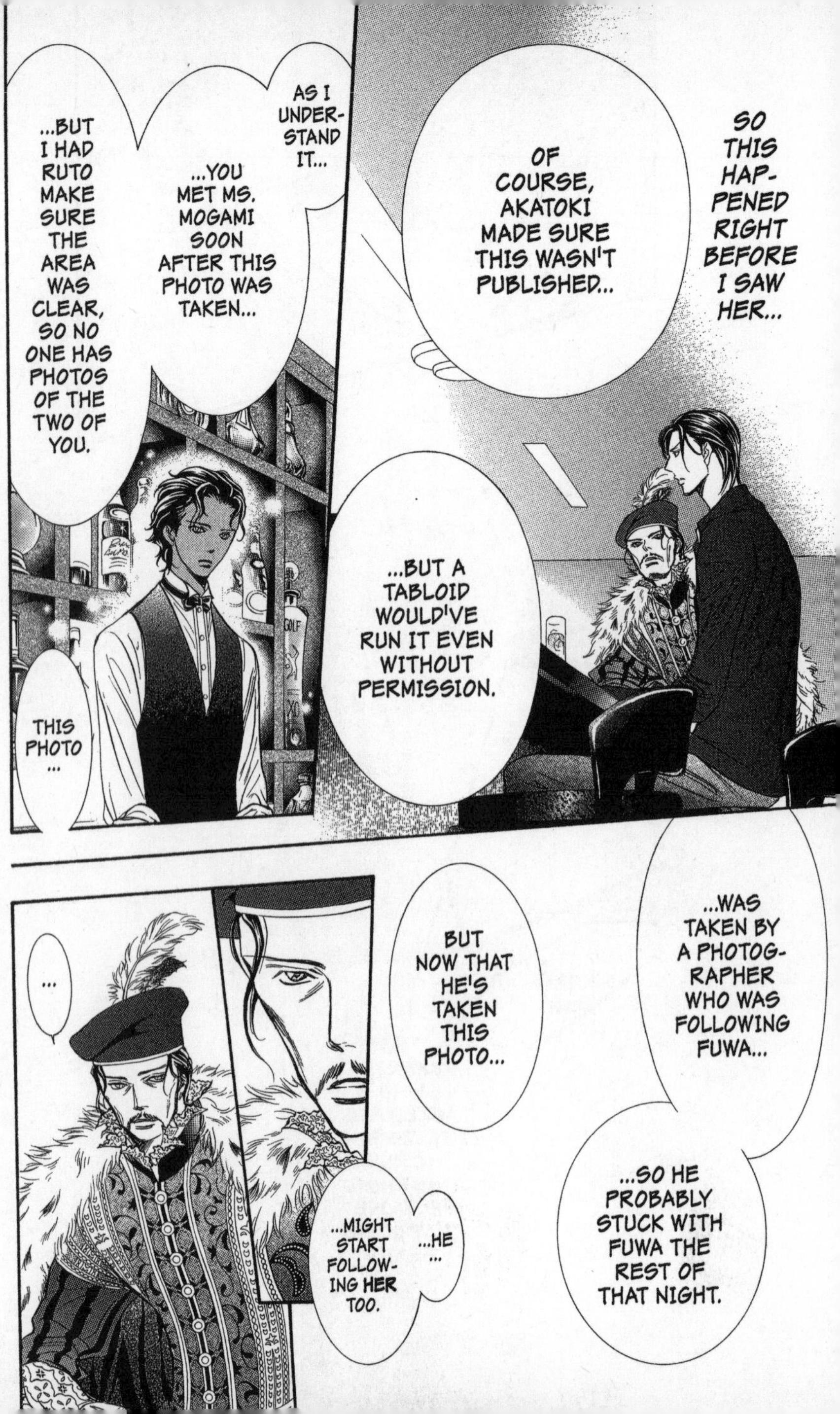
SO THIS HAP-PENED RIGHT BEFORE I SAW HER...
OF COURSE, AKATOKI MADE SURE THIS WASN'T PUBLISHED...
...BUT A TABLOID WOULD'VE RUN IT EVEN WITHOUT PERMISSION.
AS I UNDER-STAND IT...
...YOU MET MS. MOGAMI SOON AFTER THIS PHOTO WAS TAKEN...
...BUT I HAD RUTO MAKE SURE THE AREA WAS CLEAR, SO NO ONE HAS PHOTOS OF THE TWO OF YOU.
THIS PHOTO ...
...WAS TAKEN BY A PHOTOG-RAPHER WHO WAS FOLLOWING FUWA...
...SO HE PROBABLY STUCK WITH FUWA THE REST OF THAT NIGHT.
BUT NOW THAT HE'S TAKEN THIS PHOTO...
...HE ...
...MIGHT START FOLLOW-ING **HER** TOO.
...

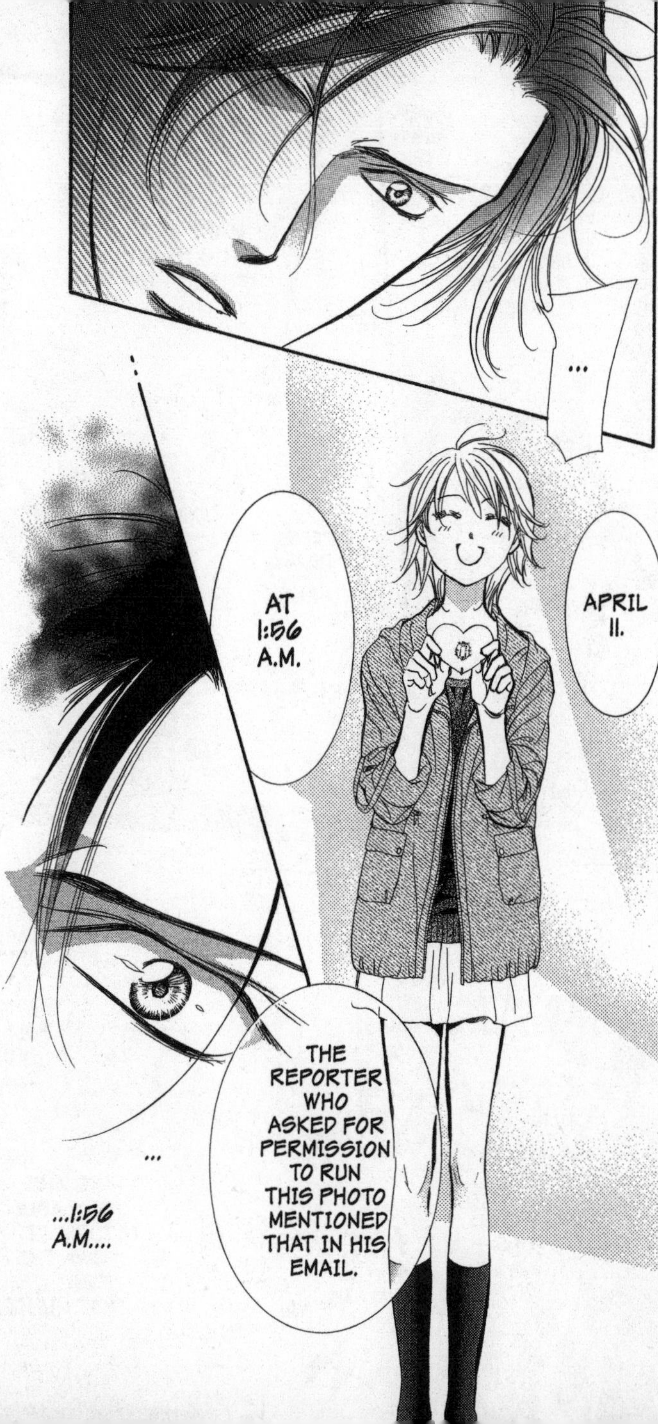
...
APRIL 11.
AT 1:56 A.M.
THE REPORTER WHO ASKED FOR PERMISSION TO RUN THIS PHOTO MENTIONED THAT IN HIS EMAIL.
...
...1:56 A.M....

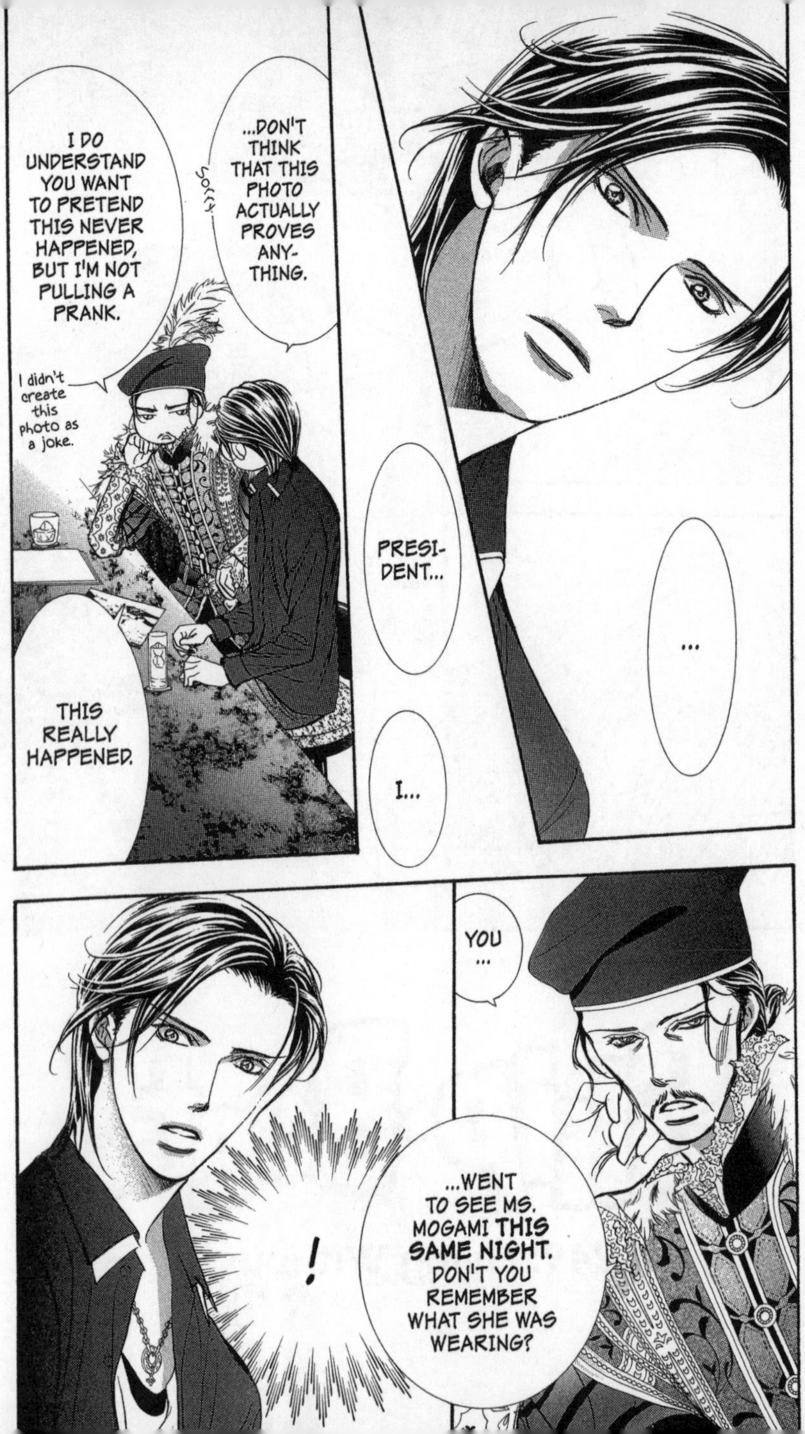

...
PRESIDENT...
I...
...DON'T THINK THAT THIS PHOTO ACTUALLY PROVES ANYTHING.
Sorry
I DO UNDERSTAND YOU WANT TO PRETEND THIS NEVER HAPPENED, BUT I'M NOT PULLING A PRANK.
I didn't create this photo as a joke.
THIS REALLY HAPPENED.
YOU ...
...WENT TO SEE MS. MOGAMI THIS SAME NIGHT. DON'T YOU REMEMBER WHAT SHE WAS WEARING?
!

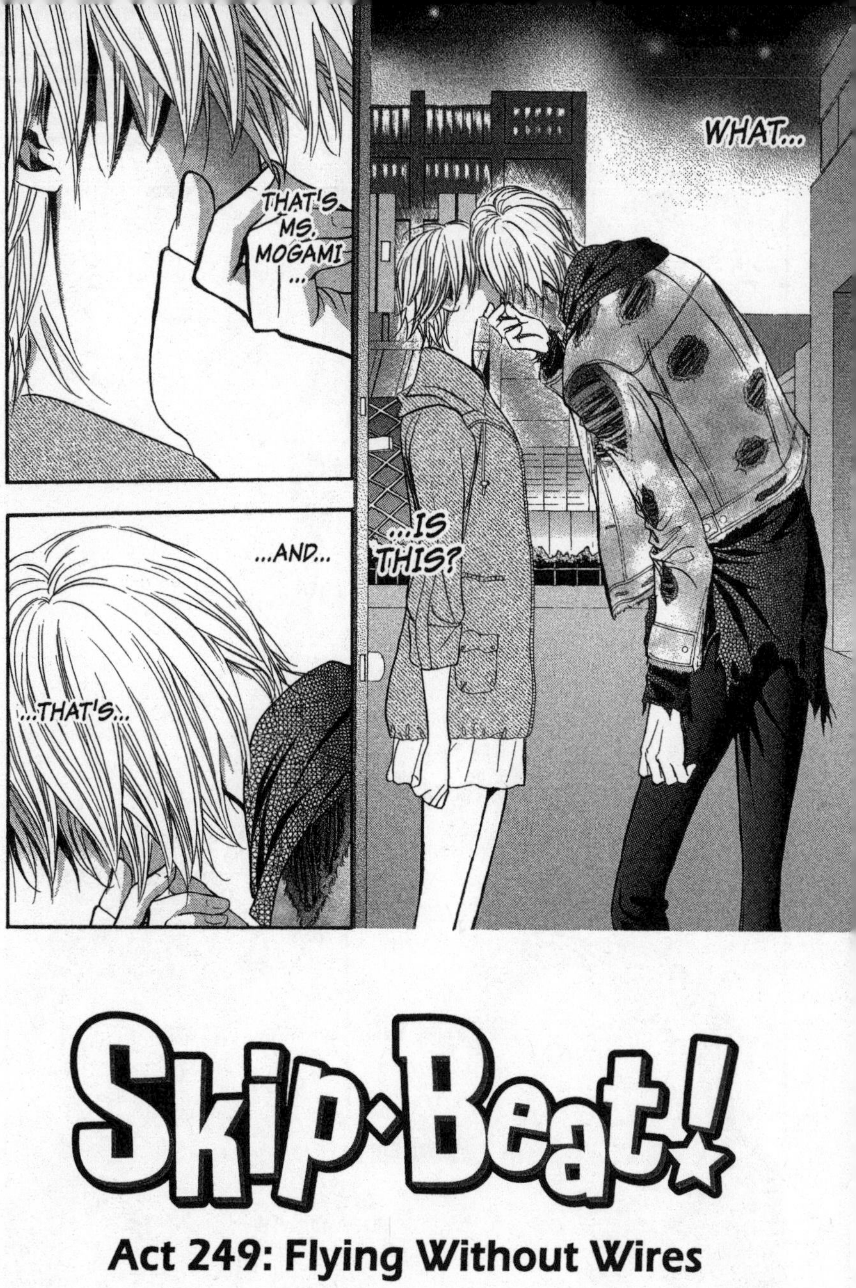
WHAT...
...IS THIS?
THAT'S MS. MOGAMI...
...AND...
...THAT'S...

# Skip·Beat!

## Act 249: Flying Without Wires

# Skip·Beat!

Volume 42

## CONTENTS

Shojo Beat

# Skip·Beat!

...REN.
HAPPY BIRTHDAY...
THIS HUNDRED-YEAR-OLD WINE IS NAMED LOTUS, JUST LIKE YOU. AND YOU SHARE A BIRTHDAY!
OOH.
REALLY ?!
THANK YOU SO MUCH.
I'LL OPEN IT ON MY BIRTHDAY NEXT YEAR.
Something to look forward to.
WHAT? JUST OPEN IT NOW!
Why do you want to wait so long?
BECAUSE...
...I can't ...
... legally drink yet.
Ren Tsuruga is still 19.
Oh!
SO HE'D COMPLETELY FORGOTTEN...
This is me...
I'd forgotten how old he was until my readers reminded me.
Thanks for telling me. (ᵕᵕ)
And so...
Clean-cut Mr. Tsuruga will not drink alcohol until he turns 20*.
But Kuon...well... You all know why.
*The legal drinking age in Japan

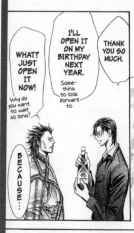

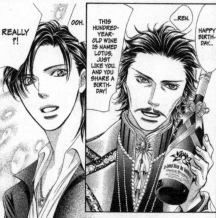

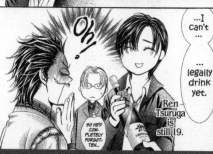

Skip·Beat!